Time Out
Madrid

Penguin Books

PENGUIN BOOKS

Published by the Penguin Group
Penguin Books Ltd, 27 Wrights Lane, London W8 5TZ, England
Penguin Books USA Inc., 375 Hudson Street, New York, New York 10014, USA
Penguin Books Australia Ltd, Ringwood, Victoria, Australia
Penguin Books Canada Ltd, 10 Alcorn Avenue, Toronto, Ontario, Canada M4V 3B2
Penguin Books (NZ) Ltd, 182-190 Wairau Road, Auckland 10, New Zealand

Penguin Books Ltd, Registered Offices: Harmondsworth, Middlesex, England

First published 1995
Second edition 1997
Third edition 1999
Fourth edition 2000
10 9 8 7 6 5 4 3 2 1

Colour reprographics by Westside Digital Media, 9 Bridle Lane, London W1
and Precise Litho, 34-35 Great Sutton Street, London EC1
Printed and bound by Cayfosa-Quebecor, Ctra. de Caldes, Km 3 08 130 Sta, Perpètua de Mogoda, Barcelona, Spain

Edited and designed by
Time Out Guides Limited
Universal House
251 Tottenham Court Road
London W1P 0AB
Tel + 44 (0) 171 813 3000
Fax + 44 (0) 171 813 6001
Email guides@timeout.com
www.timeout.com

Editorial

Editor Nick Rider
Deputy Editor Lesley McCave
Contributing Editors Harvey Holtom, Nick Lyne
Researcher Lola Delgado Muller
Proofreader Angela Jameson
Indexer Marion Moisy

Editorial Director Peter Fiennes
Series Editor Ruth Jarvis
Deputy Series Editor Jonathan Cox

Design

Art Director John Oakey
Art Editor Mandy Martin
Senior Designer Scott Moore
Designers Benjamin de Lotz, Lucy Grant
Picture Editor Kerri Miles
Deputy Picture Editor Olivia Duncan-Jones
Picture Admin Kit Burnet
Scanning & Imaging Dan Conway
Ad make-up Glen Impey

Advertising

Group Advertisement Director Lesley Gill
Sales Director Mark Phillips
International Sales Manager Mary L Rega
Advertisement Sales (Madrid) Bear Publishing
Advertising Assistant Catherine Shepherd

Administration

Publisher Tony Elliott
Managing Director Mike Hardwick
Financial Director Kevin Ellis
Marketing Director Christine Cort
General Manager Nichola Coulthard
Production Manager Mark Lamond
Production Controller Samantha Furniss

Features in this guide were written and researched by: Introduction Nick Lyne. **History** Nick Rider. **Madrid Today** Harvey Holtom. **Architecture** Harvey Holtom. **Accommodation** Mary de Sousa. **Sightseeing** Nick Lyne, Harvey Holtom, Robert Latona, Nick Rider. **Museums** Harvey Holtom, Nick Rider. **Restaurants** Nick Lyne, Mary de Sousa, Debbi Christophers. **Tapas** Nick Lyne, Vicky Hayward. **Cafés & Bars** Harvey Holtom. **Shops & Services** Harvey Holtom, Natalie Reed. **By Season** Nick Lyne. **Bullfighting** Harvey Holtom, Nick Rider. **Children** Harvey Holtom. **Film** Nick Lyne. **Flamenco** Nuria Barrios, Larry Lilue. **Galleries** Nick Lyne. **Gay & Lesbian** Juan Ignacio Durán. **Music: Classical & Opera** Harvey Holtom. **Music: Rock, Roots & Jazz** Nick Lyne. **Nightlife** Debbi Christophers, Natalie Reed. **Sport & Fitness** Harvey Holtom. **Theatre & Dance** Harvey Holtom, Stuart Green. **Trips Out of Town** Nick Lyne, Robert Latona, Nick Rider, Vicky Hayward. **Directory** Nick Lyne, Nick Rider.

The Editor would like to thank the following: Miguel Angel Delgado of the Consorcio de Transportes de Madrid, Adelaída Riego and Outline SL, Elena Garrido of the Museo Nacional del Prado, Gema Sesé of the Museo Thyssen-Bornemisza, María Luisa Ferrer, Museo de América, María José Rivas and Manuela Rodríguez of the Museo Municipal de Madrid, Antonio Pareja and the Junta de Castilla La Mancha, Alicia Moreno Espert, Consejera de Cultura, Comunidad de Madrid, Beatriz Barchino of the Real Academia de Bellas Artes de San Fernando, Miguel Angel Villena of *El País*, Javier Villán of *El Mundo*, Press department, Teatro de la Abadía, Press department, Teatro de la Comedia, Auditorio Nacional de Música, Ana Rosa Ruíz, Asociación Cultural por la Danza, Jesús Cimarro, Frutos Secos F Illanas, Umberto Asumendi, Javier Lanza, Stuart Green, Colin Stobbart, Trisha Ballsrud, Thisbe Burns, Nuria Barrios, Sol Abajo, Katrina Wekwerth, Maggi Riach, all the contributors and especially Harvey, Paloma Portero López and Ethel Rimmer.

Maps on pages 303-313, 315-16 supplied by the Consorcio de Transportes de Madrid.

Map on page 314 by Mapworld, 71 Blandy Road, Henley-on-Thames, Oxon RG9 1QB.

Photography by Sol Abajo except: pages 9, 13, 17, 23, 24, 27 **AKG London**; pages 25 **Associated Press**; pages 7, 20 **Ayuntamiento de Madrid-Museo Municipal**; page 16 **Ayuntamiento de Madrid-Museo Municipal/Real Academia de Bellas Artes de San Fernando**; page 239 **Empics**; page 69 (top) **Ermita de San Antonio de la Florida**; page 197 **Kobal Collection**; page 101 **Museo de America**; pages 91, 93, 94 **Museo Nacional del Prado**; page 96 **Museo Thyssen-Bornemisza**; page 215 **Javier del Real**; page 271 **Jorge García Sánchez**; page 245 **Compañia Nacional del Teatro Clasico**.

Contents

Introduction

Outwardly, Madrid has changed a good deal in the five years since the first *Time Out* guide to the Spanish capital appeared. The city's restaurants have become far more diverse, its music and club scenes far more internationally oriented – this year's big thing now arrives here just as quickly as it does in London or New York – and new suburbs on the city fringes are far more prominent features of the urban fabric. Inwardly, though, Madrid simultaneously (and thankfully) still clings to many of its time-honoured ways of doing things.

This city has its share of monuments and museums – not to mention some of the finest art collections in the world – but to really get the most out of it you need to take time to tramp its streets, sit in its many bars and restaurants, and try to get to know some of the people who live here. Which in large part is what this guide seeks to help you to do.

Madrid is in many ways a city of extremes. Its inhabitants seem to lead double lives: during the long, cold winter, they return to their inward-looking Castilian roots; but the summer is long and hot, so they go all Mediterranean, open up pavement bars and stay out all night partying, or just chatting.

Madrileños work long hours, but then create a parallel city that lives by night and in which a different set of rules apply. Recently, one of the prominent political currents in Madrid has been a kind of 'respectable' conservatism – in place of the plain belligerence of the old-style Spanish right – which has made much of its disapproval for wild late-night behaviour and proposed an unheard-of strictness in closing times for bars and clubs; however, the same people who sometimes support this kind of thing are perfectly capable of breaking the rules when *they* want to go out. More and more Madrileños are moving out to the suburbs, yet they are still in love with the shabby charm of the city centre, and pour back into it at weekends. Maybe they suffer from an identity crisis; if so, they seem to thrive on it. But then they always have done.

Catapulted in the 16th century from being an overlooked market town to capital of the world's greatest empire – a post it managed to hold onto for barely 100 years – Madrid then slid into sleepy decline for another couple of centuries. Unlike their cousins in Barcelona or Bilbao, Madrileños cannot even lay claim to a proper regional identity. Most are descended from immigrants from Spain's impoverished rural areas, drawn here from the 1920s onwards. Their children made good, went to university and got decent jobs, and re-invented themselves. And today, in the sprawling suburban house-with-garden developments of Pozuelo or Majadahonda, some are reinventing themselves yet again.

The return of democracy to Spain in the late 1970s sparked a boom that turned Madrid into one of the world's entertainment capitals. Per head, Madrid must have more restaurants and bars than any other European city, and Madrileños seem to spend more time in them than fellow Europeans.

The city also beats its European rivals in that its centre is both compact and – for all the suburban growth – still overwhelmingly residential. Madrid's city centre displays rude health, and its inhabitants an infectious zeal for getting the most out of its noisy, bustling life. Most visitors to Madrid allow themselves to be seduced by its chaotic blend of backstreet bars, home-cooking eateries, and corner shops – as well as the art. Perhaps more important, though, is simply to feed off the buzz of a capital city lost in the throes of change, and yet, often, actually enjoying it.

ABOUT THE TIME OUT CITY GUIDES

The *Time Out Madrid Guide* is one of an expanding series of *Time Out* City Guides, now numbering over 30, produced by the people behind London and New York's successful listings magazines. Our guides are all written and updated by resident experts who have striven to provide you with all the most up-to-date information you'll need to explore the city or read up on its background, whether you're a local or a first-time visitor.

THE LOWDOWN ON THE LISTINGS

Above all, we've tried to make this book as useful as possible. Addresses, telephone numbers, websites, transport information, opening times, admission prices and credit card details are all included in our listings. And, as far

There is an online version of this guide, as well as weekly events listings for more than 30 international cities, at http://www.timeout.com

as possible, we've given details of facilities, services and events, all checked and correct as we went to press. However, owners and managers can change their arrangements at any time. Also, in Madrid, small shops and bars often do not keep precise opening hours, and may close earlier or later than stated according to the level of trade. Similarly, arts programmes are often finalised very late. Before you go out of your way, we'd advise you whenever possible to phone and check opening times, ticket prices and other particulars. While every effort has been made to ensure the accuracy of the information in this guide, the publishers cannot accept responsibility for any errors it may contain.

PRICES & PAYMENT
The prices we have listed should be treated as guidelines, not gospel; fluctuating exchange rates and inflation can cause prices to change rapidly. We have noted where venues such as shops, hotels and restaurants accept the following credit cards: American Express (**AmEx**), Diners Club (**DC**), MasterCard (**MC**) and Visa (**V**). Many businesses also accept other cards, including Switch or Delta and JCB. In addition, some shops, restaurants and attractions take travellers' cheques issued by a major financial institution (such as American Express).

THE LIE OF THE LAND
Mail addresses in Spain include a five-digit postcode, which for Madrid always begins *28* and is written before the name of the city (as in *28014 Madrid*). We have given these codes for organisations or venues you might need to write to, such as the hotels on *pages 37 to 53*. We have also divided the city into areas – simplified, for convenience, from the full complexity of Madrid's geography – and the relevant area name is given with each venue listed in this guide (for areas used in central Madrid, *see page 57*). With all places listed in central Madrid we also give a map reference, which indicates the page and square on which an address will be found on our street maps at the back of the book (from page 304).

TELEPHONE NUMBERS
It is necessary to dial provincial area codes with all numbers in Spain, even for local calls. Hence all normal Madrid numbers begin 91, whether or not you're calling from outside the city. From abroad you must dial 34 (Spain) + 91.

ESSENTIAL INFORMATION
For all the practical information you might need for visiting the city, including emergency phone numbers and details of local transport, turn to the **Directory** chapter at the back of the guide. It starts on *page 274*.

MAPS
The map section at the back of this book includes an overview map of the city, detailed street maps of the whole of the old city   the centre of Madrid – with a comprehensive street index, a large-scale locality map for planning trips out of town and maps of the local rail and Metro networks. The map section begins on page 301.

LET US KNOW WHAT YOU THINK
We hope you enjoy the *Time Out Madrid Guide*, and we'd like to know what you think of it. We welcome tips for places that you consider we should include in future editions and take note of your criticism of our choices. There's a reader's reply card at the back of this book for your feedback – or you can email us at madridguide@timeout.com.

Introduction

In Context

Call the USA

"feel free to call"

1-800-COLLECT

1 8 0 0
COLLECT

When in Ireland
Dial: 1-800-COLLECT (265 5328)

When in N. Ireland, UK & Europe
Dial: 00-800-COLLECT USA (265 5328 872)

Member of
Dublin Tourism

The **Palacio del Buen Retiro** in the 1660s. *See p12.*

History

Catapulted centre-stage by one man's decision, Madrid is a city that has often pondered its role in the world.

Madrid is an accidental city. To some extent it was the first of the purpose-built capitals, a precursor of Canberra, Brasilia or Washington DC. These new cities, though, were selected by national congresses and committees; Madrid became capital of Spain through the choice of one man, King Philip II.

In the 17th century, after Madrid had become the capital of the Spanish Empire, an attempt was made to give it an ancient past. Several writers developed the story of its descent from a Roman city called *Mantua Carpetana*.

These accounts, however, were almost entirely the product of wishful thinking. The area around Madrid has one of the longest histories of continuous settlement of anywhere in Europe, and is extraordinarily rich in prehistoric relics, many of which can now be seen in the Museo Arqueológico Nacional. Later, there were Roman towns nearby at Alcalá de Henares (*Complutum*) and Toledo (*Toletum*), and Roman villas along the valley of the Manzanares. There is, though, no real evidence that there was ever a local Mantua, or that any of these settlements was the origin of modern Madrid.

The story of *Mantua Carpetana*, however, served to obscure the sheer insignificance of Madrid before Philip II moved his Court here in 1561, and above all the embarrassing fact that it had been founded by Muslims. Specifically, in the reign of Mohammed I, fifth Emir of Córdoba, in about 860.

FRONTIER FORTRESS

Following their eruption into the Iberian peninsula in 711 the Arab armies did not occupy the inhospitable lands north of the Sierra de Guadarrama, but established a frontier more or less along the old Roman road linking Mérida, Toledo and Saragossa. The original *Al-Kasr* (a word absorbed into Spanish as *Alcázar*) or fortress of Madrid was one of a string of watchtowers built north of this line in the ninth century, as Christian raids into *Al-Andalus* became more frequent. The rocky crag on which it stood, where the Palacio Real is today, was ideal for the purpose, since it had a view of the main tracks south from the Guadarrama. It also had excellent water, from underground streams within the rock. Madrid's original Arabic name, *Mayrit* or *Magerit*, means 'place of many springs'.

Mayrit became more than just a fortress, with an outer citadel or *Al-Mudaina* (later hispanicised as Almudena), the eastern wall of which ran along the modern Calle Factor, and a wider town or *Medina* bounded by the Plaza de la Villa and Calle Segovia. A section of wall, the **Muralla Arabe** on Cuesta de la Vega, and the remains being excavated next to the Palacio Real are the only remnants of Muslim Madrid visible in the modern city. Citadel and *Medina* consisted of a mass of narrow alleys, like the old quarters of North African cities today. They did, though, have a sophisticated system for channelling the underground springs, which would serve Christian Madrid for centuries.

Mayrit was attacked by Christian armies in 932 and 1047, and in the 970s was used by the great minister of Córdoba, Al-Mansur, as a base for his celebrated 100 campaigns against the north. By the 11th century it had about 7,000 people, among them Abul-Qasim Maslama, mathematician, astronomer, translator of Greek literature and experimenter in magic.

CHRISTIAN CONQUEST

In the 11th century the Caliphate of Córdoba disintegrated into a mass of petty princedoms called *taifas*, and *Mayrit* became part of the Emirate of Toledo. In 1086 Alfonso VI of Castile was able to take advantage of this situation to conquer Toledo, and with it Madrid. The town's main mosque became the church of Santa María de la Almudena, which would survive until the 19th century.

For many years, however, Madrid would remain in the front line. In 1109 it was again besieged, by a Moorish army that camped below the Alcázar in the place known ever since as the *Campo del Moro* ('Field of the Moor'). A new wall was built, enclosing the area between the Alcázar and Plaza Isabel II, Plaza San Miguel and Plaza Humilladero.

Nevertheless, by 1270 the Castilians had taken Córdoba and Seville. Christian Madrid, however, was a humble place that grew very slowly. Its population was probably less than

3,000. Only in 1202 was Madrid given its *Fuero*, or Royal Statutes. It was a very rural town, and most of the population who worked did so on the land. Madrid did acquire some large religious houses, notably the Friary of San Francisco, where San Francisco el Grande stands today, supposedly founded by Saint Francis of Assisi himself in 1217.

Madrid was still not entirely Christian. Many Muslims, known as *Mudéjares*, had stayed in the conquered areas, retaining their own laws and religion. They were particularly prized by the Castilian monarchs for their skills as builders and masons (*see page 30*). In Madrid they were confined to the area known as the Morería (*see page 66*). Medieval Madrid also had a smaller Jewish population, concentrated outside the walls in Lavapiés.

Very little of medieval Madrid is visible today precisely because it was so undistinguished, and so was largely discarded in later centuries. The most important remaining buildings are the *Mudéjar* towers of **San Nicolás de los Servitas** and **San Pedro el Viejo**. Most of the local notables lived around the **Plaza de la Villa**, where the Torre de los Lujanes still stands today.

During the Middle Ages Madrid did acquire its future patron saint, San Isidro. He was a local farm labourer, believed to have died in 1172, who with his wife Santa María de la Cabeza was known for great piety and a series of miraculous and saintly acts, among them that of never failing to give food to another member of the poor. The cult of Isidro, remarkable for the very lowly status of its central figure, became extremely popular locally. Once Madrid had become the Spanish capital the couple would both be canonised, as the only husband-and-wife saints in history.

> **'That Madrid was not a very prized royal possession was shown when it briefly became Armenian territory.'**

Madrid did finally begin to play more of a role in the affairs of Castile in the 14th century. In 1309 the *Cortes* or Parliament met here for the first time. Medieval Castile did not have a fixed capital, but instead the Court followed the king around the country, and the *Cortes* met in many different towns at different times.

In the 14th and 15th centuries Castile was dogged by a series of social revolts and civil wars, between monarchs, the nobility, and rival claimants within the royal family itself. Against this backdrop Madrid began to gain popularity

as a royal residence, as a country retreat more than as a centre of power. King Pedro 'the Cruel' (1350-69) first began to turn the old Alcázar into something more habitable. That Madrid was not a very prized royal possession, however, was shown when it briefly became Armenian territory. In 1383 Leo V of Armenia lost his kingdom to the Turks, and as consolation Juan I of Castile gave this Christian hero three of his own estates, among them Madrid. Later it reverted to Castilian sovereignty. Madrid was most favoured by Juan II (1407-54) and Enrique IV (1454-74), who gave it the title *muy noble y muy leal* ('very noble and very loyal').

In addition, political instability did not prevent there being substantial economic progress in 15th-century Castile, which enabled Madrid for the first time to become a reasonably prosperous trading centre. Its trade outgrew the old market in Plaza de la Villa, and in the 1460s an area east of the 12th-century wall was built up as a ramshackle new market square, the origin of the **Plaza Mayor**. A new town wall was built, not for defence but so that taxes could be levied in the new parts of the town. Its eastern entrance was a new gate, the **Puerta del Sol**.

At the end of the 15th century a new era was opening up in Castilian and Spanish history. In 1476 Enrique IV's sister Isabel and her husband Fernando of Aragon – Ferdinand and Isabella – succeeded in bringing the civil wars to an end. Through their marriage they united the different Spanish kingdoms, although each retained its own institutions for another two centuries. Within Castile they imposed their authority on the aristocracy, establishing an absolute monarchy and a professional army that enabled them to intervene in the wars of Renaissance Italy. The earnestly devout Isabella was also one of the instigators of the militant sense of religious mission that would mark Imperial Spain. Detesting the religious coexistence of medieval Spain, she ordered the expulsion of all Jews in 1492 and the forcible conversion of the *Mudéjar* Muslims in 1502. The Inquisition, established in 1478, was reinforced to police these measures. Also in 1492 came the conquest of Muslim Granada, which won Ferdinand and Isabella the title 'Most Catholic Kings' from the Pope. In this same year, of course, they also sponsored Columbus' first voyage to America.

Madrid retained a degree of royal favour, helped by connections with key figures at Isabella's Court, such as Cardinal Cisneros, the austere Franciscan, born north of Madrid at Torrelaguna, whom she made head of the Church in Spain in 1495. It continued its modest growth, and at the end of the Middle Ages had a population of around 10-12,000.

Madrid's godfather, **King Philip II**.

SUDDENLY, A CAPITAL

On 11 May 1561 the small-time aristocrats who ran the town of Madrid received a letter from their king, Philip II, informing them that he, the entire royal household and all their hundreds of hangers-on would shortly be coming to stay. They immediately set about panic buying of food stocks from surrounding towns, using the money set aside for the *fiesta* of Corpus Christi, much to the irritation of the local population. No one quite realised, though, that this transformation was intended to be permanent.

In the previous 50 years the Spanish monarchy had also been transformed. Ferdinand and Isabella were succeeded by their grandson Charles of Habsburg (1516-56), who through his father Philip, Duke of Burgundy, also inherited Burgundy (the Netherlands and large parts of eastern France) and the Habsburg lands in central Europe, and would in 1519

receive the title of Holy Roman Emperor, as Charles V. He would also, of course, acquire ever-larger territories in America. Spain thus became part, and increasingly the centre, of a European and worldwide empire.

When he first visited Spain in 1517 Charles appointed French-speakers to many state posts. This led in 1520 to the revolt of the *Comuneros*, in which the towns of Castile, Madrid among them, rose up against foreign influence and the encroachment of royal power on their traditional freedoms. However, after this had been suppressed in 1521, Charles came to value Spain – above all Castile – more and more, as the most loyal part of his empire.

Charles and his successors had an immense sense of the greatness of their dynasty and their imperial mission, believing that their vast territories had come to them through Providence and that it was their right and duty to defend both them and the Catholic faith. This would involve continual and ever more costly wars, against the French, the Muslim Turks and the northern Protestants. This idea of mission combined perfectly with the crusading, military spirit already imbued in the Castilian Church, army and aristocracy.

Charles V made no attempt to give Castile a capital. However, on his visits to Spain he did spend considerable time in Madrid, hunting at El Pardo and giving the town another grand title, *Imperial y Coronada* ('Imperial and Crowned'). In 1525, after his victory at Pavia, he had his great enemy Francis I of France brought to Madrid and imprisoned in the Torre de los Lujanes.

In 1556 Charles abdicated and retired to the monastery of Yuste, in the Sierra de Gredos (*see page 269*). Austria and the title of Holy Roman Emperor went to his brother Ferdinand, but Spain and Burgundy were passed to Charles' son, Philip II (1556-98).

The fundamental figure in Madrid's history, Philip was a deeply pious, shy, austere man. Factors personal and political led him to feel a need for a permanent capital. His father had travelled incessantly about his many dominions, and led his armies into battle. Philip, in contrast, ruled his inheritance from behind a desk, as a kind of 'King-Bureaucrat', sometimes dealing with over 400 documents a day. This extraordinary exercise in paperwork naturally required a permanent base.

Moreover, in the 1540s Charles V had introduced Burgundian state ritual into the relatively informal Court of Castile. Every appearance of the monarch – such as meals, in which food could only be served to the royal family by gentlemen-in-waiting, exalted Dukes and Marquises, on their knees – followed a set ceremonial order, in a ritual etiquette that became ever more elaborate in succeeding generations as the Habsburgs amplified their idea of their own grandeur. The number of court attendants mushroomed, making an itinerant court all the more impractical.

Precisely why Philip chose Madrid as his capital, a town without a cathedral, a college or a printing press, remains unclear. In the 1540s, as Crown Prince, he had already ordered the extension of its Alcázar. The fact that Madrid was near the dead centre of the Iberian peninsula almost certainly appealed to Philip, who was fascinated by geometry and Renaissance ideas of a king as the 'centre' of the state, but his choice made no economic sense at all, since it would give Spain the only major European capital not on a navigable river.

Valladolid and Toledo were both more obvious candidates, but this in itself seems to have been held against them. In contrast Madrid – which for centuries would normally be referred to in Spain as *la Corte*, the Court, never as a city in its own right, which indeed it wasn't – would be a capital of the monarchy's own creation, a pure expression of royal power.

BOOM TOWN OF A GOLDEN AGE

Having established his ideal capital, Philip strangely did little to build or plan it. After the completion of the Alcázar his attention shifted to **El Escorial**, where he increasingly spent his time. Royal piety was demonstrated by the endowment of new houses for religious orders, such as the **Descalzas Reales**. Philip II founded 17 convents and monasteries in Madrid, Philip III 14 and Philip IV another 17, and they would cover a third of the city until the 19th century. A wider city wall was put up in 1566, and the **Puente de Segovia** in the 1580s. Philip's favourite architect, Juan de Herrera, planned the rebuilding of the **Plaza Mayor**, but the only part built during his reign was the Casa de la Panadería in 1590. Philip's idea of a capital seemed more like a collection of royal establishments than a living city.

Reality, however, was more powerful than this rudimentary concept. The establishment of the Court and aristocracy in Madrid, the great centres of consumption and patronage, made it a magnet for people from all over Spain and abroad. The population went from under 20,000 in 1561 to 55,000 in 1584 and close to 85,000 by 1600. Building did not keep up with the influx, and a law decreed that in any house of more than one storey the upper floor could be requisitioned to house members of the Court. In response, to avoid this imposition people simply put up houses with only one floor, and much of the new Madrid grew as a mass of shabby, low buildings slapped together out of mud.

This improvised capital did not impress foreign visitors. Lambert Wyts, a Flemish aristocrat who arrived in 1571, said that it was 'the foulest and filthiest town in Spain'. Thick mud made it impossible to ride a horse down the main streets in winter until a few cobbles were put down in the 1580s. There were no drains of any kind, and the streets were full of waste thrown out of the houses every night, producing an 'unbearable stench'.

> ## '...in this Babylon, of every four things one sees, one cannot believe even two.'

From the start Madrid took on a characteristic that would stay with it to this day – that it was a city of outsiders, in which at least 50 per cent of the population was from somewhere else. Another trait for which Madrid would be repeatedly condemned was that it was a city that consumed but did not produce anything. The trades that did develop in Madrid – carpenters, shoemakers, jewellers, fanmakers, laceworkers – were overwhelmingly oriented to servicing the Court and aristocracy.

The economic frailty of Madrid reflected that of Castile as a whole. The gold and silver of Mexico and Peru seemed to give the Habsburg kings limitless potential wealth. The demands of their wars, however, were immediate, and could only be met by loans from foreign bankers. The result was soaring, uncontrollable debts, which not even American gold could match. Also, the country's political hierarchy had been built on the basis of giving the aristocracy, the *hidalgos* or lesser gentry and the Church immense privileges, including exemption from taxation. This meant that the always-increasing war taxes hit precisely and only the few productive sectors of the population. Young men of working age were also continually being drawn off for the army.

Man with a sad countenance

Philip II may have launched the city as a capital, but a more pervasive presence in Madrid is his grandson King Philip IV, whose gloom-laden face looks out from so many Velázquez portraits. He ruled for over 40 years (1621-65), and the grandest buildings, plays, celebrations and public displays of the Golden Age were all created for him.

A central figure in Philip's life was the Count of Olivares, appointed one of his gentlemen in waiting when the Prince was ten, in 1615. Olivares became Philip's mentor in all things, and later his chief minister, with the unique title of Count-Duke, *el Conde Duque*. Olivares overriding aim was to reverse the slide in the power and prestige of the Spanish empire seen since the great days of Philip II: for this, the solitary figure at the heart of the monarchy, the King, had to be able to play his part. The Count-Duke put Philip through an intensive programme of education, in languages, philosophy, politics and the arts, designed to make him into the grandest, most cultured prince in Europe. In some areas the course was very successful: Philip IV gained an abiding love of theatre and painting, and became the greatest art connoisseur and collector of his day. Aided by Velázquez, appointed court painter when only 23 years old in 1623, he built up a huge art collection that forms the core of the modern Museo del Prado.

Otherwise, however, the raw material that Olivares had to work with was terribly unsuitable. Philip IV was shy, weak-willed and indecisive, furtively pleasure-loving, prone to lethargy and depression and, like his father Philip III, racked by feelings of guilt and inadequacy when he looked towards the example set by his great ancestors. Olivares wrote frequent memoranda to his charge reminding him of his responsibilities, which only made him feel worse.

To bolster the prestige of the monarchy, and the King's own confidence, Olivares pursued a policy of keeping up appearances to an extraordinary degree. In 1632 he began the construction of a huge new royal residence on the eastern side of Madrid, the **Palacio del Buen Retiro** or 'Good Retreat'. More than one palace it was a complex of palatial buildings, with huge formal gardens, centred on a great courtyard for royal ceremonies (see pages 12 and 82-3). Olivares' aim in building it was to make an emphatic statement of the greatness of the monarchy he served, creating a self-contained compound in which the Court could be displayed at its maximum splendour. Louis XIV took the idea as his model for Versailles.

The Retiro was an essentially theatrical building, and the Court theatre was central to it. Philip IV had a special fascination for elaborate sets and visual tricks, and an

For a country with the social system of Castile, constant imperialism was near suicidal; in time, it would lead to the eradication of the growth visible under Ferdinand and Isabella, and a catastrophic decline in the rural population.

One aspect of Spain during its 'Golden Century' was its intense Catholic faith. This was also, though, the golden age of the *pícaro*, the chancer, the figure living on his wits seen in the *picaresque* novels of the period. In a society that valued aristocracy, status and military or state service over productive activity, and in which the real economy was rapidly dwindling, their numbers naturally multiplied.

The mecca for all *pícaros* was Madrid, the one place where ex-soldiers, landless peasants and drifters would be most likely to find a niche, as servants or bodyguards, or by gambling, prostitution, thieving or many other means. The great poet and satirist Quevedo wrote a whole book cataloguing the varieties of Madrid's low life and how they acquired cash. It also contained a great many of the very poor, living off the charity provided by the huge number of religious houses in the city.

Pícaros were not only found among the poor. Madrid also drew in thousands at the other end of society, often *hidalgos* with estates run to ruin, who came hoping to attach themselves to some lordly patron and so break into the circles of the Court. For them, maintaining appearances, presenting an image of aristocracy, was everything. In 1620 Madrid acquired its first guidebook, the 'Guide and advice to strangers who come to the Court, in which they are taught to flee the dangers that there are in Court life', by Antonio Liñán y Verdugo, a lawyer from Cuenca. He warned provincials who might have to do business in Madrid that in 'this Babylon', 'of every four things one sees, one cannot believe even two', for everything was just 'fabulous appearances, dreamed-up marvels, fairy-tale treasures, and figures like actors on a stage'.

Italian craftsman, Cosimo Lotti, was brought in to create extravagant productions with mechanical devices that dwarfed the human actors. Writers such as Calderón created dramas, mostly on mythological themes, to fit. Productions spread out to feature the Retiro's giant lake, with battles between life-size ships, sea-monsters appearing from the depths, and angels flying through the air.

Philip IV combined devout Catholicism with an active if guilt-ridden sex life, and is believed to have fathered 30 illegitimate children. The Habsburg Court was not, though, one like that of Louis XIV of France, where royal mistresses were displayed in semi-queenly style; it was far too formal and decorous for that, and the King's affairs had to be carried on very much below stairs. As difficulties mounted, the Court retreated more and more into rigid ritual; Philip personally added new intricacies to the already elaborate Court etiquette, as if he thought he could stave off disaster by ceremony. A Dutch visitor wrote in 1655, 'the King of Spain adopts such a degree of gravity that he walks and behaves like a statue'. The only residents exempt from etiquette were the royal dwarfs and clowns, of whom Philip IV was especially fond, to the extent of having Velázquez paint portraits of every one of them.

And yet, this man who behaved like a human monument was also a compulsive confessor. Today he would be an automatic candidate for therapy. He wrote a scholarly history of Italy, and in the preface indiscreetly described how intimidated he was by state business. Later, he was beset by dread that the decline of his empire was divine punishment for his own failings and sexual misdeeds. He corresponded for years with a nun in a convent in Soria, Sister María de Agreda, to whom he confided everything from problems of state to worries about sexual impotence. 'I fear myself more than anything else', he wrote to her, '...Oh, Sister María, I fear my weakness will prevent me from achieving the good things you desire'.

This volatile mass naturally needed entertainment. One source was the theatre, in the *corral* theatres that began to be built in the 1570s (*see page 244*), the focus of the extraordinary literary vitality of the city at this time. There were also *fiestas* and royal ceremonies. And, even foreigners who complained about the mud and the stink were impressed by the variety of luxuries that could be had in Madrid, from Italian lace to 'fresh' fish, brought caked in ice on a five-day journey from the Basque coast.

BAROQUE THEATRE

In 1571 came the greatest success of Philip II's reign with the defeat of the Turkish fleet off Lepanto in Greece. In 1580, he also became King of Portugal. He appeared to be at the height of his strength. However, suspensions of payments on his debts were becoming frequent occurrences, and in the 1560s a rebellion had broken out in the Netherlands that would develop into a morass into which Spanish armies and wealth would disappear without trace. His dispute with England, leading to the catastrophe of the Armada, and interventions in France's religious wars were equally costly.

As problems mounted without any ever being resolved, a gnawing frustration spread through Castilian society, and scapegoats were sought. The former Muslims (*Moriscos*), nominally converted to Catholicism in 1502, were put under increasing pressure and then expelled from Spain in 1609, and the Inquisition – if not the all-pervading force of Protestant caricatures – was given great powers to investigate deviations from Catholic orthodoxy.

Philip II died in 1598 at El Escorial, aged 71. His son Philip III (1598-1621) and grandson Philip IV (1621-65) had neither the intelligence, confidence or ordinarily the motivation to carry on with the awesome burden of work he had set as an example. Philip III began the practice of ruling through a favourite or *valido*, the Duke of Lerma. Spain's impoverished state, aggravated by a devastating plague in 1599, was impossible to ignore, and Lerma responded by making peace with England and the Dutch.

He also committed the ultimate injury to Madrid by moving the Court to Valladolid, in 1601. The main stated reason was that this would help revive the economy of northern Castile, although Lerma also stood to benefit personally. He also argued that Madrid, in any case, was so overrun with undesirables that it had become intolerable. The monarchy's purpose-built capital was out of control, and it would be best to write it off and start again.

Within a few months Madrid was so deserted that 'it appeared as if the Moors or the English had sacked and burnt it'. By 1605 the population had fallen back to just 26,000, little more than before Philip II's arrival in 1561. However, the Valladolid experiment did not work, and it became evident that Madrid had acquired a momentum that was difficult to disregard. In 1606 the Court returned, amid huge rejoicing, and only a year later the population was already back to 70,000.

It was after the definitive establishment of Madrid as capital, with Philip III's brief declaration *'Sólo Madrid es Corte'* ('Only Madrid is the Court'), that more was at last done to give it the look of a grand city. The Plaza Mayor was finally completed in 1619, followed by the Ayuntamiento or city hall and the Buen Retiro palace (*see page 12* **Man with a sad countenance**). The aristocracy, too, began to build palaces around the city once they were assured they would not have to move on again, and Madrid acquired several much more elaborate baroque churches.

'Habsburg Madrid functioned like a giant theatre.'

The Plaza Mayor was the great arena of Habsburg Madrid. Able to hold a third of the city's population at that time, it was the venue for state ceremonies, bullfights, executions, *autos-da-fé* (the ritual condemnation of heretics), mock battles, circus acts and carnival *fiestas*, as well as still being a market square. Particularly lavish entertainments were staged in the plaza in 1623 for the Prince of Wales, the future King Charles I, who arrived in Madrid under the bizarre alias of 'Tom Smith' in a fruitless attempt to negotiate a marriage with the sister of Philip IV.

Habsburg Madrid functioned rather like a giant theatre, a great backdrop against which the monarchy could display itself to its subjects and to the world. On either side were royal estates, which determined the shape of the city left in the middle and its peculiar north-south pattern of growth. Several times a year royal processions were held, nearly always along a similar route: from the Retiro along Calle Alcalá to Puerta del Sol, Calle Mayor and the Alcázar, then back again via Calle Arenal and Carrera de San Jerónimo, with stops for ceremonies in the Plaza Mayor and High Masses in various churches. For the occasion, buildings were covered in garlands, and temporary arches erected along the route with extravagant decoration extolling the virtues of the dynasty. As the Spanish monarchy slid towards economic collapse the lavishness of these ceremonies only increased, maintaining an illusion of power and opulence.

Away from this ceremonial route, the Habsburgs built few squares and no grand avenues, and old Madrid continued to develop along the tangled street plan it retains today. Even so, the opulence of the Court – and the poverty outside the capital – still attracted more people into the city, and in about 1630 Madrid reached its maximum size under the Habsburgs, with possibly as many as 170,000 inhabitants. In 1656 it was given its fifth and final wall, roughly surrounding the area now considered 'old Madrid', and which would set the limits of the city for the next 200 years.

The centre of all the Court pomp was for many years King Philip IV (*see page 12* **Man with a sad countenance**). Throughout the 1620s and 1630s, while the Court maintained its image of grandeur, his *valido* the Count-Duke of Olivares struggled to maintain the Spanish empire against threats on every side. In the 1620s Spain won a series of victories, and for a time it seemed the rot had been stopped. In 1639, though, a Spanish fleet was destroyed by the Dutch, and in 1643 the French crushed the Spanish army at Rocroi in Flanders. Naval defeats made it ever more difficult for Spain to import gold and silver from America. Olivares sought to extend taxation in the non-Castilian dominions of the crown, which led in 1640 to revolts in Portugal and Catalonia. Portugal regained its independence, and the Catalan revolt was only suppressed after a 12-year war.

By mid-century the effects of endless wars on Castile were visible to all, in abandoned villages and social decay throughout the country. Even Madrid went into decline, so that by 1700 the city's population had fallen back to about 100,000. In the 1660s, the total collapse of the Spanish empire seemed an immediate possibility. Castile, the first world power, had been left poorer than many countries it had tried to dominate.

HABSBURG TWILIGHT

In the Court, meanwhile, life became ever more of a baroque melodrama. Of Philip IV's 12 legitimate children by his two wives, only two girls survived adulthood – the youngest the Infanta Margarita, the little princess in Velázquez' *Las Meninas*. In 1661, however, when Philip was already prematurely aged, the Queen, Mariana of Austria, had a son, conceived, the King wrote to his friend the nun Sister María, 'in the last copulation achieved with Doña Mariana'.

The new heir, the future King Charles II, chronically infirm from birth, provided the dynasty with scant consolation. The Habsburgs' marked tendency to ill-health had been accentuated by their habit of marrying cousins or nieces. The formidable Habsburg jaw, the growth of which can be followed through the

family portraits, had in Charles become a serious disability. He was unable to eat solid food. Because of this – or more likely, due to the endless cures he was subjected to for his countless ailments – he suffered from uncontrollable diarrhoea, which detracted from the stately dignity of Court ceremonies.

In 1665 Philip IV died, leaving as regent his widow Mariana. Born in Vienna, she chose as her adviser her confessor Father Nithard, an Austrian Jesuit who was the first of many foreigners to attempt to ban bullfighting. She was forced to dismiss him by Juan José de Austria, one of Philip IV's healthier illegitimate children, who himself had ambitions on the throne. Mariana then took a less pious tack by promoting a good-looking and totally corrupt groom, Fernando Valenzuela, before being obliged to get rid of him too.

> ### 'With the pathetic last words *Me duele todo'* ('It hurts everywhere'), he finally died, and the Spanish Habsburg dynasty came to an end.'

In the meantime, the economy and government continued to slide. Concern centred again on the need for an heir, and Charles was married off twice, despite a general belief that he was both impotent and sterile. As it became evident that the throne of the Spanish empire would soon become vacant, the Court was overrun with bizarre intrigues, with different factions and the agents of European powers all waiting on Charles' final demise. In 1695 the French Ambassador reported that the King 'appeared to be decomposing', and could not walk more than 15 paces without assistance. Even so, Charles resisted everything his 'healers' threw at him until the age of 38. In 1700, though, with the pathetic last words *Me duele todo'* ('It hurts everywhere'), he finally died, and the Spanish Habsburg dynasty came to an end.

BOURBON MADRID

Philip V (1700-46), first Bourbon King of Spain, secured his throne in 1714, after the 12-year War of the Spanish Succession. He was the grandson of Louis XIV of France and María Teresa, daughter of Philip IV of Spain. Castile, abandoning its more usual francophobia, gave him complete support. The alternative, Archduke Charles of Austria, was supported by Catalonia and the other Aragonese territories, to whom he had promised a restoration of their traditional rights. Twice, in 1706 and 1710, Charles' British, Dutch, Portuguese and Catalan army took Madrid, but was unable to hold it.

The **Calle Mayor** decorated to receive King Charles III in 1760.

Once victorious, Philip reformed his new kingdom along lines laid down by his illustrious grandfather in France. In 1715 the remaining rights of the former Aragonese territories were abolished, so that it is from this date that 'Spain' can formally be said to exist.

A French king brought with him other innovations. Philip V, raised at Versailles, and his Italian second wife Isabella Farnese were not taken with Madrid or its gloomy Habsburg palaces, and so built their own Franco-Italian villa at **La Granja** (*see page 255*). They were not overly upset when the entire Alcázar burnt down in 1734, and a new Palacio Real was commissioned from Italian architects. Philip V and his administrator of Madrid the Marqués de Vadillo also sponsored many buildings by a local architect, Pedro de Ribera (*see page 31*).

Reform led to economic recuperation and a recovery in Spain's population. Madrid again had 150,000 inhabitants by 1760, and 180,000 by 1800. People still came and went, but it also acquired a more stable resident population, with a merchant community and a testy artisan and working class.

Even so, in many ways Madrid had changed little. Its main function was still to serve the Court, whose ceremonies set the calendar. They were as lavish as ever, particularly the night processions with candles all along the ceremonial route, creating an effect of 'indescribable grandeur'. Until the 1770s the amount spent annually by the Crown in Madrid was greater than the entire budget of the Spanish navy.

Within the Court itself the Bourbons introduced a much lighter style. Isabella Farnese was highly educated, and particularly interested in the arts and music. One Italian musician at Court was Domenico Scarlatti, who arrived in 1729 as music teacher to Bárbara de Braganza, the Portuguese wife of the future King Fernando VI. Scarlatti spent the last 28 years of his life here, and wrote most of his 555 harpsichord sonatas for her and her Court.

Fernando VI (1746-59) was a shy but popular King who gave Spain its longest period of peace for over 200 years. Childless, he was succeeded by his half-brother Charles III (1759-88). Previously King of Naples for 20 years, he too was unimpressed by Madrid. However, more than any of his predecessors he set out to improve the city, becoming known as Madrid's Rey-Alcalde or 'King-Mayor'.

Charles was fascinated by Enlightenment ideas of progress, science and the applied use of reason. No democrat, he sought to bring about rational improvement from the top. Reforms were undertaken in the bureaucracy and armed forces, and to improve trade with Spanish America. He challenged the privileges of the religious orders, and expelled the Jesuits from Spain in 1767 for their refusal to co-operate.

In Madrid, Charles first undertook to do something about the mud in winter, suffocating dust in summer and foul smells at all times noted by every visitor to the city. A 1761 decree banned the dumping of waste in the streets, and

Charles' Italian engineer-architect Francesco Sabatini began building sewers and street lighting. A string of major buildings was erected, of which the **Casa de Correos** in Puerta del Sol and the **Puerta de Alcalá** are the best-known. A later queen of Spain remarked that it sometimes seemed as if *all* the monuments of Madrid had been built by Charles III.

Charles III's grandest project was the **Paseo del Prado**. He sent scientific expeditions to every corner of his empire, and planned to exhibit the fruits of their varied researches in a Museum of Natural Sciences – now the Museo del Prado – and the adjacent **Jardín Botánico**.

Popular reaction to the King's improvements was mixed, some being resented as foreign impositions. A decree of Charles III's Italian minister Squillace provoked one of history's first fashion revolts. In 1766 he banned the traditional long cape and wide-brimmed hat and ordered the use of the international three-cornered hat, with the argument that the capes were used by criminals to conceal weapons. In what became known as the *Motín de Esquilache* (Squillace Riot), a mob marched on the Palacio Real, and forced the repeal of the decree.

> **'*Majos* and *majas* most often hailed from Lavapiés, and were notorious for not being deferential to anybody.'**

This period also saw the emergence of a special subculture in Madrid, the *majos* and *majas* – the word means 'fine' or 'pretty' –, also known as *manolos* and *manolas*. A *majo* wore embroidered shirts, a short jacket with a swathe of buttons and a hairnet, and carried a knife; *majas* wore mid-calf skirts with a mass of petticoats, embroidered bodices, intricately braided hair and, on top, a dramatic lace mantilla. Drawn from trades such as porters, cigarette makers or market traders, *majos* and *majas* most often hailed from Lavapiés, and were notorious for not being deferential to anybody. Their cocky elegance intrigued the upper classes, so that even one of the grandest *dames* of the day, the Duchess of Alba, used to dress up as a *maja*. This is the vibrant world seen in the early Madrid paintings of Goya, who lived in the city from 1778.

Reform and improved trade did create a feeling of well-being in late 18th-century Madrid. Nevertheless, Spain was still a very feudal society, and the real economy remained backward and frail. And, in an absolute monarchy, a great deal depended on each monarch. Charles IV (1788-1808), whose rather dozy face was immortalised by Goya, had none of his father's energy or intelligence. Also, he chose as his minister the corrupt Manuel Godoy. After the French Revolution, Spain joined other monarchies in attacking the new regime; in 1795, however, Godoy made peace and then an alliance with France, leading to an unpopular war with Britain. Then, in 1808, when Godoy was vacillating over changing sides once again, he was forestalled by anti-French riots that proclaimed Charles IV's son Fernando as King in his place. Napoleon sent troops to Madrid, assuming this decrepit state would be as easy to conquer as any other.

WAR & ROMANTICISM

The second of May 1808, when the people of Madrid rose up against the French army in hand-to-hand fighting through the streets, has traditionally been seen as the beginning of modern Spanish history. Left to themselves the authorities in the city would certainly have capitulated. The ferocity of popular resistance astonished the French, who couldn't understand why a people never included in government should care so much about who ruled them.

Napoleon made his brother, Joseph Bonaparte, King of Spain. In Madrid he tried in a well-meaning way to make improvements, among them some squares for which the city has since been very grateful, notably the Plaza de Oriente and the Plaza Santa Ana. However, this did nothing to overcome the animosity around him. In 1812 the Duke of Wellington and his army arrived to take the city, in a battle that destroyed much of the Retiro Palace. The French were finally driven out of Spain in 1813.

The suffering and devastation the war caused in Spain is seen with matchless vividness in Goya's *Disasters of War*. As well as the fighting itself, the year 1812 brought with it a catastrophic famine, which in Madrid killed over 30,000 people.

And there's no help for it, by Goya.

The shock of this upheaval initiated a period of instability that continued until 1874, although it could be said it only really ended with the death of Franco. Spain withdrew into its own problems, with one conflict following another between conservatives, reformists, revolutionaries and other factions. Each struggled to impose their model on the State and create a political system that could accommodate, or hold back, the pressures for modernisation and some form of democracy.

During the war a *Cortes* had met in Cádiz in 1812, and given Spain its first-ever Constitution. This assembly also gave the world the word 'liberal'. However, when Fernando VII (1808-33) returned from French captivity in 1814, his only thought was to cancel the Constitution and return to the methods of his ancestors. His absolute rule, though, was incapable of responding to the bankruptcy of the country. The regime was also trapped in the futile struggle to hold on to its American colonies, by then in complete rebellion.

In 1820 a liberal revolt in the army forced Fernando to reinstate the Constitution. He was saved three years later, ironically by a French army, sent to restore monarchical rule. Meanwhile, defeat at Ayacucho in Peru (1824) left Spain with only Cuba, Santo Domingo and Puerto Rico of its former American empire.

In 1830 Fernando VII's wife María Cristina gave birth to a daughter, soon to be Queen Isabel II (1833-68). Previously, the most reactionary sectors of the aristocracy, the Church and other ultra-conservative groups had aligned themselves behind the king's brother Don Carlos. When Fernando died in 1833, Carlos demanded the throne, launching what became known as the Carlist Wars. To defend her daughter's rights María Cristina as, Regent, had no choice but to look for support from liberals, and so was obliged to promise some form of constitutional rule.

For the next 40 years Spanish politics was a see-saw, as conservative and liberal factions vied for power, while the Carlists, off the spectrum for most people in Madrid, occasionally threatened at the gates. Madrid was the great centre for aspiring politicians, and the problems of Spain were discussed endlessly in its salons and new cafés, which multiplied rapidly at this time. This was the era of Romanticism, and writers such as the journalist Larra and poet José Espronceda were heavily involved in politics. Similarly, many of the politicians of the day were also writers.

Much of the time, though, these reformers were shepherds in search of a flock, for there were no true political parties. The only way a faction could really hope to gain power was with the support of a General with troops at his back.

The *pronunciamiento*, or coup, was the main means of changing governments, and soldiers identified with particular sides – Espartero, Serrano and Prim for the progressives, Narváez and O'Donnell (a descendant of Irish soldiers) for the conservatives – were the heroes of their followers. Later, many from both sides had monuments or streets named after them in Madrid, together with civilian politicians such as Bravo Murillo, Argüelles, Cea Bermúdez and Martínez de la Rosa. The clashes between them were never decisive, and it was later said that Spain had gone through 70 years of agitation without ever experiencing a revolution.

CHANGE COMES SLOWLY

This political instability did not mean that life in Madrid was chaotic. Visitors to Madrid in the early 1830s found a small, sleepy, shabby city, seemingly sunk in the past. Convents and palaces still occupied nearly half its area.

It was around this time that Spain acquired its romantic aura. A growing number of foreigners visited the country, drawn by its timeless, exotic qualities. The English traveller George Borrow, who arrived in 1836, described Madrid's population as 'the most extraordinary vital mass in the entire world'. Another visitor was the French writer Prosper Merimée, who in 1845 wrote his novel *Carmen*. This would fix the image of Spain forever, above all when given music by Bizet, who himself never visited Spain at all.

The 1830s, however, also saw the single most important change in old Madrid during the 19th century. In 1836 the liberal minister Mendizábal took advantage of the Church's sympathy for Carlism to introduce his law of *Desamortización* or Disentailment, which dissolved most of Spain's monasteries. In Madrid, the Church lost over 1,000 properties. Most were demolished remarkably quickly, and an enormous area thus became available for sale and new building.

Some urban reformers saw this as an opportunity to give Madrid broad, airy avenues, following the always-cited example of Paris. Some major projects were undertaken, the most important the rebuilding of the Puerta del Sol, in 1854-62. However, most of the local traders who benefited from *Desamortización* lacked the capital to contemplate grand projects, and built separate blocks without challenging the established, disorderly street plan. The districts of old Madrid took on the appearance they have largely kept until today, with great numbers of tenement blocks. They allowed Madrid to grow considerably in population, without going outside its still-standing wall of 1656.

A few factories had appeared in the city, but for the most part the industrial revolution was passing Madrid by. Constitutional governments expanded the administration, and the ambitions of the middle class were focused on obtaining official posts rather than on business ventures. They employed a great many servants, for labour was very cheap.

Two more major changes arrived in the 1850s. In 1851 Madrid got its first railway, to Aranjuez, followed by a line to the Mediterranean. Railways would transform Madrid's relationship with the rest of the country, opening up a realistic possibility of its fulfilling an economic function. Equally important was the completion of the *Canal de Isabel II*, bringing water from the Guadarrama, in 1858. Madrid's water supply, still part-based on Moorish water courses, had been inadequate for years. The canal, inaugurated with a giant spurt of water in Calle San Bernardo, removed a crippling obstruction to the city's growth.

> ## 'Madrid attracted intellectuals from throughout the country, from threadbare bohemians to university professors.'

Madrid's population was by this time over 300,000. Steps were finally taken for it to break out of its old walls, and in 1860 a plan by Carlos María de Castro was approved for the *Ensanche* ('extension') of Madrid, in an orderly grid pattern to the north and east (*see page 81*). However, as with earlier rebuilding, the plan came up against the chronic lack of large-scale local investors. The only major development undertaken quickly was the section of Calle Serrano bought up by the flamboyant speculator the Marqués de Salamanca, whose name was given to the whole district. Moreover, even he was unable to sell many properties to Madrid's conservative-minded upper classes at a viable price.

Meanwhile, the political situation was deteriorating once again, after a long period of conservative rule that began in 1856. Isabel II had become deeply unpopular, surrounded by an aura of sleaze and scandal. In September 1868, yet another military revolt deposed the government and, this time, the Queen as well.

There followed six years of turmoil. The provisional government invited an Italian prince, Amadeo of Savoy, to be King of a truly constitutional monarchy. However, in December 1870 General Prim, strongman of the new regime, was assassinated. Carlist revolts broke out in some parts of the country, while on the left new, more radical groups appeared. At the end of 1868 a meeting in Madrid addressed by Giuseppe Fanelli, an Italian associate of Bakunin, led to the founding of the first

anarchist group in Spain. The *Cortes* itself was riven by factions, and Amadeo decided to give up the struggle and go back to Italy.

On 12 February 1873 Spain became a Republic. Rightist resistance became stronger than ever, while many towns were taken over by left-wing juntas, who declared them autonomous 'cantons', horrifying conservative opinion. To keep control, Republican governments relied increasingly on the army. This proved fatal, and, on 3 January 1874 the army commander in Madrid, General Pavía, marched into the Cortes, sent its members home, and installed a military dictatorship.

THE RESTORATION

At the end of 1874 the army decided to restore the Bourbon dynasty, in the shape of Alfonso XII (1874-85), son of Isabel II. The architect of the Restoration regime, however, was a civilian politician, Antonio Cánovas del Castillo. He established the system of *turno pacífico* or peaceful alternation in power between a Conservative Party, led by himself, and a Liberal Party made up of former progressives. Their readiness to co-operate with each other was based in a shared fear of the social tensions visible during the previous six years. The control of these 'dynastic parties' over the political system was made sure by election-rigging and occasional repression.

In the late 1870s the wealthy of Madrid set out on a building boom. They finally overcame their reluctance to leave the old city, and the Salamanca area became the new centre of fashionable life. Most of the district's new apartment blocks had lifts, first seen in Madrid in 1874. In earlier blocks upper floors had been let cheaply, so that rich and poor had often continued to live side by side. With lifts, however, a top floor could be as desirable as a first, and this kind of class mixing faded.

Government and official bodies, too, undertook a huge round of new building. The **Banco de España**, the **Bolsa**, the main railway stations and even the municipal markets are all creations of the 1880s. Madrid also acquired a larger professional middle class, with many more doctors, engineers, journalists and architects. It attracted intellectuals from throughout the country, from the threadbare bohemians seen in the plays of Valle-Inclán, always on the lookout for something to pawn, to professors at the university, transferred to Madrid from Alcalá de Henares in 1836.

Madrid was also receiving an influx of poor migrants from rural Spain, with over 200,000 new arrivals between 1874 and 1900. The main work available for them was in building, for men, and domestic service for women.

The café era

Madrid's first true cafés appeared in the years after the Napoleonic invasion. Similar places were opening all across Europe at the time, but in few cities did they take on so much importance as in Madrid, a city where, as Pérez Galdós wrote in his novel *Tormento*, 'going for a stroll counted as an occupation'. As the writer Lorenzo Díaz has put it, 'the whole of Madrileño life in the 19th century revolved around the café'.

As well as for 'café society' in general, Madrid's cafés were the venues for *tertulias*. A *tertulia* is an informal gathering of friends to talk, differing from a simple chat in that it keeps roughly to a topic. It can be held anywhere, from a shop to a park bench. The first true literary and intellectual *tertulia* in Madrid, however, is considered to be the one that met in the Café del Príncipe, in the street of the same name, and was attended by Romantic writers such as Larra, Espronceda and Tomás Bretón. Based in a very Spanish love of talk for its own sake, *tertulias* became ever more central to the cultural life of Madrid as the 19th century went on. Their true golden age, though, was in the years between the 1874 Restoration and the Civil War.

Most of the writers of Spain's 'Silver Age' had a regular *tertulia*, and any new arrival in the city could soon find out exactly where

they had to go to find the main figures of the day and hear them hold forth on matters sacred and profane. Some figures were better known for their part in *tertulias* than anything else. A legendary character of pre-1936 Madrid was Ramón Gómez de la Serna, who presided over the gathering at the Café Pombo in Calle Carretas, credited with introducing surrealism into Spain and attended by Buñuel and García Lorca.

The real *tertulia* tradition was severely damaged by the Civil War, although a trace of it can be found in Camilo José Cela's 1940s novel *La Colmena*. A huge number of Madrid's classic cafés also disappeared between the 1950s and '70s, but a few, such as the **Gijón** and the **Comercial** (see pages 154, 157) still survive.

Economic growth was reflected in the appearance of yet more small workshops rather than factories. There were also many with next to no work, and the 1880s saw the beginning of a worsening housing crisis, with the growth around Madrid of shanty towns, regarded with fear by respectable opinion.

One of the many remedies put forward made Madrid the site of a curiously modern experiment in planning, the *Ciudad Lineal* or 'Linear City', proposed in the 1890s by the engineer Arturo Soria. His idea was that new housing should be organised around a means of transport, the railway line along Calle Alcalá. Each area would consist of small houses with gardens, of different sizes for residents of different incomes, thus ensuring social homogeneity. However, few affluent residents were ever drawn to the *Ciudad Lineal*.

Despite this poverty, the established order seemed in little danger in the first decades of the Restoration. The events of 1868-74 had discredited the old Romantic idea of the unity of

the people in pursuit of democracy. In 1879 the Spanish Socialist Party, the PSOE, was founded in the Casa Labra taberna (*see page 137*). Nevertheless, for a long time the level of agitation in the capital was very limited.

THE SILVER AGE

Just before the end of the century, however, the preconceptions on which Spanish political life had been based received a shattering blow. The Restoration regime presented itself as having returned the country to stability and some prestige in the world. In the 1890s, however, Spain was involved in colonial wars against nationalists in Cuba and the Philippines. In 1898, the government allowed itself to be manoeuvred into war with the United States. In a few weeks, almost the entire Spanish navy was sunk, and Spain lost virtually all its remaining overseas territories.

Known simply as 'The Disaster', this was a devastating blow to Spain's self-confidence. The regime itself was revealed as a decrepit, incompetent state, based on a feeble economy. Among intellectuals, this sparked off an intense round of self-examination and discussion of Spain's relationship with the very concept of modernity. Politically, it signalled the beginning of the end of the cosy settlement of 1874.

Although the intellectual debates of this time centred on Spain's apparent inability to deal with the modern world, the problems of the regime were not due to the country being backward. Rather, they spiralled out of control because after 1900 the country entered an unprecedented period of change.

Sudden economic expansion was set off by three main factors. One, ironically, was the loss of the colonies, which led to large amounts of capital being brought back to the country. Most important was World War I, which provided unheard-of opportunities for neutral Spain in the supply of goods to the Allied powers. Then, during the worldwide boom of the 1920s, Spain benefited hugely from foreign investment.

Within a few years Spain had one of the fastest rates of urbanisation in the world. The economic upheaval caused by the world war led to runaway inflation, spurring a massive movement into the cities. Madrid did not grow as rapidly as industrial Barcelona, which had become the largest city in the country. Nevertheless, after taking four centuries to reach half a million, it doubled its population again in only 30 years, to just under a million by 1930. Only 37 per cent of its people had been born in the city.

The most visible manifestation of this growth was a still-larger building boom. Bombastic creations such as the **Palacio de Comunicaciones** were symptomatic of the expansive mood. Most important was the opening of the **Gran Vía** in 1910, a project that had first been discussed 25 years previously, which would transform the heart of the old city with a new grand thoroughfare for entertainment, business and banking.

Another fundamental innovation was electricity. The city's trams were electrified in 1898, and the first Metro line, between Sol and Cuatro Caminos, opened in 1919. Electricity allowed Madrid, far from any other source of power, finally to experience an industrial take-off in the years after 1910. It was still far behind Barcelona as an industrial city, but was much more important as a base for major banks. Larger companies and new industries brought with them more aggressive styles of working, and a more industrial working class. Many lived in shabby slum districts in the outskirts, or 'misery-villes' of shanties that mushroomed around the city. At the same time, expansion in banking and office work was also reflected in the large number of white-collar workers.

Madrid was also, more than ever, the mecca for intellectuals and professionals from around the country. This was the background to the enormous vigour of the city's intellectual life at this time, the 'Silver Age' of Spanish literature. From writers of 1898 such as Antonio Machado and Baroja to the poets of the 1927 generation, Rafael Alberti and García Lorca, the city welcomed an extraordinary succession of literary talent, and painters, scientists and historians. From the 1910s onward –and despite a relatively lax dictatorship in the 1920s – Madrid's cafés were full of talk, forums for discussion multiplied, and any number of newspapers and magazines were published. The sheer range of activity was remarkable, above all by comparison with the near silence that fell upon the city in the 1940s.

In politics, this urban expansion made it impossible for the 'dynastic parties' to control elections in the way they were able to do in small towns and rural areas. In 1910, a Republican-Socialist coalition won elections in Madrid for the first time. Tensions came to a head in 1917, with a general strike throughout the country. In the following years the main focus of conflict was in Barcelona, where virtual urban guerrilla warfare broke out between the anarchist workers' union the CNT and employers and the State. In 1923 the Captain-General of Barcelona, General Primo de Rivera, suspended the constitution and declared himself Dictator, under King Alfonso XIII.

In Madrid, this was first greeted with relative indifference. However, by his action Primo de Rivera had discredited the King and the old dynastic parties, without putting anything in their place. A widespread movement against the monarchy developed in the '20s, based in a sentiment that a society that felt increasingly mature should not have a ramshackle, discredited government imposed upon it.

In 1930 Primo de Rivera resigned, exhausted. The King appointed another soldier, General Berenguer, as new Prime Minister. In an attempt to move back towards some form of constitutional rule, the government decided to hold local elections on 12 April 1931. They were not expected to be a referendum on the monarchy. However, when the results came in it was seen that republican candidates had won sweeping majorities in all of Spain's cities.

THE SECOND REPUBLIC

On 14 April 1931, as the results of the local elections became clear, the streets of Spain's cities filled with people. In Madrid, a jubilant mass converged on the Puerta del Sol. It was these exultant crowds in the streets that drove the King to abdicate and spurred republican politicians into action, for they had never expected their opportunity to arrive so soon.

The second Spanish Republic arrived amid huge optimism, expressing the frustrated hopes of decades. Among the many schemes of its first government, a Republican-Socialist coalition, was a project for Madrid, the *Gran Madrid* or 'Greater Madrid' plan, intended to integrate the sprawling new areas around the city's edge. A key part of it was the extension of the Castellana, then blocked by a racecourse above Calle Joaquín Costa. This was demolished, and the Castellana was allowed to snake endlessly northward, forming one of the modern city's most distinctive features. Also completed under the Republic was the last section of the Gran Vía, from Callao to Plaza de España, site of Madrid's best art deco architecture.

Possibilities of further change and renovation, however, would be entangled in the accelerating social crisis that overtook the Republic. The new regime aroused expectations difficult to live up to at the best of times. Instead, its arrival coincided with the onset of the world-wide depression. Moreover, Spain's own partly unreal 1920s boom had exceeded the real capacity of the country's economy. Activity slowed down, and unemployment spread.

At the same time, labour agitation and republican legislation brought wage increases for those in work. This caused panic among many employers, who became easy fodder for a belligerent, resurgent right. The optimistic harmony of April 1931 broke down. Tension was even more intense in the countryside, where agrarian reform was bogged down by conservative opposition.

As frustration grew among workers, tendencies grew apace that called for the end of republican compromise in a second, social, revolution, especially the anarchist CNT and the Communist Party. Even the Socialist Party was radicalised. On the right, similarly, the loudest voices – such as the fascist Falange, founded in 1933 by José Antonio Primo de Rivera, son of the former dictator – demanded authoritarian rule as the only means of preserving social order. The vogue for extremism was fed by the mood of the times, in which Nazism, Italian Fascism and Soviet Communism appeared as the most dynamic international models.

In 1933 the coalition between Socialists and liberal republicans broke up. With the left split, elections were won by conservative republicans backed by the CEDA, a parliamentary but authoritarian right-wing party. Reform seemed to come to a dead halt. In October 1934 the CEDA demanded to have ministers in the government, and a general strike was called in response. It was strongest in the mining region of Asturias, where it was savagely suppressed by army units commanded by a rising general called Francisco Franco.

Left-wing parties were subjected to a wave of repression that radicalised their supporters still further. In new elections in February 1936, however, the left, united once again in the *Frente Popular* (Popular Front), were victorious. In Madrid the Front won 54 per cent of the vote.

A liberal-republican government returned to power, with Manuel Azaña as President. By this time, however, the level of polarisation and of sheer hatred in the country was moving out of control. Right-wing politicians called almost openly for the army to save the country. The military had already laid their plans for a coup.

WAR, REVOLUTION & SIEGE

On 18 July the Generals made their move, with risings all over Spain, while German and Italian aircraft ferried Franco's colonial army from Spanish Morocco to Andalusia. In Madrid, troops failed to seize the city and barricaded themselves inside the Montaña barracks, the site of which is now in the Parque del Oeste.

The coup was the spark for an explosion of tension. The workers' parties demanded arms. On 20 July, as news came that the army had been defeated in Barcelona and many other cities, the Montaña was stormed and its defenders massacred, despite the efforts of political leaders to prevent it.

'Among left-wing militants the mood was ecstatic: factories, schools and public services were all taken over.'

With the right apparently defeated, Madrid underwent a revolution. Among left-wing militants the mood was ecstatic: factories, schools, the transport system and other public services were all taken over, and although the government remained in place it had little effective power. Among right-wingers trapped in the city, feelings were naturally very different. The aristocrat Agustín de Foxá wrote that 'it wasn't Spain any more. In the Gran Vía, in Alcalá, the mob had camped out.' Ad-hoc militias and patrols were the only power on the streets, and, amid the paranoia and hatred that were the other side of revolutionary excitement, summary executions of suspected rightists were common.

Meanwhile, the war still had to be fought. During the summer fighting mostly consisted of skirmishes in the Guadarrama. A far more serious threat was approaching, however, in the shape of Franco's regular troops, advancing from Seville preceded by stories of reprisals more terrible than anything done by the 'red terror' in Madrid. The militias seemed powerless to stop them.

Defeat for the Republic seemed inevitable. German planes bombed the city. On 6 November, Franco's advance guard were in the outskirts, and the government left for Valencia, a move widely seen as desertion.

Without a government, however, a new resolve was seen in the city. In the southern suburbs the troops were resisted street by street. Women, children, the old and the unmilitary joined in building trenches and barricades, and comparisons were immediately drawn with 2 May 1808. On 9 November the first foreign volunteers, the International Brigades, arrived, doing wonders for morale. Madrid, the Imperial Court, had become the front line of international democracy. After savage fighting, above all in the Ciudad Universitaria, Franco halted the frontal assault on Madrid in late November 1936.

Madrid saw little more direct fighting. From the Casa de Campo, where the remains of trenches and bunkers still exist today, the army settled in to a siege. Attempts to push them back north and south of Madrid were unsuccessful. The city was regularly bombed, and bombarded by artillery, who took their sights from the Gran Vía, 'Howitzer Avenue'.

People adapted to the situation. One could go to war by tram, and combatants were taken their lunch on the line along the Gran Vía. Right-wingers were scarcely harassed after the first few months. The siege, however, ground down the spirit of November 1936. Shortages were acute; particularly terrible was the severe winter of 1937-8, when doors and furniture were burnt for fuel. The powerful role established by the Communists, won through the Republic's dependence on the Soviet Union as its only source of arms, alienated many who were not Party supporters.

Franco, meanwhile, was advancing on other fronts. During 1937 his forces overran the Basque Country and Asturias, and in March 1938 they reached the Mediterranean near Castellón. In January 1939 they conquered Catalonia. In Madrid, fighting broke out behind Republican lines between the Communists, committed to fight to the end, and groups who wanted to negotiate a settlement with Franco. Those in favour of negotiation won, but found Franco with no intention to compromise. On 28 March the Nationalist army entered Madrid.

THE LONG DICTATORSHIP

Madrid emerged from the Civil War physically and psychologically battered. Throughout the city, hundreds of buildings stood in ruins. Buildings, however, could be rebuilt fairly quickly; healing the damage done to the city's spirit would take decades.

Vultures over Madrid, by John Heartfield.

The Madrid of the 1940s was the sombre antithesis of the expansive city of ten years previously, or its current outgoing, vivacious self. A great many Madrileños had lost someone close to them, to bombs, bullets, firing squads or prison camps. The black market rather than art and literature dominated café conversation, and the figures of earlier years were mostly in exile, or keeping indoors.

The existence of 'two Spains' (right-left, traditional-liberal, rich poor) was all too apparent. As the victors marched in they wasted no time in rounding up members (or just suspected sympathisers) of 'enemy' groups, anarchists, Communists, union members and liberals. Some were turned in by neighbours, which created a sordid atmosphere of bitterness and distrust. During the early '40s, while the rest of the world was wrapped up in World War II, thousands were executed in Spain. Others paid the price of defeat by serving as forced labour on fascist landmarks such as the **Valle de los Caídos**, Franco's vast victory monument and tomb (*see page 251*).

Madrid's loyalty to the Republic almost led to it losing its capital status, as voices were raised calling for a more 'loyal' city to represent the country. Franco actually went to Seville to look into the feasibility of moving the capital there. Tradition and financial interests bore more weight, however, and the capital stayed put.

The Falange, official party of the regime, produced extravagant plans to turn Madrid into a Spanish version of Imperial Rome, along the lines of schemes drawn up by Albert Speer for Hitler. However, a dire lack of funding and galloping inflation scotched all but a few of these nouveau-Imperialist notions (*see page 34* **Franquista kitsch**). The economy was in a desperate state, and Spain went through a period of extreme hardship, the *años del hambre* or 'hunger years'. Many people remember not having eaten properly for ten years after 1936. This poverty also led to the phenomenon that would most shape the face of Madrid in the post-war decades: massive immigration from Spain's rural provinces.

Madrid has grown faster than any other European capital this century. A 'big village' of just over half a million at the turn of the century, and 950,000 in 1930, it passed the three million mark by 1970.

Until the 1950s, migrants arriving in Madrid found few real opportunities for work, in an economy that was internationally isolated and excluded from Marshall Aid and the other reconstruction packages of post-war Europe. After 1945 many in Spain and abroad assumed that the Franco regime would shortly go the way of its former friends in Germany and Italy.

Most European countries continued to shun the regime, at least in public, but in 1953, as the Cold War intensified, Franco was saved by the US government's 'our son-of-a-bitch' policy in choosing allies. A co-operation treaty gave the regime renewed credibility and cash in exchange for air and sea bases on Spanish soil, and later President Eisenhower flew in to shake the dictator's hand.

For those not devoted to the regime, life under Franco was often a matter of keeping one's head down and getting on with things. Football and other means of escapism played an enormous part in people's lives. The late 1950s were the golden years of Real Madrid, whose successes were loudly trumpeted to boost the prestige of the regime.

The national Stabilisation Plan of 1959 gave the fundamental push to Madrid's development, and brought Spain definitively back into the Western fold. Drawn up by technocrats from the Catholic lay organisation the Opus Dei, the plan revolutionised the country's economy, and especially that of the Madrid region. In the 1960s, tourism began to pump money into Spain, and Madrid trebled in size to became an industrial powerhouse. Quiet tree-lined boulevards were widened to make way for cars, and elegant Castellana palaces were replaced by glass-sheathed monoliths. Madrid took on much more of the look, and feel, of a big city.

Francoist style: a parade in the 1940s.

A NEW ERA

In the 1960s, too, opposition to the regime revived in the shape of labour unrest, while in the north the Basque organisation ETA was becoming active. The oil crisis of 1973 coincided with the assassination by ETA of Franco's Prime Minister, Admiral Carrero Blanco, when a bomb planted beneath a Madrid street launched his car right over a five-storey building. The regime, weakened by labour and student protests, now had to deal with rising unemployment, inflation and a moribund Franco. The transition to democracy had begun.

Franco died in November 1975, closing a parenthesis of nearly 40 years in Spanish history. A new age, uncertain but exciting, dawned. In July 1976 King Juan Carlos, chosen by Franco to succeed him, named a former Falange bureaucrat, Adolfo Suárez, as Prime Minister. Nobody, however, knew quite what was going to happen.

To widespread surprise, Suárez initiated a comprehensive programme of political reform. Clandestine opposition leaders surfaced, parties were legalised and famous exiles began coming home. The first democratic elections since 1936 were held in June 1977, and a constitution was approved in late 1978. Suárez' centrist UCD (Centre-Democratic Union) won the national elections, but local elections in Madrid in 1979 were won by the Socialists, led by Enrique Tierno Galván as Mayor.

The 'other' Spain, though, had not disappeared, and was getting nervous. Hard-core Francoists were horrified at the thought of Socialists and/or Communists coming to power.

Many of the 'old guard' still held influential positions in the armed forces, and were not inclined to give them up easily.

On 23 February 1981 democrats' worst nightmares appeared to come true when a Civil Guard colonel called Tejero burst into the Cortes with a squad of men, firing his pistol into the air. Tanks were in the streets in Valencia, and there was uncertainty everywhere. In Madrid, however, troops stayed in their barracks. A little after midnight, King Juan Carlos appeared on TV and assured the country that the army had sworn him its allegiance and that the coup attempt would fail. The next day, people poured onto the streets to demonstrate support for freedom and democracy.

The wolf had shown his teeth, but they were not as sharp as had been feared. Moreover, the coup attempt helped significantly to win Felipe González and the socialist PSOE their landslide victory in the elections of November 1982.

'The *Movida* was simply the discovery by young Spaniards that they could have the party right here.'

The late 1970s and early '80s saw the arrival of democracy and free speech, the decriminalisation of drug use and the breakdown of old sexual conventions. Long-repressed creative impulses were released. The compulsorily staid Madrid of earlier years gave way to an anything-goes, vivacious city: an explosion of art, counter-culture and nightlife, creativity and frivolity that was known as the *Movida* – very roughly translatable as 'Shift' or 'Movement'.

Madrid's *Movida* propelled some to international fame, such as fashion designer Sybilla, artists like Ouka Lele and, above all, Pedro Almodóvar, who began making films in clubs. For many, though, the *Movida* was simply the discovery by young Spaniards that, after decades in which their country had seemed a hostile place it was best to get out of, they could have the party right here.

The Socialists used control of Madrid's Ayuntamiento – led by the very fondly remembered Tierno Galván – to renovate the city's infrastructure, with long-overdue facelifts in squares and parks. Mayor Tierno also provided unprecedented support for all sorts of progressive causes and the arts, and launched a whole string of new festivals.

If Tierno Galván's local administration was happy to be regarded as godfathers to the *Movida*, the national government of Felipe González was still more eager to be seen as leaders of a reborn country. Decades of international isolation ended with Spain's entry into the European Community in 1986. This had a near-immediate effect on the economy, and in the late '80s the country was the fastest-growing member of the EU. The González governments achieved major improvements in some areas – health, the transport system – but frustrated the expectations of many of their supporters, often giving the impression they believed modernisation would solve all Spain's problems more or less by itself.

The apotheosis of the country's transition was the 'Year of Spain' in 1992, with the Barcelona Olympics, Expo '92 in Seville and, least successful of the three, Madrid's year as Cultural Capital of Europe. Afterwards, a different mood became apparent. Spain's boom pre-'92 had postponed the effects of the international downturn at the end of the '80s, but it hit Madrid with a vengeance in 1993. Breakneck growth had created its own problems, and land speculation sent property prices through the roof. At the same time, the Socialists, inseparable from the boom, began to be dragged down by a staggering stream of revelations of corruption.

Disenchantment with the Socialists and a newly cautious mood that followed the brash over-confidence of the boom years were major factors behind the rise of the re-formed right of the *Partido Popular* (PP). Even before Spain's great year, in 1991, the PSOE had lost control of the Madrid city administration to the PP.

Tony Blair and **José María Aznar** confer.

BUSINESS AS USUAL?

The 1990s in Spain were markedly different in feel and content from the preceding decade. Led by the deliberately bland José María Aznar, the *Partido Popular* ably connected with the groundswell of discontent provoked by the later years of Socialist administrations. In the 1993 election Felipe González, long the great survivor of Spanish politics, lost his overall majority, but staggered on for another three years by means of a pact with Catalan nationalists. Next time, however, in 1996, the winners were the PP, even though they too still had to rely on pacts with minority parties to be able to form a sustainable government. The PSOE was sent into opposition for the first time in 14 years.

In Madrid the PP had already made its mark on local life. Having rallied voters by denouncing the sleaze and corruption that overwhelmed the PSOE and the Socialists' irresponsible – as many saw it – spending of taxpayers' money, the PP felt it had a clear mandate to cut back and balance the books. In Madrid, this meant cuts in budgets for arts festivals, a tightening up on licences for new bars and clubs and a general attack on the supposed excesses of the nightlife scene. The mayor, José María Alvarez de Manzano, also lays much stress on encouraging traditional Spanish culture. In another field, the PP city administration has greatly concerned itself with traffic, embarking on a giant programme of tunnel and car-park construction.

Key events

c860 Madrid founded during the reign of Emir Mohammed I of Córdoba.
1085-6 Alfonso VI of Castile conquers Toledo and Madrid.
1109 Madrid besieged by Moorish army.
1202 Madrid given *Fuero* (Statutes); population c3,000.
1212 Battle of Navas de Tolosa: decisive defeat of Moslems in Spain.
1309 First Cortes held in Madrid.
c1360 King Pedro the Cruel rebuilds the Alcázar of Madrid.
1476 Isabella becomes unchallenged Queen of Castile after battle of Toro.
1492 Conquest of Granada; expulsion of Jews from Spain; Discovery of America.
1520-1 Madrid joins Comuneros revolt.
1547 Birth of Cervantes, in Alcalá de Henares.
1561 Philip II moves Court to Madrid from Toledo; population c20,000.
1562 Lope de Vega born in Madrid.
1563-84 Building of El Escorial
1566 Beginning of Dutch Revolt
1574 First permanent theatre opened in Madrid, the *Corral de la Pacheca*.
1588 Defeat of the Armada against England.
1599-1600 Plague and famine throughout Castile.
1601-6 Court moved to Valladolid.
1605, 1615 Don Quijote published, in two parts.
1609 Expulsion of the former Muslims, the *Moriscos*, from the whole of Spain.
1617-9 Completion of Plaza Mayor.
1632-40 Buen Retiro palace built; population of Madrid c150-170,000.

1640 Revolts break out in Portugal and Catalonia.
1643 Battle of Rocroi: Spanish army in Flanders decisively defeated by the French.
1660 Death of Velázquez.
1665 Philip IV succeeded by Charles II, aged four.
1700 Charles II dies without an heir.
1701-14 War of the Spanish Succession: Philip V, first Bourbon King of Spain. Population of Madrid c100,000.
1715 Decree of *Nova Planta*; Spain created as one state.
1734 Alcázar of Madrid destroyed by fire.
1761 Charles III bans waste dumping in Madrid streets.
1775-82 Paseo del Prado created.
1778 Goya moves to Madrid from Aragon.
1800 Population of Madrid c180,000.
1808-12 Madrid under French occupation.
1812 Cortes in Cádiz agrees first Spanish constitution; disastrous famine in Madrid.
1814 Fernando VII abrogates constitution.
1810-24 Latin American Wars of Independence.
1820 Military coup begins three years of liberal rule.
1823 French army restores Fernando VII to full power.
1833 Carlist Wars begin on death of Fernando VII; constitutional government established in Madrid, with limited powers.
1836 Main decree on Disentailment of Monasteries; University of Alcalá de Henares moved to Madrid.
1851 Railway line to Aranjuez inaugurated.
1854-62 Puerta del Sol rebuilt.

Leading figures in the arts bemoan what they see as the PP's philistine approach to culture, and residents' groups protest vociferously about the havoc caused by interminable roadworks, but many people have applauded these changes. It has long been thrown in the face of the PP by those to its left that the Party is directly descended from the Franco regime, and the PP's more extreme supporters do occasionally show their heads. Aznar, however, constantly emphasises his image as a practical, modernising, non-ideological, 'managerial' prime minister, and in EU affairs his closest ally is Mr Tony Blair. That the dire warnings about the PP no longer bore much electoral weight was born out in the elections of March 2000, which saw Aznar swept back to power with an overall majority, and left the PSOE and other left-wing parties in complete disarray.

The macroeconomic numbers show Spain's economy as booming, and the PP has adroitly cultivated its image as the Party that looks as if it knows how globalisation and the future will work, another vital factor in convincing voters to back them. The Socialists, meanwhile, remain in the midst of a profound identity crisis, shocked at the electoral appeal of conservative policies that they themselves had in many ways encouraged. In Madrid, the PP's Mayor Alvarez de Manzano, despite being seen as a joke by much of the press, will continue to run the city in his old-fashioned style until at least 2003.

1858 Canal de Isabel II water system inaugurated.
1860 Plan for *Ensanche* of Madrid approved.
1868 Revolution overthrows Isabel II.
1871 Amadeo of Savoy becomes King of Spain. First trams in Madrid, drawn by mules.
1872 Population of Madrid 334,000.
1873 February: Amadeo abdicates; Republic declared.
1874 January: Republic becomes military dictatorship after coup. December: Alfonso XII declared King.
1879 Spanish Socialist Party (PSOE) founded.
1898 Spanish-American War: disaster for Spain. Madrid's tramlines electrified.
1900 Population of Madrid 539,835.
1907 First registration of motor vehicles in Madrid.
1910 Building of Gran Vía initiated.
1917 General Strike in the whole of Spain.
1919 First Madrid Metro line opened.
1923 Primo de Rivera establishes a dictatorship
1929-31 Barajas airport opened.
1930 Fall of Primo de Rivera; Madrid's population officially 952,832.
1931 14 April: Proclamation of the Second Spanish Republic.
1931-3 *Gran Madrid* plan approved.
1934 October: General Strike against entry of right-wing ministers into government, bloodily suppressed in Asturias by General Franco.

1936 February: elections won by Popular Front; 18 July: military uprising against left-wing government; 9 November: Francoist forces launch assault on Madrid.
1939 1 April: Franco declares war over.
1946-50 UN imposes sanctions on Spain.
1953 Co-operation treaty with USA.
1950-60 Population of Madrid passes two million.
1959 Stabilisation Plan opens up Spanish economy.
1961 First violent attack by Basque nationalists of ETA.
1970 Juan Carlos declared Franco's successor; population of Madrid 3,146,000.
1975 20 November: Death of Franco.
1977 15 June: First democratic general election.
1979 April: Enrique Tierno Galván, elected Socialist Mayor of Madrid.
1980 Pedro Almodóvar's first feature, *Pepi, Luci, Bom, y otras chicas del montón.*
1982 Socialists win national elections.
1986 1 January: Spain joins the European Community.
1991 Popular Party takes over Madrid city council.
1992 Madrid, European City of Culture; Barcelona Olympics; Expo '92 in Seville.
1996 *Partido Popular* wins power in central government in Spain-wide elections.
2000 *Partido Popular* re-elected with overall majority.

Madrid Today

Citadel of tradition, city of café life and literature…
but Madrid is changing fast.

In its time Madrid has seen periods of great change, and spells of relative demographic, economic and cultural stagnation. The dawn of the new Millennium finds it once again in ebullition, undergoing a series of crucial changes, some apparent, others less so, that could transform its fibre radically.

The city is becoming more like its counterpart European capitals, both in terms of an ever-more cosmopolitan population and in the growth of new suburbs. Only a decade or so ago, Madrid was one of the 'whitest' and most homogeneous capitals anywhere. Nowadays Africans, Latin Americans and Asians are very much in evidence (*see page 29* **New faces in town**). Strangely, Spain is not an obvious candidate to receive large numbers of immigrants, as unemployment nationally stands at around fifteen per cent.

This figure is, though, misleading, as it includes all persons registered as out of work, not necessarily those genuinely looking for it. One explanation for this paradoxical situation is that, after two decades in which modern Spanish families have been notably obsessed with education, young people here have very high expectations, and are often ready to wait rather than take something that doesn't match their qualifications. Immigrant labour finds its way into those areas of the economy to which Spanish

workers no longer have any pretensions – low-paid, physical work where safety regulations, work contracts and rights are frequently ignored.

Neighbourhoods such as Lavapiés, with a lot of old, sometimes substandard housing at low rents, are increasingly multicultural. For many Madrileños this is exciting, something that's enriching their city; for others it's profoundly unfamiliar, a threat to the character of the place.

WELCOME TO THE 'BURBS

Less apparent to visitors, who naturally tend to spend their time amid the attractions of the old centre, is the rapid growth of suburbia. This is one more apparent paradox in a city with zero population growth and an ageing population. Previously, Madrid has never been a 'doughnut' city like so many in northern Europe and North America, with a centre largely vacated at night; it still isn't, but the tendency has visibly arrived.

Suburban sprawl is certainly related in part to the prohibitive price of buying properties within Madrid itself. It could also be that the current phenomenal building boom in outer Madrid can be partially explained by a rush to put hitherto undeclared savings into something more solid than cash before the upheaval that will come with the arrival of the Euro in 2002. *El País* and *El Mundo* both carry fat property supplements each week, with endless pages on new out-of-town developments. 'Quality of life', represented by a new house with garden in a leafy, tranquil setting is the bait, and plenty of young Madrileño professionals are more than willing to take it up. Many are ever-less inclined to take on an old flat in the city, wanting, as they do, everything to be new and in working order when they move in.

These developments lead, implicitly, to an Anglo-American, car-based way of life, with all the trappings such as shopping malls, ring-road cinema complexes and so on. And, places like Aravaca, or especially Pozuelo (pictured, *page 28*), to the west of the Casa de Campo, already have some of the biggest malls and multiplexes in Europe. Quite what the implications are for the social fabric in all this is anybody's guess. Spaniards are used to seeing their culture as very solid, and often think they can always carry it with them. However, this is also a society where people have been used to living on top of one another, and where a big part of daily interaction has involved spending time in big groups. How this will carry over into the relative isolation of suburban living remains to be seen.

POLICY

These changes, of course, have much to do with the political and economic context. The pegging of the peseta to the low-valued Euro suits Spanish exporters as much as it does visiting tourists and outside investors. José María Aznar's *Partido Popular* government has been keen to claim responsibility for this success, and attribute it to their globalising agenda – flexible labour legislation, economic liberalisation, privatisation. Deregulation of the labour market certainly favours the contracting of immigrant labour, and globalisation also encourages the adoption of lifestyles previously seen as foreign.

The same party has also dominated municipal politics in Madrid for over a decade. Turnout in recent local elections has been very low, and opposition is vociferous but ineffective. Many complain about the council's cultural policy, or the apparently futile crusade against nightlife, but the opposition lacks a clear alternative agenda. Much criticism centres on Mayor Álvarez de Manzano, given to verbal incontinence when he airs his views on issues such as immigration or domestic violence. Perhaps, though, his homespun prejudices reflect the views of more people than his opponents care to admit.

At the same time, for all these changes, many of the facets of life that make Madrid unique remain, and for ordinary Madrileños getting on with life, in spite of all the globalising influences, remains the order of the day. Café and bar culture, the *marcha* or 'scene' – often the aspects of life here that most impress visitors – are still very much in evidence. 'Doughnutting' may be in the air, but Madrid's old centre with its narrow streets is still a lively and lived-in place, buzzing with streetlife all year round. It will take a lot really to change it.

New faces in town

Spain has been a country of emigrants, and in Madrid 'immigrant' used to refer to incomers from elsewhere in Spain. This has changed radically since 1995, as citizens from the world over, impelled by economic desperation or conflict in their own countries, have come in search of a perhaps illusory Spanish El Dorado.

With a very low birth-rate, Spain does need new hands, and the annual quota of 25,000 work and residency permits falls far short of the demands of the economy. The flow goes on illegally. Maghrebis and West Africans resort to precarious boats in dramatic attempts to cross the Gibraltar straits, frequently with a tragic outcome. Eastern Europeans get in on tourist visas and stay, often hoping to move on to the US or Canada. Others, from Andean countries, the Dominican Republic or the Phillipines come with visas to work in domestic service.

Officially, non-EU immigrants still make up only 1.9 per cent of the region's population, but the real figure is much higher. The signs are everywhere. Adverts for Money-Gram are in Rumanian and Cyrillic script, Afro-Caribbean hairdressers' shops are ever-more common and phone centres offering 'Colombia 67ptas min' are ubiquitous. Africans and Bulgarians schlep gas bottles up apartment blocks, Peruvian women look after middle-class kids, Moroccans dig holes in the roads and many Chinese run 'Todo a 100' shops (see page 161).

Reactions to this new phenomenon run the gamut, via downright hostile and grudgingly accepting. The activities of a gang of homeless Maghrebi teenagers who appeared, without any other family members, in Lavapiés and were responsible for a spate of muggings, have given a bad reputation to a whole community. African women are often assumed to be prostitutes, Rumanian Gypsies scroungers. At an institutional level, the authorities are aware they have a problem, and precious little experience. How Madrid as a whole faces up to this new situation will be a big challenge.

Architecture

Grey-slate pointed spires, neo-Moorish brickwork, art deco flourishes: Madrid's architectural mix is as quirky as the city itself.

Visitors familiar with the architectural splendours of other European cities can be disappointed by Madrid. Eleven centuries of history, along with the city's one-time status as hub of an immense empire, are only palely reflected in the modern metropolis. Constrained by its walls until the 1860s, Madrid rebuilt itself so many times over the top of existing constructions that by the late 19th century it was pretty much a modern city.

Madrid has a special history, and its architecture shows a very individual, eccentric mixture of styles. Traces survive of most of its past epochs – periods of Moorish, Flemish, Italian, French and American influence are all reflected to a greater or lesser degree. A 'typical' Madrileño architectural identity is hard to find, but the city can claim one, typically unusual, style as its own, neo-*mudéjar* (*see page 33* **Moorish fantasies**). Also, Madrid has many monuments that are complete one-offs.

SMALL-TOWN MADRID

To start at the beginning, a segment of the **Muralla Arabe**, the first town wall built by the Moors, can be found on Cuesta de la Vega, near the Almudena cathedral. Some remains of the original Muslim fortress are also now being excavated next to the **Palacio Real**.

For centuries after they were conquered from their Moorish rulers, Madrid and most of Castile continued to have large populations of Muslims living under Christian rule, the *Mudéjares*. The Castilian monarchs were greatly in thrall to their superior building skills, especially in bricklaying and tiling, and throughout the Middle Ages many of the country's most important buildings were built using techniques and styles that had originated in Muslim Andalusia. Hallmarks of the *Mudéjar* style are Moorish arches and intricate geometric patterns in brickwork, which can be seen on the 12th-century tower of Madrid's oldest surviving church, **San Nicolás de las Servitas**, built by Arab craftsmen (the body of the church was later rebuilt). Madrid's other *Mudéjar* tower, on **San Pedro el Viejo**, was built 200 years later in the 14th century.

Other medieval buildings in Madrid, such as the 15th-century Torre de los Lujanes in **Plaza de la Villa**, were much plainer in style, reflecting the town's humble status before 1561.

THE HABSBURG CAPITAL

The establishment of Madrid as capital, first in 1561 and definitively in 1606 (*see pages 9-15*), utterly transformed the town and its architecture. Since it was above all a royal seat, 'the Court', the tastes of successive rulers were of special importance. Philip II's favourite architect, Juan de Herrera, was the first to leave a stamp on the city. He and his royal master had little idea of urban planning, but their major constructions – the **Puente de Segovia** (1584), the first stages of the **Plaza Mayor**, the widening of Calles Atocha, Segovia and Mayor – gave Madrid a shape that lasts to this day.

> ## 'It's known as Castilian baroque, but few of its features are especially Castilian.'

El Escorial (*see page 249*), designed by Herrera and the older architect Juan Bautista de Toledo, firmly established the 'Herreran' or 'Court' style – austere, rigid and typically employing grey slate for rooftops and the ubiquitous pointed turrets – that would be near-obligatory for major buildings in Madrid until the very end of the Habsburg era in 1700, despite all changes in fashion in the rest of Europe. Now a symbol of the 'Madrid of the Austrias', it is also known as Castilian baroque, but few of its features are especially 'Castilian': the slate pinnacles were taken from Flanders, which appealed to the Flemish-born Charles V and his son Philip.

Herrera's chief disciple, Juan Gómez de Mora, modified his master's legacy with a less monolithic, lighter style. He was responsible for the completion of the **Plaza Mayor** in 1619, where his original plan is still recognisable in the slate spires, high-pitched roofs and dormer windows, and the 1630 **Casa de la Villa**, the City Hall. Gómez de Mora was also structurally innovative, as seen in the massive cellars and housing blocks along Cava San Miguel, which back on to and complete the Plaza Mayor. Due to the abrupt drop in the level of the land he was obliged to build up to eight storeys high for these blocks to meet the rest of the square, making them the tallest buildings in Madrid

until the 20th century. However, he fell out of favour with Philip IV's minister the Count-Duke of Olivares; in 1636 Gómez was accused of stealing a Titian from the royal collection, and sent off to design drainage ditches in Murcia.

His great rival in Madrid was Gian Battista Crescenzi, an Italian who nevertheless adopted the 'Court style' – with some Italian flourishes – to please his Spanish masters. Both architects probably worked, at different times, on the **Palacio de Santa Cruz** near the Plaza Mayor, built in 1629-43 and now the Foreign Ministry. It shows clear Italian baroque influences, with a façade much more richly shaped than anything Herrera would have tried. Crescenzi, with Gómez' former assistant Alonso Carbonell, also undertook the largest single building scheme of Habsburg Madrid, the Palacio del Buen Retiro (*see pages 7 and 12*), only parts of which survive.

Meanwhile, the overall impression that Madrid – capital of the first worldwide empire – left on the 17th-century visitor was one of chaos, dirt and haphazard growth. The Habsburgs commissioned much that was noble and even palatial, but did not really configure a true city. Another reason why much building was unimpressive was the increasingly rickety state of the economy, which led to bricks and mortar being favoured over expensive stone.

BOURBON RENEWAL

The expiry of the Spanish Habsburgs with King Charles II in 1700 was followed by war, and the arrival of the Bourbons, under Philip V. If anything symbolizes the new dynasty's architectural achievements, it was their efforts to embellish and dignify Madrid.

The Bourbons were French, and Philip V's second wife, Isabella Farnese, was Italian, and these two influences would long predominate in the dynasty's tastes in buildings. Nevertheless, Philip V's administrator in Madrid, the Marqués de Vadillo, saw to it that many projects went to a local architect, Pedro de Ribera, among them the 1722 Hospice, now the **Museo Municipal**, the Cuartel Conde Duque barracks, now the **Centro Cultural Conde Duque**, the **Puente de Toledo** and many churches. Ribera's buildings, while still based in the Herreran tradition, feature exuberant baroque façades centred on elaborately-carved entrance porticos, which lend a touch of fantasy absent in Habsburg Madrid. Many Ribera entrances have been retained in buildings that have since been rebuilt, as in the 1734 Palace of the Dukes of Santoña at C/Huertas 3, now occupied by the Cámara de Comercio. In his churches, such as **San José** on Calle Alcalá, Ribera introduced a delicately ornate baroque style into Madrid's religious architecture.

Elsewhere in 18th-century Madrid the influence of French and Italian architects was far more apparent. After the old grey-spired Alcázar burnt down in 1734 Philip V commissioned a new **Palacio Real** from a group mainly of Italian architects led by Filippo Juvarra and Giambattista Sacchetti. Responsible for many projects was Charles III's 'chief engineer', Francesco Sabatini. The great exponents of the sober, 'pure' neo-classicism of the later years of Charles III's reign, however, were Spaniards: Ventura Rodríguez, who had also worked on the Palacio Real, and Juan de Villanueva, architect of the **Museo del Prado** and the **Observatorio**. Like the greatest project of the King's reign, the Paseo del Prado – of which these buildings were part – they clearly reflect Enlightenment ideals of architecture and urban planning.

OPEN HOUSE: THE 19TH CENTURY

Joseph Bonaparte's brief reign (1808-13) saw the first demolition of convents and monasteries, to be replaced by squares such as **Plaza Santa Ana**. On the whole, though, the first half of the 19th century was a time of architectural stagnation in Madrid. After the great clearance of monasteries began in the 1830s, many of the buildings that replaced them were simply constructed apartment and tenement blocks, such as the *corralas* (*see page 78*). Public buildings of this time, such as the 1840s **Cortes** or the **Teatro Real** (*see page 216*), were often in a conservative neo-classical style.

Greater changes came to Madrid after 1860, with the demolition of the walls and Carlos María de Castro's plan for the city's extension or *ensanche* (*see pages 19 and 81*). Areas covered by the plan are easy to spot on a map by their grid street pattern. Chief among them is the **Barrio de Salamanca**, still the most self-consciously grand *barrio* of the *ensanche*. Its wealthiest residents built opulent mansions in a completely eclectic mix of styles – French Second Empire was one of the most popular – some of which still stand on Calles Velázquez and Serrano. Other *ensanche* districts – Chamberí, Argüelles, Delicias – have in common a rational urban layout, wide thoroughfares and plainer, regular-sized blocks.

Public buildings of the first years of the Bourbon Restoration were as eclectic as Salamanca mansions. Madrid's own revivalist style, neo-*mudéjar* (*see page 33* **Moorish fantasies**), was used for official buildings, bullrings, churches, homes and factories. One of the most extraordinary constructions of the time, Ricardo Velázquez' **Ministerio de Agricultura** in Atocha, is in contrast a remarkable combination of Castilian brickwork

and extravagant, French Beaux Arts-style sculpted decoration. This was also the great period of cast-iron architecture in Madrid, with fine structures such as the city markets and the **Estación de Atocha**.

Art nouveau (called *modernismo* in Spain), so characteristic of Barcelona in the early 20th century, aroused little interest in Madrid, but there are a few examples of the style. The iced-cake-like **Sociedad General de Autores** (1902), by Jose Grasés Riera, is the best known, but the lower-key Casa Pérez Villamil at Plaza Matute 6, off Calle Huertas, is also impressive.

FORWARDS & BACKWARDS

As the *ensanche* was built up and Madrid's economy boomed from the 1900s to the 1920s, the city's architects looked for inspiration forwards and backwards in time, and both inside and outside Spain. The **Gran Vía**, a slightly weird monument to cosmopolitanism (*see page 72*), was born of this thinking.

> ## 'The Gran Vía became grander, and more eccentric, as it progressed.'

An all-modern thoroughfare through Madrid's old centre, the Gran Vía obliterated 14 old streets, and became grander, and more eccentric, as it progressed. Writer Francisco Umbral has said it recalls New York or Chicago, but its first building of any standing, the 1905 Edificio Metrópolis, was very French in inspiration. No.24 shows neo-Renaissance influence, the 1930s Palacio de la Música cinema (No.35) has distinctly baroque touches, and the 1929 **Telefónica** building is a New York skyscraper in miniature.

The 1930 apartment block at Gran Vía 60 is a classic of Madrileño cosmopolitanism, by Carlos Fernández Shaw, who in 1927 also built a futuristic petrol station on C/Alberto Aguilera (two blocks west of San Bernardo Metro). Also working at this time was the very original Antonio Palacios, main architect of the **Palacio de Comunicaciones** (1904-18) – a remarkable hotchpotch of Spanish, American and Viennese art nouveau influences – and the more subtle **Círculo de Bellas Artes**

During its brief existence the Spanish Republic further encouraged rationalist, rather self-consciously modern architecture, as in the earliest parts of the **Nuevos Ministerios**. Art deco architecture was in vogue, in office blocks like the Capitol building on Gran Vía (corner of Calle Jacometrezo) or the curious model housing district of **El Viso**, which has some of the most unusual domestic architecture in Madrid.

Moorish fantasies

Around 1870 an architectural style emerged in Madrid that the city can claim as its very own, neo-*mudéjar*. It would turn up in all kinds of structures, but the first example of the style was the new bullring commissioned to replace the plain 18th-century one that stood near the Puerta de Alcalá. In the revivalist atmosphere of the 19th century, architects Ricardo Rodríguez Ayuso and Lorenzo Alvarez Capra decided not to look to Gothic or Egyptian traditions for inspiration, but searched for something to revive closer to home. They opted for the styles and superb bricklaying techniques that had been employed by the Muslim *Mudéjar* master builders of medieval Castile.

Neo-*mudéjar* uniquely incorporated Moorish horseshoe arches, arabesque tiling and interlaced brickwork together with a modern use of glass and cast iron. The 1870s bullring no longer stands, but the style became near-obligatory for *plazas de toros* throughout Spain, and Madrid's next ring at **Las Ventas**, completed in 1934, sports many neo-*mudéjar* features. The style was extended to many other buildings. Perhaps the best in Madrid is the **Escuelas Aguirre**, also by Ayuso and Alvarez Capra, at the intersection of Calles Alcalá and O'Donnell on the north side of the Retiro park. Its most outstanding feature is a slim minaret-style tower, with a glass and iron lookout-gallery on top. Another splendid Arab inspired tower is

the giant spire of the **Santa Cruz** church at the top of Calle Atocha (No. 6, by Plaza Benavente), built in 1899-1902.

Other impressive neo-*mudéjar* structures scattered around Madrid include the former water tower that is now the **Sala del Canal de Isabel II** exhibition space, and the Castellana façade of the **ABC-Serrano** shopping mall (see page 161). In La Latina there is the giant **Iglesia de la Paloma** church, focus for one of Madrid's most historic *fiestas* (see page 187), completed in 1911 by Alvarez Capra with neo-Gothic elements in its twin-towered frontage. The style was also used for more everyday buildings, as in the block of flats at Calle Barquillo 21 in Chueca, which displays a remarkable façade combining diamond-pattern brickwork and neo-Moorish plaster details, complemented by elaborate iron-work balconies.

Civil war and the arrival of the Franco regime brought much destruction, and had an immediate impact in architecture. Falangist thinking on architecture was dominated by nostalgia for a glorious past, and so Madrid acquired monster constructions that looked straight back to imperial Spain (*see page 34* **Franquista kitsch**).

By the 1950s the regime's ideological enthusiasms were fading, although it still sought to impress. Built with no pretence at neo-baroque or anything similar is the tacky 32-floor 1957 **Torre de Madrid** on Plaza de España, which could have been lifted from any Latin American city of the same era. These years, though, also saw the beginnings of real modernity in Madrid, most notably with Francisco Cabrero and Rafael Aburto's Casa Sindical at Paseo del Prado 18-20, built in 1948-9 for the Francoist labour unions and now the Health Ministry. This was a forerunner of much later rationalist architecture in the city.

Until the 1960s the state of the Spanish economy still limited the scope for building. When the economy did improve, Madrid opened up to international influences, but much of its newest buildings were dreary apartment blocks, built for an exploding population in the era of *desarrollismo* (development).

MODERN TIMES

As Spanish society and the economy opened up with the rebirth of democracy in the late 1970s, one effect of the retro-obsessions of the Franco years was that Spanish architects – and the public – felt little inclination to look back with nostalgia or add neo-classical fronts to new buildings, and welcomed modernity with gusto. The most influential contemporary architects in Madrid have been Alejandro de la Sota and Francisco Sáenz de Oiza, both active from the 1950s, and Sáenz's gifted and very original protégé Rafael Moneo.

Franquista kitsch

In modern Spain the fascist dictatorship that ruled this country for 36 years can often seem strangely remote in time. The Franco regime, however, made a determined effort to glorify its achievements through architecture, and its mark is still visible in Madrid. Francoist attitudes to architecture were eminently retro, a mix of ideas borrowed from other Fascists in Germany and Italy and a mentality that looked to Spain's imperial Golden Age as a reference point in everything. The result was a series of grandiose, bombastic constructions that, wittingly or not, embrace kitsch with relish.

The archetypal product of Francoist architecture has to be the **Valle de los Caídos**, Franco's tomb, a combination of baroque and Universal Studios-horror (see page 251), but the foremost example within Madrid is the **Ministerio del Aire**, the Air Ministry, at the top of Calle Princesa in Argüelles. The original 1942 plan of architect Luis Gutiérrez Soto was inspired by German projects, but by the time the ministry was finally completed in 1957 it was more like a pastiche Escorial, Herreran pinnacles and all. Not for nothing was it dubbed the *Monasterio del Aire*. Near to it is the **Arco del Triunfo**, Franco's monument to his own victory.

Down Princesa in Plaza de España is perhaps Francoism's most manic creation, the **Edificio España** (pictured), a megalomaniac colossus designed by the brothers Joaquín and José María Otamendi in 1948-53. It was conceived in line with a fashionable American idea of containing a 'small city' in one huge block, with shops, offices, a hotel and apartments; outside, though, it was given all sorts of neo-Herreran decorative touches, as a Castilian baroque skyscraper.

The architects responsible for these buildings had often worked in very different styles in earlier times. In 1930 Gutiérrez Soto, for example, had designed the Barceló cinema in Chueca (now the **Pachá** disco), an art deco classic; Joaquín Otamendi had earlier worked with Antonio Palacios on the also overblown (but non-Herreran) **Palacio de Comunicaciones**.

The affluent *Barrio de Salamanca* also contains a good many retro constructions from the era, above all in its huge churches. A typical example is the 1952 **San Francisco de Borja** at the corner of Calles Serrano and Diego de León, vast in scale and ambition, and based on 17th-century Jesuit baroque churches in Madrid, Toledo and Rome.

An important factor in building during the 1980s was the coming of the Socialists to power in the city council, in 1979, and in the government in 1982. The Ayuntamiento of Mayor Tierno Galván committed itself to the regeneration of public spaces, and so facilitated the emergence of one of the characteristic features of modern Madrid – daringly imaginative 'grand revamps' of long-decrepit historic buildings. An outstanding example is the **Estación de Atocha**: the 1880s cast-iron railway terminal, run-down and grime-caked, was transformed by Rafael Moneo into a spectacular multi-purpose space. The **Reina Sofía** and **Thyssen** museums – also by Moneo, something of a specialist in far-reaching renovations – were similarly rebuilt, and the **Centro Cultural Conde Duque** was created out of Ribera's 1720s barracks, making use even of cracks in the old façade to good effect.

Outside the public domain the most vigorous contributions to Madrid since the '80s have been the skyscrapers that line the upper Castellana, by the **AZCA** area, such as the Catalana Occidente insurance company building (no.50), the superb white 1988 **Torre Picasso** by Minoru Yamasaki, and the spectacular leaning **Torres KIO** at Plaza Castilla. With Madrid's expansion much recent building has been on the city's edge. The **Feria de Madrid** complex (*see page 279*) is a new corporate showcase, and Manuel Delgado and Fernando Vasco's **Estadio de la Comunidad de Madrid** is a dramatic structure in the form of a tilted oval plate (*see page 236*).

> ▶ For details of buildings highlighted in this chapter, see pages 56-88 and 89-109.

Accommodation

Accommodation 37

Feature boxes

Accommodation

From downright luxurious to old and atmospheric, Madrid can always offer somewhere to rest a weary head.

Finding somewhere to stay is never a real problem in Madrid. In the very heart of the old city there are plenty of mid-range and budget hotels, all within walking distance of the artistic 'Golden Triangle' (the Prado, Thyssen and Reina Sofía), the old streets of Los Austrias or the buzzing nightlife zones of Plaza de Santa Ana, Sol or Chueca. Finding something more than anonymous comfort without spending a sizeable amount can be harder, but is not impossible. At the top end of the range, heavy hitters like the **Ritz** (*see page 38*) and **Palace** (*see page 38*) remain the essence of glamour. It's Madrid's mid-range hotels, many of them part of big chains, which are often well-equipped but lacking in any distinctive flavour.

The budget traveller looking for a clean, well-located room, on the other hand, can pick up some great bargains. More and more Madrid *hostales* have woken up to the idea of air-conditioning, a lifesaver in a city where temperatures regularly pass 40°C in summer. And there are still a few quirky finds, such as the **Mónaco** (*see page 47*) and the **Paris** (*see page 45*), which are well-priced to boot.

Apart from the areas around Sol in the old city – preferred by most tourist travellers – Madrid's other big hotel area is up the Castellana in Salamanca, Chamberí or Chamartín, the preferred location for business hotels. Even if you're not here on business, you might prefer the extra space and facilities that they can provide. Hotels with swimming pools are surprisingly hard to find in Madrid (for those that *do* have them, *see page 49* **Best pools**). If you're driving, try to find a hotel with garage parking. This will be both safer and more convenient, as parking in central Madrid is severely restricted (*see page 278*), even though using a hotel car park will often be charged for as an extra on your bill.

STARS, PRICES & DISCOUNTS

Hotel prices in Madrid, which long lagged behind the rest of Europe, have been catching up fast. However, price rises are not uniform across the board, and it's still possible to find excellent bargains, even in five-star establishments. The official local star ratings, from one to five, are based on fairly arbitrary criteria, and not an entirely reliable guide to

quality. This can work in your favour, as four-star hotels sometimes have services equal to or even better than more expensive five-stars. The other main local differentiation is that between *hoteles* and *hostales*. Anywhere called a hotel should have bathrooms in all rooms, whereas *hostales* or *pensiones* (virtually interchangeable terms) may not, even though many have now added

Booking a room

If you arrive in Madrid without a room and don't feel like looking around yourself, these agencies can make bookings for you. With the **www.madridandbeyond.com** site you can also book ahead online, and the large Spanish hotel chains such as NH (**www.nh-hoteles.es**) and Tryp (**www.trypnet.com**) have websites with online reservation for all their (mid-range) hotels. For information on renting a room longer-term, *see page 289*.

Brújula

Estación de Atocha (91 539 11 73). Metro Atocha RENFE/bus all routes to Atocha. **Open** 8am-10pm daily. **Map** p310 H10.
A private agency (the name means 'Compass') with offices at both main rail stations that books rooms in hotels of all categories in Madrid and its region. There is a 400ptas booking fee; you are given a map, and directions to the hotel.
Branch: Estación de Chamartín (91 315 78 94), **Open** 7.30am-11pm daily.

Viajes Aira

Terminals 1 & 2, Barajas Airport (91 305 42 24/91 305 84 19).
Open 8am-midnight daily.
Viajes Aira have two hotel reservation desks in the arrivals areas at Barajas. They do not deal with all hotels in Madrid, but mainly have rooms in mid-range categories (about 10,000-20,000ptas a double). There is no booking fee. Once you've made the booking, you must find your way to the hotel yourself.

showers in at least some rooms. *Hostales*, also, will usually have only limited facilities in terms of bars, lounges and so on.

All hotel and *hostal* bills are subject to seven per cent IVA (Value-Added Tax) on top of the basic price, which is normally quoted separately on bills, although a few hotels now include it in their listed prices. One thing to note is that many upper-range Madrid hotels, geared to business clients, offer user-friendly discounts at weekends, Christmas, during Easter and in August. Consequently, they sometimes provide a better all-round deal than places apparently further down the scale. Many hotels also reduce prices at some other times of the year (often October-November), and it's always worth enquiring whether any special rates may be available.

The hotels and *hostales* listed here, apart from apartment hotels and youth hostels, are divided according to the basic price of a **double room at standard rates, without IVA**. Given the frequency of discounts, these prices should be taken as a **guideline** only. Prices quoted are per room, not per person, and unless stated otherwise do not include breakfast. The cheap B&B hotel doesn't really exist in Madrid: most hotels will offer coffee, a roll and maybe some juice as breakfast, but this is rarely included in the room price, and the amount charged for it can be unreasonably expensive. It's often better to do like the city's natives, and have breakfast in a café.

Grand luxury (over 40,000ptas)

Most of Madrid's top hotels are on or not far from the city's great spine, the Paseo del Prado, Recoletos and the Castellana.

Huertas & Santa Ana

Hotel Palace

Plaza de las Cortes 7, 28014 (91 360 80 00/ fax 91 360 81 00/www.palacemadrid.com). Metro Banco de España/bus 9, 14, 27, 37, 45. **Rates** 56,000-72,000ptas single; 63,000-79,000ptas double; 100,000ptas junior suite; 185,000ptas executive suite; 525,000ptas royal suite. **Credit** AmEx, DC, MC, V. **Map** p310 G8. This colossal 465-room monster, which, along with the Ritz (*see below*), makes up Madrid's traditional duo of classic grand hotels, first opened its doors in 1913. Now owned by the Westin group (and so officially the Westin Palace), it seeks to combine old-world elegance with up-to-the-minute facilities, such as a smart new fitness centre. The lounge areas and stunning lobby have maintained an air of real sumptuousness, and it has deliciously comfortable (and surprisingly reasonably priced) bars and restau-

rants, open to non-residents. A popular meeting-point for politicians from the parliament across the road, it has a reputation as a place to let your hair down, and its bubbling, moving-and-shaking atmosphere keeps the crowds coming back. Staff are as smoothly professional as you would expect. **Hotel services** *Air-conditioning. Babysitting. Bar. Beauty salon. Business services. Currency exchange. Disabled: adapted rooms. Gym. Hairdresser. Laundry. Limousine service. No-smoking floor/rooms. Parking. Restaurant.* **Room services** *Dataport. Hairdryer. Mini-bar. Radio. Room service (24hr). Safe. Telephone. TV (satellite). Video on request.*

Hotel Villa Real

Plaza de las Cortes 10, 28014 (91 420 37 67/ fax 91 420 25 47/www.derbyhotels.es). Metro Banco de España/bus 9, 10, 14, 27, 45. **Rates** 34,900ptas single; 41,600ptas double. **Credit** AmEx, DC, MC, V. **Map** p310 G8. When architects Fernando Chueca Goitia and José Ramos designed this intimate hotel of 115 rooms in 1989, they set out to capture the feeling of its neighbouring competitors-to-be, the Palace (*see above*) and the Ritz (*see below*). Refurbished again in 1998, it has a flavour of former eras, with neo-classical embellishments in the lobby; the rooms are not quite as elegant, but very comfortable, and the hotel is ideally situated for the museums, Sol and Atocha. **Hotel services** *Air-conditioning. Babysitting. Bar. Beauty salon. Business services. Concierge. Disabled: adapted rooms. Laundry. Limousine service. Massage. No-smoking rooms. Parking. Restaurant. Sauna.* **Room services** *Dataport. Hairdryer. Mini-bar. Radio. Room service (24hr). Safe. Telephone. TV (satellite).*

Salamanca & the Retiro

Hotel Ritz

Plaza de la Lealtad 5, 28014 (91 701 67 67/ fax 91 701 67 76/www.RITZ.es). Metro Banco de España/bus 9, 14, 27, 37, 45. **Rates** 49,000-69,000ptas single/double; from 99,000ptas suite. **Credit** AmEx, DC, MC, V. **Map** p310 H7. Madrid's most elite hotel stands on a small green plaza on one side of the Paseo del Prado. It was built in 1910 thanks to a personal intervention by King Alfonso XIII, who had been embarrassed during his wedding in 1906 because his official guests had not been able to find any hotel in the city of the standard they expected. Regularly placed in surveys among the ten best hotels in the world, it's still gorgeous, right down to the hand-made carpets and fine linen sheets; the service is matchless; and the restaurant, serving Spanish and French cuisine, is superb. The rooms have all been renovated in their original belle époque style, and the hotel's garden terrace, a fashionable Madrid meeting point, is truly lovely. Smaller and more intimate than the Palace (154 rooms), the Ritz has shaken off its slightly stuffy image and now welcomes celebs that it once shunned. Also, special weekend rates and occasional offers make this oasis of luxury more accessible than you might think.

Hotel services *Air-conditioning. Babysitting. Bar. Beauty salon. Business services. Concierge. Garden. Gym. Hairdresser. Laundry. Limousine service. No-smoking floor/rooms. Parking. Restaurant. Sauna.* **Room services** *Dataport. Hairdryer. Mini-bar. Radio. Room service (24hr). Safe. Telephone. TV (satellite). Video on request.*

Hotel Villa Magna

Paseo de la Castellana 22, 28046 (91 576 75 00/ fax 91 431 22 86/hotel@villamagna.es). Metro Rubén Dario/bus all routes to Paseo de la Castellana. **Rates** 60,000ptas single; 67,000ptas double; 100,000-107,000ptas suite. **Credit** AmEx, DC, MC, V. **Map** p306 I2.

They say you get what you pay for, and here you pay for service: there isn't a request you could dream up that the staff wouldn't rally round to fulfil. Business folk and affluent tourists flock to this modern 182-room hotel, as well as the stars – U2, Naomi Campbell and Madonna have all stayed here. Visually it's a bit unprepossessing: the exterior is plain, rooms are unremarkable, and the glitzy main floor suggests '70s Miami Beach chic, but it's the comfort and convenience of Villa Magna that attract. It also houses a very fine restaurant, **Le Divellec** (*see chapter* **Restaurants**).

Hotel services *Air-conditioning. Babysitting. Bar. Beauty salon. Business services. Concierge. Disabled: adapted rooms. Garden. Gym. Hairdresser. Laundry. Limousine service. No-smoking floor/rooms. Parking. Restaurant. Sauna.* **Room services** *Dataport. Hairdryer. Mini-bar. Room service (24hr). Safe. Telephone. TV (satellite). Video.*

Chamberí

Hotel Orfila

C/Orfila 6, 28010 (91 702 77 70/ 91 702 77 72/www.hotelorfila.com). Metro Alonso Martínez or Colón/bus 7, 21. **Rates** 41,000ptas single; 50,000ptas-67,000ptas double; 100,000ptas junior suite; 160,000ptas suite. **Credit** AmEx, DC, MC, V. **Map** p306 H4.

A newcomer in the glamour league, this small mansion in a tranquil residential area off the Castellana has been transformed into a quietly elegant five-star hotel. Built in the 1880s as a private home for an artistic family, the house also contained a theatre and a literary salon in the 1920s. The hotel, with 28 rooms and four suites, retains the original nineteenth century façade, carriage entrance and main stairway, and has been very tastefully refurbished. It represents a nice option for those who want five-star style and treatment without the hurly-burly of a big hotel. The stylish restaurant, **El Jardín de Orfila**, conjures up the atmosphere of a 1920s tea salon, with tables in a wonderful garden patio, a young, up-and-coming chef and a cocktail wizard behind the bar.

Hotel services *Air-conditioning. Babysitting. Bar. Garden. Laundry. Lifts. Limousine service. Parking. Restaurant.* **Room services** *Dataport. Room service (24hr). Telephone. TV. Video on request.*

The elegant patio of **Hotel Orfila**.

Hotel Santo Mauro

C/Zurbano 36, 28010 (91 319 69 00/fax 91 308 54 77/www.ac-hoteles.com). Metro Rubén Dario/bus 5, 7, 40, 147. **Rates** 34,000ptas single; from 46,200ptas double. **Credit** AmEx, DC, MC, V. **Map** p306 H2.

Built in the 19th century as an aristocratic palace, this hotel with just 36 rooms – each one different – is the last word in restrained chic, a strong contender for the most beautiful hotel in Madrid. While the lounges, restaurant (in the old library) and bar have retained their original flavour, with lofty ceilings and marble fireplaces, the bedrooms have been stylishly decorated in contemporary colours. A hotel since the early '90s – previously it housed embassies – it sits in a quiet, tree-filled area near Chamberí, with gracious gardens, and has welcomed many famous names seeking luxury and privacy. The former stables have been converted into duplexes.
Hotel services *Air-conditioning. Babysitting. Bar. Business services. Concierge. Garden. Gym. Laundry. Limousine service. No-smoking floor/rooms. Parking. Restaurant. Sauna. Safe. Swimming pool.* **Room services** *Dataport. Hairdryer. Mini-bar. Radio. Refrigerator. Room service (24hr). Telephone. TV (satellite). Video on request.*

Smooth comfort (22-40,000ptas)

Sol & Gran Vía

Hotel Arosa

C/de la Salud 21, 28013 (91 532 16 00/ fax 91 531 31 27/arosa@hotelarosa.com). Metro Sol/bus all routes to Puerta del Sol. **Rates** 14,425ptas single; 22,295ptas double. **Credit** AmEx, DC, MC, V. **Map** p309 E7.

With Puerta del Sol and Gran Vía at opposite ends of the street, this 139-room hotel couldn't be better placed for exploring. The immediate area is not the classiest, but the street is quiet, and the spacious reception, restaurant and bar area on the recently renovated second floor come as a pleasant surprise. Rooms are clean and spacious, families are welcome, and friendly and attentive staff mean guests, especially British and American, keep coming back.
Hotel services *Air-conditioning. Bar. Concierge. Laundry. Parking. Restaurant.* **Room services** *Dataport. Hairdryer. Mini-bar. Radio. Room service (7am-11pm). Safe. Telephone. TV (satellite). Video on request.*

Hotel Emperador

Gran Vía 53, 28013 (91 547 28 00/fax 91 547 28 17/hemperador@sei.es). Metro Gran Vía/bus all routes to Gran Vía. **Rates** 21,000ptas single; 26,200ptas double. **Credit** AmEx, DC, MC, V. **Map** p309 E6.

An immaculately maintained 50-year-old hotel that's ideally placed in the centre of town. Rooms are spacious, with original furnishings in impeccable shape, and pleasantly quiet despite the traffic below. Bathrooms have all been redone in the last few years,

and staff are very helpful. Its greatest plus, though, is its wonderful rooftop pool, a real distinction among Madrid hotels (*see p241*). Although it has 241 rooms, you need to book early, as it's very popular. This stretch of the Gran Vía is not really problematic, but be careful with bags, especially at night.
Hotel services *Air-conditioning. Bar. Babysitting. Beauty salon. Business services. Concierge. Disabled: adapted rooms. Gym. Laundry. Limousine service. Sauna. Swimming pool.* **Room services** *Hairdryer. Mini-bar. Radio. Room service (7am-midnight). Safe. Telephone. TV (cable).*

Hotel Santo Domingo

Plaza de Santo Domingo 3, 28013 (91 547 98 00/ fax 91 547 59 95/www.hotelsantodomingo.com). Metro Santo Domingo/bus all routes to Gran Vía. **Rates** 17,775ptas single; 26,350ptas double. **Credit** AmEx, DC, MC, V. **Map** p309 D6.

Don't be put off by the murky salmon-coloured exterior of this 120-room former apartment block, or its sad sidestreet. It was taken over by the Barcelona Style chain in the early 1990s, when the interior was transformed with warm yellow walls, old paintings and statuary. Rooms are small but individually styled and comfortable; those on the fifth floor have tiny balconies with great views over the rooftops to the city's green edges. The Palacio Real is around the corner, and it's two minutes from the Sol shopping area.
Hotel services *Air-conditioning. Bar. Babysitting. Disabled: adapted room. Laundry. Limousine service. Parking. Restaurant.* **Room services** *Hairdryer. Mini-bar. Radio. Room service (7am-midnight). Safe. Telephone. TV (satellite).*

Hotel Tryp Ambassador

Cuesta de Santo Domingo 5-7, 28013 (91 541 67 00/fax 91 559 10 40/www.trypnet.com). Metro Opera or Santo Domingo/bus 25, 39, 44, 133, 147. **Rates** 24,000ptas single; 30,000ptas double. **Credit** AmEx, DC, MC, V. **Map** p309 D7.

Hidden away in a side street close to the Teatro Real is this luxurious 181-room branch of the Tryp chain. The rooms are large and very different one from another, and all have a lot of light. Plácido Domingo laid his head in suite 403 after singing at the opening gala of the opera house. The hotel also has a glass atrium, classy bar and eating area, and don't miss the cool patio garden, overseen by Curro the parrot. Staff are helpful, and multilingual.
Hotel services *Air-conditioning. Bar. Concierge. Laundry. No-smoking floor/rooms. Restaurant.* **Room services** *Dataport. Hairdryer. Mini-bar. Radio. Room service (7.30am-midnight). Safe. Telephone. TV (satellite).*

Huertas & Santa Ana

Gran Hotel Reina Victoria

Plaza de Santa Ana 14, 28012 (91 531 45 00/ fax 91 522 03 07/www.trypnet.com). Metro Sevilla or Sol/bus all routes to Puerta del Sol. **Rates** 24,000ptas single; 30,000ptas double. **Credit** AmEx, DC, MC, V. **Map** p309 E/F8.

Hotel Santo Mauro combines style with antique opulence. *See p41.*

Overlooking a square that's a magnet for foreigners, tapas-seekers and the local night-time crowd (*see page 75*), this 202-room hotel has a great history. It was a favourite put-up of bullfighters and their number-one fan Ernest Hemingway in bygone days, and a restored replica of the room used by the legendary *torero* Manolete is kept as a memorial. Otherwise, the hotel is unremarkable, in decor or amenities, but the bar is a great place to get a taste of the inner world of bullfighting and its larger-than-life characters. **Hotel services** *Air-conditioning. Bar. Babysitting. Business services. Concierge. Laundry. Parking. Restaurant.* **Room services** *Dataport. Mini-bar. Radio. Room service (8am-5pm, 8.30pm-midnight). Telephone. TV.*

Hotel Suecia

C/Marqués de Casa Riera 4, 28014 (91 531 69 00/ fax 91 521 71 41/hotelsuecia@genio.infor.es). Metro Banco de España/bus all routes to C/Alcalá. **Rates** 20,600ptas single; 25,800ptas double. **Credit** AmEx, DC, MC, V. **Map** p310 G7.

In a peaceful part of the old city, next to the Círculo de Bellas Artes and with other good restaurants close by, the Suecia (Sweden) is also minutes from Sol or the museums. Its rooms, 128 in all, are small-ish but comfortable, and the hotel has a spacious lobby and a seventh-floor terrace that, while not huge, is a relaxing place for a nap and a sunbathe. **Hotel services** *Air-conditioning. Bar. Babysitting. Concierge. Laundry. No-smoking floor/rooms. Parking. Restaurant.* **Room services** *Hairdryer. Mini-bar. Room service (7.30am-11pm). Safe. Telephone. TV (satellite).*

Salamanca & the Retiro

Hotel Alcalá

C/Alcalá 66, 28009 (91 435 10 60/ fax 91 435 11 05/www.nh-hoteles.es). Metro Príncipe de Vergara/bus all routes to C/Alcalá. **Rates** 20,900ptas single; 24,100ptas double. **Credit** AmEx, DC, MC, V. **Map** p310 I6.

Near the Retiro, this is one of the friendliest hotels in town. Many of its staff have worked here for years, and polished wood floors and fittings add to the warm atmosphere. Its 146 rooms have been well refurbished, and inside rooms overlook an attractive courtyard. One room on each floor has been decorated in the bright colours and naïf style (bright red poppies growing from bedsteads, for example) of hip designer Agatha Ruiz de la Prada. **Hotel services** *Air-conditioning. Bar. Babysitting. Concierge. Laundry. No-smoking floor/rooms. Parking. Restaurant. Safe.* **Room services** *Dataport. Hairdryer. Mini-bar. Radio. Room service (7am-11pm). Telephone. TV (satellite).*

Hotel Wellington

C/Velázquez 8, 28001 (91 575 44 00/fax 91 576 41 64/www.hotel-wellington.com). Metro Retiro/bus 1, 9, 19, 51, 74. **Rates** 29,750-37,500ptas single/double. **Credit** AmEx, DC, MC, V. **Map** p307 J2.

A moment's walk from the Retiro and the shops of Calle Goya, this 272-room upscale hotel is distinctly swish, but its rates are a little lower than those of others with similar facilities. It has a hand-

some entrance and surprisingly intimate lobby, and a faithful international business clientele. During San Isidro in May (*see p186*) many bull-fighters stay here, as it's the best-situated upper-range hotel for Las Ventas bullring.
Hotel services *Air-conditioning. Babysitting. Bar. Beauty salon. Business services. Hairdresser. Laundry. Limousine service. No-smoking rooms. Parking. Restaurant. Sauna. Swimming pool.* **Room services** *Dataport. Hairdresser. Mini-bar. Radio. Room service (24hr). Safe. Telephone. TV (satellite).*

Chamberí

Gran Hotel Conde Duque

Plaza Conde del Valle Suchil 5, 28015 (91 447 70 00/fax 91 448 35 69/condeduque@ hotelcondeduque.es). Metro San Bernardo/bus 21, 147. **Rates** 16,900ptas single; 27,000ptas double. **Credit** AmEx, DC, MC, V. **Map** p305 E3.
The 143 rooms of this 40-year-old hotel were rebuilt and tastefully redesigned in 1992. Service is smooth, and travellers who are not too bothered about being close to the city centre and the big museums will find the location refreshing, as it's on a small square on the fringes of Chamberí that's regularly full of students and local families socialising. A tea lounge adds to the refined air of the place, and it's attractive from the outside, too.
Hotel services *Air-conditioning. Babysitting. Bar. Business services. Laundry. Limousine service. Parking. Restaurant.* **Room services** *Dataport. Hairdryer. Mini-bar. Radio. Room service (24hr). Safe. Telephone. TV (satellite).*

Chamartín

Hotel Eurobuilding

C/Padre Damián 23, 28036 (91 345 45 00/ fax 91 345 45 76/www.nh-hoteles.es). Metro Cuzco/bus 11, 40, 150. **Rates** 29,700-32,700ptas single/double; 60,000ptas suite; 103,000ptas imperial suite. **Credit** AmEx, DC, MC, V.
The very name conjures up images of glossy corporate blankness, but for business travellers in this twin-tower, 469-room giant, very near Real Madrid's Estadio Bernabéu and the Palacio de Congresos, is actually pretty hard to beat. Located in a residential and business neighbourhood with very few tourists in sight, it offers almost every imaginable service and facility, and has perhaps Madrid's best hotel pools, both indoor and outdoor (both open to non-residents; *see p241*). Apartment-size suites are available for long stays.
Hotel services *Air-conditioning. Babysitting. Bar. Beauty salon. Business services. Concierge. Disabled: adapted rooms. Gym. Laundry. Limousine service. No-smoking rooms/two floors. Parking. Restaurant. Swimming pool.* **Room services** *Dataport. Mini-bar. Room service (24hr). Safe. TV (satellite). Telephone. Video on request.*

Upper-mid (14-22,000ptas)

Sol & Gran Vía

Hotel Carlos V

C/Maestro Vitoria 5, 28013 (91 531 41 00/ fax 91 531 37 61/recepcion@hotelcarlosv.com). Metro Sol/bus all routes to Puerta del Sol. **Rates** *incl breakfast* 12,381ptas single; 15,583ptas double. **Credit** AmEx, DC, MC, V. **Map** p309 D/E7.
This hotel, with 67 unexceptional rooms, is in the pedestrianised shopping area north of Sol. The entrance is clean and bright, and there's an attractive second-floor lounge and restaurant area. Go for the fifth-floor rooms, with balconies.
Hotel services *Air-conditioning. Bar. Concierge. Laundry. Parking.* **Room services** *Dataport. Hairdryer. Mini-bar. Room service (8am-11pm). Safe. Telephone. TV (satellite).*

Hotel Opera

Cuesta de Santo Domingo 2, 28013 (91 541 28 00/fax 91 541 69 23). Metro Opera/bus 3, 25, 39. **Rates** 10,300ptas single; 14,600ptas double. **Credit** AmEx, DC, MC,V. **Map** p309 D7.
Smoked glass and wood panelling in the entrance give this unassuming three-star a business feel, and the 79 rooms are clean and well stocked, if unexciting. Plus points are location (facing the Teatro Real on a quiet street next to the Palacio Real and Plaza de Oriente), very friendly staff, and an adjoining restaurant that serves an above-average *menú del día*.
Hotel services *Air-conditioning. Bar. Babysitting. Disabled: adapted room. Laundry. Limousine service. Restaurant.* **Room services** *Hairdryer. Mini-bar. Radio. Room service (24hr). Safe. Telephone. TV (satellite). Video on request.*

Huertas & Santa Ana

Hotel Asturias

C/Sevilla 2, 28014 (91 429 66 76/fax 91 429 40 36/ www.chh.es). Metro Sevilla/bus all routes to C/Alcalá. **Rates** *incl breakfast* 13,500-14,600ptas single; 14,100-15,400ptas double; 17,100ptas suite. **Credit** AmEx, DC, MC, V. **Map** p309 F7.
Two hundred metres from Sol, this 170-room hotel, opened in 1875, was spruced up in the mid-1990s. It is good value, especially considering its location, which is ideal for both nightlife and sightseeing. Ask for an inside room, as the streets on either side are noisy.
Hotel services *Bar. Disabled: adapted room. Laundry. Restaurant.* **Room services** *Safe. Telephone. TV.*

Argüelles

Aparto-hotel Rosales

C/Marqués de Urquijo 23, 28008 (91 542 03 51/ www.apartohotel-rosales.com). Metro Argüelles/ bus 21, 74. **Rates** 17,000ptas single; 19,000ptas double; 22,500-25,000ptas apartments. **Credit** AmEx, DC, MC, V. **Map** p304 B/C 3.

This establishment, half-way between a conventional hotel and an aparthotel, is a little disorientating when you first enter, thanks to an overuse of smoked mirrors. Nevertheless, its facilities are quite smart, and it's well-positioned in an upscale area, with the cafés of Paseo del Pintor Rosales and Parque del Oeste close by. The rooms and studio apartments are all well-furnished, and comfortable.
Hotel services *Air-conditioning. Café. Concierge. Parking. Restaurant.* **Room services** *Room service (24hr) Telephone. TV (cable).*

La Florida & the Manzanares

Hotel Florida Norte
Paseo de la Florida 5, 28008 (91 542 83 00/ 91 547 78 33). Metro Príncipe Pío/bus 39, 46, 74, C. **Rates** 13,000-14,000ptas single; 18,500ptas double; 21,500ptas triple; 24,500ptas suite. **Credit** AmEx, DC, MC, V. **Map** p308 A6.
This 399-room hotel near the Manzanares is a very popular package choice, but is another that doesn't overflow with character. It was built in the early '70s, and the decor hasn't changed much since: piped music dominates the huge, bustling lobby, and leather chairs and gleaming chrome and glass add to the effect. Rooms are well-equipped with modern

The shady garden at **Residencia de El Viso**.

facilities, but plain. However, it's in an interesting, unusual and handy location, near the river, San Antonio de la Florida, the Casa de Campo, the Parque del Oeste and the Príncipe Pío train and bus stations.
Hotel services *Air-conditioning. Café. Laundry. Parking. Restaurant.* **Room services** *Dataport. Room service (24hr). Telephone. TV.*

Chamberí

Hotel Zurbano
C/Zurbano 79, 28003 (91 441 55 00/fax 91 441 32 24/www.nh-hoteles.es). Metro Gregorio Marañón/ bus 12, 45, 147. **Rates** 17,900ptas single; 21,700ptas double. **Credit** AmEx, DC, MC, V.
In a quiet area to the north of Chamberí, near Nuevos Ministerios, this 260-room hotel is divided between two buildings. Although it's near the top end of this price bracket, it still represents very good value, and makes a good choice for anyone who prefers to be slightly off the tourist trail. It's contemporary in style, decorated with bleached wood and modern Spanish art, and the bedrooms are spacious. There's also a good restaurant and bar, Metro and bus connections are a short walk away, and there are well-priced weekend rates.
Hotel services *Air-conditioning. Babysitting. Bar. Business services. Concierge. Laundry. No-smoking floor/rooms. Parking. Restaurant.* **Room services** *Dataport. Hairdryer. Mini-bar. Radio. Room service (7am-midnight). Safe. Telephone. TV (satellite).*

Chamartín

Hotel Don Pío
Avda Pío XII, 25, 28016 (91 353 07 80/ 91 353 07 81). Metro Pío XII/bus 16, 29, 150. **Rates** 11,250-17,000ptas single; 15,000-23,000ptas double. **Credit** AmEx, MC, V.
This small but well-equipped newcomer is aimed at business clients, and looks the part from outside. Inside, however, it also gives a welcome feeling of warmth and luxury. The 41 spacious rooms are arranged round a pretty glass-roofed patio containing the café-restaurant. All rooms have modem and fax points, and all the marble-finish bathrooms have hydromassage baths. The location in north Madrid can seem remote, but it's opposite the Pío XII Metro station and just 15 minutes from the airport. Another local attraction is a decent public swimming pool, close by on the same road.
Hotel services *Air-conditioning. Business service. Café. Concierge. Laundry. Restaurant. Parking.* **Room services** *Dataport. Mini-bar. Room service (7am-12.30am). Telephone. TV (Cable).*

El Viso

Residencia de El Viso
C/Nervión 8, 28002 (91 564 03 70/fax 91 564 19 65/elviso1@jazzfree.com). Metro República Argentina/bus 7, 16, 19, 51. **Rates** 11,000ptas single; 18,000ptas double. **Credit** AmEx, DC, MC, V.

This art deco cube, with tiny windows, stands in the leafy 1930s model housing community of El Viso, one of the most unusual parts of the city. Until recently it was a family home. It's now an intimate 12-room hotel offering a different experience from that provided by most Madrid hotels. The location makes it feel miles from the centre, but it takes only a few minutes to get there; rooms are not quite as special as the art deco touches in the public rooms, such as a great staircase, but still stylish and comfortable. Its best feature by far, though, is the garden patio and eating area – ideal for cool, quiet moments, when the city seems far away. **Hotel services** *Air-conditioning. Babysitting. Bar. Garden. Laundry. Limousine service. Restaurant.* **Room services** *Dataport. Radio. Telephone. TV (satellite).*

Lower-mid (7-14,000ptas)

Los Austrias

Hostal Madrid

C/Esparteros 6, 2°, 28012 (91 522 00 60/fax 91 532 35 10). Metro Sol/bus all routes to Puerta del Sol. **Rates** 6,500ptas single; 9,500ptas double; 10,000-15,000ptas apartment. **Credit** MC, V. **Map** p309 E7.
An original and enterprising *hostal* a few steps from either Sol or the Plaza Mayor. As well as 15 well maintained rooms, all with bathrooms and TVs, it now has four new apartments, which are a real bargain: they can accommodate two to four people, and each one has a kitchenette and washing machine. Excellent value in general, the Madrid attracts a youngish clientele – the owners are young and welcoming too, and provide discount drinks' passes to clubs and a range of other information; guests are also given keys so that they can come and go as they please, and late-risers are never hustled out. A second floor, with no lift. **Hotel services** *Air-conditioning. Safe.* **Room services** *Telephone. TV.*

Sol & Gran Vía

Hotel París

C/Alcalá 2, 28014 (91 521 64 91/fax 91 531 01 88). Metro Sol/bus all routes to Puerta del Sol. **Rates** *incl breakfast* 9,000ptas single; 12,000ptas double. **Credit** AmEx, DC, MC, V. **Map** p309 E7.
This characterful 120-room hotel, a riot of tacky china animals, velvet and crystal right on Puerta del Sol, is actually one of the most historic hotels in Madrid. It has presided over Sol since the 1890s, and before the creation of the Ritz, the Palace and the like it was also one of the city's smartest hotels. Nowadays, the wooden-floored (often creaky) rooms are sparsely furnished; not all have air-conditioning, and the outside rooms are noisy, but a delightful interior courtyard adds a breath of fresh air. Staff are also super-friendly, and it's still a bargain for the price. **Hotel services** *Air-conditioning. Bar. Disabled: adapted room. Laundry. Restaurant.* **Room services** *Radio. Room service (24hr). Safe. Telephone. TV.*

The best # Hotels

For an all-out splurge

The **Ritz** (see page 38), naturally, where you can sleep between fine linen, have every whim answered and relax in one of the city's prettiest gardens; or the **Santo Mauro** (see page 41), for more secluded luxury, dazzlingly beautiful decor, and a pool.

For business efficiency

The **Eurobuilding** (see page 43) will connect you up to every contemporary gadget, or try the **Palace** (see page 38) if you want to catch the eye of any local movers and shakers.

For families with kids

The **Arosa** (see page 41) offers families a warm welcome and the **Emperador** (see page 41) and **Eurobuilding** (see page 43) have great pools and above-average babysitting services. At another price level, the apartments at **Hostal Madrid** (see page 45) could solve a lot of your problems.

For a romantic weekend

The **Ritz** and **Santo Mauro** win again (see pages 38 and 41), but for a louche time it has to be the **Mónaco** (see page 47).

For a special welcome

Hostal Madrid and **Hostal Persal** (see page 45) both offer service well above the norm for their price bracket, with loads of extras and owners willing to go the extra metre for their guests.

For perfumed gardens

The **Ritz** (see page 38), again, but another oasis in the city can be found at the **Residencia de El Viso** (see page 44).

For a real view

The roof of the **Emperador** (see page 41) has no challengers. And there's a pool up there too.

Huertas & Santa Ana

Hostal Persal

Plaza del Angel 12, 28014 (91 369 46 43/fax 91 369 19 52/hostal.persal@mad.servicom.es). Metro Sol or Anton Martin/bus 6, 26, 32. **Rates** *incl IVA* 5,800ptas single; 8,700ptas double; 12-17,700ptas trebles-quintuples. **Credit** AmEx, DC, MC, V. **Map** p309 E8.
The top end of the *hostal* world, the Persal is big, with 85 rooms, and has been imaginatively and com-

prehensively overhauled in 1998-2000. It could easily hold its own with a one or two-star hotel: rooms, all with bathrooms, are much more attractive and comfortable than in many *hostales*, and the hard-working staff are especially welcoming and helpful. It also has some very large rooms that are a real bargain if you're travelling as a family or a group. Plus, it's also on one of Huertas' most attractive (and sometimes busiest) squares.
Hotel services *Air-conditioning. Café. Concierge. Laundry. Parking. Safe.*
Room services *Telephone. TV.*

Hotel Inglés

C/Echegaray 8, 28014 (91 429 65 51/fax 91 420 24 23). Metro Sevilla or Sol/bus all routes to Puerta del Sol. **Rates** 8,500ptas single; 12,000ptas double. **Credit** AmEx, DC, MC, V. **Map** p309 F7/8.
This 58-room hotel dates from 1853, and has more character than many Madrid hotels, with an ornate, Victorian-style lobby lined with leather sofas and numerous pictures of the hotel in former eras. Calle Echegaray can get noisy, but the rooms overlooking the street are pleasant and get lovely morning light; go for an inside room if you want something quieter. Rooms are well equipped and there's a pleasant breakfast room, making the hotel good value, even though the staff seriously need a charm injection.
Hotel services *Air-conditioning. Café. Laundry. Parking. Safe.* **Room services** *Telephone. TV.*

Hotel Mora

Paseo del Prado 32, 28014 (91 420 05 64/fax 91 429 15 69). Metro Atocha/bus all routes to Atocha. **Rates** *incl VAT* 6,762ptas single; 8,875ptas double. **Credit** AmEx, DC, MC, V. **Map** p310 G7.
Built in the 1930s, this 62-room hotel was fully renovated in the 1990s, and is fresh, clean and bright. The entrance is attractive, and, although everything else is a bit more functional, the place is often buzzing. It can be hard to get a room, for not only is the Mora good value but it's also opposite the Prado and not far from Atocha station. Staff, on the other hand, make little effort to be friendly.
Hotel services *Air-conditioning. Safe.* **Room services** *Telephone. TV (satellite).*

Hotel Santander

C/Echegaray 1, 28014 (91 429 95 51/ fax 91 369 10 78). Metro Sevilla or Sol/bus all routes to Puerta del Sol. **Rates** *incl IVA* 7,000ptas-8,000ptas single/double. **Credit** MC, V. **Map** p309 F7.
An antique but well-maintained and cosy lobby welcomes you into this charming old hotel of just 35 rooms, in the heart of Huertas. With lots of high ceilings, generous bathrooms and individual furniture, this is something of a gem, and the corner room, number 105, is particularly spacious and well lit. Some rooms face on to the Carrera de San Jerónimo and can be noisy,but the staff are friendly, making the Santander more likeable than many of its competitors.
Hotel services. *Laundry. Safe.* **Room services** *Room service (8am-7pm). Telephone. TV.*

A stopover since 1853, **Hotel Inglés**.

Chueca

Hostal-Residencia Santa Bárbara

Plaza de Santa Bárbara 4, 3°, 28004 (91 446 93 08/ fax 91 446 23 45). Metro Alonso Martínez/bus 3, 7, 21, 40, 149. **Rates** 6,200ptas single; 8,300ptas double. **Credit** MC, V. **Map** p306 G4.
A fairly ordinary *hostal* with rather drab furnishings, the Santa Bárbara is nevertheless clean and well-located, right on the plaza of the same name in the Alonso Martínez section of Chueca. All of its 13 rooms have bathrooms, and guests can also make use of a TV lounge.
Hotel services *Air-conditioning.* **Room services** *Room service (9am-5pm). Telephone.*

Hotel Mónaco

C/Barbieri 5, 28004 (91 522 46 30/fax 91 521 16 01). Metro Chueca or Gran Vía/bus 3, 40, 149. **Rates** *incl IVA* 7,440ptas single; 10,700ptas double. **Credit** AmEx, MC, V. **Map** p309 F6.
The Mónaco is an eccentric monument among Madrid's hotels. It was originally built as an apartment block, in 1918, but within a year it had become a brothel, and from then until the 1950s was the most fashionable house of ill repute in the city. Among those entertained there were Mussolini's son-in-law and foreign minister Count Ciano and countless famous bullfighters. It was also a particular favourite of King Alfonso XIII, who on his regular visits would bring with him a

whole string quartet, which would accompany the royal exertions from behind a curtain. In 1959 it became the Hotel Mónaco, but much of the fabulous decor and some of the louche atmosphere were retained, helped along (until recently) by amiably eccentric staff. The highlights are the 'special rooms', such as no.20, the former King's room, with raised bath and an alcove where the quartet used to play, no.123, with a grand canopy with full-length mirror above the bed, or no.127, a riot of shocking-pink fake-baroque curtaining in plaster, but there are other tarty touches throughout the hotel, such as the red-leather clad cafetería. The Mónaco's camp decadence is widely known, and over the years it's been used as a backdrop for fashion or video shoots by magazines and music companies from across Europe and beyond. In a city with so many bland hotels, it should be treasured. Should be: the problem is that the Mónaco is not under any kind of preservation order, but is entirely privately owned, and the current owners don't seem to have any idea of what to do with it. The place is becoming increasingly run-down and neglected, and one reader has even reported part of a bathroom ceiling collapsing, without this producing any reaction from the management. It's a shame; the Mónaco is still a hotel 'with character', and staying there can be an experience, but be warned that you might get more 'character' than you would really wish for.
Hotel services *Air-conditioning. Bar. Safe.*
Room services *Telephone. TV.*

Malasaña & Conde Duque

Hostal Sil

C/Fuencarral 95, 3°, 28004 (91 448 89 72/ fax 91 447 48 29). Metro Bilbao/bus 3, 21, 40, 147, 149. **Rates** from 4,500ptas single; 7,900ptas double. **Credit** MC, V. **Map** p305 F3.
This 21-room *hostal* at the more salubrious northern end of Fuencarral, is run by a friendly middle-aged couple with occasional help from their English-speaking children. All the very well-kept rooms have air-conditioning and most have baths, and the *hostal* offers good value for money.
Hotel services *Air-conditioning.* **Room services** *Telephone. TV.*

Salamanca & the Retiro

Hotel-Residencia Don Diego

C/Velázquez 45, 28001 (91 435 07 60/ fax 91 431 42 63). Metro Velázquez/bus 1, 74, 89. **Rates** 7,600ptas single; 10,500ptas double. **Credit** AmEx, DC, MC, V. **Map** p307 J2.
A very strange arrangement, this, reached by a lift above private apartments, with just one forlorn man sitting downstairs at a scruffy desk to represent the establishment. The 58 basic rooms are clean, though and all have TV, air-conditioning and some other electrical extras. Not pretty, not charming, but it's difficult to stay in this classy shopping district for less.

Hostal Delvi: pleasant, ultra-cheap, and right on the Plaza Santa Ana. *See p49.*

Hotel services *Air-conditioning. Laundry.*
Room services *Dataport. Room service (8am-11pm). Safe. Telephone. TV (satellite).*

Argüelles

Hotel Tirol

C/Marqués de Urquijo 4, 28008 (91 548 19 00/fax 91 541 39 58). Metro Argüelles/bus 1, 21, 44, 74, C. Rates *incl breakfast* 12,100ptas single; 13,500ptas double. Credit MC, V. Map p304 B/C3.
This 95-room hotel is in an area with relatively few options, and conveniently placed for the Plaza de España, the Parque del Oeste and the university district. Not the most characterful building, but the rooms are spacious and clean, and prices are reasonable.
Hotel services *Air-conditioning. Bar. Laundry. Parking. Safe.* Room services *Telephone. TV (satellite).*

Budget (7,000ptas & under)

As in other Spanish cities, in Madrid there are areas where cheap hotels are bunched together. The most important is around Plaza de Santa Ana and streets nearby such as Calle Cervantes, in the heart of the Huertas bar and nightlife area. There is another cluster in Chueca and Malasaña, on either side of Calle Fuencarral. The hotels around the main train stations are in general not as pleasant as more centrally placed establishments at the same price.

Many basic hotels are in single apartments in blocks, where addresses will often be identified as *izq* (*izquierda*, left) or *dcha* (*derecha*, right) after the floor number. Some budget hotels do not have someone on the door 24 hours a day, so check how to get back in at night.

Los Austrias

Hostal Riesco

C/Correo 2, 3°, 28012 (91 522 26 92). Metro Sol/bus all routes to Puerta del Sol. Rates 4,000ptas single; 5,800ptas double. No credit cards. Map p309 E7.
Heavy on the decoration, this 22-room *hostal* just off Puerta del Sol is for those who really want to stay in the absolute centre of the city. All rooms have bathrooms, and several have flower-decorated balconies. It has been run by the same family for over 25 years, and the lady of the house, if sometimes severe, is efficient. A third floor, but with a lift.
Hotel services *Air-conditioning.*
Room services *Telephone.*

Huertas & Santa Ana

Hostal Armesto

C/San Agustín 6, 1°, 28014 (91 429 90 31). Metro Antón Martín/bus 6, 9, 26, 32. Rates 5,500ptas single; 6,500ptas double. Credit MC, V. Map p310 G8.

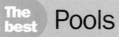

The best Pools

Apartamentos Juan Bravo
You might think you were in Benidorm.
See page 52.

Hotel Emperador
A real star – Madrid's only rooftop hotel pool with panoramic views. See page 41.

Hotel Eurobuilding
Pools indoors and out. See page 43.

Hotel Santo Mauro
The palatial alternative. See page 41.

Hotel Wellington
Not quite the same, but still opulent.
See page 42.

A six-room *hostal* right in the centre of Huertas, with baths in each room, and owned by a wonderfully friendly woman and her husband. A treat for those with inside rooms is a view over the garden of an old palace next door, giving a feel of old Madrid.

Hostal Bruña

C/Moratín 50, 28014 (91 429 47 01). Metro Antón Martín/bus 6, 26, 32. Rates 4,500ptas single; 5,300ptas double. No credit cards. Map p310 G8.
A sparklingly clean gem of a *hostal* run very professionally by a family who look out for all the details; the lobby and the rooms, all with TV and bathroom, are spacious and excellently maintained. It's one of the best options in this price range, in a perfect spot for museum- or café-browsing.
Hotel services *Air-conditioning.*
Room services *TV.*

Hostal Cervantes

C/Cervantes 34, 2°, 28014 (91 429 83 65/fax 91 429 27 45). Metro Antón Martín/bus 9, 10, 14, 27, 34. Rates *incl VAT* 5,500ptas single; 7,000ptas double. Credit MC, V. Map p310 G8.
Just round the corner from the Armesto (*see above*), and equally close to the Huertas-Santa Ana bar scene, this 12-room hostel is bright and clean and has a relaxed atmosphere, kept up by friendly, helpful owners. All of its rooms have their own bathrooms and firm beds, and there's a lift.
Room services *Room service (9am-5pm). TV.*

Hostal Delvi

Plaza de Santa Ana 15, 3°, 28012 (91 522 59 98). Metro Sevilla or Sol/bus all routes to Puerta del Sol. Rates 2,000ptas single; 4,000ptas double.
No credit cards. Map p309 F8.
Anyone who wants to be in the middle of things could do no better than stay on the Plaza de Santa Ana itself. This pleasant and ultra-cheap third-floor *hostal* (with

no lift) has eight rooms, all different in size. Some have showers, one has its own toilet, and several have space for three people. If you prefer a bit more peace and quiet, ask for a room facing the side street, away from the main square. The owner is friendly and obliging.

Hostal Filo
Plaza de Santa Ana 15, 2°, 28012 (91 522 40 56).
Metro Sevilla or Sol/bus all routes to Puerta del Sol.
Rates 2,200ptas single; from 3,800ptas double.
No credit cards. Map p309 F8.
In the same building as the Delvi, but one floor down, the Filo has 20 high-ceilinged rooms with great furniture and lots of light. The owner seems grumpy, but is no dummy, and over the years has acquired just enough English to deal with his guests. Only four rooms actually face the square. Three rooms have showers, but four toilets are shared by all guests. Some rooms have space for three people.
Hotel services *Air-conditioning.*
Room services *Telephone. TV.*

Hostal Martín
C/Atocha 43, 3°, 28012 (91 429 95 79).
Metro Antón Martín/bus 6, 26, 32.
Rates 5,800ptas single; 6,800ptas double; 9,100ptas triple. **Credit** AmEx, DC, MC, V.
Map p310 G9.
This 26-room *hostal* on Calle Atocha itself has a pleasantly rough-and-tumble family feel, but is clean, with large air-conditioned rooms all of which

The best Youth Hotels

Hostal Benamar
A backpacker's standby near the heart of the Chueca and Malasaña nightlife scenes. See page 51.

Hostal Madrid
A young friendly team who know what their guests want; even better now they've added trendy, well-equipped apartments. See page 45.

Hostal San Antonio
A relaxed but on-the-ball owner and a great location make this a favourite for younger travellers. See page 50.

Hostal Valencia
A *hostal* in the centre of town that you can treat as a home, and where you can be sure of a friendly welcome. See page 50.

Hotel Monaco
Something to write home about: catch up with your disreputable fantasies, but don't bother looking for the mini-bar. See page 47.

have bathrooms attached. Parking is available nearby, and the laid-back owners will book you in to other hotels if you're moving on.
Hotel services *Air-conditioning.* **Room services** *Telephone. TV.*

Hostal-Residencia La Coruña
Paseo del Prado 12, 3°, 28014 (91 429 25 43).
Metro Banco de España/bus 9, 14, 27, 37, 45.
Rates 3,000ptas single; 5,000ptas double.
No credit cards. Map p310 G7.
You'd have to camp inside the Prado Museum itself – or put up at the Ritz – to get closer to the Goyas. The six clean rooms, with two shared bathrooms, have high ceilings, chandeliers and plain furniture, and the friendly owners are delighted to have guests. One of the best-value budget *hostales*, but note that it's closed in August. A third floor, with no lift.
Room services *TV.*

Hostal-Residencia Sud-Americana
Paseo del Prado 12, 6°, 28014 (91 429 25 64).
Metro Banco de España/bus 9, 14, 27, 37, 45.
Rates *incl VAT* 2,600ptas single; 5,000ptas double.
No credit cards. Map p310 G7.
In the same building as the Coruña (*see above*), and so sharing its advantages as far as location is concerned (but on the sixth floor, so more of a hike upstairs). This charming old-fashioned *hostal* has eight rooms with washbasins, one shared bathroom, and some fantastic features: tasteful, vintage furniture, chandeliers, high ceilings and creaky wooden floors. The elderly couple running it are utterly charming too. It closes in August, though.

Hostal San Antonio
C/León 13, 2°, 28014 (91 429 51 37). Metro Antón Martín/bus 6, 9, 26, 32. **Rates** 3,500ptas single; 5,500ptas double. **No credit cards. Map** p309 F8.
A clean, quiet and cool new-style *hostal* in the heart of the main Huertas drags – tranquil by day, buzzing on weekend nights – that's imaginatively run by a friendly young woman. Rooms are comfortable and generously-sized for this bracket, and all now come with air-con and their own bathrooms.
Hotel services *Air-conditioning.*
Room services *TV.*

Hostal Valencia
C/Espoz y Mina 7, 4°, 28012 (91 521 18 45).
Metro Sol/bus all routes to Puerta del Sol.
Rates 3,500ptas single; from 5,500ptas double.
No credit cards. Map p309 E8.
This tiny *hostal* has a very homely feel and a laid-back atmosphere, which is helped along greatly by its amiable young owner's attempts to jazz up the old apartment. It's youth-oriented in style, so you don't have to worry about negotiating with a grumpy doorman if you get back late. The rooms, five doubles and one single, all with bathrooms, are comfortable and spacious, their walls washed in warm primary colours; there's also a fridge and washing machine for guests' use, the owner speaks

A cut above the rest (and dogs are not essential): the **Hostal Valencia**. *See p50.*

English and other languages, all guests have their own key, and the location is great for Sol and Santa Ana. A fourth floor, with no lift.
Room services *TV.*

Hostal Villamáñez

C/San Agustín 6, 2°, 28014 (91 429 90 33).
Metro Antón Martín/bus 6, 9, 26, 32.
Rates 6,000ptas double; 7,300ptas triple.
No credit cards. Map p310 G8.
This *hostal* is on the floor above the Armesto (*see above*), bang in the centre of town. The eight rooms all have bathrooms and plenty of plain, cheap furniture, and the recent addition of air-conditioning makes it a good budget option for summer.
Hotel services *Air-conditioning. Safe.* **Room services** *Telephone. TV.*

Pensión Jaén

C/Cervantes 5, 3° 28014 (91 429 48 58).
Metro Antón Martín/bus 9, 10, 14, 27, 34.
Rates 3,500ptas single; from 4,500ptas double.
Credit MC, V. **Map** p309 F8.
The genial owners are the main plus at this tiny, basic *hostal* of just eight rooms in a fairly quiet spot close to Plaza Santa Ana. All rooms have showers, and some have their own toilet and/or bath. No lift.
Hotel services *Safe.* **Room services** *Telephone. TV.*

Pensión Olga

C/Zorrilla 13, 28015 (91 429 78 87). Metro Banco de España or Sevilla/bus 9, 10, 27, 34. **Rates** 4,400ptas single; 5,880ptas double; 7,500ptas triple.
Credit V. **Map** p310 G7.
With warmly decorated lounges that are invitingly comfortable after a hard day's sightseeing, this 20-room, family-owned *hostal* offers slightly more sophisticated service than many of the others in this bracket, even though the rooms themselves (all with baths) are quite basic. It's very well-located on a quiet side street by the Cortes, just at the back of the Museo Thyssen.
Hotel services *Safe.* **Room services** *Telephone. TV.*

Lavapiés – Atocha

Hostal Rivera

Paseo de Santa María de la Cabeza 2, 1°, 28045 (91 527 37 17). Metro Atocha/bus all routes to Atocha.
Rates 2,500ptas single; 3,500ptas double.
No credit cards. Map p310 H10.
In a good spot for travellers arriving at Atocha by train, the Rivera is a small, family-run, friendly, no-nonsense traditional *hostal*. It's also very near the Reina Sofía. Its nine very low-priced rooms all have washbasins, but share one bathroom; it may not have air-con, but the Rivera, two floors up in an old block (with no lift), stays relatively cool in summer. Some of the family speak English, and it's better than most Atocha cheap hotels.

Chueca

Hostal Benamar

C/San Mateo 20, 2°, 28004 (91 308 00 92).
Metro Tribunal/bus 3, 37, 40, 149. **Rates** 2,500ptas single; 4,000ptas double. **Credit** MC, V.
Map p306 G4.
Budget travellers wanting to be in the thick of the Chueca-Alonso Martínez-Malasaña night action will be delighted by this airy, light *pensión*, a backpackers' favourite. The 22 sparklingly clean rooms all have wash basins, but no baths, and there are four bathrooms. There is, though, a TV lounge, and some of the rooms now have air-conditioning. The friendly owner speaks a little English.
Hotel services *Air-conditioning (some rooms).*

Hostal-Residencia Gloria

C/Conde de Xiquena 4, 28004 (91 522 04 42).
Metro Chueca/bus 27, 37, 45, 53.
Rates 2,300ptas single; 4,000ptas double.
No credit cards. Map p306 H5.
A tidy but basic 14-room hostel on a quiet street on the smarter side of hip Chueca. There are few facilities and it's a bit dark, but it's very popular, with regulars who have been coming here for years.

Salamanca & the Retiro

Hostal Retiro/Hostal Narváez

*C/O'Donnell 27, 4° & 5°, 28009 (91 576 00 37).
Metro Ibiza or Príncipe de Vergara/bus 2, 15, 28, C.
Rates from 3,500ptas single; 5,900ptas double.*
No credit cards.
You can practically roll out of bed and into the
Retiro from either these two *hostales*, one above the
other, both run by the same family, and in an
untouristy area of Salamanca. The 30 rooms all
have showers, and are bright and recently painted.
The lift is another bonus.
Room services *TV.*

Apartment hotels

Apartment hotels are generally made up of
self-contained small flats, with limited kitchen
facilities, plus reception and maid service.
They are handy for slightly longer stays,
and usually offer reduced weekly, monthly or
longer-term rates (*see also page 43* **Aparto-
hotel Rosales**).

Apartamentos Juan Bravo

*C/Juan Bravo 58-60, Salamanca, 28006 (91 402 98
00/fax 91 309 32 28). Metro Diego de León/bus 26,
29, 52, 61, C. Rates per week from 42,000ptas
studio; from 56,000ptas apartment.*
No credit cards. Map p307 L2.
These 300 apartments, in a residential area on the
eastern edge of Salamanca some way from tourist
attractions, are showing their age, and some of the
hallways are very dark. None of that matters too
much come summer, though, as there's a great
swimming pool at the back.
Hotel services *Air-conditioning. Laundry. Parking.
Swimming pool.* **Room services** *Refrigerator. Safe.
Telephone.*

Apartamentos Turísticos Príncipe

*C/Príncipe 11, Huertas, 28012 (902 11 33 11/fax 91
429 42 49). Metro Sevilla or Sol/bus all routes to
Puerta del Sol. Rates per night 9,000ptas two-person
studio; 12,000ptas four-person studio; 16,000ptas
four-person suite; 20,000ptas four-person apartment.*
Credit AmEx, DC, MC, V. **Map** p309 F8.
A comfortable, very well-maintained apartment
hotel, very handily placed just off Plaza Santa Ana,
the Príncipe offers apartments (36 in total), ranging
in size from studios to family flats and top-floor
attics with large balconies, all of them with baths,
washing machines and kitchenettes. In the entrance,
there also a grand crystal chandelier.
Hotel services *Air-conditioning. Laundry.* **Room
services** *Dataport. Telephone. TV.*

Aparthotel Tribunal

*C/San Vicente Ferrer 1, Malasaña & Conde Duque,
28004 (91 522 14 55/fax 91 523 42 40/
www.ourworld.compuserve.com/homepages/ma_
ventura). Metro Tribunal/bus 3, 40, 149. Rates per*

*night 9,500ptas single studios; 12,600ptas doubles;
per week 56,000ptas single studios; 66,500ptas
doubles; per month 160,000ptas single studios &
doubles.* **Credit** AmEx, DC, MC, V. **Map** p305 F4.
A neon sign leads you off Calle Fuencarral to this
unprepossessing 111-apartment block. Its major
attribute is its prime location, which makes it the
perfect place to lay one's head between late nights
in the heart of party land, so despite having few
frills, it's very popular. The studio apartments are
large but utilitarian; all have small but fully
equipped kitchens.
Hotel services *Air-conditioning. Laundry.* **Room
services** *Radio. Telephone. TV.*

Youth hostels

To get a bed in one of Madrid's two official
hostels it can be necessary to book, but you
can try your luck and turn up at the door to see
what they have left for the night. Reservations
need to be made in writing 15 days in advance,
and sent to the hostels or the Instituto de
Albergues Juveniles, Central de Reservas,
C/Alcalá 32, 28014 Madrid (91 580
42 16/fax 91 580 42 15), which also accepts
reservations by fax. IYHF cards are required,
and you can stay a maximum of three nights
consecutively, and six nights in total during a
two-month period.
   There is a 1.30am curfew at both hostels,
although if you want to stay out any later the
staff are often prepared to be flexible and
provide some means of getting back in. Doors
reopen at 8am. Note that in summer Spanish
youth hostels are often heavily booked by
school parties, who tend to set the atmosphere.

Albergue Juvenil
Richard Schirmann

*Casa de Campo, 28011 (91 463 56 99).
Metro Lago/bus 31, 33, 39, 65.*
Rates *per person, incl breakfast* 1,700ptas; 1,200ptas
under-26s with youth card. **No credit cards.**
Bookings for this hostel are only taken for groups
of ten or more, but individuals are welcome to turn
up at the door. Its main attraction is its location,
in the middle of the Casa de Campo, which is a long
way from the city centre, but a great setting if
you're into nature. The hostel has its own bar and
library, and is quite comfortable and well maintained. All rooms have from two to six beds, and
bathrooms are shared by two rooms. It's a bit of a
walk from the Lago Metro station (to get to the
hostel, walk along Paseo de los Castaños away
from the lake, and look for signs for Albergue
Juvenil). Prostitutes and kerb-crawlers congregate
along these roads at night, so it's a good idea to
ask about the best way of getting back after dark.
Staff seem a little jaded.
Hotel services *Café. Disabled: adapted rooms.
Garden. Laundry. Telephone. TV.*

Albergue Juvenil
Santa Cruz de Marcenado
C/Santa Cruz de Marcenado 28, Malasaña & Conde Duque, 28015 (91 547 45 32/fax 91 548 11 96). Metro Argüelles/bus 2, 21, 44, 133, C. **Rates** *per person, incl breakfast* 1,700ptas; 1,200ptas under-26s with youth card. **Credit** V. **Map** p305 D3.
Individuals or groups of less than ten who wish to book a bed at a Madrid youth hostel should write or fax to this hostel, in a quiet street near the Centro Cultural Conde Duque. It's modern and quite well fitted-out, with 72 beds split between rooms for four to eight people, with male- and female-only floors. Reception staff are matronly but friendly, and some speak a little English.
Hotel services *Disabled: adapted rooms. Laundry. Lift. TV.*

Campsites

There is a fair sprinkling of campsites all around the Madrid region, and towards the Guadarrama and Gredos mountains (*see pages 263-72*). Although distances may be inconvenient, sites further away from the city are in more attractive locations and tend to have better facilities than those on the outskirts of Madrid. A full list of local sites is available from tourist offices; all are open year-round.

Camping Alpha
Carretera N-IV, km 12.4, 28906 Getafe, Madrid (91 695 80 69). Bus 441, 442, 446 from Atocha to Getafe; train Cercanías C-4 from Atocha to Parla; by car N-IV to Getafe, km 12.4. **Rates** *per night* 695ptas adults; 600ptas under-15s; 780ptas tent or caravan; 690-2,000ptas vehicles; 670ptas electricity. *bungalows* 6,800ptas 1 or 2 people; 7,800ptas 3 people; 8,800ptas 4 people; *rooms* 4,500ptas single; 5,000ptas double. **Credit** MC, V.
The site south of Madrid near Getafe opened 20 years ago, when its pine trees probably made it a little oasis. It has slowly been surrounded by an industrial estate and is close to a motorway, but once inside by the pool it's easy to forget all that. Along with as camping and caravan space, bungalows for two to six people are available. There are tennis, basketball and football facilities, a children's play area and a large pool, and when civilisation calls Madrid is just a 15-minute whizz down the N-401.

Camping La Fresneda
Carretera M-608, 28791 Soto el Real, between Soto del Real and Manzanares el Real (91 847 65 23). Bus 724 from Plaza de Castilla to Colmenar Viejo. **Rates** 575ptas per person, per car or per tent; 525ptas per child. **Credit** AmEx, MC, V.
This high-grade campsite is about a 45-minute drive north of Madrid near Manzanares el Real (*see p267*), just south of the fabulous rock formation of La Pedriza, and 500m from the Embalse de Santillana, a reservoir where you can fish (with a licence). La Fresneda has a laundry, two swimming

pools, a tennis court and a small football pitch, and activities available include mountain bike hire, pony trekking and hiking trips with guides.

Camping Madrid
Carretera de Burgos (N-1), km 11, 28050 (91 302 28 35). Bus 151, 154, 155 from Plaza de Castilla; by car exit 12 from N-I. **Rates** *per night* 600ptas per person or per car; 450ptas under-12s; 6-700ptas per tent; 1,000ptas per caravan; 450ptas per motorcycle; 450ptas electricity. **Credit** AmEx, MC, V.
Recently renovated, this site is in the northern outskirts of Madrid and reasonably well connected by road with the centre, although difficult to reach by public transport. It's quite peaceful and nicely situated, and has a swimming pool, restaurant and bar, supermarket and free hot showers.

Camping Osuna
Avenida de Logroño s/n, 28042 (91 741 05 10). Metro Campo de las Naciones or Canillejas/bus 105, 115. **Rates** *per night* 690ptas per person; 600ptas under-10s; 690ptas per tent; 690ptas per car; *rooms* 5,265ptas for two people. **No credit cards.**
The closest campsite to central Madrid, and the only one within reasonable distance of any Metro stations. It's pleasantly situated amid parks in part of the 18th-century gardens of the Capricho de la Alameda de Osuna (*see p88*) and facilities include a bar/restaurant, currency exchange, shop, playground and 17 rooms available to rent in case you've forgotten your tent. On the downside, it's near the airport, so can be noisy.

Caravaning El Escorial
Carretera de Guadarrama a El Escorial, km. 3.5 (91 890 24 12). Bus 664 from Moncloa; by car N-VI, exit 47. **Rates** *per night* 700ptas per person, per car or per tent; 2,100ptas per plot; 675ptas under-12s; 500ptas electricity. **Credit** MC, V.
This luxury campsite, in the mountains about 45 minutes from Madrid, is set in 40 hectares (99 acres) of grounds and boasts four swimming pools and tennis, basketball and five-a-side football courts. Very popular with Spaniards, it also has a restaurant, café-bar, a laundrette, supermarket and disco.

Soto del Castillo
C/Soto del Rebollo s/n, 28300 Aranjuez (91 891 13 95). Bus Aisa from Estación Sur de Autobuses (Metro Méndez Alvaro) to Aranjuez; train Cercanías from Atocha. **Rates** 475ptas per person; 400ptas under-16s; 425-525ptas per tent; 400ptas per car; 325ptas per motorcycle; from 550ptas per caravan; from 600ptas motorhome; 525ptas electricity. **Credit** MC, V.
In a bend of the Tagus near the Royal Gardens of Aranjuez (*see p257*), this site has a lovely setting, with plenty of shade. Facilities include a restaurant, supermarket, social club, children's park and swimming pool, and bikes and canoes can be hired. It's a short walk from Aranjuez, a little under an hour's drive from Madrid, and well served by public transport. Rates vary according to the season.

Sightseeing

Feature boxes

Introduction

Madrid is a book that you read with your feet...

Sightseeing

Madrid is a city that has managed to pack a lot in over the years, in time and in space, and this density and variety within a very compact area has always been one of the city's essential characteristics. This makes things very convenient for the visitor. Madrid's most famous attraction, the Prado, and its two other major art museums (the Thyssen and the Reina Sofía) are all alongside the same avenue – the southern continuation of the Paseo de la Castellana – and together form the *Paseo del Arte* or 'art promenade'. And, in spite of all the recent growth on the city's outskirts, most of its other historic attractions are not far away either, as they too fall inside the area of 'old Madrid', which until the 19th century made up the entire city – between Glorieta de Bilbao and the Puerta de Toledo and Atocha, from north to south, and between the Palacio Real and Plaza de Cibeles, from west to east.

Visitors in the 1630s saw it as a sprawling city, but old Madrid was built to a human scale, and is manageable by foot. Trying to get anywhere by car within the old city is usually a waste of time, and even though there are good public transport links, unless you're in a real hurry you often find it's just as easy to walk, which, of course, also allows you to take in other things along the way. A map is handy,

but even visitors who prefer to wander without a specific destination in mind needn't lose out, for wherever they are in the city centre some of Madrid's eclectic sights will be within reach.

Despite its compactness, Madrid is a city of *barrios* or neighbourhoods, each with its own identity. The major districts are well established on the map, and in most cases are neatly divided by easy-to-identify main arteries. Elsewhere, or within them, though, a group of just a few streets might be considered by some to have a special feel – and so its own name – or there might be different alternative names to choose from for the same district. There are often long-running arguments about where one *barrio* ends and another begins, and some locals habitually refer to the place they live by the name of the nearest Metro station. The qualities that give a *barrio* its character are elusive: even new arrivals to the city soon form an attachment to their particular patch, but a myriad of details make up the vital differences. The division into areas we have followed throughout this Guide is a simplification of the intricate geography of Madrid, for convenience and comprehensibility. However, while you are here you may sometimes come across other names being used for smaller areas, sub-districts and other corners of the city.

Concessions & free entry days

Admission is free to most of the monuments administered by Spain's *Patrimonio Nacional*, which includes the Palacio Real, Descalzas Reales, the Encarnación and San Antonio de la Florida, on at least one day a week, usually **Wednesday**, (officially) for European Union citizens only. At other times there are reduced, concessionary prices for students, under-18s and over-65s. Admission is also free for all visitors to the state museums (which does not include the Museo Thyssen) on **Saturday afternoons** and **Sundays**, and entry to these museums is **free** at all times for anyone under 18 or over 65. There are reduced prices for students. For further details, see page 89.

HOLES IN THE GROUND
Since the early '90s Madrid has been a city of building schemes and tunnelling projects, associated particularly with Metro extensions and road and car park construction. The disruption they cause is never bad enough to ruin a visit to the city, but can be frustrating when you come upon them unannounced. In 2001-2, big construction sites are most likely to turn up along the route of Metro line 10, between Gregorio Marañón and the Casa de Campo. Large-scale renovation and improvement schemes including the renovation of whole squares are also underway in many parts of the old city, especially Lavapiés.

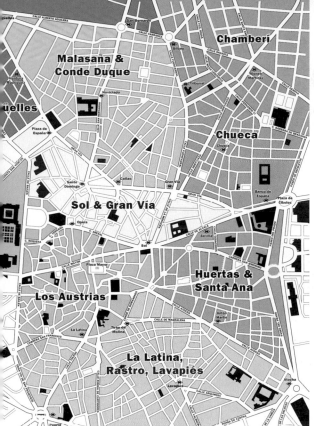

life went on pretty much as normal. Madrid continued to be slammed for seediness and lack of amenities, even by visitors such as 19th-century Romantics who found its people utterly fascinating.

The last half of the 19th century saw major infrastructure improvements. The walls came down, the railway came in and the Canal de Isabel II brought an (almost) unlimited supply of water down from the sierra. In the 1880s, finally, the wealthy became the first Madrileños to begin to move outside the limits of the Habsburg city, to the Salamanca district, the new hub of fashionable society. These transform-ations paved the way for a demographic upheaval as country people migrated from rural Spain into the big cities. In the 20th century Madrid sprawled out into entirely new areas miles beyond the old city, with factories, dormitory towns and a manic radial road system, and this mushrooming suburban spread is continuing apace in the 21st century (*see pages 28-9*).

BUILDING THE CITY

Propelled by royal whim into becoming the seat of Court and empire, this former Moorish town above the Manzanares was never in a hurry to become like any other European capital. It wasn't until the 17th century that Madrid acquired its first monumental flourishes. From the moment it became Spain's capital in 1561, observers and aspiring urban planners have complained endlessly about its lack of grandeur and a suitably orderly structure. Meanwhile, the shabby city walls put up in 1656 to ensure that tolls and taxes were charged on incoming goods continued to mark its limits until well into the 1860s.

Under the 18th-century Bourbons new monuments, churches and convents were added. Between the 1760s and 1780s King Charles III sought to dignify his capital with promenades, fountains and arches, street lighting and the city's first sewers. A couple of streets away from Charles' monuments, though,

Nevertheless, old Madrid, much of it rebuilt in the 19th century after the clearance of the city's monasteries, has remained very much the city's centre, the site of its most important attractions, cinemas and cultural and government institutions and a great many of its most popular restaurants, cafés and night-time venues. Only the business world has truly managed to move outside it, up the great spine of the Castellana. Many locals may now spend much of their workaday time in the newer, outer districts, or driving around the city periphery, but for visitors to Madrid, especially, the old city remains the great focus of attention. *Barrios* such as Huertas, Malasaña or Chueca continue to develop new life and draw in a steady flow of new residents, and this vibrancy and movement within an accessible, walkable core – far more intact and alive than in most cities at the end of the 20th century – is one of Madrid's permanent attractions.

Hubs of the City

Vital anchors to help you place yourself on the map.

Sightseeing

Every city has its essential reference points. If you drive into Madrid one of the first things you're likely to notice, after the M-30 and M-40 ring roads, is the **Paseo de la Castellana**, the great north-south avenue that cuts through the city almost from top to bottom, connects the old town to the new northern business districts and forms one of Madrid's most unusual features. On foot, on the other hand, you're far more likely to begin with the **Puerta del Sol** (*see page 59*), which is very literally the centre of the city, in that all street numbers in the city count up outwards from Sol, and it contains *kilómetro cero*, the point from which distances from Madrid to other parts of Spain are measured. Equally, Sol is also the main hub of the transport system.

Puerta del Sol is also a neutral meeting point for many of the districts of the old city – the old town of the early Habsburgs, Huertas, the streets leading up to Malasaña and Chueca to the north. East of Sol, the Calle de Alcalá runs down to another vital point on the map, **Plaza de Cibeles**, symbol of Madrid for Spaniards and the junction of the old city, the Castellana and the new city built up from the 19th century. To the west, Calle Mayor leads from Sol towards the **Plaza Mayor**, core of Madrid throughout its imperial golden age.

Three plazas

Plaza de Cibeles

Metro Banco de España/bus all routes to Plaza de Cibeles. **Map** p310 H7.

Midway between the Puerta del Sol and the Retiro park, this four-way intersection and its statue and fountain signify Madrid to Spaniards as much as Nelson's Column, the Eiffel Tower or the Empire State Building identify their particular cities. It is surrounded by some of the city's most prominent buildings. Clockwise from the most imposing of the four, the **Palacio de Comunicaciones** or post office, they are the **Banco de España** (for both, *see p63*), the Palacio Buenavista (now the Army headquarters) and the Palacio de Linares, which now houses the **Casa de América** (*see p107*). The Ventura Rodríguez statue in the middle is of *Cybele*, a Graeco-Roman goddess of fertility and symbol of natural abundance, on a chariot drawn by lions. The goddess and the fountain around her have traditionally been the gathering point for victorious

Real Madrid fans (Atlético supporters soak themselves in the fountain of Neptune, by the Museo Thyssen) and the place where wins by the Spanish national football team have been celebrated. Following the theft of Cybele's arm in one bout of revelry during the 1994 World Cup it was proposed that the (repaired) statue should be closed off to such activities, but Real fans (and the team) once again took over the goddess after their European Cup triumphs in 1998 and 2000. North of Cibeles the Paseo del Prado changes name to Paseo de Recoletos, shortly to become the Castellana, Madrid's endless north-south artery.

Plaza Mayor

Metro Sol/bus all routes to Puerta del Sol. **Map** p309 D8.

Madrid's grand main plaza was the city's hub for centuries. It began life in the 15th century as a humble market square, then called *Plaza del Arrabal* (Square outside the Walls). After Madrid was made capital of Spain by Philip II in the 1560s, Juan de Herrera drew up plans for it to be completely rebuilt, but the only part constructed immediately was the **Casa de la Panadería** (the Bakery). Dominating the square, with two pinnacle towers, it was completed under the direction of Diego Sillero in 1590. In the early 1990s, in a move that would not even be contemplated in most countries, this historic edifice was decorated with some striking, vaguely hippyish murals. The rest of the plaza was built by Juan Gómez de Mora for Philip III, and completed in 1619. Large sections had to be rebuilt after a disastrous fire in 1790. Bullfights, carnivals and all the great festivals and ceremonies of imperial Madrid were held here (*see p14*). At its centre is a 1616 statue of Philip III on horseback by Giambologna and Pietro Tacca, which stood originally in the Casa de Campo and was moved here in the last century.

The ample expanse of the square can be enjoyed in different ways at different times. Weekday mornings are calm, a perfect time to study the architecture or enjoy breakfast in one of the attractive (but expensive) cafés. Jewellery, hats, fans and other souvenirs can be bought in the plaza's shops, many of which retain their traditional façades. On Sunday mornings the plaza bustles with a stamp and coin market (*see p182*); other activities include the serving of giant paellas and free *cocido* to long lines of Madrileños during the **San Isidro** fiestas. For Christmas, it houses a traditional fair with stalls for both events, *see pp186 and 189*). From the south side of the Plaza, Calle Toledo runs down towards La Latina and Lavapiés, and the Rastro market.

Greeting the sun in **Puerta del Sol**.

Puerta del Sol

Metro Sol/bus all routes to Puerta del Sol.
Map p309 E7.

It's nearly impossible to visit Madrid and not pass through this semicircular space, if only because it is very much the hub of the public transport system. From here, too, Calles Arenal and Mayor lead away to the opera house, the Palacio Real and the Plaza Mayor, while to the east Calle Alcalá and Carrera de San Jerónimo run to the Huertas area, the Paseo del Prado and the main museums. It is called a *puerta* (gate) because this was indeed the main, easternmost gate of 15th-century Madrid. Under the Habsburg kings it was surrounded by churches and monasteries, and the space between them eventually supplanted the Plaza Mayor as the city's main meeting place. It was rebuilt in its present form in 1854-62. It still is Madrid's most popular meeting point, particularly the spot by the monument with the symbols of Madrid, a bear and a *madroño* or strawberry tree, at the junction with Calle Carmen. Across from there is the square's most important building, the **Casa de Correos**, built in 1766 by Jaime Marquet as a post office for Charles III. Today it houses the Madrid regional government, the Comunidad de Madrid. It was altered significantly in 1866 when the large clock tower was added; this is now the building's best-known feature, since it's the clock the whole country looks to on New Year's Eve, when

Madrileños crowd into the square to await the 12 chimes (*see p189*). In the 1990s the tower developed a precarious incline due to rot in its timbers, but it was rebuilt and unveiled once again in 1998. In front of it is *kilómetro cero*, the mark from which distances from Madrid are measured.

The Castellana

Madrid may not have a Thames or Seine to dominate the urban layout – the city's own humble river, the Manzanares, has never been more than an accessory in local affairs (*see page 69*) – but it has something similar, its own peculiar 'river' – except that it's a road, the Castellana. Look at any map of Madrid and you see it, a long, sometimes curving, sometimes dead-straight strip, running north-south for miles right through the city. At different points it is called, from south to north, the Paseo del Prado, Paseo de Recoletos and then Paseo de la Castellana, which opens up into a four-lane highway. It is as if, in a city where people had so often complained of the lack of grand avenues, somebody had suddenly decided to silence the critics with one single thoroughfare such as they'd never seen before.

This endless strip developed gradually rather than out of one decision. The most attractive section, and the one that most new arrivals in Madrid first become familiar with, is the oldest, the **Paseo del Prado**, from Atocha up to Plaza de Cibeles. Once an open space between the city wall and the Retiro – *prado* means 'meadow' – it was given its present form in 1775-82, to a design chiefly by José de Hermosilla, as the most important of Charles III's attempts to give his shabby capital the kind of urbane dignity he had seen in Paris and Italy. The King intended it to be a grand avenue lined by centres of learning and science (*see page 16*). The form of the main section, from Cibeles to Plaza Cánovas del Castillo and originally called *Salón del Prado*, was modelled on the Piazza Navona in Rome, with three fountains by Ventura Rodríguez: Cibeles at the most northerly point

Sightseeing

The **Plaza Mayor**, seen at (relative) peace, and bustling during San Isidro.

Tours

Sightseeing

Bus tours

Open-top buses

Three companies currently offer open-top bus tours on similar routes around Madrid, with multilingual commentary and taking in all the main sights in the city centre and parts of Salamanca and the Retiro. As a way to get your bearings they're useful, and allow you to see some architectural details (especially on Gran Vía) that are hard to see from ground level. All pass through Sol, the Gran Vía and Plaza de España, which are good places to board. Tickets, bought on board, allow you to get off and on buses (of the same company) as many times as you like on the same day. The companies currently have the same daytime prices: 1,600ptas adults; 800ptas under-15s and over-65s; free under-6s.

Bus companies

Madrid Vision *(91 302 03 68/91 767 17 43/www.trapsa.com/madridvision/ index.htm).* **Tours** *9.45am-7pm daily.* **Credit** *V.*
Sol Open Tours *(902 30 39 03/ 91 522 11 20/solopentours.com).* **Tours** *10am-6.30pm daily.* **No credit cards.*
TouristBus *(91 892 90 48).* **Tours** *10am-11.45pm daily.* **No credit cards.* There is a reduced price of 1,000ptas (800ptas, under-15s, over-65s) after 8.30pm.

Coach tours

Both these companies offer a standard range of coach-with-guide tours: bullfights, evening tours with flamenco shows and so on. They also offer the same time-worn menu of tours of the towns around Madrid (Toledo, Segovia, Aranjuez and others), for 5,000-10,700ptas.

Companies

Juliá Tours *Gran Vía 68, Sol & Gran Vía (91 559 96 05). Metro Santo Domingo/ bus all routes to Gran Vía.* **Open** *8am-8.30pm Mon-Sat; 8am-4.30pm Sun.* **Tickets** *tours within Madrid 2,750ptas-13,200ptas.* **No credit cards.* **Map** *p309 D6.*
Pullmantur *Office: C/Orense 16, Cuatro Caminos (91 556 11 14). Metro Nuevos Ministerios/bus 5, 149, C.* **Open** *9am-1.30pm, 4.30-7.30pm Mon-Fri, 9am-1.30pm Sat; closed Sun.* **Tickets** *tours within Madrid 2,750-10,000ptas.* **Credit** *AmEx, V. Bus terminal: Plaza de Oriente 8, Los Austrias (91 541 18 05). Metro Opera/ bus 3, 25, 39, 148.* **Map** *p308 C7.*

Walking tours

Descubre Madrid

C/Mayor 69, Los Austrias (91 588 29 06/07). Metro Sol/bus all routes to Puerta del Sol. **Open** *July-Sept 8.30am-2.30pm Mon-Fri; closed Sat, Sun. Oct-June 8.30am-2.30pm Mon, Tue, Thur, Fri; 8.30am-2.30pm,*

and Neptune to the south, with a smaller figure of Apollo in the middle. The southern stretch of the Paseo, tapering down to Atocha, has another statue, the Four Seasons, in front of the Museo del Prado.

In the 19th century the Paseo del Prado was the great promenade of Madrid. Virtually the entire population, rich and poor, took a turn along it each evening, to see and be seen, pick up on the latest city gossip, make assignations, and show off their clothes and carriages.

The tree-lined boulevard still has many attractions today, despite the traffic, most notably Madrid's 'big three' great art museums (for details of which, *see pages 89-99*). As well as Charles III's creations such as the **Jardín Botánico** *(see page 63)* and the **Museo del Prado** itself, there are, at the very bottom, the **Centro de Arte Reina Sofía** and **Atocha** station *(see page 63)*. On the south side of the

Botanical Gardens there are the second-hand bookstalls of the **Cuesta de Moyano** *(see page 163)*. Further up, by the statue of Neptune there is the **Museo Thyssen**, almost opposite such important elements in local life as the **Bolsa** *(see page 63)* and the **Hotel Ritz**. To the left, looking up, streets lead off into Huertas and the old city, while to the right is the tranquil district of the Retiro.

The continuation north of Cibeles, **Paseo de Recoletos**, was mostly added in the 1830s and 1840s. It is a bit more businesslike than its predecessor, but still green and elegant, with fashionable cafés such as **El Espejo** and the **Café Gijón** *(see pages 154-5)*. The curiously grand marble palace a little further north on the right, now the **Banco Hipotecario**, was once the residence of the Marqués de Salamanca, 19th-century Madrid's huckster-in-chief *(see page 81)*.

60 Time Out Madrid Guide

4-6pm Wed; closed Sat, Sun. **Tickets** *On foot* 500ptas. *By bus* 950ptas. **No credit cards. Map** p309 D8.

Run by the city tourist board, this service offers walking and bus tours covering every aspect of Madrid, its architecture, literary life, little-known figures and so on. Most of the many itineraries are available only in Spanish, but even if you don't speak much of the language they can be interesting, and some include sights and buildings otherwise difficult to get into.

Old Madrid Walking Tours

Tours depart from Plaza Mayor 3, Los Austrias (91 588 16 36). Metro Sol/bus all routes to Puerta del Sol. **Tours** *Velázquez y el Palacio del Buen Retiro:* 10am in English & Spanish, Wed; *Madrid de Velázquez: Oct-April* 8pm, *May-July* 9pm, in English & Spanish, Fri; *Madrid de los Austrias:* 10am in English, noon in Spanish, Sat. **Tickets** 500ptas; 400ptas concessions. **No credit cards. Map** p309 D8.

Also run by the city office, these interesting tours give a good introduction, in English, to different aspects of Golden Age Madrid. The Velázquez (Fri) and Austrias (Sat) tours start at the tourist office in the Plaza Mayor (see page 287); the Retiro tour (Wed) begins at the Paseo del Prado entrance to the Museo del Prado. You are asked to be at the departure point half an hour in advance; tours last about two hours.

Other adventures

Medios Publicitarios Hinchables

C/Gutiérrez Solana 6, Cuatro Caminos (91 563 38 84/908 81 50 53). Metro Santiago Bernabéu/bus 14, 27, 43, 150. **Open** *July, Aug* 9am-3pm Mon-Fri; closed Sat, Sun. *Sept-June* 9am-2pm, 5-8pm Mon-Fri; closed Sat, Sun. **Tickets** 25,000ptas for 1hr 30min flight.

Balloon trips over Madrid and the Guadarrama, by appointment only, departing from Villanueva del Pardillo, west of Madrid near Las Rozas. Trips longer than two hours can be arranged.

Trapsatur

Office C/San Bernardo 23, Malasaña & Conde Duque (91 541 63 20/ www.trapsa.com). Metro Noviciado/ bus 147. **Open** 7.30pm-9.30pm Mon-Sat; 7.30am-4.30pm Sun. **Tickets** *To El Escorial* 5,950ptas, 8.45am, 3.45pm daily; *To Toledo & El Escorial* 12,000ptas, 8.45am daily. **Credit** AmEx, MC, V. **Map** p305 E4.

Flights in four-seater light aircraft (so bookings can be made for groups of three), from Cuatro Vientos airfield southwest of the city. They do not actually fly over Madrid, but skirt the city on the way north. Flights over El Escorial last about 45min, and 90min flights take in Segovia. Transport is provided between the office and Cuatro Vientos.

At the north end of Recoletos on the right stands the huge building housing the **Biblioteca Nacional** and, behind it, the **Museo Arqueológico Nacional**. The most ambitious project of the reign of Isabel II, it was commissioned in 1865, but only completed in 1892. It overlooks the **Plaza de Colón**, where, at Columbus' feet, a cascading wallof water, beautifully cool in summer, conceals the entrance to the **Centro Cultural de la Villa** arts centre (*see pages 107 and 243*).

In 1860, when he designed Madrid's *Ensanche* ('extension'; *see page 19*), Carlos María de Castro took the significant decision, since the Paseo del Prado and Recoletos were already there, to continue along the same route with the main avenue of the new district. Thus the Castellana was born. Until the Republic of 1931 demolished Madrid's old racetrack it reached only as far as Calle Joaquín Costa. Today it snakes away freely northwards, through thickets of office blocks. It also contains, near the junction with Calle Juan Bravo (location of the **Museo de Esculturas al Aire Libre**, for which *see page 64*), Madrid's 'beach' of upmarket terrace bars, at the height of fashion in the mid-1990s (*see page 231*). To the east is the Salamancadistrict, heart of affluent Madrid, and thecity's most upscale shopping area.

In the 1970s and '80s banks and insurance companies vied with each other to commission in-vogue architects to create prestige corporate showcases along the upper Castellana. Constructions to see and judge include the **Bankinter** building at no.29, and **Bankunión** at no.46. The junction with Calle Joaquín Costa is marked by the Kafkaesque grey bulk of the enormous **Nuevos Ministerios** government buildings (*see page 64*).

Inescapable: **Museo del Prado**. *See p90.*

Beyond that, a huge branch of the Corte Inglés signals your arrival at the **AZCA** complex (*see page 64*), a monument to '80s corporate taste. A little further up again, opposite each other, are Real Madrid's **Estadio Bernabéu** (*see page 64*) and the **Palacio de Congresos** conference centre. By this time, the view up the Castellana is dominated by the two leaning towers officially known as the **Puerta de Europa** at Plaza Castilla. These remarkable smoked-glass blocks, 15° off perpendicular, are perhaps the greatest monument to Spain's 1980s boom, begun with finance from the Kuwait Investment Office (so that the towers are more often called the **Torres KIO**) and left unfinished for years after a financial scandal in 1992. With their phallic fountain in the middle, they have now joined the landmarks of modern Madrid.

Sights along the Castellana are listed here from bottom to top, south to north. The Metro system partly avoids the avenue, but the 27 bus runs up and down the whole stretch, the Paseo del Prado, Recoletos and the Castellana.

Estación de Atocha
Glorieta del Emperador Carlos V. Metro Atocha/bus all routes to Atocha. **Map** p310 H10.
Madrid's classic wrought-iron and glass main rail station was built in 1888-92, to a design by Alberto del Palacio. It remained much the same, gathering a coating of soot, until the 1980s, when Rafael Moneo – he of the Museo Thyssen – gave it a complete renovation in preparation for Spain's golden year of 1992. Entirely new sections were added for the AVE high-speed train to Andalusia and the *Cercanías* local rail network, and an indoor tropical garden was installed. Even if you're not catching a train, a visit to Atocha is worthwhile to see this imaginative blend of old and new.

Jardín Botánico
Plaza de Murillo (91 420 30 17). Metro Atocha/bus all routes to Atocha. **Open** *Oct-Apr* 10am-dusk daily. *May-Sept* 10am-9pm daily. **Admission** 250ptas; 125ptas concessions. **Map** p310 H9.
Madrid's luscious botanical gardens were created for Charles III by Juan de Villanueva and the botanist Gómez Ortega in 1781. They are right alongside the Paseo del Prado, just south of the Prado museum, but inside this deep-green glade, with over 30,000 plants from around the world, it's easy to feel that city life has been put on hold. Ideal for a stroll or a moment's peace in spring, early summer or autumn.

Bolsa de Comercio de Madrid
Plaza de la Lealtad 1 (91 589 26 00). Metro Banco de España/bus 9, 27, 34, 37, 45. **Open** *exhibition space* 10am-2pm Mon-Fri; closed Sat, Sun. **Admission** free. **Map** p310 H7.
In the same plaza as the Hotel Ritz, Madrid's stock exchange is a landmark as well as a business centre. Enrique María Repullés won the competition to design the building in 1884, with a neo-classical style chosen to reflect that of the nearby Prado. The building has two distinct areas. One, the trading area; the second, open to the public, houses an exhibition on the market's history. *See also p279.*

Banco de España
Plaza de Cibeles. Metro Banco de España/bus all routes to Cibeles. **Map** p310 G7.
A grandiose pile designed in 1882 by Eduardo Adaro and Severiano Saínz de la Lastra to house the recently created Bank of Spain. The eclectic style was most influenced by French Second-Empire designs, with a few Viennese touches. The decorative arched window and elaborate clock above the main entrance are best appreciated from a distance.

Palacio de Comunicaciones (Correos)
Plaza de Cibeles (91 521 65 00). Metro Banco de España/bus all routes to Plaza de Cibeles. **Open** 8.30am-9.30pm Mon-Fri; 9.30am-9.30pm Sat; 8.30am-2pm Sun. **Map** p310 H7.
Recent arrivals in Madrid often refuse to believe that this extraordinary construction, dwarfing the Plaza de Cibeles and regularly compared to a sand-castle or a wedding cake, can be just a post office. However, that's what it is. Madrid's main post office was designed in 1904 by Antonio Palacios and Joaquín Otamendi and completed in 1918, and is the best example of the extravagant style favoured by Madrid's elite at their most expensive. The design

Estación de Atocha. *See p63.*

was influenced by Viennese art nouveau, but also features many traditional Spanish touches. Its sheer quality-kitsch style has made it a much loved institution. Customers who come to buy stamps or post a parcel are treated to a grand entrance (with oversized revolving door), a Hollywood film-set staircase, soaring ceilings, stunning columns and grand marble floors. For details of mail services, *see p280*.

Museo de Esculturas al Aire Libre

Paseo de la Castellana 41. Metro Rubén Darío/bus 5, 7, 27, 45, 150. **Map** p307 I2.

An unconventional museum, this 1970s space at the junction of the Castellana with Calle Juan Bravo was the brainchild of engineers José Antonio Fernández Ordoñez and Julio Martínez Calzón. Designing a bridge across the avenue, they thought the space underneath would be a good art venue, and sculptor Eusebio Sempere convinced fellow artists to donate their work. The result, often unappreciated by all except a few skateboarders, is one of the most original modern spaces in Madrid. All the major names in late 20th-century Spanish sculpture are represented – Pablo Serrano, Miró, Chillida – and much of their work is spectacular, especially the dynamic stainless-steel *Mon per a infants* ('A world for children') by Andreu Alfaro and the spectacular cascade by Sempere that forms a centrepiece to the whole 'museum'.

Nuevos Ministerios

Paseo de la Castellana 67. Metro Nuevos Ministerios/ bus 5, 12, 27, 40, 45.

A seemingly endless, bunkerish building that contains a complex of government ministries, begun in 1932 and one of the largest projects bequeathed by the Spanish Republic to Madrid. It was designed by a team led by Secundino Zuazo, chief architect of the *Gran Madrid* plan (*see p22*), in a monolithic '30s rationalist style; then, after the victory of Franco, the same architect added to the still-unfinished building curving, traditionalist details more to the taste of the new regime. Inside it has a park-like garden, open to the public, that's often frequented by local office workers taking a break from the city.

Urbanización AZCA

Paseo de la Castellana 95 & Avda General Perón. Metro Nuevos Ministerios or Santiago Bernabéu/ bus 5, 27, 40, 147, 150.

Known to some as 'Little Manhattan', this glitzy skyscraper development was first projected during the Franco regime's industrial heyday in the '60s, but gained extra vigour in democratic Spain's 1980s boom to become a symbol of Madrid yuppiedom. The most striking of its giant blocks are the circular **Torre Europa** and the **Torre Picasso**, designed by Japanese architect Minori Yamasaki in 1988 and, at 157m (515ft), Madrid's tallest building. Between them is Plaza Picasso, a well-maintained park. Amid the office blocks, there are a chic shopping mall, restaurants and other facilities to allow workers to spend their whole day here without needing to venture outside. As to the name, don't try to figure it out, as the letters AZCA apparently don't stand for anything at all.

Estadio Santiago Bernabéu

Paseo de la Castellana 144. Metro Santiago Bernabéu/bus 14, 27, 147, 150.

The temple of Real Madrid football club, designed in the '40s and named after the club's long-time chairman. A colossal grey structure, it resembles a stack of cans each larger than the next, with swirling stairwells at each corner. It has capacity for 105,000 fans. *See also p237*.

Jardín Botánico, a green refuge. *See p63.*

The Old City

Art deco avenues and baroque spires, crowded shops and time-worn alleys, enclosed monasteries, a gay village and any number of places to eat, drink and talk: Madrid's historic core contains them all.

Austrias to Gran Vía

Los Austrias

The area between Sol, the Palacio Real and San Francisco el Grande contains within it the oldest part of the city, and so is commonly known as the 'Madrid of the Austrias' or 'Habsburg Madrid', although in truth Philip II and his dynasty can scarcely claim responsibility for very much of it. At its core is the greatest monument they did build, the **Plaza Mayor**, archetypal creation of the Castilian-baroque style (*see page 31*). Battered and sometimes burnt over the years, the Plaza has been expensively restored since the 1980s. But then, the Plaza Mayor has seen it all: executions, riots, bullfights, wild carnival revels and the nastier doings of the Inquisition. Today, it welcomes coin and stamp collectors for their Sunday market, dance bands during *fiestas* and tourists all year long, with a unique selection of traditional shops and pavement cafés that are sometimes overpriced, but pleasant nonetheless.

In the south-west corner of the plaza there is a tourist office (*see page 287*) and an arch, the **Arco de los Cuchilleros** (Knifemakers' Arch), with a spectacular bank of steps that leads down through Calle de los Cuchilleros to the Plaza de la Puerta Cerrada, decorated with some engaging 1970s murals. The street leading away on the opposite, south, side of this plaza is Calle Cava Baja, home to the most celebrated *mesones*, temples to Madrid's hefty traditional cuisine (*see p124-7*). Directly south of the Plaza Mayor in Calle Toledo stand the twin baroque towers of **San Isidro** (*see page 68*), perhaps Madrid's most important historic church.

To the south-east, where Calle Atocha runs up to the Plaza Mayor in the Plaza de la Provincia, is another major work of Castilian baroque, the squatly proportioned **Palacio de Santa Cruz** of 1629-43, the work of several architects (*see page 31*). Despite its grand appearance it was originally the Court prison, with a dungeon so deep prisoners had to rub their rags with lard and set them alight to stop themselves going blind, although it now has a more dignified role

San Pedro el Viejo. *See p71.*

as the Foreign Ministry. In former times executions often took place in the **Plaza de la Cebada**, just a tumbrel ride away.

The area between Plaza de la Cebada, Mayor and the Palacio Real really is the oldest part of the city, the site of the Muslim town and of most of medieval Madrid. This may not be immediately apparent today, even though most of the streets still follow their original medieval lines. Like several other parts of the old city, this area has been smartened up recently, and become something of a leisure area for the over-30s, with wine bars and smartish restaurants. Getting a sense of medieval or early Habsburg Madrid requires an exercise of the imagination (*see page 66* **Walk 1: Madrid of another age**). Tucked away in sidestreets are **San Pedro el Viejo** and, across Calle Mayor, **San Nicolás de los Servitas** (for both, *see page 71*), the only two

Walk 1: Madrid of another age

In terms of bricks and mortar, there is little left of the Madrid that Philip II saw when he decided to make this market town the capital of the Spanish Empire. The 16th-century exteriors that once fronted its interconnecting squares – Paja, Plaza de la Cruz Verde, Plaza de los Carros – were mostly replaced in the 19th century. Nevertheless, these intimate plazas and most of the winding streets of the district of 'Los Austrias' still follow their original Arab and medieval courses, and with a little imagination a walk around these alleys can still be evocative of the atmosphere of the Habsburg city, and the medieval town before it (this walk is marked in **yellow** on the maps on pages 308-9).

A natural place to begin is the **Plaza Mayor**, the centre of Madrid life for four centuries. The steps from the Arco de Cuchilleros, in the south-west corner, lead down to Calle Cuchilleros, where on the left there is the 18th-century **Casa Botín**, the oldest restaurant in the city (if not the world, see page 126). Continue across the Puerta Cerrada into **Calle Cava Baja** (pictured), and you will be walking along the line of the 12th-century wall, although it's now lined with restaurants specialising in traditional Madrileño cuisine. Cut right up Calle Almendro, and take the first right again down the narrow Pretíl de San Sebastián. At the end is the pretty **Calle del Nuncio**, now home to two of the many new wine bars that have sprung up in the area. Turn left, and on the Costanilla de San Pedro is the dusty 17th-century church of **San Pedro el Viejo**, with its 14th-century minaret-like *Mudéjar* tower.

Carry on past San Pedro through Calle Príncipe de Anglona, veer left and you'll enter the **Plaza de la Paja** (Straw Square), which as the grain and fodder market was at the heart of medieval Madrid, and probably marked the southernmost point of the Arab wall. The only substantial buildings that outlived 19th century reconstruction are **San Andrés** and the **Capillas del Obispo** and **San Isidro**.

On the south side of San Andrés there is what appears to be one, albeit rambling square, but which traditionally consists of several sections with different names. As well as the Plaza de la Cebada (Barley Square), once the site for public executions, and the Plaza de San Andres, there is the **Plaza de la Puerta de Moros** ('Moors' Gate') – site of the gateway to the Muslim quarter or *Morería* under Christian rule. From there head down Carrera de San Francisco towards **San Francisco el Grande**, beautifully lit at night, and the cavernous dome of which can be seen in several of Goya's skylines. To the right of the church, continue along Travesía de las Vistillas to Calle de la Moreria, which winds back over C/Bailén down to **Plaza de la Moreria**. The knot of streets between here and Plaza de la Paja and Puerta de Moros formed the *Morería*, to which Madrid's community of *Mudéjar* Muslims were confined for four centuries (see page 8). The little Plaza de la Morería (also called Plaza del Alamillo) was the site of the Mosque and the *Aljama*, the Muslim community courts. Today it is more a shady, bar-lined side street than a square.

Alamillo ends at **Calle Segovia**. Cross over it, and head up through Calle del Rollo and over Calle Sacramento. Turn right and then left up through Calle del Codo (Elbow Street), stopping off, in Plaza Conde de Miranda, at the 17th-century **Convento de las Carboneras**, a closed order of nuns who sell own-baked biscuits through a grill in the wall (see page 174). This little alley leads round into the **Plaza de la Villa**, with the city hall. It began life as the Arab souk, and so continued to be Madrid's main square until the creation of the Plaza Mayor. At night, especially in winter, it is just possible to imagine it as it was in the 17th century.

medieval *Mudéjar* towers in Madrid. If you continue down Calle Segovia beneath the viaduct you will pass Madrid's oldest relic, a forlorn fragment of the **Muralla Árabe** (Arab Wall; *see page 68*), embedded in a rocky ridge.

Back into town along Calle Mayor is the **Plaza de la Villa** (*see page 70*), the city's oldest square, and so still home to the city hall, the **Casa de la Villa**. In pre-Habsburg Madrid this was also the preferred place for residences of the local élite, one of which, the **Torre de los Lujanes**, is still there. Together with the third construction on the square, the **Casa de Cisneros**, they make up a compendium of the history of Madrid from provincial town to imperial capital.

The Calle Mayor was the main thoroughfare of Madrid for centuries. Cross-streets between Mayor and Arenal offer an odd mixture of bookbinders and picture-framers, liturgical outfitters and Galician restaurants. The western end of Mayor, near the Palacio Real, has several old palaces, and **Casa Ciriaco**, one of the city's most famous restaurants (*see page 114*).

Calle Mayor runs out west into Calle Bailén, connected southwards to a splendid 1930s concrete viaduct offering views of the sierra and the Casa de Campo. However, the viaduct's notoriety as a suicide point has led the city authorities to place giant glass panels all along it, giving it a very strange look and feel without doing that much to reduce the suicide rate. At the southern end of the viaduct is the hill and park of **Las Vistillas** (*see page 70*), with more great views and cafés from which to observe them, and the giant church of **San Francisco el Grande**.

In the opposite direction, Calle Bailén runs up past the **Almudena** cathedral and the **Palacio Real** (*see page 68*) to dip through a tunnel under the now-pedestrianised **Plaza de Oriente** (*see page 70*). On the esplanade between the cathedral and the palace archaeological excavations are finally under way of some of the remains of the original Muslim fortress and of the foundations of Philip II's Alcázar, covered over by the building of the later Palacio Real. Some of the masonry uncovered, including some impressive Moorish arches, is currently visible through the fence around the dig; in future (from around 2003), the excavations will be permanently open to public view as part of a visit to the Palacio Real. Behind the palace, the delightful **Campo del Moro** gardens run down towards the Manzanares and the Paseo de la Florida (*see page 69* **The unknown river**).

On the east side of Plaza de Oriente is Madrid's opera house, the **Teatro Real** (*see page 216*). From here Calle Arenal, originally a stream bed, leads back to the Puerta del Sol. Off Arenal, in the alleyway next to the glitzy-tacky Joy Eslava disco that snakes around the little

church of **San Ginés**, there are bookstalls that have been bringing in the browsers since 1850, and the Chocolatería San Ginés, an institution for late-night revellers in need of sustenance (*see page 234*).

Basílica de San Francisco el Grande

Plaza de San Francisco s/n (91 365 38 00). Metro La Latina/bus 3, 17, 35, 60, 148, C. **Open** *Oct-May* 11am-1pm, 4-7pm Tue-Sat; closed Sun. *June-Sept* 11am-1pm, 5-8pm Tue-Sat; closed Sun. **Admission** 100ptas. **Map** p308 C9.

This huge, multi-tiered church between Puerta de Toledo and the Palacio Real is difficult to miss. A monastery on the site, reputedly founded by Saint Francis of Assisi, was knocked down in 1760; in its place Francisco Cabezas and later Francesco Sabatini built this neo-classical church from 1761 to 1784. Most challenging was the construction of the dome, with a diameter of 33m (108ft). So unusual (and potentially unstable) was it that it has recently needed extensive restoration work. Inside there is an early Goya, *The Sermon of San Bernardino of Siena* of 1781, and several frescoes by other artists. Visitors are not admitted during weddings.

Campo del Moro

Paseo de la Virgen del Puerto (91 542 00 59). Metro Opera or Príncipe Pío/bus 25, 33, 39, 46, 75, C. **Open** *Oct-Mar* 10am-6pm Mon-Sat; 9am-6pm Sun, public holidays. *Apr-Sept* 10am-8pm Mon-Sat; 9am-8pm Sun, public holidays. **Map** p308 B7.

Before or after a visit to the Palacio Real it's worth wandering around the pleasant formal garden below it, towards the river, though sadly, access is now only possible from the Paseo Virgen del Puerto side, and so to reach the entrance you have to walk down Cuesta de San Vicente or Cuesta de la Vega. As a reward you will see two fine monumental fountains. Nearest the palace, is *Los Tritones*, originally made in 1657 for the palace in Aranjuez (*see p257*); the other is *Las Conchas*, designed in the 18th century by Ventura Rodríguez. Both were moved here in the 1890s. The Campo del Moro also contains a Museum of Royal Carriages, which has been closed for renovation for so long that hardly anyone remembers what's inside it.

Catedral de la Almudena

C/Bailén 10 (91 542 22 00). Metro Opera/bus 3, 25, 39, 148. **Open** 9am-9pm daily. **Map** p308 C7/8.

If ever a project looked like it would last for ever, this was it. For centuries, Church and State could not agree whether Madrid should have a cathedral. When they did, in the 1880s, it took 110 years to complete. In 1883 work began on a neo-Gothic design by the Marqués de Cubas, but this scheme went off course after only the crypt, accessible from Calle Mayor, was completed. Another architect, Fernando Chueca Goitia, took over in 1944, and introduced a neo-classical style. It has failed to attract popular affection over the years, but was finally finished in 1993 – an achievement marked by a visit from the

Regal retreat: the palatial gardens of the **Campo del Moro**. *See p67.*

Pope. Until 1870, when it was knocked down by liberal urban reformers, the site contained the church of Santa María de la Almudena, formerly the main mosque of Muslim Madrid.

Iglesia-Catedral de San Isidro (La Colegiata)

C/Toledo 37 (91 369 20 37). Metro La Latina or Tirso de Molina/bus 17, 23, 31, 35, 65.
Open 7.30am-1pm, 6.30-8.30pm Mon-Sat; 9am-2pm, 5.30-8.30pm Sun, public holidays.
Map p309 D8.
This giant church was built as part of the *Colegio Imperial*, centre of the Jesuit order in Spain, in 1622-33. The high-baroque design was by Pedro Sánchez (himself a member of the order), inspired by the mother church of the Jesuits, the Gesù in Rome; the façade was completed by Francisco Bautista in 1664. In 1768, after Charles III's dispute with the Jesuits (*see p16*), the church was separated from the college, dedicated to San Isidro and altered by Ventura Rodríguez to accommodate the remains of the saint and his spouse, brought from the Capilla de San Isidro (*see p70*). It was Madrid's 'provisional' cathedral from 1885 until the completion of the Almudena in 1993; nevertheless, although it has not formed part of the Jesuit college for centuries, it is still often popularly known as *la Colegiata*.

Muralla Arabe (Arab Wall)

Cuesta de la Vega. Metro Opera/ bus 3, 14, 31, 50, 65. **Map** p308 B8.
Until the 1980s, this crumbling stretch of ninth-century rampart, the only substantial relic of Madrid's Muslim founders, was virtually ignored by the city.

As some recompense the Tierno Galván city administration renamed the area around it the **Parque Emir Mohammed I**. It's occasionally used as a venue in summer arts festivals (*see p188*).

Palacio Real (Palacio de Oriente)

Plaza de Oriente, C/Bailén s/n (91 542 00 59/91 454 88 00/guided tours 91 454 88 03). Metro Opera/ bus 3, 25, 39, 148. **Open** 9am-6pm Mon-Sat; 9am-3pm Sun, public holidays; closed during official acts; *guided tours (phone to book)* 9am-2pm Mon-Fri.
Admission 900ptas; 350ptas concessions.
Free to EU citizens Wed. *Guided tours* 1,000ptas.
Temporary exhibitions 500ptas; 250ptas concessions.
Guided tours of permanent & temporary exhibits 1,300ptas. **No credit cards**. **Map** p308 C7.
You are unlikely to catch sight of Spain's royal family here, as this 3,000-room official residence is only visited by them for occasional state functions requiring additional grandeur. The rest of the time the palace, commissioned by Philip V after the earlier Alcázar was lost to a fire in 1734, is open to view. The architects principally responsible for the final design, which reflects the taste of the Spanish Bourbons, were Italian – Giambattista Sacchetti and Francesco Sabatini, with contributions by the Spaniard Ventura Rodríguez. Filippo Juvarra, Philip V's first choice, had planned a palace four times as large, but after his death the project became a little less ambitious. Completed in 1764, the late-baroque palace is built almost entirely of granite and white Colmenar stone, and, surrounded by majestic gardens, contributes greatly to the splendour of the city.

Inside, you must keep to a fixed itinerary, but are free to set your own pace rather than follow a tour.

The unknown river

Madrid's river, the Manzanares, has often been disparaged. Quevedo called it 'a ditch learning to be a river', and a visiting French aristocrat once made the much-repeated quip, upon seeing the regal Puente de Segovia, that since the city had such a fine bridge, then maybe it should now get a river. In the years after the Civil War people still swam in it. The river was neglected, though, from the 1950s to the '70s, and, lined for long stretches by the M-30, it became heavily polluted.

The Socialist city administration of the early 1980s initiated a major clean-up, and a pleasant walk was opened along the stretch of the river from the Puente del Rey, by the entrance to the Casa de Campo, north to Puente de los Franceses. Beside the river there is one of the lesser-known artistic jewels of Madrid, **San Antonio de la Florida**, just beside it there's a great stop-off spot in the Asturian cider-house **Casa Mingo** (see page 121), and across the river in the district of **Ribera del Manzanares** there are more pleasant restaurants, some with riverside terraces in summer. Further south, there are some more, if less attractive, riverside walks by Madrid's two historic bridges.

Ermita de San Antonio de la Florida

Glorieta de San Antonio de la Florida 5 (91 542 07 22). Metro Príncipe Pío/ bus 41, 46, 75. **Open** 10am-2pm, 4-8pm Tue-Fri; 10am-2pm Sat, Sun; closed Mon, public holidays. **Admission** 300ptas; 150ptas concessions. Free to all Wed; to EU citizens Sun. **Map** p304 A4.

This plain neo-classical chapel was completed by Felipe Fontana for Charles IV in 1798. Quite out of the way, north of Príncipe Pío station on the Paseo de la Florida, outside the Parque del Oeste, it is famous as the burial place of Goya, and for the unique frescoes of the miracles of Saint Anthony (pictured top right), incorporating scenes of Madrid life, which he painted here in 1798. In contrast to the rather staid exterior, the colour and use of light in Goya's images are stunning; featuring a rare mix of elements, including his unique, simultaneously ethereal and sensual 'angels', they are among his best and most complex work, and have been reborn through a major restoration programme begun for the 250th anniversary of Goya's birth in 1996. Forming a pair, with the Ermita, on the other side of the

road into the park is a near-identical second chapel, built in the 1920s in order to allow the original building to be left as a museum. There are free guided tours of the Ermita, in Spanish and English, at 11am and noon on Saturdays.

Puente de Segovia

C/Segovia. Metro Puerta del Angel/bus 25, 31, 36, 39, 65, 138, C. **Map** p308 A8.
When travelling by car over this stone bridge (pictured below) it's hard to imagine that it was commissioned by Philip II from Juan de Herrera and completed in 1584, to make it easier for the King to get to El Escorial (see page 249). It's best appreciated from a distance, along the river's edge. As has often been noted, its elegant arches make it much grander than the Manzanares flowing beneath it.

Puente de Toledo

Glorieta de Pirámides.
Metro Marqués de Vadillo or Pirámides/bus 23, 35, 36, 116, 118, 119.
Built by Pedro de Ribera for Philip V in 1718-32, south of the old city, this was only the second major bridge over the Manzanares after the Puente de Segovia. It has suffered from the fumes and noise of the M-30, which it straddles. However, the bridge has been restored and closed to traffic, and there's a riverside park along the east side. A good place to see in a Sunday morning amble from the Rastro down Calle Toledo, and across to the very different *barrio* west of the river.

The entrance into the palace is awe-inspiring: you pass up a truly vast main staircase, and then through the main state rooms, the Hall of Halbardiers and Hall of Columns, all with soaring ceilings and frescoes by Corrado Giaquinto and Giambattista Tiepolo. In the grand Throne Room there are some fine 17th-century sculptures commissioned by Velázquez, which were saved from the earlier Alcázar. Other highlights are the extravagantly ornate private apartments of the palace's first resident, Charles III, again decorated by Italians, especially the 'Gasparini Room' the King's dressing room, covered in mosaics and rococo stucco by Mattia Gasparini, and the 'Porcelain Room', similar to the one in Aranjuez, its walls covered entirely in porcelain reliefs. A later addition is another giant, the State Dining Room, redesigned for King Alfonso XII in 1880, and still used for official banquets. There are also imposing collections of tapestries, table porcelain, gold and silver plate and finally clocks, a particular passion of the little-admired King Charles IV. Also very interesting are two sections with separate entrances off the palace courtyard: the **Real Armería** (Royal Armoury), with a superb collection of ceremonial armour, much of it actually worn by Charles V and other Habsburgs, and which has recently been very finely restored; and the engaging rooms of the **Real Farmacia**, the Royal Pharmacy, one of the oldest in Europe, and wholly dedicated to attending to the many ailments of Spain's crowned heads for several centuries. In future years an opportunity to view the excavations of the older Alcázar and Muslim fortress beneath the palace (*see p67*) will also form part of the visit. The palace is closed to the public when official receptions or ceremonies are due, so it's a good idea to check before visiting. On the first Wednesday of each month the Royal Guard stages a ceremonial Changing of the Guard in the courtyard, at noon.

Parque de las Vistillas

C/Beatriz Galindo. Metro La Latina/bus 3, 31, 50, 65, 148. **Map** p308 B/C8/B9.
The biggest reason to head for these gardens, just south of the Palacio Real along Calle Bailén, is the view. Easily seen from this high open spot are the Almudena, the whole of the Casa de Campo and the peaks of the Guadarrama. There's also a peaceful terrace bar, and the park is often used for neighbourhood events, concerts and dances during *fiestas* and in summer (*see pages186 and 188*).

Plaza de Oriente

Metro Opera/bus 3, 25, 39, 148. **Map** p308 C7.
Curiously, Madrid owes this stately square that seems ideally to complement the Palacio Real not to the Bourbon monarchs but to Spain's 'non-King', Joseph Bonaparte, who initiated the clearing of the area during his brief reign (1808-13). After his departure it was left as a dusty space for many years before being laid out in formal style in 1844. Most recently, it has been dug up again while Calle Bailén has been sent into a tunnel. The plaza is now fully pedestrianised, and so its avenues effectively extend

up to the walls of the palace. At the centre of the square is a fine equestrian statue of King Philip IV that once stood in the courtyard of the Buen Retiro (*see p12*). It was made by the Italian sculptor Pietro Tacca, who on the insistence of the Count-Duke of Olivares was required to create the first-ever monumental bronze statue featuring a rearing horse, rather than one with four feet on the ground, a remarkable feat achieved with engineering assistance from Galileo. On the opposite side from the palace is the **Teatro Real** opera house (*see p216*). Its reopening in 1997 has led to a certain revitalisation of the area's street- and nightlife, and there are several pavement cafés with fine views of the palace. Now a distant memory are the rallies Franco addressed here from the palace balcony, for which devotees were bussed in from all over the country.

Plaza de la Villa

Metro Opera or Sol/bus all routes to Puerta del Sol. **Map** p309 D8.
This historic square, the market square of Muslim and early medieval Madrid, contains three distinguished buildings all in different styles. Dominating it is the **Casa de la Villa** or City Hall, designed in Castilian-baroque style by Juan Gómez de Mora in 1630, although financial problems prevented it being completed until 1695. The façade was also altered by Juan de Villanueva in the 1780s. It contrasts nicely with the **Casa de Cisneros**, which was built as a palace by a relative of the great Cardinal Cisneros in 1537. It was restored in 1910, and now also houses municipal offices. Opposite the Casa de la Villa is the simple **Torre de los Lujanes**, once the residence of one of Madrid's aristocratic families, from the 1460s. It is believed that King Francis I of France was kept prisoner in the tower by Charles V after his capture at the Battle of Pavia in 1525.

San Andrés, Capilla del Obispo & Capilla de San Isidro

Plaza de San Andrés 1 (91 365 48 71). Metro La Latina/bus 17, 23, 35, 60. **Open** 8am-1.30pm, 6-8pm Mon-Thur, Sat, Sun; 8-11am, 6-8pm Fri. **Map** p308 C8.
The large church of San Andrés in the heart of old Madrid dates from the 16th century, but was badly damaged in the Civil War in 1936 and subsequently rebuilt in a relatively simple style. Attached to it, though (but with separate entrances), are two of Madrid's most historic early church buildings. The **Capilla del Obispo** (Bishop's Chapel, 1520-35) on Plaza de la Paja, is the best-preserved Gothic building in the city and contains finely carved tombs and a 1550 altarpiece by Francisco Giralte. Further towards Plaza de los Carros is the **Capilla de San Isidro**, built in 1642-69 by Pedro de la Torre to house the remains of the saint, which were later transferred to the **Iglesia-Catedral de San Isidro**. The problem is that both chapels have been under long-running restoration and neither is regularly open to the public. However, their permanent opening is promised, so it could be worth calling by to check.

Las Descalzas Reales. *See p74.*

San Nicolás de los Servitas

Plaza San Nicolás (91 559 40 64).
Metro Opera/bus 3, 25, 39, 148. **Open** 8.30am-2pm
Mon; 8.30-9.30am, 6.30-8.30pm Tue-Sat; 10am-2pm,
6.30-8.30pm Sun. **Map** p308 C7.
The oldest surviving church in Madrid, only a few
minutes from Plaza de Oriente. The 12th-century
tower is one of two *Mudéjar* towers, built by Muslim
craftsmen living under Christian rule, in the city.
Most of the rest of the church was rebuilt in the 15th
and 16th centuries. To see it on days other than
Monday, go to the priory behind the church on
Travesia del Biombo and ask the monks there to
open it for you. It's best to phone first if you can.

San Pedro el Viejo

Costanilla de San Pedro (91 365 12 84).
Metro La Latina/bus 31, 35, 50, 65. **Open** 6-8pm
daily (phone first to check). **Map** p309 D8.
The other *Mudéjar* brick tower in Madrid, from the
14th century. Again, the rest of the church dates
from much later, rebuilt in the 17th century.

Sol & Gran Vía

The **Puerta del Sol** is where most of the main
streets (and many bus routes) of old Madrid
converge, and where all newcomers from the rest
of Spain come at least once to feel sure they've
arrived. If you stop for a couple of minutes you
can check out the statue of Madrid's totemic bear
and strawberry tree (*madroño*) symbol, at the end
of Calle Carmen, and the Tio Pepe sign over
the eastern end of the square that has been there
longer than practically any of its other fixtures,
and so also ranks as a symbol.

Famously, people have come to Sol to find
out what's going on. Until the 1830s the block
between Calle Correo and Calle Esparteros was
occupied by the monastery of San Felipe el
Real, the steps and cloister of which were, in
Habsburg Madrid, one of the recognised
mentideros – literally, 'pits of lies', or gossip-
mills – where people came to pick up on the
latest news, anecdotes or scurrilous rumours.
In a city with no newspapers, but where who
was in or out of favour with the powerful was
of primary importance, they were a major social
institution, and rare was the day when at least
one of the great figures of Spanish literature
such as Cervantes, Lope or Quevedo did not
pass by here. The steps of San Felipe were also
overlooked by one of the largest brothels of the
era, another attraction for men about town.

Sol is also where Napoleon's Egyptian
cavalry, the Mamelukes, charged down on the
Madrileño crowd on 2 May 1808, as portrayed
in one of Goya's most famous paintings. Today,
revellers turn out in the Puerta del Sol on New
Year's Eve to eat their lucky grapes, one for
each chime of the clock (*see page 189*).

Sightseeing

The New Year's Eve clock rises out of Charles III's elegant 1766 post office, the **Casa de Correos**, now the seat of the Madrid regional government. In the Franco era, however, it had much grimmer connotations, as the Interior Ministry and police headquarters.

The area between Sol, Arenal, Alcalá and the Gran Vía forms central Madrid's main pedestrian axis and shopping centre, above all **Calle Preciados**. There are banks and shoe shops, stores such as **El Corte Inglés** and the **Fnac** (*see pages 160-1*) and stacks of offices, as well as cafeterias and fast food temples for employees on their lunch break.

Running almost alongside Preciados up to Gran Vía is **Calle Montera**, happily shabby, lined with cheap, vaguely out-of-date and often quirky shops and the main area for street prostitution in the city centre. At the top, parallel with Gran Vía, is Calle Caballero de Gracia, with a 19th-century oratory that lays on special masses for the working girls, many from the Dominican Republic, who operate along the

street. While seedy, this area is not generally dangerous, and is heavily policed. Care should be taken walking around late at night, though, especially if you're on your own.

The area north and east of Sol is dominated, however, by its two great avenues, **Calle Alcalá** and the **Gran Vía**. Alcalá follows the centuries-old main route into Madrid from the east, and in the 18th century, when it was lined by aristocratic palaces, was described as the grandest street in Europe. It is still pretty grand today, with a wonderful variety of 19th- to early 20th-century buildings, from the dignified 1882 **Banesto** building (corner of Calle Sevilla) to the cautiously modernist **Círculo de Bellas Artes** (*see page 73*). There are also fine older constructions along the street, such as the austere neo-classical Finance Ministry, built as the **Aduana** or Customs administration by Francesco Sabatini in 1761-9, and, alongside it, the **Real Academia de Bellas Artes de San Fernando** (*see page 99*). At the point where Alcalá and Gran Vía meet there is Pedro de Ribera's exuberantly baroque

Madrid's grand avenue

Fourteen streets disappeared for ever when the Gran Vía (pictured left and below) was scythed out of the urban tangle in 1910 so that motor traffic could reach Cibeles from Calle Princesa. Intended to be a broad modern boulevard, it got grander still when World War I made neutral Madrid a clearing house for international money. With the economy booming, developers and architects set out to embrace modernity as hard as they could, and to show that, if you wanted something impressive, they could provide it. In following decades, each 'generation' sought to keep up with the times and add their own stamp. The result is unique, and a walk up the Gran Vía reveals a fascinating collection of 20th-century architectural eccentricities.

church of **San José**, of 1730-42, with a plaque inside to commemorate the fact that Simón Bolívar was married here in 1802.

The Gran Vía, on the other hand, is a child of the 20th century, sliced through the old city – albeit with a rather rusty knife, for its construction took over 20 years – after 1910. Although an interloper, it has a style all of its own (*see below*). It completely transformed the core of old Madrid, with a new, grand avenue full of bustle for banking, shopping, offices and, above all, cinemas. Love it or hate it, no one can deny that it's lively. On Sundays, it's packed with people queuing under the enormous hand-painted film posters around Plaza Callao.

To the north-west, the Gran Vía runs out into the sprawling space of the **Plaza de España**. South of the avenue there are some surprising corners of Habsburg Madrid tucked away, most especially the closed nunneries of the **Descalzas Reales** and the **Encarnación** (for both, *see page 74*). Just north of the Encarnación, occupying the site of another convent, is the old 19th-century

Palacio del Senado (Senate), now made redundant by its back-to-back counterpart in granite and smoked glass by Santiago Goyarre.

Círculo de Bellas Artes

C/Alcalá 42 & C/Marqués de Casa Riera 2 (91 360 54 00). Metro Banco de España/bus all routes to Cibeles. **Open** *Café* 9am-2am Mon-Thur, Sun; 9am-4am Fri, Sat. *Exhibitions* 5-9pm Tue-Fri; 11am-2pm Sat, Sun; closed Mon. **Admission** 100ptas. **Map** p310 G7.
Enormous windows giving on to the Calle Alcalá allow passers-by a look into one of Madrid's most stunning clubs, built in 1919-26 by Antonio Palacios. Entry is not restricted to members, provided you pay the modest fee. As well as a beautifully airy main floor café, with a gracious pavement terrace, the Circulo offers a plethora of classes, exhibitions, lectures and concerts, plus an annual Carnival Ball. There is also a cosy, dark library. *See also pp107, 118, 145, 214, 216 & 242.*

Plaza de España

Metro Plaza de España/bus all routes to Plaza de España. **Map** p305 D5.
This expanse at the end of the Gran Vía could be called the Franco regime's very own plaza, as it was

Sightseeing

Spanish urban reformers had often compared Madrid unfavourably to Paris, and as the first address on the Gran Vía they got an entire Parisian building, the **Edificio Metrópolis**, designed by Jules and Raymond Février in 1905. It is offset by the stacked cupolas of the Grassy building (the one with the Piaget sign).

As you move away from Alcalá the buildings become taller, and grander. When the **Telefónica** building (pictured) by the Gran Vía Metro went up in 1929 everyone was thrilled by how modern (ie, un-Spanish) it seemed. At 81m (265ft) tall, it was certainly conspicuous, and as Madrid's first skyscraper it had a huge impact. It was designed by Ignacio de Cárdenas, with the help of a New York engineer called Louis Weeks.

The section of the street from Callao to Plaza de España was completed under the Republic. On the corner of Calle Jacometrezo is Madrid's best art deco building, the 1932 **Edificio Carrión**, better known simply as the **Capitol**, designed by Luis Martínez Feduchi and Vicente Eced. The same section is also full of the Gran Vía's lavish 1920s movie palaces with their spectacular hand-painted signs, a tradition that scarcely survives anywhere else outside India.

The last part of the Gran Vía is the work of the Franco era, when the Telefónica was finally upstaged by the 1948-53 **Edificio España** in the Plaza de España. A baroque skyscraper, it sums up the contradictions of the regime – obsessed with 'eternal values', but desirous to show the world that it, too, could build a skyscraper as big as anyone else's (see also page 34).

mainly laid out in the 1940s and is flanked by two classic buildings of the type sponsored by the regime when out to impress, the '50s-modern Torre Madrid (1957) and the humungous Edificio España of 1948-53 (*see p34*). The three statues in the middle – of Cervantes, Don Quixote and Sancho Panza – are by Teodoro Anasagasti and Mateo Inurria, from 1928. The square around them is big, but noisy and not a particularly relaxing place to sit.

Real Monasterio de las Descalzas Reales

Plaza de las Descalzas 3 (91 542 00 59/information 91 454 88 00). Metro Callao or Sol/bus all routes to Puerta del Sol. **Open** 10.30am-12.45pm, 4-5.45pm Tue-Thur, Sat; 10.30am-12.45pm Fri; 11am-1.45pm Sun, public holidays; closed Mon. **Admission** 700ptas; 300ptas concessions. Free to EU citizens Wed. **Map** p309 D7.

Those who chance upon this atypical monastery-museum often feel amazed at their find, for few expect to come across such a place in the middle of one of Madrid's busiest shopping areas, close to the Gran Via and the major stores. The convent of the *Descalzas Reales* (literally, 'the Royal Barefoot Sisters') is the most complete 16th-century building in Madrid, and still houses an enclosed community of nuns. It was first built as a palace for Alonso Gutiérrez, treasurer of Charles V, but was converted into a convent in 1556-64 by Antonio Sillero and Juan Bautista de Toledo after Philip II's widowed sister Joanna of Austria decided to become a nun. Founded with royal patronage, the Descalzas became the preferred destination of the many widows, younger daughters and other women of the royal family and high aristocracy of Spain who entered religious orders. Hence it also acquired an extraordinary collection of works of art, given as bequests by the novices' families – paintings, sculptures, tapestries and *objets d'art*. Equally lavish is the baroque decoration of the building itself, belying its sternly austere façade, with a grand painted staircase, frescoed ceilings and 32 chapels, only some of which can be visited.

The largest non-Spanish contingents in its art collection are Italian, with Titian, Luini, Angelo Narddi and Sebastiano del Piombo, and Flemish, with Brueghel (an *Adoration of the Magi*), Joos Van Cleve and Rubens. The Descalzas is also an exceptional showcase of Spanish baroque religious art, with works by Gaspar Becerra, Zurbarán, Claudio Coello and others. From another epoch, there is even a tiny painting attributed to Goya. In addition, as you walk round you can catch glimpses of the nuns' courtyard vegetable garden, virtually unchanged since the convent was built, and closed to the public. The monastery was seen by very few until the 1980s, when it was restored and partially opened as a museum. It can be visited only with official tours, and while the guides rarely speak English, the wealth of things to see makes up for this. Tours leave about every 20min, and last about 45min.

Real Monasterio de la Encarnación

Plaza de la Encarnación s/n (91 547 05 10/ information 91 454 88 00). Metro Opera or Santo Domingo/bus 25, 39, 148. **Open** 10.30am-12.45pm, 4-5.45pm Tue-Thur, Sat; 10.30am-12.45pm Fri; 11am-1.45pm Sun, public holidays; closed Mon. **Admission** 475ptas; 275ptas concessions. Free to EU citizens Wed. **Map** p308 C6.

This understated monastery was once a *Casa de Tesoro* (treasury), connected to the nearby Alcázar by a concealed passageway. It was endowed as a monastery in 1611 by Philip III and his wife Margaret of Austria, and rebuilt to a design by Gómez de Mora. However, the only part of his convent that remains is the façade, as much of the rest was damaged by fire in 1734 and rebuilt in a classical-baroque style in the 1760s by Ventura Rodríguez. It still contains a community of around 20 nuns, but most of the building is open to the public. Although not as lavishly endowed as the **Descalzas Reales**, it contains a great many pieces of 17th-century religious art, the most impressive of them Jusepe Ribera's shimmering *chiaroscuro* portrait of *John the Baptist*. The Encarnación's most famous and memorable room, however, is the *reliquario* (relics room). In its glass casements are displayed some 1,500 saintly relics, bone fragments and/or former possessions of saints and martyrs, in extravagantly bejewelled copper, bronze, glass, gold and silver reliquaries. Even more amazing is the solidified blood of San Pantaleón, kept inside a glass orb. The blood reportedly liquifies each year from midnight on the eve of his feast day (27 July) until the stroke of midnight on the day itself, 28 July. The wait for this to happen is an annual local news item.

Huertas to La Latina

Huertas & Santa Ana

Spain has the greatest number of bars and restaurants per capita of any city in the world, and you can get the impression that around half of the 17,000-plus that there are in Madrid are crowded into the wedge-shaped swathe of streets between Alcalá and Calle Atocha. Oddly enough, this clearly delimited area has an identity problem, for the authorities can never agree on a name, but if anyone suggests a pub crawl down Huertas, or a jar in Santa Ana, it will always bring you – and several thousand others on any weekend – to the right place.

This was once the haunt of Madrid's Golden Age literary set, which explains the district's fussy alternative name, the *barrio de las letras* ('the district of letters'). Here were the theatres that provided them with a living, along with whorehouses and low dives. It still is Madrid's

A historic literary hub, the **Teatro Español**.

Sightseeing

most distinctive theatre district. Close by, but not too close, lived the nobles who might have tossed a couple of ducats your way if you buttered them up in a sonnet. Otherwise there were feuds, libellous exchanges and duels to fall back on.

Lope de Vega's charming old house, the **Casa-Museo Lope de Vega** (*see page 103*), with its tiny garden, is on the street named after his enemy, Cervantes. The author of *Don Quixote* lived around the corner on Calle León, but was buried in the enclosed convent of the **Trinitarias Descalzas** (the 'Barefoot Trinitarians') on Calle Lope de Vega, which seems deliberately confusing. Coming upon the massively plain, slab-like brick walls of the Trinitarias amid the Huertas bars can come as a great surprise, and gives a vivid impression of what old Madrid must have looked like before the great clear-out of religious houses in the 1830s, of which it is a rare survivor.

A reverential nod is in order to Madrid's **Ateneo** on Calle del Prado, the cultural institution that has been a major centre of discussion and thought at many times in its history, most notably in the years running up to the Republic of 1931 (*see page 284*). In the old days, Ateneo members could also find any number of cafés nearby with a suitably literary atmosphere. There are still a few around, such as the **Salón del Prado** (*see page 149*).

To the south, the Huertas area is bounded by splendidly seedy Calle Atocha, with cheap *pensiones* and two enormous sex centres. It is also home to the **Teatro Monumental** concert hall (*see page 216*) and, at the bottom, towards Atocha station, the macro-disco **Kapital** at no.125 (*see page 227*).

Very different is the **Carrera de San Jerónimo**, which borders the north of the district. Once part of the 'Ceremonial Route' of the Habsburg and Bourbon monarchs (*see page 14*), today it is one of the centres of official Madrid. On one side is the **Congreso de los Diputados**, Spain's Parliament building, while opposite is the **Hotel Palace**, where politicians go to mingle and relax (*see page 38*). Further up the hill is **Lhardy**, the classic Franco-Spanish restaurant founded in 1839 (*see pages 123 and 138*). North of San Jerónimo, behind the Congreso, is the grandish 1856 **Teatro de la Zarzuela**, the city's most characterfully distinguished music theatre.

To the south of Carrera de San Jerónimo several streets run back towards Huertas proper. On Calle Echegaray is **Los Gabrieles**, a bar and venue sheathed in perhaps the world's most photographed wall-to-wall tiles. An equally popular alternative is **Viva Madrid**, around the corner (*see page 155*). Last but in no way least there is the core of the district, **Plaza Santa Ana**. Like Plaza de Oriente this popular square was bequeathed to Madrid by poor, unappreciated Joseph Bonaparte, who tore down yet another superfluous convent to do so. Somebody should thank him: lined by some of the city's most popular bars and pavement terraces, Santa Ana has long been one of Madrid's favourite places for hanging out for an entire afternoon or three.

Here is the once-elegant **Hotel Reina Victoria**, the traditional bullfighters' hangout, and fine bars such as **Cervecería La Moderna** and the **Cervecería Alemana** (*see page 147*), perhaps the best-known Hemingway haunt in Madrid. In the adjoining Plaza del Angel is **Café Central**, Madrid's best jazz club (*see page 223*). On the eastern side of the plaza is the distinguished **Teatro Español**, on a site that has been a theatre continuously since 1583, when the *Corral del Príncipe* opened its doors to the *mosqueteros* (groundlings), whose reactions were so violent they sometimes forced terrified playwrights to change plots mid-play.

Congreso de los Diputados (Las Cortes)

Plaza de las Cortes (91 390 67 50/91 390 65 25). Metro Banco de España or Sevilla/bus 9, 14, 27, 34, 45. **Open** *guided tours 10.30am, 12.30pm Sat; closed Mon-Fri, Sun, public holidays & Aug.* **Admission** free. **Map** p310 G7.
Spain's Cortes, the Parliament, was built in 1843-50 by Narciso Pascual y Colomer on the site of a

recently demolished monastery, which has led to no end of problems, as the plot is too cramped to accommodate the legislators' ancillary offices. A classical portico gives it a suitably dignified air, but the building is best distinguished by the handsome 1860 bronze lions that guard the entrance. Tourists are welcome on the popular free Saturday guided tours. Given demand, it's best to phone ahead; groups of more than 15 can book to visit on weekdays.

La Latina, Rastro, Lavapiés

South of Sol and the Plaza Mayor, between San Francisco el Grande and Atocha, the streets slope sharply downhill towards the *rondas* of Atocha, Valencia and Toledo. The districts within this area – commonly divided up by locals into La Latina, Rastro, Lavapiés and Embajadores – have traditionally been considered the arch-repositories of Madrid's *castizo* identity (*see page185*). To some extent they still are, but since the end of the 1990s Lavapiés in particular has also taken on a new characteristic: as Spanish families have moved out to more modern housing elsewhere, and Madrid has become a significant recipient of non-Spanish immigration – from China, Pakistan, north and west Africa – this is becoming the city's most multicultural neighbourhood.

These districts have always been the kind of place where newcomers to the city could find a niche. Historically they were known as the *barrios bajos*, in the double sense of low-lying

Walk 2: Exploring Lavapiés

Tatty, atmospheric Lavapiés (pronounced *La-va-**pee**-yes*) shows Madrid's past, present and future. Once the Jewish quarter, long the main working-class area and still home to a large gypsy community, Lavapiés is now the most racially mixed neighbourhood in the city. It has also acquired something of a (sometimes exaggeratedly) bad reputation (see page 78), but it's still a rewarding place to explore, and, while this walk (marked in **blue** in the map on pages 309-10) is not recommended to

anyone at night, by day, so long as you're reasonably alert, nothing unwanted need happen to you.

A natural starting point is **Plaza Tirso de Molina**. At its eastern end is the **Teatro Nuevo Apolo**, with a quirky façade that mixes art deco and neo-*mudéjar*. On the southern side of the plaza is the present headquarters of the CNT anarchist workers' union, a reflection of Lavapiés' long association with left-wing politics.

Calle Mesón de Paredes is named after the long-gone inn of one Señor Paredes, inventor of the *emparedado*, a type of sandwich. For refreshment today, though, there is the historic **Taberna de Antonio Sánchez** at no.13 (see page 140). Mesón de Paredes once boasted all manner of shops, but nowadays what most strikes the eye is the number of *venta al mayor* (wholesale) signs, indicating shops offering a wide range of bargain-basement jackets, T-shirts, jewellery and other accessories, and mostly Chinese-run. Turn right down Calle Abades to avoid the mugger's hotspot at Calle Cabestreros and reach **Calle Embajadores** ('Ambassadors', so called because all Madrid's foreign embassies were once moved down here during a 17th-century outbreak of the plague).

Just by the corner, in amid the urban disorder, there is the splendid baroque church of **San Cayetano**, built by a variety of architects, including Ribera and Churriguera, between 1678 and 1761. Despite the many hands involved in its construction, its façade is one of the most finely worked in Madrid. Opposite, a plaque recalls that this was the

and full of low life – the closer to the river, the shabbier the surroundings. In imperial Madrid, most of the food brought to the city came in through the **Puerta de Toledo** (*see page 78*), and many of the tasks that the upper classes wanted neither to see nor smell, such as slaughtering and tanning, were concentrated here. Consequently, these districts became home to Madrid's first native working class. In the 18th century the *majos* and *majas* from these streets were admired by the intelligentsia for their caustic wit (*see page 17*), and the Madrileño tradition of sharp, sarcastic, uppity humour has continued to this day.

La Latina takes its name from the nickname of Beatriz Galindo, teacher of Latin and confidante to Queen Isabella. At the end of the 15th century she paid for a hospital to be built on the square that bears her name. Its site is now occupied by the **Teatro La Latina**, stronghold of traditional Spanish entertainment. The district is relatively quiet except during its grand *fiestas*, around the time of **La Paloma** in August (*see page 189*).

On the eastern edge of La Latina is the **Rastro**, Madrid's time-honoured Sunday flea market (*see page 179*). It runs all the way down Ribera de Curtidores to the Ronda de Toledo from **Plaza Cascorro**, with its monument honouring a young soldier raised in a nearby orphanage, who volunteered for a suicide mission in Cuba in the 1890s. A true cultural

house of the great architect Pedro de Ribera himself, during the 1730s. Further down Embajadores on the left there is the bustling district market of **San Fernando**, surrounded by likeable cafeterias.

Below the market a new square has been created between Embajadores and Mesón de Paredes, the **Plaza Agustín Lara**, which, after much reconstruction, should be finally completed during 2001. On its south side are the ruins of the 18th-century church and school of the **Escuelas Pías de San Fernando**, destroyed in the Civil War. Facing the ruins from Mesón de Paredes is Madrid's most famous *corrala* tenement block (see page 78). At the bottom of Embajadores, near Ronda de Valencia, there is the hefty neo-classical pile of the **Tabacalera**, built in 1792 as a distillery but the state tobacco factory since 1809. It figures large in Lavapiés' history, as it once employed a fifth of Madrid's working population, especially the sassy *cigarreras*, counterparts of Carmen in Seville, who are amply represented in local literature.

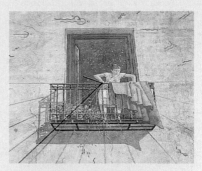

Nearby, on the corner of Calle Miguel Servet, is the art deco municipal bathhouse, where showers can still be had for just 25ptas.

Calle Miguel Servet itself offers **La Mancha en Madrid** tapas bar (see page 140), Arab cafés and **La Tienda de las Hamacas**, selling Mexican hammocks. Calle Amparo, off to the right, has several Arab and oriental food shops. The top end of Servet leads into Calle Valencia and, further up, the **Plaza de Lavapiés**. At the top right-hand corner is the gloriously down-at-heel **Nuevo Café Barbieri** (see page 150); in the bottom, eastern corner there is **Calle Argumosa**. Pretty, broad and tree-lined, Argumosa has a dozen pavement cafés, and neo-hippyish shops. Restaurant stops include the vegetarian **Granero de Lavapiés**, at no.10 (see page 125). At the far end a turn left will take you into **Calle Doctor Fourquet**, home to several art galleries, especially the highly respected **Helga de Alvear**. It also leads conveniently to Calle Santa Isabel and the **Reina Sofía**.

phenomenon, the Rastro is also a district with a strong identity, moulded by centuries of acting as an emporium for goods of all kinds. To avoid the crowds, and the pickpockets, avoid Sundays: the wicker furniture dealers will still be open, and so will the junk shops and purveyors of fine antiques.

If, on the other hand, instead of trying to make your way down the Rastro, you head from Plaza Cascorro slightly eastwards down Calle Embajadores, you will enter Lavapiés proper. Since the rapid changes in the area, Lavapiés is sometimes portrayed, in local conversations and the press, as an urban crisis zone to be avoided (*see pages 28-9 and 286*). This is one of the areas with a high incidence of petty crime, commonly associated with gangs of North African boys living on the streets, who have especially bad relations with the district's Chinese shopkeepers. However, these images have a tendency to get out of proportion: there are places in Lavapiés it's probably best to steer clear of (the small square halfway down Mesón de Paredes, by Calle Cabestreros, is the most obvious), but it would be a shame if this led anyone to avoid the whole *barrio*, for this web of sloping, winding streets remains one of the most characterful parts of old Madrid (*see page 76* **Walk 2: Exploring Lavapiés**).

Another aspect of Lavapiés, particularly the section around Plaza de Lavapiés and towards Calle Atocha, is that it's also home to a lot of *guiris* – young northern Europeans and Americans. This is also one of Madrid's upcoming hip zones, with galleries, fringe theatres, cafés and cheap restaurants and bars, associated with a more on-the-cusp style than the more conventional bar life of Huertas.

Plaza Tirso de Molina, with its statue of the Golden Age dramatist whose name it bears, is the main crossroads between these *barrios bajos* and the city centre proper. From there, Calle Mesón de Paredes, with Calle Embajadores one of the two main arteries of historic Lavapiés, winds off down the hill. Along Mesón de Paredes today there are, as well as some of Madrid's most historic *tabernas*, shops selling tropical fruit, Moroccan tea houses, Halal butchers, African fabric stores and any number of Chinese-owned wholesale stores selling discount jewellery and T-shirts.

Also on Mesón de Paredes, near the bottom by Calle Sombrerete, is **La Corrala**, the city's best surviving example of an 1880s courtyard tenement, garnished as tradition requires with freshly washed sheets and underwear billowing from the balconies. After the demolition of Madrid's monasteries in the mid-19th century many streets in these districts were rebuilt with

these distinctive, open-balconied tenements. *Corralas* always faced an inner patio, multiplying the noise and lack of privacy that have rarely bothered Spaniards, and became a characteristic of neighbourhood life. This *corrala*, restored in the 1980s, is used in summer as a setting for a season of Madrileño *zarzuela* comic operas (*see page 217*). A later *corrala*, not easily visible from the street, is at Calle Embajadores 60.

The **Plaza de Lavapiés** is believed to have been the centre of Madrid's medieval Jewish community, expelled, like all others in her dominions, by the very pious Queen Isabella in 1492. Today the recently renovated square has several good cafés and restaurants. The narrow, very steep streets between the plaza and Calle Atocha are much more tranquil than those around Mesón de Paredes and, with exuberant boxes of geraniums on virtually every balcony, often strikingly pretty. Despite all the changes in the area, these closely packed streets of old apartments, shops and small workshops still convey the essence of a very distinctive urban way of life. There are some attractive restaurants, such as the vegetarian **Elquí** (*see page 124*) and cool shops like **Pepita is Dead** (*see page 170*), and some of the old workshops have been turned into new venues such as the **Sala Trángulo** fringe theatre (*see page 245*). At the top of the area by Calle Atocha is the **Filmoteca** film theatre, in the old Cine Doré (*see page 198*).

Running away from the south-east corner of the Plaza de Lavapiés is **Calle Argumosa**, with more shops and restaurants and outdoor-terrace bars that make a popular summer alternative to more expensive and more hectic places further into town. Argumosa leads towards Atocha and the **Centro de Arte Reina Sofía**, the opening of which has led to the appearance nearby of attractive one-off shops (**Lola Fonseca**, *see page 172*) and galleries (*see page 203*). Close by, filling a big stretch of Calle Santa Isabel, is the 17th-century **Convento de Santa Isabel**, sponsored, like the Encarnación, by Margaret of Austria, wife of Philip III, and one of the largest religious houses to escape the liberals' axe in the 1830s.

Puerta de Toledo

Glorieta de la Puerta de Toledo.
Metro Puerta de Toledo/bus all routes to Puerta de Toledo. **Map** p308 C10.
Slightly swallowed up in the traffic at the meeting point of the old city and the roads in from the south-west, this neo-classical gate was one of the monuments commissioned by Napoleon's brother Joseph in his brief span as King of Spain. After his departure it was rejigged to honour the delegates from the Cortes in Cádiz, and then King Fernando VII.

North of Gran Vía

Chueca

The *barrio* of Chueca, bounded by the Gran Vía, Calle Fuencarral and the Paseo de Recoletos has been through several transformations. In the 18th century Calle Hortaleza was the site of the *Recogida*, a refuge for 'public sinners' where women could be confined for soliciting on the street, or merely on the say-so of a male family member. Release was only possible through marriage or a lifetime tour of duty in a convent.

In the 19th century it became a more respectable, affluent district, but by the 1970s and early '80s it was a shabby, declining area. Since then, though, Chueca has undergone a spectacular revival, due, above all, to it having become *the* gay centre of Madrid.

The **Plaza de Chueca** itself is the hub of the district and of the Chueca scene. With the **Berkana** gay bookshop and bars such as the **Café Acuarela** and **Truco** (*see pages 208 and 213*), the plaza and its terraces are packed with buzzing crowds on hot summer nights, and the only limitation on the scene could be whether the plaza can actually hold any more people. On the back of the gay scene many more

Plaza de Chueca – hip and happening.

restaurants, trendy shops, cafés and clubs have opened up too, and Fuencarral, the borderline between Chueca and Malasaña, is now the heart of Madrid's club-fashion scene. Many gay venues have acquired a growing crossover fashionable status among the hip non-gay crowd (to the extent that some gays now find some Chueca clubs too 'diluted'). Whatever, Chueca has established itself as a booming free zone for socialising of all kinds, not just gay.

The north side of the district, above Calle Fernando VI, is not really Chueca proper and is often known as **Alonso Martínez**, after the Metro station. It's not so much part of 'gay Chueca' either, although it too has many new restaurants and bars. Instead, it's one of the foremost preserves of Madrid's teen scene. Streets such as Fernando VI or Calle Campamor and Plaza Santa Bárbara are lined with bars and clubs catering to a 16-25 crowd, and on weekend nights the roads are packed too, with noisy (but safe) crowds of kids.

Towards Recoletos, Chueca also becomes more commercial and more upmarket by day. Calle Barquillo is full of electrical shops, while Calle Almirante and its cross-street Calle Conde de Xiquena are an important fashion shopping zone. Off Almirante in Calle Tamayo y Baus is one of Madrid's most important theatres, the **Teatro María Guerrero** (*see page 244*).

This area is also part of official Madrid, with the giant **Palacio de Justicia** on Calle Bárbara de Braganza. It was formerly the Convento de las Salesas, built in 1750-8 under the patronage of Queen Bárbara, wife of Fernando VI. It has housed law courts since 1870. Its refined classical baroque contrasts nicely with the art nouveau of the **Palacio Longoria**, a few streets away. On the west side of Chueca are two of Madrid's most engaging museums, the **Museo Municipal** and **Museo Romántico** (*see pages 100 and 105*), while to the south, toward Calle Alcalá, there is an isolated relic of Philip II's Madrid, the **Plaza del Rey** and venerable 1580s **Casa de las Siete Chimeneas**, originally designed by Juan de Herrera, architect of El Escorial.

Sociedad General de Autores (Palacio Longoria)

C/Fernando VI, 6 (91 349 95 14). Metro Alonso Martínez/bus 3, 14, 37, 40. **Map** p306 G4.
Given the extraordinary output of Catalan Modernist architects such as Gaudí in Barcelona in the early 20th century, it is remarkable, to non-Spaniards at least, that there is not a single example of their work in Madrid. The only thing at all like it is this building in Chueca, designed by José Grasés Riera in 1902 as a residence for banker Javier González Longoria. The façade looks like it was formed out of wet sand, moulded by an expert in giant cake decoration: if a building could be considered voluptuous, this would be it. It

was once thought Catalan architecture influenced Grasés, but Héctor Guimard and French art nouveau seem to have been a more direct inspiration. It is now owned by the Spanish writers' and artists' association.

Malasaña & Conde Duque

By day, Malasaña, between Calles Fuencarral and San Bernardo, is a quiet *barrio* that offers an eyeful of 19th-century Madrid: grannies watering their geraniums on wrought-iron balconies, idiosyncratic corner shops. By night, though, this has long been an epicentre of Madrid's bar culture. It's not as trendy or as adventurous as Chueca; rather, Malasaña is associated with laid-back cafés, rock bars and cheap, grungy, studenty socialising – most of all in one of modern Madrid's great curiosities, the *litrona* scene, when hundreds of kids sit out on the street (*see page 232*).

In a very different era this area was the centre of resistance to the French on 2 May 1808. The name of the district comes from a 17-year-old seamstress heroine, Manuela Malasaña, shot by the invaders for carrying concealed weapons (her scissors) or ammunition to the Spanish troops – there are various versions of her exploits. The name of the main square, **Plaza Dos de Mayo**, also recalls that day. Where the square is today was then the Monteleón artillery barracks, from where the artillery captains Daoíz and Velarde galvanised the resistance of the people. The last remaining part of the barracks, a gate, stands with a monument to the two men in the square.

This plaza gained a tough reputation in the 1980s, but Malasaña is one area where urban renovation schemes have been most successful. Plaza Dos de Mayo itself can be covered on Saturday and Sunday mornings with cans, bottles and malodorous evidence of the previous night's partying, but once this has been cleaned up children cavort in the new play area, while a complete cross-section of the city enjoys its many *terraza* outdoor cafés.

The streets between Fuencarral and San Bernardo abound with great cafés, bars and restaurants. There are also indications – such as the broad-arched doorways for carriages – that the 19th-century well-to-do once lived here. One of the most rewarding streets is **Calle San Vicente Ferrer**, with jewellery shops and a delightful 1920s tile display advertising the long-defunct pharmacy Laboratorios Juanse. Other old ceramic signs on the **Calle San Andrés** feature a little boy signalling that his chamber pot is full, and a dramatic, reclining vamp. Calle de la Palma and Calle Divino Pastor, with craft and jewellery shops, are equally worth a stroll. To the north is Glorieta de Bilbao, site of one of Madrid's best traditional cafés, the **Café Comercial** (*see page 157*).

The atmosphere gets more mobile as you approach the streets near Fuencarral that lead down to the Gran Vía, such as **Corredera Baja de San Pablo**. This is an area of cheap restaurants, wholesale produce dealers in white aprons, shops selling nothing but light bulbs, and working-class people who have known each other all their lives. Recent additions are club-style fashion shops, especially towards or on Calle Fuencarral (*see page 169*). At the corner of the Corredera Baja and Calle Ballesta there is an unusual brick church, built by Felipe III for his Portuguese subjects in Madrid. Later it was set aside for German Catholic émigrés, and is still known as **San Antonio de los Alemanes**. It is rarely open to visitors. Just a block away along Calle del Pez, often unnoticed amid the shops, bars and theatres that surround it, is the slab-walled convent of **San Plácido**, another of Madrid's surviving religious houses.

The area west of Calle San Bernardo is most commonly known as **Conde Duque**, after its finest monument, the **Centro Cultural Conde Duque**, which occupies the giant barracks (*cuartel*) built in 1717-54 by Pedro de Ribera for King Philip V's royal guard. It was wonderfully renovated by the Tierno Galván city council in the 1980s as an arts centre (*see pages 107*). Slightly hidden next to it is one of Madrid's least-seen treasures, the **Palacio de Liria**.

Otherwise, Conde Duque is a continuation of Malasaña, with a similar – if less grungy – mix of old *tabernas*, new cafés, clubs, restaurants and stylish new bars – such as the happening **Café de la Palma** (*see page 220*). The **Plaza de las Comendadoras** is one of the district's centres, with delightful open-air *terrazas*.

Palacio de Liria

C/Princesa 20 (91 547 53 02/fax 91 541 03 77). Metro Ventura Rodríguez/bus 1, 2, 44, 74, 133, C. **Open** *guided tours* 10.45am, 11.30am, 12.15pm Fri only. **Admission** free. **Map** p305 D3.
This sober, neo-classical palace, completed in 1783 and refurbished in the 1910s by Edwin Lutyens, is still very much the private property of Spain's première aristocrat, the Duchess of Alba. The extraordinary collection inside includes work by Rembrandt, Palma Vecchio, Titian and Rubens, and one of the most important Goyas in private hands, his portrait of the earlier Duchess of Alba in red and white. The problem is, the current Duchess has no need to open her palace to public view. Space on the Friday guided tours has to be requested in advance, **in writing** (letters can be sent by fax). This is not as impossible as it might seem: the waiting list for groups is over a year long, but if there are just one to three of you the helpful staff do their best to fit you in, possibly in about two to three weeks (call to check). So, if you can plan your trip a little ahead, it's worth trying.

Outside the Old City

Beyond old Madrid there are broader vistas, smart shopping routes, likeable *barrios* and the city's delicious range of parks.

Salamanca & the Retiro

Salamanca

In the mid 19th century, as it became evident that Spanish cities needed to expand beyond their old walls, attempts were made to ensure that this happened in an orderly way. Madrid and Barcelona had plans approved for *ensanches* ('extensions'; *see page 19*). Carlos María de Castro's 1860 plan for Madrid envisaged the expansion of the city north and east in a regular grid pattern, with restrictions on building height, and public open spaces at regular intervals within each block to ensure a healthy harmonious landscape.

The problem, however, was that for a good while few of Madrid's middle classes seem to have had the money or motivation to invest in such a scheme, and preferred to stay within the cramped, noisy old city. That Madrid's *ensanche* got off the ground at all was due to a banker, politician and speculator notorious for his dubious business practices, the Marqués de Salamanca.

The marquis had previously built his own vast residence, now the **Banco Hipotecario**, on Paseo de Recoletos in 1846-50. It had the first flushing toilets in Madrid, an amenity he later offered to residents in his new housing developments. He spent one of several fortunes he made and lost in his lifetime on building a first line of rectangular blocks along Calle Serrano, from Calle Goya up to Ramón de la Cruz. However, his ambitions overstretched his resources, the apartments proved expensive for local buyers, and he went terminally bankrupt in 1867. Nevertheless, it is to the rogue Marqués, not the old Castilian university town, that Madrid's smartest *barrio* owes its name.

It was only after the Restoration of 1874 that Madrid's wealthy really began to appreciate the benefits of wider streets and residences with more class than the musty old neighbourhoods could supply. Once the idea caught on, though, the exodus proceeded apace, and the core of Salamanca was built up by 1900.

The wealthiest families of all built individual palaces along the lower stretch of the Castellana, in a wild variety of styles – French imperial, Italian Renaissance, neo-*mudéjar*. Only a handful of these extravagances remain – the Palacio de Linares, now the **Casa de América**, is perhaps the best preserved on the Castellana itself (*see page 107*). The block on Calle Juan Bravo between Calles Lagasca and Velázquez contains another magnificent example, the neo-baroque palace of the **Marqueses de Amboage**, now the Italian Embassy. From the Calle Velázquez side it's possible to get a good view of the extraordinarily lush gardens. Other mansions are scattered around the district, tucked in between apartment blocks. Those who could not quite afford their own mansion moved into giant apartments in the streets behind. The *Barrio de Salamanca* has been the centre of conservative, affluent Madrid ever since.

Salamanca is a busy area, with streets that often boom with traffic, and so the best time to explore it is Saturday morning, when the shops are open but traffic has slackened. Streets

1980s corporate glass and 1880s curlicues: two sides of **Salamanca**'s architecture.

(namely Calles Jorge Juan, Ortega y Gasset, Goya and Juan Bravo) yield top designers, art galleries and dealers in French wines, English silver or superior leather goods. Salamanca also has its own social scene, based around Calle Juan Bravo, with shiny, smart bars and discos. Towards the east end of Calle Goya there is a more affordable shopping area, as well as the **Palacio de Deportes** for basketball games (*see page 236*). On the very eastern flank of Salamanca is Madrid's temple of bullfighting, **Las Ventas**.

Art buffs are advised to head for the marble tower with sculpture garden at Calle Castelló 77, base for the **Fundación Juan March**'s first-rate collection of modern art, and which hosts great contemporary art shows, free classical concerts and so on (*see pages 108 and 217*). At the north end of Serrano is the eclectic (but temporarily closed) **Museo Lázaro Galdiano** (*see page 99*), from where a short walk west along Calle María del Molina and then up the quiet, leafy Calle del Pinar leads to an institution of near-legendary significance in 20th-century Spanish cultural life, the **Residencia de Estudiantes**, where Buñuel, Dalí and García Lorca all first met. It is still an important cultural and exhibition centre (*see page 109*).

Calle Claudio Coello, parallel to Calle Serrano, is the city's most elegant centre for private art galleries. The blocks of Serrano, Claudio Coello and Lagasca below Calle Ortega y Gasset are the oldest part of Salamanca, the first section built up by the Marqués in the 1860s. Streets here are narrower, traffic less intense, and shops closer together, making them more amenable for strolling, browsing and snacking. There are charming buildings with intriguing details – such as the glass-galleried block on the corner of Claudio Coello and Calle Ayala. The block between Claudio Coello and Lagasca on Calle Ayala also contains the **Mercado de la Paz**, Salamanca's market. It's a cut above other Madrid markets, with a superb range and quality of produce (*see page 176*). Nevertheless, it still has cafeterias offering excellent *menús del día* for 1,000ptas.

Plaza de Toros de Las Ventas

C/Alcalá 237 (91 356 22 00).
Metro Ventas/bus 21, 53, 74, 146.
More than 22,000 spectators can catch a bullfight in this, Spain's largest arena, completed in 1929. Like most early 20th-century bullrings it is in neo-*mudéjar* style, with much use of ceramic tiles in a design that could almost be called playful. Around it there is ample open space to accommodate the crowds and food vendors, so it's easy to get a good look at the exterior. It's not necessary to go to a *corrida* to see the ring from within, too, for when the bulls are back on the ranch concerts are often held here, and

alongside the ring there is the **Museo Taurino** (*see p103*). The bullfight season runs from May to October. *See also pp190-2.*

The Retiro & its *barrios*

Salamanca abuts on to Madrid's overburdened lung, the Retiro park. When Philip II ruled Madrid, this whole area was just open country, apart from the church of **San Jerónimo** (*see page 85*) and a few other royal properties. It was made into gardens – unprecedented in size for the era, the 1630s – as part of the **Palacio del Buen Retiro**, built by the Conde Duque de Olivares for Philip IV to impress the world (*see pages 7 and 12-13*). Gardeners were brought from across Europe to create the park and its lake, and to ensure that the gardens would have shade and flowers throughout a Madrid summer.

After the death of Philip IV in 1665 relatively little use was made of the Retiro, although the palace gained a new lease of life when the Alcázar burned down in 1734, as it became the primary royal residence in Madrid until the Palacio Real was completed in 1764. However, in 1808 Napoleon's troops made it into a barracks, and when the British army arrived in 1812 to fight over Madrid, much of it was destroyed.

On the north side of the park, forming a bridge between it and Salamanca, is the **Puerta de Alcalá** (*see page 84*), still imposing despite being surrounded by the hectic traffic of the Plaza de la Independencia. The districts around and south of the Retiro are in some ways similar to Salamanca, but less emphatically affluent and more mixed. The elegant streets between the park and the Paseo del Prado make up Madrid's most concentrated museum district, with, as well as the Museo del Prado itself, the **Museo del Ejército** and several others (*see page 103*).

Just south-west of the park, right on Glorieta de Atocha, is one of the area's biggest but least-known sights – the magnificently grandiose 1880s **Ministry of Agriculture**, by Ricardo Velázquez, the same architect who designed the delicate exhibition halls inside the Retiro itself.

Sabatini's **Puerta de Alcalá**. *See p84.*

The Retiro

The Retiro is a jewel among parks. Covering nearly 122 hectares (300 acres), its gardens retain a good deal of the regal air they were given when they were first laid out as part of the Buen Retiro palace in the 1630s. Charles III first opened sections of the gardens to the public in 1767, but it was only after the fall of Isabel II in 1868 that they became entirely free to the citizens of Madrid. After it became a park the Retiro acquired most of its many statues, particularly the giant 1902 monument to King Alfonso XII that presides over the lake.

Since it was made open to all, the Retiro has found a very special place in the hearts and habits of the people of Madrid. On a Sunday morning stroll, especially before lunch, you will see multi-generational families watching puppet shows; dog owners and their hounds; children playing on climbing frames; vendors hawking everything from *barquillos* (traditional wafers) to etchings; palm and tarot readers; buskers from around the world; couples on the lake in hired boats; kids playing football; elderly men in leisurely games of *petanca* (boules); cyclists; runners, and a good many bench-sitters who want nothing more than to read the paper. In the week it's much emptier, and it's easier to take a look at some of its 15,000 trees, the rose garden or the exhibition spaces.

The Retiro also contains several interesting buildings. At the south end of the park is the **Observatorio Astronómico**, one of Charles III's scientific institutions, completed after his death in 1790. Beautifully proportioned, it is the finest neo-classical building in Madrid, designed by Juan de Villanueva. It still contains a working telescope, which can only be seen by prior request. One room is also open to the public. Also an important part of the Retiro are its fine exhibition spaces, the **Palacio de Cristal** (pictured above), the **Palacio de Velázquez** and the **Casa de Vacas**. Added in the 19th century, they were extensively renovated during the 1980s (see pages 107 and 109).

The greatest curiosity of the park, though, is Madrid's monument to the Devil, Lucifer himself, in the moment of his fall from heaven. Known as the *Angel Caído* ('Fallen Angel'; pictured left), this bizarrely unique statue is on the avenue south of the Palacio de Cristal.

Observatorio Astronómico

C/Alfonso XII, 3 (91 527 01 07). Metro Atocha/bus all routes to Atocha. **Open** 9am-2pm Mon-Thur; guided tours 11am Fri; closed Sat, Sun. **Admission** free. **Map** p310 I9/10.

Parque del Retiro

Main entrance Plaza de la Independencia (Puerta de Alcalá). Metro Atocha, Ibiza or Retiro/bus all routes to Puerta de Alcalá. **Open** 24hrs daily. **Map** p310 I6-10/ p311 I-K 6-9.

The Casa de Campo

Madrid is often promoted as the European capital with most parkland within its central area. Yet, aside from the Retiro, the first-time visitor is more likely to be struck by the absence of parks in the city centre. What they have overlooked is the **Casa de Campo**, a sprawling 1,820-hectare (4,500-acre) woodland on the other, western side of the River Manzanares.

Once a royal hunting estate, the Casa de Campo was only opened to the public under the Republic in 1931. Five years later it became a key site for Franco's forces in the Civil War battle for Madrid, its high ground being used to shell the city centre and the university. Remains of trenches still exist.

Today, the Casa is home to the **Parque de Atracciones** funfair and the **Zoo** (see pages 194-5), as well as, near Lago Metro, **swimming pools** and tennis courts (see page 240), and a large lake. There is also a pleasant **youth hostel** (see page 52). The cafés that ring the lake make a fine place for a straightforward outdoor lunch, and the boating lake itself has been cleaned up and repaired. Row boats can be hired (pictured), and cyclists should note that most of the park's roads are closed to cars on Sundays until 3pm.

Once you stray away from the criss-crossing roads much of the park is surprisingly wild, and it's possible to have a real country walk through its woods and gullies. A favourite way to visit is via the **Teleférico**

cable car from **Parque del Oeste** (see page 85), which runs over the trees almost to the middle of the Casa, where there are viewpoints, an (admittedly undistinguished) bar-restaurant and picnic spots.

Couples seeking seclusion favour the Casa de Campo, by day and night, and the area by the Teleférico has been a gay cruising spot, although police have been cracking down on this. In contrast, one peculiar feature of the modern Casa is that Madrid's *Partido Popular* city authorities seem near-set on turning the roads from Lago Metro to the Zoo into a semi-official prostitution zone, virtually 'encouraging' prostitutes to move there from the city centre. Consequently, by night, and often by day, there are bunches of female and transvestite prostitutes along these roads, displaying their assets pretty outrageously to cruising drivers. One very Spanish aspect of this is that many of the other users of the park, by day at least, don't let this bother them, but carry on lunching, cycling or whatever, regardless.

Casa de Campo

Metro Batán or Lago/bus 33, 41, 75/ Teleférico (cable car) from Paseo del Pintor Rosales.
Four special bus routes (Z-1 to Z-4) also run from the city centre to the Zoo on Saturdays, Sundays and public holidays.

A few blocks east from there along the (traffic-ridden) Paseo Reina Cristina, a turn right down Calle Julián Gayarre leads to the **Real Fábrica de Tapices**. On Julián Gayarre there is also the much rebuilt **Basilica de Atocha** and the odd, often deserted, **Panteón de Hombres Ilustres**, containing the elaborate tombs of once-celebrated Spanish politicians of the 19th century.

Puerta de Alcalá

Plaza de la Independencia. Metro Retiro/ bus all routes to Plaza de la Independencia. **Map** p310 H/I6.

A short distance along Calle Alcalá from Cibeles, in the middle of another traffic junction, stands one of the most impressive monuments built for King Charles III, a massive neo-classical gate designed by his favourite Italian architect Francesco Sabatini to provide a grand entrance to the city. It was built in 1769-78, using granite and stone from Colmenar. Possible to miss in daytime traffic, it is unavoidably impressive at night.

Real Fábrica de Tapices

C/Fuenterrabia 2 (91 434 05 50). Metro Menéndez Pelayo/bus 10, 14, 26, 32, 102, C. **Open** *guided tours only* 10am-2pm Mon-Fri (last tour approx 1pm); closed Sat, Sun. **Admission** 300ptas.

Goya created some of his freshest images as designs for Madrid's royal tapestry factory, founded in 1721. In his day the factory was in Plaza Santa Bárbara in Chueca, but it has been at this location since 1889. The hand-working skills and techniques used, though, are entirely the same, and on the tours one gets a clear idea of the intricate, painstaking work carried out in its two sections, the carpet room and the tapestry room. Goya designs are a mainstay of the production today (as well as maintaining carpets for royal palaces and the Ritz), but the factory also does work for private clients (for a considerably high price). Although the tours are normally in Spanish, if you phone or call in advance an English-speaking guide can usually be arranged for you.

San Jerónimo el Real

C/Moreto 4 (91 420 30 78). Metro Atocha or Banco de España/bus 9, 10, 14, 19, 27, 34, 45. **Open** *July-Sept* 9am-1.30pm, 6-8pm daily. *Oct-June* 9am-1.30pm, 5.30-8pm daily. **Map** p310 H8.

Founded in 1464 and rebuilt for Queen Isabella in 1503, this church near the Retiro was particularly favoured by the Spanish monarchs, and used for state ceremonies. Most of the original building was destroyed in the Napoleonic Wars, and the present church is largely a reconstruction carried out between 1848 and 1883. Controversially, it is now proposed that it should be taken over by the Prado (*see p90*).

Other Districts

North & west

Argüelles & Moncloa

West of Conde Duque lie the districts known as Argüelles and Moncloa. **Argüelles**, properly speaking, is the grid of streets between Plaza de España, Calle Princesa, Plaza de Moncloa and Paseo del Pintor Rosales. The Paseo, above the **Parque del Oeste** (*see page 86*), is known for its pleasant *terrazas*, open-air bars that are ideal for taking the air on summer evenings.

In the southern corner of the district, just off Plaza de España, is the **Museo Cerralbo** (*see page 99*). In the opposite, northern corner, unmissable at the end of Calle Princesa, stands one of the biggest, most significant creations of the Franco regime, the **Ministerio del Aire** or Air Ministry, built in the 1950s, but in kitsch-Castilian baroque style (*see page 34*).

Alongside the Ministry is the Plaza de Moncloa, with Moncloa Metro station and the departure points for many bus services to towns north and west of Madrid. There is also the fake-Roman triumphal arch Franco had built to commemorate winning the Civil War.

Viewpoints

Madrid's skies and sky-scapes have been celebrated in local folklore and movies like *Women on the Verge of a Nervous Breakdown*, but, unless you know someone with a roof terrace or stay in a hotel with one (such as the **Hotel Emperador**, see page 41), it's surprisingly difficult to see them. Travellers on the Teleférico across the Casa de Campo enjoy splendid views of the skyline from the west: the best time to go is near sunset, when the Palacio Real and Almudena are bathed in an orange glow. For views in the opposite direction, north to the Guadarrama, the café at **Las Vistillas** is unbeatable (see page 151).

Faro de Madrid

Avda de los Reyes Católicos (91 544 81 04). Metro Moncloa/bus 16, 46, 61, 132, 133, C. **Open** 10am-1.45pm, 5-6.45pm Tue-Fri; 10.30am-5.15pm Sat, Sun; closed Mon. **Admission** 200ptas; 100ptas concessions. **Map** p304 B1.

If heights aren't a problem, the best way to get an overview of Madrid is from this tower, built for 1992, exactly 92m (302ft) high and giving an (almost) 360° view. The tower may be closed for repairs at some point in 2000-2001.

Teleférico de Madrid

Paseo del Pintor Rosales (91 541 74 59). Metro Argüelles/bus 21, 74 to Casa de Campo. Metro Lago/bus 33. **Open** *Apr-Sept* 11am-dusk daily. *Oct-Mar* noon-dusk daily. **Tickets** 535ptas return; 375ptas one way; free under-3s; 300ptas return over-65s. Free Wed. **Map** p304 B3.

These six-person cable cars connect the Casa de Campo and Parque del Oeste. The trip takes you right over the Casa, with great views of the Palacio Real, the Manzanares and the city skyline. Closing times vary with sunset; also, there's often a break in service around 2-4pm, when, if you've reached the Casa, you're expected to stay for lunch. See also pages 84 and 86.

Sightseeing

Cooling off in **Parque del Oeste**.

To the north of the plaza, **Moncloa** district is occupied mostly by the sprawling campus of the Universidad Complutense, the **Ciudad Universitaria**. Consequently, the streets just south and east have plenty of studenty bars. Within the university are specific attractions, too, notably the **Museo de América** (*see page 101*) and the **Faro de Madrid** observation tower (*see page 85*).

Parque del Oeste

C/Rosales & Paseo de Moret. Metro Argüelles, Moncloa or Príncipe Pío/bus 21, 46, 74, 133. **Map** p304 A1-C5.
A special method to reach this park is with the **Teleférico** from the Casa de Campo (*see p85*). This park, designed by Cecilio Rodríguez in the 1900s, is one of Madrid's most attractive spaces. Particularly beautiful in spring is *La Rosaleda*, the rose garden. The park formed part of the front line in the Civil War and was virtually destroyed, but has since been completely relaid. The Montaña del Príncipe Pío, at its southern end, is one of the highest points in Madrid, with great views of the Palacio Real and Casa de Campo. This was the site of the Montaña barracks, the Nationalists' main stronghold at the start of the Civil War (*see p22*), before it was demolished and the hill incorporated into the park. Bizarrely, it is now home to the **Templo de Debod**, a genuine Egyptian temple from the fourth century BC presented to Spain by Egypt after it had been removed from its original site to make way for the Aswan Dam. Below the Teleférico stop a path leads to the river and the **Ermita de San Antonio de la Florida**, with its Goya frescoes (*see p69*). The fountain below the Teleférico used to preside over the roundabout at Príncipe Pío station, but was moved to the park in 1994. In its place by the station there is now the **Puerta de San Vicente** – an entirely new, quite convincing reconstruction of the 18th-century gate that once stood on this side of the city. On Sundays Madrid's Andean community take over the Parque del Oeste, with volleyball tournaments and picnics; after dark, the park roads around the fountain have, like the Casa de Campo, become a prostitution zone, particularly at weekends.

Chamberí

Directly north of Malasaña is the *barrio* of Chamberí. This was one of the first working-class districts outside the walls to be built up in the second half of the 19th century. Consequently central Chamberí became one of the few areas outside the old city on the list of those generally considered to have genuine *castizo* character.

As befits a *barrio* with a proper identity, Chamberí has its own bar crawl, with good tapas bars a Calles Cardenal Cisneros and Hartzenbush (*see page 142*). There's also the pleasant, circular **Plaza de Olavide**, ringed with easy-going pavement cafés. On the north side of Chamberí is Madrid's water system, the Canal de Isabel II. On Calle Santa Engracia, a neo-*mudéjar* water tower has been converted into a unique photography gallery, the **Sala del Canal de Isabel II** (*see pages 33 and 109*).

Tetuán, Prosperidad & the north

North of Chamberí are **Cuatro Caminos** and **Tetuán**, arranged along Calle Bravo Murillo, both modern, working areas, and above them **Chamartín**, which contains the major business area of modern Madrid. For the visitor the main point of interest is the local market, the **Mercado de Maravillas** at Calle Bravo Murillo 122, just north of Cuatro Caminos, the largest in the whole city. On Sunday mornings, too, a mini-'*rastro*' gets going on Calle Marqués de Viana.

Across the Castellana, north-east of Nuevos Ministerios, is **El Viso**, an anomaly in high-rise Madrid. It was developed in the 1920s as a model community on garden-city lines, on the fringes of the city at that time, and some of its individual houses are museum-worthy examples of art deco architecture. The district has retained its desirable (and expensive) status. Further east again is **La Prosperidad**, also once a model housing development, although most of its early buildings have been replaced by modern blocks. Within it is the **Auditorio Nacional** (*see page 215*).

South of centre

The barrios of southern **Embajadores**, **Delicias**, **Arganzuela** and **Legazpi** occupy a triangular chunk of land just south of the old city, bordered by the Manzanares, the M-30 motorway and the rail lines from Atocha. Low rents attract a fair number of resident foreigners. Conventional attractions are few – the **Museo Ferroviario** and the **Parque Tierno Galván**, with the **IMAX** and **Planetario** (*see page 193*) – but the area contains the **Estación Sur** bus station, and two symbols of the city, the **Atlético Madrid** stadium and, alongside it, the Mahou brewery.

Viva Vallecas

Although long part of Madrid, Vallecas continues to consider itself distinct from the rest of the capital – combining the streetwise savvy of the Madrileño with a strong sense of neighbourhood pride. Vallecas doesn't have famous monuments, but it's a very characterful, friendly place, it has some fine places to eat and drink that are cheaper than others in the centre, and, if you're looking for a blast of Madrileño neighbourhood atmosphere, there's nowhere better.

Central Vallecas is easy to find your way around, spread along the *barrio*'s main artery, the **Avenida de la Albufera**, which is followed by Metro line 1 between Puente de Vallecas and Portazgo stations. One great way to get to know the district is to plan a visit around a game by Vallecas' very own football team, the battling **Rayo Vallecano**, at its ground, officially the Estadio Teresa Rivero, by Portazgo Metro. In the 2000-1 season Rayo, whose cool strip resembles a Red Stripe beer can, celebrated holding onto First Division status for two years running. A visit to a Rayo game is not like a trip to that sometimes-silent football megalith the Bernabéu, home of Real Madrid; it's more fun, more of a neighbourhood *fiesta*, with fans of all ages (pictured), *bocadillos* and wineskins being passed round, cheerful abuse being yelled and the whole rounded off by repeated playing of the ineffable *Himno del Rayo*, a kind-of *paso doble*. While the hard core of Real's support has a disturbing tendency to play around with fascist insignia, Rayo fans pay homage to the *barrio*'s nature with banners of Che Guevara, the hammer and sickle, Bob Marley and marihuana leaves. It's much cheaper, too – the ground is small enough so that you never miss a thing, and lately the team isn't bad either (for more on seeing games, see page 237).

Rayo's Sunday games used to be played at noon, an acceptance of the club's humble status, but now, with the team enjoying greater success, matches are played at the more normal Sunday time of 5pm. This gives more time to explore Vallecas and its bars and eating places. By Nueva Numancia Metro, **La Isla de Vallecas** (Avda Albufera 69, 91 437 30 26, open 8am-midnight daily) is an easy-going place for a drink, and **El Fosforito** (C/Picos de Europa 14, 91 328 09 14, open 10.30am-midnight daily), just around the corner up a side street, has great tapas and hosts a flamenco *peña* on Saturday nights. Vallecas' attractive main place for strolling is **Calle Peña Gorbea**, known locally as *el Búlevar*, which runs parallel to the southern side of the Albufera and has a tree-lined central promenade with pavement cafés. Pay homage to the bust of Angeles Rodriguez Hidalgo, *La abuela rockera* or 'rocking granny', who was a familiar figure on the local rock scene until she died aged 93. The *Bulevar* is the site of Vallecas' annual 'water battle' on the penultimate Sunday in July, despite the efforts of the local council to ban it. The water fight began when a group of locals called for independence from Madrid in 1980, citing the need for a port. The rest is history.

For finer food, one of the very best places to eat in the district is **La Cervecera** (C/Monte Perdido 61, 91 477 91 55, open 10am-1am daily), a couple of blocks south of the *Búlevar*, with wonderful tapas and *raciones* (get there early or late; at 2pm on Sunday it's invariably packed). Afterwards, cross over the Albufera again and go up through the back streets to the **Parque del Cerro del Tío Pío**, known as the *Siete Tetas*, 'seven breasts', thanks to its man-made hills. It has a café, and the view of the Madrid skyline is especially dramatic at sunset.

Vallecas has always been a centre of heavy rock and the punk scene in Madrid, and its best-known club reflects this. **Hebe** (C/Tomás Garcia 5, no phone, open 7pm-3am Mon-Thur, Sun; 7pm-4am Fri, Sat), a little south of the *Bulévar*, is an amiably shabby place that has been packing them in for 20 years with live gigs, comedy nights and talent nights, and makes a great place to finish off the day.

Sightseeing

Just south of the river is the **Parque de San Isidro**, containing a charming 18th-century hermitage dedicated to the saint, the traditional focus of the *Romería* (Procession) *de San Isidro*. The park still fills with life and crowds during the **San Isidro** *fiestas* every May (*see page 186*). At other times it's very tranquil; the view from the hill of San Isidro is familiar as one painted many times by Goya, and is still quite recognisable, despite the tower blocks.

Vallecas

Vallecas, beyond the M-30 south-east of the city, was already an industrial suburb in the 1930s, and manages still to be one of the areas of Madrid with a firm sense of its own identity. It doesn't lay much claim to being traditionally *castizo*, even though many of its residents came here as overspill from the centre. Rather, to say Vallecas in Madrid is to immediately suggest the post-Civil War, post-1950s working class. Vallecas is known for a strong sense of neighbourly solidarity. It has its own football team, **Rayo Vallecano**, forever struggling to keep up with its money-laden neighbours (*see page 87* **Viva Vallecas**). Car stickers proclaim 'Independence for Vallecas' (spelt 'Vallekas' by hipper natives, who have their own punky sense of cool). It also has a pleasant tree-lined main drag, more than enough to mark it out from other areas around it. There have been problem areas near Vallecas, such as **Entrevías**, on its south side, home to some of Madrid's largest Gypsy communities. Even this area is being transformed, though, with the construction of Madrid's new regional assembly building, the **Asamblea de Madrid**, and a promised influx of civil servants.

Outer limits

The south

Carabanchel, **Leganés**, **Getafe**, **Móstoles**, **Alcorcón** – Madrid's southern industrial belt, virtually all of it built up from nothing since the 1960s. Areas still within the city such as **Orcasitas** blend into the towns of the *extrarradio*, the outskirts, and concrete flyovers and tower blocks make up the urban landscape.

These areas are due to be better connected with the rest of Madrid with the construction of a new Metro line, *Metrosur*, in 2000-3 (*see page 275*). Central city dwellers also come down here for entertainment. **Alcorcón** holds a flamenco festival (*see page 202*), and **Fuenlabrada** has a clutch of teen-macro-discos. The popularity of hard rock in these suburbs is also attested to by Calle AC/DC in Leganés, inaugurated by the Aussie rock legends themselves in 2000. On it

is a converted bullring that has become one of the most important music venues in Madrid, the **Cubierta de Leganés** (*see page 220*).

The northern suburbs

The northern and western *extrarradio* offers a radical contrast to the south. The thing to do for those with the necessary cash in Madrid in the last 20 years or so has been to adopt the Anglo-Saxon way of life and move out of city flats to house-and-garden developments like **Puerta de Hierro**, north of the Casa de Campo, named after the 1753 'Iron Gate' to the royal hunting reserve of El Pardo. Its posh residences, though, are no match for **La Moraleja**, off the Burgos road, an enclave for executives and diplomats.

The growing districts to the east are not nearly so lush. The area along the A2 motorway towards the airport is intended to be Madrid's major commercial development zone, with the **Feria de Madrid** trade fair complex and the **Parque Juan Carlos I**. Oddly enough, the area already contains, swallowed up in the urban spread, one of Spain's most appealing and neglected 18th-century gardens, the **Capricho de la Alameda de Osuna**.

Capricho de la Alameda de Osuna

Paseo de la Alameda de Osuna (info 010). Metro Canillejas/bus 101, 105. **Open** *Oct-Mar* 9am-6.30pm Sat, Sun, public holidays; closed Mon-Fri. *Apr-Sept* 9am-9pm Sat, Sun, public holidays; closed Mon-Fri.
One of Madrid's most unusual, little-known parks, in a very unusual location, north of the Barcelona road between the Feria and the airport. These French-style gardens were designed by Marie Antoinette's gardener J-B Mulot for the Duchess of Osuna, a great hostess and friend of Goya, in the 1790s. Legends abound about the revels held here in the duchess's day; two of Goya's early macabre 'black paintings', the *Witches' Sabbath* and *Witchcraft Scene* (both in the **Museo Lázaro Galdiano**), were commissioned for her house here (long demolished). The gardens are wonderfully cool and peaceful, a romantic fantasy with an artificial lake with islands in the middle. They were left to decay for years until restoration began in 1974. They have recently been restored once again, but note that they are still only open at weekends. A campsite is nearby (*see p53*).

Parque Juan Carlos I

Avda de Logroño & Avda de los Andes. Metro Campo de las Naciones/bus 101, 105, 122.
This huge park, Madrid's newest green (and brown) space, lies between the airport and the Feria de Madrid trade fair centre. With time it should become one of the city's more attractive places, but it has taken a while for any trees to grow to provide shade. That said, current draws include a series of different gardens within a circle of olive trees, an artificial river and other water features.

Museums

A spectacular concentration of great art – plus rare but unknown treasures, quirky private collections and sometimes-bizarre takes on history.

With the Prado, the Reina Sofía and the Thyssen-Bornemisza museums – all within walking distance of each other – Madrid possesses a truly remarkable concentration of great art. This 'big three' of major art palaces easily contain enough world-class works to keep any attentive visitor busy for days, and naturally tend to dominate one's attention. But, they are not the be all and end all of Madrid's art and museum holdings, and visitors willing to take a little time can also find real gems in far less well-known collections.

Fine works by classic Spanish, Flemish and Italian painters can also be seen at the Museo Cerralbo (see page 99) and the Real Academia de Bellas Artes de San Fernando (see page 99), while the Museo Romántico (see page 100) and above all the Museo Lázaro Galdiano (see page 99), two museums currently undergoing renovation to differing degrees, both have impressive collections. Elsewhere, the Basílica de San Francisco el Grande (see page 67), the Palacio Real (see page 68), the Real Monasterio de las Descalzas Reales (see page 74) and most of all the Ermita de San Antonio de la Florida (see page 69), all detailed in the previous chapter, contain works by major Italian and Spanish painters, and most especially Goya. Between them, the works by El Greco, Dürer, Velázquez, Titian, Arcimboldo, Goya and others in these museums and monuments make a nice complement to those in the three majors.

Outside the fine arts field, the Museo Arqueológico Nacional (see page 102), the Museo de Antropología (see page 102), the Museo del Ejército (see page 103) and the Museo Naval (see page 105) all have very distinctive – in some cases distinctly odd – collections, while the Museo de América (see page 101) has the finest collection of pre-Columbian artefacts anywhere outside the Americas. The Casa-Museo de Lope de Vega (see page 103), the great dramatist's former house, is a charming corner of old Madrid, and interest in the city itself is catered for in the Museo Municipal (see page 105), the Museo de la Ciudad (see page 103) and the new Museo de San Isidro (see page 105). Of the special interest museums, some of the best are the Museo de Ciencias Naturales (see page 106) and the Museo Ferroviario railway museum (see page 107). Together with the Cosmocaixa (see page 193), these museums are likely to be of particular interest to children.

Spain's national cultural authorities have an ongoing policy of museum renovation, which affects different places at different times. Two Madrid museums due to undergo work involving at least partial closure in 2001-2 are the Museo Romántico and the Museo Municipal, and the Museo Lázaro Galdiano will be closed completely for some time. Far and away the most ambitious scheme now in progress, though, is the grand plan for the Prado (see page 90). The Reina Sofía and Museo Thyssen-Bornemisza also each have more limited plans for expansion (see pages 97 and 98).

TICKETS & TIMES

The Spanish national museums (which includes all the majors, except the Thyssen) have a standard adult entry charge of 500ptas. There are discounts for students, and admission is free to everyone, Spanish or otherwise, under 18 or over 65 – something not appreciated by many foreign visitors, who assume they have to pay (ID is usually required). Admission to the national museums is free for everyone on Saturday afternoons and Sunday mornings (when they are often very full), and some less frequented museums are still free at all times. For more on entry concessions, see page 56.

Most museums are shut on Mondays, with the exception of the Reina Sofía, which closes on a Tuesday. Many of the national museums offer volunteer guides free of charge, but they rarely speak English. To have a personal English-speaking guide you will normally have to pay. Only the major museums always have catalogues and so on in English; similarly, most exhibits are labelled only in Spanish, with a few exceptions such as the Thyssen and the Museo Taurino (see page 103).

The Big Three

A joint ticket, the **Paseo del Arte** voucher, is available that gives entry to all three of these museums for 1,275ptas, a reduction overall of 25 per cent. After visiting one museum with the ticket you can visit the other two at any time within the same calendar year. Although sometimes under-advertised, the Paseo del Arte is available from the ticket desks at all three museums; you only have to ask. Each museum

The Prado Plan

The Prado has been undergoing constant renovation ever since the 1980s, but in a piecemeal fashion, with no clear final goal. Its main problem has been lack of space, so that only some 1,000 of its almost 3,400 works could be on display at any one time. However, with the approval by the Ministry of Culture of a comprehensive plan in 1997, ratified two years later after much controversy and wrangling, clear lines have finally emerged as to where the Prado is going as the new millennium unfolds.

With Rafael Moneo, Madrid's specialist in spectacular renovations (see page 34), as lead architect, the plan foresees a dramatic expansion of the Prado from two to five buildings, increasing exhibition space by 50 per cent to allow for the permanent display of a further 500 works and readier access to those in store. This involves turning the central part of the Barrio del Retiro effectively into the *Barrio del Prado*, something that has been strongly resisted by the district's often-wealthy residents.

The refurbishment of the main Juan de Villanueva building is now, by and large, finished, as is the re-ordering of the main collection. Already part of the Prado was the **Casón del Buen Retiro** on Calle Felipe V, which has housed the museum's collection of Spanish 19th-century art. The building – which contains, in the former ballroom of the Retiro palace, Luca Giordano's fresco T*he Order of the Golden Fleece* – is currently having three new floors dug beneath it out of the earth, to be able to show more of these holdings, and may re-open some time in 2001. The church of **San Jerónimo el Real** (see page 85) is, very controversially, also due to be taken over by

the museum, with an all-new cube-shaped, glass-fronted building by Moneo alongside it to create new room for the Prado's offices and, in the church, an entirely separate space for temporary exhibitions. The biggest changes are due to come in 2001-2, when the Prado is scheduled to take over the building now occupied by the **Museo del Ejército** (see page 103), the largest surviving part of Philip IV's Palacio del Buen Retiro (see page 12), despite strong opposition from local residents, voices among the military and even Madrid's Mayor Alvarez de Manzano. In this context the recent appointment of former Defence Minister Eduardo Serra Rexach as president of the Prado's trustees was probably a politic move. This is the most ambitious and most exciting part of the whole plan, involving the return of the giant Velázquez equestrian portraits of the Habsburg monarchs and paintings such as *The Surrender of Breda* to the room for which they were painted, the *Salón de Reinos* or Throne Room of Philip IV's palace, and the substantial restoration of this hall to its original 1630s appearance. The Palacio should eventually also house the sumptuous jewellery collections, such as the *Tesoro del Delfín*, and other paintings and artefacts associated with the setting.

While work has gone on some temporary redistribution of works was often necessary, but with the completion of most of the alterations in the main building the Prado's most famous masterpieces are now all on view. It has also been promised that for the time being temporary shows will be small-scale, so as not to take up space needed by the permanent collection.

---

also has its own 'friends' tickets, giving unlimited entry for one year, which are more expensive, and more widely publicised. A better deal is the 6,000ptas annual museums ticket, available from any national museum, which gives unlimited entry to all the main museums, with the exception of the Thyssen.

The Prado

Madrid's most celebrated attraction occupies a giant neo-classical edifice begun by Juan de Villanueva for King Charles III in 1785, extending alongside the gorgeous tree-lined boulevard of the same name. King Charles had

intended it to be a museum of natural sciences, in line with his own interests, but when it eventually opened in November 1819 it was as a public art museum, one of the first in the world. The idea of using the building to display the royal art collection had actually first been mooted by Spain's 'non-king', Joseph Bonaparte, but surprisingly – given his lack of any democratic impulses – it was later taken up by the restored King Fernando VII.

The Spanish royal collection itself remains the core of the Prado, and reflects the shifting tastes and alliances of Spain's kings from the 15th to the 17th centuries. Naturally, there is a comprehensive display of works by the Court

The **Prado** displays Velázquez on the grand scale – *The Surrender of Breda...*

painters Diego de Velázquez and Francisco de Goya. Close ties with Italy, France and especially the southern, Catholic, Netherlands led to the presence of superb works by Titian, Rubens and Hieronymus Bosch, among others.

Conversely, such choices caused some gaps in the collection. The Spanish monarchs' unfamiliarity with artists predating the High Renaissance is evident, and hostilities with England, Holland and other Protestant states also led to little representation of artists from these countries, although more recent acquisitions have somewhat made up for this.

Royal collecting had begun centuries earlier; and in the 1500s Queen Isabella already possessed a large number of Flemish paintings. Under Charles V (1516-56) and Philip II (1556-98), Italian and Flemish painting still dominated the royal collections. Titian was favoured by both Kings, and Philip II's eclectic taste led him to purchase several paintings by Bosch, among them one of the Prado's most popular, the enigmatically surreal triptych *The Garden of Earthly Delights* (recently cleaned and restored), which Philip kept in his bedroom at El Escorial. The white face beneath a hat in the 'Hell' panel is believed to be Bosch's self-portrait.

Philip IV (1621-65) was the greatest of the Habsburg art collectors, and the leading connoisseur of his day (*see pages 12-13*). Flemish influence was still very strong, and Philip IV was a major patron of Rubens. The latter was contemptuous of Spanish painters until he saw the work of the young Velázquez, who would serve Philip IV as Court painter for nearly 40 years, from 1623 to 1660. Velázquez also supervised the acquisition of other works for Philip IV, adding nearly 2,000 paintings by Renaissance and 17th-century masters,

including some by Van Dyck that had belonged to Charles I of England and were acquired after his execution by Philip's agents.

The 1734 fire that destroyed the old Alcázar of Madrid took with it over 500 works of art. However, more were bought or commissioned to replace these losses. Spain's first Bourbon King, Philip V (1700-46), brought with him one of the Prado's most extraordinary possessions, the *Tesoro del Delfín*, the 'Treasures of the Grand Dauphin'. The Grand Dauphin, eldest son of Louis XIV of France and father of Philip V of Spain, accumulated a massive art collection, part of which was left to Philip. The 'Treasure' consists mostly of 16th-17th-century Italian

...and the small: *Las Meninas.*

objets d'art, such as rock crystal vases studded with semi-precious stones and with gold and silver trimmings. Currently in the basement of the main museum, this is due to be relocated in the Palacio del Buen Retiro in the next few years (*see page 90* **The Prado Plan**).

The last monarch to add significantly to the royal collection was Charles IV (1788-1808), the employer of Goya, possibly the least respectful Court painter who ever lived. The collection would from then on be supplemented by later purchases and works seized from religious houses following their dissolution in the 1830s.

HIGHLIGHTS

The Prado contains such a high concentration of masterpieces that it is really impossible to do it justice in one visit, or in just a brief survey – decent illustrated guides run to around 300 pages. Its layout can be confusing, although the free maps given out at the entrance – regularly updated while the renovation programme goes on – do help, and reorganisation carried out so far has made for a more rational arrangement of its pictures. The layout could, however, still change a little as the Prado plan proceeds.

The main entrance is the Puerta de Goya, at the north end. If, as most people do, you go up the steps to enter on the first floor, the first rooms you see contain French and Italian 16th and 17th century painting, with fine works by Georges de la Tour and Artemisia Gentileschi among others, followed, on the left, by several rooms of Flemish works (Rubens, Brueghel, Van Dyck). Stretching ahead on the right is a a

long gallery with Spanish paintings of the same period, which leads to one of the Prado's very greatest attractions, the Velázquez rooms.

In the great hall in the centre of this floor are the massive state portraits painted by Velázquez of Philip IV and his Court, with their air of melancholic grandeur, and his wonderful *Surrender of Breda* (known in Spanish as *Las Lanzas*, 'The Lances'), which are all due to move to the Palacio del Buen Retiro at some point (*see page 90* **The Prado plan**). Pride of place, though, is taken by *Las Meninas*, often described as the greatest painting in the world, because of its complex interplay of perspectives and realities. Velázquez paints himself at the left of the picture, supposedly painting a portrait of the King and Queen, who appear bizarrely in a 'mirror' at the end of the room, but in whose place stands every spectator, watched forever by Velázquez, the little Infanta Margarita and other figures in the painting. Different but equally impressive are his extraordinary *Los Borrachos* ('The Drunkards') and the portraits of the royal dwarves.

The rooms devoted to the other great Spanish painter most associated with the Prado, Goya, are at the far, south, end of the first floor and in the newly-refurbished rooms on the floor above. Every stage of his career is superbly represented in the Prado: his sarcastic portraits of the royal family and the aristocracy, and the renowned *Majas*. An important recent addition to the Goya collection is his portrait of the *Marquesa de Chinchón*. There are also his tremendous images of war, such as the

Panel 1 of Botticelli's *The Story of Nastagio degli Onesti*, another of the **Prado**'s holdings.

masterpiece *The Third of May*, depicting the executions carried out by the French in Madrid in 1808. Still more fascinating are the *Pinturas Negras* or 'Black Paintings', the turbulent images executed in his last years. Witchcraft, violence and historical drama combine in an astonishing array of monstrous images, many originally painted on the walls of his home, the Quinta del Sordo, between 1819 and 1823. On the second floor there are his earlier, lighter, portraits and the carefree tapestry cartoons he designed for the royal palaces. Here too are European paintings from the 18th century, few of which were previously exhibited.

The ground floor contains earlier painting and sculpture: remarkable Spanish Romanesque murals and Gothic altarpieces, the Italian Renaissance (masterpieces by Botticelli, Rafael, Titian, Caravaggio and many others), 15th century Flemish painting, with the world's greatest collection of Hieronymus Bosch, El Greco, and German paintings that include Dürer's extraordinary 1498 *Self-portrait*. Also on this floor are Classical and Renaissance sculpture, and the vault that currently houses the *Tesoro del Delfín*, until its eventual transfer to the Palacio del Buen Retiro (*see page 90* **The Prado plan**).

For the museum's cafeteria, *see page 104* **Necessary sustenance**.

Museo del Prado

Paseo del Prado s/n, Retiro (91 330 29 00/ 91 420 37 68/http://museoprado.mcu.es). Metro Atocha, Banco de España/bus 9, 14, 27, 34, 37. **Open** 9am-7pm Tue-Sat; 9am-2pm Sun; closed Mon. **Admission** 500ptas; 250ptas students; free under-18s, over-65s, & for all Sat 2.30-7pm & Sun. *Paseo del Arte Ticket* 1.275ptas. **Credit** (shop only) AmEx, DC, MC, V. **Map** p310 H8.

The Thyssen

The third point of Madrid's 'Golden Triangle' was completed with the official opening of the Thyssen-Bornemisza Museum on 10 October 1992. Widely regarded as the most important private collection in the world, it provides a rich complement and contrast to the different areas of art on show in the Prado and the Reina Sofía.

Baron Hans-Heinrich Thyssen-Bornemisza's invaluable collection originally came to Spain on a nine-and-a-half-year loan, but a purchase agreement for the 775 paintings was signed in 1993. The Baron's fourth wife, Carmen Tita Cervera, a former Miss Spain, no doubt influenced his final decision, as did Madrid's offer to house it in the Palacio de Villahermosa, an early 19th-century pile that was empty and available at the time. It had been converted into offices in the 1960s, and architect Rafael Moneo completely rebuilt the interior. This (hugely

Goya's dark *The Sabbath*, from the **Prado**.

expensive) conversion is itself one of the most remarkable features of the museum. Terracotta-pink walls, skylights and marble flooring provide a luminous setting for the collection, and rarely is it possible to see old master paintings so perfectly lit.

This inimitable collection was begun by the present Baron's father in the 1920s. On his death in 1947, however, his 525 paintings were dispersed among his heirs. His son Baron Hans-Heinrich then proceeded to round the collection up once more, buying them back from his relatives, and emulated his father's vocation with a passion, first acquiring old masters, and then turning towards contemporary art in the 1960s. His desire to keep the collection together led him to search for a larger home for his paintings, as his own Villa Favorita in Lugano in Switzerland could only accommodate about 300 pictures. Hence the attraction of the Villahermosa, although a part of the collection, mostly early medieval and Renaissance works, is exhibited in the 14th-century Pedralbes Monastery in Barcelona.

THE COLLECTION

The Thyssen-Bornemisza offers an extraordinary lesson in the history of Western art. You begin on the second floor, with the 13th century and the early Italians (exemplified by Duccio di Buoninsegna's *Christ and the Samaritan Woman*), and work your way downwards through all the major schools until you reach the ground floor and the likes of Roy Lichtenstein's *Woman in Bath*, or the basement café and Renato Guttuso's 1976 *Caffè Greco*. Alternatively, head for a favourite period, guided by the free plan provided.

The Thyssen-Bornemisza fills some of the gaps in the Prado or the Reina Sofía's collections. Unlike either of these two, it includes substantial holdings of 17th-century Dutch painting, Impressionism, German Expressionism, Russian Constructivism, geometric abstraction and pop art.

The Thyssen's detractors say the collection is a ragbag, catch-all collection of every kind of style, put together without discrimination or an eye to quality. However, one of its great attractions is that, while it is extraordinarily broad in scope, it is also recognisably a personal collection reflecting a distinctly individual taste, as seen in the wonderful room dedicated to early portraits, with works by Antonello da Messina and Hans Memling. Equally quirky is the section on early North American painting, including a *Presumed Portrait of George Washington's Cook* by Gilbert Stuart, and works by American artists rarely seen in Europe such as Thomas Cole, Frederick Remington and Winslow Homer.

The museum also has its share of real masterpieces. Among the old masters, the works of Duccio, Van Eyck and Petrus Christus stand out. The museum's most famous painting is the great Florentine master Domenico Ghirlandaio's idealised *Portrait of Giovanna Tornabuoni* (1488), in the portrait room. Two rooms further on is Vittore Carpaccio's allegorical *Young Knight in a Landscape* from 1510, another gem. From among the masters of the Flemish School is the sublime *Annunciation* diptych by Van Eyck, more a three-dimensional sculptural relief than a painting. The Thyssen

is exceptionally strong in the German Renaissance, with many works by Cranach the Elder, a remarkable series of portraits by different artists and Albrecht Dürer's *Jesus among the Doctors*, portraying an idealised, almost effeminate Christ pressed upon by diabolical doctors.

From the later 16th century and baroque there are superb paintings such as Titian's *Saint Jerome in the Wilderness*, Mattia Preti's unsettling *A Concert* and Caravaggio's magnificent *Saint Catherine of Alexandria*. There are also representative works by El Greco, Rubens, Guercino, Tintoretto and Jusepe Ribera, and a Bernini marble, *Saint Sebastian*.

The first floor, below, begins with several rooms of 17th-century Dutch pictures – perhaps the least interesting section of the Thyssen – followed by the most varied part of the museum, with such things as a sombre *Easter Morning* by Caspar David Friedrich, a Goya portrait of his friend *Asensio Juliá*, a great selection of Impressionists (Monet, Manet, Renoir, Degas dancers, two beautiful and little-known Van Goghs, and Gauguin and Cézanne), and even Constable's 1824 *The Lock* – although not jumbled together, but carefully ordered and arranged. The collection is generally strong in German art of all kinds, with several rooms of Expressionists and powerful works by Emil Nolde, Ernst Ludwig Kirchner, Otto Dix, Max Beckmann and the *Blue Rider* group artists Kandinsky and Franz Marc.

Also present, on the ground floor, are more familiar modern masters – Braque, Mondrian, Klee, Max Ernst and Picasso, in the shape of his 1911 *Man with a Clarinet*, among others. The last few rooms concentrate on the USA, with a fabulous Georgia O'Keeffe, *New York with Moon*, a *Hotel Room* by Edward Hopper and Robert Rauschenberg's 1963 *Express*, but also on show are *Large Interior, Paddington* by Lucian Freud and an early David Hockney, *In Memoriam Cecchino Bracci*.

Personal, eclectic and fun, the Thyssen-Bornemisza collection shows a range of work that it would otherwise be physically impossible to reach – without unlimited time, travel and privileged access to many private collections and museums. A full tour of the museum takes at least two hours. Temporary shows are also a feature of the museum, and in recent times have included an important retrospective of El Greco, another of Giorgio Morandi and a show on landscape painting from Breughel to Van Gogh. Also worth looking out for are the occasional *Contextos* exhibits, in which a single painting from the museum is shown alongside other works from the same era, to place it in context.

Fit for a grand baron, the **Thyssen**.

Sightseeing

Palma Vecchio, Ghirlandaio, Franz Marc and Van Gogh, all from the **Thyssen**.

The Thyssen also has an expansion plan, under which it is due to take over two adjoining buildings on the north-west corner of the block. This project was to have been completed to coincide with the museum's tenth birthday in 2002, but little progress has been made as the architectural competition was declared void. For the museum's cafeteria, *see page 104* **Necessary sustenance**.

Museo Thyssen-Bornemisza

Palacio de Villahermosa, Paseo del Prado 8, Huertas & Santa Ana (91 420 39 44/ www.museothyssen.org). Metro Banco de España/bus 9, 14, 27, 34, 37. **Open** 10am-7pm Tue-Sun; closed Mon. **Admission** 700ptas; 400ptas students, over-65s; free under-12s; *Paseo del Arte Ticket* 1,275ptas. *Temporary exhibitions* 500ptas; 300ptas students, over-65s. *Both* 900ptas; 500ptas students, over-65s. **Credit** AmEx, DC, MC, V. **Map** p310 G7.

The Reina Sofía

Two glass and steel lift-shafts, designed by British architect Ian Ritchie, now run up the façade of this immense, slab-sided building, formerly the San Carlos Hospital, built in 1776-81 by Francesco Sabatini for King Charles III. The views provided by the lifts are an appetiser to this spectacular art space.

Madrid's national museum of modern art boasts a giant area of exhibition space, only surpassed in Europe by the Centre Pompidou and the Tate Modern. The hospital closed in 1965, and the initial conversion was carried out from 1977 to 1986, when Queen Sofía first opened the new facility named after her. It was initially only a temporary exhibition space, and more renovation – with the addition of the lifts – continued until 1990, when it finally opened as a museum with a permanent collection.

Its great jewel is unquestionably Picasso's *Guernica*, his impassioned denunciation of war and fascism commemorating the 1937 destruction of the Basque town of Guernica by German bombers supporting the Francoist forces in the Spanish Civil War – although some art historians, sometimes encouraged by Picasso himself, have seen it more in formal terms, as a reflection on the history of Western painting using elements from the work of the old masters. It has been in the Reina Sofía since 1992, when it was transferred here from the Casón del Buen Retiro (*see page 90* **The Prado Plan**) amid great controversy. Picasso refused to allow the painting to be exhibited in Spain under the Franco regime, and it was only in 1981 that it was finally brought to Spain from the Museum of Modern Art in New York. The artist had intended that it should be housed in the Prado – of which the Casón is at least an

annexe – and his family bitterly opposed the change of location. The acquisition of *Guernica* hugely boosted the prestige of the Reina Sofía, but the conflictive saga of its final resting place has continued: Bilbao, capital of the Basque province of Vizcaya, which contains the town of Guernica, has staked a claim on the picture for its Guggenheim Museum. However, since the painting belongs to the Spanish State any such move is very unlikely.

The rest of the permanent collection, which came mainly from the old Museo Español de Arte Contemporáneo in Moncloa, has been much criticised. For many, the Reina Sofía's claim to be an international centre for contemporary art is frankly fallacious. At best, it is pointed out, it is a reasonable collection of Spanish contemporary art, with some thin coverage of non-Spanish artists. It certainly contains works by practically all the major Spanish artists of the 20th century – Picasso, Dalí, Miró, Juan Gris, Julio González, Tàpies and Antonio Saura are all present – but even here the representation of individual artists is often patchy, with few major works.

In response, an active acquisitions policy was adopted in the early 1990s that sought to fill some gaps in the range of Spanish art, and add works by major foreign artists. Representative pieces by Donald Judd, Anish Kapoor, Bruce Nauman, Tony Cragg, Ellsworth Kelly and Julian Schnabel were all added, along with Picasso's 1928 *Figura*. However, since the *Partido Popular* government came to power in 1996 (and given the demands made on the State arts budget by restoration at the Prado), the Reina Sofía's purchasing budget has been cut drastically, and now amounts just to a miniscule 375 million pesetas (around £1.5 million/$2.25 million), supplemented a little by donations from private patrons. Director José Guirao, who was replaced by Juan Manuel Bonet in June 2000, attempted to continue the acquisitions policy, but focussed resources on the Spanish collection with early pieces by Miró and Gris. Promises have also been made to pay greater attention to Latin American art.

THE COLLECTION

The permanent collection is on the second and fourth floors; temporary exhibitions are presented on the ground (Floor 1) and third floors. On each of the permanent-collection floors there are additional rooms for the temporary display of works from the collection not normally on show. The second floor begins with a selection entitled 'The Turn of the Century', looking at the origins of modernism in Spanish art, placing haphazardly together artistic currents from different parts of Spain –

Sightseeing

One of the world's most airy art spaces, the **Reina Sofía**.

Basque painters such as Zuloaga, Regoyos and Echevarría, Catalan Modernists such as Rusiñol, Nonell and Casas – even though they have relatively little in common. Next is the first avant-garde, with pieces by Uruguayan Joaquín Torres García and other artists who worked in Spain such as Picabia and the Delaunays, followed by a room dedicated to Juan Gris. Then comes the major draw for most visitors, the Picasso rooms, divided into pre- and post-Civil War, with *Guernica* in the centre.

Miró, Julio González and Dalí have rooms of their own. Paintings by the latter include The *Great Masturbator* and *The Enigma of Hitler*. Several of the works by Miró are from his later life, the 1970s. After a room on international surrealism (Ernst, Magritte) there follows one on Luis Buñuel, and then the final displays on this floor take you to the end of the Civil War in 1939, looking at Spanish art of the 1930s.

The fourth floor runs from Spain's post-war years up to the present day, starting with figurative art and the beginnings of abstraction in Spain, taking in Tàpies, Mompó, Oteiza, Palazuelo and Equipo 57. For international context there are also works by Bacon, Henry Moore and Lucio Fontana alongside Saura and Chillida. Later rooms feature pop art, figurative work by Arroyo, and minimalism, with pieces by Ellsworth Kelly, Dan Flavin and Barnett Newman. Overall, though, the collection of non-Spanish art remains very limited.

The immensity of the building, with its tranquil inner courtyard, is a great advantage for the exhibition of monumental pieces. The garden has been used to house large installations, as has the plaza, Plaza Sanchéz Bustillo, in front of the museum. Inside, long halls, high-vaulted ceilings and masses of windows give it an airy, spacious feel. Plans are also afoot to expand the museum, using the courtyard on Ronda de Atocha and Calle Argumosa. The design of French architect Jean Nouvel consists of three steel-and-glass constructions united under one roof, but work on this project will not begin until 2001.

The Reina Sofía is also a major international centre for large-scale temporary exhibitions of contemporary art, in which role it has won universal praise – so much so that it's often said that its temporary shows are far more important than anything on permanent display (except *Guernica*). Exhibitions of international artists and collections – in painting, sculpture, photography, prints and more – are shown on the ground (the 'first') and third floors, the most impressive exhibition spaces in Madrid. At any given time there may be three quality shows in progress at the centre; lately, they have included comprehensive exhibitions on Man Ray, Roberto Matta, Louise Bourgeoise and Antoni Tàpies. Shows have become a little staid and 'classical' of late, but smaller exhibits of cutting-edge installations and new media work do appear, in *Espacio Uno* on the ground floor.

The Reina Sofía also serves as a venue for many other activities. It runs the Palacio de Cristal and Palacio de Velázquez exhibition halls in the Retiro (*see page 109*), which are used to present dynamic shows of sculpture and installations. It's also home to Madrid's principal contemporary music centre, the Centro para la Difusión de la Música Contemporánea (*see chapter* **Music: Classical & Opera**), has exceptional book, music art and video libraries, and contains a very superior art-oriented book and souvenir shop. For the cafeteria, *see page 104* **Necessary sustenance**.

Museo Nacional
Centro de Arte Reina Sofía

*C/Santa Isabel 52, Lavapiés (91 467 50 62
/www.museoreinasofia.mcu.es). Metro Atocha/bus all
routes to Atocha.* **Open** 10am-9pm Mon, Wed-Sat;
10am-2.30pm Sun; closed Tue. **Admission** 500ptas;
250ptas students, free under-18s, over-65s, & for all
Sat 2.30-9pm & Sun. *Paseo del Arte* Ticket 1,275ptas.
Credit (shop only) AmEx, DC, MC, V.
Map p310 G10.

Other museums

Fine & decorative arts

Colección Permanente del
Instituto de Crédito Oficial (ICO)

*C/Zorrilla 3, Huertas & Santa Ana (91 420 12
42/www.ico.es). Metro Banco de España/bus all
routes to Plaza de Cibeles.* **Open** 10am-7pm Tue-Sat;
10am-2pm Sun. **Admission** free. **Map** p310 G7.
The ICO, a State credit bank, began to invest in art
in the 1980s, and inaugurated this exhibition space
for its collection in 1996. It has three main parts –
most important is Picasso's *Suite Vollard*, a mile-
stone in 20th-century prints, from 1927-37; there is
also a fine selection of modern Spanish sculpture,
and some international painting from the 1980s. The
bank has bought little since the museum's inauguration, so changes come in the form of temporary
shows, such as a recent tribute to Luis Buñuel.

Museo Cerralbo

*C/Ventura Rodríguez 17, Argüelles (91 547 36 46).
Metro Plaza de España/bus all routes to Plaza de
España.* **Open** *Sept-June* 9.30am-2.30pm Tue-Sat;
10am-2pm Sun. *July, Aug* 10am-2pm Tue-Sat;
10.30am-1.30pm Sun. **Admission** 400ptas; 200ptas
students, free under-18s, over-65s, & for all Wed &
Sun. **No credit cards. Map** p304 C5.
This sumptuous late 19th-century mansion houses
the personal collection of its former owner Enrique
de Aguilera y Gamboa, the 17th Marqués de
Cerralbo. A man of letters, reactionary politician and
fanatical collector, he travelled throughout Europe
and Asia in pursuit of pieces to add to his collection,
which he left to the Spanish State on his death in
1922. One curious feature of the museum stems from
the fact that in his will the Marqués stipulated that
the collection should be displayed exactly as he had
arranged it. This means in a way that is anathema
to modern museum thinking, with paintings in three
levels up the walls. Also, few items are labelled.
However, in among the many paintings there are El
Greco's *The Ecstasy of Saint Francis of Assisi* – the
real highlight – and works by Zurbarán, Alonso
Cano and other Spanish masters. As well as the actual exhibits, a major attraction of the house is the
opportunity it gives to see a near-intact aristocratic
residence of the Restoration era, especially the centrepiece of the ground floor, the lavish ballroom. The
upper level has a much more masculine air, and this

is where you find the Marqués' astonishing collection of European and Japanese armour, weapons,
watches, pipes, leatherbound books, clocks and
other curiosities. Guided tours in Spanish are available, but must be requested in advance.

Museo Lázaro Galdiano

*C/Serrano 122, Salamanca
(91 561 60 84/www.flg.es). Metro Gregorio
Marañón/bus 9, 12, 19, 51, 89.* **Currently
closed for renovation. Map** p307 J1.
Another, more important private legacy, this little
known, extraordinarily eclectic collection of 15,000
paintings and *objets d'art* was accumulated over 70
years by the financier José Lázaro Galdiano (1862-
1947). Its holdings include – with many lesser items
– paintings by Goya and Bosch, and wonderful
Renaissance ornamental metalwork. The four-storey
Salamanca mansion and its gardens are also a sight
in themselves. The museum will, however, be closed
for at least two years from October 2000, while an
extensive renovation programme is carried out.

Museo Nacional
de Artes Decorativas

*C/Montalbán 12, Retiro (91 532 64 99/www.mec.es).
Metro Banco de España/bus all routes to Plaza de
Cibeles.* **Open** 9.30am-3pm Tue-Fri; 10am-2pm Sat,
Sun, public holidays. **Admission** 400ptas; 200ptas
students, free under-18s, over-65s, & for all Sun.
No credit cards. Map p310 H7.
Founded in 1871 primarily for teaching purposes,
the National Museum of Decorative Arts consists of
objets d'art, furniture and tapestries from all over
Spain. Since 1932 it has been housed in a small
palace by the Retiro, former home of the Duchess of
Santoña. Of its 58 display rooms, the most prized is
the tiled kitchen on the fifth floor, painstakingly
transferred from an 18th-century Valencian palace.
Its 1,604 painted tiles depict a domestic scene of that
era, with a huddle of servants making tea for the
lady of the house. The museum also has a wealth of
other curiosities, including graphically shaped jewel
cases from the 'Dauphin's Treasure', the rest of
which is in the Prado (*see p91*), 19th-century dolls'
houses, antique fans, an ornate 16th-century four-
poster bedstead and a Sèvres jug given to Queen
Isabel II by Napoleon III. The museum has also
taken part in the PHotoEspaña programme (*see
p186*) hosting some special shows on historical
themes. Guided tours are available, usually in
Spanish only, if requested in advance

Museo de la Real Academia de
Bellas Artes de San Fernando

*C/Alcalá 13, Sol & Gran Vía (91 522 14 91/
Calcografía Nacional 91 532 15 43). Metro Sevilla or
Sol/bus all routes to Puerta del Sol.* **Open** 9am-
2.30pm Mon, Sat, Sun, public holidays; 9am-7pm
Tue-Fri. *Calcografía Nacional* 10am-2pm Mon, Sat,
Sun, public holidays; 10am-2pm, 4-8pm Tue-Fri.
Admission 400ptas; 200ptas students; free under-
18s, over-65s, & for all Wed. *Calcografía Nacional*
free. **No credit cards. Map** p309 F7.

Founded in 1794, the San Fernando Royal Academy of Fine Arts is the oldest permanent artistic institution in Madrid. The eclectic display collection is partly made up of works donated by aspiring members in order to gain admission to the academy, of varying quality. Its greatest possessions, though, are its thirteen works by Goya, an important figure in the early years of the institution, shown in a special room that was renovated for the 250th anniversary of his birth in 1996. They include two major self-portraits, a portrait of his friend the playwright Moratín, a large portrait of Charles IV's hated minister Godoy, and *El Entierro de la Sardina* ('Burial of the Sardine'), a Carnival scene that foreshadows his later, darker works. Another of the academy's most prized possessions is the Italian mannerist Giuseppe Arcimboldo's *Spring*, a playful, surrealistic portrait of a man made up entirely of flowers. It was one of a series on the four seasons painted for Ferdinand I of Austria in 1563: *Summer* and *Winter* are still preserved in Vienna, but the whereabouts of *Autumn* is unknown. There are also important portraits by Velázquez and Rubens, and several paintings by Zurbarán; among the later works the best-known are some Picasso engravings and a Juan Gris, the most surprising the extraordinarily colourful fantasies of the little-known Múñoz Degrain, and the De Chirico-esque work of Julio Romero de Torres.

The academy also has a valuable collection of plans and drawings, such as those of Prado architect Juan de Villanueva, and rare books. In the same building is the **Calcografía Nacional**, a similarly priceless collection and archive of engraving and fine printing, which has on show many of the original plates for the great etching series of Goya.

Museo Romántico

C/San Mateo 13, Chueca (91 448 10 45/ www.mec.es). Metro Tribunal/bus 3, 37, 40, 149. **Open** 9am-3pm Tue-Sat, 10am-2pm sun, public holidays. Closed Aug. **Admission** 400ptas; 200ptas students; free under-18s, over-65s, & for all Sun. **No credit cards. Map** p306 G4.

This rather weather-beaten museum has been undergoing slow restoration in recent years, but it now seems that the green light has been given for thorough structural repairs to go ahead from some time in 2001. This may mean that the upper floor will be closed, during which time a selection of the exhibits will be moved temporarily downstairs. The museum is (until now) a slightly grimy but charming reflection of the Romantic era in 19th century Spain – its previous neglect and creaking floor adding to its nostalgic feel. The period is evoked through furniture, paintings, ornaments, early pianos and memorabilia associated with various writers, most especially the journalist Larra. The Romántico is another museum set up by a private collector, the Marqués de Vega-Inclán, an antiquarian who was responsible for the first conservation of many of Spain's historic monuments and also inspired the creation of the Parador hotel chain (*see*

p257). A whole – rather unexciting – section is dedicated to him on the ground floor downstairs. The house itself, from 1770, is of great interest. Gracing its chapel is the museum's most valuable painting, Goya's luminous *Saint Gregory the Great*.

Museo Sorolla

Paseo del General Martínez Campos 37, Chamberí (91 310 15 84/www.emcu.es/nmuseos/sorolla). Metro Gregorio Marañón or Iglesia/bus 5, 16, 61. **Open** 10am-3pm Tue-Sat; 10am-2pm Sun. **Admission** 400ptas; 200ptas students; free under-18s, over-65s, & for all Sun. **No credit cards. Map** p306 H1.

The former home of painter Joaquín Sorolla is a must. Often thought of as a neo-impressionist, Sorolla is perhaps better described as an exponent of 'luminism', the celebration of light. Built for him in 1910, the mansion still exudes a very comfortable old-world elegance, even though it could now benefit from restoration (plans to this effect are apparently pending approval). Visitors enter through the deliciously peaceful, Moorish-inspired garden, a cool haven for locals who just want to sit and contemplate the fountains. Inside, notice the skylights, essential elements in the home of an artist renowned for his iridescent, sun-drenched paintings. His studio contains a curious Turkish bed, decrepit but still in one piece, where he apparently took his siestas. Around the rooms are his collections, ranging from exotic to kitsch, including a very large collection of traditional Spanish ceramics. The ground floor has been preserved to give the visitor a feel of Sorolla's life, while the upper floor has been converted into a gallery. In his exquisite large portrait of the singer Ráquel Méller, her white dress shimmers with flecks of green, violet, ochre and pink; beside it is a picture of Sorolla's family, lying on a sea of deep green grass. The few men as subjects are usually portrayed toiling away, while women and young boys are seen at play or rest. It's easy to dismiss Sorolla, for his leisured themes, and for painting pictures that are incorrigibly greeting cardish – as indeed they are used throughout the world – but few people fail to find his world at least a little seductive, or to admire his spectacular use of light.

Museo Tiflológico

C/La Coruña 18, Tetuán (91 589 42 00/ www.museoonce.es). Metro Estrecho/bus 3, 43, 64, 126, 127. **Open** 10am-2pm, 5-8pm Tue-Fri; 10am-2pm Sat. **Admission** free.

Run by the ONCE, the powerful Spanish organisation for the blind and partially sighted, this special museum presents exhibitions of work by visually-impaired artists (the name comes from the French *tiphlologique*, for all things connected with visual problems, from the Greek *tiflos*, sightless). In contrast to the norm in most museums, work here is intended to be touched, and is generally sculptural, three-dimensional, rich in texture and highly tactile. As well as temporary shows the museum has a large permanent collection of instruments devised to help the blind over the years, and a series of scale models of monuments from Spain and around the world.

The Madrid Codex

The great works of art that hang in Madrid, by Velázquez, Goya, Bosch or Picasso, are world-famous and globally recognised images. The city also contains, however, another artefact that is all but unique, and yet is curiously little known. This is the Madrid Codex, preserved in the **Museo de América** in Moncloa (see below), one of only four Mayan illustrated manuscripts in existence.

It consists of a single folding document of 56 pages of bark paper, each one densely painted on both sides, and is believed to have been made in the Yucatán peninsula some time in the 15th century. At the time of the Spanish conquest of Mexico there were hundreds of such books, but the missionary friars, believing that they were the work of the devil and, rightly, that they played an important part in maintaining Mayan culture, destroyed as many as they could lay their hands on. Today, the only other Mayan codices that have survived are the Dresden and the Paris, kept in those cities, and the Grolier, in Mexico City. The Madrid Codex itself is believed to have been brought to Spain by none other than the conqueror of Mexico Hernán Cortés in the 1520s, although it disappeared for centuries until it was discovered in a private collection in the 19th century. It is sometimes known as the *Trocortesiano*, a combination of the names of Cortes and the collector Juan de Tro, who first brought it to light in 1866.

The Codex, like its fellows, is a kind of almanac, detailing the many ceremonies and rituals that marked the Mayan year. On nearly each page there are complex images, surrounded by texts and numbers in the Mayan glyph writing system. There are images of deities, such as the long-nosed rain god Chac (pictured); there are also astronomical tables, plotting the movements

of Mars, birds, animals and scenes of human sacrifice, hunting, trading, playing music and beekeeping. Made far too little of by the museum, and by Madrid in general, the Codex is a remarkable product of a completely alien civilisation.

Archaeology & anthropology

Museo Africano

C/Arturo Soria 101, Arturo Soria (91 415 24 12/ www4.planalfa.es/mcombonianos). Metro Arturo Soria/bus 11, 70, 114, 201. **Open** guided tour only 11.30am Sun. Call for appointment, Mon-Sat. Closed July-Sept. **Admission** free.

'Museum' is really too grand a term to describe this collection of African artefacts. It has been assembled over more than 30 years by the Combonian Missionaries, an order founded by Italian priest Father Daniel Comboni. Its most prized hoard is a collection of tribal masks, but it also has unusual musical instruments to complement its knives, machetes, terracotta figures, gourds and implements for traditional magic. There is also a fine collection of recordings of African music.

Museo de América

Avda de los Reyes Católicos 6, Moncloa (91 543 94 37/ www.mec.es). Metro Moncloa/bus all routes to Moncloa. **Open** 10am-3pm Tue-Sat; 10am-2.30pm Sun, public holidays. **Admission** 500ptas; 250ptas students; free under-18s, over-65s, & for all Sun. **No credit cards**.

An oddly mixed experience. First the positives: Madrid's Museum of the Americas contains the finest collection of pre-Columbian American art and artefacts in Europe, a combination of articles brought back at the time of the Conquest or during the centuries of Spanish rule over Central and South America with later acquisitions and others donated by Latin American countries in the modern era. The museum fell victim to one of Madrid's longest-ever renovation programmes, lasting a full 12 years from 1982 to 1994. The reopening of its galleries, now beautifully lit and equipped, was eagerly awaited. The collection includes near-matchless treasures: there is the *Madrid Codex*, one of only four surviving Mayan illustrated glyph manuscripts anywhere in the world (*see page 101* **The Madrid Codex**); the *Tudela Codex* and illustrated manuscripts from central Mexico describing the events of the Spanish Conquest; superb carvings from the Mayan city of Palenque, sent back to Charles III by the first-ever modern survey expedition to a pre-Hispanic American ruin in 1787; and the 'Gold of the Quimbayas', a series of exquisite gold figures from the Quimbaya culture of Colombia, presented to Spain by the Colombian government. All the main pre-Columbian cultures are represented – further highlights include Aztec obsidian masks from Mexico, Inca stone sculptures and funeral offerings from Peru, and finely modelled, comical and sometimes highly sexual figurines from the Chibcha culture of Colombia, which give a vivid impression of the lives of their makers. There are also exhibits from the Spanish colonial period, such as the remarkable *Entry of the Viceroy Morcillo into Potosí* (1716) by the early Bolivian painter Melchor Pérez Holguín, a series of paintings showing in obsessive detail the range of racial mixes possible in colonial Mexico, and a collection of gold and other objects from the galleons Atocha and Margarita, sunk off Florida in the 18th century and only recovered in 1988.

The negative side of the museum is that, during the long years of closure the decision was taken to arrange the collection not in the apparently too-conventional way, by countries and cultures, but thematically, so that rooms are dedicated to topics such as 'the family', 'communication' and so on, with artefacts from every period and country alongside each other. Some may find this stimulating, but many of the supposed 'connections' drawn between objects from different cultures and eras are frankly banal, and in general unless you already have some knowledge of the many pre-Columbian cultures it is confusing and uninformative. After all these years of waiting, it seems an opportunity lost. Frustrating, but still a superb, intriguing collection; temporary shows are also often interesting.

Museo de Antropología/Etnología

C/Alfonso XII, 68, Atocha (91 539 59 95). Metro Atocha/bus all routes to Atocha. **Open** 10am-7.30pm Tue-Sat; 10am-2pm Sun. **Admission** 400ptas; 200ptas students; free under-18s, over-65s, & for all Sat 2.30-7.30pm & Sun. **No credit cards. Map** p310 H10.

This three-storey edifice near the Retiro is officially now called the Museo de Antropología, although confusingly Museo de Etnología is built into the façade. Either way, it makes an attractive, conveniently-sized museum. The interior is structured around a grand open hall that allows a view of all the several levels of the building, where each floor is devoted to a specific region or country. The first level has an extensive collection from the Philippines (a former Spanish colony), dominated by a 6m (20ft) dugout canoe. Among the bizarre highlights are a 19th-century Philippine helmet made from a spiky blowfish, shrunken human heads from Peru, and the skeleton of Don Agustín Luengo y Capilla, a resident of Extremadura who attracted scientific attention by being 2.25m (7ft 4in) tall. Even more enticing is a shrivelled tobacco leaf-skinned mummy, said to have once been in Charles III's Royal Library. The latter two are in the annexe to the first level.

Museo Arqueológico Nacional

C/Serrano 13, Salamanca (91 577 79 12/ www.man.es). Metro Colón or Serrano/bus all routes to Plaza de Colón. **Open** 9.30am-8.30pm Tue-Sat; 9.30am-2.30pm Sun, public holidays. **Admission** 500ptas; 250ptas students; free under-18s, over-65s, & for all Sat 2.30-8.30pm & Sun. **No credit cards. Map** p310 I5.

One of Madrid's oldest museums, sharing the same giant building overlooking the Plaza de Colón as the Biblioteca Nacional (*see p284*) and Museo del Libro (*see p105*), the Archaeological Museum was set up in 1867. It traces the evolution of human cultures from prehistoric times up to the 15th century, and the collection of artefacts includes finds from the Iberian, Celtic, Greek, Egyptian, Punic, Roman, Paleochristian, Visigothic and Muslim cultures. Remarkably, the great majority of them came from excavations carried out within Spain, illustrating the extraordinary continuity and diversity of human settlement in the Iberian peninsula. Some of the most interesting relics are from the area around Madrid itself, such as the many 4,000-year-old neolithic campaniform (bell-shaped) pottery bowls found south of the city at Ciempozuelos. If you wish to tour the whole museum in chronological order you should begin a visit with the basement, which holds paleontological material including skulls, tombs and a mammoth's tusks, still attached to its skull. The ground floor holds the museum's most famous possession, the Iberian sculpture the *Dama de Elche*, an enigmatic figure whose true gender is a mystery. Further up, the usual definition of archaeology is stretched somewhat to include interesting exhibits on post-Roman Visigothic and Muslim Spain, with wonderful ceramics and fine metalwork from Moorish Andalusia. A series of rooms has recently been reopened with pieces from the Middle Ages and later eras, after having been closed for many years. In the garden, steps lead underground to a reproduction of the renowned Altamira prehistoric cave paintings in Cantabria, which can be an acceptable substitute for visiting the caves themselves.

Casa-Museo de Lope de Vega: the garden.

Bullfighting

Museo Taurino
*Patio de Caballos, Plaza Monumental de Las Ventas,
C/Alcalá 237, Ventas (91 725 18 57). Metro
Ventas/bus all routes to Ventas.* **Open** *Mar-Oct*
9.30am-2.30pm Tue-Fri; 10am-1pm Sun. *Nov-Feb*
9.30am-2.30pm Mon-Fri. **Admission** free.
Its location beside the stables in the Las Ventas
bullring makes this little museum easy to find – let
your nose lead you to it. If this fails, head towards
the right side of the bullring entering from Calle
Alcalá. It was renovated a few years ago, and only
six bulls' heads remain from the original museum,
which then seemed to be mostly a homage to the
bull. The present museum celebrates more the man
and the bullfight itself. There are sculptures and
portraits of famous matadors, and *trajes de luces*
(suits of lights), including the pink and gold outfit
worn by the legendary Manolete on the afternoon of
his death in the ring in 1947 (alongside the blood-
transfusion equipment that was used in attempts to
save him). Among the 18th-century paintings is a
portrait of torero Joaquín Rodríguez Costillares, once
thought to be by Goya but now labelled as anonymous. It's an old-fashioned, shabby museum, but is
one of few in Madrid with labelling in Spanish and
English. Plans to move the museum to another part
of the bullring are still very much up in the air.

Literary & historical

Casa-Museo de Lope de Vega
*C/Cervantes 11, Huertas & Santa Ana
(91 429 92 16). Metro Antón Martín/bus 9, 14, 27,
34, 37.* **Open** 9.30am-2pm Tue-Fri; 10am-2pm Sat.
Admission 200ptas; 100ptas students, over-65s,
group of 20 or more; free Wed.
No credit cards. Map p310 G8.
Spain's most prolific playwright and poet Félix Lope
de Vega Carpio (1562-1635) spent the last 25 years
of his life in this simple, tranquil three-storey house,
oddly enough on a street now named after his rival
Cervantes. The house and charming garden are

themselves the most interesting things to see,
remarkable survivors from the Golden Age. The
furniture and ornaments, obtained from a variety of
sources, are approximations to Lope de Vega's
household inventory rather than the actual originals.
However, even the garden –much loved by Lope,
and where he used to sit after a day's writing –
contains the same fruit trees and plants he detailed
in his journals. The house can be visited with guided tours; some guides speak English, and if possible
call by in advance to check when one will be available (catalogues and brochures are also available).
The tour begins at the tiny chapel on the second
floor. Lope de Vega, whose tumultuous life had
included numerous love affairs, scandals and service in the Spanish Armada, became a priest in 1614.
His tiny alcove of a bedroom has a window that
opens to the chapel so he could hear mass from his
bed, as Philip II did at El Escorial. Just outside his
alcove was the room where the women of the household met to sew and chat. It has no chairs, only a low
platform or *tarima* with silk cushions propped round
a brazier, Moorish-style, as was customary in 16th-
century Castile. In the children's bedroom on the top
floor, you can see a quaint belt of amulets draping a
small chair by a crib, of a type that was often given
to children to ward off the evil eye. The house also
holds within it 1,500 antique books, all from the 16th
and 17th centuries and based on Lope's own library.

Museo de la Ciudad
*C/Príncipe de Vergara 140, Prosperidad
(91 588 65 99). Metro Cruz del Rayo/bus 1, 29, 52.*
Open *mid Sept-mid July* 10am-2pm, 4-6pm Tue-
Fri;10am-2pm Sat, Sun. *Mid July-mid Sept* 10am-2pm,
5-7pm Tue-Fri. **Admission** free.
Opened in 1992 in a new building in the north of
Madrid near the Auditorio Nacional (*see p215*), this
museum seeks to show Madrid's history and future
projects in store for the city. The collection, though,
is patchy, and the historical material inferior to that
in the Museo Municipal (*see p105*). Informative but
often heavy-going exhibits deal with the development of city services –the Metro, gas, water and so
on. Its temporary exhibitions on Madrid-related
topics are often more interesting, and visitors short
of time for sightseeing can at least see scale models
of Madrid's more emblematic buildings.

Museo del Ejército
*C/Méndez Núñez 1, Retiro (91 522 06 28).
Metro Banco de España/bus 9, 14, 27, 34, 37.*
Open 10am-2pm Tue-Sun. **Admission** 100ptas;
50ptas students, under-18s, over-65s; free Sat.
No credit cards. Map p310 H8.
Spain's Army Museum holds a truly massive and
often surprisingly sumptuous collection of military
memorabilia, which includes some very rare treasures. The building it has occupied for many years
is one of the only remaining parts of the Buen Retiro
palace (*see p12*), and its *Salón de Reinos* ('Hall of the
Kingdoms') retains most of its original decoration,
some of it by Velázquez. Within the next few years

Sightseeing

Necessary sustenance

To do Madrid's great art repositories justice requires giving each of them at least two hours of your time, so you'll probably want and/or need a break on the way. Each of the three majors has its own café-restaurant, of varying degrees of attractiveness.

Cafetería del Museo del Prado

91 330 28 00. **Open** 9.30am-6pm Tue-Sat; 9.30-1pm Sun. **Average** 1,500ptas. **No credit cards. Map** p310 H8.
A straightforward bar and self-service cafeteria down in the basement of the giant museum. The food isn't innovative – bocadillos, grills, pasta and so on, but good value, and it's a relaxing space. It's only accessible from inside the museum.

Cafetería del Museo Thyssen

91 429 27 32. **Open** 10am-7pm Tue-Sun. **Average** 2,000ptas. **Set lunch** 1,500ptas. **Credit** AmEx, MC, V. **Map** p310 G7.
This cool, attractive bar-restaurant offers more sophisticated fare than the other museum cafés, with high-quality tapas and a slightly Italian orientation to the menu. It's consequently a bit more expensive, but it's also more comfortable than the others, especially on a hot day, and worth it. You can enter the café, in the basement, without going into the museum. Also, in the evenings from July to September a *terraza*-branch of the **Paradís** (see p123) opens in the cool patio above (9pm-midnight daily), serving interesting light dishes.

Cafetería del Centro Reina Sofía

91 467 50 62. **Open** 10am-8pm Mon, Wed-Sat; 10am-1pm Sun. **Average** 1,500ptas. **Set lunch** 1.200ptas. **Credit** MC, V. **Map** p310 G10.
The once-shabby Reina Sofía café has recently been revamped, and is now an attractive, airy space with a comfortable bar and a separate dining area where the daily menus – of fairly standard modern-Spanish fare – are served. You do not need to enter the museum to use it.

OUTSIDE THE MUSEUMS

If on the other hand you prefer to step outside to get your refreshment, below are some places within a few steps of the major museums. If you're ready to walk up the hill to Plaza Santa Ana, you can find many more.

Restaurants

For refined food, there's a clear choice between the multi-national inventions of **Asia Society** (see page 119) and the more Spanish specialities of **Viridiana** (see page 133). Other favourite venues nearby are the enormously popular **Champagnería Gala** (see page 120) and **La Vaca Verónica** (see page 123). The very pleasant **Finca de Susana**, well-placed for the Thyssen, has an exceptional-value menú (see page 121), and the budget choice for Reina Sofía goers is **Restaurante Económico – Soldemersol** (see page 124).

Cafés, Bars & Tapas

El Brillante (see page 139) serves visitors to the Reina Sofía as well as it does train-travellers from Atocha, while a little further up the Paseo del Prado a short detour up Calle Moratín will take you to **La Platería**, with quality tapas and wines (see page 138). Just around a corner from there on Calle Lope de Vega is the Plaza de Jesús, with three great bars, **La Fábrica** (see page 137), **Los Gatos** (see page 149) and **La Dolores** (see page 154), with tapas that cover the range from earthy to refined. Or, for a much calmer atmosphere and an outside table, there's **El Botánico** (see page 159), right on the other side of the Prado towards the Retiro park.

---

it is due to be taken over by the Prado (*see p90* **The Prado plan**), but no dates have been fixed, and the Army Museum's own administration still seem oddly unaware of what's in store, as if they are hoping to stage a last-ditch defence of their palace. When the transfer happens the museum will most probably be moved to the eminently suitable setting of Toledo's Alcázar.

In the meantime, this rambling, disorderly collection remains in Madrid. Spain had a professional army earlier than most European countries, and the museum accordingly goes back further than the norm. Its more remarkable treasures include *La Tizona*, said to be the sword of the semi-legendary Castilian hero El Cid, and which, the story goes, he won in battle by slaying its owner King Bucar of Morocco; another sword that was used by the last Muslim king of Granada; a fragment of the cross planted by Columbus on his arrival in the New World; and a quite spectacular Arab tent used by the Emperor Charles V on military campaigns in the 1530s. Toy soldier enthusiasts can see a whole room devoted to miniatures, while the rifle room contains enough weaponry to make any gun-freak drool.

Even more curious is a small room dedicated to a handful of Spanish heroines, with romanticised paintings of women such as seamstress Manuela Malasaña, killed by French soldiers in 1808 when she tried to defend herself with a pair of scissors (*see p80*), and others who enlisted in wars disguised as men. There are rooms and rooms dedicated to the Spanish army in the 19th century, while the 20th century sections give a strong impression that the museum has been set aside as a space where the more intransigent and elderly members of the Spanish military could live on unmolested, in return for their (grudging) acceptance of democracy: the rooms on Franco and the Civil War are completely celebratory, and this must surely be one of the only museums in the world today that unabashedly commemorates the Nazis' fight against Bolshevism, with a gung-ho room on the *División Azul*, the 'Blue Division' of Spanish fascist volunteers who fought with the German Army in Russia in World War II. A strange place. English-speaking guides can be arranged a week in advance (7,500ptas).

Museo del Libro

Biblioteca Nacional, Paseo de Recoletos 20, Salamanca (91 580 78 00). Metro Colón/bus all routes to Plaza de Colón. **Open** 10am-9pm Tue-Sat; 10am-2pm Sun, public holidays. **Admission** free. **Map** p306 I5.

Spain's national library, the Biblioteca Nacional (*see p284*), possesses such a wealth of printed matter that it has been described as the Prado of Paper. It has over three million volumes, among them every work published in Spain since 1716, Greek papyri, Arab, Hebrew and Greek manuscripts, Nebrija's first Spanish grammar, bibles, and drawings by Goya, Velázquez, Rembrandt and many others. Given the precious and fragile nature of the texts, access was limited to scholars, but in 1996 the administration opened this museum to allow the public a glimpse of the library's riches. The displays are conceived as interactive, steering visitors through bibliographical history via multimedia applications including laser shows, video and holographs.

Museo Municipal

C/Fuencarral 78, Chueca (91 588 86 72/smuseosm@munimadrid.es). Metro Tribunal/bus 3, 37, 40, 149. **Open** *Sept-July* 9.30am-8pm Tue-Fri; 10am-2pm Sat, Sun. *Aug* 9.30am-2.30pm Tue-Fri, 10am-2pm Sat, Sun. **Admission** 300ptas; 150ptas under-18s, over-65s; free Wed & Sun. **Credit** (shop only) MC, V. **Map** p306 G4.

A highlight of Madrid's municipal museum is its façade and exuberantly ornate entrance by Pedro de Ribera, one of the finest examples of baroque architecture in Madrid. The building was first commissioned as a hospice, the Hospicio de San Fernando, and completed in 1722. The museum collection was inaugurated in 1929; in 2000 it handed over a sizeable chunk of its stocks covering pre-historic settlement in the area and Roman, Moorish and medieval Madrid to the new Museo de San Isidro (*see right*).

Chronologically, the collection now begins with *Madrid de los Austrias* on the ground floor and continues through to the 19th century, with many unusual maps, manuscripts, paintings and artefacts, among them the oldest comprehensive map of Madrid, by Pedro Teixeira (1656). Fascinating, also, is an 1833 model of the city that occupies an entire room. There are also some noteworthy paintings, by Goya, Sorolla and Eugenio Lucas, and in the patio there is a pretty baroque fountain, the *Fuente de la Fama* ('Fountain of Fame'), also by Ribera. Its temporary shows often make an interesting complement to a visit, and there is a great book and souvenir shop (*see p162*). This is another museum for which a modernisation plan is foreseen, significant changes in 2001-2 include the rearrangement of the collection and the provision of wheelchair access.

Museo Naval

Paseo del Prado 5, Retiro (91 379 52 99). Metro Banco de España/bus all routes to Cibeles. **Open** 10.30am-1.30pm Tue-Sun. **Admission** free. **Map** p310 H7.

Judging from the baritone hum of voices in the high-ceilinged rooms of this museum, most of its visitors are male. Amid its collection of navigational instruments, muskets, guns and naval war paintings are spoils from the expeditions of Columbus and other early mariners. Glass displays enclose primitive weapons, some of which, like the swords lined with sharks' teeth from the Gilbert Islands, promise greater damage than their Western counterparts. The most impressive room is dominated by a huge mural-map that traces the routes taken by Spain's intrepid explorers: in front of it are two equally impressive 17th-century giant globes. The room also holds the museum's most valuable possession, the first known map of the Americas by a European. Dating from 1500, the parchment paper drawing by royal cartographer Juan de la Cosa is believed to have been made for Ferdinand and Isabella. Worth a look also is the room occupied by items salvaged in 1991-3 from the 'Nao San Diego', which went down in the China Seas in 1600.

Museo de San Isidro

Plaza de San Andrés 2, Austrias (91 366 74 15). Metro La Latina/bus 17, 18, 31, 60. **Open** 9.30am-8pm Mon-Fri; 10am-2pm Sat, Sun, public holidays. **Admission** free. **Map** p308 C8.

Madrid's newest museum, dedicated to the city's Patron Saint, the well-digger and labourer San Isidro. It occupies an early 16th-century mansion first built for the Lujanes family, and owned by the Counts of Paredes for generations. It was knocked down only in the 1970s, and has been entirely rebuilt to house the museum. Apparently, it sits on the spot where the good Isidro supposedly lived and performed one of his most famous miracles: when his son, Illán, fell into a well, Isidro made the water rise and thus was able to rescue the unfortunate lad. The well – or *a* well, anyway – is preserved inside the house, as is the chapel built in 1663 on the spot

Sightseeing

where Isidro supposedly died. According to legend, he was originally buried here too. This is, then, a museum that deals in legends as much as any solid artefacts, but it's a project that Madrid's PP city council has been very devoted to.

Since the museum is still in its infancy, the current material on show is a little limited. The finds from local archaeological digs, formerly in the Museo Municipal (*see left*) and housed in the basement, are of first interest. They cover settlement in the Madrid region from lower Palaeolithic times, through the Roman Villas along the Manzanares river, the Muslim era, when Madrid proper was founded (something that Madrileños still cannot get their heads around), and up to the 16th century. When the Museum opened in May 2000 it also hosted two temporary shows, one of pieces loaned from the Museo Municipal on the life and works of San Isidro and another on *Madrid antes de ser Corte* ('Madrid, before becoming a Capital'). This is likely to be the embryo of a future permanent display.

The natural world

Museo de Ciencias Naturales

C/José Gutiérrez Abascal 2, Salamanca (91 411 13 28/www.mncn.csic.es). Metro Gregorio Marañón/bus all routes to Paseo de la Castellana. **Open** 10am-6pm Tue-Fri; 10am-8pm Sat; 10am-2.30pm Sun, public holidays. **Admission** 400ptas; 300ptas 4-14s, over-65s. *Special exhibitions* 500ptas; 300ptas 4-14s, over-65s; 250ptas groups. **No credit cards.**

Don't confuse the street name with that of a larger street called José Abascal, across the Castellana from this museum. The Museum of Natural Sciences is made up of two buildings, behind a sloping garden. The building to the north was inaugurated in 1994, and has one of the more dynamic and interactive displays in Madrid. The history of the earth and of all living creatures is illustrated via audio-visual presentations and hands-on exhibits, in imaginative, often child and family-oriented displays, which the museum hopes to make even funkier in the future. The second building contains a simpler, more old-fashioned presentation of fossils, dinosaurs and geological exhibits. The two-level exhibition area is dominated by the replica of a Diplodocus, surrounded by real skeletons of a Glyptodon (giant armadillo) and other extinct animals. The most distinguished skeleton here, though, is that of the *Megatherium americanum*, a bear-like creature from the pleistocene period unearthed in Luján, Argentina, in 1788. Small-scale temporary shows are held annually, and every 18 months or so they let their hair down with a huge year-long one; throughout 2001 there will be 'Living with Volcanoes'.

Museo de la Ciencia y Tecnología

Paseo de las Delicias 61, Delicias (91 530 31 21). Metro Delicias/bus all routes to Paseo de las Delicias. **Open** 10am-2pm, 4-6pm Tue-Sat; 10am-2.30pm Sun, public holidays. **Admission** free.

This little museum, tacked on to the side of the railway museum (*see p107*), is worth a look at if you are visiting the latter. Its small collection of scientific instruments includes navigation equipment, and some interactive experimental devices such as Magdeburg's hemispheres, Gravesande's ring and an example of dynamic paradox. There are also old radios, televisions, phonographs, cameras and a lovely old linotype machine. The museum's curators, however, ought to think a lot more about how to make the museum more interesting for children, given the competition these days.

Museo Geominero

C/Rios Rosas 23, Cuatro Caminos (91 349 57 59/www.itge.mma.es). Metro Rios Rosas/bus 3, 12, 37, 45, 149. **Open** 9am-2pm Mon-Sat. **Admission** free.

The most striking thing about this geological and mining museum is the splendid stained-glass roof overhead – the best vantage point to see it is from beside the 450kg (992lb) block of rose-coloured quartz that stands in the centre of the vast hall. Surrounding it above are three narrow exhibition floors. The collection was begun in 1865, and is suitably old-fashioned.

Stamps & coins

Museo Casa de la Moneda

C/Doctor Esquerdo 36, Salamanca (91 566 65 44/ www.fnmt.es/museo). Metro O'Donnell/bus all routes to O'Donnell. **Open** 10am-2.30pm, 5-7.30pm Tue-Fri; 10am-2pm Sat, Sun. **Admission** free.

Unless you're a coin collector, this museum will probably be of little interest, and the fact that some of its many rooms are poorly lit, if not in virtual darkness, doesn't help. However, the size and scope of this collection, begun in the 18th century, place it among the most important in the world. The history of coins is represented in chronological order, and complemented by displays of seals, bank notes, engravings, rare books and medals – the holdings of 16th- to 18th-century sketches and drawing from Spain, Italy and Flanders amount by themselves to some 10,000 items. Temporary exhibitions are frequent, usually related to numismatic themes.

Museo Postal y de Telecomunicaciones

Palacio de Comunicaciones, C/Montalbán, Retiro (91 396 25 89/www.correos.es). Metro Banco de España/bus all routes to Plaza de Cibeles. **Open** 9am-2pm, 5-7pm Mon-Fri, 9am-2pm Sat. **Admission** free. **Map** p310 H7.

And one for stamp collectors. Although small, this museum contains a huge wealth of stamps from all over the world. There are also exhibits on the history of the mail and telecommunications, including a mock-up of the Hispasat satellite, antique switchboards, morse code machines, telephones, postmen's uniforms, post horns, bicycles, seals, scales and 19th-century lion's-head mailbox slots.

Transport

Museo del Aire

Carretera de Extremadura N-V, km 10.5 (91 509 16 90). Bus from Príncipe Pío to Alcorcón/by car Carretera de Extremadura/train Cercanías line C-5 to Cuatro Vientos, then bus 139. **Open** 10am-2pm Tue-Sun. **Admission** 100ptas; free students, over-65s, & for all Wed. **No credit cards.**

Spain's air museum, on one side of the military air-base at Cuatro Vientos, on the south-west road out of Madrid, is a suitably gung-ho collection of historic aircraft, models, uniforms, photos and other relics from the Spanish and some foreign air forces. Some civil aircraft and artefacts are included, including a 1930s Autogiro, an early form of helicopter invented by the Spaniard La Cierva. Star attractions, though, are the De Havilland Dragon Rapide that was hired by Spanish aristocrats in England to fly Franco secretly from the Canaries to Spanish Morocco just before the Civil War in 1936, and a recently-added modern flight simulator.

Museo Ferroviario de Madrid (Antigua Estación de Delicias)

Paseo de las Delicias 61, Delicias (91 506 83 33/www.ffe.es/delicias). Metro Delicias/bus all routes to Paseo de las Delicias. **Open** 10am-3pm, Tue-Sun. Closed Aug. **Admission** 500ptas; 250ptas students, 4-12s, over-65s; free Sat. **No credit cards.**

Concealed behind the national railway offices is the elegant old station of Delicias, with ironwork by no less than Gustave Eiffel. Now disused, it houses an evocative collection of old engines, railway models and antique railway equipment and memorabilia. A recent addition is a room entirely of clocks, with, in prime position, the one that marked time when Spain's first-ever train chugged from Barcelona to Mataró. You can climb onto trains, have a drink in an old restaurant car or watch historic film footage of Spanish railways. It's a good museum for kids, with occasional children's theatre performances.

Exhibition spaces

Madrid's many exhibition spaces offer a very varied diet of temporary shows, large and small, as counterpoint to the museum exhibits.

Casa de América

Palacio de Linares, Paseo de Recoletos 2, Salamanca (91 595 48 00/tour reservations 91 595 48 09/www.casamerica.es). Metro Banco de España/bus all routes to Plaza de Cibeles. **Open** *exhibitions* 11am-7pm Tue-Sun; *palace tours* by appointment Sat, Sun. **Admission** *exhibitions* free; *palace tours* 300ptas; 150ptas under-14s, over-65s. **Map** p310 H6.

The Casa de América was opened in 1992, Columbus' year, in the 1872 mansion the Palacio de Linares to showcase the arts of Latin America, and to promote cultural contacts between these countries and Spain. As well as exhibitions of artists from all the Latin American countries – established names

and young unknowns – it offers film seasons, music, theatre, talks and other events. There are also print and video libraries, a good bookshop, and a fine Paradis café-restaurant in the beautiful garden (*see p123*). New Latin American art has a vitality often lacking elsewhere, and is not to be missed.

Centro Cultural Casa de Vacas

Parque del Retiro (91 409 58 19). Metro Retiro/bus all routes to Puerta de Alcalá. **Open** 11am-3pm, 5-9.30pm daily. **Admission** free. **Map** p311 I7.

The Casa de Vacas, next to the boating lake in the Retiro, resembles nothing so much as a kind of suburban Spanish dream house. Run by the city, it houses an unpredictable variety of shows, ranging from children's books to wildlife photography and, recently, a retrospective of the designs of wacky fashion queen Agatha Ruíz de la Prada. With such a range, it's always worth looking in when you're in the park.

Centro Cultural Conde Duque

C/Conde Duque 11, Malasaña & Conde Duque (91 588 58 34). Metro Noviciado or Ventura Rodríguez/bus 1, 2, 44, 133, C. **Open** 10am-2pm, 5.30-9pm Tue-Sat; 10.30am-2.30pm Sun. **Admission** free. **Map** p305 D3.

The Cuartel Conde Duque, a magnificent 18th-century edifice built as a barracks for Philip V's Guard by Pedro de Ribera, now functions as a multi-purpose exhibition space, concert venue and base for a wide variety of other services. There are three big granite-walled galleries, and three huge patios that used to be showing sculpture. It hosts about 12 large exhibitions a year, with both single artist and group shows, and historical shows also feature frequently. The main patio also hosts many festival events (*see p187*).

Centro Cultural de la Villa

Jardines del Descubrimiento, Plaza de Colón, Salamanca (91 575 60 80). Metro Colón/bus all routes to Plaza de Colón. **Open** 10am-9pm Tue-Sat; 10am-2pm Sun. **Admission** free. **Map** p306 I4.

Behind the deafening but refreshing water cascade in Plaza Colón, below the Columbus monument, is the city council's only purpose-built cultural centre (rather than a restyled older building). It offers theatre, zarzuelas in summer, concerts, a café and a spacious gallery, which has welcomed group and individual shows by many important Hispanic artists. *See also chapter* **Theatre & Dance.**

Círculo de Bellas Artes

C/Marqués de Casa Riera 2 (91 360 54 00/902 42 24 42). Metro Banco de España/all routes to Plaza de Cibeles. **Open** *exhibitions* 5-9pm Tue-Sat; 11am-2pm Sat, Sun. **Admission** 100ptas. **No credit cards. Map** p310 G7.

This great multifunctional cultural and social centre, housed in its own fine and very large building since 1926, has spruced itself up at the end of the 1990s, gone after outside funding, and become far more dynamic. It plays a major part in every area of the arts in Madrid, more so than many heavily subsidised institutions, and, apart from a theatre

Sightseeing

and concert hall and a wonderful café, has four impressive exhibition spaces that show work in all media. An annual new-media event to look out for is the *Salón Digital*, organised by the New York School of Visual Arts every January. *See also pp73, 118, 145 and 216.*

Fundación Arte y Tecnología

C/Fuencarral 1, Sol & Gran Vía (91 531 29 70/www.telefonica.es). Metro Gran Vía/bus all routes to Gran Vía. **Open** 11am-2pm, 5-8pm Tue-Fri; 10am-2pm Sat, Sun. **Admission** free. **Map** p309 E6.

The mega-rich, privatised national phone company Telefónica uses the big main space here to show selections from its permanent collection of Spanish art, including work by Eduardo Chillida, Luis Fernández, Miró, Picasso and Tàpies. It has a permanent show – criticised by some as incomplete – based around post-Civil War Spanish artists of the so-called Madrid and Paris Schools, who went into internal or external exile. A second temporary space acts as a meeting point for art and technology, with shows of multi-media- and technology-based installations – sometimes weird, but never boring.

Fundación La Caixa

C/Serrano 60, Salamanca (91 426 02 02). Metro Serrano/bus 1, 9, 19, 51, 74. **Open** 11am-8pm Mon, Wed-Sat; 11am-2.30pm Sun. **Admission** free. **Map** p307 I3.

The Catalan savings bank la Caixa is the largest and richest in Spain, and its cultural foundation's branch in Madrid is famous for its high-quality exhibitions covering many fields. Featured recently have been Russian Symbolists, Indigenous Art in Alaska, Latin-American art in the Constantini Collection and photographer Harry Callahan; upcoming shows include one on Tibetan Monasteries, and an exhibition by Turner Prize nominee Gillian Wearing.

Fundación Carlos de Amberes

C/Claudio Coello 99, Salamanca (91 435 22 01/www.fcamberes.org). Metro Núñez de Balboa/bus 9, 19, 51, 61. **Open** 10am-8pm Tue-Fri; 11am-2pm, 5.30-8.30pm Sat, 11am-2.30pm Sun, public holidays. **Admission** free. **Map** p307 J2.

The Carlos de Amberes (Charles of Antwerp) charitable foundation, which formerly administered a church and a hospital, was founded centuries ago when Spain still ruled over present-day Belgium, and it has always maintained its links with the area. In recent years it has presented excellent exhibitions, very often but not always connected with the Low Countries: Ansel Adams, Magritte, Spanish and Flemish cartography, Rembrandt engravings and Tintin have been some of the themes covered.

Fundación Juan March

C/Castelló 77, Salamanca (91 435 42 40/www.march.es). Metro Núñez de Balboa/bus 1, 29, 52, 74. **Open** 10am-2pm, 5.30-9pm Mon-Sat; 10am-2pm Sun. **Admission** free. **Map** p307 K2.

Wild design by Agatha Ruíz de la Prada, at the **Centro Cultural Casa de Vacas**. *See p107.*

Set up in 1955 by Juan March, one of Spain's richest men, this is one of the most important private art foundations in Europe. It organises a great many art exhibitions each year, sometimes in collaboration with other museums, galleries and collectors, which are regularly among the most interesting in Madrid. They are presented in the Fundación's own space and in other centres throughout Spain and abroad. In Madrid there are usually three major shows each year, often retrospectives of first-rank artists such as Kandinsky, Picasso or, recently, Chagall, reconsiderations of lesser-known figures such as Amadeo de Souza-Cardoso or Lovis Corinth, or group shows on particular movements or schools. The foundation's own collection contains over 1,300 works of art by some of the best contemporary Spanish artists, some of which are permanently exhibited in the Madrid building. The March is also a major patron of music (*see p217*).

Fundación Mapfre Vida

Avda General Perón 40, Tetuán (91 581 1596/www.maprfrevida.com). Metro Santiago Bernabeu/bus 40, 27, 14, 5, 147, 150 y 120. **Open** 10am-9pm Mon-Sat; noon-8pm Sun. **Admission** free.

This private foundation sponsored by the insurance giants Mapfre Vida regularly holds exhibitions of 20th century Spanish (especially Catalan) artists who have been overlooked or undervalued. In recent times Pablo Gargallo, Julio Romero de Torres, José Gutiérrez Solana, Eugenio Granell and Isidre Nonell have all featured, as well as French Symbolism and early 20th-century Spanish photography.

Fundación Santander Central Hispano

C/Marqués de Villamagna 3, Salamanca (91 575 14 30). Metro Serrano/bus 5, 27, 45, 150. **Open** 11am-2pm, 5-9pm, Tue-Sat; 11am-2.30pm Sun. **Admission** free. **Map** p306 I3.

The art foundation of the giant Banco Santander Central Hispano has a collection of more than 800 works by Spanish artists, among them Broto, García Sevilla and Chillida. It also houses temporary shows of Spanish art and recently showed Fernando Botero's private collection, and an interesting collective exhibition on Catalan Modernism.

Institut Français

C/Marqués de la Ensenada 12, Chueca (91 319 49 63). Metro Colón/bus all routes to Plaza de Colón. **Open** 10am-1pm, 4-8pm Mon-Fri; 10am-1pm Sat. **Admission** free. **Map** p306 H4.

The French Institute in Madrid presents a varied programme of exhibitions of painting, photography and sculpture by artists from both sides of the Pyrenees, as well as film showings and frequent performances of dance, theatre and music.

Instituto de México en España

Carrera de San Jerónimo 46, Huertas & Santa Ana (91 369 29 44/www.embamex.es). Metro Banco de España or Sevilla/bus 9, 14, 27, 34, 37, 45. **Open** 10am-3pm, 5-7pm Mon-Fri. **Admission** free. **Map** p309 F7.

The cultural centre of the Mexican Embassy hosts several exhibitions each year of work by artists, craftspeople and photographers from or connected with Mexico. Recent interesting exhibitions have featured graphic artist Jan Hendrix, photographer Laura Cohen and painter Gabriela Rosado.

Palacio de Cristal

Parque del Retiro (91 574 66 14). Metro Retiro/bus all routes to Puerta de Alcalá. **Open** *Oct-May*10am-6pm Mon, Wed-Sat, 10am-4pm Sun. *June-Sept* 11am-8pm Mon, Wed-Sat, 11am-6pm Sun. Closed Tue. **Admission** free. **Map** p311 J8.

This beautiful, luminescent 1880s glass and wrought-iron structure in the Retiro has recently been regained as a lovely, luminous space for viewing art, generally large installations. The re-opening featured Russian artists Ilya and Emilia Kabakov, and since then the Cuban Alexis Leyva, 'Kcho' and Iranian Siah Armajani have shown here.

Palacio de Velázquez

Parque del Retiro (91 573 39 40). Metro Retiro/bus all routes to Puerta de Alcalá. **Open** *Oct-Apr* 10am-6pm Mon, Wed-Sat, 10am-4pm Sun. *May-Sept* 11am-8pm Mon, Wed-Sat, 11am-6pm Sun. Closed Tue. **Admission** free. **Map** p311 J8.

Built by Ricardo Velázquez for a mining exhibition in 1883, this pretty brick and tile building amid the trees of the Retiro is topped by large iron and glass vaults. Serving as an annexe to the Reina Sofía, its galleries are wonderfully airy, and it hosts very good touring shows. Recent exhibitions have included powerful installations by Catalán sculptor Jaume Plensa, thought-provoking pieces by Annette Messager and paintings by Miguel Ángel Campano.

La Residencia de Estudiantes

C/Pinar 21-23, Salamanca (91 563 6411/www.residencia.csic.es). Metro Gregorio Marañón/bus 7, 14, 27, 45, 150. **Open** 11am-3pm, 4-9pm Mon-Fri; 11am-3pm, 5-8pm Sat; 11am-3pm Sun. **Admission** free.

From its foundation in 1910 until 1936 the Residencia de Estudiantes was the most vibrant cultural centre in Madrid, and a powerful innovative force in Spain as a whole. *La Resi* – as the name suggests, a student residence, but with a much broader remit as well – organised visits to Madrid by leading artists and scientists of the day, such as Einstein, Keynes, Marie Curie, Stravinsky and Le Corbusier, and was active in the propagation of avant-garde ideas from the world over. Forever associated with it are its most famous early residents, García Lorca, Buñuel and Dalí, who all first met here. This atmosphere of intellectual freedom came to an abrupt halt in 1936 with the Civil War, and the Residencia languished in inactivity until the late '80s, when it was resurrected as a private foundation under the auspices of the CSIC, Spain's official council for scientific research. It has once again become a centre of excellence, hosting talks by major international literary, scientific and artistic figures, conferences and exhibitions, poetry recitals, films and concerts, and its exhibition halls have recently been extended. Events and exhibits here often have some connection with figures associated with the Residencia, especially the famous three.

Sala de las Alhajas/Caja de Madrid

Plaza de San Martín 1, Sol & Gran Vía (91 379 24 61). Metro Opera or Sol/bus all routes to Puerta de Sol. **Open** 11am-8pm Tue-Sat; 11am-2pm Sun, public holidays. **Admission** free. **Map** p309 D7.

Run by the local savings bank's arts foundation, the *Sala de las Alhajas* ('Jewel Room') is a significant artistic reference point, but will be closed for renovation until autumn 2001.

Sala del Canal de Isabel II

C/Santa Engracia 125, Chamberí (91 445 20 00). Metro Ríos Rosas/bus 3, 12, 37, 45, 149. **Open** 11am-2pm, 5-9pm Tue-Sat; 11am-2pm Sun. **Admission** free.

This water tower, built in elaborate neo-*mudéjar* style in 1907-11 and considered one of the finest pieces of industrial architecture in Madrid (*see p33*) has been imaginatively transformed into a unique exhibition space, specialising in photography. Its shows are often world-class, if at times not-so.

Eat, Drink, Shop

Restaurants

Guts, roasts, fabulous fish and, lately, innovative salads and creative departures with herbs: there's never been a bigger choice for diners in Madrid.

Madrid has traditionally been a repository of the best of Spanish food, with restaurants offering the cuisines of all the country's very different regions (*see page 130* **Tour de Spain**). Madrid's own traditional specialities (*see page 124* **Hearty eating: Madrileño classics**) are humble food, with plenty of beans and lentils, and much use of offal. Worth looking out for – despite the distance from the sea – are fish and shellfish, which are outstandingly good here.

This city has been slow to accept new cooking styles – many Madrileños are a stick-in-the-mud lot, and know what they like. In Madrid's finest restaurants, the dominant style has for some time been a mix of contemporary Spanish (especially Basque) and international (above all French) influences, but elsewhere indigenous cooking has had little to challenge it.

At the end of the 1990s, however, things began to change pretty quickly, with a proliferation of eating-places that try to offer something brighter, lighter and more varied than the traditional fare. Serving a younger generation, some restaurants are opting for a more fun approach to eating; elsewhere, younger Spanish cooks open to international influences are taking an adventurous look at their own traditions, and at the same time the city has welcomed a rapid influx of restaurants offering good non-Spanish – especially Japanese – or even multi-national cuisine. A few new-style places have a faddish tendency to go in for novelty for its own sake, but as a result of all these changes diners in Madrid now have a greater range to choose from than ever before.

Even so, one thing to understand about food in Madrid is that the important thing – as with much socialising here – is to go out. Spain is, after all, a country that gives snacking (as in tapas) near-equal status with full-scale dining, and as places to eat restaurants as such are only part of a varied whole. And, for all the new arrivals, they are still offset against a mass of restaurants serving traditional Spanish cooking in all its forms, and which put the prime emphasis on quality ingredients over innovations in technique. This no-nonsense approach to eating can be refreshing for jaded palates arriving from other cities less self-assured than Madrid when it comes to food.

PRACTICALITIES

A pretty comprehensive range of eating-places at all price levels can be found within a short distance of each other inside the old city. Madrid's first-ever restaurant streets, Calles Cuchilleros and Cava Baja in Los Austrias, still contain the city's most historic *mesones* or inns (*see page 124* **Hearty eating: Madrileño classics**). Lately, Chueca has been an upcoming area for new restaurant openings, as for much else that's fashionable in Madrid. The only big exception to this concentration in the old city comes with Madrid's top-flight restaurants, many of which are in affluent Salamanca, or the business district further up the Castellana, towards Chamartín. Many are geared to a business clientele, and tend to be filled by suited men at lunchtime.

TIMING AND THE *MENU*

Madrileños rarely lunch before two, and often have dinner after 11pm on hot summer nights, although 9-10pm is more usual at other times. You will find it hard to order a full meal in a restaurant before 8.30pm (tapas bars serve food at other times, *see pages 135-43*). Also, despite growing flexibility in opening times, there are still relatively few city restaurants open on Sunday evenings, and some places still close for all or part of August. We've listed annual closing dates where possible, but during August it's a good idea to phone to check.

Madrid eats differently for lunch and dinner. Fewer and fewer Madrileños get home for lunch, but many still expect home-style cooking for their midday meal, not just a sandwich on the hop. Restaurants and bars meet this demand with *menú del día* two- or -three-course set lunches, for around 1,000-2,000ptas, with a choice of dishes for each course. In the evenings set-price menus are less common (although they are becoming more widely available), prices are usually higher, and people tend to pick and choose more.

► For more places to eat, see chapters **Tapas** and **Cafés & Bars**. For restaurants popular with a gay clientele, see page 208, and for places where you can eat or snack late at night, see page 234.

The best *menús*

Upscale

Pride of place has to go to **Le Divellec** (see page 132) – its set menus are not cheap, but spectacular; next in line is **El Olivo** (see page 133) – a chance to initiate yourself in the myriad possibilities of olive oil; and the Pacific-Rim eclecticism of **Asia Society** (see page 119) is very worth checking out.

Mid-range

La Nunciatura offers fine modern Spanish food in the historic heart of Los Austrias (see page 117); for something more conventionally traditional, **Bar Salamanca** (see page 114) and **Casa Marta** (see page 115) both offer quality food in unfussy settings. In Chueca, **La Dame Noire** and **Divina la Cocina** (see page 127) are two gay faves that both offer excellent set-price menus of sophisticated modern cuisine. Perhaps the best modern menú of all, though, is the exceptional value one at **La Finca de Susana** (see page 121).

Bargain-basement

Belmar (see page 123) is a legendary favourite among Lavapiés thrifties, accompanied by **El Nueve** in Chueca (see page 129), and for a vegetarian choice there's **Elquí** (see page 124), but even they are challenged by Finca de Susana.

Good *menús* are exceptional bargains, and if you want to eat cheaply and well, lunch is the time to do it. Even many gourmet restaurants offer set-meal formulas, which make it possible to sample their creations for much less than their à la carte prices might suggest (*see above*).

BOOKING, CHILDREN AND TIPPING

It's advisable to book in pricier, fashionable restaurants, especially at weekends, and increasingly useful to do so for dinner in mid-range places as well, but in all restaurants it's still far more common than in many countries for people just to ask for a table at the door.

The only places that commonly have a dress code are the prestige restaurants in Salamanca and the business district, where a dressy formality reigns. Children are welcome almost anywhere, if, again, rather less so in the smarter business restaurants. Very few restaurants in Spain have no-smoking areas, but you can ask (*¿hay mesas para no fumadores?*). Normally, you just have to put up with it.

Bills include seven per cent *IVA* tax (VAT), which very occasionally is not included in prices on the menu. Service (*servicio*) is sometimes included in the bill (*la cuenta*), but more often tipping is at your discretion. There is no percentage rule nor any absolute obligation to tip, but it is welcomed, and it's reasonable to leave about five to ten per cent, up to and not over 1,000ptas.

THE VEGETABLE QUESTION

A tenet often observed in Spanish – above all Castilian – food is that, if an ingredient is good, it's best appreciated on its own, without any accompanying mush to obscure the flavours. However, a Castilian meal of two pure-meat or fish courses without a green leaf in sight can come as a shock to anyone accustomed to having vegetables provided automatically. In most restaurants, if you want greenery you should order it separately, as a first course or side salad, since main courses will normally come without vegetables (except perhaps *patatas fritas*, chips). For vegetarian restaurants, *see page 133* **Vegetariana**.

WINES

In cheap restaurants house wine – commonly a Valdepeñas, from La Mancha, although this region also produces several quality labels – can be pretty poor, and locals often mix it with lemonade (*gaseosa*), if they don't just prefer beer. Of the quality wines, the well-known Riojas have in recent years been surpassed by those of other areas, notably Navarra, Ribera del Duero and Rueda. Also rapidly improving are Toro reds and Basque Txacoli whites.

AVERAGES

Average prices listed in this chapter are for a three-course meal of a *primer plato* (starter), a main course (*segundo plato*) and dessert (*postre*), without wine, beer or water. The set menus given, however, do often include a drink.

Los Austrias

La Abacería de la Villa

C/de la Villa s/n, near Plaza de la Villa (91 541 78 76). Metro La Latina/bus 3, 148. **Open** 11am-4.30pm, 8-11.30pm Tue-Thur; 11am-4.30pm, 8pm-1am Fri, Sat; 11am-4.30pm Sun; closed Mon. **Average** 3,000ptas. **Credit** AmEx, DC, MC, V. **Map** p308 C8.

You would never stumble upon this restaurant, on a little street winding up from Plaza de la Cruz Verde, but for classic local dishes made with imaginative touches it can't be beaten. A small menu offers deep-fried puffs of *idiazábal* cheese, a deliciously soft rice with foie, or maybe scrambled eggs with boletus mushrooms or *morcilla*. Manolo, in

Eat, Drink, Shop

The menu

For ingredients and dishes normally eaten as tapas, see pages 138-9.

Basics

Primer plato (entrante) first course; **Segundo plato** second or main course; **Postre** dessert; **Plato combinado** quick, one-course meal, with several ingredients served on the same plate; **Aceite y vinagre** oil and vinegar; **Agua** water; **Con gas/sin gas** fizzy/still; **Pan** bread; **Vino** wine (**tinto** red, **blanco** white, **rosado** rosé); **Cerveza** beer; **La Cuenta** the bill; **Servicio incluído** Service included; **Propina** tip.

Cooking styles & techniques

Adobado marinated; **Al ajillo** with olive oil and garlic; **Al chilindrón** (usually chicken or lamb) cooked in a spicy tomato, pepper, ham, onion and garlic sauce; **A la marinera** (fish or shellfish) cooked with garlic, onions and white wine; **A la parilla** charcoal-grilled; **Al pil-pil** (Basque) flash-fried in sizzling oil and garlic; **A la plancha** grilled directly on a hot metal plate; **A la romana** fried in batter; **Al vapor** steamed; **Asado (al horno de leña)** roast (in a wood oven); **Crudo** raw; **En salsa** in a sauce or gravy; **Escabechado, en escabeche** marinated in vinegar with bay leaf and garlic; **Estofado** braised; **Frito** fried; **Guisado** stewed; **Hervido** boiled; **(en) Pepitoria** casserole dish, usually of chicken or game, with egg, wine and almonds; **Relleno** stuffed.

Huevos (Eggs)

Huevos fritos fried eggs (sometimes served with chorizo); **Revuelto** scrambled eggs; **Tortilla asturiana** omelette with tomato, tuna and onion; **Tortilla francesa** plain omelette; **Tortilla de patatas** Spanish potato omelette.

Sopas y potajes (Soups & stews)

Caldo (Gallego) broth of pork and greens; **Fabada** rich Asturian stew of beans, chorizo and *morcilla*; **Gazpacho** cold soup, usually of tomatoes, red pepper and cucumber; **Purrusalda** (Basque) soup of salt cod, leeks and potatoes; **Sopa de ajo** garlic soup; **Sopa castellana** garlic soup with poached egg and chickpeas; **Sopa de fideos** noodle soup.

Pescado y mariscos (Fish & shellfish)

Almejas clams; **Atún, bonito** tuna; **Bacalao** salt cod; **Besugo** sea bream; **Bogavante** lobster; **Caballa** mackerel; **Calamares** squid; **Camarones** small shrimps; **Cangrejo, Buey de mar** crab; **Cangrejo de río** freshwater crayfish; **Dorada** gilthead bream; **Gambas** prawns; **Kokotxas** (Basque) hake cheeks; **Langosta** spiny lobster; **Langostinos** langoustines; **Lubina** sea bass; **Mejillones** mussels; **Mero** grouper; **Merluza** hake; **Ostras** oysters; **Pescadilla** whiting; **Pescaditos** whitebait; **Pulpo** octopus; **Rape** monkfish; **Rodaballo** turbot; **Salmonete** red mullet; **Sardinas** sardines; **Sepia** cuttlefish; **Trucha** trout; **Ventresca de bonito** tuna fillet; **Vieiras** scallops.

Carne, aves, caza y embutidos (Meat, poultry, game & charcuterie)

Bistec steak; **Buey, vacuno** (cuts **solomillo, entrecot**) beef; **Butifarra** Catalan sausage; **Callos** tripe; **Capón** capon; **Cerdo** pork, pig; **Chorizo** spicy sausage, served cooked or cold; **Choto** kid; **Chuletas, chuletones, chuletillas** chops; **Cochinillo** roast suckling pig; **Cocido** traditional stew of Madrid (see page 124 **Hearty eating: Madrileño**

---

charge, takes his job seriously, and is happy to recommend dishes. The larger parent restaurant in Salamanca serves adventurous larger dishes. **Branch:** C/Castelló 83, Salamanca (91 578 26 05)

Bar Salamanca

C/Cava Baja 31 (91 366 31 10). Metro La Latina/bus 18, 31, 35, 50, 65. **Open** 1-4.30pm, 9pm-midnight Wed-Sat; 1-4.30pm Sun; closed Mon, Tue. **Set menus** 1,200ptas, 2,000ptas. **No credit cards.** **Map** p309 D8.

A tiny family-run restaurant surrounded by more expensive *mesones* (*see p124* **Hearty eating**). Great local dishes, good-value set menus and some of the best *croquetas* and stuffed artichokes in town.

Casa Ciriaco

C/Mayor 84 (91 548 06 20). Metro Opera or Sol/bus all routes to Puerta del Sol. **Open** 1.30-4.30pm, 8.30-11.30pm Mon, Tue, Thur-Sun. Closed Wed & Aug. **Average** 2,500ptas. **Credit** MC, V. **Map** p308 C8.

Over 70 years' worth of kitschy memorabilia and paintings donated by former clients hang around the walls of this historic tavern. Founded in 1917, Casa Ciriaco was a meeting place for the intelligentsia in pre-Civil War days. From the staple Castilian fare, try the chicken *pepitoria*, trout *en escabeche*, the *cocido* on Tuesdays and the paella on Sundays. You can also sample fine Valdepeñas wine, with a meal or with tapas eaten in the beautiful old tiled bar.

Eat, Drink, Shop

classics); **Codillo** knuckle (normally pig's); **Codornices** quails; **Conejo** rabbit; **Cordero** lamb; **Costillas** ribs; **Estofado de ternera** veal stew; **Faisán** pheasant; **Gallina** chicken; **Hígado** liver; **Jabalí** wild boar; **Jamón ibérico** cured ham from Iberian pigs; **Jamón serrano** cured ham; **Jamón york** cooked ham; **Lacón** gammon ham; **Lechazo, cordero lechal** milk-fed baby lamb; **Liebre** hare; **Lomo (de cerdo)** loin of pork; **Morcilla** black blood sausage; **Pato** duck; **Pavo** turkey; **Perdiz** partridge; **Pollo** chicken; **Riñones** kidneys; **Salchichas** frying sausages; **Sesos** brains; **Ternera** veal (in Spain it is slaughtered later than most veal, so is a bit more similar to beef).

Arroz y legumbres (Rice & pulses)

Alubias, judías white beans; **Arroz a banda** rice cooked in shellfish stock; **Arroz negro** black rice cooked in squid's ink; **Fideuà** seafood dish similar to a paella, but made with noodles instead of rice; **Fríjoles** red kidney beans; **Garbanzos** chickpeas; **Habas** broad beans; **Judiones** large haricot beans; **Lentejas** lentils; **Paella de mariscos** shellfish paella; **Pochas (caparrones)** new-season kidney beans.

Verduras (Vegetables)

Acelgas Swiss chard; **Alcachofas** artichokes; **Berenjena** aubergine/eggplant; **Calabacines** courgettes/zucchini; **Cebolla** onion; **Champiñones** mushrooms; **Col** cabbage; **Ensalada mixta** basic salad of lettuce, tomato and onion; **Ensalada verde** green salad, without tomato; **Espárragos** asparagus; **Espinacas** spinach; **Grelos** turnip leaves; **Guisantes** peas; **Habas** broad beans; **Judías verdes** green beans; **Lechuga** lettuce; **Menestra** braised mixed

vegetables; **Patatas fritas** chips; **Pepino** cucumber; **Pimientos** sweet peppers; **Pimientos de piquillo** slightly hot red peppers; **Pisto** mixture of cooked vegetables, similar to ratatouille; **Setas** forest mushrooms; **Tomate** tomato; **Zanahoria** carrot.

Fruta (Fruit)

Arándanos bilberries; **Cerezas** cherries; **Ciruelas** plums; **Fresas** strawberries; **Higos** figs; **Macedonia** fruit salad; **Manzana** apple; **Melocotón** peach; **Melón** melon; **Moras** blackcurrants; **Naranja** orange; **Pera** pear; **Piña** pineapple; **Plátano** banana; **Sandía** watermelon; **Uvas** grapes.

Postres (Desserts)

Arroz con leche rice pudding; **Bizcocho** sponge cake; **Brazo de gitano** ice-cream or custard swiss roll; **Cuajada** junket (served with honey); **Flan** crème caramel; **Helado** ice-cream; **Leche frita** custard fried in breadcrumbs; **Membrillo** quince jelly (often served with cheese); **Tarta** cake; **Tarta de Santiago** sponge-like almond cake; **Torrijas** sweet bread fritters.

Quesos (Cheeses)

Burgos, Villalón, Requesón white, cottage-like cheeses, often eaten as dessert; **Cabrales** strong blue Asturian goat's cheese; **Idiazábal** Basque sheep's milk cheese; **Mahón** usually mild, creamy cow's milk cheese from Menorca; **Manchego (tierno, añejo, semi, seco)** hard sheep's-milk cheese (young, mature, semi-soft, dry); **Tetilla** soft cow's milk cheese; **Torta del Casar** tangy sheep's milk cheese from Extremadura.

Casa Gallega

Plaza de San Miguel 8 (91 547 30 55). Metro Opera or Sol/bus all routes to Puerta del Sol. **Open** *1-4pm, 8pm-midnight, Tue-Sun; closed Mon.* **Average** 5,000ptas. **Credit** AmEx, DC, MC, V.
Map p309 D8.
This long-running Galician showcase is now pricey, but considering the quality of the food (especially the shellfish), a meal here is usually worth the expense. As well as the seafood on ice in the windows, there are Galician standards – *caldo, lacón con grelos* (gammon ham with greens) and a big range of Galician wines. Great tapas are on offer, too, in the basement bar.
Branch: C/Bordadores 11 (91 541 90 55).

Casa Marta

C/Santa Clara 10 (91 548 28 25).
Metro Opera/bus 3, 25, 39, 148. **Open** *1.30-4pm, 9pm-midnight Mon-Sat. Closed Sun & Aug.*
Average 3,000ptas.
Set menu 1,200ptas. **Credit** AmEx, DC, MC, V.
Map p308 C7.
After 70 years as a tavern and tapas bar, Casa Marta, in a tiny street off Plaza de Santiago, was converted into a restaurant in the 1990s. Stews and hearty Castilian fare are the mainstay, and marvellously handled. Dishes such as scrambled eggs with serrano ham, chorizo, brains and sheep's stomach are certainly not for the faint-hearted, but there are gentler things on offer, too.

Eat, Drink, Shop

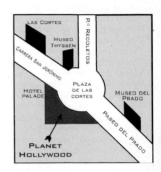

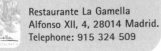

El Estragón

Costanilla de San Andrés 10 (91 365 89 82). Metro La Latina/bus 31, 50, 65. **Open** 1.30-5pm, 8.30pm-midnight, daily. **Average** 2,500ptas. **Set menus** *lunch* 1,200ptas, *dinner* 2,475ptas. **Credit** AmEx, DC, MC, V. **Map** p308 C8.

This pleasant vegetarian restaurant is a welcome addition to the restored Plaza de la Paja nearby. With its good music, friendly service and quality food, it's no wonder it's popular, especially with expats. A great place for meeting people.

Kalas

C/Amnistía 6 (91 559 17 55). Metro Opera/bus 3, 148, N13. **Open** 1.30-5pm, 9.30pm-midnight Mon-Fri; 9.30pm-midnight Sat; closed Sun. **Average** 2,500ptas. **Set lunch** 1,500ptas. **Credit** AmEx, DC, MC, V. **Map** p309 D7.

Part of the wave of small restaurants offering fresh modern food springing up in the city, Kalas has a menu that combines healthy ingredients and generous portions. What it does best are huge tasty brunches, including the popular lunchtime-after-the-night-before combination of salmon, scrambled eggs and Bloody Mary. The evening menu, unusually, offers choices to suit meat-eaters and vegetarians alike, and the staff are friendly and charming.

Maldeamores

C/Don Pedro 6 (91 366 55 00). Metro La Latina/bus 3, 60, 148. **Open** 1.30-4.30pm, 9pm-12.30am daily. Closed mid Aug. **Average** 5,000ptas. **Credit** AmEx, MC, V. **Map** p308 C9.

One of the first (and best) of the new model restaurant/bars *a la moda* in Madrid, Maldeamores serves food with upfront style. With softly modern decor and gorgeous bar staff (turning out killer cocktails), it's a smart operation; the chef draws on his South American origins and ten years' travelling to produce dishes such as black lasagne with smoked salmon and seafood, *huevos Maldeamores* (a fancy take on bacon, egg and chips), or sushi, prawns and seaweed. The interesting wine list offers New World and European labels. Prices, though, can mount up.

Marechiaro

C/Conde de Lemos 3 (91 547 00 42). Metro Opera/bus 3, 148, N13.. **Open** 2-4pm, 9pm-midnight Mon-Fri; 9pm-1am Sat; closed Sun. **Average** 2,500ptas. **Credit** MC, V. **Map** p308 C8.

A speedy duo of Italians are in the running for producing the best pizza in the city, from this laid-back restaurant near the Teatro Real. The pizzas, turned out from a real wood-fired oven, are a heavenly mix of thin tasty crust and fresh ingredients. The menu also offers properly cooked pasta and salads – all against a soundtrack of the best in dreadful Italian 1970s pop. Pizzas can be ordered to take away, too.

Masaniello

C/Cava Baja 28 (91 364 54 86). Metro La Latina/bus 18, 23, 31, 50, 65. **Open** 9pm-1am Tue; 2-4pm, 9pm-1am Wed-Sun; closed Mon. **Average** 3,000ptas. **Credit** DC, MC, V. **Map** p309 D8.

Stylish munchies at **Maldeamores**.

Good generous portions of basic, unadventurous Italian food are served up in this cosy bistro, on a street otherwise full of temples to Madrid's own most sacred dishes. For a big change from Castilian meat, try the *papardelle Masaniello* or *calzone*.

La Nunciatura

C/del Nuncio 19 (91 366 25 91). Metro La Latina/bus 31, 50, 65. **Open** 1-4pm, 9pm-1am, Tue-Sun; closed Mon. **Average** 3,500ptas. **Set menus** *lunch* 1,700ptas, *dinner* 2,800ptas. **Credit** AmEx DC, MC, V. **Map** p309 D8.

With tasteful decor, music and lighting, La Nunciatura is perfect for a romantic dinner amid the old streets of Los Austrias. The cooking is Spanish with international tinges; try crab croquettes, and the Basque speciality *bacalao al pil-pil*; the rice pudding ice-cream is something special, too.

Palacio de Anglona

C/Segovia 13 (91 366 37 53). Metro La Latina/bus 31, 50, 65. **Open** 1.30-4pm, 8.30pm-1am Mon-Thur, Sun; 1.30-4pm, 8.30pm-2am Fri, Sat. **Average** 3,500ptas. **Credit** AmEx, MC, V. **Map** p309 D8.

A large, three-level bar and restaurant with modern decor, young staff and imaginative, light pasta, pizza and other internationally oriented dishes at very accessible prices. It's long been a favourite with students, wandering foreigners and late-night eaters, and is nearly always full till closing time.

La Taberna del Alabardero

C/Felipe V, 6 (91 541 51 92). Metro Opera/bus 3, 25, 39, 148. **Open** 1-4pm, 9pm-midnight daily. **Average** 6,000ptas. **Credit** AmEx, DC, MC, V. **Map** p308 C7.

Close to the Palacio Real and the opera, this Taberna has a claim to fame in that it's owned by a priest, but its Basque food is of high standing as well. You can order a selection of *raciones* at the bar or on the *terraza*, or enjoy a full meal at tables further inside. The five-course gourmet menu for 5,500ptas is a veritable feast.

El Tormo

Travesía de las Vistillas 13 (91 365 53 35). Metro La Latina/bus 3, 60, 148. **Open** 1-4pm, 9-11pm Tue-Sat; 1-4pm Sun. Closed Mon & mid July-mid Sept. **Average** 4,000ptas. **No credit cards.** **Map** p308 C9.

Eat, Drink, Shop

A one-off foodie experience. The Racionero family dish up fare from La Mancha, as made centuries ago: *morteruelo* (hot game pâté), *guiso de cordero* (lamb stew), *ajoarriero* (salt cod and potato purée) and rice with honey. There are just five tables and no choice of menu, so it's best to go in a group. Note too that it only opens if it has prior bookings.

El Viajero
Plaza de la Cebada 11 (91 366 90 64). Metro La Latina/bus 17, 18, 23, 35, 60. **Open** 2-4.30pm, 9pm-12.30am Tue-Sat; 2-4.30pm Sun; closed Mon. **Average** 3,500ptas. **Set lunch** *Tue-Fri only* 1,500ptas. **Credit** AmEx, DC, MC, V. **Map** D9
El Viajero opened up at the meeting-point of Austrias, La Latina and the Rastro in 1994, and soon became one of the area's most fashionable spots. There's splendid meat from Uruguay, hormone-free, and *chorizo criollo*, a barbecued smoked sausage. For vegetarians there are good pizzas and pastas, and after eating you can enjoy spectacular views from its ultra-popular rooftop bar. It gets crowded, so book or arrive early, especially for a table on the roof. *See also p225.*

Sol & Gran Vía

Café del Círculo de Bellas Artes
C/Alcalá 42 (91 360 54 00/902 42 24 42). Metro Metro Banco de España/bus all routes to Cibeles. **Open** 9am-2am Mon-Thur, Sun; 9am-3am Fri, Sat; *lunch served* 1.30-4pm daily; restaurant closed Aug. **Admission** 100ptas. **Set lunch** 1,500ptas. **Credit** AmEx, DC, MC, V. **Map** p310 G7.
The Círculo de Bellas Artes – officially a cultural association (*see p73 and p145*)– has long opened its wonderful café to non-members for a nominal entry fee of 100ptas. More recently, it has also begun to offer an attractive – and very popular – set lunch menu too. It's based in light, modern Spanish food, with interesting salads and pasta dishes; plus, you get to eat in one of Madrid's most gracious spaces.

Caripén
Plaza de la Marina Española 4 (91 541 11 77). Metro Santo Domingo/bus 25, 39, 147, N13. **Open** 9pm-3am Mon-Sat; closed Sun. **Average** 4,500ptas. **Credit** MC, V. **Map** p308 C6.

Multi-purpose night haunt **El Viajero**.

Presided over by fakely grouchy French chef Daniele Bouté and his icily glamorous wife Françoise, this is a favourite late-night haunt of TV and media folk. Showmanship aside, there is an excellent kitchen turning out a small but beautifully prepared menu, highlights of which include perfect mussels, crêpes with caviar, mouthwatering meat and a sublime thin pastry apple tart. Can turn into a party, on the right night with the right people.

Don Paco
C/Caballero de Gracia 36 (91 531 44 80). Metro Gran Vía/bus all routes to Gran Vía. **Open** 2-4.30pm, 9.30-11.30pm, Mon-Sat. Closed Sun & Aug. **Average** 4,000ptas. **Set menu** 1,600ptas. **Credit** AmEx, DC, MC, V. **Map** p309 F7.
One of the best Andalusian restaurants in Madrid, tucked away in a narrow street between Alcalá and Gran Vía. Service is excellent, the atmosphere is very friendly, and the slightly-Sevillano decor has the right balance of tiles and brickwork. Try the prawn omelette (*tortilla de gambas*), oxtail stew (*rabo de buey*) or sweetbreads (*mollejas*) in sherry. At lunchtime there's an excellent-value set menu.

Gula Gula
Gran Vía 1 (91 522 87 64). Metro Banco de España or Sevilla/bus all routes to Gran Vía. **Open** 1-4.30pm, 9.30-11.30pm Mon-Wed, Sun; 1-4.30pm, 9.30pm-midnight Thur-Sat. **Average** 4,000ptas. **Credit** AmEx, DC, MC, V. **Map** p310 G7.
A campily gay restaurant that's also a favourite for a girls' night out. A visit to Gula Gula ('Greedy, Greedy') is more about the drag queen or boy in leather shorts who shows you to your table than the food, but the latter has its plusses: an enormous and very good eat-as-much-as-you-like salad buffet, followed by so-so second courses. The nightly show cleverly targets straight 'tourists' with a just-to-the-edge risqué performance that leaves them laughing without getting uncomfortable (be ready to join in the choreographed show tunes section)
Branch: C/Infante 5 (91 420 29 19).

Kawara
C/Aduana 23 (91 532 89 03). Metro Sol/bus all routes to Puerta del Sol. **Open** 1.30-4pm, 8-11pm, daily. Closed Aug. **Average** 3,500ptas. **Credit** MC, V. **Map** 309 E7.
Just off Calle Montera is this little-known Japanese restaurant, popular with the city's Japanese community. Prices and quality are excellent; service and explanations impeccable (in English). The decor, however, is austerely basic.

Larios Café
C/Silva 4 (91 547 93 94). Metro Santo Domingo/bus all routes to Gran Vía and Callao. **Open** 8pm-1am Mon-Thur, Sun; 8pm-3am Fri, Sat. **Average** 3,000ptas. **Credit** AmEx, MC, V. **Map** p309 D6.
Not a place to go in your combats and trainers, Larios Café is now one of *the* places to see and be seen. Prices at the bar are high to fit the sleek decor, but the mainly Cuban food is reasonably priced and,

The best Top chefs

Asia Society
A cleverly eclectic interloper in the Madrid scene. See page 119.

Cabo Mayor
Exquisite variations on Basque seafood in a delightful setting. See page 134.

El Cenador del Prado
Innovative reworkings of Spanish traditions. See page 120.

Le Divellec
Fine cuisine from a Parisian chef. See page 132.

Nodo
Spanish-Japanese fusion food: clever, and stylish too. See page 133.

La Taberna de Liria
A little gem. See page 132.

Zalacaín
The top of the top-range. See page 133.

with ups and downs, can be pretty good. Dishes to look out for include *mero a la crema marina* (halibut in cream sauce with cockles), avocado salad and refried beans. Also, 1,001 ways with yucca.

Musashi
C/Conchas 4 (91 559 29 39). Metro Callao/bus all routes to Plaza del Callao. **Open** 1.30-4pm, 8.30-11.30pm, Tue Sun; closed Mon. **Average** 2,000ptas. **Set menus** 900ptas, 1,200ptas. **Credit** MC, V. **Map** p309 D7.
A low-priced Japanese restaurant can sound like a contradiction in terms, but the Japanese locales around Madrid take good advantage of the quality of fresh fish in the city. This little place just south of the Gran Vía has no pretensions to elaborate decor but does offer attentive service and good sushi at reasonable prices.

El RTE
C/Veneras 3 (91 559 35 08). Metro Santo Domingo/ bus all routes to Plaza del Callao. **Open** 1-4pm, 9pm-12.30am daily. **Average** 5,000ptas. **Set lunch** 2,000ptas. **Credit** AmEx, DC, MC, V. **Map** p309 D6.
There's a down-to-earth approach at this spacious restaurant, where the emphasis is on barbecued meats and fish. Top-quality ingredients means there's no need for a hiding place behind sauces, and the prime cuts of tuna are superb. At lunchtime the place is popular with office types and even the odd senator. Evenings tend to attract a clientele that knows its meat and fish.

La Vaca Argentina
C/Caños del Peral 2 (91 541 33 18). Metro Opera/bus 3, 25, 39. **Open** 1-4.30pm, 9pm-12.30am daily. **Average** 5,000ptas. **Credit** AmEx, DC, MC, V. **Map** p309 D7.
The largest city-centre branch of a chain that has struck a cord with carnivorous Madrileños by offering prime steaks, cooked Argentinian-style on an open grill, in smart, comfortable surroundings. To go with the meat there are salads, Argentinian wines and own-made, very sweet desserts. Several branches – most notably Paseo del Pintor Rosales and Ribera de Manzanares – also have popular outdoor *terrazas*.
Branches: C/Bailén 20 (91 365 66 54); C/Prim 13 (91 523 52 70); Paseo del Pintor Rosales 52 (91 559 66 05); Ribera de Manzanares 123 (91 559 37 80); C/Gaztambide 50 (91 543 53 83).

Huertas & Santa Ana

Artemisa
C/Ventura de la Vega 4 (91 429 50 92). Metro Sevilla/bus all routes to Puerta del Sol. **Open** 1.30-4pm, 9pm-midnight, daily. **Average** 2,500ptas. **Set menu** 1,350ptas. **Credit** AmEx, DC, MC, V. **Map** p309 F7.
One of the city's longest-established vegetarian restaurants; it's always busy, thanks to a combination of a central location and low prices. However, the cooking and the range of dishes on the menus (organic gazpacho, veg curry) can be routine.
Branch: C/Tres Cruces 4 (91 521 87 21).

Asia Society
C/Lope de Vega 37 (91 429 92 92). Metro Antón Martín/bus 10, 14, 27, 37, 45.. **Open** 1-4pm, 9pm-12.30am Tue-Sat; closed Mon, Sun. **Average** 4,500ptas. **Set lunch** 2,300ptas. **Credit** MC, V. **Map** p310 G8.
New York chef Jamie Downing has brought the energy of his home town and a touch of Asian delicacy to Madrid with this exciting restaurant. The imaginative menu regularly offers a great starter of satay with peanut sauce, while main courses include a fine duck and noodles and lightly fried tofu with shiitake mushrooms. Understated decor and helpful service also work to make this one of the nicest settings in which to eat Pacific-rim-inspired food.

El Caldero
C/Huertas 15 (91 429 50 44). Metro Antón Martín/bus 6, 26, 32. **Open** 1.30-4pm Mon, Sun; 1.30-4pm, 9pm-midnight Tue-Sat. **Average** 3,500ptas. **Credit** AmEx, DC, MC, V. Map F8
One of a handful of restaurants in Madrid serving the food of Murcia. The star turns are *dorada* baked in a salt crust, and *arroz al caldero* (rice cooked in a rich fish and shellfish stock). First courses might be *habas con jamón* (broad beans with ham) or *salazones* (cold salt-dried tuna and roe). This restaurant is very good value and has been recommended by *Time Out* readers.

Eat, Drink, Shop

A place in the shade

Perhaps the best expression of Madrid's Mediterranean mindset, café and restaurant terraces are the setting for open-air eating, music, socialising and general living for long months each summer. For other café and late-night bar *terrazas*, see pages 150-1 and chapter **Nightlife**.

Opportunities to eat a full meal outside are, though, a little limited in the city centre: the **Plaza Mayor** is an obvious option, but the splendour of the setting is often offset by sub-standard food and service, and exploitative prices. One *terraza* better than the rest is **El Soportal**.

Not far away, the **Pasaje Matheu** – an alley between Calles Espoz y Mina and Victoria, just south of Puerta del Sol – is another, cheaper and more rumbustious place for outdoor eating. It's home to a line of *terraza* bar-restaurants including a branch of **Las Bravas** (see page 137), but they all seem to mingle into one giant outdoor eatery. Don't be put off by the *pasaje*'s touristy feel: OK, so it looks like a Benidorm backstreet, and the waiters practise their English on you, loudly and badly. But, as well as all the tourists, you'll find dozens of Spaniards there, and if you're in the mood it's fun.

Much more elegant, however, is the **Paradís-Casa de América**, the branch of the Paradís chain (see page 120) in the Casa de América on Plaza de Cibeles, where light, modern Catalan food is served in the lovely garden of a Salamanca mansion.

Away from the centre and the crowds, **La Plaza de Chamberí** is a good option, in the square of the same name. A few streets to the west is another Chamberí plaza, the circular **Plaza de Olavide**, with bargain *terrazas* that fill up with local families at weekend lunchtimes.

There are more favourite areas on either side of the Parque del Oeste, and towards the river (see pages 69 and 86). A classic place to eat al fresco in Madrid is Paseo del Pintor Rosales, with **Los Porches**, a branch of **La Vaca Argentina** (see page 119) and several more tranquil *terrazas*. On the opposite side of the Parque del Oeste, beside San Antonio de la Florida (see page 69) and the river, is the eternally popular **Casa Mingo**.

The Colonia de Manzanares, reached by crossing the river at San Antonio de la Florida and walking north (to the right), is a charming, low-key district between the river and the Casa de Campo with several restaurants that have tables near the riverbank, including another **Vaca Argentina** and **Leocadio**. After eating, you can relax with a stroll along the Manzanares.

Finally, inside the Casa de Campo itself, by the exhibition area (see page 279), there are several regional restaurants, with garden terraces and cleaner, cooler air than the city centre, such as **A Casiñā** and **Currito**. Much cheaper are the cafés along the Casa's lake, especially popular in the early evening or for Sunday lunch (see page 84).

El Cenador del Prado

C/del Prado 4 (91 429 15 61). Metro Antón Martín/bus 6, 9, 26, 32. **Open** 1.30-4pm, 9pm-midnight Mon-Fri; 9pm-midnight Sat; closed Sun. **Average** 4,500ptas. **Set menu** 3,450ptas. **Credit** AmEx, DC, MC, V. **Map** p309 F8.

The Herranz brothers produce imaginative, modern Spanish regional cuisine at this restaurant just off Plaza de Santa Ana, with specialities such as *patatas con almejas* (potatoes with clams), and a very good *menú de degustación* (gourmet menu). With a lush green conservatory and soothing decor, the Cenador has the feel of an oasis amid the Huertas streets; service is very smooth, and despite its prestige the usual crowd is fashionable rather than formal.

Champagnería Gala

C/Moratín 22 (91 429 25 62). Metro Antón Martín/bus 6, 26, 32. **Open** 2-4.30pm, 9pm-1.30am, daily. **Average** 1,800ptas. **No credit cards. Map** p310 G8.

As well as champagne, this laid-back 'Champagnerie' specialises in Catalan paellas and *fideuàs*, a similar dish made with noodles instead of rice: there are 14 of each to choose from, including vegetarian options. Some can be a tad disappointing, but the setting is so attractive you often don't notice: an airy, semi-glass-covered patio, filled with plants. Run by a group of women, Gala has been much appreciated by *Time Out* readers.

Donzoko

C/Echegaray 3 (91 429 57 20). Metro Sevilla/bus all routes to Puerta del Sol. **Open** 1.30-3.30pm, 8.30-11.30pm, Mon-Sat. **Average** 3,000ptas. **Credit** AmEx, DC, MC, V. **Map** p309 F7.

Conveniently close to Plaza de Santa Ana, this roomy Japanese restaurant has all that you would expect: discreet decor, correct service and beautifully presented sushi and tempura.

A Casiña

*Avda del Angel, Casa de Campo
(91 526 34 25). Metro Lago/bus 31, 33,
36, 39.* **Open** 10am-midnight Mon-Sat;
10am-4pm Sun; *lunch served* 1.30-4pm
daily; *dinner served* 8.30-11.30pm Mon-
Sat. **Average** 5,500ptas. **Credit** AmEx, DC,
MC, V.
A smart Galician bar-restaurant that
specialises in seafood dishes and tapas.
Pricey, but excellent.

Casa Mingo

*Paseo de la Florida 34 (91 547 79 18).
Metro Príncipe Pío/bus 41, 46, 75.* **Open**
11am-midnight daily. **Average** 1,500ptas.
No credit cards. Map p304 A4.
A big, boisterous, bare-wood Asturian cider
house, a favourite with students and others
for decades. The menu doesn't change
much: staples are spit-roasted chicken, nose-
bending *cabrales* cheese and *morcilla*,
accompanied by salads bizarrely served in
a kind of army mess tin covered in cling wrap
(they're made up each day) and dry cider.
A great lunch.

Currito

*Pabellón de Vizcaya, Casa de Campo (91
464 57 04). Metro Lago/bus 31, 33, 36, 39.*
Open 1.30-4pm, 9-11.30pm Mon-Sat; 1.30-
4pm Sun. **Average** 6,500ptas. **Credit** AmEx,
DC, MC, V.
Currito serves Basque cuisine, including fine
grilled fish and meat.

La Plaza de Chamberí

*Plaza de Chamberí 10 (91 446 06 97). Metro
Iglesia/bus 3, 16, 40, 61, 147.* **Open** 1-4pm,
8.45-11.45pm Mon-Sat. **Average** 4,000ptas.
Credit AmEx, DC, MC, V. **Map** p306 G2.
La Plaza offers interesting modern Spanish
food, on a pleasant neighbourhood square.

Leocadio

*C/Bahía 17, Colonia de Manzanares (91 547
10 36/91 547 83 20). Metro Príncipe Pío,
then bus/bus 41, 75.* **Open** 11.30am-
11.30pm Tue-Sun; closed Mon & Aug.
Average 4,000ptas. **Credit** AmEx, MC, V.
A big tent-like *terraza* near the river where you
can sample the food of Navarre, with
excellent freshwater fish and meats.

Los Porches

*Paseo del Pintor Rosales 1, Argüelles
(91 548 13 36). Metro Argüelles/bus 21, 44,
74, C.* **Open** noon-5pm, 8pm-midnight daily.
Average 5,500ptas. **Credit** AmEx, DC, MC, V.
Map p304 B4
An elegant restaurant with an (expensive)
international menu and a leafy terrace with
views of the Casa de Campo.

El Soportal

*Plaza Mayor 33, Austrias (91 366 39 66).
Metro Sol/bus all routes to Puerta del Sol.*
Open 1-4pm, 8pm-midnight, daily. **Average**
5,000ptas. **Credit** AmEx, DC, MC, V.
Map p309 D8.
A good choice on the Plaza Mayor,
specialising in fish and meat grills.

La Finca de Susana

*C/Arlabán 4 (91 369 35 57). Metro Sevilla or Sol/bus
all routes to Puerta del Sol.* **Open** 1-3.45pm, 8.30-
11.45pm, daily. **Average** 2,500ptas. **Set lunch** *Mon-
Fri* 995ptas. **Credit** AmEx, DC, MC, V. **Map** p309 F7.
Susana's place must be one of the best-value restaurants in Madrid. The set lunch is exceptional, and
the main menu is also very reasonable. The only dif-
ficulty is in choosing from the wide-ranging list, with
plenty of vegetarian options and modishly light
dishes; hits include char-grilled vegetables with
two sauces, and mammoth *arroces* (paella-like rice
dishes). The only snag is you can't book, so get there
before 9.30pm or be ready to join the queue.

Lhardy

*Carrera de San Jerónimo 8 (91 521 33 85). Metro Sol/
bus all routes to Puerta del Sol.* **Open** 1-3.30pm, 8.30-
11pm Mon-Sat; 1-3.30pm Sun. Closed Aug. **Average**
6,000ptas. **Credit** AmEx, DC, MC, V. **Map** p309 E7.

This landmark restaurant, opened in 1839, is credited with having introduced French haute cuisine
into the culinary wilds of Madrid. Founder Emile
Lhardy was supposedly enticed here by none other
than *Carmen* author Prosper Mérimée, who told him
there was no other decent restaurant in the city.
Today it's rated as much for its history and belle
époque decor as for the (expensive) food. The menu
is as Frenchified as always, although there's also a
very refined *cocido*, good game and *callos*, and an
excellent, if pricey, wine list. *See also p138.*

Paradís Madrid

*C/Marqués de Cubas 14 (91 429 73 03). Metro
Banco de España/bus all routes to Plaza de Cibeles.*
Open 1.30-4pm, 9pm-midnight Mon-Fri; 9pm-
midnight Sat; closed Sun. **Average** 6,000ptas.
Credit AmEx, DC, MC, V. **Map** p310 G7.
Paradís Madrid offers new-wave, light Catalan food:
fish and seafood rices, *bacallà amb gambes* (salt cod

Eat, Drink, Shop

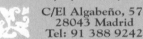

with prawns), with fine oils and infusions. It has a stylish wine bar, and prices – especially for wines – reflect the smart setting. There is also another branch of the Paradís in the very pretty garden of the Casa de América, on Plaza de Cibeles.
Branches: Paradís-Casa de América, Paseo de Recoletos 2 (91 575 45 40).

Do Salmón

C/León 4 (91 429 39 52). Metro Antón Martín/bus 6, 26, 32. **Open** 1-4pm, 9pm-midnight, Tue-Sun; closed Mon. **Average** 3,000ptas. **Credit** AmEx, MC, V. **Map** p309 F8.
Plain, straightforward, very good Galician food in an unpretentious setting. Start with a plate of the tetilla cheese or *entremeses*, and follow with *pulpo a feira* or, for the ravenous, *codillo* (boiled shoulder of ham with potatoes, turnips and chorizo). The house Ribeiro wine, drunk out of white ceramic bowls, is perfectly quaffable, but you should try the Albariño if you're feeling flush.

La Vaca Verónica

C/Moratín 38 (91 429 78 27). Metro Antón Martín/bus 6, 26, 27, 32, 45. **Open** 2-4pm, 9pm-midnight Mon-Fri; 9pm-midnight Sat; closed Sun. **Average** 3,500ptas. **Set menu** 1,900ptas. **Credit** AmEx, DC, MC, V. **Map** p310 G8.
Hidden away at the bottom of Huertas, very near the major museums, 'Veronica the Cow' has a relaxed bistro feel. Interesting fresh pasta dishes, some with seafood, imaginative salads and home-made

El Cenador del Prado. *See p120.*

La Finca de Susana. *See p121.*

desserts, plus friendly service, have kept it popular for years. The full menu is oddly pricey, but some good-value set menus compensate.

La Latina, Rastro, Lavapiés

Albaraka

C/Mesón de Paredes 56 (91 530 05 14). Metro Lavapiés/bus all routes to Embajadores. **Open** 8am-midnight daily. **Average** 1,500ptas. **No credit cards. Map** p309 E10.
A Moroccan café that opens all day to serve mint tea and cakes, and offers meals as well in an upstairs room from midday through to the evening. It's popular with local Maghrebis and with Madrileños looking for authentic Moroccan cooking. A side of the 'new' Lavapiés that goes against the stereotypes.

Asador Frontón I

Plaza Tirso de Molina 7 (entrance at C/Jesús y María 1; 91 369 16 17). Metro Tirso de Molina/bus 6, 26, 32, 35. **Open** 1-4pm, 9pm-midnight Mon-Sat; 1-4pm Sun. **Average** 5,500ptas. **Credit** AmEx, MC, DC, V. **Map** p309 E8.
Two restaurants set up by former pelota star Miguel Ansorena, serving classic Basque grills. Their fame is justified by first-class ingredients and meat and fish grilled to perfection. Don't be put off by the giant-sized chops – they are served cut into strips that you can share. The branch has a broader menu.
Branch: C/Pedro Muguruza 8 (91 345 36 96).

Belmar

C/Lavapiés 6 & C/Cabeza 12 (91 528 55 46). Metro Tirso de Molina/bus 6, 26, 32. **Meals served** 8am-1am daily. Closed Aug. **Average** 1,500ptas. **Set menu** 1,000ptas. **No credit cards. Map** p309 E9.
A great budget bar-restaurant with half a dozen tables near Tirso de Molina, serving a set menu and a selection of dishes from around the regions. Packed at lunchtime; if you can't get a table, or don't want a full meal, it also does good tapas.

Casa Lastra Sidrería

C/Olivar 3 (91 369 08 37). Metro Antón Martín/bus 6, 26, 32. **Open** 8pm-midnight Mon; 1-5pm, 8pm-midnight Tue, Thur-Sat; 1-5pm Sun; closed Wed. **Average** 3,500ptas. **Set lunch** 2,000ptas. **Credit** AmEx, DC, MC, V. **Map** p309 E9.

Eat, Drink, Shop

This hugely popular Asturian restaurant and cider house is known for massive portions. Recommended starters include *fabes con almejas* (white beans with clams) and *chorizo a la sidra* (chorizo in cider); good mains are *entrecot al cabrales* (entrecote with a powerful blue cheese sauce), *merluza a la sidra* (hake in cider) or, in winter, an excellent *fabada*. Wash it all down with *sidra natural* (still cider) or wines from an extensive list. For dessert, try *carbayón* (made from almonds and sweetened egg yolks). Expect queues at weekends.

Elquí

C/Buenavista 18 (91 468 04 62). Metro Antón Martín/bus 6, 26, 32. **Open** 1.45-4pm Tue-Thur, Sun; 1.45-4pm, 9-11.30pm Fri, Sat; closed Mon & Aug. **Average** (dinner Fri, Sat only) 1,500ptas. **Set lunch** 950ptas. **No credit cards. Map** p309 F9.
The first self-service vegetarian restaurant in Madrid has a great value all-you-can-eat lunch buffet for 950ptas. It is only open in the evening on Fridays and Saturdays, when it offers a brief à la carte menu, still at a good price. Dishes include veggie moussaka and (believe it or not) something interesting with tofu. Elquí serves organic wines, but, who invented the rule that vegetarians don't smoke or drink coffee? (instead, there are herb teas).

El Granero del Lavapiés

C/Argumosa 10 (91 467 76 11). Metro Lavapiés/bus 27, 34, C. **Open** 1-4pm Mon-Thur, Sun; 1-4pm,.8.30-11pm Fri, Sat. Closed mid Aug. **Average** 2,000ptas. **Set menu** 1,200ptas. **Credit** MC, V. **Map** p309 F10.
Normally open only at lunchtimes, this is one of the most popular restaurants among local vegetarians. Choices on the menu range from broccoli with carrot mayonnaise to *cardos con almendras* (cardoon – a type of edible thistle considered particularly healthy – with almonds). Food is served in an attractive, sunny dining room.

La Pampa

C/Amparo 61 (91 528 04 49). Metro Lavapiés/bus 27, 34, C. **Open** 1.30-4.30pm, 9pm-12.30am Tue-Sat; 1.30-4.30pm Sun; closed Mon. **Average** 3,000ptas. **Credit** AmEx, DC, MC, V. **Map** p309 E9.
A carnivore's den (like most Argentinian restaurants), La Pampa also offers non-meat dishes and very sweet desserts. *Empanada de choclo* (maize pastry) and *pascualina* (a type of spinach pie) make interesting appetizers, and the hefty mains include *asado de tira* (a cross-the-ribs cut of steak). Wines are generally stout and unsophisticated.

Hearty eating: Madrileño classics

Despite recent moves to broaden tastes, many of Madrid's residents love nothing better than to pile into an old-fashioned restaurant, at least a few times each year, for a lengthy meal of their own traditional hearty, powerful, wintry cuisine.

The city's foremost dish is *cocido*, a kind of grand stew. In a real *cocido completo*, all the ingredients are cooked slowly together in the same pot, but served as separate courses: first broth and noodles, as a soup, then the vegetables (chickpeas, cabbage, leeks, turnips, onions and more), and finally the meat (beef, pig's trotters, chorizo, *morcilla*). This is not a quick meal. Castilian lamb and pork roasts, *besugo a la madrileña* (sea bream in white wine and garlic), garlic soup and lentil stews are other standards. The classic places to find these dishes are the old *mesones* or inns around Cava Baja, located below the Plaza Mayor.

Also ultra-Madrileño are offal dishes – *callos a la madrileña* (tripe in a hot tomato sauce, with chorizo and *morcilla*), *orejas* (pigs' ears), *sesos* (brains) and other things that other cultures shy away from. Here, they are a long-standing and much-loved part of traditional cooking.

La Bola Taberna

C/de la Bola 5, Sol & Gran Vía (91 547 69 30). Metro Opera or Santo Domingo/bus 3, 25, 39, 147. **Open** 1-4pm, 9pm-midnight Mon-Sat; 1-4pm Sun. **Average** 4,000ptas. **No credit cards. Map** p309 D6
Home to the city's most authentic *cocido*, La Bola is still run (though no longer owned) by the family who founded it in the 19th century. The tiled interior is almost unchanged, and the *cocido*, served only at lunchtime is cooked in the traditional manner on a wood fire in big earthenware pots. Very popular.

La Botillería de Maxi

C/Cava Alta 4, Austrias (91 365 12 49). Metro La Latina/bus 17, 18, 23, 35, 60. **Open** 1-4pm, 8.30pm-midnight Tue-Sat; 12.30-6pm Sun; closed Mon & Aug. **Average** 2,500ptas. **Set menus** 1,100-1,400ptas. **No credit cards. Map** p309 D8.
A mecca for offal fans, with a sawdust-sprinkled floor. A good *callos a la madrileña* has been known to convert even fervent offal haters, and Maxi's Is acknowledged as the best there is. If you really can't face it, there's also cheese, good *jamón serrano* and a simple set menu.

Restaurante Económico – Soldemersol

C/Argumosa 9 (no phone). Metro Atocha, Lavapiés/bus all routes to Atocha. **Open** 1-5pm, 8pm-midnight, daily. Closed mid Aug-mid Sept. **Average** 1,000ptas. **No credit cards.** Map F10

Often known as the *Económico*, this tiled eaterie is an institution among those in need of a cheap meal. There's a good choice of solid fare, with vegetarian options. Service is friendly, but scatty – two elderly brothers run the show, while an ancient lady, apparently their mother, can just be made out amid the steam of the kitchen. Arrive early on Sunday lunchtimes when after-Rastro crowds pack the place.

Tuttiplen

C/Salitre 48 (no phone). Metro Lavapiés/bus 6, 26, 32. **Open** 1.30-4pm, 8.30-11.30pm, Mon, Tue, Thur-Sun; closed Wed. **Average** 2,000ptas. **Credit** MC, V. **Map** p309 F9.

If you suffer from chronic impatience don't come here – it's the antithesis of fast food, with a chef who prepares each dish from scratch in the tiny kitchen. However, it's worth waiting for the vast salads, delicious crepes and diet-destroying puddings. Popular with Lavapiés' boho, artsy crowd for its good, cheap food and friendly, relaxed atmosphere.

Chueca

Al-Jaima

C/Barbieri 1 (91 523 11 42). Metro Gran Vía/bus all routes to Gran Vía. **Open** 1.30-4.30pm, 9pm-midnight, daily. **Average** 3,000ptas. **Set menu** *for groups* 2,500ptas. **Credit** AmEx, DC, MC, V. **Map** p309 F6.

The owners of Al-Jaima are Spanish and Egyptian, and it presents North African food together with nominally Spanish dishes adapted from Moroccan cuisine. It's excellent value, with the option (if you book) of eating from low Moroccan tables.

El Bierzo

C/Barbieri 16 (91 531 91 10), Metro Chueca/bus 3, 37, 40, 149. **Open** 1.30-4pm, 8-11.30pm Mon-Sat; closed Sun. **Set menus** 1,500ptas, 2,500ptas. **No credit cards.** **Map** p309 F6.

No-nonsense home-cooking in the heart of Chueca. It's one of the last of the old neighbourhood eateries that still attracts a truly local clientele. Try the mixed veg, lentils with rice, or great beef ribs.

Café Xpress

C/Barquillo 44 (91 310 40 05). Metro Chueca/bus 3, 37, 40, 149. **Open** 9am-2am Mon-Thur, Sun; 10am-3am Fri, Sat. **Average** 4,500ptas. **Set menu** *Mon-Fri* 2,000ptas. **Credit** AmEx, MC, V. **Map** p306 H5.

Service gets there at **Soldemersol**. See p125.

If you want to mingle with Madrid's fashpack then Café Xpress is the place to go. If you want to make like a fashionista, nibble at a plate of the excellent char-grilled vegetables, or cheese *crujientes* (upmarket cheese spring rolls). If not, head for the carpaccio with parmesan or superb *chipirones* (baby squid). A full menu is available throughout the day and into the night. Service can be snooty.

Carmencita

C/Libertad 16 (91 531 66 12). Metro Banco de España or Chueca/bus 3, 37, 40, 149. **Open** 1-4pm, 9pm-midnight Mon-Fri; 9pm-midnight Sat; closed Sun. **Average** 4,000ptas. **Set menu** 1,400ptas. **Credit** AmEx, MC, V. **Map** p306 G5.
Dating back to 1850, Carmencita's labyrinthine, old-world interior has long been a favourite with the famous, and continues to attract discreet gatherings of the well-known. Not that that's the only reason to go there. The food is Basque-based these days, but traditional Madrileño dishes such as *callos*, partridge and squid are still highlights on the menu.

Chez Pomme

C/Pelayo 4 (91 532 16 46). Metro Chueca/bus 3, 37, 40, 149. **Open** 1.30-4pm, 8.30-11.30pm, Mon-Sat. Closed Sun & Aug. **Average** 1,800ptas. **Set menu** 1,100ptas. **Credit** V. **Map** p309 F6.

▶ ## Hearty eating: Madrileño classics (continued)

Botín

C/Cuchilleros 17, Austrias (91 366 42 17/ 91 366 30 26). Metro Sol/bus all routes to Puerta del Sol. **Open** 1-4pm, 8pm-midnight daily. **Average** 5,000ptas. **Set menu** 4,430ptas. **Credit** AmEx, DC, MC, V. **Map** p309 D8
Founded in the 1720s and claimed to be the oldest continually-functioning restaurant in the world, Botín is certainly the most historic of the old taverns. A visit to this institution was an obligatory call for Hemingway and many others who have passed through Madrid, but today it's also the most touristy of the *mesones*. The big speciality is Castilian roasts, rather than *cocido*.

Casa Lucio

C/Cava Baja 35, Austrias (91 365 32 52). Metro La Latina/bus 17, 18, 23, 35, 60. **Open** 1-4pm, 9pm-midnight Mon-Fri, Sun; 9pm-midnight Sat. Closed Aug. **Average** 6,000ptas. **Credit** AmEx, DC, MC, V. **Map** p309 D8.
The most reliable of the historic inns. A mixed political, artistic and business clientele comes here for Castilian roasts, *cocido*,

novelties such as *judías con faisán* (beans with pheasant), a sprinkling of Basque dishes, and... egg and chips. Service is brisk, and booking absolutely essential. To spot celebs, insist on the main restaurant, not the annexe over the road.

Casa Humanes – Freiduría de Gallinejas

C/Embajadores 84, Embajadores (91 517 59 33). Metro Embajadores/bus all routes to Embajadores. **Open** 11am-11pm Mon-Sat; closed Sun & Aug. **Average** 1,000ptas. **No credit cards.**
One of the last full-time havens for lovers of one of the fundamentals of Madrid's traditional cuisine – offal. The city used to have many such bustling, tiled fried-offal cafés, the local answer to the fish and chip shop for the working classes, but today they're hard to find. There's no better place to sample the delights of deep-fried *mollejas* (sweetbreads), *entresijos* (stomach), *gallinejas* (lamb's chitterlings), *criadillas* (bulls' testicles) and other delicacies. For dessert, try the great freshly-baked apples.

El Landó

Plaza de Gabriel Miró 8, Austrias (91 366 76 81). Metro La Latina/bus 31, 50, 65. **Open** 1.30-4pm, 9pm-midnight Mon-Sat; closed

This vegetarian restaurant in Chueca is popular with the local gay clientele. The menus have a home-cooking feel, and are more interestingly varied than those of some more basic and austere vegetarian eating-places. The set menu is excellent value.

La Dame Noire

C/Pérez Galdós 3 (91 531 04 76). Metro Chueca or Tribunal/bus 3, 40, 149. **Open** 9pm-1am Mon-Thur, Sun; 9pm-2.30am Fri, Sat. **Average** 5,000ptas. **Set dinner** 2,300ptas. **Credit** AmEx, DC, MC, V. **Map** p306 G5.

Not a place for shy, retiring types, La Dame Noire is a temple of kitsch, with scarlet decor broken up by fans, gilt, candles, cherubs… But even this doesn't overshadow the food. It operates a set-price formula (without wine); all very Gallic, with Burgundy snails (dripping in garlic butter), steak tartare and tarte tatin among the offerings. If you're lucky, Jean Luc, one of the owners, may wear his trousers that match the embossed wallpaper. Which is nice.

Divina la Cocina

C/Colmenares 13, corner C/San Marcos (91 531 37 65). Metro Banco de España or Chueca/bus all routes to Gran Vía. **Open** 1.30-4pm Mon; 1.30-4pm, 9pm-midnight Tue-Thur; 1.30-4pm, 9pm-12.45am Fri, Sat;

closed Sun. **Set menu** *lunch* 2,200ptas, *dinner* 3,200ptas. **Credit** AmEx, DC, MC, V. **Map** p310 G6.

The Divine Kitchen, run by a group of gay men, is enormously popular. With cool modern decor, it offers excellent value set menus for lunch and dinner, with a big choice of imaginative dishes. It can have its off days, but most of the time the duck and fish dishes are superb, puddings are heavenly, and the setting is extremely comfortable and relaxing.

La Gastroteca de Stéphane y Arturo

Plaza de Chueca 8 (91 532 25 64). Metro Chueca/bus 3, 40, 149. **Open** 2-3.30pm, 9-11pm Mon-Fri; 9-11pm Sat. Closed Sun & Aug. **Average** 6,000ptas. **Credit** AmEx, DC, MC, V. **Map** p306 G5

Stéphane Guérin's cooking is characterful modern French, while her husband's front-of-house style is very Spanish, making this very comfortable place in Chueca interestingly offbeat. Favoured dishes include black olive sorbet, skate cooked a variety of ways, and profiteroles with honey ice-cream. The wine list is one of the most international in town.

Kikuyu

C/Bárbara de Braganza 4 (91 319 66 11). Metro Colón/bus all routes to Plaza de Colón. **Open** 2-4pm,

Sun & Aug. **Average** 6,500ptas. **Credit** AmEx, DC, MC, V. **Map** p308 C8

Something of a well-kept secret, on a plaza next to the gardens of Las Vistillas, the Landó has the same owners as Casa Lucio, but is much more discreet. This is as good as it gets in traditional Madrileño cooking: some diners go for a cholesterol orgy, with egg and chips as a starter, followed by tripe to die for, set off by superb wines. With big, crowded tables of enthusiastic diners, it can get noisy, so it's not a place for a meal à deux. Try and raise a posse instead, to enjoy the restaurant at its best.

Malacatín

C/de la Ruda 5, La Latina (91 365 52 41). Metro La Latina/bus 17, 18, 23, 35, 60. **Open** 1.30-3.30pm Mon-Sat; closed Sun & Aug. **Set lunch** 2,500ptas. **No credit cards**. **Map** p309 D9.

People wax lyrical over the *cocido* at this century-old restaurant near the Rastro. It's made to order (ring the day before) and served at wooden trestle tables, for lunch only, in two sittings, at 2.30pm and 3.30pm. At other times you can have tapas at the bar (also available between 7.30pm and 11pm Monday to Friday). If you decide to go the whole hog, you might well need a siesta afterwards. The price includes wine.

Posada de la Villa

C/Cava Baja 9, Austrias (91 366 18 60). Metro La Latina/bus 17, 18, 23, 35, 60. **Open** 1-4pm, 8pm-midnight Mon-Sat; 1-4pm Sun. Closed Aug. **Average** 6,000ptas. **Credit** DC, MC, V. **Map** p309 D8.

The most picturesque of the old *mesones*, with a domed oven and high-beamed roof. All the traditional Madrileño dishes are served, plus fine wood-roasted lamb and suckling pig, and now-rare traditional puddings such as *bartolillos* (small pastries filled with custard, then fried).

Viuda de Vacas

C/Cava Alta 23, Austrias (91 366 58 47). Metro La Latina/bus 17, 18, 23, 35, 60. **Open** 1.30-4.30pm, 9.30pm-midnight Mon-Wed, Fri, Sat; 1.30-4.30pm Sun; closed Thur & Sept. **Average** 2,500ptas. **Credit** MC, V. **Map** p309 D8.

One of the most authentic of the old-town taverns, with a wood-fired brick oven, tiles, oak beams and a spiral staircase. The excellent-value menu features all the standards, and, while the decor is self-consciously scruffier, the food is pretty much on a level with that of pricier rivals nearby. It's worth noting that Viuda de Vacas gets crowded, and unfortunately the owners don't take reservations.

Eat, Drink, Shop

9pm-midnight Mon-Sat. Closed mid Aug. **Average** 4,500ptas. **Credit** AmEx, DC, MC, V. **Map** p306 H5.
Fashionable with Madrid's art crowd, Kikuyu accordingly headlines on design, with slick decor featuring slate floors and interior patios tastefully decorated with plants. To go with the ambience, the food is also fashionably modern and global, combining Mediterranean touches with others from around the world, and plenty of vegetarian dishes.

El Nueve

C/Santa Teresa 9 (91 319 29 46). Metro Alonso Martínez/bus 3, 21, 37, 40, 149. **Open** 1.45-4pm Mon, Tue, Sat, Sun; 1.45-4pm, 9-11pm Wed-Fri. Closed Aug. **Average** 1,500ptas. **Set lunch** 1,150ptas. **No credit cards. Map** p306 H4.
On the north side of Chueca, the Nueve is a big, functional bar that's packed them in for decades with cheap, plentiful food such as *cocido* and *fabada*.

El Pepinillo de Barquillo

C/Barquillo 42 (91 310 25 46). Metro Chueca/bus 3, 37, 40, 149. **Open** 1pm-1am daily. **Average** 2,500ptas. **No credit cards. Map** p306 H5.
You'll know you're in the right place if there is a monstrous gherkin (*pepinillo*) speared with a giant toothpick hanging from the roof. These quirks aside, the Pepinillo offers an excellent range of imaginatively prepared salads; highlights include the goat's cheese platter and, of course, the many different ways with peppers. It can get cramped, so go early (that's before 10pm) for dinner.

El Puchero

C/Larra 13 (91 445 05 77). Metro Bilbao or Tribunal/bus 3, 37, 40, 149. **Open** 1.45-4pm, 9pm-midnight Mon-Sat; closed Sun & Aug. **Average** 4,000ptas. **Credit** AmEx, MC, V. **Map** p306 G3.
Checked tablecloths, white-aproned waitresses and a spread of traditional dishes with specials such as *perdiz estofada* (braised partridge), mark the style of this easily missed Castilian restaurant, in a basement. It also has good Ribera del Duero house wine.
Branches: C/Padre Damián 37 (91 345 62 98); C/Fuente del Berro 8 (91 401 20 46).

Ribeira Do Miño

C/Santa Brígida 1 (91 521 98 54). Metro Tribunal/bus 3, 40, 149. **Open** 1-4pm, 8pm-midnight Tue-Sun;

Simply divine: **Divina la Cocina.** See p127.

World on a plate

Madrid's tastes have been diversifying at a rapid rate, and consequently more and more international eating-places have opened up to satisfy them.

American
Hard Rock Café (see page 132).

Arab & North African
Albaraka (see page 123); **Al-Jaima** (see page 125).

French
Caripén (see page 118); **La Dame Noire** (see page 127); **La Gastroteca de Stéphane y Arturo** (see page 127); **Le Divellec** (see page 132); **El Olivo** (see page 133).

Global
Maldeamores (see page 117); **Asia Society** (see page 119); **Kikuyu** (see page 127); **Nodo** (see page 133).

Indian
Adrish (see page 131).

Italian
Marechiaro (see page 117); **Masaniello** (see page 117); **Palacio de Anglona** (see page 117).

Japanese
Kawara (see page 118); **Musashi** (see page 119); **Donzoko** (see page 120).

Latin American
El Viajero (see page 118); **Larios Café** (see page 118); **La Vaca Argentina** (see page 119); **La Pampa** (see page 124); **Zara** (see page 130); **Pizzeria Mastropiero** (see page 132).

closed Mon. **Average** 3,500ptas. **No credit cards. Map** p306 G4.
A wonderful value, plain and simple Galician *marisquería*, hung with fishing nets. The thing to go for is a *mariscada* (shellfish platter) for two, for 3,500ptas: with mussels, crab, langoustines, prawns and more, it's truly a meal in itself. Service is bustling, and the tables are regularly packed. There are a few cheap fishless dishes, and good Ribeiro house wine. Recommended by several *Time Out* readers.

Salvador

C/Barbieri 12 (91 521 45 24). Metro Chueca/bus 3, 37, 40, 149. **Open** 1.30-4pm, 9-11.30pm, Mon-Sat. Closed Sun & Aug. **Average** 4,000ptas. **Credit** AmEx, DC, MC, V. **Map** p309 F6.

Eat, Drink, Shop

Tour de Spain

As far as many Spaniards are concerned, there is not really such a thing as 'Spanish' food. Every part of the country has its own distinctive cuisine and its own treasured specialities; and, since the population of Madrid hails from all over Spain, its restaurants can almost form a culinary map of Iberia.

Within this variety, there are some simple dishes that have spread all over the country. Straightforward, often cheap dishes that don't fit into any one style – plain stews, potato *tortillas*, grilled fish – are often referred to as *comida casera* (home cooking). Some restaurants specialise in a type of food, particularly seafood. Basque, Galician and Catalan cooking all feature seafood prominently.

Andalusia

Andalusian standards are gazpacho, *pescadito frito* (flash-fried small fish) and *rabo de toro* (braised bull's tail). Also from this region and neighbouring Extremadura comes the finest *jamón ibérico*, cured ham from the Iberian breed of pig. Properly cured ham, from pigs fed on acorns to give the meat a distinctive earthy-sweet flavour, is now an expensive luxury.

Restaurants: **Don Paco** (see page 118); **La Giralda** (see page 132).

Asturias

The northern region of Asturias, green and cool, is renowned for sturdy mountain food. *Fabada*, a rich stew of beans, onions, chorizo and black pudding (*morcilla*), is the classic dish; other specialities are strong cheeses, rice puddings and pastries, and fish soups and stews. Cider (*sidra*) rather than wine is the local drink, and traditional Asturian cider is coarse and strong.

Restaurants: Casa Lastra Sidrería (see page 123); **Casa Portal** (see page 132); **Casa Mingo** (see page 121 **A place in the shade**).

Basque Country, Navarra, La Rioja

Basque cooking has long been considered the most sophisticated in Spain, and many of Madrid's finest restaurants have Basque chefs. The Basque Country offers a wide-ranging cuisine, with very original fish dishes, and much use of crab (*txangurro* in Basque). From inland Navarra and La Rioja come vegetable dishes such as *menestra de habas* (mixed vegetables in wine and herbs), fine

---

In former times the artistic regulars of Chicote cocktail bar (*see p145*) often wandered over to eat at this Castilian restaurant. The clientele is less exotic these days, but the bullfight photos on the walls remain unchanged. The big speciality here is *rabo de toro* (bull's tail), but the other traditional dishes are also excellent.

Sarrasín

C/Libertad 8 (91 532 73 48). Metro Chueca/ bus 3, 37, 40, 149. **Open** 1-4pm, 9pm-midnight, Mon-Sat; closed Sun & first two weeks Aug. **Set menus** 1,250ptas lunch, 1,800ptas dinner. **Credit** MC, V. **Map** p306 G5.

One of a number of gay-run restaurants in Chueca that offer only set price formulas. The food is well prepared, simple and modern, without too many surprises; service is attentive, if sometimes a little over-speedy, and the restaurant is very popular with a gay and non-gay clientele. *See p208.*

Tienda de Vinos (El Comunista)

C/Augusto Figueroa 35 (91 521 70 12). Metro Chueca/bus 3, 40, 149. **Open** 1-4.30pm, 9pm-midnight Mon-Sat; 9pm-midnight Sun. Closed mid Aug-mid Sept. **Average** 1,500ptas. **No credit cards. Map** p306 H5.

An eternally popular budget bar-restaurant, still commonly known as *El Comunista* because of its role as a leftist meeting point years ago under Franco (*Tienda de Vinos* is all you'll see above the door). It serves traditional staples such as *estofado de ternera* (beef stew) and grilled fish; service is famously deadpan (don't take it personally), and the food can be hit-and-miss, but the great atmosphere, decor that's a real piece of old Madrid and very friendly prices more than make up for it.

Zara

C/de las Infantas 5 (91 532 20 74). Metro Gran Vía/bus all routes to Gran Vía. **Open** 1-5pm, 8-11.30pm Mon-Fri; closed Sat, Sun & Aug. **Average** 3,000ptas. **Set menu** 2,500ptas. **Credit** AmEx, DC, MC, V. **Map** p309 F6.

Zara offers simple Cuban food and ace cocktails, served beneath a pseudo-bamboo roof for that touch of Caribbean colour. Forget the average set menu and try the 'Typically Tropical' dishes, such as *arroz a la cubana* (rice with tomato sauce and fried egg), banana omelette or *frijoles negros* (refried black beans). Very friendly service and amenable prices make Zara a popular place and mean that queues can be long, especially at night.

meats, and freshwater fish options like *trucha a la navarra* (trout with ham).
Restaurants: **La Taberna del Alabardero** (see page 117); **Asador Frontón I** (see page 123); **Carmencita** (see page 126); **Oter Epicure** (see page 133); **Zalacaín** (see page 133); **Cabo Mayor** (see page 134); **Currito** (see page 121 **A place in the shade**); **Leocadio** (see page 121 **A place in the shade**).

Castile

The food of Spain's central *meseta* is stout stuff. Most famous are the roasts of milk-fed lamb and suckling pig cooked in wood-fired ovens, most associated with Segovia (see pages 253-5), and the superb Castilian lentil and bean stews. Also to be found, though, are less well-known specialities from specific areas such as Cuenca, and the mountain plateau of El Bierzo in León.
Restaurants: **Casa Ciriaco** (see page 114); **Casa Marta** (see page 115); **El Tormo** (see page 117); **El Puchero** (see page 129); **Salvador** (see page 129); **La Playa** (see page 134).

Catalan & Mediterranean

Spain's Mediterranean coastline, from Catalonia through Valencia and the Balearic islands to Murcia, embraces sea and mountain. Catalonia is the source of some of the most inventive modern cooking in Spain, with light, varied dishes that mix seafood, meat and vegetables to a degree rarely seen in Castile. The Mediterranean shoreline, above all Valencia, is also the home of the classic paella, but this is only one of hundreds of variations and other rice dishes found along the coast.
Restaurants: **El Caldero** (see page 119); **Champagneria Gala** (see page 120); **Paradís Madrid** (see page 121).

Galicia

There are hundreds of Galician bar-restaurants around the city, many of them straightforward neighbourhood places. Most have tapas bars at the front, and many are seafood *marisquerías*. As well as fish and shellfish, Galician standards are *caldo gallego* (a heavy broth of swiss chard, potatoes, gammon ham and chorizo), *lacón* (gammon ham) and *empanadas*, savoury pies with meat or fish fillings.
Restaurants: **Casa Gallega** (see page 115); **Do Salmón** (see page 123); **Ribeira Do Miño** (see page 129); **A Casiña** (see page 121 **A place in the shade**).

Malasaña & Conde Duque

Adrish

C/San Bernardino 1 (91 542 94 98). Metro Noviciado or Plaza de España/bus all routes to Plaza de España. **Open** 1.30-4pm, 8.30pm-midnight Mon-Thur, Sun; 1-30-4pm, 8.30pm-1am Fri, Sat. **Average** 2,500ptas. **Set menus** 2,350-5,000ptas. **Credit** MC, V. **Map** p305 D4.
Not far from the Plaza de España, this Indian restaurant offers a menu that stretches a bit beyond the obvious clichés. Chicken *chap* (a tandoori dish with almonds) and dried-fruit kabli nan are among the interesting dishes baked in the clay oven.

La Dama Duende

C/de la Palma 63 (91 532 54 41/reservations mobile 619 21 91 80). Metro Noviciado/bus 147. **Open** 9pm-1am Mon-Sat; closed Sun. **Average** 4,500ptas. **Credit** AmEx, DC, MC, V. **Map** p305 E4.
Inventive and traditional cooking, pleasant decor and a relaxed, neighbourhood atmosphere have made this women's-run restaurant very popular. The menu is seasonal: pheasant salad, cod fillets in cream and ox medallions with onion jam are among the delights. Lunch is served only for groups (phone to reserve).

La Granja

C/San Andrés 11 (91 532 87 93). Metro Bilbao or Tribunal/bus 3, 21, 40, 147, 149. **Open** 1.30-4.30pm, 9pm-midnight Mon, Wed-Sun; 1.30-4.30pm Tue. **Average** 1,500ptas. **Set menu** 1,100ptas. **Credit** AmEx, MC, V. **Map** p305 E4.
With ultra-reasonable prices and a varied menu, La Granja is a great budget stop-off for vegetarians in Malasaña. Its paella, stuffed peppers and soya burgers are great, and there are also home-made cakes. Very popular, so arrive early to get the full choice.

La Isla del Tesoro

C/Manuela Malasaña 3 (91 593 14 40). Metro Bilbao or San Bernardo/bus 21, 147. **Open** 1-4pm, 9-11.30pm Mon-Sat; 1-4pm Sun. **Average** 2,500ptas. **Set lunch** 1,300ptas. **Credit** MC, V. **Map** p305 E/F3.
A vegetarian restaurant that breaks the rules. There's no meat, but neither is there the no-drinking, no-smoking code that often comes as part and parcel. The menu features a strange, seemingly random distinction between *entradas*, *primeros* and *segundos*, but the food is interesting, portions are generous, and there are chocolate cakes to die for. The *menú del día* features offerings from a different nation – France, Mexico, Indonesia – each day.

Eat, Drink, Shop

La Musa

C/Manuela Malasaña 18 (91 448 75 58). Metro Bilbao/bus 3, 21, 147, 149. **Open** 9am-5pm, 6pm-midnight daily; *lunch served* 1.30-4.30pm, *dinner served* 8.30pm-midnight daily. **Average** 1,500ptas. **Set lunch** *Mon-Sat* 1,200ptas, *Sun* 1,600ptas. **Credit** AmEx, DC, MC, V. **Map** p305 E3

A light, bright and popular bar-restaurant with friendly young staff, a clean, plain-wood look and art work around the walls. The frequently changing fare consists of excellent Castilian/Spanish dishes with contemporary touches that make them lighter and more varied. The set lunch menu costs a little more than some, but is still good value. A choice of a fish or meat main course may be turkey *albóndigas* (meatballs), or John Dory grilled with lemon. Similarly imaginative tapas are available at the bar. A very enjoyable place.

Pizzería Mastropiero

C/San Vicente Ferrer 34 (no phone). Metro Tribunal, Noviciado/bus 3, 40, 147, 149. **Open** 8pm-1am Mon-Thur, Sun; 8pm-2.30am Fri, Sat. **Average** 1,500ptas. **No credit cards.** Map p305 E4.

A good, if cramped, Argentinian pizzeria in Malasaña. The 20 or so pizzas come small (750ptas) or large (1,500ptas), and there are also pastries, quiches and cheap wine.

El Restaurante Vegetariano

C/Marqués de Santa Ana 34 (91 532 09 27). Metro Noviciado or Tribunal/bus 3, 40, 147, 149. **Open** 1.30-4pm, 9pm-midnight Tue-Sat; 1.30-4pm Sun; closed Mon. **Average** 2,000ptas. **Set lunch** 1,000ptas. **Credit** MC, V. Map p305 E4.

The menu at the imaginatively named 'Vegetarian Restaurant' – one of the longest-established veggie cafés in town – changes every three months, and sometimes features interesting things such as roast Mediterranean vegetables with houmous, and a good *sopa de pepinos* (cucumber soup).

La Taberna de Liria

C/Duque de Liria 9 (91 541 45 19). Metro Ventura Rodríguez/bus 1, 2, 44, 133, C. **Open** 1-3pm Mon-Fri. **Dinner served** 9.15-11pm Mon-Sat. Closed Sun & Aug. **Average** 5,000ptas. **Credit** AmEx, DC, MC, V. **Map** p305 D4.

Sophisticated cooking and a very comfortable atmosphere are the attractions of this smart little restaurant. Chef Miguel López Castanier's menu reflects his Franco-Spanish origins, and might include beef in a rich basil sauce, fine pasta salads or fish dishes such as *dorada* (gilthead bream) in garlic and almonds; on the dessert menu are his fabulously moreish sorbets. His wife Sonia is very helpful.

Salamanca & the Retiro

Casa Portal

C/Doctor Castelo 26 (91 574 20 26). Metro Ibiza/bus 15, 26, 61, 63, C. **Open** 1.30-5pm, 8pm-midnight Mon-Sat; closed Sun & Aug. **Average** 4,000ptas. **Credit** MC, V. **Map** p311 K6.

This traditional Asturian restaurant, with fine cheeses piled in the window, has been serving its clients *fabada* (including variants with partridge and clams), fish, shellfish, soups, tortillas and great cider for 50 years. Choose between the sawdust-strewn bar at the front, or the more formal dining room behind it.

Le Divellec

Hotel Villa Magna, Paseo de la Castellana 22 (91 587 12 34). Metro Rubén Darío/bus all routes to Paseo de la Castellana. **Open** 1-4pm, 8.30pm-midnight Mon-Sat; closed Sun. **Average** 10,000ptas. **Set menus** 5,000-7,500ptas. **Credit** AmEx, DC, MC, V. **Map** p306 I2.

The Villa Magna is one of Madrid's best hotels (*see p39*), and has sought to establish one of the best restaurants in the city. French chef Jacques Le Divellec, whose Paris flagship has two Michelin stars, is an expert in seafood, and his cuisine emphasises simple preparation and subtle sauces; his lobster with truffles, and sea bass baked in salt, are superb. With set menus to moderate (slightly) the high prices, this can be a wonderful place for a treat. From May to October there are tables in a garden.

La Galette

C/Conde de Aranda 11 (91 576 06 41). Metro Retiro/bus all routes to Puerta de Alcalá. **Open** 2-4pm, 9pm-midnight Mon-Sat; 2-4pm Sun. Closed mid Aug. **Average** 2,500-3,000ptas. **Credit** AmEx, DC, MC, V. **Map** p310 I6.

An unusual 'vegetarian' restaurant, in that it offers a few meat and fish dishes for accompanying carnivores, but it's by far the most plush of Madrid's vegetarian eating-places. The all-vegetarian main menu offers an international range of dishes showing oriental and Caribbean influences.
Branch: C/Bárbara de Braganza 10 (91 319 31 48).

La Giralda

C/Claudio Coello 24 (91 576 40 69). Metro Serrano/bus 1, 9, 19, 51, 74. **Open** 1-4pm, 9pm-midnight Mon-Sat; 1-4pm Sun. **Average** 5,000ptas. **Credit** AmEx, DC, MC, V. **Map** p307 J5.

The quaint-ish decor of tiles and wine barrels of this Andaluz taberna is new and a bit brash, but the flavours of the bull's tail, fried fish and *salmorrejo* (thick gazpacho) are strong and good. It also has two smaller branches in Chamberí, with excellent tapas.
Branches: C/Maldonado 4 (91 577 77 62); C/Hartzenbush 12-15 (91 445 17 43).

Hard Rock Café

Paseo de la Castellana 2 (91 436 43 40). Metro Colón/bus all routes to Plaza de Colón. **Open** 12.30pm-2am daily. **Average** 2,500ptas. **Credit** AmEx, DC, MC, V. **Map** p306 I4.

On a prime site by the Plaza Colón, with the usual interior filled with all the rock memorabilia you'd expect, burgers just like they make 'em at your local HRC – and queues just as long. Full of young Spaniards in love with the US of A, and young Americans who like to 'travel' as little as possible.

Vegetariana

In the last few years the number of enjoyable vegetarian restaurants in Madrid has increased rapidly, and many of the new-style, modern 'crossover' restaurants also offer far more options than a traditional Castilian eating-house. Just about any bar-restaurant will serve tortilla and salad, but with other choices it's worth remembering that a lot of vegetable dishes may come sautéd with ham, and lentil and bean stews might be made with a meat stock, so it's advisable to check when you order (ask *¿lleva tocino?*, does it have pig fat in it).

Los Austrias
El Estragón (see page 117).

Huertas & Santa Ana
Artemisa (see page 119).

La Latina, Rastro, Lavapiés
Elquí (see page 124); El Granero de Lavapiés (see page 124).

Chueca
Chez Pomme (see page 126).

Malasaña & Conde Duque
La Granja (see page 131); La Isla del Tesoro (see page 131); El Restaurante Vegetariano (see page 132).

Salamanca & the Retiro
La Galette (see page 132).

Chamberí
EcoCentro (see page 134).

Nilo
C/José Ortega y Gasset 8 (91 431 60 60). Metro Núñez de Balboa/bus 1, 9, 19, 51, 74.. **Open** 1.30-3.30pm, 9.30-11.30pm Mon-Sat; closed Sun. **Average** 3,500ptas. **Credit** AmEx, DC, MC, V. **Map** p307 J3.
In the battle between food and decor the decor just about wins here, but it's a tough contest. Nilo is part of the traditional Salamanca delicatessen chain Mallorca (*see p175*), but you would never know it from the feather topped blinds, candy-coloured chandeliers and cool furniture in its high-design rooms. The food is well prepared Mod Med, but it's the look that makes this special. Service can be patchy.

Nodo
C/Velázquez 150 (91 564 40 44). Metro República Argentina/bus 7, 16, 19, 51, C. **Open** 1.30-4pm, 9pm-midnight Mon-Thur; 1.30-4pm, 9pm-1am Fri-Sun. **Average** 4,500ptas. **Credit** AmEx, DC, MC, V.

It's hard to remember you're in Madrid in this chic haven to minimalism and all things Eastern, right at the northern end of Salamanca. The food style could be called Eastern-fusion, or Mediterranean-Japanese (as in *tataki* with Málaga garlic soup). The menu runs from delicately cooked parcels of steamed fish to sophisticated versions of Spanish classics, as in the creamy *revuelto* with *setas* (scrambled eggs with wild mushrooms). Puddings are spectacular (try the white chocolate bombe), the crowd is young and lively, and prices are lower than you might expect.

El Olivo
C/General Gallegos 1, corner of Juan Ramón Jiménez 37 (91 359 15 35). Metro Cuzco/bus 5, 40, 150. **Open** 1-4pm, 9pm-midnight, Tue-Sat. Closed Mon, Sun & Aug. **Average** 6,500ptas. **Set menus** 3,950-5,950ptas. **Credit** AmEx, DC, MC, V.
It took a Frenchman to show off Spain's olives and their oil to their utmost advantage, but Madrileños have taken to Jean-Pierre Vandelle's olive-green dining room, with its trolley loaded with different oils and bar stocked with over 120 different sherries. Specialities include *salmón y mero* (salmon and grouper marinated in oil), salt cod cooked four different ways and a fine *tarta de manzana* (apple tart).

Oter Epicure
C/Claudio Coello 71 (91 431 67 70). Metro Velázquez or Serrano/bus 9, 19, 51, 61. **Open** 1-4.30pm, 8.30pm-midnight Mon-Sat. Closed Aug. **Average** 7,000ptas. **Credit** AmEx, DC, MC, V. **Map** p307 J3.
A smart, rather self-conscious foodie citadel with a modern Basque/Navarrese-based menu of well-presented dishes such as wild mushroom and duck pâté canneloni, or swirls of sole filled with spinach cream. Most impressive is the wine list, and an area is given over for tasting from its many labels. Service is attentive, if a bit stiff, and prices are high.

Viridiana
C/Juan de Mena 14 (91 523 44 78). Metro Banco de España or Retiro/bus all routes to Puerta de Alcalá. **Open** 1.30-4pm, 9pm-midnight Mon-Sat; closed Sun & Aug, Easter, Christmas. **Average** 11,000ptas. **Credit** AmEx, V. **Map** p310 H7.
A short walk from both the Prado and the Thyssen, hung with stills from Buñuel films, Viridiana offers excellent seasonal food backed up by an exceptional wine cellar. The refined menu features inventive combinations such as *cabracho con relleno de almejas* (scorpion fish stuffed with clams and dressed with olive oil) or *solomillo de buey con trufas negras* (steak with black truffles). Service and atmosphere are pleasantly informal considering the standard of this restaurant.

Zalacaín
C/Alvarez de Baena 4 (91 561 59 35). Metro Gregorio Marañón/bus 12, 16, 40, 147. **Open** 1.15-4pm, 9pm-midnight Mon-Fri; 9pm-midnight Sat; closed Sun & Aug. **Average** 12,000ptas. **Set menu** 13,500ptas. **Credit** AmEx, DC, MC, V.

Budget choices

The number of budget options increases greatly at midday, when many restaurants become much cheaper via the *menú del día* (see page 113 **The best** *menús*).

Los Austrias
Bar Salamanca (see page 114); **Kalas** (see page 117); **El Viajero** (see page 118).

Sol & Gran Vía
Musashi (see page 119).

Huertas & Santa Ana
Artemisa (see page 119); **Champagneria Gala** (see page 120).

La Latina, Rastro, Lavapiés
Albaraka (see page 121); **Belmar** (see page 123); **Elquí** (see page 123); **El Granero de Lavapiés** (see page 124); **Restaurante Económico – Soldemersol** (see page 125); **Tutiplen** (see page 125).

Chueca
El Bierzo (see page 125); **El Nueve** (see page 129); **Sarrasín** (see page 130); **Tienda de Vinos (El Comunista)** (see page 130).

Malasaña & Conde Duque
La Granja (see page 131); **Pizzeria Mastropiero** (see page 132).

Other districts
Casa Humanes – Freiduría de Gallinejas (see page 126 **Hearty eating**); **Casa Mingo** (see page 121).

Under master chef Benjamín Urdaín and proprietor Jesús María Oyarbide Zalacaín has been the première restaurant in Madrid for the last two decades, and the only one with three Michelin stars. The setting is seamlessly luxurious, the seasonal, Basque-based cooking is superb, and the wine list offers an exceptional selection of fine Spanish vintages. Prices can be controlled just a little with the set gourmet menu of five courses plus dessert. The only drawback could be the strict jacket-and-tie dress code.

Chamberí

EcoCentro
C/Esquilache 4 (91 553 55 02). Metro Cuatro Caminos/ bus all routes to Cuatro Caminos. **Open** 1am-midnight daily. **Average** 2,000ptas. **Set menu** 1,450ptas. **Credit** AmEx, DC, MC, V.

The enormous ground-floor restaurant at this mutifaceted vegetarian and organic products centre offers a very wide choice of dishes. To drink there are organic wines, natural beers and a selection of herb teas; the shop above has food, books, music and health and beauty products.

La Playa
C/Magallanes 24 (91 446 84 76). Metro Quevedo/bus 16, 37, 61, 149. **Open** 1-4.30pm, 8.30pm-midnight Mon-Sat; 1-4.30pm Sun. Closed Aug. **Average** 3,500ptas. **No credit cards. Map** p305 E2.

A (very) old-fashioned family restaurant in Chamberí, with high-quality Castilian dishes, especially steaks, which are fast-cooked red-rare at your table. All the ingredients are expertly selected, which means relatively high prices. The elderly white-jacketed waiters come from another era, and are very charming.

Chamartín

Cabo Mayor
C/Juan Ramón Jiménez 37, Chamartín (91 359 89 87). Metro Cuzco/bus 5, 40, 150, 150 with stripe. **Open** 1.30am-4pm, 9pm-midnight Mon-Sat; closed Sun & Aug, & Easter week. **Average** 7,000ptas. **Credit** AmEx, DC, MC, V.

The most consistently impressive of all the new-wave Spanish restaurants in Madrid that appeared in the 1980s. The mainly-seafood menu features modern Basque and northern Spanish dishes, combining fish and vegetables in light but luxurious offerings such as a superb lobster salad. To follow, there are equally wonderful desserts. The slightly nautical interior is pleasantly chic, the atmosphere is more laid-back than in the stuffier top-flight Madrid restaurants, and an extra attraction is a neat pavement patio (evenings only) in summer.

Cabo Mayor: fine food in an unstuffy setting.

Tapas

Tapas have now spread as far as Sydney and San Francisco, but the Spanish capital is still the place to find the original, and the best...

El Almendro 13. *See p136.*

Eat, Drink, Shop

The fact that tapas are one of Spain's great export successes has not escaped notice in their native land. They've become more sophisticated at home too, and more expensive. A crop of new-style, 'gourmet' tapas bars has appeared in Madrid (*see page 142* **Smart tapas**), while on the other hand there are now few bars around that offer much for free in the way of tapas, other than an olive or two or a bit of sausage. An evening's *tapeo* can quite easily cost more than going to a restaurant for a full meal.

The word *tapa* itself means 'lid', and the custom supposedly comes from Andalusia, where a small dish used to be placed over a glass of wine to keep out the flies. Small servings of food were placed on the lid to accompany the drink. Since then it has become a culinary genre all of its own, with some bar-top cabinets resembling elaborate still-lifes.

Since Madrid's population includes so many non-natives, there are bars and tapas here from every corner of Spain. Galician bars highlight octopus, prawns and seafood, traditionally with white Ribeiro wine served in little ceramic bowls. Asturian bars specialise in cider (*sidra*), theatrically poured from above the head to separate out sediment, accompanied by blood sausage, *morcilla*, or *cabrales* goat's cheese. Andalusian bars offer cold dry fino sherry with *mojama* (dry-cured tuna) or sardines. Madrid's own specialities are *patatas bravas*, offal, and snails in a hot sauce. And modern Madrid also has places offering other snacks – especially Arab and Middle-Eastern.

Eating tapas is also a ritual with its own customs attached, and its own verb, *tapear*. If there's a group of you, rounds should be paid for in strict rotation. As with many of life's essentials in Spain, traditionally at least, there should be no hurrying involved. And be ready to do as locals do: many tapas come with spare

▶ For other bars more suited to having coffee, drinking or a night out – but which also may serve tapas – see chapters **Cafés & Bars** and **Nightlife**.

parts – olive stones, prawn shells – which involve using your fingers, and all can be dropped on the floor (except in upmarket places; check what others are doing first).

Los Austrias

The old streets below the Plaza Mayor to the west are now the main growth area for stylish tapas bars in Madrid (*see page 142* **Smart tapas**). The area also has plenty of old-style bars, so this is the first choice for a *tapa*-trail.

El Almendro 13

C/Almendro 13 (91 365 42 52). Metro La Latina/ bus 17, 18, 23, 31, 35. **Open** 1-4pm, 7pm-midnight daily. **No credit cards. Map** p309 D8.
Skilfully restored, but retaining an old Madrid feel, this comfortable hangout is one of the old centre's most popular. White wines, sherries and beer are the drinks to go for, and the must-try *tapa* is *pisto manchego* with fried eggs and bacon.

As de los Vinos –
La Casa de las Torrijas

C/de la Paz 4 (91 532 14 73). Metro Sol/bus all routes to Puerta del Sol. **Open** 9.30am-4pm, 5-11.30pm Mon-Thur; 9.30am-4pm, 6pm-midnight Fri, Sat. Closed Sun & Aug.
No credit cards. Map p309 E8.
Since who-knows-when this historic old *taberna* near was El Anciano Rey de los Vinos, the 'Old Man, King of Wines'. It was famed for its wines, and an unusual speciality, *torrijas* – bread soaked in wine and spices, coated in sugar and deep fried. In 1998 it changed name to the 'Ace of Wines' (which might be overdoing it), but, not to worry, everything else stayed the same. Plenty of alternatives to *torrijas* for those with less of a sweet tooth, such as fried *bacalao* (cod), *callos* or *albóndigas*, at low prices.

Casa Lucás

C/Cava Baja 30 (91 365 08 04). Metro La Latina/ bus 17, 18, 23, 31, 35. **Open** 1-4pm, 8pm-midnight daily. **No credit cards. Map** p309 D8.
Warm decor and open brickwork make Lucás a treat in winter, with its satisfying *caldo* broth, and other delights such as mushroom pasties and mini steaks.

Casa Paco

Plaza de la Puerta Cerrada 11 (91 366 31 66). Metro La Latina/bus 17, 18, 23, 31, 35. **Open** 1.30-4pm, 8.30pm-midnight Mon-Sat. Closed Sun & Aug. **No credit cards. Map** p309 D8.
A classic old-town tavern with top-quality (if expensive) *Manchego* cheese and *jamón serrano*.

Desahogo Taberna

Plaza de San Miguel (91 559 08 97). Metro Sol/ bus all routes to Puerta del Sol. **Open** 1-4pm, 8pm-midnight Tue-Sat; 1-4pm Sun; closed Mon. **No credit cards. Map** p309 D8.
The Plaza de San Miguel is now host to a couple of interesting eateries, and is growing in popularity.

One for old Labour, **Casa Labra**. *See p137*.

Desahogo has Asturian-inspired tapas that match its other imaginative creations well. Part of the cutting edge of the wine and tapas scene.

El Pulpito

Plaza Mayor 10 (91 366 21 88). Metro Sol/bus all routes to Puerta del Sol. **Open** 9.30am-1am daily. **No credit cards. Map** p309 D8.
A pleasant bar that's one of the least touristy on Plaza Mayor, with a big outside *terraza* from Easter to November like the other plaza bars. Despite the name ('The Little Octopus'), *pulpo* isn't always the best thing to have: try the *albóndigas* or *callos*.

La Taberna de Cien Vinos

C/del Nuncio 16 (91 365 47 07). Metro La Latina/bus 17, 18, 23, 31, 50. **Open** 1-3.45pm, 8-11.45pm Tue-Sun; closed Mon. **No credit cards. Map** p309 D8.
The name ('100 wines') might be a bit of an exaggeration, but this lovely, plain stone *taberna* has a range that isn't far off, plus a good choice of *pinchos* and larger dishes.

La Torre del Oro

Plaza Mayor 26 (91 366 50 16). Metro Sol/bus all routes to Puerta del Sol. **Open** 11am-2am daily. **No credit cards. Map** p309 D8.
Don't be put off by the postcards of Seville and bull-fight accoutrements on the walls – this Andalusian bar is no tourist trap. The Andaluz waiters yell at each other and punters with manic glee, whether or not you understand a word, and there's excellent fino sherry, and great prawns and *pescaditos* (white-bait). Another good Plaza Mayor *terraza*.

Sol & Gran Vía

Almimás

C/Montera 32 (91 522 09 00). Metro Gran Vía/bus all routes to Puerta del Sol. **Open** noon-midnight daily. **No credit cards. Map** p309 E7.
A Syrian-run bar with a fine mix of Mediterranean Arab specialities: falafel, doner kebab, baklava and mint tea. Not much seating, but it's excellent value.

Las Bravas

Pasaje Matheu 5, off C/Victoria (91 521 51 41).
Metro Sol/bus all routes to Puerta del Sol.
Open 12.30-4pm, 7.30pm-midnight daily.
No credit cards. Map p309 E7.
There are several branches of this legendary institution around Sol. It claims actually to have invented *patatas bravas*, and while others may now do better versions, here they're still very cheap. There's also fine *pulpo* and *orejas*. Several branches have outside tables.
Branches: throughout the Sol area.

Casa Labra

C/Tetuán 12 (91 531 00 81). Metro Sol/bus all routes to Puerta del Sol. **Open** 9.30am-3.30pm, 6-11pm Mon-Sat; 1-4pm, 8-11pm Sun. **Credit** AmEx, DC, MC, V. **Map** p309 E7.
Founded in 1860, this *taberna*-restaurant was the birthplace of the Spanish Socialist Party in 1879. It is also known for its *soldaditos de pavia* and great *croquetas*, and, as it's so busy at lunchtimes, this is one of few bars where you pay as you order.

Huertas & Santa Ana

Plaza de Santa Ana is one of Madrid's favourite tapas haunts – especially for foreigners – with a ring of bars with tables outside in summer.

Bar Viña P

Plaza de Santa Ana 3 (91 531 81 11). Metro Sol/bus all routes to Puerta del Sol. **Open** 1-4.30pm, 8pm-12.30am daily. **No credit cards. Map** p309 E/F8.

The Asturian cider ritual: **El Garabatú**.

The place for *montados, gambas al ajillo,* asparagus, stuffed mussels, *almejas* and other tapas for around 1,000ptas a *ración*.

Casa Alberto

C/Huertas 18 (91 429 93 56). Metro Antón Martín/bus 6, 26, 32. **Open** *Bar* noon-12.30am Tue-Sat; noon-4pm Sun. Closed Mon & two weeks in Aug.
No credit cards. Map p309 F8.
Founded in 1827, Alberto's still retains its 19th-century red-painted tavern façade, behind which you can choose from a fine range of freshly made tapas – *caracoles, calamares,* prawns – and larger dishes.

Casa de Pontevedra

C/Victoria 2 (91 523 08 01). Metro Sol/bus all routes to Puerta del Sol. **Open** *Bar* 10.30am-midnight daily. *Restaurant* 10.30am-4.30pm, 8pm-midnight daily.
No credit cards. Map p309 E7.
A bar offering Galician specialities, with great *pulpo a feira, empanadas, pimientos rellenos* (stuffed peppers) and Ribeiro and Albariño white wines.

Cervecería La Moderna

Plaza de Santa Ana 12 (91 420 15 82).
Metro Sevilla or Sol/bus 6, 26, 32, 50. **Open** noon-12.30am Mon-Thur, Sun; noon-1.30am Fri, Sat. **Credit** AmEx, DC, MC, V. **Map** p309 E/F8.
La Moderna, as its name suggests, has no pretensions to antiquity. The decor is contemporary, and the tapas are great (if a little pricey), with an imaginative use of herbs, and a big choice of farmhouse cheeses (*quesos artesanales*). House wines are also above average. A popular Santa Ana *terraza*.

La Fábrica

C/Jesús 2 (91 369 06 71). Metro Antón Martín/bus 9, 10, 14, 34, 45. **Open** 11am-1am Mon-Thur, Sun; 11am-2am Fri, Sat. **Credit** AmEx, MC, V. **No credit cards. Map** p310 G8.
This pleasant, roomy *taberna* at the bottom end of Huertas specialises in canapés, many topped with smoked fish or top-notch charcuterie. Wines hail from Rioja, Ribera del Duero and Penedès.

El Garabatú

C/Echegaray 5 (91 429 63 90).
Metro Sevilla or Sol/bus 6, 26, 32, 50. **Open** noon-12.30am Mon-Thur, Sun; noon-1.30am Fri, Sat. **No credit cards. Map** p309 F8.
A basic old Asturian bar-restaurant with earthy tapas such as *chorizo a la sidra* (in cider), *fabada* and nose-bending *cabrales* cheese, and Asturian cider to go with it. Also try the hearty *menú de día* out the back.

El Lacón

C/Manuel Fernández y González 8 (91 429 36 98).
Metro Sevilla or Sol/bus all routes to Puerta del Sol. **Open** noon-4pm, 8pm-midnight Mon-Thur, Sun; noon-4pm, 8pm-1.30am Fri, Sat. Closed Aug.
Credit AmEx, DC, MC, V. **Map** p309 F8.
A big, down-to-earth Galician bar-restaurant with excellent pulpo, mussels and *empanadas*. Larger dishes, and a *menú* for 1,200ptas, are served at big tables inside. It sometimes closes on Mondays.

Eat, Drink, Shop

Tips on tapas

There are three basic sizes of tapa portion: a *pincho* (more or less a mouthful), a *tapa* (a saucerful or so) and a *ración* (a small plateful). Some bars offer *media raciones* (a half-*ración*). If there's something you like the look of that isn't identifiable on the menu or the list behind the bar, just point to it. Bread – *pan* – normally comes automatically, but if not, just ask. Normally, you let a tapas bill mount up and pay when you've finished, not when you order; it's usually about 25 per cent more expensive if you sit at a table rather than eat at the bar. For more food terminology, see pages 114-5.

Basics

Bocadillo sandwich in a roll or part of a French loaf; **Cazuelita** small hot casserole; **Montados** canapé-style mixed tapas, often a slice of bread with a topping; **Pincho/pinchito** small titbit on a toothpick, or mouthful-sized *tapa*; **Pulga/pulguita** small filled roll; **Ración** a portion (small plateful); **Tabla** platter (of cheeses, cold meats); **Tosta** slice of toast with topping; **Una de gambas, chorizo**… one portion of prawns, chorizo…; **Por unidad** per item.

Carne, aves y embutidos (Meat, poultry & charcuterie)

Albóndigas meat balls; **Alitas de pollo** chicken wings; **Callos** tripe; **Cecina** dry-cured beef; **Chistorra** Navarrese sausage with paprika; **Chorizo** spicy sausage, eaten cooked or cold; **Criadillas** bulls' testicles; **Flamenquines** ham and pork rolls in breadcrumbs; **Longaniza, fuet** mild but chewy, often herby, salami-type sausages; **Mollejas** sweetbreads; **Morcilla** a black, blood sausage; **Oreja (de cerdo)** pig's ear; **Pincho moruno** grilled meat brochette; **Riñones al Jerez** kidneys cooked in sherry; **Salchichón** a large, fatty, soft, salami-type sausage; **San Jacobo** fried ham and cheese escalope; **Sobrasada** soft Mallorcan paprika sausage; **Torrezno** grilled pork crackling; **Zarajo** grilled sheep's intestine on a stick.

Pescado y mariscos (Fish & shellfish)

Ahumados smoked fish; **Almejas** clams; **Anchoas** salted conserved anchovies; **Anguilas** eels; **Angulas** elvers; **Berberechos** cockles; **Bienmesabe** marinated fried fish; **Boquerones en vinagre/fritos** pickled fresh anchovies; **Calamares a la romana** squid rings fried in batter; **Calamares en su tinta** squid cooked in their ink; **Carabineiros** large red ocean prawns; **Centollo** spider crab; **Chanquetes** tiny fish, served deep fried; **Chipirones en su tinta** small Atlantic squid in their ink; **Chopito** small cuttlefish; **Cigalas** crayfish; **Croqueta de bacalao** salt cod

Lerranz

C/Echegaray 26 (91 429 12 06).
Metro Sevilla or Sol/bus all routes to Puerta del Sol.
Open 1.30-4pm, 8.30pm-1am daily.
Credit AmEx, MC, V. **Map** p309 F8.
One of the smarter tapas bar in Huertas, sometimes even a tad snooty, but one that offers a very wide range from traditional country bread with various toppings to *pulpo con papas y ali-oli* (octopus with potatoes and garlic mayonnaise) and interesting salads. Try also the set lunch for 1,500ptas.

Lhardy

Carrera de San Jerónimo 8 (91 522 22 07).
Metro Sol/bus all routes to Puerta del Sol.
Open *Bar* 9.30am-3pm, 5-9.30pm Mon-Sat; 9.30am-3pm Sun. **Credit** AmEx, DC, MC, V. **Map** p309 E7.
Madrid's most historic restaurant is also the aristocrat of tapas bars. Serve yourself consommé from a silver samovar, try knock-out croquettes, or order finos and a hot pastry-boat with kidneys (*barquitos de riñones*). Taking tapas at Lhardy is a cheaper way of seeing this institution than eating in the restaurant. *See also chapter* **Restaurants**.

Muddy's

C/Alameda 6 (91 420 34 84). Metro Atocha/bus 9, 10, 14, 27, 34, 45. **Open** 11am-2am Mon-Sat; 11am-3pm Sun. **No credit cards. Map** p310 G9.
Owner Diego used to run a blues bar called Downtown, and has kept the idea with this nicely refurbished, bare-brick bar. Tables at the back, terrific tapas, a good crowd of regulars, and blues and the occasional unplugged gig to entertain the ears.

La Oreja de Oro

C/Victoria 7 (91 531 33 66). Metro Sol/bus all routes to Puerta del Sol. **Open** 10am-midnight daily. Closed Aug. **No credit cards. Map** p309 E7.
'The Golden Ear' specialises in an old Madrileño delicacy: fried pigs' ears, big plates of them. They have other things, but if you've come all this way…

La Platería

C/Moratín 49 (91 429 17 22). Metro Antón Martín/bus all routes to Atocha. **Open** 7.30am-1am Mon-Fri; 9.30am-1am Sat, Sun. **No credit cards. Map** p310 G8.
As well as serving good-quality tapas such as *jamón ibérico*, tuna steaks on toasted bread and

croquette; **Fritura de pescado** flash-fried fish; **Gambas al ajillo** prawns fried with garlic; **Gambas en gabardina** prawns deep-fried in batter; **Huevas** fish roe; **Mojama** dried and salted tuna fish; **Navajas** razorfish; **Nécora** swimming crab; **Percebe** goose neck barnacle; **Pulpo a feira/a la gallega** octopus with paprika and olive oil (pictured); **Quisquillas** shrimps; **Salpicón** cold chopped salad, often with some shellfish; **Soldaditos de Pavía** strips of salt cod, fried in light batter; **Tigres** mussels cooked with a spicy tomato and béchamel sauce; **Zamburiñas** small scallops.

Vegetales (Vegetable tapas)

Aceitunas, olivas (adobados, rellenos) olives (pickled, stuffed); **Almendras saladas** salted almonds; **Pan con tomate** bread rubbed with fresh tomato and olive oil; **Patatas bravas** deep-fried potatoes with hot pepper sauce; **Perdiz de huerta** lettuce hearts; **Pimientos de Padrón** fried, hot small green peppers; **Queso en aceite** cheese marinated in olive oil; **Setas** forest mushrooms.

Other tapas

Caracoles snails; **Croquetas** potato croquettes (which may be made with chicken, ham, tuna, and so on); **Empanada** flat pies, usually with a tuna filling; **Empanadilla** small fried pasties, usually with a tomato and tuna filling; **Ensaladilla rusa** salad of potatoes, onions, red peppers, usually tuna and other ingredients in mayonnaise, now a completely Spanish dish, but still called a Russian salad; **Huevos rellenos** stuffed cold hard-boiled eggs; **Migas (con huevo frito)** fried breadcrumbs (with fried egg); **Pisto manchego** stir-fried vegetables with meat (usually ham) and egg.

pulguitas, La Platería also offers breakfasts and chocolate *napolitanas*. The wine list is extensive: the house wine is a young Ribera, but there are also *crianza* Riojas, Priorat, Penedès and cava.

La Toscana

C/Manuel Fernández y González 10, corner C/Ventura de la Vega 22 (91 429 60 31). Metro Sevilla/bus all routes to Puerta del Sol. **Open** 1-4pm, 8pm-midnight Tue-Sat. Closed Mon, Sun & two weeks Aug. **Credit** AmEx, MC, V. **Map** p309 F8.
Morcillo (stewed beef on the bone) is the house speciality at La Toscana, which boasts plenty of table space and *raciones* for around 1,000ptas. There are also good egg *revueltos*, and decent salads.

La Trucha

C/Manuel Fernández y González 3 (91 429 58 33). Metro Sevilla or Sol/bus all routes to Puerta del Sol. **Open** 12.30-4pm, 7.30pm-midnight Mon-Sat; closed Sun. **Credit** AmEx, DC, MC, V. **Map** p309 F8.
A bar-restaurant with a wide range of tasty traditional tapas and *raciones*, 'The Trout' and its nearby branch are invariably packed at peak times.

As well as smaller dishes there's a *menú del día*. A very enjoyable introduction to Madrid for new arrivals, with outside tables.
Branch: C/Núñez de Arce 6 (91 532 08 82).

La Latina, Rastro, Lavapiés

One of the best areas for traditional, gutsy Madrileño tapas is the Rastro, where the bars are at their most atmospheric (and fullest) on a Sunday morning.

Bar Castilla

C/Mesón de Paredes 24 (91 467 54 56). Metro Tirso de Molina/bus 6, 26, 32, 65. **Open** 9am-midnight Mon-Fri, Sun; closed Sat. **No credit cards. Map** p309 E9.
One for *croqueta* fans: on a Sunday morning there's a choice of over 100 kinds (nine for 500ptas) in this tiny bar. Also good for *chipirones en su tinta*.

El Brillante

Glorieta del Emperador Carlos V, 8 (91 528 69 66). Metro Atocha/bus all routes to Atocha. **Open** 6.30am-1am daily. **No credit cards. Map** p310 H9.

On the edge of Lavapiés facing Atocha station, this is the first link in a no-nonsense chain of big café-bars with quality food at swallowable prices. It was established by the station in pre-AVE days, to fortify travellers pre- or post- long journeys to the south, and still has takeaway snacks for the train. There's also a huge variety of fresh *bocadillos*, tapas and hot meals. An ideal call-in, it's always busy, especially early morning when it fills with arrivals from Atocha and revellers ending a night with hot chocolate and *churros*. It's standing only in the bar, but outside there's one of Madrid's largest *terrazas*. **Branches:** throughout the city.

Hip haunt in Lavapiés, **El Tío Vinagre**.

Café Melo's

C/Avemaría 44 (91 527 50 54). Metro Lavapiés/bus 2, 26, 27, 32. **Open** 9am-2am Tue-Sat. Closed Mon, Sun & Aug. **No credit cards. Map** p309 E9.
An attractive little Lavapiés bar known for its delicious fresh *croquetas*, *zapatillas* (sandwiches of Galician country bread, cheese and ham) and *empanadas* with rich fillings.

Los Caracoles

Plaza de Cascorro 18 (91 365 94 39). Metro La Latina/bus 17, 18, 23, 35, 60. **Open** 10am-4pm, 7-10.30pm Mon-Sat; 10am-4pm Sun, public holidays. **No credit cards. Map** p309 D9.
Genial host Don Amadeo welcomes everyone to his bar at the top of the Rastro. It gets hugely busy on Sunday lunchtimes, and is famous for its house speciality – snails, cooked Madrileño-style in a rich broth with chorizo and paprika. If that doesn't appeal there are plenty of other tapas, and ice-cold beer or cheerfully cheap red wine to go with them.

Cayetano

C/Encomienda 23 (91 527 77 07). Metro La Latina or Tirso de Molina/bus 17, 23, 26, 35. **Open** 9.30am-3.30pm, 5.30-11.30pm Mon, Wed-Sun; closed Tue. **No credit cards. Map** p309 E9.
Another good Rastro stop off, this time for shellfish – especially prawns in their shells – and wine.

Los Hermanos

C/Rodas 28 (91 468 33 13). Metro La Latina or Puerta de Toledo/bus 17, 18, 23, 35, 60. **Open** 7am-11pm Mon-Fri; 7am-5pm Sun. Closed Sat & Aug. **No credit cards. Map** p309 D10.
Right next to the Rastro is this bar with a strong local feel, generous complimentary tapas and a huge range of *raciones* such as *jamón de jabugo* and Madrileño offal such as *criadillas* and *callos*. Sundays there's a *menú* for 1,200ptas (900ptas weekdays), but expect it to be packed with post-Rastro crowds.

La Mancha en Madrid

C/Miguel Servet 13 (no phone). Metro Embajadores/bus 6, 27, 32, 57, 27. **Open** 1-4.30pm, 8.30pm-1am daily. **No credit cards. Map** p309 E10.
Popular with *guiris* (young foreigners) and surviving *progres* (the Spanish mix of hippie and lefty who flourished in the last years of Franco): an easygoing atmosphere, well-served cold beer, decent wines,

imaginative tapas – farmhouse cheeses, quality ham and meats, fish in *escabeche* – and walls festooned with posters and information about walks in the hills, concerts, demonstrations and other activities.

La Taberna de Antonio Sánchez

C/Mesón de Paredes 13 (91 539 78 26). Metro Tirso de Molina/bus 6, 26, 32, 65. **Open** noon-4pm, 8pm-midnight Mon-Sat; noon-4pm Sun. **No credit cards. Map** p309 E9.
Madrid's most historic and best-preserved *taberna*, founded by a bullfighter in the heart of Lavapiés in 1830. It has scarcely changed since, from its zinc bar to the bits and pieces around the walls. Its owners have all been involved in the bullfighting world, and long *tertulias* (*see p20*) between critics, *toreros* and aficionados are still held here. It has also been patronised by writers and artists, among them the painter Ignacio Zuloaga, who left a fine portrait of the first Antonio Sánchez. For all its fame, though, this is still a local place, and the friendly owners are happy to chat about its history. Superior tapas – *callos*, *morcilla*, smoked fish – and full meals are available.

La Taberna del Avapiés

C/Lavapiés 5 (91 539 26 50). Metro Tirso de Molina/bus 6, 26, 32, 65. **Open** 7.30pm-1am Mon; 1-3pm, 7.30pm-1am Tue-Thur; 1-3pm, 7.30pm-2am Fri, Sat; 1-5pm Sun. **No credit cards. Map** p309 E9.
Once a cocktail bar, this place offers a great selection of charcuterie and imaginative tapas. Service is attentive, and the atmosphere youthful and relaxed.

El Tío Vinagre

C/San Carlos 6 (91 527 45 93). Metro Lavapiés or Tirso de Molina/bus 6, 26, 32, 50, 65. **Open** 8pm-1am Mon-Fri; 12.30-4pm, 8pm-1am Sat; 12.30-5pm Sun. Closed Aug. **No credit cards. Map** p309 E9.
Lavapiés has drawn younger bar owners recently, and a crowd to match. Run by a group of women, 'Uncle Vinegar' is notably female-friendly, and has decent wines and unusual tapas such as cod in olive oil, *cecina*, and chorizo and *cecina* of venison.

Chueca

La Bardemcilla

C/Augusto Figueroa 47 (91 521 42 56). Metro Chueca/bus all routes to Callao. **Open** noon-4.30pm, 8pm-2am daily. **Credit** AmEx, MC, V. **Map** p306 G5.
A fixture on the Chueca scene, this spacious – but still sometimes crowded and noisy – bar is owned

by leading Spanish film actor Javier Bardem, and run by his sister. It's no Planet Hollywood, though, for the interior is hip and stylish. Imaginative tapas and good wines, and the bar is equally popular as a starting-off point for many a night's revelries.

El Bocaíto

C/Libertad 6 (91 532 12 19). Metro Chueca/bus 3, 37, 40, 149. **Open** 1-4pm, 8-30pm-midnight Mon-Fri; 8.30pm-midnight Sat. Closed Sun & Aug. **No credit cards. Map** p306 G5.
Madrileños rate this pricey tapas bar highly. Energetic, jokey waiters dish up *huevas* (fish roes), a variety of *revueltos*, pâtés, salads, pastries, mushroom kebabs and other unusual tapas. There's no seating, so it's not a place for leisurely eating.

Santander

C/Augusto Figueroa 25 (91 522 49 10). Metro Chueca/bus 3, 40, 149. **Open** 10.45am-4pm, 7-11pm Mon-Sat. Closed Sun & Aug. **No credit cards. Map** p306 G5.
One of the largest tapas ranges in Madrid, with around 100 to choose from, including *brandada* (salt cod and potato purée), stuffed mussels and a huge range of *montados* (canapés). Prices are low, too.

Taberna de Pelayo

C/Pelayo 8 (91 532 80 31). Metro Chueca/bus 3, 40, 149. **Open** 11am-5pm, 7pm-1am Tue-Sun; closed Mon. **No credit cards. Map** p306 G5.
Part of the revival of Chueca, this self-consciously rustic bar specialises in oven-cooked chorizo and *lomo*. Good beer, vermouth and a small but select range of wines have guaranteed its success so far.

La Tradicional

C/Santo Tomé 5 (91 310 15 03). Metro Colón/ bus 3, 37, 40, 149. **Open** 11am-midnight Mon-Thur, Sun; 11am-1.30am Fri, Sat. **No credit cards. Map** p306 H5.
Excellent value, big portions of traditional staples such as chickpeas, sardines or *albóndigas*, washed down with well-priced local wines. Take your time and sit at a window table watching the world go by.

Malasaña & Conde Duque

Albur

C/Manuela Malasaña 15 (91 594 27 33). Metro Bilbao/bus 147, 149. **Open** noon-midnight Mon-Wed, Sun; noon-1.30am Thur-Sat. **No credit cards. Map** p305 F3.
As Malasaña smartens up, new-model tapas enter the equation. This intimate bar has a small selection of tapas, including very fine *morcilla* blood sausage, with a fair variety of wines to go with them.

Casa do Campañeiro

C/San Vicente Ferrer 44 (91 521 57 02). Metro Noviciado or Tribunal/bus 3, 40, 147, 149. **Open** 1.30pm-2am daily. **No credit cards. Map** p305 E4.
Galician bar with wonderful tiles and traditional wines and tapas – *pimientos de Padrón* and shellfish.

La Fortuna

Plaza de los Mostenses 3 (91 547 30 98). Metro Plaza de España/bus all routes to Plaza de España. **Open** noon-midnight daily. Closed Aug & Sun in July. **No credit cards. Map** p305 D5.
An old-fashioned bar near the Plaza de España worth a visit to sample bargain fine wines by the jug, fried *boquerones*, roast chorizo and meaty tapas.

El Maño

C/de la Palma 64 (91 521 50 57). Metro San Bernardo/bus 147. **Open** noon-4pm, 7.30pm-midnight Thur-Sun; closed Mon-Wed. **No credit cards. Map** p305 E4.
This likeable bar opened in the '90s as part of the revival in the Conde Duque area, but its owners kept the locale's attractive 1920s decor. There's a good selection of wines, innovative tapas, friendly service, and plenty of room at the bar if tables are full.

Mesón Los Toledanos

Travesía de Conde Duque 5 (91 541 11 55). Metro Noviciado/1, 2, 44, 133, C. **Open** 7am-11.30pm Mon-Fri, Sun. Closed Sat & Aug. **No credit cards. Map** p305 D4.
A down-to-earth tapas bar near the Cuartel Conde Duque with a great spread of *chipirones, caracoles,* very hot chorizo, marinated trout (*trucha en escabeche*) and other earthy dishes.

Taberna 9

C/San Andrés 9 (no phone). Metro Tribunal/bus 3, 40, 147, 149. **Open** 6pm-1am Mon-Thur; 6pm-2.30am Fri, Sat; closed Sun. **No credit cards. Map** p305 F4.
Flamenco and Cuban salsa blare out from this laid-back modern tapas bar. Inside, there's excellent-quality meats and cheese, and well-priced canapés.

Salamanca & the Retiro

Upmarket – and prices reflect it – but there are some great, long-established bars, and the local clientele demand high standards.

Alkalde

C/Jorge Juan 10 (91 576 33 59). Metro Serrano/bus 1, 9, 19, 51, 89. **Open** 1-4.30pm, 8.30pm-midnight daily. Closed Sat & Sun during July & Aug. **Credit** AmEx, DC, MC, V. **Map** p307 J5.
An old-fashioned Basque bar that's quite expensive, but has great *chistorra*, tortilla with peppers, *morcilla, jamón, empanadillas* and *chipirones en su tinta*.

Hevia

C/Serrano 118 (91 562 30 75). Metro Gregorio Marañón/bus 9, 16, 19, 51. **Open** 9.30am-1am Mon-Sat. Closed Sun & Aug. **Credit** AmEx, DC, MC, V. **Map** p307 J1.
A buzzy tapas bar in Salamanca's affluent heart that uses excellent ingredients, put together in pretty much whichever canapé-combination you wish. Not cheap, but service by the white-jacketed waiters is great; the clientele can be as plush as the locale. Also one of the district's most transited *terrazas*.

Eat, Drink, Shop

Smart tapas

A new, more polished style of *tapeo* – tapa-sampling – has emerged in Madrid with the opening of a string of bars – which generally use the more historic name *tabernas* – above all in Los Austrias, which all offer a similar combination of tradition, modernity, comfort and a refined approach to food. Much care is taken to create a contemporary look, but one that fits in with the historic surroundings: bare brick, or rag-rolled pastel shades. Their food reveals far more care for ingredients, originality and presentation than your neighbourhood bar will offer, and wine lists are extensive. This is where you can sample the best of recent Spanish wines. Prices, though, are higher too.

Aloque

C/Torrecilla del Leal 20, Lavapiés (91 528 36 62). Metro Antón Martín/bus 6, 26, 32, 57. **Open** 7.30pm-1am Mon-Thur, Sun; 7.30pm-2am Fri, Sat. Closed Aug. **Credit** MC, V. **Map** p309 F9.
One new-style *taberna* not in the Austrias bar zone. When this little bar opened a few years ago it was a pioneer in selling quality wines with original snacks, in an area full of plain, humble bars. A blackboard shows the day's wines, from a range of over 200 labels. The menu is seasonal, but all year there are great canapés such as *solomillo* with pepper sauce or marinated salt cod, and fine cheese pies.

La Corolla

C/del Almendro 10, Austrias (91 364 52 32). Metro La Latina/bus 17, 18, 23, 31, 35. **Open** noon-4pm, 8pm-midnight Tue-Sun; closed Mon & Aug. **Credit** AmEx, MC, V. **Map** p309 D8.

Friendly, lively, invariably crowded, this *taberna* has a full range of Spanish wines, from a cheap, very drinkable Valdepeñas to the finest Riberas. To eat there are loads of canapés, with varied combinations of cheese, salmon, anchovies, avocado and other tasty things.

El Madroño

Plaza de Puerta Cerrada 7, Austrias (91 364 56 29). Metro La Latina/bus 17, 18, 23, 31, 35, 65. **Open** 9am-2am Mon-Thur, Sun; 9am-2.30am Fri, Sat. **Credit** AmEx, MC, V. **Map** p309 D8.
A new *taberna* opened by the family that ran the old El Madroño pastelería in Lavapiés, long one of Madrid's most original cake shops, known for unusual specialities such as beetroot cakes and the strawberry-ish *Licor de Madroño* liqueur. Some (including the *licor*) are still available at this bar, along with hot and cold canapés, great meat *pinchos* and *raciones*, and a good *menú*. The wine range is smaller, but well-chosen.

Matritum

C/Cava Alta 17, Austrias (91 365 82 37). Metro La Latina/bus 17, 18, 31, 35, 65. **Open** 1-5pm, 8.30pm-midnight Tue-Sun; closed Mon. **No credit cards**. **Map** p309 D8.
A pleasant, warmly decorated *taberna*, Matritum (pictured) – Latin for Madrid – serves choice wines from Ribera del Duero, Penedès, Priorat and other regions, and has excellent *raciones* as well as canapés. Its *croquetas*, with ham, prawns or Roquefort, are superb, as is the potato gratin with five cheeses and chickpeas with spinach.

José Luis

C/Serrano 89-91 (91 563 09 58). Metro Núñez de Balboa/bus 9, 19, 51, 89. **Open** 9am-1am Mon-Sat; noon-1am Sun, public holidays. **Credit** AmEx, DC, MC, V. **Map** p307 J2.
Classic Salamanca bars with cocktail-type tapas from a list little changed since the 1950s (smoked salmon tartare, melted Brie and pâté, small steak canapés and mixed *montados*), delicious cakes, and a yuppyish crowd. Tables outside in summer.
Branches: C/Rafael Salgado 11 (91 458 01 83); C/San Francisco de Sales 14-16 (91 441 20 43); Paseo de La Habana 4-6 (91 562 31 18).

Peláez

C/Lagasca 61 (91 575 87 24). Metro Serrano/bus 1, 74, 89. **Open** 10am-midnight Mon-Sat. Closed Sun & Aug. **No credit cards**. **Map** p307 J4.

An old bar that has been turning out creative tapas – *huevas*, *montados*, *mojama*, smoked fish tortillas – since the 1960s. In the evenings it's often packed.

North & west

Chamberí

Another area with a tapas round of its own – Calles Cardenal Cisneros and Hartzenbush are lined with cheapish bars.

Bodegas La Ardosa

C/Santa Engracia 70 (91 446 58 94). Metro Iglesia/bus 3, 37, 149. **Open** 10am-3.30pm, 6-11pm daily. Closed two weeks Aug. **No credit cards**. **Map** p306 G2.

Taberna Bilbao

Costanilla de San Andrés 8, Austrias
(91 365 61 25). Metro La Latina/bus 17,
18, 23, 31, 35, 65. **Open** 1-4pm, 8pm-
midnight daily. *July, Aug* from 8.30pm.
No credit cards. Map p308 C8.
Not the cheapest but high on quality, Taberna
Bilbao offers Basque tapas and a huge range
of wines. For a real taste of Euskadi, try a
glass of *txacoli* (from the *taberna*'s own
vineyards) and *delicias de idiazábal* (smoked
idiazábal cheese, fried in light batter).

Taberna la Salamandra

C/Alfonso VI, 6, Austrias
(91 366 05 15). Metro La Latina/bus 17,
18, 23, 31, 35. **Open** 1.30-4pm, 8.30pm-
1am daily. Closed two weeks Aug.
Credit AmEx, MC, V. **Map** p308 C8.
A very pleasant *taberna*, La Salamandra
takes its name both from the lizard, iron
reproductions of which lurk on the walls, and
a machine used to gratinée food, known as a
salamandra. One of the best canapés of
many on offer is *solomillo con queso fundido*,
a mini-steak with melted cheese on garlic
toast. The warm salads are also excellent,
and there's plenty for wine buffs, too.

La Taberna del Zapatero

C/del Almendro 27, Austrias
(91 364 07 21). Metro La Latina/bus 17,
18, 23, 31, 35. **Open** 1.30-4pm,
8,30pm-midnight daily. **No credit cards.**
Map p309 D8.
One Austrias nouveau-taberna that gives you
plenty of room in which to get expansive – set
as it is on two floors of what was formerly a
shoe warehouse. Choose from a long and
sophisticated wine list, and such culinary
delights as chorizo in cider, stuffed tomato
and home-made *pisto manchego*.

La Tasca de Jesús

C/Cava Alta 32, Austrias
(91 366 61 61). Metro La Latina/
bus 17, 18, 23, 31, 35. **Open** noon-5pm,
8pm-1am Tue-Sun; closed Mon.
No credit cards. Map p309 D8.
Not a place to linger: it's too small.
However, a well-thought out selection of
wines and simple but exquisitely prepared
tapas more than compensate.

El Tempranillo

C/Cava Baja 38, Austrias (
91 364 15 32). Metro La Latina/bus 17, 18,
23, 31, 53, 65. **Open** noon-4pm, 8pm-
midnight daily. Closed two weeks Aug.
Credit AmEx, MC, V. **Map** p309 D8.
In bullring ochre and bare brick, with flamenco
guitar on the sound system, El Tempranillo
offers an impressive range of labels from
nearly every wine-producing region in Spain.
The tapas are addictive too: try the *Boletus
Edulis* of wild mushrooms in scrambled egg,
or any of the cured meats.

A classic and ever-popular red-fronted *taberna*:
among the dishes on offer are brilliant *patatas
bravas*, marinated sardines, shellfish and loads of
yummy fried things.

Mesón do Anxo

C/Cardenal Cisneros 6 (91 446 17 43). Metro Bilbao/
bus 3, 21, 147, 149. **Open** noon-midnight Tue-Sun;
closed Mon. **No credit cards. Map** p305 F3.
A modern bar offering a good range of tapas,
among them wild mushrooms, fine calamares and,
for the staunch carnivores among you, grilled meat
sold by weight.

Taberna 2

C/Sagasta 2 (91 532 21 43). Metro Bilbao/bus 21,
147, 149. **Open** *Oct-May* 11am-3pm, 6pm-midnight
Mon-Thur; 11am-3pm, 6pm-2.30am Fri, Sat. *June,*
July, Sept noon-4pm, 7.30pm-12.30am Mon-Thur;
noon-4pm, 7.30-2.30pm Fri, Sat. Closed Sun & Aug.
No credit cards. Map p305 F3.
A good-value wine bar serving pungent Asturian
cabrales cheese, and cheap *montados* of *sobrasada*.

Taberna Los Madriles

C/José Abascal 26 (91 593 06 26).
Metro Alonso Cano/bus 3, 5, 12, 37, 149. **Open**
11am-4pm, 7pm-12.30am Mon-Sat; closed Sun.
Credit AmEx, MC, V.
Modern, but imitating the old-style Madrid *taberna*,
Los Madriles is all white tiles, adorned with photos
of its regulars – as children. The range of tapas
in not huge but very choice: *gambas al ajillo* and
cullos are great, but the star snack is *pincho los
madriles*, of red pepper and anchovies. There are
tables outside in summer.

Eat, Drink, Shop

Cafés & Bars

Whether scruffy or elegant, cheap or expensive, Madrid's range of watering holes is unbeatable.

Any precise distinction between 'cafés', 'bars' and related refreshment-points is pretty blurry in this city. But, whatever name they go by, Madrid is full of them – from small, shabby, neighbourhood bars with tongue-rasping wine to splendid 1890s grand cafés. Madrileños spend a large amount of their time and income in cafés and bars, so getting acquainted with them means you're getting to grips with Madrid itself. Whether you want to quench a thirst, have a quiet coffee or go on a bender, you'll find a place to suit your needs.

'Official' opening times can be very elastic, and those given here should be taken as guidelines (dates of summer schedules are especially variable). Neighbourhood bars mostly close around midnight – later at weekends – but in the city centre all bars tend to stay open later.

Refined relaxation at **Café de Oriente**.

Los Austrias

The historic heart of Madrid offers a choice of old-fashioned tiled *tabernas*, relaxing cafés and an ever-growing contingent of upscale tapas-and-wine bars (*see pages 142-3*).

Café de los Austrias

Plaza de Ramales, off Plaza de Santiago (91 559 84 36). Metro Opera/bus 3, 25, 39, 148. **Open** 9am-1.30am Mon-Thur; 9am-3am Fri, Sat; 5pm-midnight Sun. **Credit** AmEx, DC, MC, V. **Map** p308 C7.
This re-creation of a 19th-century café – actually just a few years old – on the site of a former nunnery is a welcome turnabout in the tendency for older-style cafés to disappear. It's big, looks out onto two old streets and a little plaza, and boasts marble tables and prints of monarchs along the walls.

Café de Oriente

Plaza de Oriente 2 (91 541 39 74). Metro Opera/bus 3, 25, 39, 148. **Open** 8.30am-1.30am Mon-Thur, Sun; 8.30am-2.30am Fri, Sat.
Credit AmEx, DC, MC, V. **Map** p308 C7.
A classic café with an aristocratic feel about it, the Oriente suffered greatly during the interminable refurbishing of the plaza of the same name outside. It survived, and is now once again a magnet for well-heeled locals and visitors alike. There is a restaurant, but visitors are mainly taken with the views over the newly-splendid Plaza de Oriente, the Palacio Real and the mountains beyond. Its very popular *terraza* tables are in place from May to October, with service from about 12.30pm onwards; if they're full, the café is deliciously comfortable inside, too.

De 1911

Plazuela de San Ginés 5, corner C/Coloreros (91 366 35 19). Metro Opera or Sol/bus all routes to Puerta del Sol. **Open** 6pm-2am daily.
No credit cards. **Map** p309 D7.
Not far from Sol, the tiny Plazuela de San Ginés is a haven of tranquillity. This is one of the nicest bars on the square, and is so named because, well, it opened in 1911. Inside, it has been finely refurbished with hand-painted tiles, and offers beers from around the world and excellent speciality coffees.

Kairos

C/del Nuncio 19 (91 364 01 25). Metro La Latina/bus 17, 31, 50, 65. **Open** 8.30pm-2.30am Mon-Thur, Sun; 8.30pm-3.30am Fri, Sat.
No credit cards. **Map** p309 D8.
Just off Calle Segovia is this well-designed, pleasant small bar, near the Café del Nuncio (*see p151*), with a faithful local clientele, fine cocktails and great coffee. It has tables outdoors from May to October.

Sol & Gran Vía

The Gran Vía and the streets around it contain some of Madrid's most distinguished cafés and cocktail bars from before the Civil War.

Bar Cock

C/de la Reina 16 (91 532 28 26). Metro Gran Vía/bus all routes to Gran Vía. **Open** *Sept-June* 7pm-3am daily. *July, Aug* 9pm-4am Mon-Sat; closed Sun.
Credit AmEx, DC, MC, V. **Map** p309 F6.
Not strictly Sol-side of the Gran Vía, but one of three cocktail bars that form a tiny city-centre triangle (the others being Chicote and Del Diego). Dark wood-

Eat, Drink, Shop

panelled walls and a high-beamed ceiling give it a subdued air that still sometimes attracts the media, theatre and fashion crowd.

Café del Círculo de Bellas Artes

C/Alcalá 42 (91 360 54 00/902 42 24 42).
Metro Banco de España/bus all routes to Cibeles.
Open 9am-2am Mon-Thur, Sun; 9am-3am Fri, Sat.
Admission 100ptas. **Credit** AmEx, DC, MC, V.
Map p310 G7.

The wonderful cultural association that is the Círculo (*see p73*) charges a nominal 100ptas for non-members to use its elegant but informal café overlooking Calle Alcalá. It's well worth this slight extra cost to be able to sit and read or chat for as long as you might wish in this magnificently airy, relaxing room, one of Madrid's most special places, amid Antonio Palacios' grand 1920s decor, with paintings, the reclining nude sculpture and fabulous chandeliers. The tapas can be great, too, and recently the Círculo has also begun to serve larger dishes and an excellent *menú*. A final touch is the very comfortable *terraza* in front, from May to October.

Del Diego

C/de la Reina 12 (91 523 31 06). Metro Gran Vía/bus all routes to Gran Vía. **Open** 7pm-3am Mon-Thur; 7pm-4am Fri, Sat. Closed Sun & Aug. **No credit cards.** **Map** p309 F6.

Founded by ex-Chicote waiter Fernando del Diego, this bar has a younger clientele and a lighter style than most traditional *coctelerías*. The atmosphere is convivial, and the cocktails are something else. Try a Diego: vodka, kirsch, peach, lime and crushed ice.

Museo Chicote

Gran Vía 12 (91 532 67 37). Metro Gran Vía/bus all routes to Gran Vía. **Open** 8am-3am Mon-Thur; 8am-4am Fri, Sat; closed Sun. **Credit** AmEx, DC, MC, V. **Map** p309 F6.

The doyen of Madrid cocktail bars, with the city's best 1930s art deco interior, and famous for never having closed during the Civil War. The seats are also original, which means that you could be sitting where ole Hemingway and other international press hacks spent their days sheltering from the artillery shells flying down the Gran Vía. Grace Kelly, Ava Gardner and just about every Spanish writer, actor or artist of the last 60 years have passed through too. The cocktail range is impressive, but expensive (prices are lower before 5pm). The waiters are gentlemen from another epoch. Grab an alcove table, and savour a treat to remember.

Huertas & Santa Ana

Despite its rivals, this is perennially Madrid's busiest, most popular bar zone. Also among the area's essential bars are **Los Gabrieles** and **Viva Madrid** (*see page 155*).

Alhambra

C/Victoria 9 (91 521 07 08). Metro Sol/bus all routes to Puerta del Sol. **Open** 10am-2am Tue-Sun; 6pm-2am Mon. **No credit cards.** **Map** p309 E7.

Dating from 1929, as confirmed on the tiles outside, this pretty *taberna* has a suitably Andaluz-Moorish look to go with its name. During the day it's tranquil, serving drinks and tapas, but at night things get lively, when a youngish crowd packs out the place and Spanish pop dominates the speakers. It also has a 'Cantina', with a lunch *menú* for 1,200ptas.

El Café del Español

C/del Príncipe 25 (91 420 43 05). Metro Antón Martín or Sol/bus all routes to Puerta del Sol. **Open** *Oct-May* noon-2am Mon-Thur, Sun; noon-3am Fri, Sat. *June-Sept* 4pm-2am Thur-Sun; 4pm-3am Fri, Sat. **Credit** AmEx, DC, MC, V. **Map** p309 F8.

Eat, Drink, Shop

The best Cafés & Bars

For admiring the architecture

Café de Oriente (see page 144), or the **Café del Nuncio** for a more casual choice (see page 151).

For a vision of heaven on earth

Círculo de Bellas Artes (see page 145). Okay, that's saying a lot, but it's pretty wonderful.

For corny Hemingway references

Museo Chicote (see page 145) and the **Cervecería Alemana** have the Ernie trail covered (see page 147).

For boozing, mingling & the like

So many: try **Montes** (see page 150), **Casa Camacho** or **Viva Madrid** (see pages 154-5).

For claiming to write great things

Café Gijón (see page 154), or **Café Comercial** (see page 157) if you want someone to listen.

For poetic moments

Café de Ruíz, on a quiet afternoon when there are orchids on the bar (see page 158).

For seeing mountains, or the stars

Las Vistillas (see page 151). Just don't expect anything fancy.

For café society in all its forms

Café Comercial (see page 157), it has to be, but **El Salón del Prado** (see page 149) and **La Sastrería** (see page 151) are contenders.

Occupying a very big, elegant space alongside the Teatro Español, looking out over Plaza Santa Ana, this airy café contrasts with the many *cervecerías* around the square. Inside, there's a wide choice of cocktails, salads and sarnies to sample, and for an added touch, take one of the deep-red plush booths.

Casa Pueblo
C/León 3 (91 429 05 15). Metro Antón Martín/ bus 6, 26, 32, 57. **Open** 9pm-2am Tue-Sun; closed Mon. **No credit cards. Map** p309 F8.
Casa Pueblo has been offering quietly formal but relaxed service for over 15 years. Excellent jazz on tape and a live pianist after midnight help make it one of Madrid's most pleasant watering holes.

Cervecería Alemana
Plaza de Santa Ana 6 (91 429 70 33). Metro Antón Martín or Sol/bus all routes to Puerta del Sol. **Open** 10.30am-12.30am Mon, Wed, Thur, Sun; 10.30am-2am Fri, Sat; closed Tue. **No credit cards. Map** p309 F8.
Built in 1904 and based (loosely) on a German bier-keller, the Alemana still serves beer in steins, if you ask for them. Hemingway (as many people might tell

you) was once a regular, and the old place is still much as it was then. It's very much on the tourist trail, but on Sunday mornings still offers an ideal setting to browse the papers; at night, though, it gets packed, and so is often not the best place to meet up.

Cervecería Santa Ana
Plaza de Santa Ana 10 (91 429 43 56). Metro Antón Martín or Sol/bus all routes to Puerta del Sol. **Open** 11.30am-1.30am Mon-Thur, Sun; 11.30am-2.30am Fri, Sat. **No credit cards. Map** p309 E/F8.
Slightly overshadowed by the Alemana next door, the Santa Ana is plainer to look at, but still has good beer. There are tables outside from Easter to October, but no tables inside at any time, and in the evenings space at the bar is highly contested. Good cheese, pâté and tapas are on offer.

Ducados Café
Plaza de Canalejas 3 (91 360 00 89). Metro Sevilla, Sol/bus all routes to Puerta del Sol. **Open** 8am-2am Mon-Thur, Sun; 9.30am-2.30am Fri, Sat. **Credit** AmEx, MC, V. **Map** p309 F7.
Despite a sleek, rather corporate appearance and theme-'Latino' feel, with bright colours and salsa on

Match of the day

Like everywhere in the world, from Almaty to Cochabamba, Madrid saw a proliferation of pubs in the 1990s, mainly Irish. According to how keen you are on Riverdance and the Coors, or nostalgic for brown beer, they offer a wonderful home-from-home atmosphere, or a silly pastiche of the real thing. One thing about them is that, thanks to satellite and cable, the pubs now allow sports-mad *guiris* in Madrid to keep up to date with the ups and downs of their football teams, and watch UK and international football, rugby, baseball (sometimes) and even the All-Ireland hurling championship. Many are among the city's more enterprising live music venues, hosting gigs from traditional Irish to rock or jazz (in particular the **Moby Dick/Irish Rover** and **Triskel Tavern**, see chapter **Music: Rock, Roots & Jazz**). Listed here are just a few of the most popular – there are plenty more.

Bo Finn
C/Velázquez 97, Salamanca (91 411 40 79). Metro Núñez de Balboa/bus 16, 19, 51. **Open** noon-1am Mon-Thur, Sun; noon-2am Fri, Sat. **Credit** AmEx, DC, MC, V. **Map** p307 J2.
In Salamanca, so a bit smarter (and more comfortable) than most, the Bo Finn has Sky sports and good food, with a 1,300ptas *menú del día.*

Kitty O'Shea's
C/Alcalá 59, Salamanca (91 575 49 01). Metro Banco de España/bus all routes to Cibeles. **Open** 10am midnight daily. **Credit** AmEx, DC, MC, V. **Map** p310 H6.
In a space that was until recently the Café Lión, one of Madrid's historic cafés, Kitty O'Shea's is a big, airy bar-restaurant with a more extensive menu than most pubs (mixing Spanish, Irish and French cooking), regular live music and an outside terrace just up the hill from Cibeles.

O'Neill's
C/Príncipe 12, Huertas & Santa Ana (91 521 20 30). Metro Sevilla/bus all routes to Puerta del Sol. **Open** noon-2am Mon-Thur, Sun; noon-3am Fri, Sat. **Credit** AmEx, DC, MC, V. **Map** p309 F8.
Just off Santa Ana, O'Neill's has live music most nights and a big basement bar with TV screens (try to get to the front, though).

The Quiet Man
C/Valverde 44, Malasaña & Conde Duque (91 523 46 89). Metro Tribunal/bus 3, 40, 149. **Open** 5.30pm-2am Mon-Thur; 1pm-3am Fri-Sun. **Credit** AmEx, DC, MC, V. **Map** p305 F4.
Malasaña's popular Quiet Man has good food, and four screens for sports viewing.

Café del Círculo de Bellas Artes. *See p144.*

the speakers, the Ducados Café is not part of any franchise chain, but a one-off. It fills up with tourists and local lunchers and after-workers, drawn by a big range of tapas, a midday *menú* for 1,250ptas, good coffee and other drinks and lots of room to sit down. It hosts occasional live music gigs in the basement.

Los Gatos
C/Jesús 2 (91 429 30 67). Metro Antón Martín/bus 14, 27, 34, 37, 45. **Open** noon-1am Mon-Thur, Sun; noon-2am Fri, Sat. **No credit cards**. **Map** p310 G8.
Overlooked on most tourist trails despite its handy location at the bottom of Huertas, not far from the Prado and the Thyssen, this veteran is a companion to near-neighbour **La Dolores** (*see p155*). Popular with the bullfighting fraternity (among many others), it retains a local feel, with excellent tapas and good, frothy beer, served at battered tables.

Naturbier
Plaza de Santa Ana 9 (91 429 39 18). Metro Antón Martín or Sol/bus all routes to Puerta del Sol. **Open** 11.30am-2am Mon-Thur, Sun; 11.30am-2.30am Fri, Sat. **No credit cards**. **Map** p309 E/F8.
Neighbour to the Cervecerías Alemana and Santa Ana on the plaza, Naturbier has another *terraza*, and is one of few places in Madrid that brews its own beer, to traditional German recipes. Always popular with students and foreigners.

Reporter
C/Fúcar 6 (91 429 39 22). Metro Antón Martín/bus 6, 26, 32, 57. **Open** noon-5pm Mon; noon-2am Tue-Thur, Sun; noon-3.30am Fri, Sat.
No credit cards. **Map** p310 G9.
Splendid cocktails and fruit juices are the major draws of this trendy, stylish Huertas cocktail-café, with low-volume jazz and occasional photo shows. It also serves tapas and meals in the afternoon.

El Salón del Prado
C/del Prado 4 (91 429 33 61). Metro Antón Martín/bus 6, 9, 26, 32. **Open** 2pm-2am Mon-Thur; 2pm-3am Fri, Sat; 2pm-1am Sun.
Credit AmEx, DC, MC, V. **Map** p309 F8.
Elegance itself, the Salón del Prado is one of the best spots around for a coffee – preferably with alcohol – after a hard day's touring. Service is formal yet friendly, and children are welcome. Chamber music concerts on Thursday nights (not July to September).

Salón de Té Sherazade
C/Santa María 16 (no phone). Metro Antón Martín/bus 6, 26, 32. **Open** 8pm-3am Mon-Thur; 8pm-4.30am Fri-Sun. **No credit cards**. **Map** p309 F8.
A sweetly scented Moroccan tea room, with arabesque decor, water pipes, delicious Arab teas and a big room at the back where an ultra-laidback (read: horizontal) crowd recline or sit Buddha style. Often packed around midnight.

La Venencia
C/Echegaray 7 (91 429 73 13). Metro Sevilla or Sol/bus all routes to Puerta del Sol. **Open** 1-3pm, 7.30pm-1.30am daily. **No credit cards**. **Map** p309 F8.
Unchangingly down at heel, the Venencia is worthy of a film set, with peeling sherry posters from no one knows when, barrels behind the bar and walls burnished gold by decades of tobacco smoke. It serves only sherry, from dry *fino* to robust *palo cortado*.

La Latina, Rastro, Lavapiés
The mixture of genuine old-style taverns, ethnic and neo-hippie bars and trendier new joints reflects the diversity of Madrid's *barrios bajos*.

El 21
C/Toledo 21 (91 366 28 59). Metro La Latina/bus all routes to Plaza Mayor. **Open** noon-3.30pm, 7-11pm Mon-Thur, Sun; noon-3.30pm, 7pm-midnight Fri, Sat. **No credit cards**. **Map** p309 D9.
A perfect Rastro stop-off, the 21 and its marble countertop seem locked in a time warp (even its bullfighting posters date back over two decades). No sign identifies the bar from the street, and most of the time it's filled with elderly locals, although a young crowd arrives at night and weekends.

La Clave
C/Calatrava 6 (91 366 48 38). Metro La Latina, Puerta de Toledo/bus 17, 18, 23, 35, 60. **Open** 9pm-1am Mon-Thur; 9pm-2.30am Fri, Sat; 9pm-1.30am Sun. **No credit cards**. **Map** p308 C9.
As much a gallery as a café, this place also hosts *tertulias* (*see p20*), and the owners publish their own arts magazine. The coffee's not bad, either, but note that the hours are artistically unpredictable.

Håga Café & Bazar
C/Avemaría 8 (no phone). Metro Antón Martín or Lavapiés/bus 6, 26, 32. **Open** *Sept-June* 6pm-midnight Mon-Thur, Sun; 6pm-2am Fri-Sat. *July, Aug* 7.30pm-1am Mon-Thur, Sun; 7.30pm-2am Fri. Sat. **No credit cards**. **Map** p309 F9.

Eat, Drink, Shop

On the terraces

Time spent sampling the city's outdoor café *terrazas*, by day or night, is an essential part of a Madrid summer. Below is a brief run-through of the city's best places to sit outside with a long drink: for some *terrazas* that are busiest late night, *see chapter* **Nightlife**, and for open-air dining, *see chapter* **Restaurants**. Most *terrazas* have their tables in place from around May (or earlier) to October; wherever you are, you will pay a bit extra for the privilege of sitting outside.

Los Austrias offers several alternatives: **Plaza Mayor**, expensive, but obligatory at least once; **Plaza Conde de Barajas**, a tiny square that's often overlooked by the crowds nearby; **Calle del Nuncio**, one of the most attractive corners of old Madrid, with Café del Nuncio and Kairos (see page 144); **Plaza de la Cruz Verde**, one of the oldest pavement spaces in the city; **Plaza de Oriente**, for elegance and grandeur; and **Las Vistillas**, where you're suddenly taken almost outside the city by magnificent views.

Huertas has another essential call in the **Plaza Santa Ana** itself. **Lavapiés**, too, has jumped on the *terraza* bandwagon, with the fast-rising popularity of El Eucalipto (see chapter **Nightlife**) and around ten more unfussily hip bars along **Calle Argumosa**, now labelled *Costa Argumosa* by some, which makes for a lively *terraceo* alternative to more expensive places further up town.

Chueca, naturally, has the **Plaza de Chueca**, hub of the gay scene and much else besides, and the incomparably less trendy **Plaza Santa Bárbara**, by Alonso

Martínez Metro. **Malasaña & Conde Duque** offer the **Plaza Dos de Mayo** – grungy, but refurbished, with half a dozen *terrazas* open most of the year, even though the famous *kiosko* in the middle has closed – and **Plaza de las Comendadoras** – slightly cheaper, and now more cool, socially speaking.

Other special places: of Madrid's parks, the **Retiro** and **Casa de Campo** both contain pleasantly simple cafés around their lakes, and, above the **Parque del Oeste**, by the eastern end of the **Teleférico** (see pages 85 and 86), is the **Paseo del Pintor Rosales**, a *paseo* lined with *terrazas* – many ice-cream bars (see page 153) – that's another favourite place to take the air. Finally, one of the most time-honoured of all places to sit at an outdoor table is the **Paseo de Recoletos**, with two of the city's most impressive cafés, the historic **Café Gijón** and **El Espejo** (see pages 154-5).

The name Håga (a neighbourhood of Gothenburg, where the owner once lived) doesn't appear above the door, but this amiably hip corner of Lavapiés is easily found – just look for an engaging tiled scene of a barber's shop, and a sign saying *Salón de Peluquería*. It's a good spot to chill out with some own-made cakes and a tea, a coffee or something stronger, if you prefer. Furnishings and decor are wackily improvised, and there's a second-hand clothes bazaar out at the back.

Montes

C/Lavapiés 40 (91 527 00 64). Metro Lavapiés/bus 6, 26, 32, 57. **Open** noon-4pm, 7.30pm midnight Tue-Sat; 11am-4pm Sun. Closed Mon & Aug. **No credit cards. Map** p309 E9.
An authentic neighbourhood bar where genial owner César has been catering to the finer palates of Lavapiés for decades. It's a walk-in-off-the-street

joint, with little more than standing room, where newly arrived Brits, Americans and other foreigners wanting to soak up atmosphere rub shoulders with local regulars. The wine selection is excellent, and the fresh tapas (some on the house) include fine *jamón*, anchovies and *cabrales* cheese.

Nuevo Café Barbieri

C/Avemaría 45 (91 527 36 58). Metro Lavapiés/bus 6, 26, 32. **Open** 3pm-2am Mon-Thur, Sun; 3pm-3am Fri, Sat. **No credit cards. Map** p309 F9.
After years of decline, the Barbieri and its columned interior were part-restored to some of their former glory in the '80s. The big old café still has an appealingly ramshackly side, and attracts a lively, young clientele. Newspapers and magazines on the bar make it an excellent spot to while away an afternoon, and it's a good place to go on your own. There is a *terraza* outside in mid-summer.

Café Comendadoras

*Plaza de las Comendadoras 1, Malasaña
& Conde Duque (91 532 11 32). Metro
Noviciado/bus 21, 147.* **Open** *Sept-June*
6pm-2am Mon-Thur, 6pm-3am Fri, Sat,
6pm-1am Sun. *June-Sept* noon-2am Mon-
Thur, noon-3am Fri, Sat, noon-1am Sun.
No credit cards. Map p305 D3.
Comendadoras is a good place to meet up if
you're en route to any festival events
presented at the Centro Conde Duque. The
Café Comendadoras has all the necessaries,
and is inexpensive; like others on the plaza it
gets crowded on hot nights, so go early.

Café Moderno

*Plaza de las Comendadoras 1, Malasaña
& Conde Duque (91 522 48 35). Metro
Noviciado or San Bernardo/bus 21, 147.*
Open *Sept-May* 6pm-2am Mon-Thur, Sun;
6pm-3am Fri, Sat. *June-Aug* 3pm-2am Mon-
Thur, Sun; 3pm-3am Fri, Sat.
No credit cards. Map p305 D3.
This slightly more elegant alternative (pictured)
has a fake art deco interior. Also fills up.

Café del Monaguillo

*Plaza de la Cruz Verde 3, Austrias (91 541
29 41). Metro La Latina/bus 31, 50, 65.*
Open 5.30pm-2.30am daily.
No credit cards. Map p308 C8.
A good stop-off in the heart of Los Austrias.

Café del Nuncio

*C/Nuncio 12 & C/Segovia 9, Austrias
(91 366 08 53). Metro La Latina/bus 31,*
50, 65. **Open** 12.30pm-2.30am daily.
Credit MC, V. **Map** p309 D8.
The Escalinata del Nuncio on Calle Nuncio
is one of the most picturesque streets in
the old city, a winding alley of steep stone
steps. The two halves of the Café del Nuncio
are at either end: both have great terraces
for taking a breather (with no traffic to
disturb you), and, inside, can be delightfully
calm and cosy even when they fill up.

La Heladería

*C/Argumosa 7, Lavapiés (91 528 80 09).
Metro Lavapiés/bus 6, 26, 32, 57, 27.*
Open 10am-1am Mon-Thur, Sun; 10am-
2am Fri, Sat. **No credit cards.**
Map p309 F10.
A great little ice-cream shop-café-*terraza*
on the Argumosa strip, serving cheap but
good coffees, beers, ices and *horchata*
and other coolers (see page 158). The
owners are ultra-friendly.

Las Vistillas

*C/Bailén 14, Austrias (91 366 35 78).
Metro Opera/bus 3, 148.* **Open** 11am-
1am Mon-Thur, Sun; 11am-3am Fri, Sat.
No credit cards. Map p308 C8.
The bar with the view. Just down from
the Palacio Real, this *terraza* is run with
absolutely no concern for any trends or
fashions but has a magnificent location
looking out over the Casa del Campo and
all the way to the Guadarrama. Las Vistillas
is situated at the corner of Bailén and
Calle de la Morería.

Vinícola Mentridana

*C/San Eugenio 9 (91 527 87 60). Metro Antón
Martín/bus 6, 26, 36.* **Open** 1pm-1am Mon-Thur, Sun;
1pm-2am Fri, Sat. **No credit cards. Map** p310 G9.
The Vinícola occupies what used to be a very dingy
old *bodega*. Its renovation has really only involved
rearranging the bar and smartening things up a bit,
so it maintains a low-key feel. They have, though,
spruced up the drinks on offer – a limited but good
range of wines, and well-pulled beer – accompanied
by some tasty tapas and *raciones*.

Chueca

On the up since the mid-'90s, in great part due
to the gay influx. Many of its bars now cater
equally to a mixed gay and non-gay crowd.
For more gay venues, *see pages 207-213.*

La Sastrería

*C/Hortaleza 74 (91 532 07 71). Metro Chueca/
bus 3, 40, 149.* **Open** 10am-2am Mon-Thur;
10am-3am Fri; 11am-3am Sat; 11am-2am Sun.
Credit MC, V. **Map** p306 G4.
Occupying a one-time tailor's shop – which is
what *Sastrería* means – this big café-bar is still decorated like one. Spacious, light and airy, it's popular
with gay men, lesbians and all others alike, and its
success shows no sign of diminishing. *See also p208.*

El Son

*C/Fernando VI, 21 (91 308 04 29). Metro Alonso
Martínez/bus 3, 37, 40, 149.* **Open** 8.30am-2am
Mon-Fri; 8.30am-1pm, 8pm-2am Sat. Closed Sun &
Aug. **No credit cards. Map** p306 H4.
Rum-lovers' paradise. 'The Sound' offers 90 labels
from Cuba, Venezuela, Barbados, Haiti, Jamaica and
the Dominican Republic, among others. Avoiding

Eat, Drink, Shop

kitsch tropical decor, its owners have done the bar out in design-bar style; the music is pure Latino – salsa, *merengue, cumbias*. Offset the effects of the rum with Colombian coffee.

Stop Madrid

C/Hortaleza 11 (91 523 54 42). Metro Gran Vía/ bus all routes to Gran Vía. **Open** *Sept-July* 12.30-4pm, 6pm-2am Mon-Sat; closed Sun. *Aug* 12.30-3.30pm, 7pm-2am Sat; closed Sun. **No credit cards. Map** p306 H4.
Housed in an old ham and *embutidos* shop from 1926, this amiable bar – an equal mix of traditional and trendy – has retained practically all of its original fit-

tings, including a marble counter and big shop windows, now used to display bottles of win. Chueca-ites and families rub shoulders inside, partaking of beer on tap, a good run of wines and all manner of things to pick at, above all first-rate Spanish ham.

Zanzíbar

C/Regueros 9 (91 319 90 64). Metro Alonso Martínez or Chueca/bus 3, 37, 149. **Open** 7pm-2am Tue-Thur, Sun; 7pm-3am Fri, Sat. Closed Mon & last two weeks Aug. **No credit cards. Map** p306 H4.
Solidarity is the theme in this bar, which seeks to sell only fair-trade products (the coffee and sugar

Cakes & coolers

If alcohol is not indispensable for you, Madrid also has cafés that specialise in teas, cakes and summer coolers such as *horchata*, *granizado* or ice-cream (see page 158). Some *chocolaterías* – serving thick, hot chocolate – are also favourite stop-offs on the Madrileño night-time round (see chapter **Nightlife**).

Bruin

Paseo del Pintor Rosales 48, Argüelles (91 541 59 21). Metro Argüelles/bus 21, 74. **Open** *mid Oct-May* noon-8pm daily; *June-mid Oct* 9am-2am daily. **No credit cards. Map** p304 B3.
One of Madrid's oldest, best-known ice-cream parlours, ideally placed near the Teleférico (*see* p85). Over 20 different flavours, and ice-cream cakes, *granizados* and *horchata*.

Café Viena

C/Luisa Fernanda 23, Argüelles (91 559 38 28). Metro Ventura Rodríguez/bus 1, 2, 44, 74, C. **Open** 8am-2am Mon-Sat; 4pm-2am Sun. **Credit** AmEx, DC, MC, V. **Map** p304 C4.
This smart, velvet-draped café specialises in Irish and other coffees, hot chocolate and cakes. It also hosts Monday-night 'Lyrical' sessions, with opera and *zarzuela*.

Compañía Infusionera de las Indias

C/de las Minas 1, Malasaña & Conde Duque (no phone). Metro Noviciado/bus 147. **Open** 6pm-midnight daily. **No credit cards. Map** p305 E4.
For a wide choice of teas from all over Asia and a laid-back, not to say chilled-out, atmosphere, try this hippie-ish tea house at the quieter end of Malasaña. In its expansive rooms you'll find carpets, cushions, armchairs and mellow music.

Embassy

Paseo de la Castellana 12, entrance C/Ayala 2 (91 576 00 80). Metro Colón/bus all routes to Plaza de Colón. **Open** *Sept-June* 9am-1am Mon-Sat, 9am-11pm Sun. *July, Aug* 9am-1am Mon-Sat; closed Sun. **Credit** AmEx, MC, V. **Map** p306 I2.
For a real traditional English tea, such as the English are supposed to enjoy, this 1930s tearoom is the place to come. Popular with prosperous Salamanca residents, especially store-cruising ladies, it has dozens of teas, and even little diamond-shaped cucumber sandwiches (plus cocktails, for when that hour comes around). It has an additional entrance at Calle Ayala 12.

Gelato Frullati

Avda Felipe II 8, Salamanca & the Retiro (91 577 09 52). Metro Goya/bus 15, 26, 29, 52, 53. **Open** 1am-1pm daily. **No credit cards.**
A genuine Italian *gelatería*, opened in 1999, Frulati has upwards of 20 fabulous flavours to take away or eat sitting outside after flexing your credit card in Salamanca. A small range of cakes and coffees is served too.

Viena Capellanes

C/Marqués de Urquijo 17, Argüelles (91 559 51 90). Metro Argüelles/bus 1, 21, 74, 44, 133, C. **Open** 8.30am-9pm daily. **No credit cards. Map** p304 C3.
The Viena chain of cake and pastry shops is scattered throughout Madrid, but this branch near Paseo Rosales has counter and table service for on-the-spot sampling of its delicious snacks and coffee. For addresses of other branches, pick up a napkin while you're here.
Branches: throughout the city.

Eat, Drink, Shop

Style in tiles

Not that long ago, tiled walls were pretty much standard decor for cheaper *tabernas* in Madrid, outside and in. Before the days of easily washable paint, they were a cheap, colourful and hygienic option for bar-owners (as well as pharmacists, butchers, poultry shops and barbers, among others). The best tile jobs were specially hand-painted, and became a genre of their own, frequently depicting scenes of local life, usually in Madrid or the owner's *pueblo* of origin, with many-coloured flourishes that are classics of lushly traditional Spanishness. Others used ready-made designs, strikingly based on old Andalusian-Moorish styles. With the advent of running water came another easy-to-clean addition – the zinc bar top – that became a standard of the Madrileño bar. Many of these bars have now disappeared, but a good handful, every one different, remain. Also possessed of fine tiles is **La Taberna de Antonio Sánchez** (see page 140).

El Anciano

C/Bailén 19, Austrias (91 559 53 32). Metro Opera/bus 3, 25, 39, 148. **Open** 10am-3pm, 5-11pm Mon, Tue, Thur-Sue. Closed Wed & Aug. **No credit cards. Map** p308 C8.
Dating back to the 1900s, this bar by the Calle Bailén viaduct was originally a sister to As de los Vinos (formerly also called El Anciano, see page 136). Kept much as it was 50 years ago – very simple – it serves good tapas, and is a great place for a drink after visiting the Palacio Real.

Angel Sierra

C/Gravina 11, Chueca (91 531 01 26). Metro Chueca/bus 3, 40, 149. **Open** noon-1.30am daily. **No credit cards. Map** p306 G5.

An archetypal old *taberna*, looking onto the Plaza de Chueca, with all the right tiled walls, zinc bar top, overflowing sink and glasses stacked on wooden slats. Yellow-ish brown paintings and a fresco on the ceiling complete the look. One thing no longer so traditional is the (often overflowing) clientele, which, with all the changes in Chueca, is now positively trendy.

Bodega de la Ardosa

C/Colón 13, Malasaña & Conde Duque (91 521 49 79). Metro Tribunal/bus 3, 40, 149. **Open** 11.30am-3.30pm, 6.30pm-12.30am daily. **No credit cards. Map** p305 F5.
The tiled *taberna* meets the Irish theme bar: the decor of this bar combines Spanish tiles and Goya with posters from Irish pubs, and it was one of the first in Madrid to serve Guinness. There's also a fine choice of other beers.

Casa Camacho

C/San Andrés 21, Malasaña & Conde Duque (91 531 35 98). Metro Tribunal/bus 3, 40, 149. **Open** 10.30am-midnight daily. **No credit cards. Map** p305 F4.
This family-run *bodega* opened in 1928 and, right in the centre of Malasaña, is a popular meet-up point for locals, foreigners and big groups of all ages. With vermouth and beers on tap, snacks and cheap wine and spirits, Camacho's serves most needs of passers-by. Going for a pee is an experience, and requires some agility – you duck under the bar and slip through a doorway at the back.

La Dolores

Plaza de Jesús 4, Huertas & Santa Ana (91 429 22 43). Metro Antón Martín/bus 6, 26

always meet the criteria) and gives support to various independent aid organisations. Coffees with alcohol, cocktails, beers and light snacks also feature. The (not very loud) speakers give out a mixture of world music, flamenco and jazz, and there's a small stage at the back for story-telling and other performances.

Paseo de Recoletos

Café Gijón

Paseo de Recoletos 21 (91 521 54 25).
Metro Banco de España/bus all routes to Cibeles.
Open 7am-2am daily.
Credit AmEx, DC, MC, V. **Map** p310 H6.

Madrid's definitive literary café, open since 1888. Despite Hemingway's view that the clientele were all snobs, it maintains its literary connections with an annual short story prize, and has tried to keep the *tertulia* tradition (*see p20*) alive with rather formalised gatherings of writers, film makers, bullfighters and so on. And, overall, it still retains far more than most the atmosphere of Madrid's great cafés of yore. Get a window seat if you possibly can, or stand at the bar, which as well as the literati attracts an in-off-the-street crowd of concierges and office workers from nearby. There's a decent-value set lunch menu; outside, the Gijón also has an equally classic, if pricey, summer terrace (from March to November only).

32, 57. **Open** 11am-1am Mon-Thur, Sun;
11am-2am Fri, Sat. **Credit** MC, V.
Map p310 G8
Dating back to the 1920s, this enormously
popular Huertas bar is very well placed for
the big museums, and draws a clientele
divided mainly between the overspill from
the district's night-haunts at weekends and
bustling bunches of local office workers
during the week. The tapas are tasty and
tempting, if a tad expensive.

Los Gabrieles
*C/Echegaray 17, Huertas & Santa Ana
(91 429 62 61). Metro Sevilla or Sol/bus
all routes to Puerta del Sol.* **Open** 1pm-
2.30am Mon-Thur, Sun; 1pm-3.30am Fri,
Sat. **No credit cards. Map** p309 F8.
Perhaps the most impressive of all the bar
tiles in Madrid, and the most famous. Until the
'70s Los Gabrieles was a brothel, run by
gypsies, with rooms in the now-inaccessible
cellar. It then became a bar, and in the *Movida*
years attracted all the city's beautiful and
famous. Now, you're more likely to find a mass
of 20-somethings, local and *guiri* (for this vital
term, see p225). It also hosts flamenco nights
on Tuesdays (see chapter **Flamenco**).

Oliveros
*C/San Millán 4, La Latina (91 354 62 52).
Metro La Latina or Tirso de Molina/bus 17,
26, 60.* **Open** noon-1.30am Tue-Thur; noon-
2am Fri, Sat; 11am-1.30am Sun.
No credit cards. Map p309 D9.
One of Madrid's oldest taverns, Oliveros
opened its doors in 1857, but stood empty
for years until 1999. Now opened anew
by Julio Oliveros, great-grandson of the
Oliveros whose name is above the door,

it has wonderful old tiles, a zinc bar, an
original soda machine on the wall, and a
dining room offering *cocina madrileña*.

Taberna Gerardo
*C/Calatrava 21, La Latina (91 365 36 46).
Metro Puerta de Toledo/bus all routes to
Puerta de Toledo.* **Open** noon-4pm, 7.30-
11.30pm Mon-Sat; noon-4pm Sun.
No credit cards. Map p308 C9.
This old La Latina bar is a place to be during
La Paloma in August (see chapter **By Season**),
but at other times it's still an essential part of
the *barrio*, with excellent sausage, ham and
cheese, fine seafood and chilled vermouth.

Viva Madrid
*C/Manuel Fernández y González 7, Huertas &
Santa Ana (91 429 36 40). Metro Sevilla or
Sol/bus all routes to Puerta del Sol.* **Open**
1pm-2am Mon-Thur, Sun; 1pm-3am Fri, Sat.
No credit cards. Map p309 F8.
The eternal rival, and near-neighbour, of Los
Gabrieles, this is another of Madrid's best-
known bars, and a favourite with visitors
and residents. It's a little expensive, but
worth it for the interior, with a vaulted ceiling,
whirring fans, beams and and fabulous tiles
of Madrid scenes from the 1900s. A classic
place to enjoy its daytime tranquillity, start
off a bar crawl or to come along later, when
it truly starts to buzz.

El Espejo
*Paseo de Recoletos 31 (91 319 11 22).
Metro Colón/bus all routes to Plaza de Colón.*
Open 9am-2am Mon-Fri; 10.30am-2am Sat, Sun.
Credit AmEx, DC, MC, V. **Map** p310 H6.
Not nearly so historic as the Gijón, although it may
look it: opened in 1978, 'The Mirror' set out to be
the art nouveau bar Madrid never had, with
positively Parisian 1900s decor. Its terrace bar on
the Paseo occupies a splendid glass pavilion
reminiscent of a giant Tiffany lamp. Fashionable
and comfortable, it has excellent tapas at reasonable
prices, particularly the *croquetas* and *tortilla*, and
the outside tables (from May to October) are a great
vantage point on city life.

Malasaña & Conde Duque

A little less grungy than in former times, these
areas boast fine cafés, old-style taverns, cool
hang-outs and rowdier bars.

Bar El 2 De
*C/Velarde 24 (91 446 55 16). Metro Tribunal/bus 3,
40, 149.* **Open** 1pm-2am Mon-Wed, Sun; 1pm-3am
Thur-Sat. **No credit cards. Map** p305 F4.
In a former haberdasher's shop on Plaza Dos de
Mayo, the 2 De has a nicely tiled bar and engraved
mirrors, smoke-stained buff walls and overhead
fans, all of which serve to attract a crowd of
Malasaña diehards all year round. To drink there's

Eat, Drink, Shop

everyday 10-3

marques de valdeiglesias 6
tel: 91 5326099
fax: 91 5319215

madrid - spain

CAMP

bar - restaurant - dance

vermouth, lager and Beamish Irish Stout on tap, plus plenty of bottled beers and a small range of wines and canapés. Music tends to be rock, blues and R&B.

Café Comercial
Glorieta de Bilbao 7 (91 521 56 55).
Metro Bilbao/bus 3, 21, 40, 147, 149.
Open 8am-1am Mon-Thur, Sun; 8am-2am Fri, Sat.
No credit cards. Map p305 F3.
A true grand café, a great institution, and one of the city's ever-popular meeting points. With heavy wooden tables and leather-lined seats, the mirrored interior of the century-old Comercial attracts all kinds of people, from huddled bunches of students and would be literary types to elderly local residents who have been taking breakfast there since before

the Civil War. Just bring a newspaper, and settle in. To show the Comercial is in keeping with the times, the previously little-used upstairs room has been turned into a cybercafé (*see p280*). There are a few outdoor tables in front from May to October.

Café Isadora
C/Divino Pastor 14 (91 445 71 54).
Metro Bilbao/bus 3, 21, 40, 147, 149.
Open 4pm-2am Mon-Thur, Sun; 4pm-2.30am Fri, Sat. **No credit cards. Map** p305 F4.
Books and old prints line the walls, giving this Malasaña café a relaxed, literary feel. The collection of Patxaráns (*see p157* **House rules**), many individually made, is worth examining, but the coffees are also excellent if you're not up for a heavy night.

House rules

Behave yourself
The civilised tradition that you only pay when you are ready to leave is still the norm in bars in Spain, and rarely abused. Spaniards commonly respect queues and wait their turn, and you can get a waiter's ear with a brisk *oiga* (literally, 'hear me', a perfectly polite way of attracting someone's attention). Madrileños often get their drinks down quickly; added to the fact that in the centre there are entire streets given over to bars, this means that at night people often move from place to place, have one drink and sample whatever the bar's speciality might be and then move on. Settling in to one place is something that's often only done when you can sit down, as at an outdoor *terraza*. Tipping is discretionary. Change is usually returned in a small dish, and in bars people generally leave just a few coins, regardless of the amount spent. Also, in neighbourhood bars, olive pits, toothpicks, paper napkins (*servilletas*) and other disposables are customarily thrown on the floor.

Coffee & tea
For breakfast, most people have a *café con leche*, a largish, milky coffee, which at that time of day comes in a cup. At later times it will often be smaller and served in a glass, and if you want a cup you should ask for a *taza grande*. A plain black espresso is a *café solo*; the same with a dash of milk is *un cortado*, while *un americano* is a *solo* diluted with twice the normal amount of water. With a shot of alcohol, a solo becomes a *carajillo*. A true Madrileño carajillo is made with coffee, sugar, some coffee beans and brandy in a glass (*un carajillo de coñac*), which is then

set alight on top so that the mixture gets mulled a little; a *carajillo* can also be just a *solo* with a shot of *coñac*, and you can equally ask for a *carajillo de whisky, de ron* (rum), *de anís* (aniseed spirit) or anything else you fancy. Also popular are Irish coffees (*café irlandés*) and a variety of other mulled spirit-and-cream combinations, labelled generically *cafés especiales*. Decaffeinated coffee is *descafeinado*.

The quality of coffee in bars varies hugely. It tends to arrive at medium temperature, so if you want it really hot you should remind the waiter *que esté bien caliente, por favor*. In summer a great café alternative is *café con hielo* – iced coffee. Tea in bars is usually awful, as most places have little idea how to prepare it. Very popular, however, are herb teas, *infusiones*, such as *menta* (mint) or *manzanilla* (camomile) and nowadays there are a few more Madrid cafés than there ever used to be – often branches of coffee shop chains – that are at least a little aware of what decent tea might be.

Beer
Wine may be more traditional in Spain, but in quantity *cerveza* has overtaken it as the national drink. Draught beer (*de barril*) is served in *cañas*, a measure that's around ¼litre (ask for *una caña, dos cañas*, and so on), in tall glasses called *tubos*, or in a *doble* (around ½litre). Some places even serve *pintas* (pints), often called *jarras*. Bottled beer usually comes in *tercios* (⅓ litre) or *botellines* (½ litre). Spain produces some good-quality beers. In Madrid, the favourite is the local Mahou, with two basic varieties, green label Mahou *clásica* and the stronger ▶

Café Manuela

C/San Vicente Ferrer 29 (91 531 70 37).
Metro Tribunal/bus 3, 40, 149. **Open** 7pm-2am
daily. **No credit cards. Map** p305 F4.
A Malasaña café that was a hive of activity for
the early-'80s scene, Café Manuela is still going
strong in post-*Movida* times. It's an obligatory
stop-off on the local round, with art nouveau decor,
many kinds of coffee and varying entertainment
throughout the week.

Café de Ruíz

C/Ruiz 11 (91 446 12 32). Metro Bilbao/bus 3, 21,
40, 147, 149. **Open** 2pm-2am Mon-Thur, Sun;
2pm-3am Fri, Sat. **Credit** MC, V.
No credit cards. Map p305 F3.

Dark wood, an amiably old-fashioned feel, coolly
relaxing music – Peggy Lee, Charles Trenet –, exuberant flowers on the bar and ultra-comfortable
seats make the Ruíz a special spot to kill a few hours
or retreat from the night-time grunge. Fine straight
coffees, milkshakes (*batidos*) and elaborately made
carajillos (*see p157* **House rules**) can be consumed
while reading a paper or planning your next move.

La Ida

C/Colón 11 (91 522 91 07). Metro Tribunal/bus 3,
40, 149. **Open** 1pm-1.30am daily. Closed last two
weeks Aug. **No credit cards. Map** p305 F5.
This cool spot on the borders of Malasaña is rather
like someone's living room. Frequented by pierced
and tattooed types from the Mercado Fuencarral

▶ # House rules
(continued)

red label *cinco estrellas*. A darker Mahou
beer (*negra*) is also available. Imported
beers are now common, too, but nearly
always cost more than Spanish brands.

Wines, spirits & other drinks

All bars have a sturdy cheap red (*tinto*) on
offer, and usually a white (*blanco*) and rosé
(*rosado*). A traditional drink of Madrid is
tinto con sifón (red with a splash of soda).
If you fancy a better wine, then most bars
listed here will have at least one decent
Rioja and probably *Cava*, Catalan sparkling
wine, but truly good wines are best sought
after in the new-style *tabernas* that take
pride in their lists (see pages 142-3).
  Sherry is *jerez*. The type virtually always
drunk in Spain is dry fino, served very cold.
A good fuller-bodied variety is *palo cortado*.
Sweet sherries have traditionally been only
for export. Red vermouth (*vermút*) with soda
is another Madrid tradition, usually as an
aperitif, and has recently come back into
fashion a little. For a powerful after-dinner
drink, try Galician *orujo*, a fiery spirit similar
to grappa or schnapps, which comes plain
(*blanco*) or *con hierbas*, with a luminous green
colour. Other *digestivos* include Patxarán, a
fruity aniseed-flavoured liqueur from Navarra,
and the more Castilian *anís*, the best of
which hails from Chinchón (*see page 258*)
and is available dry (*seco*) or sweet (*dulce*).

Non-alcoholic drinks

Low- and alcohol-free beers (Laiker, Buckler,
Kaliber) have an important niche in the
market, and other favourites for non-alcohol
drinkers are the Campari-like but booze-free
Bitter Kas, and plain tonic (*una tónica*), with

ice and lemon. Fresh orange juice, *zumo
de naranja*, is often available, but strangely
expensive in a country with so many oranges.
Trinaranjus is the best-known bottled juice
brand; favourite flavours are orange,
pineapple (*piña*) and peach (*melocotón*).
Mosto is grape juice, served in small glasses,
sometimes with ice and a slice. A great and
unappreciated Spanish speciality, though,
are its traditional summer refreshers: most
unusual is *horchata*, a milky drink made by
crushing a root called a *chufa*. It has to be
drunk fresh, from a specialised shop, as
it curdles once made. The same places
also offer *granizados* – crushed ice with
fresh lemon, orange or coffee – which when
properly made are fabulous. Mineral water
(*agua mineral*) can be ordered anywhere,
either fizzy (*con gas*) or still (*sin gas*).

Food

At any time of day, you can accompany
your coffee or drink with something to eat.
For breakfast, many places have *churros*
or *porras*, sweet deep-fried sticks of batter,
or fresh pastries such as croissants,
napolitanas (soft, glazed pastries filled with
chocolate or egg custard), *sobaos* (a buttery
sponge) or *madalenas* (sponge cakes). For
more on bar food, *see chapter* **Tapas**.

Tobacco

A cigarette is still an automatic
accompaniment to a drink for a majority
of Spaniards. In bars, cigarettes (*cigarros*)
are sold in machines. Spaniards differentiate
between black tobacco (*tabaco negro*) and
international-style light tobacco (*rubio*). If
you want to pass for a native, try Ducados
or their stronger brothers Habanos, full-
flavoured black tobacco. Popular Spanish
rubio brands are Fortuna, LM and Nobel.

A cool customer at **Bar El 2 De**. *See p155.*

around the corner (*see p169*), La Ida serves beer by the hectolitre, wine, tea, coffee and toasted canapés. The music – lots of jazz, a bit of everything – is mellow and doesn't spoil conversation. It gets livelier at night, when the punters spill out onto the pavement.

El Maño
C/Jesús del Valle 1 (91 531 36 85). Metro Noviciado/bus 147. **Open** 8pm-1.30am Mon-Sat; 12.30-4pm Sun. **No credit cards. Map** p305 E4.
For years this bodega was a pleasant, scruffyish place serving cheap wine, beer and simple tapas to a local clientele. More recently, as this side of town has gone a little upmarket, El Maño has had a lick of paint and diversified its fare, and now frequently gets packed. House wine is just over 125ptas a glass, and there are varieties from all over Spain for 150-300ptas. Tapas worth trying are the own-made pâté and the platter of *ahumados* (smoked fish). There are no outside tables, but the wide doors open right onto the street.

Mendocino Café
C/Limón 11 (91 542 91 30). Metro Noviciado/bus 147. **Open** 4pm-midnight Tue-Thur; 4pm-2am Fri; noon-2am Sat; noon-midnight Sun. Closed Aug. **No credit cards. Map** p305 D4.
An extremely relaxing café just around the corner from the Centro Conde Duque, the Mendocino is great for conversation, playing board games (in English or Spanish) or just sitting down to read. Tastefully done in blue, with discreet lighting and non-intrusive music, the café serves snacks, salads, soups and brunch at weekends, and also holds poetry readings from time to time.

El Parnasillo
C/San Andrés 33 (91 447 00 79). Metro Bilbao/bus 3, 21, 40, 147, 149. **Open** 3.30pm-3am Mon-Thur, Sun; 3.30pm-3.30am Fri, Sat. **No credit cards. Map** p305 F3.
A smart café with a relaxed atmosphere, pleasant, almost classical decor and a full range of alcohol-boosted coffees and cocktails, especially *mojitos* and *caipirinhas*. Long frequented by writers, artists, journalists and intellectuals, El Parnasillo was very much at the centre of Madrid's 1970s-'80s cultural renewal, to the point that it was bombed by a far-right group. Don't panic, though – there's little danger of that happening now.

El Pez Gordo
C/del Pez 6 (91 522 32 08). Metro Callao or Noviciado/bus 147 & all routes to Callao. **Open** *June-Aug* 8pm-1.30am Tue-Fri; 1pm-1.30am Sat, Sun; closed Mon. *Sept-May* 8pm-1.30am Tue-Fri; 1pm-1.30am Sat, Sun; closed Mon. **No credit cards. Map** p305 E5.
A simply decorated, friendly bar with nice snacks, the 'Fat Fish' is regularly busy thanks to its good wines, well-served beer and laid-back atmosphere. Try the *migas* (fried breadcrumbs) or the gutsy *empanadas* from León, with a glass of red – fabulous. Film and theatre posters, many from the Alfil fringe theatre down the road, adorn the walls.

Salamanca & the Retiro

Balmoral
C/Hermosilla 10 (91 431 41 33). Metro Serrano/bus 1, 9, 21, 53, 74. **Open** 12.30-3pm, 7pm-2am Mon-Sat; closed Sun. **Credit** AmEx, DC, MC, V. **Map** p307 I4.
The Balmoral keeps itself to itself. Behind a slightly daunting exterior you will find not only a bizarre Scottish theme (tartan carpet, the Monarch of the Glen, hunting prints), but a clientele ranging from crusty older locals to bikers. Excellent cocktails and impeccable service, too, even if prices are a bit steep.

El Botánico
C/Ruiz de Alarcón 27 (91 420 23 42). Metro Banco de España/bus all routes to Plaza de Cibeles. **Open** 8am-11pm daily. **No credit cards. Map** p310 H8.
A world away from the tourist trail around the Prado, which it sits directly behind (you can see the museum and the Jardín Botánico from its outside tables), the Botánico is a calm, smart, roomy café.

Café del Arte
C/Alcalá 113 (91 576 6361). Metro Príncipe de Vergara or Retiro/bus 15, 29, 52, 146. **Open** 7.30am-11.30pm Mon-Thur; 9am-2am Fri, Sat; 9am-11.30am Sun. **Credit** MC, V. **Map** p307 K5.
A good stop-off after a hectic afternoon's shopping in Salamanca, with (partial) views of the Retiro. Regular art exhibitions complement the café design.

Café y Té
C/Goya 18 (91 578 29 67).
Metro Velázquez/bus 1, 21, 53, 74. **Open** 6am-1.15am Mon-Thur, Sun; 6am-4am Fri, Sat. **Credit** AmEx, DC, MC, V. **Map** p307 J4.
A very American-looking café chain that started out in Barcelona. The design, with a half-on-the-street, half-inside feel, makes it very much a quick stop-off, but a fine range of coffees and attentive service from uniformed waiters are temptations to stay on a bit longer and relax.

Eat, Drink, Shop

Shops & Services

Mega-malls to tiny corner shops, chic clubwear and high fashion to traditional Spanish tack: the shops and markets of Madrid offer a near-limitless variety.

Ever since the 1980s, middle-class Madrileños have taken to shopping as a leisure activity with gusto. Years ago buying anything was more of a parochial, low-key affair, but economic booms and the middle-class move to the suburbs have changed things enormously, as out-of-town malls pop up like mushrooms.

In Madrid's old centre, meanwhile, shopping has become far more diverse. Fears that the new big fish would gobble up the little ones are not without foundation, but in among all the big new international stores there are still plenty of enterprising individuals running small, idiosyncratic shops. All manner of services are offered by the malls, but they still compete with traditional specialists. This diversity in era and style is one of the great features of Madrid.

THE SHOPPING MAP

The area around **Calle Preciados**, between Sol and Gran Vía, is still considered by most Madrileños to be the city's shopping heart, with branches of many big stores. To the south, the streets of **Los Austrias** and the Plaza Mayor have many individual, traditional or eccentric shops, with good spots for souvenir-buying.

East of the centre, well-heeled **Salamanca** is also Madrid's smartest shopping zone, with the major names in Spanish and international fashion, and antique galleries, design stores, fine food shops and more. There are more designer outlets in **Chueca**, which also has many hip, gay-oriented shops (*see page 212*). These spill over onto **Calle Fuencarral**, the 'border' of Malasaña, and the main drag for street and club fashion (*see page 169*), thanks above all to the very trendy Mercado Fuencarral. **Malasaña** has art, design and gift shops, and another small cluster of one-off shops is in **Lavapiés**, near the Reina Sofía. A very different experience can be had at the **Rastro** (*see page 179*), the Sunday flea market.

THE SUNDAY OPENING DRAMA

Traditionally the only shops allowed to open on Sundays in Madrid were bakeries, *pastelerías* (cake shops) and shops around the Rastro. Since the 1980s demands have arisen from big retailers for them to be permitted to trade on Sundays as well, but this has met with fierce opposition from small traders, fearful of being unable to compete unless they abandon their

one day off. A mid-'90s 'truce' allowed 'large spaces' (big stores and malls) to open on eight Sundays (usually including all four prior to Christmas) and four other holidays each year. Shops selling 'cultural goods' (books, CDs, videos) can also open every Sunday.

In mid-2000, however, a new Sunday trading law was introduced that permits small and medium-sized businesses to open for up to 12 hours on any Sunday. How this will work out in practice is still to be seen, but it may mean that **in future some shops listed in this chapter as being closed on a Sunday may open for at least part of the day**. The law may also be further revised once again.

SALES & TAX REFUNDS

Sales normally run through January, February, July and August. The rate of value-added tax (IVA) depends on the product – seven per cent on most things, 16 per cent on some classed as luxuries. In many stores non-EU residents can request a tax-free cheque on purchases of over 15,000ptas, which can be cashed at the airport on departure to reclaim VAT. Shops in the scheme have a 'Tax-Free' sticker on the door.

One-stop shops

El Corte Inglés

C/Preciados 1-4, Sol & Gran Vía (phone for all branches 91 418 88 00/Tel-entradas ticket phoneline 902 40 02 22/www.elcorteingles.com). Metro Sol/bus all routes to Puerta del Sol. **Open** 10am-9.30pm Mon-Sat; 11am-9pm first Sun of every month except Aug. **Credit** AmEx, DC, MC, V. **Map** p309 E7.

A Spanish institution if ever there was one, this retailing giant has long been the most complete department store in the country. There are 19 outlets in Madrid alone, between stores and out-of-town hypermarkets (called **Hipercor**). They provide a comprehensive range of goods and services, from key-cutting and shoe repair to furniture and holidays, and now offer online shopping and home delivery as well. Most branches have good supermarkets, and information points with multilingual staff.

Several branches now specialise: Castellana 85 has things for children, toys, sports and computers and IT; C/Serrano 47 mainly has fashion, jewellery and cosmetics; and C/Princesa 42 has gourmet food counters and a superior café. This Preciados branch, C/Fuencarral 118 and C/Goya 76 sell books, CDs, videos and so on, and so can open every Sunday (*see p160*). Also, the Corte Inglés has a ticket phoneline for booking seats at some events (*see p171*). **Branches**: throughout the city.

Fnac

C/Preciados 28, Sol & Gran Vía (91 595 61 00). *Metro Callao/bus 44, 75, 133, 146, 147.* **Open** 10am-9.30pm Mon-Sat; noon-9.30pm Sun, public holidays. **Credit** AmEx, MC, V. **Map** p309 E7.

Not a complete one-stop shop, but this huge French-owned emporium has an enormous range of books, CDs (excellent for World Music), videos, magazines, Spanish and foreign press, computers and software, mostly at discount prices and displayed in a convenient, ultra-modern fashion. There are some books in English and French, and a very handy desk selling concert and theatre tickets (with no commission). It also hosts readings and other cultural events.

Marks & Spencer

C/Serrano 52, Salamanca (91 520 00 00). *Metro Serrano/bus 1, 9, 19, 51, 74.* **Open** 10am-9pm Mon-Sat; closed Sun. **Credit** MC, V. **Map** p307 J2.

M&S is well established in Madrid, and successful with Spaniards as well as British residents and visitors, who will be pleased to know that store cards and vouchers from back home can be used here. The overvalued pound has made M&S expensive of late. **Branch**: Centro La Vaguada (91 730 38 74).

Smart Salamanca's **ABC Serrano** mall.

Tienda de Regalos – Todo a 100

C/Fuencarral 22, Chueca (no phone). Metro Gran Vía/bus 3, 40, 149. **Open** 9.30am-9pm Mon-Sat; closed Sun. **No credit cards**. **Map** p309 E6.

The *Todo a 100* is an ever-spreading phenomenon of modern Madrid. Often owned and run by Chinese immigrants, and with impossible-to-miss signs announcing *Todo a 100ptas, 500, 1,000*, they have, yes, all their stock at fixed, low prices: generally a wild variety that runs from weird and wonderful kitsch ornaments to more practical items such as stationery, cosmetics and children's toys. They can also be great standbys for cheap kitchenware, openers and so on. This one is central; there are others in every part of town.

After-hours

Useful for finding things out-of-hours are the many Chinese-run all-purpose stores that have proliferated all over central Madrid in recent times. For 24-hour pharmacies, *see page 284*.

7-11

C/Arenal 9, Los Austrias (no phone). *Metro Opera/bus 3, 148.* **Open** 24hrs daily. **No credit cards**. **Map** p309 D7.

General stores for non-sleepers. Many 7-11 shops are attached to petrol stations.

Vip's

Gran Vía 43, Sol & Gran Vía (91 559 66 21). *Metro Callao or Santo Domingo/bus 1, 44, 74, 133, 148.* **Open** 9am-3am daily. **Credit** AmEx, DC, MC, V. **Map** p309 D6.

The most central branch of the Vip's chain, which has others all over town. These multi-purpose emporia are bland but handy, offering things you might need late at night or on a Sunday afternoon: restaurants (usually with a pizzería and a kids' menu), cafés, supermarkets (pricey), books, cosmetics, CDs, toys, film processing and newsstands. Central branches include Calle Serrano 41, Calle Velázquez 84 & 136 and Calle Fuencarral 101.

Centros comerciales/malls

There are many more big malls in the suburbs around Madrid's edge, mainly reachable by car.

ABC Serrano

C/Serrano 61 & Paseo de la Castellana 64, Salamanca (91 577 50 31). Metro Rubén Darío/bus 5, 9, 14, 27, 51. **Open** 10am-9.30pm Mon-Sat; closed Sun. **Map** p307 J2.

A chic Salamanca mall inside the neo-*mudéjar* building that once housed the ABC newspaper. Inside it has five levels of fashion, design, gift and craft shops, plus cafés and restaurants. Its rooftop summer terrace bar, also called ABC Serrano (open till late), is popular with a well-heeled crowd. There are also loads of parking spaces.

Eat, Drink, Shop

Centro Comercial La Vaguada (Madrid 2)

Avda Monforte de Lemos 36, Barrio del Pilar (information 91 730 10 00). Metro Barrio del Pilar/bus 49, 83, 128, 132. **Open** 10am-10pm daily; *leisure area only* 10am-3am Mon-Sat; closed Sun.

The biggest mall more-or-less within Madrid – some 350 outlets, a **Corte Inglés** (*see p160*), plus an entertainments floor (cinemas, a disco, a bowling alley, a mini-fairground). A drawback is its location – a long way from the centre – but it has a fast Metro link.

El Jardín de Serrano

C/Goya 6-8, Salamanca (91 577 00 12). Metro Serrano/bus 9, 19, 21, 51, 53. **Open** 10am-10pm Mon-Sat; closed Sun. **Map** p307 J4.

A small but ultra-chic mall. The 20 or so shops mainly offer high-fashion clothes and accessories.

Antiques

The clusters of antiques shops, galleries and *almonedas* (auction houses which also sell in the normal fashion) around the Rastro cover the spectrum from junk to genuine antiques, with some shops specialising in particular eras or styles. Calle del Prado in Huertas also houses a smattering of antique shops, but truly opulent antiques will be found in Salamanca, where Calle Claudio Coello has many prestigious shops.

Galerías Piquer

C/Ribera de Curtidores 29, Rastro (no phone). Metro Puerta de Toledo/bus 3, 17, 23, 35, C. **Open** 10.30am-2pm, 5-8pm Mon-Fri; 10.30am-2pm Sat, Sun. **Map** p309 D9

Twenty different antique shops in one space in the Rastro, and great for browsing. Opening times may be different for the various shops.

Nuevas Galerías

C/Ribera de Curtidores 12, Rastro (no phone). Metro La Latina/bus 17, 18, 23, 35. **Open** 9am-2pm, 5-8pm Mon-Sat; 9am-2pm Sun. **Map** p309 D9

There are 11 different antique shops in this Rastro arcade. Opening times may differ from shop to shop.

Books

Fnac (*see page 161*) has an excellent general selection. A traditional centre of the book trade is **Calle de los Libreros** ('Booksellers' Street') off Gran Vía, with many specialist bookshops.

La Casa del Libro Espasa Calpe

Gran Vía 29, Sol & Gran Vía (91 521 21 13). Metro Gran Vía/bus all routes to Gran Vía. **Open** 9.30am-9.30pm Mon-Sat; closed Sun. **Credit** AmEx, DC, MC, V. **Map** p309 E6.

Madrid's most comprehensive bookshop, this five-storey monster – part of a publishing house – has good English and English-teaching sections. **Branch**: C/Maestro Victoria 3 (91 521 48 98).

Crisol

C/Juan Bravo 38, Salamanca (91 423 82 80). Metro Diego de León/bus 26, 29, 52, 61, C. **Open** 10am-10pm Mon-Sat; 11am-3pm, 5-9pm Sun, public holidays. **Credit** AmEx, DC, MC, V. **Map** p307 K2.

A major bookshop chain with a bit of everything. There are good English-language, press, music and stationery sections, and a ticket desk. There's a branch in the **Círculo de Bellas Artes** (*see p73*). **Branches**: throughout the city.

Librería de Mujeres

C/San Cristobal 17, Austrias (91 521 70 43). Metro Sol/bus all routes to Puerta del Sol. **Open** 10am-2pm, 5-8pm Mon-Fri; 10am-2pm Sat; closed Sun. **Credit** V. **Map** P309 D7.

The only specialised women's bookshop in Madrid, with its own publishing house, *Horas y Horas*.

La Tienda de Madrid

Museo Municipal, C/Fuencarral 78, Malasaña & Conde Duque (91 531 16 44). Metro Tribunal/bus 3, 37, 40, 149. **Open** *Sept-June* 10am-2pm, 4.30-8pm Mon-Fri; 10am-2pm Sat, Sun. *Mid July-mid Sept* 10am-2pm daily. **No credit cards**. **Map** p305 F4.

This shop in the Museo Municipal is ideal for readers interested in any aspect of Madrid's history, architecture and culture. Virtually all the books are in Spanish, but many are beautifully illustrated. There's also an original range of souvenirs, all related in some way to Madrid.

English-language books

Booksellers

C/José Abascal 48, Chamberí (91 442 79 59). Metro Alonso Cano/bus 3, 12, 37, 149. **Open** 9.30am-2pm, 5-8pm Mon-Fri; 10am-2pm Sat; closed Sun. **Credit** AmEx, DC, V.

As well as a full range of English-language literature, press from both sides of the Atlantic and everything an English teacher might need, Booksellers has a fine children's section and a range of videos in English. There's also a useful noticeboard.

The International Bookshop

C/Campomanes 13, Sol & Gran Vía (91 541 72 91). Metro Opera or Santo Domingo/bus 3, 25, 39, 510. **Open** 11am-2.30pm, 4.30-8.30pm Mon-Fri; 11am-2.30pm, 4.30-7.30pm Sat; closed Sun. **No credit cards**. **Map** p309 D7.

This popular, mainly second-hand shop buys and sells books in English, French, German, Italian, Portuguese and Spanish. Included are classics, bestsellers, travel guides, biographies, poetry, drama, history and sport. There's also a noticeboard advertising rooms to let, language classes and other services, mostly offered by or for resident foreigners.

Pasajes

C/Génova 3, Chueca (91 310 12 45/ pasajes@infornet.es). Metro Alonso Martínez/bus 3, 7, 21. **Open** 10am-2pm, 5-8pm Mon-Fri; 10am-2pm Sat; closed Sun. **Credit** MC, V. **Map** p306 H4.

A pleasant, well-lit bookshop with material in English, French, German and Spanish, plus some books in Italian and Portuguese: fiction, general non-fiction, children's books, language learning materials, maps, audio books and videos.

Second-hand & rare

Bookshops dealing in rare and antique books are concentrated around Calle Huertas. A great place to find cheap second-hand books is the **Cuesta de Moyano**, on Calle Claudio Moyano, by the Jardín Botánico (**Map** p310 H9). It has a line of kiosks selling second-hand books, from rare editions to remainders. There are some that are open all week, but they're busiest on Sunday mornings.

Librería del Prado

C/del Prado 5, Huertas & Santa Ana (91 429 60 91). Metro Antón Martín/bus 6, 26, 32. **Open** 10am-2pm, 5-8pm Mon-Fri; 10am-2pm Sat; closed Sun. **Credit** AmEx, MC, V. **Map** p309 F8.
Books from the 18th and 19th centuries, plus manuscripts, postcards and the like. Prices are reasonable.

Travel & maps

Perseo

C/Fernández de los Ríos 95, Moncloa (91 549 31 07). Metro Moncloa/bus all routes to Moncloa. **Open** 9.30am-2pm, 4.30-8.30pm Mon-Fri; 10am-2pm Sat; closed Sun. **Credit** MC, V. **Map** p304 C1.
For maps and travel guides to Spain.

Desnivel

Plaza Matute 6, Huertas & Santa Ana (91 429 97 40/www.libreriadesnivel.com). Metro Antón Martín/bus 6, 26, 32. **Open** 10am-1.30pm, 4-8pm Mon-Sat; closed Sun. **Credit** AmEx, MC. V. **Map** p309 F8.
An excellent, centrally located travel and adventure bookshop with a comprehensive stock of maps and books on every part of Spain and further afield. Desnivel publishes its own walking and climbing-guides – particularly good on the Madrid region and the Sierras – and is a good place to get information about organised walks, hikes and so on.

La Tienda Verde

C/Maudes 23 & 38, Cuatro Caminos (91 534 32 57). Metro Cuatro Caminos/bus all routes to Cuatro Caminos. **Open** 9.30am-2pm, 4.30-8.30pm Mon-Fri; 9.30am-2pm, 5-8pm Sat; closed Sun. **Credit** AmEx, DC, V.
Madrid's best general travel book and map shops.

Children

Clothes

Adult chains such as **Zara** (*see page 169*) also have imaginative children's lines.

C&A

C/Conde de Peñalver 8, Salamanca (91 576 48 51). Metro Goya/bus 21, 26, 53, 61. **Open** Sept-July 10am-9pm Mon-Sat; closed Sun. *Aug* 10am-1.30pm, 5.30-9pm Mon-Sat; closed Sun. **Credit** AmEx, MC, V. **Map** p307 L4.
Still going strong in Spain, C&A offer perhaps the best deals in kids' clothes and shoes in town, with exceptional bargains during sales.
Branch: C/Bravo Murillo 8, Tetuán (91 570 32 02).

Max Kinder

C/Carretas 19, Austrias (91 522 80 50). Metro Sol/bus all routes to Puerta del Sol. **Open** 10am-8.30pm Mon-Sat; closed Sun. **Credit** MC, V. **Map** p309 E8.
The kiddies' version of fashion store Max Moda (opposite at no.8) has a good, well-priced range of trendy wear for kids from three months to 16 years.

Prénatal

C/Fuencarral 17, Malasaña & Conde Duque (91 521 64 24). Metro Gran Vía/bus 3, 40, 146, 149. **Open** Sept-mid-June 10am-1.45pm, 5-8pm Mon-Sat; closed Sun. *Mid-June-Sept* 10am-1.45pm, 5-8.30pm Mon-Sat; closed Sun. **Credit** AmEx, DC, MC, V. **Map** p309 E6.
Everything for parents and kids: maternity wear, clothes for kids up to about eight; pushchairs, feeding bottles and toys. Quality stuff, but at a price.
Branches: throughout the city.

Z

C/Bravo Murillo 140, Tetuán (91 534 76 92). Metro Estrecho/bus 43, 66, 124, 127. **Open** mid Sept-mid June 10am-2pm, 5-8.30pm Mon-Sat; closed Sun. *Mid June-mid Sept* 10am-2pm, 5.30-9pm Mon-Sat; closed Sun. **Credit** MC, V.
Colourful, affordable and trendy-ish kiddies' clothes.

Toys

Check out also the Paseo de la Castellana 85 branch of **El Corte Inglés** (*see page 160*).

Bazar Mila

Gran Vía 33, Sol & Gran Vía (91 531 87 28). Metro Callao/bus all routes to Callao. **Open** 9.30am-8.30pm Mon-Sat; closed Sun. **Credit** AmEx, DC, MC, V. **Map** p309 E6.
A traditional toy shop with a window full of giant teddies, train sets, model kits and dolls' houses.

Don Juego

C/Alcalá 113, Salamanca (91 435 37 24). Metro Príncipe de Vergara/bus 15, 52, 146. **Open** 10am-2.30pm, 5-8.30pm Mon-Sat. Closed Sun & last two weeks Aug. **Credit** MC, V. **Map** p307 K5.
A great little shop selling board games and puzzles, among them Ma Jong and solitaire.

Imaginarium

C/Núñez de Balboa 52, Salamanca (91 577 33 55). Metro Núñez de Balboa or Velázquez/bus 1, 21, 74. **Open** 10am-2pm, 5-9pm Mon-Sat; closed Sun. **Credit** AmEx, V. **Map** p307 J3.

Eat, Drink, Shop

A toy shop with a difference – there are no war toys, and the emphasis, as the name suggests, is on educational and interactive games and toys for young children. There are branches in many local malls.

Cleaning & laundry

Truly self-service *lavanderías* (laundrettes) are hard to find: in most there will be an attendant who will assume that customers (especially male ones) want her to do their washing for them, for a small charge, and will often proceed as if this is the case without asking. *Tintorerías* are dry cleaners, but generally offer other clothing care services (including repairs) as well.

Lavandería MC

C/Pelayo 44, Chueca (91 319 48 81). Metro Chueca/bus 3, 40, 149. **Open** 10am-8pm Mon-Sat; closed Sun. **No credit cards. Map** p306 G5.
A friendly launderette, with an attendant. A service wash and dry costs 1,400ptas, an ironing service is also available, and the staff speak some English.

Lavomatique

C/Cervantes 1, Huertas & Santa Ana (no phone). Metro Antón Martín/bus 6, 9, 26, 32. **Open** 9am-8pm Mon-Sat; closed Sun. **No credit cards. Map** p309 F8.
A self-service, coin-operated laundry that charges 500ptas per load. The same family also runs a good dry cleaners nearby, **Tintes Saigón**.
Branch: Tintes Saigón C/León 14 (91 429 49 85).

Tinte Rapi-Seco

C/Gaztambide 35, Malasaña & Conde Duque (91 543 30 32). Metro Moncloa/bus 2, 16, 44, 61, C. **Open** 8.30am-8pm Mon-Fri; 8.30am-2pm Sat; closed Sun. **No credit cards. Map** p304 C1.
A good dry cleaner that gives a discount of 10% if you pay in advance. A suit costs 810ptas.

Design & household

Adamante

C/Raimundo Lulio 5, Chamberí (91 447 61 84). Metro Iglesia/bus 3, 40, 147. **Open** 10.30am-2pm, 5-8.30pm Mon-Sat; closed Sun. **Credit** MC, V. **Map** p306 G2.
A good and very reasonably-priced range of furniture and household objects, including both the functional and the decorative.
Branch: C/Infantas 19 (91 522 58 05).

Aldaba

C/Belén 15, Chueca (91 308 38 33). Metro Chueca/bus 3, 37, 40, 149. **Open** *Sept-June* 10am-2pm, 5-8.30pm Mon-Sat; closed Sun. *July, Aug* 10am-2pm, 6-9pm Mon-Sat; closed Sun. **Credit** MC, V. **Map** p306 H4.
A roomy shop on the trendy side of Chueca, with some fine lamps, household items and ornaments.

Arena

C/Conde de Xiquena 7, Chueca (91 522 75 56). Metro Chueca/bus 37. **Open** 10.30am-2pm, 5-8.30pm Mon-Sat; closed Sun. **Credit** AmEx, DC, MC, V. **Map** p306 H5.

Eat, Drink, Shop

BD Ediciones de Diseño. *See p166.*

Furniture, lamps, clocks and a whole mix of other household goods, hand-made or restored and decorated by designer Begoña Robles. Her style is fun and modern, but not gratuitously wacky or over the top. Her workshop is at the back of the shop.

BD Ediciones de Diseño

C/Villanueva 5, Salamanca (91 435 06 27). Metro Serrano/bus 1, 9, 19, 51, 74. **Open** 9.30am-1.30pm, 4.30-8pm Mon-Fri; 10am-1.30pm Sat. Closed Sun & Aug. **Credit** AmEx, DC, MC, V. **Map** p307 J5.
A high-style design shop much frequented by designers and architects, with furniture and other work by major Spanish designers such as Oscar Tusquets and international names like the Memphis group. Wonderful to look at, and suitably expensive.

Garage Regium

C/Pradillo 5, Prosperidad (91 411 05 99). Metro Concha Espina/bus 16, 29, 52, 122. **Open** *Sept-June* 11am-9pm Tue-Sun; closed Mon. *July, Aug* 11am-9pm Tue-Sat; closed Mon, Sun. **Credit** AmEx, DC, MC, V.
From plastic kitsch to ultra-chic minimalism, this shop/café/restaurant is a showcase for the type of furniture, lighting and accessories that wins design awards, with a focus on items combining functionality with humour, sleek lines and new materials.

La Oca

Ronda de Toledo 1, Rastro (91 366 35 31). Metro Puerta de Toledo/bus all routes to Puerta de Toledo. **Open** 10am-2pm, 5-8.30pm Tue-Fri; 10.30am-2.30pm, 5-8.30pm Sat; 11.30am-3pm Sun; closed Mon. **Credit** AmEx, MC, V.
This designer kitchen and household emporium by the Rastro is part of a failed mall, Mercado Puerta de Toledo, but has survived alone. The range is substantial, and it's a great place for browsing.

PlazAarte

C/Costanilla de los Capuchinos 5, corner C/San Marcos, Chueca (91 522 85 93). Metro Chueca/bus 3, 40, 149. **Open** *Sept-June* 11.30am-3pm, 5.30-9pm Mon-Sat; closed Sun. *July, Aug* 6-9.30pm Mon-Thur; 11.30am-2pm, 6-9.30pm Fri, Sat; closed Sun. **Credit** AmEx, MC, V. **Map** p309 F6.
A trendy Chueca shop specialising in contemporary design items for the home, which also acts as a gallery space for the designers who sell there.

Vinçon

C/Castelló 18, Salamanca (91 578 05 20). Metro Velázquez/bus 21, 29, 52, 53. **Open** 5-8.30pm Mon; 10am-2pm, 5-8.30pm Tue-Sat; closed Sun. **Credit** AmEx, MC, V. **Map** p307 K4.
The Madrid outpost of the classic Barcelona design store, housed in a suitably stylishly renovated old factory that's filled with furniture, home and garden accessories and attractive gift ideas.

Fashion

Designers

If your credit cards are prepared for a major workout, **Salamanca** is littered with designer boutiques. **Calle José Ortega y Gasset** and **Calle Juan Bravo**, in particular, host a string of familiar names such as Versace, Chanel, Kenzo, Calvin Klein, Armani and so on. Home-grown Spanish fashion is enjoying a boom as well, with more and more young designers creating fresh and very wearable designs at pretty accessible prices.

Adolfo Domínguez

C/Ortega y Gasset 4, Salamanca (91 576 00 84). Metro Núñez de Balboa/bus 1, 9, 19, 51, 74. **Open** 10.15am-2pm, 5-8.30pm Mon-Sat; closed Sun. **Credit** AmEx, DC, MC, V. **Map** p307 J3.
Adolfo Domínguez won his fame by bending the rules, and dressing Spanish trendsters and politicians alike in simple, comfortable, original clothes. Recently they've sometimes been a little staid, but he has a younger sports range at competitive prices. **Branches**: throughout the city.

Agatha Ruiz de la Prada

C/Marqués de Riscal 8, Chamberí (91 310 44 83). Metro Rubén Darío/bus 5, 7, 14, 27, 150. **Open** 10am-2pm, 5-8pm Mon-Sat; closed Sun. **Credit** AmEx, MC, V. **Map** p306 I3.
A 'veteran' of the *Movida* scene, Agatha Ruiz creates an off-the-wall brand of couture that features the kind of ultra-bright colours and naif heart and flower motifs more commonly found in children's paintings. She also has a range of accessories.

Movida fashion queen **Sybilla** can still strike exciting notes. *See p168.*

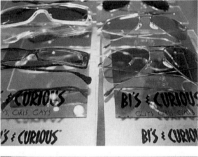

Mitsuoko. *See p169.*

Amaya Arzuaga

C/Lagasca 50, Salamanca (91 310 52 77/
91 319 43 79). Metro Serrano/bus 1, 9, 19, 21, 51,
53. **Open** 10am-9pm Mon-Sat.
Credit AmEx, DC, MC, V. **Map** p307 J4.

An all-new store to showcase rising star Arzuaga's
work. One of the new jewels in Spain's fashion
crown, she has attracted attention around the world
with her sexy, young and innovative designs, using
an exciting mix of fabrics and textures.

Jesús del Pozo

C/Almirante 9, Chueca (91 531 36 46). Metro
Chueca or Colón/bus 3, 37, 40, 149. **Open** *Sept-May*
11am-2pm, 5-8pm Mon-Sat. *June-Aug* 11am-2pm,
5.30-8.30pm Mon-Sat. Closed Sun & two weeks Aug.
Credit AmEx, MC, V. **Map** p306 H5.

Designer del Pozo's exquisite locale has a feel of spa-
ciousness, his clothes exude sober elegance, and the
range covers shirts, trousers, tops, dresses, suits and
wedding dresses, plus accessories and cosmetics.

María José Navarro

C/Conde de Xiquena 9, Chueca (91 523 47 98).
Metro Chueca or Colón/bus 37, 40, 149, all routes to
Paseo de Recoletos. **Open** 10.30am-2pm, 5-8.30pm
Mon-Sat; closed Sun & two weeks Aug.
Credit AmEx, MC, V. **Map** p306 H5.

Aimed at independent, professional women who
favour practicality and style over the whims of fashion, Navarro offers well-tailored simple yet modern
suits and separates, and glamorous but equally
unfussy evening wear in sensuous fabrics.

Pedro del Hierro

C/Serrano 24, Salamanca (91 575 69 06).
Metro Serrano/bus 1, 9, 19, 51, 74.
Open 10am-8.30pm Mon-Sat; closed Sun. **Credit**
AmEx, DC, MC, V. **Map** p310 I6.

One of the classics of current Spanish design, using
modern fabrics and bright colours to create attractive and practical men's and women's clothes

Pedro Morago

C/Almirante 20, Chueca (91 521 66 28).
Metro Chueca or Colón/bus 37, 40, 149, all routes to
Paseo de Recoletos. **Open** *Sept-July* 10.30am-2pm, 5-
8.30pm Mon-Sat; closed Sun. *Aug* 10.30am-2pm, 5-
8.30pm Mon-Fri; 10.30am-2pm Sat; closed Sun.
Credit AmEx, MC, V. **Map** p306 H5.

Purveyor of trendy togs to the city's style-conscious
footballers and many famous faces from the movie
world, Pedro Morago carries on a crusade against
the conservative dress habits of Spanish men with
his sleek jackets. Check out that cloth.

Purificación García

C/Serrano 28, Salamanca (91 435 80 13).
Metro Serrano/bus 1, 9, 19, 51, 74.
Open 10am-8.30pm Mon-Sat; closed Sun. **Credit**
AmEx, DC, MC, V. **Map** p307 J4.

A Galician designer who's now attracting increasing international attention, García dresses men and
women in a discreetly stylish urban wardrobe that
combines natural fibres with new fabrics and classic styling with a contemporary look.
Branches: throughout the city.

Eat, Drink, Shop

Chic and cheerful; bright, fun T-shirts at **El Tintero**. *See p170.*

Sybilla

C/Jorge Juan 12, Salamanca (91 578 13 22).
Metro Retiro or Serrano/bus 1, 9, 19, 51, 74.
Open 10am-2pm, 4.30-8.30pm Mon-Fri; 11am-3pm,
5-8.30pm Sat; closed Sun & Aug.
Credit AmEx, DC, MC, V. **Map** p307 J5.
Once labelled the *maga* (sorceress) of Spanish
design, Sybilla was a celebrity of the *Movida*. Her
international take-off has not been as spectacular as
was expected, but she still produces exciting ranges
of accessories, shoes and bags and striking but
wearable clothes, all available here.

Fashion stores

Compañía Multihispana

C/Hortaleza 30, Chueca (91 532 38 33). Metro
Chueca/bus 3, 40, 149. **Open** 5-8pm Tue-Fri; closed Sun. *July Aug also* 11am-
2pm Sat. **Credit** AmEx, DC, MC, V. **Map** p309 F6.
A cut above most of the shops in the streets nearby,
Compañía Multihispana stocks selected items from
young, mainly Spanish designers, with a focus on
Amaya Arzuaga and Home-Less.

Disidente

C/Arenal 8, Austrias (91 531 99 83).
Metro Opera/bus 3, 25, 39, 148.
Open 10.30am-2pm, 5-8.30pm Mon-Sat; closed Sun.
Credit AmEx, MC, V. **Map** p309 D7.
On the first floor of an otherwise uninspiring city
centre mini-mall, Disidente is worth a look for its
varied stock of reduced end-of-line designer wear.
There are some wonderful bargains to be had.

Ekseption

C/Velázquez 28, Salamanca (91 577 43 53).
Metro Velázquez/bus 1, 9, 19, 51, 74.
Open 10.30am-2.30pm, 5-9pm Mon-Sat; closed Sun.
Credit AmEx, DC, MC, V. **Map** p307 J4.
With selected items from the collections of some of
the most fêted designers of the moment such as
Prada, Marni, Van Noten, Miu Miu and Chloë,
Ekseption is a fashion victim's paradise. A spacious,
sleek space, it has women's clothes only, and shoes
and accessories. Great reductions for end-of-season
sales; otherwise it's scarily pricey.
Branch: C/Concha Espina 14 (91 562 55 87).

Factory

Carretera de la Coruña (N-VI), exit 19, Las Rozas
(902 15 75 02). **Open** 11am-9pm Mon-Sat, & first
Sun of every month except Aug.
Credit AmEx, DC, MC, V.
Two giant warehouse spaces, with racks and racks
of clothes and shoes from many quality Spanish and
foreign labels, for around 40% under normal prices.
On exit roads north and south of Madrid, they're
designed to be mainly accessible by car, but free
buses run during the 1-31 July sales (when prices are
even cheaper), from Príncipe Pío, to Las Rozas, and
from Sol and Atocha to Getafe.
Branch: Carretera de Andalucia (N-IV), exit 17
(902 15 75 02).

L'Habilleur

Plaza de Chueca 8, Chueca (91 531 32 22). Metro
Chueca/bus 3, 37, 40, 149. **Open** 11am-2pm, 5-9pm
Mon-Sat; closed Sun. **Credit** MC, V. **Map** p306 G5.
Despite its smart, sophisticated appearance and
matchlessly trendy location on Plaza de Chueca, this
sister branch of a Paris shop offers heavily reduced
prices on end-of-line items from cool labels such as
Plein Sud and John Richmond. Mens- and womens-
wear and accessories, all chosen with a great eye.

Chain links

Blanco

C/Mayor 14, Austrias (91 366 44 26).
Metro Sol/bus all routes to Puerta del Sol.
Open 10am-9pm Mon-Sat; closed Sun.
Credit AmEx, DC, MC, V. **Map** p309 D7.
Cheap, fun fashion for groovy young party girls,
which can sometimes be a little on the tacky side.
Branch: throughout the city.

Mango

C/Princesa 75, Malasaña & Conde Duque
(91 534 54 20). Metro Argüelles/bus 1, 21, 44, C.
Open 10.30am-9pm Mon-Sat; closed Sun.
Credit AmEx, MC, V. **Map** p304 C2.
Immensely popular with trendy teens and young
working women, and with branches opening across
the world, Mango has a full range of smart and
casual wear that looks good and doesn't cost a bomb.
Branches: throughout the city.

Eat, Drink, Shop

Zara

C/Princesa 45, Malasaña & Conde Duque (91 541 09 02). Metro Argüelles/bus 1, 21, 44, 133, C. **Open** 10am-8.30pm Mon-Sat; closed Sun. **Credit** AmEx, DC, MC, V. **Map** p304 C3.
With branches all over Spain and abroad, Zara is a mega-success of Spanish retailing. Whatever top designers produce each season, Zara copies at a fraction of the price within a few weeks. It's the fashion fallback for a big slice of the Spanish population – men, women and small kids are all catered for. Check buttons, zips and seams, though, when buying. **Branches**: throughout the city.

Street & club fashion

The recent explosion in club culture in Madrid has also brought a boom in street and clubwear, with new shops coming and going as quickly as the many club nights on offer. The opening of **Mercado Fuencarral** has consolidated the Calles Fuencarral-Hortaleza area as the hip streetwear heartland, but there are interesting shops in many parts of town.

Chill Out

C/Martín de los Heros 17, Argüelles (91 542 34 06). Metro Plaza de España or Ventura Rodríguez/ bus 1, 2, 44, 74, 133 C. **Open** 10.30am-2pm, 5.30-9pm Mon-Sat; closed Sun. **Credit** AmEx, MC, V. **Map** p304 C4.
A funky little shop with psychedelic decor (fuchsia walls and a fake-fur counter), club- and streetwear, great colourful tops for girls, and wacky accessories.

Fun and games at **Fiestas Paco**. *See p170.*

Flip

C/Mayor 19, Austrias (91 366 44 72). Metro Sol/bus all routes to Puerta del Sol. **Open** 10am-9pm Mon-Sat; closed Sun. **Credit** AmEx, MC, V. **Map** p309 D7.
Formerly a second-hand jeans store, Flip has also jumped on the clubwear bandwagon and now offers funky labels like gsus, Miss Sixty and Spanish Custo. Good accessories too – shades, bags and hats.

Glam

C/Fuencarral 35, Malasaña & Conde Duque (91 522 80 54). Metro Chueca or Gran Vía/bus 3, 40, 149. **Open** 10am-2pm, 5-9pm Mon-Sat; closed Sun. **Credit** AmEx, MC, V. **Map** p305 F5.
Glam by name and glam by nature, with glitzy club and party wear – think slinky dresses and bustiers, and just about anything shiny, with lots of PVC and leather. An institution among up-for-it clubbers, Glam sells imports from London and its own brand.

Loreak Mendian

C/Argensola 5, Chueca (91 319 47 16). Metro Alonso Martínez or Colón/bus 21, 37. **Open** 11am-2pm, 5-8.30pm Mon-Sat; closed Sun. **Credit** AmEx, MC, V. **Map** p306 H4.
Basque designer Mendian does a great line in simple yet cool streetwear for boys and girls. Other labels such as Pure and Carhartt are also stocked.

Mercado Fuencarral

C/Fuencarral 45, Malasaña & Conde Duque (91 521 41 52). Metro Tribunal/bus 3, 40, 149. **Open** 10am-9pm Mon-Sat; closed Sun. **Credit** varies. **Map** p305 F5.
The epicentre of the Madrid club and youth fashion scene, this three-floor complex contains over 40 shops, selling clothes, shoes, music, books, cosmetics and more, plus a hip hairdresser, a tattooist and a Net café. Shops to look out for include **Smikke**, with accessories by local designers, and the slightly classier (and more expensive) clothes at **Doble Aa**; for fun second-hands and cheaper stuff, head for the top floor. There's also **AMA Records** (*see p180*). The Mercado houses a club, the **Sala Mix** (*see chapter* **Nightlife**), which hosts film shows, theatre and exhibits, and stool squatters at the café enjoy cool music from the **Cabina Central**. The noticeboards and flyer racks are great places to find out about new things in the local scene.

Mitsuoko

C/Fuencarral 59, Malasaña & Conde Duque (91 701 08 35). Metro Chueca/bus 3, 40, 149. **Open** 10.30am-9pm Mon-Sat; closed Sun. **Credit** MC, V. **Map** p305 F5.
A spacious, two-storey 'press-fashion-design café', with men's and women's lines from a cosmopolitan array of labels. It's leisure wear for young professionals, and after the tiring business of trying it all on you can relax with a plate of sushi in the café.

No Comment

C/Fuencarral 39, Malasaña & Conde Duque (91 531 19 57). Metro Chueca or Gran Vía/bus 3, 40, 149. **Open** 10.30am-9pm Mon-Sat; closed Sun. **Credit** AmEx, MC, V. **Map** p305 F5.

Eat, Drink, Shop

No Comment sells some of the coolest labels of the moment such as Pash, W&L.T. and E-Play, with a focus on casual gear and lots of combat trousers.

Odd!

C/León 35, Huertas & Santa Ana (91 429 05 70).
Metro Antón Martín/bus 6, 26, 32, 57. **Open** 10.30am-2pm, 5.30-9pm Mon-Fri; 11am-2pm, 6-9pm Sat; closed Sun. **Credit** AmEx, MC, V. **Map** p309 F8.
Run by four brothers and sisters, Odd! stocks bright, hip clothes for men and women, at good prices.

Pepita is Dead – Cristina Guisado

C/Doctor Fourquet 10, Lavapiés (91 528 87 88).
Metro Atocha/bus all routes to Atocha.
Open 11am-2pm, 5-8.30pm Mon-Sat; closed Sun. **Credit** AmEx, MC, V. **Map** p310 G 9/10.
A little shop run very personally by designer Cristina Guisado. She originally sold only her own designs, but now has new and second-hand '60s and '70s clothes.

Plastic People

C/Apodaca 6, Chueca (91 521 71 54).
Metro Bilbao or Tribunal/bus 3, 37, 40, 149.
Open 11am-2.30pm, 5.30-9pm Mon-Sat; closed Sun & Aug. **Credit** AmEx, MC, V. **Map** p305 F4.
An exceptionally friendly shop that began life in Ibiza. It sells Total's glitzy clubwear, skirts and dresses by Rectangle Blanc and Viva Maria's wickedly sacrilegious underwear with images of Mary and Jesus.

Supreme

C/Martín de los Heros 24, Argüelles (91 541 00 42).
Metro Plaza de España/bus all routes to Plaza de España. **Open** 10am-9pm Mon-Sat; closed Sun. **Credit** AmEx, DC, MC, V. **Map** p304 C4.
A funky little shop outside the Fuencarral heartland, but which has a neon skateboarder sign to guide you in. Inside you'll find a white-painted brick cave with smart streetwear from supremely cool labels such as Duffer of St George, Boxfresh and Sylvia Rielle.

El Tintero

C/Gravina 5, Chueca (91 308 14 18). Metro Chueca/bus 3, 37, 40, 149. **Open** 10.30am-2pm, 5-9pm Mon-Fri; 11am-2.30pm, 5.30-9pm Sat; closed Sun. **Credit** AmEx, DC, MC, V. **Map** p306 H5.
Stylish printed T-shirts with bright, witty designs.

Fashion accessories

Dress & costume hire

Cornejo

C/Magdalena 2, Lavapiés (91 530 55 55).
Metro Tirso de Molina/bus 6, 26, 32, 65.
Open *Sept-June* 9am-2pm, 3-6pm Mon-Fri; closed Sat, Sun. *July, Aug* 8am-3pm Mon-Fri; closed Sat, Sun. **No credit cards. Map** p309 E8.
Dress yourself up in 15th-century garb, as a clown or a Roman Emperor at this historic costume-hire shop. The stock is enormous, and prices start at 10,000ptas for a weekend. Cornejo also hires out wedding dresses and formal attire.

Fiestas Paco

C/Toledo 52, La Latina (91 365 27 60).
Metro La Latina/bus 17, 18, 23, 35, 60. **Open** 9.30am-2pm, 5-8.30pm Mon-Sat; 11am-3pm Sun. **Credit** MC, V. **Map** p309 E8.
All manner of party stuff is available at this wacky shop, including masks, disguises, decorations, tricks, jokes and goodies. It also has leaflets and information about clowns, magicians and other kinds of entertainers for private parties.

Embroidery

Carmelitas Descalzas de Aravaca

Carretera de Aravaca a Húmera, km 1.5 (91 307 18 74). Bus 657 from Moncloa, 563 from Aluche.
Open *Sept-June* 10am-noon, 4-7pm Mon-Fri. *July, Aug* 10am-1pm, 5-8pm Mon-Fri; closed Sat, Sun & Easter. **No credit cards.**
Something you will not find in the Gran Via. Take a piece of cloth of your choice along to the Barefoot Carmelite Nuns, and have it hand-embroidered as you wish. You pick it up a few days later. Designs, as one might expect, are traditional. Prices vary, but are very low for the quality of the work.

Lingerie & underwear

Corsetería La Latina

C/Toledo 49, La Latina (91 365 46 22).
Metro La Latina/bus 17, 18, 23, 35, 60. **Open** 10am-1.30pm, 5-8pm Mon-Fri; closed Sat, Sun & Aug. **Credit** AmEx, DC, MC, V. **Map** p309 D9.
Corsets, bras, girdles and suspenders for a race of giants. Walking up Calle Toledo it's difficult to resist gawping at the window display in sheer amazement.

¡Oh, qué Luna!

C/Ayala 32, Salamanca (91 431 37 25).
Metro Serrano/bus 1, 74. **Open** 10am-2pm, 5-8.30pm Mon-Fri; 11am-2pm, 5-8.30pm Sat; closed Sun. **Credit** AmEx, DC, MC, V. **Map** p307 J4.
Ultra-smart, sexy lingerie and housewear, for those who lounge around the house in silky negligées and dressing gowns. Bed linen and swimwear, too.

Woman's Secret

C/Velázquez 48, Salamanca (91 578 14 53).
Metro Velázquez/bus 1, 9, 19, 51, 74. **Open** *Sept-June* 10.15am-8.30pm Mon-Sat; closed Sun. *July, Aug* 10.15am-2pm, 5-8.30pm Mon-Sat; closed Sun. **Credit** AmEx, DC, MC, V. **Map** p307 J4.
A great choice of quality underwear at very decent prices, as well as swimwear and skincare products. **Branch:** throughout the city.

XXX

C/San Marcos 8, Chueca (91 522 17 70). Metro Chueca/bus 3, 40, 149. **Open** 5-9pm Mon; noon-2pm, 5-9pm Tue-Fri; 11.30am-2pm, 5.30-9pm Sat; closed Sun. **Credit** AmEx, MC, V. **Map** p309 F6.
Stylish men's underwear, in the heart of gay Chueca. The Barquillo branch also has undies for women. **Branch:** C/Barquillo 41 (91 310 38 60).

Jewellery & accessories

Concha García

C/Goya 38, Salamanca (91 435 49 36). Metro Goya/bus 21, 29, 52, 53. **Open** 10.30am-2pm; 5-8.30pm Mon-Sat; closed Sun. *July, Aug* 10.30am-2pm; 5.30-9pm Mon-Fri; 10.30am-2pm Sat; closed Sun. **Credit** AmEx, DC, MC, V. **Map** p307 K4.

A showcase for contemporary and ethnic jewellery design, Concha García has a fresh, modern approach to jewellery and the use of non-precious metals. There's a broad range of styles on display, from the work of some top Spanish and European designers to beautiful ethnic jewellery. Prices are usually very reasonable, and she also presents regular exhibitions of new work by independent jewellers.

Tickets & travel

Advance ticket sales for concerts, theatres and other events are now a very competitive business in Madrid. A Spanish peculiarity is the large-scale role of savings banks: Caja de Cataluña and Caja Madrid have the most advanced telesales operations, followed by the ubiquitous **Corte Inglés** (see page 160). **La Caixa** bank has Servicaixa machines in some branches, through which you can buy tickets for a number of events by credit card (or by phone, 902 33 22 11). The **Crisol** chain of bookshops (see page 162) sells tickets for other events, the **Fnac** (see page 161) ticket desk is good for many concerts and theatres (at list price), and the **Madrid Rock** record store (see page 181) has rock and pop gig tickets. Also, event organisers such as Forocio have begun to go into travel and other youth-oriented fields. For the customer, it's always well worth looking around.

La Guía del Ocio

The local listings magazine (see p290) has an online ticket sales service for theatres and cinemas in Madrid, Barcelona and beyond, at www.guiadelocio.com.

Tel-entradas/Caja de Cataluña

Tel-entradas phoneline 902 10 12 12. **Open** 24hrs daily.
Credit AmEx (some venues) DC, MC, V.
The Caja de Cataluña savings bank has a ticket sales service through which you can book tickets for many Madrid theatres, venues and concerts. Happily, there is no commission fee. Tickets can be bought at any Caja branch or by credit card with the Tel-entradas phone line (staff usually speak some English). Tickets can be collected from the nearest branch of the Caja or picked up at the venue before the performance. Its main associated venues include Centro Cultural Conde Duque, Círculo de Bellas Artes, Teatro La Abadía and especially many smaller theatres.

Tele-entradas de Caja Madrid

Tele-entradas phoneline 902 48 84 88. **Open** 24hrs daily.
Credit AmEx (some venues) DC, MC, V.
This 24-hour service sells tickets for various venues and can attend to English speakers. You will hear a recorded message in Spanish: to be put through to an operator, state the name of the show or venue you're interested in. Tickets can be collected at the box office or, if booked more than 24 hours ahead, at a Caja Madrid branch. It's good for bigger local venues, such as the Auditorio Nacional, Teatro de la Zarzuela, Teatro María Guerrero, Teatro de la Comedia and Teatro Real, and many other theatres.

Travel & related agencies

For TIVE, the official student and youth travel agency, see page 291.

Forocio

C/Mayor 6, 4°, Austrias (91 522 56 77). Metro Sol/bus all routes to Sol. **Open** 10am-8pm Mon-Fri; closed Sat, Sun. **Credit** DC, MC, V. **Map** p309 E7.
A multi-purpose agency aimed at young foreigners, Forocio runs 'International Parties' in the Palacio de Gaviria (see chapter **Nightlife**) and other venues, and offers other services such as flat-hunting, car-hire, Interrail and student cards, language exchanges, budget flights and tours. English and other languages are spoken.

Viajes Zeppelin

Plaza de Santo Domingo 2, Sol & Gran Vía (91 532 51 54). Metro Santo Domingo/bus all routes to Callao. **Open** 9am-8pm Mon-Fri; 10am-1pm Sat; closed Sun.
Credit AmEx, DC, MC, V. **Map** p309 D6.
A good place for cheap European charter deals and long-haul youth fares. Popular, so you may have to queue, but service is fast and friendly.

Eat, Drink, Shop

Lola Fonseca

C/Santa Isabel 50, Lavapiés (91 530 65 22).
Metro Atocha/bus all routes to Atocha.
Open 10am-2pm, 4.30-8.30pm Mon-Sat; closed Sun.
Credit AmEx, DC, MC, V. **Map** p310 G9.
Lola Fonseca produces her own brand of art, in the shape of her beautiful, intricately printed and hand-painted silk scarves. Work in progress can be seen stretched over screens at the back of the shop.

Piamonte

C/Piamonte 16, Chueca (91 522 45 80). Metro Chueca/
bus 3, 37, 40. **Open** 10.30am-2pm, 5-8.30pm Mon-Sat;
closed Sun. **Credit** AmEx, MC, V. **Map** p306 H5.
A wide range of accessories – with a focus on contemporary jewellery from national and international names – as well as funky bags and leather goods.
Branch: C/Lagasca 28 (91 575 55 20).

Scooter

Callejón de Jorge Juan 12, Salamanca (91 575 15 76).
Metro Colón/bus all routes to Plaza de Colón.
Open 10.30am-8.30pm Mon-Fri; 10.30am-2.30pm,
4.30-8.30pm Sat; closed Sun.
Credit AmEx, DC, MC, V. **Map** p307 J5.
An elegant French boutique in a Salamanca alleyway (off Calle Jorge Juan, near the corner of Calle Velázquez), Scooter has great accessories – scarves, bags, beads, bangles – together with some clothing.

Shoes & leather

Great places for any budding Imelda Marcos are the *Zapaterías de muestrarios* – shops specialising in end-of-line footwear, where good-quality, name-label shoes cost from 5,000ptas. There's a whole clutch of them on Calle Augusto Figueroa in Chueca. Some also have good lines in bags and belts.

Antigua Casa Crespo

C/Divino Pastor 29, Malasaña & Conde Duque (91
521 56 54). Metro San Bernardo/bus 21, 147, 149.
Open 10am-1.30pm, 4.30-8pm Mon-Fri; 10am-1.30pm
Sat. Closed Sun & late Aug. **No credit cards.**
Map p305 E3.
The most famous espadrille shop in Madrid, with every kind of traditional *alpargata*, in every size, in a shop that is itself a museum piece.

Camper

C/Preciados 23, Sol & Gran Vía (91 531 78 97).
Metro Callao/bus 44, 75, 133, 146, 147.
Open 10am-8.30pm Mon-Sat; closed Sun. **Credit**
AmEx, DC, MC, V. **Map** p309 E7.
Camper boots and shoes were made for walking, combining comfort and practicality with a very individual chunky, casual style. They're now sought-after world-wide, but are still significantly cheaper if bought in Spain.
Branches: throughout the city.

Excrupulus Net

C/Almirante 7, Chueca (91 521 72 44).
Metro Chueca/bus all routes to Paseo de Recoletos.
Open 11am-2pm, 5.30-8.30pm Mon-Sat; closed Sun.
Credit AmEx, DC, MC, V. **Map** p306 H5.
Cutting-edge Catalan and Mallorcan shoe design, with a good range of Muxart's attractive, completely original men's and women's shoes, and a small selection of accessories. Not cheap, though.

Loewe

C/Serrano 26 & 34, Salamanca (91 577 60 56).
Metro Serrano/bus all routes to Plaza de Colón.
Open 9.30am-8.30pm Mon-Sat; closed Sun.
Credit AmEx, DC, MC, V. **Map** p307 I4.
The world-famous, élite Spanish leather goods company. Prices are very high.
Branches: throughout the city.

Ana Millán. *See p173.*

Some of the irresistible confections of old-world **La Duquesita**. *See p174.*

Nuevos Guerrilleros
Puerta del Sol 5, Sol & Gran Vía (91 521 27 08).
Metro Sol/bus all routes to Puerta del Sol.
Open 9.30am-2pm, 4.30-8.30pm Mon-Sat; closed Sun.
Credit AmEx, MC, V. **Map** p309 E7.
A bargain-basement store with a giant stock of cheap and cheerful men's and women's shoes, with occasionally wacky designs. An army of assistants awaits customers in the vast interior. The original Guerrilleros, from which these shops split away (guerrilla movements were ever thus), is a similar operation that still has shops in Calle Montera and many other locations.
Branches: C/Marcelo Usera 41, Usera (91 475 66 48); C/Alcalá 339, Ciudad Lineal (91 367 88 26); C/General Ricardos 71 (91 471 28 05).

Repairers

Every market and most *barrio* streets have a shoe repairer – look out for *rápido* or *reparación de calzados* signs.

Aldao
Gran Vía 15, Sol & Gran Vía (91 521 69 25). Metro Gran Vía/bus all routes to Gran Vía. **Open** 10am 2pm, 5-8.30pm Mon-Fri; 10am-2pm Sat; closed Sun.
Credit AmEx, DC, MC, V. **Map** p309 F6.
A jeweller, silversmith and watch-seller in one. You can hand in broken watches at both branches, although Calle Velázquez is the specialist in repairs.
Branch: C/Velázquez 43 (91 431 46 50).

Calzados LG
Gran Vía 11, Sol & Gran Vía (91 531 82 73).
Metro Gran Vía/bus all routes to Gran Vía. **Open** 9.30am-2pm, 4.30-8pm Mon-Fri; 9.30am-2pm Sat; closed Sun. **Credit** AmEx, MC, V. **Map** p309 F6.
Artisan shoemakers LG have a full repair service.
Branch: C/Lope de Rueda 57 (91 573 30 30).

Restauraciones Peña
C/Ave María 8, Lavapiés (91 369 39 97). Metro Antón Martín/bus 6, 26, 32. **Open** 9.30am-1.30pm, 4.30-8pm Mon-Fri; 9.30am-1.30pm Sat; closed Sun & Aug. **No credit cards. Map** p309 F9.
All kinds of leather goods – bags, cases, jackets and coats – repaired, cleaned or restored, quickly, cheerfully and with great skill.

Florists

Ana Millán
C/Hortaleza 55, Chueca (91 522 32 83). Metro Chueca/bus 3, 40, 149. **Open** 10am-1.45pm, 5-8.30pm Mon-Fri; 10am-2pm Sat. Closed Sun & Aug.
Credit AmEx, DC, MC, V. **Map** p306 G5.
Ana Millán is a florist that also sells sexy men's and women's underwear. An oddly effective combination.

Martín Floristas
C/San Sebastián 1, corner of C/Huertas 2, Huertas & Santa Ana (91 429 13 32).
Metro Antón Martín/bus 6, 26, 32, 57. **Open** 10am-2pm, 5-8pm Mon-Fri; 10am-2pm Sat; closed Sun.
Credit AmEx, DC, MC, V. **Map** p309 E8.
For more than a century this family business has provided Madrileños with cut flowers, floral arrangements and plants for indoors and out.

Food & drink

Chocolates, cakes & sweets

Antigua Pastelería del Pozo
C/del Pozo 8, Huertas & Santa Ana (91 522 38 94).
Metro Sol/bus all routes to Puerta del Sol.
Open 9.30am-2pm, 4.40-8pm Mon-Fri; 9.30am-2pm Sat; closed Sun & part of July-Aug.
No credit cards. Map 309 E7.
This wonderful old *pastelería* has been here since 1830, and the decor and counter are both original. Cakes and pastries are baked on the premises, and the old boys serving have a lovely yesteryear manner.

Casa Mira
Carrera de San Jerónimo 30, Huertas & Santa Ana (91 429 88 95). Metro Sevilla/bus all routes to Puerta del Sol. **Open** *Feb-Oct* 10am-2pm, 5-9pm Mon-Sat, 10.30am-2.30pm, 5.30-9pm Sun, public holidays. *Nov-Jan* 9.30am-2pm, 4.30-9pm daily. Closed part of July, Aug. **No credit cards. Map** p310 G7.
With 150 years behind it, Casa Mira is a specialist in *turrón*, the nougat that's an essential part of a Spanish Christmas (but available all year). There's also a big choice of chocolates, marzipan, cakes and savouries. Expect long queues at Christmas time.

Eat, Drink, Shop

Convento de las Carboneras

Plaza Conde de Miranda 3, Austrias (91 548 37 01).
Metro Sol/bus all routes to Puerta del Sol.
Open 9.30am-1pm, 4-6.30pm Mon-Fri; closed Sat,
Sun. **No credit cards. Map** p309 D8.

Buy cakes and biscuits with an extra aura of sanc-
tity from the nuns of the Carboneras convent (*see*
p66), who make their own Castilian specialities –
mantecados, eggy *yemas*, almond biscuits. This is a
closed convent, so you buy them through a grill.

La Duquesita

C/Fernando VI, 2, Chueca (91 308 02 31). Metro
Alonso Martínez/bus 3, 21, 37. **Open** 9.30am-
2.30pm, 5-9pm Tue-Sat; 9.30am-3pm, 5-9pm Sun;
closed Mon & July. **Credit** MC, V. **Map** p306 H4.

This fabulous little *pastelería* hasn't changed much
since it opened in 1914 (it's been used for period-
piece filming), and sells wonderful chocs and cakes,
and a huge range of pre-Christmas *turrones*.

Horno San Onofre

C/San Onofre 3, Chueca (91 532 90 60). Metro Gran
Vía/bus 3, 40, 46, 146, 149. **Open** 8am-9.30pm
Mon-Sat; 9am-9pm Sun. **Credit** AmEx, DC, MC, V.

This fine old establishment is not to be missed.
Everything is baked on the premises, including seasonal cakes (*torrijas* at Easter, *turrones* at
Christmas, *Roscón de Reyes* for 6 January). The *tarta*
de Santiago (a traditional sponge cake) is excellent,
as are the savouries such as *empanada gallega*.
Branches: Hernani 7 (91 554 33 96); C/Hortaleza 8
(91 531 83 76); C/Mayor 73 (91 559 62 14).

La Mallorquina

Puerta del Sol 8, Sol & Gran Vía (91 521 12 01).
Metro Sol/bus all routes to Puerta del Sol.
Open 9am-9.15pm daily. Closed mid July, Aug.
No credit cards. Map p309 E7.

A splendid slice of local life. On the ground floor is
a bustling pastry shop, with own-baked cakes and
savouries. Above, there's a café full of señoras chatting over coffee and the best *napolitanas* in town.

El Riojano

C/Mayor 10, Austrias (91 366 44 82). Metro Sol/bus
all routes to Puerta del Sol. **Open** *Sept-June* 9am-
2pm, 5-9pm daily. *July, Aug* 9am-2pm, 5-9pm Mon-
Sat; closed Sun. **Credit** MC, V. **Map** p309 D7.

From a hundred kinds of cheese...

Patrimonio Comunal Olivarero. *See p175.*

Since 1885 this delightful *pastelería* has been serving
cakes, pastries, glacé fruits and seasonal goodies.
All are made in the traditional way, and presentation and the original decor are marvellous.

Delicacies

In **La Cebada** market (*see page 176*) there is a
very good cheese stand, no.20/21, **Magerit**, and
an excellent place to buy olives is **F Illanas**,
stalls 33-44, in the **Mercado de Chamberí**,
Calle Alonso Cano 10 (91 446 95 89).

For more information on cheeses, check out
www.cheesefromspain.com, and for *Jamón*
Serrano try www.consorcioserrano.com.

La Boulette

Mercado de La Paz, stands 63-68, C/Ayala 28,
Salamanca (91 431 77 25). Metro Serrano/bus 1, 9,
19, 51, 74. **Open** 9am-2pm, 5-8pm Mon-Fri; 9am-
2pm Sat; closed Sun. **Credit** MC, V. **Map** p307 J4.

Inside Salamanca's La Paz market, La Boulette has
nearly 400 cheeses on offer, from Spain and elsewhere, and a similarly vast selection of charcuterie.

Cuenllas

C/Ferraz 3, Argüelles (91 547 31 33). Metro Plaza
de España/bus 74, all routes to Plaza de España.
Open 9am-2pm, 5-8.30pm Mon-Fri; 9am-3pm Sat;
closed Sun. **Credit** AmEx, DC, MC, V. **Map** p304 C5.

Not really for those on a tight budget, but an excellent
selection of meats and cheeses from Spain, pasta, grappa from Italy, brandies, Scotch, pâtés and more besides.
Branch: C/Virgen del Lluc 4 (91 404 19 02).

González

C/León 12, Huertas & Santa Ana (91 429 56 18).
Metro Antón Martín/bus 6, 9, 26, 32. **Open**
10.30am-3pm, 6-11pm Tue-Sat; closed Sun.
Credit AmEx, DC, MC, V. **Map** p309 F8.
This traditional local grocery store has been
turned into a smart deli with a wide range of fine
foods. There's a wine bar, with a great selection,
and which hosts art exhibitions; out front there's
a whole range of select cheese (they do their own
curing) and charcuterie, preserves, coffees, fruit,
nuts, olive oils and much more besides. The cold-
store chamber dates from 1924 and is reputedly
the oldest of its kind in Madrid.

Jamonería Ferpal

C/Arenal 7, Austrias (91 521 51 08).
Metro Sol/bus all routes to Puerta del Sol.
Open *Sept-July* 9.45am-8.45pm Mon-Sat; closed Sun.
Aug 9.45am-2pm, 5.30-9pm Mon-Sat; closed Sun.
Credit AmEx, DC, V. **Map** p309 D7.
Right in the city centre, and with a superb selection
of *embutidos*, hams and cheeses.

A Lareira

C/Fernando el Católico 78, Moncloa (91 543 74 80).
Metro Moncloa/bus 16, 44, 61, C. **Open** 9am-
2.30pm, 5-8.30pm Mon-Fri; 9am-2.30pm Sat; closed
Aug. **Credit** AmEx, DC, MC, V. **Map** p304 C2.
A bewildering range of products from northern
Spain: powerful cheeses from Cantabria and
Asturias, crisp Ribeiro and Albariño white wines
and *orujo* (a very strong grain spirit) from Galicia,
morcillas and chorizos from León, and many
different kinds of honey. Try the *hogazas* (huge
loaves of bread from Galicia).

Mallorca

C/Serrano 6, Salamanca (91 577 18 59). Metro
Retiro/bus all routes to Puerta de Alcalá. **Open** 9.30am-
9pm daily. **Credit** AmEx, DC, MC, V. **Map** p310 I6.
The Mallorca shop-cafés, dotted around Madrid, are
multi-purpose gourmet establishments where you
can call in for coffee, have a drink and a quick meal
or pick up every kind of luxury foodstuff. They have
a great choice of cakes and sweets, excellent charcuterie and ready-prepared dishes, and fine cheese,
wines and cava. Beautiful presentation, too, even if
the prices are to match.
Branches: throughout the city.

Mantequerías Bravo

C/Ayala 24, Salamanca (91 576 76 41). Metro
Serrano/bus 1, 9, 19, 51, 74. **Open** 9.30am-2.30pm,
5.30-8.30pm Mon-Fri; 9.30am-2.30pm Sat; closed Sun
& Aug. **Credit** AmEx, DC, MC, V. **Map** p307 J4.
This superbly stocked shop sells a vast range of
Spanish foods – wonderful meats and cheeses –,
wines and spirits, freshly roast and ground coffees,
teas and a host of imports (even English mustard and
cream crackers). Bravo also has its own delivery
network, within Spain and abroad.
Branch: Paseo Gral Martínez Campos 23
(91 448 09 18).

Mozzarella

*C/Hortaleza 49, Chueca (91 532 49 35). Metro
Chueca or Tribunal/bus 3, 40, 149.* **Open** 10am-
2pm, 5-8.30pm Mon-Fri; 10am-2pm Sat. Closed
Sun & Aug. **Credit** AmEx, MC, V. **Map** p306 G5.
A small shop crowded with a vast array of
different cheeses, from France, Switzerland, Italy
and Spain, including some wonderful but little-
known Spanish regional varieties. Pâtés, fresh
pasta and oil are also specialities.

Museo del Jamón

*Carrera de San Jerónimo 6,
Huertas & Santa Ana (91 521 03 46).
Metro Sol/bus all routes to Puerta del Sol.*
Open 9am-midnight Mon-Sat; 10am-midnight Sun,
public holidays. **Credit** MC, V. **Map** p309 E7.
The 'Ham Museums' around the city centre may
not be the cheapest place to stock up on Spanish
hams and cheeses, but are certainly the most
spectacular. You can sample the stock at the bar
or in their giant restaurants.
Branches: throughout the city.

Patrimonio Comunal Olivarero

*C/Mejía Lequerica 1, Chueca (91 308 05 05). Metro
Alonso Martínez/bus 3, 21, 37, 40, 149.* **Open**
10am-2pm, 5-8pm Mon-Fri; 10am-2pm Sat; closed
Sun & Aug. **Credit** MC, V. **Map** p306 G4.
This Chueca shop stocks just about every kind of
olive oil. It's a vast range from all over Spain,
includes several varieties sold only through this
shop, at all grades and in quantities from two-litre
bottles up to five-litre tins. There are also many
attactive gift-style bottles.

...to monsters of the deep...

Deliveries

La Casita de los Arroces
(91 571 65 65). **Open** 11am-4.30pm daily.
No credit cards.
Half a dozen or so varieties of paella at 700-1,650ptas
per person (minimum order 2,350ptas). You keep the
paellera (the paella pan) as a souvenir.

Sushi Ya
C/Cadarso 15, Sol & Gran Vía (902 23 13 23).
Metro Plaza de España/bus all routes to Plaza de
España. **Open** 1pm-4pm, 8pm-midnight Mon-Sat;
closed Sun. **No credit cards. Map** p304 C5.
Smartly presented sushi and other Japanese dishes.
Sushi plus salad for two is about 4,500ptas; there's
also a takeaway service on the premises.

Telecubata
91 447 76 65. **Open** 7pm-3am Mon-Thur, Sun; 7pm-
5am Fri, Sat, public holidays. **No credit cards.**
You're planning a party or a tête-à-tête in your *pen-*
sión room, and you realise the cocktails are missing.
Never fear, Telecubata (a *cubata* is a rum and cola)
will speed to the rescue with a party pack of booze,
ice, mixers, soft drinks, cups and condoms. Prices
vary, but start at 875ptas for a bottle of spirits; minimum order is 1,400ptas. They also send crisps,
olives and the like if you really want to impress.

Telepescaíto
91 767 05 13. **Open** *Sept-May* noon-4pm, 7.30pm-
midnight daily. *June-Aug* noon-4pm, 7.30pm-
midnight Tue-Sun; closed Mon. **Credit** MC, V.
Flash-fried whitebait (950ptas) and other Andaluz
dishes, plus chilled *fino* if you wish, to your door.
The drawback is that it's based in north Madrid, far
from the centre; minimum order 2,500ptas.

Markets

The market (*el mercado*) is for those who want
to shop for food the traditional way, who are
prepared to try out phrases like *¿Quién da la*
vez? or *¿Quién es el último/la última?* (both mean
'Who's the last in the queue?'). There's always
an astounding range of quality and prices –
mountains of fruit and vegetables, wet fish
stands, piles of cheeses and all manner of pork
products, as well as hawkers in the doorways
with bags of garlic bulbs at 100ptas.

All the following markets are open from
around 9am-2pm and 5-8pm (15 May-15 Sept till
8.30pm) Mon-Fri, and 9am-2pm Sat.

Anton Martín
C/Santa Isabel 5, Lavapiés (91 369 06 20). Metro
Antón Martín/bus 6, 26, 32, 57. **Map** p309 F9.

La Cebada
Plaza de la Cebada s/n, La Latina (91 365 91 76).
Metro La Latina/bus 17, 23, 35, 60. **Map** p309 D9.
Central, ugly to look at, but very good price-wise.

...and luscious fruit: all at Madrid's markets.

Chamartín
C/Bolivia 9, Chamartín (91 459 49 48). Metro
Colombia/bus 7, 14, 16, 29, 51.

Maravillas
C/Bravo Murillo 122, Tetuán (91 534 84 29). Metro
Alvarado/bus all routes to Cuatro Caminos.
Out of the way but the biggest market in the city,
with a near-unbeatable range of fresh fish.

La Paz
C/Ayala 28, Salamanca (91 435 07 43). Metro
Serrano/bus 1, 9, 19, 51, 74. **Map** p307 J4.
Salamanca's market has the most varied and refined
selection of any in Madrid.

San Miguel
Plaza de San Miguel, Austrias (91 548 12 14). Metro
Sol/bus all routes to Puerta del Sol. **Map** p309 D8.
Very central, but of more interest for its fine
wrought-iron architecture than its stalls

Supermarkets

Madrid's booming hypermarkets are mostly on
the main roads around the edge of the city, and
accessible only by car. If you're mobile and need
to stock up, look for ads for Alcampo, Continente
or Pryca. **El Corte Inglés** branches (*see page*
160) also have (pricey) supermarkets. For
information on Sunday opening, *see page 160.*

Champion
C/Valencia 2, Lavapiés (91 467 42 08). Metro
Lavapiés/bus 27, 34, C. **Open** 9.15am-9.15pm Mon-
Sat; closed Sun. **Credit** MC, V. **Map** p309 F10.
The inner-city outlets of the French-owned Carrefour
group (also owners of the Continente and Pryca
stores in Spain), Champion stores are good general
supermarkets that open all day and serve all needs.
Branches: throughout the city.

Sebaco
C/Bravo Murillo 16, Tetuán (91 447 37 71). Metro
Quevedo/bus 16, 37, 61, 149. **Open** 9.30am-9pm
Mon-Sat; closed Sun. **Credit** MC, V.

Pleasant, roomy supermarkets with a fairly upmarket range of products, especially imported cheeses. **Branches**: throughout the city.

Vegetarian & health foods

Central Vegetariana

C/de la Palma 15, Malasaña & Conde Duque (91 447 80 13). Metro Tribunal/bus 3, 40, 147, 149. **Open** 10am-2pm, 5-8pm Mon-Fri; 10am-1.30pm Sat; closed Sun & Aug. **Credit** MC, V. **Map** p305 E4.
Organic foods, herbal medicines and cosmetics.

El Linar

C/Huertas 5, Huertas & Santa Ana (91 429 64 25). Metro Antón Martín/bus 6, 26, 32, 57. **Open** 10am-2pm, 5-8pm Mon-Fri; 10am-2pm Sat; closed Sun. **Credit** AmEx, DC, MC, V. **Map** p310 G8.
A full range of wholefoods and environmentally friendly cosmetics, cleaning materials and literature.

Wine & drink

A *bodega* (literally a cellar) can be anything from an old tavern to a superbly stocked wine shop. The following are some of the best.

Bodegas Lafuente

C/Luchana 28, Chamberí (91 448 13 52). Metro Bilbao/bus 3, 21, 40, 147. **Open** 10am-2pm, 5-8.30pm Mon-Sat; closed Sun. **Credit** MC, V. **Map** p306 G3.
Laid out like a supermarket, this cavernous wine and spirits store has a prodigious range of Spanish and foreign labels, some at near-wholesale prices. Self-service, but the helpful staff know their stock. **Branch**: C/San Bernardo 10 (91 521 25 39).

Lavinia

C/José Ortega y Gasset 16, Salamanca (91 426 06 04/lavinia@lavinia.es). Metro Nuñez de Balboa/bus 1, 9, 19, 51, 74, 89. **Open** 10am-9pm Mon-Sat; closed Sun & first two weeks Aug.
Credit AmEx, DC, MC, V. **Map** p307 J3.
A true wine palace, Lavinia describes itself as the largest shop in Europe dedicated exclusively to wine, and it's a claim that would be hard to challenge. The selection of Spanish, European, New World and other wines is simply astonishing, all laid out in a big, well-designed space in the heart of smart Salamanca. The multi-lingual staff are also highly knowledgeable, and can make up cases to fit your exact requirements. No wine lover should miss this place.

Mariano Aguado

C/Echegaray 19, Huertas & Santa Ana (91 429 60 88). Metro Sevilla/bus all routes to Puerta del Sol. **Open** 9.30am-2pm, 5.30-8.30pm Mon-Fri; 9.30am-2pm Sat; closed Sun & Aug. **No credit cards. Map** p309 F8.
The name of this quiet, slightly solemn establishment only appears embossed in the doorstep, so it's easy to miss. It's oriented to the wine connoisseur, but not expensive, and always has lesser-known but good-quality wines from Rioja, Navarra and Rueda.

Mariano Madrueño

C/Postigo de San Martín 3, Sol & Gran Vía (91 521 19 55). Metro Callao/bus all routes to Plaza del Callao. **Open** 9.30am-2pm, 5-8pm Mon-Fri; 10.30am-2pm Sat. Closed Sun & Aug. **Credit** AmEx, MC, V. **Map** p309 D7.
A fabulous old *bodega*, with wrought-iron columns and carved wooden shelves. Its selection of wines and spirits is enormous, drawn from all over Spain.

Gifts & specialities

Ceramics & crafts

Antigua Casa Talavera

C/Isabel la Católica 2, Sol & Gran Vía (91 547 34 17). Metro Santo Domingo/bus 147. **Open** 10am-1.30pm; 5-8pm Mon-Fri; 10am-1.30pm Sat; closed Sun. **No credit cards. Map** p309 D6.
Perhaps the best place in town for truly traditional Spanish ceramics, every inch of shelving in this delightful old shop is piled high with brightly patterned ceramics from different parts of Spain, all handmade in traditional regional designs.

El Arco de los Cuchilleros

Plaza Mayor 9, bajos, Austrias (91 365 26 80). Metro Sol/bus all routes to Puerta del Sol. **Open** 11am-8pm Mon-Thur, Sun; 11am-9pm Fri, Sat. **Credit** AmEx, MC, V. **Map** p309 D8.
A very attractive shop, with an interesting selection of modern craftwork and especially fine ceramics and textiles. It has a gallery space that hosts exhibits by Spanish craftworkers and designers, and despite its location, just off Plaza Mayor, prices are reasonable.

El Bazar de Doña Pila

C/Divino Pastor 31, Malasaña & Conde Duque (mobile 655 23 91 84). Metro San Bernardo/bus 21, 40, 147. **Open** 10am-1.30pm, 5-8.30pm, Mon-Sat. **No credit cards. Map** p305 E3.
A little Malasaña shop with a varied range that includes original ceramics, glass and board games, by craft designers from Spain and many other countries. It also hosts occasional exhibitions.

Cántaro

C/Flor Baja 8, Sol & Gran Vía (92 547 95 14). Metro Plaza de España/bus all routes to Gran Vía. **Open** 10am-2pm, 5-9pm Mon-Sat. Closed Sun & Aug. **Credit** AmEx, DC, MC, V. **Map** p305 D5.
A big range of Spanish ceramics, from traditional designs to contemporary tableware. Discounts are given for big purchases (and there's a 10% reduction for readers showing this guide).

Dom

C/Piamonte 10, Chueca (91 522 77 34). Metro Chueca/bus 3, 37, 40, 149. **Open** 11am-2pm, 5-9pm Mon-Sat; closed Sun. **Credit** MC, V. **Map** p306 H5.
Fun, funky, well-priced gifts and household objects: furry fluorescent money-box buddhas, lava lamps and inflatable furniture, which can fit into your luggage. It also has a groovy gift-wrapping service.

Eat, Drink, Shop

Expresión Negra

C/Piamonte 15, Chueca (91 319 95 27).
Metro Chueca/bus 3, 37, 40, 149.
Open 11am-2pm, 5-8.30pm Mon-Sat; closed Sun.
Credit AmEx, DC, MC, V. **Map** p306 H5.
A superior stockist of contemporary African hand-
icrafts; richly coloured throws and textiles, metalwork and contemporary clothing using African
fabrics, plus funky, eye-catching lamps, briefcases
and objects made from recycled tin cans.

Hablando en Plata

*Plaza General Vara del Rey, 11, Rastro (91 365 01
34). Metro Puerta de Toledo/bus 3, 17, 23, 35, C.*
Open 10.30am-2pm, 5-8pm Mon-Fri; 10.30am-2pm
Sat; 9.30am-3.30pm Sun. **Credit** DC, MC, V.
Map p309 D9.
A treasure trove of craftwork from around the
world, among them Tuareg kilims, Moroccan ceram-
ics and Indian silver jewellery and textiles.

Popland

*C/Manuela Malasaña, 7, Malasaña & Conde Duque
(91 446 38 95). Metro Bilbao/bus 21, 147, 149.*
Open 11am-2.30pm, 5-9pm Mon-Sat; closed Sun &
two weeks Aug. **Credit** AmEx, DC, MC, V.
Map p305 F3.
Kitsch glorious kitsch, Popland sells original '60s
and '70s memorabilia, plastic handbags and sports
bags, huge sunglasses, film T-shirts and posters, as
well as more recent bits and pieces, with a throw-
back feel and easy listening muzak on the stereo.

Tarasca

*C/Divino Pastor 14, Malasaña & Conde Duque (91
446 56 71/91 446 56 81). Metro Bilbao or
Tribunal/bus 3, 37, 40, 147, 149.* **Open** 11am-2pm,
5.30-8.30pm Mon-Fri; 11am-2.30pm Sat; closed Sun.
Credit AmEx, DC, MC, V. **Map** p305 E3.
Tarasca sells ironwork and metal design by Spanish
designers and craftworkers, from furniture to small
sculptures, clocks, candlesticks and jewellery.

Miscellaneous/unclassifiable

Almirante 23

C/Almirante 23, Chueca (91 308 12 02).
Metro Chueca/bus 5, 14, 27, 37, 53. **Open** 11am-
2pm, 5-9pm Mon-Sat; closed Sun. **Credit** AmEx, DC,
MC,V. **Map** p306 H5.
In the living room of a ground-floor flat, this great
junk shop has loads of old postcards and prints.

Belloso

*C/Mayor 23, Austrias (91 366 42 58). Metro Sol/bus
all routes to Puerta del Sol.* **Open** 9.45am-2pm, 4.45-
8pm Mon-Fri; 9.45am-2pm Sat; closed Sun. **Credit**
AmEx, DC, MC, V. **Map** p309 D7.
One of the most spectacular of many similar shops
around the Calle Mayor. Since 1893, this shop has
been selling everything a loyal Catholic could wish
for, from rosaries, nativities, crucifixes and statues
of the Virgin to enough grand altarpieces and
cassocks to fit out a cathedral.

Galeán

C/Carretas 31 & 33, Austrias (91 521 18 94).
Metro Sol/bus all routes to Puerta del Sol. **Open**
9.30am-1.30pm, 5-8pm, Mon-Fri; 10am-2pm Sat;
closed Sun. **Credit** MC, V. **Map** p309 E8
Calle Carretas has its share of eccentric shops, and
this is a classic example: it sells every possible type
of oilcloth (popular as hard-wearing table coverings),
some with engaging designs, combined with a
bizarre range of orthopaedic equipment.

Macarrón

*C/San Agustín 7, Huertas & Santa Ana
(91 429 68 01). Metro Antón Martín/bus 9, 19, 27,
37, 45.* **Open** 9am-1.30pm, 4.30-8pm Mon-Fri; 10am-
1.30pm Sat; closed Sun & Aug.
Credit AmEx, DC, MC, V. **Map** p310 G8.
The official art materials supplier to the Círculo de
Bellas Artes, patronised in its day by Dalí and
Picasso. The staff are helpful and well informed.

Manuel Riesgo

*C/Desengaño 22, Malasaña & Conde Duque (91 531
19 56). Metro Gran Via/bus all routes to Gran Via.*
Open 10am-7pm Mon-Fri; 10am-1.30pm Sat; closed
Sun & mid Aug. **Credit** MC, V. **Map** p309 E6.
This incredible shop has some 25,000 products (pig-
ments, essences, oils, waxes and the like) for use in
the fields of beauty, pharmaceuticals and art.

Perfumería & Cuchillería Arturo Viñas

C/Atocha 62, Lavapiés (91 369 34 95).
Metro Antón Martín/bus 6, 26, 32. **Open** 9.30am-
2pm, 5.30-8.30pm Mon-Fri; 9.30am-2pm Sat; closed
Sun. **No credit cards.** **Map** p309 F8.
Arturo Viñas began selling perfumes from a stall in
1920, and opened this shop five years later. It's still
run by his family, but along with scents now offers
a huge range of kitchen knives, cleavers, razors and
penknives. A uniquely spectacular display.

Santería La Milagrosa

*C/San Alberto 1, corner C/Montera 21, Sol &
Gran Via (906 42 11 29). Metro Gran Via or
Sol/bus all routes to Puerta del Sol.* **Open** 11am-
9pm Mon-Sat; closed Sun. **Credit** DC, MC, V. **Map**
p309 E7.
A prominent product of the Cuban influx into
Madrid, a shop dedicated to the Afro-Cuban cult of
Santería (or voodoo, if you prefer). Lotions, potions,
candles and incense, promising effects ranging from
attracting back an errant lover or wealth and for-
tune to creating good vibes in the home.

Hair & beauty

Cosmetics & perfumes

Make Up & Art

C/Lagasca 34, Salamanca (91 577 28 54).
Metro Serrano/bus 1, 9, 19, 21, 51, 53. **Open**
10.30am-2.30pm; 5-8.30pm Mon-Sat; closed Sun.
Credit AmEx, MC, DC, V. **Map** p307 J4.

A world of its own: the Rastro

The Rastro, Madrid's bustling Sunday flea market, thought to date back five centuries, is as much a mass hang-out spot as a place for serious shopping. Around it there are any number of bars and cafés, from which noisy crowds spill out onto the streets every Sunday. Stalls set up from 7am, and real bargain-seekers arrive around 9am; the best time to come is from about 11am to 2-3pm.

Market stalls are packed in all the way down the Rastro's main street, Calle Ribera de Curtidores, and in summer the crowds get very hot, too. The Rastro has also sprawled out to take over much of the surrounding neighbourhood. A good starting point, though, is Plaza de Cascorro, from where Ribera de Curtidores winds all the way down to Ronda de Toledo.

Stalls at the top end focus mainly on cheap clothes, jewellery, gifts and hippy gear, while those further down generally offer a more miscellaneous hotch-potch, from pottery, electrical parts, birds, paintings, religious ornaments and second-hand leather jackets to old comics and plain junk. The streets between Calles Ribera de Curtidores and Toledo have many antiques stalls and shops, from cluttered junk shops to smarter affairs, and a few antiques arcades (see page 162). Of individual shops, **El 8** (C/Mira el Rio Alta 8, 91 366 94 07) and **El Transformista** (C/Mira el Rìo Baja 18, 91 539 88 33) sell 1950s-'60s furniture and collectors' items. Plaza General Vara del Rey contains a clutch of cheap second-hand clothes outlets.

Haggling sometimes works in the Rastro, at stalls and in the antique shops, but isn't all that widely practised. Note, also, that while the Rastro isn't a dangerous place, with such packed crowds, pickpocketing is rife. Try not to look careless, don't walk around with open bags or wallets in a back pocket, and be aware of anyone sticking too close behind you. When the crowds get a bit too much, head for Plaza de Humilladeros, for a drink at one of its easygoing *terrazas*.

El Rastro

C/Ribera de Curtidores, Rastro. Metro La Latina, Puerta de Toledo/bus 17, 18, 23, 35, 60, 148, C. **Open** dawn-approx 2pm Sun, public holidays.

A classy option for the luxury products fiend, stocking cosmetics, skin-care products, candles and beautifully packaged, divinely scented bathtime goodies.

Sephora

C/Alberto Aguilera 62, Malasaña & Conde Duque (91 550 20 50). Metro Argüelles/bus 1, 21, 44, 133, C. **Open** 10am-9.30pm Mon-Sat, & first Sun of every month. **Credit** AmEx, MC, DC, V. **Map** p304 C3.
Sephora offers a spectacular stock of fragrances, cosmetics and beauty accessories, and its own kaleidoscopic make-up range. There's a 'lowest price in town or your money back' guarantee on all perfumes, too.

Hairdressers

Alta Peluquería Vallejo

C/Santa Isabel 22, Lavapiés (91 527 44 48). Metro Antón Martín/bus 6, 26, 32. **Open** 9am-2pm, 4.30-8.30pm Mon-Fri; 9am-1.30pm Sat; closed Sun. **No credit cards. Map** p310 G9.
A traditional gentlemen's barber. It's friendly, cheap (1,100ptas) and offers good basic cuts.

Jofer

C/Galileo 56, Chamberí (91 447 51 60). Metro Quevedo/bus 2, 12, 16, 61. **Open** 8am-10pm Mon-Sat; closed Sun. **Credit** AmEx, DC, MC, V. **Map** p305 D1.
Well-priced unisex hair and beauty salons, offering the full range: cut and blow dry, colouring, waxing, sunbeds and so on. In most of their centres, of which there are around 20 in Madrid, you don't need an appointment. Prices vary between shops, but are generally very reasonable.
Branches: throughout the city.

Sally Whitmore/mobile hairdresser

91 859 50 35.
Vidal Sassoon-trained and formerly of Trevor Sorbie's London salon, Sally Whitmore is an English hairdresser who will travel anywhere in the Madrid area. She's often booked up, so recommends calling at least 48 hours ahead. Minimum charge per visit is 3,000ptas. She may be changing phone numbers shortly, but will have a detour on this number, and advertises in the local English-language press.

It's a Spanish thing: *lo típico*

The Spanish have a favourite word, *hortera*, which means 'tacky' or 'in bad taste'. As the capital of Spain, Madrid is also capital of all things traditionally-Spanish, and the city has a great collection of shops that are stuffed to overflowing with *horteradas*, pieces of *hortera*dom. Classic examples include tablecloths with maps of Spain, flamenco dancer dolls in full polka dot costumes, or little metal Don Quixotes. The range of 'typical Spanish' products also includes, though, some things that are actually very finely made, such as traditional hand-made shawls.

Almoraima

Plaza Mayor 12, Austrias (91 365 42 89).
Metro Sol/bus all routes to Puerta del Sol.
Open 10.30am-2.30pm, 4-8pm Mon-Fri;
10.30am-2.30pm Sat; closed Sun & Jan,
Feb. **Credit** AmEx, DC, MC, V. **Map** p309 D8.
Traditional fans of all descriptions (pictured).

Bisutería Otero

C/Mayor 28, Austrias (91 366 54 80).
Metro Sol/bus 3 and all routes to Puerta del
Sol. **Open** 10am-1.30pm, 5.30-9pm Mon-Fri;
10am-1.30pm Sat; closed Sun. *July, Aug,*
Sept 10am-1.30pm, 5.30-9pm Mon-Fri;
5.30-9pm Sat; closed Sun.
No credit cards. Map p309 D7.
Over a century old, Bisutería Otero has a wide selection of plastic beads and bracelets, and also does a fine line in peinetas (tall combs that are worn with a mantilla) and other gypsy-style *atrezzo*. The old shop itself is truly delightful.

Caramelos Paco

C/Toledo 55, La Latina (91 365 42 58).
Metro La Latina/bus 17, 18, 23, 35, 60.
Open *Sept-June* 9.30am-2pm, 5-8.30pm
Mon-Sat; 11am-3pm Sun. *July, Aug* 9.30am-
2pm only Sat. **Credit** MC, V. **Map** p309 D9.
All manner of boiled sweets – replicas of hams, sausages, figurines, and lollipop models of umpteen football team badges. At no.52 there is the party shop run by the same proprietors (see page 170).

La Casa de los Chales

C/Maiquez 3, Salamanca (91 409 72 39).
Metro Goya or O'Donnell/bus 2, 28, 30, C.
Open 9.30am-1.45pm, 5-8.30pm Mon-Sat;
closed Sun. **Credit** MC, V.
Originally selling fabrics, this shop now specialises in *mantones de Manila*, traditional fringed and embroidered shawls. They come in all colours and beautiful designs, and the price range is enormous.

La Casa de las Escayolas

C/León 5, Huertas & Santa Ana (91 429 48
50). Metro Antón Martín/bus 6, 26, 32, 57.
Open 10am-2pm, 5-8pm Mon-Fri; 10am-2pm
Sat; closed Sun. **Credit** AmEx, MC, V.
Map p309 F8.
A shop devoted to the plaster statue trade, with reproductions of many classic works of sculpture. Take home a scale model of Michelangelo's *David*, and delight your friends and family by painting him in the lurid colours of your choice. Nearby at no.19 is Escayolas Inma, its eternal rival.

Eat, Drink, Shop

Massages

Masajes a 1,000

C/Carranza 6, Malasaña & Conde Duque (91 447 47
77). Metro Bilbao/bus 21, 147, 149.
Open 7am-midnight daily. **Credit** AmEx, MC, V.
Map p305 E3.
The ideal way to unwind after a hard day's sight-seeing or shopping, Masajes a 1,000 offers massages starting at, yes, 1,000ptas for ten minutes, or you can splash out with a full hour. Also a complete range of beauty treatments, manicures and facials.
Branches: throughout the city.

Tattooing & body piercing

Mercado Fuencarral (*see page 169*) also has a tattoo and piercing centre.

Mao & Cathy

Corredera Alta de San Pablo 6, Malasaña & Conde
Duque (91 523 13 33). Metro Tribunal/bus 3, 40,
149. **Open** 3.30-8pm Mon; 11am-2pm, 3.30-8pm Tue-
Sat; closed Sun. **No credit cards. Map** p305 F4.
One of Madrid's longest-standing tattoo and body-piercing parlours. Prices start at around 5,000ptas.

Music

The **Fnac** (*see page 161*) has a very comprehensive music department.

AMA Records

Mercado Fuencarral, C/Fuencarral 45, Malasaña &
Conde Duque (91 522 64 03). Metro Tribunal/bus 3,
40, 149. **Open** 10am-9pm Mon-Sat; closed Sun.
Credit AmEx, MC, V. **Map** p305 F5.

Casa Jiménez

C/Preciados 42, Sol & Gran Vía (91 548 05 26). Metro Callao/bus all routes to Plaza del Callao. **Open** *Sept-June* 10am-1.30pm, 5-8pm Mon-Sat. Closed Sun & Aug, & Sat pm July. **Credit** AmEx, DC, MC, V. **Map** p309 E7.
One of the most famous shops in Madrid (and Spain) for *mantones* and *mantillas* – traditional lace and embroidery shawls. Superb – but wearable – pieces of skilled and patient work cost from 5,000ptas.

Efectos Militares y Civiles G Bodas

C/Mayor 15, Austrias (91 365 88 00). Metro Sol/bus 3 and all routes to Puerta del Sol. **Open** 9.30am-1.30pm, 5-8pm Mon-Fri; 9.30am-1.30pm Sat; closed Sun & Aug. **Credit** AmEx, DC, MC, V. **Map** p309 D7.
This supplier of military stripes, banners and insignia also has lead soldiers and other necessities for the military-minded. There's a Guardia Civil, a miniature Franco (obviously popular with the clientele) and – the Pope (?).

Guantes Luque

C/Espoz y Mina 3, Huertas & Santa Ana (91 522 32 87). Metro Sol/bus all routes to Puerta del Sol. **Open** 10am-1.30pm, 5-8pm Mon-Sat; closed Sun. **Credit** MC, V. **Map** p309 E8.
This traditional glovemaker, run by the same family for over a century, sells only gloves, with a huge variety of styles and prices.

Objetos de Arte Toledano

Paseo del Prado 10, Huertas & Santa Ana (91 429 50 00). Metro Banco de España/bus 9, 14, 27, 34, 37. **Open** 9.30am-8pm Mon-Sat; closed Sun. **Credit** AmEx, DC, MC, V. **Map** p310 G7.
If you're near the Prado, pop into this palace of hispano-tack across the way, selling everything from flamenco dolls to full-size suits of armour, as well as Lladró porcelain and Majorica pearls. Outside on Paseo del Prado you can get the ultimate in kitsch – a poster of a torero or a flamenco singer with your name on it.

Seseña

C/de la Cruz 23, Sol & Gran Vía (91 531 68 40). Metro Sol/bus all routes to Puerta del Sol. **Open** 10am-2pm, 4.30-8pm Mon-Fri; 10am-2pm Sat; closed Sun. **Credit** AmEx, DC, MC, V. **Map** p309 E7/8.
One that's much more distinguished: this long-established business is the only one left in the city specialising in traditional Madrileño capes. Ideal for the aspiring dandy, they're beautifully made, wonderfully warm, and expensive.

Specialising in the latest sounds in dance music, AMA is run by DJ crew Jazzin' Club, and has the hottest info on the Madrid party and club scene.

Del Sur

C/Caños del Peral 9, Austrias (91 541 96 93). Metro Opera/bus 3, 25, 39. **Open** 10.30am-2pm, 5-8.30pm Mon-Sat; closed Sun. **Credit** MC, V. **Map** p309 D7.
One of the most complete and well-priced record shops in the city. It has all types of music, with a recently expanded section for dance and electronics.

El Flamenco Vive

C/Conde de Lemos 7, Austrias (91 547 39 17/ www.elflamencovive.com). Metro Opera/bus 3, 25, 39. **Open** 10.30am-2pm, 5-9pm Mon-Sat; closed Sun. **Credit** AmEx, DC, MC, V. **Map** p308 C8.
As well as a superb selection of flamenco CDs and tapes, 'Flamenco Lives' has books on the genre

(some in English), flamenco clothing and other paraphernalia, and has a web and mail-order service.

Madrid Rock

Gran Vía 25, Sol & Gran Vía (91 523 26 52). Metro Gran Vía /bus all routes to Gran Vía. **Open** 10am-10pm daily. **Credit** AmEx, MC, V. **Map** p309 E6.
The city's biggest general record store. It has a broad stock, good clear-out offers and sells concert tickets.

Manzana

Plaza del Carmen 3, Sol & Gran Vía (91 521 40 61). Metro Sol/bus all routes to Puerta del Sol. **Open** 10.15am-2pm, 5-8.30pm Mon-Fri; 11am-2.45pm, 5-8.30pm Sat; closed Sun. **Credit** AmEx, DC, MC, V. **Map** p309 E7.
A great stock of Latin music (salsa, cumbias, merengue), and goodish jazz, blues and world music sections. Also – a lot of good stuff on vinyl.

Eat, Drink, Shop

Musical instruments

There are several more small shops selling fine handmade instruments in the Huertas area.

Garrido Bailén

C/Bailén 19, corner C/Mayor 88, Austrias (91 542 45 01). Metro Opera/bus 3, 25, 39, 148. **Open** 10am-1.30pm, 4.30-8.15pm Mon-Fri; 10am-1.45pm Sat; closed Sun. **Credit** AmEx, DC, MC, V. **Map** p308 C8.
Possibly the world's best musical instrument shop. It has everything from tiny ocarinas to Alpine horns, electronic keyboards and drum machines, and every kind of traditional Spanish musical instrument.

Guitarrería F Manzanero

C/Santa Ana 12, La Latina (91 366 00 47). Metro La Latina/bus 17, 18, 23, 35, 60. **Open** 10am-1.30pm, 5-8pm Mon-Fri; closed Sat, Sun. *July* 10am-1.30pm Mon-Fri; closed Sat, Sun. **Credit** AmEx, DC, MC, V. **Map** p309 D9.
The very friendly Félix Manzanero has been making all kinds of guitars (beginners', semi-pro, professional) for around 45 years. Fans will also love the display of old and rare string instruments.

Opticians

Grand Optical

Puerta del Sol 14, Sol & Gran Vía (91 701 49 80). Metro Sol/all routes to Puerta del Sol. **Open** 10am-9.30pm Mon-Sat; closed Sun. **Credit** AmEx, DC, MC, V. **Map** p309 E7.
Part of the same group as the UK's Vision Express, Grand Optical has the same three-year guarantee on all glasses. Glasses take an hour, graduated sunglasses take three, and there's also a wide range of contacts.

Photocopying

Most stationers (*papelerías*) or printers (*imprentas*) also have faxes and photocopiers.

Repografías Cuarta Línea

C/Duque de Alba 13, La Latina (91 369 40 21). Metro Tirso de Molina/bus 6, 26, 32, 65. **Open** *Sept-July* 9am-2pm; 4.30-8pm Mon-Fri; closed Sat, Sun & two weeks Aug, *rest Aug* 9am-3pm Mon-Fri; closed Sat, Sun. **Credit** AmEx, MC, V. **Map** p309 D9.
A very good stationery shop, which does laser printing, colour copies, enlargements and so on.

Photographic

Fotocasión

C/Carlos Arniches 22, Rastro (91 467 64 91). Metro Puerta de Toledo/bus all routes to Puerta de Toledo. **Open** 4.30-8.30pm Mon; 9.30am-2pm, 4.30-8.30pm Tue-Fri; 9.30am-2pm Sat, Sun. **Credit** MC, V. **Map** p309 D10.
A treasure trove for photographers and camera collectors. Owner José Luis Mur is a walking encyclopaedia on anything and everything to do with

cameras; he also has great offers on spare parts, new and second-hand cameras, and other materials.

Foto Sistema

Gran Vía 22, Sol & Gran Vía (91 521 20 63). Metro Gran Vía/bus all routes to Gran Vía. **Open** 9.30am-8pm Mon-Fri; 9.30am-2pm Sat; closed Sun. **Credit** AmEx, DC, MC, V. **Map** p309 F6.
A good-quality one-hour developing service for colour, black and white, slides and enlargements. **Branches**: throughout the city.

Sport

Supporters Shop

C/Goya 50, Salamanca (91 575 88 68). Metro Goya/bus 21, 53. **Open** 10am-2pm, 5-8.30pm Mon-Fri; 10.30am-2.30pm, 5.30-8.30pm Sat; closed Sun & Aug. **Credit** DC, MC, V. **Map** p307 K4.
Want a Coventry City shirt? Prefer the chequered Croatian national strip, or Boca Juniors? It's all here: shirts and memorabilia from some 525 clubs from around the world. The boss knows his football, too.

Tornal Moya Deportes

Ronda de Valencia 8, Lavapiés (91 527 54 40). Metro Embajadores/bus 27, C, all routes to Embajadores. **Open** 10am-2pm, 5-8.30pm Mon-Sat; closed Sun. **Credit** MC, V.
This big, well-laid-out shop stocks top-name sportswear, trainers, walking boots, swimwear, sunglasses, tennis rackets, football shirts and backpacks.

Stamps & coins

Stamp & coin market

Plaza Mayor, Austrias. Metro Sol/bus all routes to Puerta del Sol. **Open** *approx* 9am-2pm Sun; closed Mon-Sat. **Map** p309 D8.
Every Sunday the Plaza Mayor is taken over by an avid mass of stamp and coin collectors buying, selling and eyeing each others' wares. It's also a Sunday-morning attraction for anyone on a stroll in the city centre, whether or not they share a fascination with tarnished old pesetas, stamps of all nations and 19th-century share certificates. There are also traders selling old magazines, second-hand books, postcards, badges and ex-Soviet bloc military regalia – even phonecards are beginning to appear. In short, just about anything collectable is here.

Tobacco & smoking

Estancos (tobacco shops; *see page 287*) are found all over town.

La Mansión del Fumador

C/Carmen 22, Sol & Gran Vía (91 532 08 17). Metro Sol/bus all routes to Puerta del Sol. **Open** 10.30am-1.30pm, 4.30-8.30pm Mon-Sat; closed Sun. **Credit** AmEx, MC, V. **Map** p309 E7.
No tobacco as such, but 1accessories such as cigar-cutters, lighters, humidifiers, pipes and ashtrays.

Art & Entertainment

By Season

Locals might get dressed up for a Madrileño *fiesta*, but all you really have to do is turn up in the right street.

According to a much-quoted survey, Spaniards rate traditional *fiestas* among their favourite leisure interests, on a par with fashion, football and music. This doesn't mean that they are obsessed with dressing up in bizarre costumes and going to Mass several times a day. However Catholic most *fiestas* may be in their origins, nowadays their most visible aspect is as occasions for partying in the street and socialising *en masse*, which is something Spaniards really are addicted to.

As well as its traditional celebrations, Madrid hosts arts and music festivals, techno-gatherings, theatrical seasons and other events through the year. In Madrid there is, however, a good deal of gloom that the city is no longer the party capital it was a decade ago. The policies of the conservative PP *Ayuntamiento* (city council) have had a powerful effect on culture in the city. Many of the city's arts festivals were founded under Socialist administrations during the 1980s, with lavish budgets; in the new climate, some have disappeared entirely, while those that remain, such as the **Veranos de la Villa** summer festival (*see page 188*), have been subjected to swingeing budget cuts. Some events, such as **Madrid en Danza** and the **Festival de Otoño** (*see pages 187 and 188*), are in a better state and remain highlights of the arts year, mainly because they are reliant not on the *Ayuntamiento* but the regional government, the *Comunidad*, which, while also controlled by the PP, has a less hostile attitude than the city council to public funding of anything with a whiff of the unconventional.

The institutional vacuum has partly been filled by private promoters, but one of the liveliest recent initiatives, the alternative jamboree **Festimad** (*see page 187*), has a cloudy future. More vibrant is the **PHotoEspaña** city-wide photography festival (*see page 187*), which has developed into a must-see event.

In the meantime, the city's assorted neighbourhood street festivals will no doubt continue, more through locals' ability to turn

▶ For more information on flamenco festivals in and around Madrid, *see page 201*.

a day off into a knees-up than to the city hall's interest or budgeting. It's a good idea to be in town for the end-of-summer *verbenas* (street parties), the time of the year when Madrid and the Madrileños really come into their own. **La Paloma** and the other *verbenas* in August are manifestations of a popular culture still in touch with its roots (for which, *see page 185* **Kings of the street**). **Dos de Mayo** and **San Isidro** are two other popular events that bring the masses onto the streets. And don't forget **Carnival**, lower-key than in some parts of Spain but a great excuse for a bash nonetheless.

Madrid also hosts a great many trade fairs, mostly at the Feria de Madrid exhibition complex (*see page 279*). Information on them is available on the Feria website, www.ifema.es.

WHAT'S ON

Advance information about arts festivals is notoriously hard to come by, as programming details are often not finalised until very late, but local listings magazines such as the *Guía del Ocio* and *Metrópoli* usually produce special pull-out supplements in the preceding weeks (for both, *see page 290*). Information is also available from tourist offices and the city council's **010** info line (for all, *see page 287*), and the *Comunidad*'s information line, **012**. Events listed below that are public holidays are marked *; for a full list of them, *see page 288*.

Spring

La Alternativa
Information Comunidad de Madrid, tourist offices & 012. **Date** Feb-Mar.
Formerly the fringe element of the Festival de Otoño (*see p188*), this lively festival of 'alternative theatre' features fringe theatre and some dance performances in the Sala Triángulo, the Teatro Alfil and various other venues (*see pp243-6*).

Día de la Mujer/ Semana de la Mujer
Various venues. Route normally starts at Plaza Jacinto Benavente, Huertas & Santa Ana. Metro Sol or Tirso de Molina. **Information** Dirección General de la Mujer (91 580 47 00) & Centro de la Mujer (91 319 36 89). **Date** 8 Mar & surrounding week.

Kings of the street

Who are those men dressed up in flat caps and dogtooth-check jackets, and why are their wives and girlfriends wearing long, tight dresses with frills at the bottom? And the carnation in the hair, and the headscarf? Why are small children so dressed up on a very hot day? These are the sort of questions you may well ask yourself if you go along to any of Madrid's more traditional *fiestas*. Well, what cockneys are to London, *castizos* (pictured) are to Madrid.

In the last quarter of the 19th century, as the city grew rapidly, a working class developed, and, like most, sought an identity to distinguish itself from the rest of society. *Castizos* were in effect descendants of the *Majos* and *Majas* painted by Goya (see page 17). Their slang and humour were celebrated in the *zarzuela* light operas, which developed in Madrid at around the same time (see page 217).

Famous for their caustic, chippy wit or *chulería* – exemplified by the action of tossing the head back and clicking the tongue, an archetypal *castizo* gesture – *castizos* lived in the tenements or *corralas*, which once made up a large part of districts such as Lavapiés or La Latina (see page 76). Chamberí is another area of the city that lays claim to be the heart of *castizo*-dom.

Much of this may all be in the past but, in a city where most people are from somewhere else, those who can trace their origins here back more than a generation or so are proud to celebrate it. The current city council, always happy to look backward, also actively celebrates the notion of *lo castizo* (*castizo*-ness), and has ensured that there is a higher *castizo* content in San Isidro and other city *fiestas*, with old-fashioned *castizo* comics, traditional dancing competitions and *zarzuelas*.

Although hardly in vogue, the concept of the *castizo* has been rescued from decline in recent years. People turn out in full regalia for the most traditional Madrid *fiestas*, San Isidro and, particularly, the August *verbenas* leading up to La Paloma. It's then you have a chance to gather round the barrel-organ and watch the experts at the *chotis*, a Madrileño version of a supposedly Scottish folk dance in which the man pivots on the spot, turning his partner – usually to the tune of the local anthem *Madrid, Madrid, Madrid* (actually written by a Mexican, Agustín Lara). The open-air *zarzuela* season at La Corrala is another major *castizo* event (see page 216). And, despite their reputation, *castizos* are a chummy lot, and will gladly tell you all about their ancestry if you ask to have your picture taken with them.

International Women's Day, 8 March, is marked with a march (usually starting at 8pm, and nearly always from Plaza Jacinto Benavente down Calle Atocha), followed by *fiestas* in bars and clubs at night, organised by women's groups. The official Dirección General de la Mujer (*see p288*) organises a week of events by female artists and performers.

Semana Santa (Holy Week)

All over Madrid. **Information** Tourist offices & 010.
Date Easter Week, Mar/Apr.

Holy Week is a less impressive event in Madrid than in southern Spain, but nevertheless there are several religious processions in the city during the week, with the traditional hooded figures of the *Penitentes* (Penitents) and huge images of Christ and the Virgin carried on the shoulders of troops of sturdy bearers. The most striking procession in Madrid is that of the brotherhood of *Jesús Nazareno el Pobre*, which winds its way around La Latina. There are also organ concerts in many churches and chapels. Easter is more important in towns around Madrid. The procession in **Toledo**, held in silence, is particularly solemn and ceremonious, and **La Granja** offers the eerie spectacle of the hooded penitents bearing huge crucifixes on their backs. In

Chinchón, on Good Friday, there is a performance of a medieval Passion Play in the Plaza Mayor. For all these towns, *see chapter* **Castilian Towns**.

Fiesta del Trabajo* (May Day)

City centre & Casa de Campo. Metro Batán or Lago/bus 33, 41, 75. **Date** 1 May.

May Day in Madrid has lost much of its political and emotional significance since the 1970s, but it still witnesses a sizeable march in the city centre, organised jointly by the Communist-led CCOO, the Socialist UGT and the anarcho-syndicalist CGT unions. Another march, by the anarchist CNT, runs through Tetuán, along Calle Bravo Murillo. After the speeches a festive spirit takes over and the crowds make for the Casa de Campo, where the UGT usually organises a big party with the *Casas Regionales* (clubs representing the different regions of Spain), with *chiringuitos* (stalls) offering beer, *bocadillos* (rolls) and traditional food and drink of all sorts.

Dos de Mayo*

District of Malasaña. Metro Bilbao, Noviciado or Tribunal/bus 3, 40, 147, 149. **Map** p305 E4. *Parque de las Vistillas. Metro Opera/bus 3, 25, 33, 39, 148.* **Information** Tourist offices & 012. **Date** 2 May. **Map** p308 C8.

The second of May 1808, when the people of Madrid rose up in an attempt to expel Napoleon's invading army (*see p17*), is a hallowed day in local legend. Today it is the official holiday of the Madrid region, the *Comunidad de Madrid*. Resistance was strongest in the Malasaña area around the Monteleón artillery barracks, which stood where the Plaza Dos de Mayo is today, and the district takes its name from the teenage heroine of the struggle, Manuela Malasaña. The modern *fiesta*, the beginning of the summer *verbena* season, is also centred here, with bands playing dance music in the Plaza Dos de Mayo, and a more mixed crowd than the young bunch who usually frequent the *barrio*'s streets. The *Comunidad* also organises concerts and dance stages around the city, particularly in the Parque de las Vistillas (*see p70*) next to the Palacio Real.

San Isidro*

Plaza Mayor and all over Madrid. **Information** Plaza Mayor tourist office & 010. **Date** one week around 15 May.

San Isidro, the humble 12th-century labourer famed for his many miracles in aid of the needy (*see p8*), is Madrid's patron saint, and the week around his day, 15 May, is the whole city's *fiesta mayor* or biggest wingding. In the **Plaza Mayor** there are concerts of dance music each night, and a giant *cocido* or traditional stew (*see p124*) is cooked up (by army cooks) for anyone who wants some on one of the Sundays of the week. These are some of the most traditional parts of the *fiesta*, with the old and the very young dressed up in *castizo* attire. On 15 May itself the tradition is to go to the **Ermita de San Isidro** in the park of the same name (*see p88*), which gets packed for this one day of the year with

Seeing the lights during **San Isidro**.

picknicking families, in modern versions of the scenes painted many times by Goya. Stalls offer bocadillos of Madrileño delicacies – *gallinejas, entresijos* and other forms of guts (*see p124*).

Another focus of activity is **Las Vistillas**, the park near the Palacio Real with a view out over the sierra (*see p70*), where there is a music stage that hosts flamenco, salsa and traditional Spanish dance bands – inevitably playing the Madrileño *chotis* – every night of the week. More improptu music stages appear in various squares around the Austrias district, while a more modern dance all-nighter with bands and DJs is consigned to the **Parque Juan Carlos I** (*see p88*). Concerts by an international range of performers – Tom Jones, the Vieja Trova Santiagüeña from Cuba, Georges Moustaki – feature at many theatres, especially the Centro Cultural de la Villa (*see p242*), there is a children's puppet theatre festival in the Retiro (*see p195*) and even the Teatro Real stages a gala. Many other events come under the San Isidro umbrella – a kids' programme, theatre, exhibitions, demonstrations of local cuisine, craft and book fairs – some of which are listed below. San Isidro is also Madrid's (and so the world's) most important bullfighting *feria*, with *corridas* every day for a whole month at **Las Ventas** (*see p192*). A full *fiesta* programme is available free from the Plaza Mayor tourist office (usually just before the first day), but get one early, as they're often in short supply.

Associated events

Feria de la Cerámica *Avda Felipe II, Salamanca.*
Metro Goya/bus 15, 21, 29, 30, 43, 63, C.
A high-quality ceramics fair that now includes work
in a range of other crafts.
Feria de la Cerámica y Cacharrería *Plaza de las*
Comendadoras, Malasaña & Conde Duque. Metro
Noviciado/bus 21, 147. **Map** p305 D3.
More of a household crockery fair, and so cheaper,
but you can still find traditional Spanish ceramics.
Feria del Libro Antiguo y de Ocasión *Paseo de*
Recoletos, Salamanca. Metro Banco de España or
Colón/bus all routes to Plaza de Colón. **Map** p310 H6.
An old and second-hand book fair usually held on
the weekends of the San Isidro week, where you
might find rare treasures or recent remainders.

Madrid en Danza

Various venues. **Information** Tourist offices & 012.
Dates mid May-mid June.
After a few years when differences between the city
hall and regional government hindered its development, this international dance festival looks to be
very much back on the rails, and the recent extension of activities to fringe venues and towns outside
Madrid has generated great public interest. Recent
editions have featured very fresh and dynamic
international programmes of contemporary dance,
combining locally-based groups such as 10 y 10 or
the flamenco ballet of Antonio Canales with the
Flanders Ballet, Barcelona's Lanònima Imperial,
Maguy Marin and British-based dancer Javier de
Frutos. Venues include the Círculo de Bellas Artes
(*see p73*), the Teatro Albéniz, Sala Cuarta Pared and
others (*see chapter* **Theatre & Dance**).

La Feria del Libro (Madrid Book Fair)

Parque del Retiro. Metro Atocha, Ibiza or Retiro/bus
all routes to Atocha or Puerta de Alcalá. **Information**
Asociación de Libreros (91 534 61 24). **Date** two
weeks end May-June. **Map** p310 I6-10/p311 I-K 6-9.
The Book Fair began as a local show 56 years ago,
but is now an international event, with appearances
by major writers from around the world, and hundreds of stands in the Retiro. Public attendance is
massive throughout the two weeks. It is one of few
events held in the Retiro, and there is opposition to
it on environmental grounds. However, for the
moment, it looks set to continue among the trees,
lakes and statues of Madrid's main park.

Summer

San Antonio de la Florida

Ermita de San Antonio de la Florida, Paseo de la
Florida 5, La Florida. Metro Príncipe Pío/bus 41,
46, 75. **Information** 91 547 07 22. **Date** 12 June.
Map p304 A4.
The hermitage of San Antonio de la Florida, with its
Goya frescoes (*see p69*), is also the place where sin-
gle women looking to find a suitable chap have tra-
ditionally gone on the saint's day, 12 June, to leave

Nacho Duato in **Madrid en Danza**.

a needle in the hope that this might get him to intervene and send one along. In former times it was a
big day out for Madrid's traditional seamstresses.
Today, there's a big street party outside.

PHotoEspaña

Various venues. **Information** 91 360 13 20/
www.photoes.ya.com. **Date** mid June-mid July.
Launched in 1998, PHotoEspaña is the biggest treat
photography lovers in Madrid have ever had. It promotes over 70 photo exhibitions in the course of a
month – from the World Press Photo exhibition to a
show on Russia in the 1920s, or on photographers
such as Pablo Genovés or Otto Steinert. All the
major art spaces take part, together with other museums, private galleries, *Cercanías* stations, colleges,
bookshops and less conventional venues. There are
also workshops, talks and prizes. One of the organisers is La Fábrica gallery in Huertas (*see p203*),
which is a good source of information.

Festimad

Círculo de Bellas Artes, C/Marqués de Casa Riera 2,
Huertas & Santa Ana. Metro Banco de España/bus
all routes to Cibeles. **Map** p310 G7.
Parque el Soto, Móstoles. Train Cercanías
C-5. **Information** 91 547 23 85/91 360 54 00.
Dates June-July.
This 'Alternative Festival' was begun in a nightclub
in 1994, with the idea of providing a focus for every-
thing to do with Madrid's alternative youth culture.

Within two years it had grown to such an extent that the Círculo de Bellas Artes (*see p73*) became the main venue for a week-long jamboree of sculpture and photography, seminars, a flea market, record launches, dance performances, film screenings, poetry readings and DJ nights and concerts by musicians of all kinds from Spain's young/indie music scene. The parallel pop-rock festival then moved out to a park in suburban Móstoles, where it continued to grow. However, organisational and money problems led to the 2000 edition being cancelled, all except for the **CineMad** week of fringe and short films, in the Mercado Fuencarral (*see p169*). The organisers determinedly state that it will bounce back in future, so it's still worth looking out for.

Fiesta Africana/World Music Getafe

C/Hospital de San José & C/General Palacios, Getafe. Bus 441, 442 from Atocha/train Cercanías line C-4 to Getafe Centro. **Information** Cultura Africana, C/San Eugenio 8, Madrid (91 539 32 67), or Getafe town council (91 681 82 12/91 681 60 62). **Date** July.
The Fiesta Africana and World Music Getafe have been held five minutes' walk from each other in the industrial suburb of Getafe since 1994, and now look set to merge. The Fiesta Africana includes batik workshops, storytelling, African cuisine and, of course, music; World Music Getafe is now a fixture on the musical calendar, with acts from Spain and across Europe, Africa, Asia and Latin America. The main venue is the old Hospital de San José, on the street of the same name off Getafe's main street, Calle Madrid, a short walk from the station.

Veranos de la Villa

Various venues. **Information** Tourist offices & 010. **Dates** July-mid Sept.
The 'Summers in the City' programme is Madrid's largest city-sponsored arts programme. Funding cuts have meant that it has become more limited virtually each year, but the occasional big name – Youssou N'Dour, Pat Metheny, Gilberto Gil, Elvis Costello – and interesting lesser-known acts still appear. Formerly it had a strongly themed programme of opera, flamenco, pop, modern dance, jazz, cinema, theatre and more; since the cuts, it has become more like an umbrella provided by the Ayuntamiento under which private venues and promoters can shelter, including events with no official participation. In future the music programme itself will probably be subcontracted to a private promoter, so that corners will be cut even further. That said, there are a few things that do not change: the main venue is the patio of the **Centro Cultural Conde Duque** (*see p107*). Concerts, from salsa to rock and pop, also take place in the Las Ventas bullring, a fabulous music venue on a summer night.

Opera is also on offer at the Conde Duque, but the classical music programme is heavily reliant on tired, but cheap, ensembles from Eastern Europe. Dance performances take place in the Conde Duque or the Teatro de Madrid, and other fixtures of the festival are theatre, the *zarzuela* programmes presented in the Centro Cultural de la Villa and La Corrala (*see p217*), and the open-air cinema season on the Paseo de la Florida (*see p198*).

Verbenas de San Cayetano, San Lorenzo & La Paloma

La Latina & Lavapiés. Metro La Latina, Lavapiés or Puerta de Toledo/bus all routes to Puerta de Toledo. **Information** Tourist offices & 010. **Date** 6-15 Aug. **Map** p309 D/E9.
In August, those who haven't managed to quit the city for the beach or mountains let their hair down at these street *fiestas*, the most traditional and *castizo* in Madrid. San Cayetano (7 August), San Lorenzo (10 August) and La Paloma (15 August) follow in quick succession, all blending into the one event. The action takes place all around the old districts of La Latina and Lavapiés, where every street and square is decked out in flowers and bunting, and many people appear in all their *castizo* finery. During the day, there are parades and lots of events for kids. The main *fiesta* really gets going after the sun goes down, and from then until the early hours the drink flows freely, stalls sell nuts, coconut, rolls, sangría and lemonade, and live bands and sound systems provide music from pop and salsa to Madrid's very own *chotis*. To take it all in, just walk around from about 9pm onwards, going down as many side streets as you can.

Autumn

Fiestas del Partido Comunista

Casa de Campo. Metro Batán or Lago/bus 33, 41, 75. **Information** Partido Comunista de España (91 300 49 69). **Date** mid Sept.
The Spanish Communist Party organises this three-day jamboree on a weekend in September in the Casa de Campo. As on May Day (*see p186*), the *Casas Regionales* provide local delicacies, and there are live bands, theatre shows and stalls set up by a range of groups. Tickets go on sale at Madrid Rock (*see p181*).

Semana Internacional de la Moda (International Fashion Week)

Feria de Madrid/IFEMA, Recinto Ferial Juan Carlos I. Metro Campo de las Naciones/bus 73, 122. **Information** 91 722 50 00/91 722 51 80/www.ifema.es. **Dates** mid Sept & mid Feb.
Fashion aficionados can delight at the sight of the world's models showing new creations by every name in Spanish fashion and many from abroad. Sections highlight lingerie, sportswear or furs; the February event covers summer- and swimwear.

Festival de Otoño (Autumn Festival)

Various venues. **Information** Comunidad de Madrid (91 580 25 75), tourist offices & 012. **Date** Oct-Dec.
Initiated in the 1980s as the Madrid International Theatre Festival, this event mushroomed under the Socialist administration into something far wider,

embracing a complete range of the performing arts. Over the years every kind of music has featured, and top names from the world of dance; at the other end of the spectrum, a huge number of fringe theatre groups, from excellent to frankly terrible, appeared in the alternative theatre festival, which has now moved to spring as **La Alternativa** (*see p184*). The Teatro Albéniz (*see p243*) hosts most events in the main festival, but many other venues are used. This is another case in which earlier overspending has been followed by a much more restrictive regime, but the festival still maintains a high level of quality in theatre and dance, and the 2000 programme featured such performers as Canada's La La La Human Steps, Odin Teatret from Denmark and Hanna Schygulla, reciting Brecht. In music, there was Paquito D'Rivera and a lot of Latin Jazz.

Festival de Jazz de Madrid
Information: CP Conciertos (91 447 64 00).
Dates Oct-Dec.
The Jazz Festival follows on at the end of the Festival de Otoño (*see above*). In addition to Madrid's usual jazz venues, major halls such as the Auditorio Nacional (*see p215*) open their doors to fine jazz musicians from the world over – Cassandra Wilson headlined in the 1999 event.

Winter

See above **Semana International de la Moda**.

Feria de Artesanía
Paseo de Recoletos, Salamanca. Metro Banco de España or Colón/bus all routes to Plaza de Colón.
Date Dec-6 Jan. **Map** p310 G/H7.
Madrid's biggest craft fair takes over the Paseo de Recoletos in the weeks before Christmas and continues to the end of the festive season, 6 January. The official stalls run from Plaza de Cibeles to Colón, but unlicensed traders, *piratas*, stretch away as far again on each side. There is plenty worth buying, but it's best to go early, as the final days are frantic.

Navidad* (Christmas)
All over Madrid. **Date** 25 Dec.
Unlike in other countries nowadays, the Christmas period still only starts in December in Madrid (for the moment, at least). Festivities centre around 24 and 31 December and 6 January, the Feast of the Three Kings, or Epiphany. Traditionally, the main Spanish Christmas decoration is a crib, not a tree, and children receive their presents from the Three Kings on 6 January, not on Christmas, although in the last few decades Father Christmas and other international trappings of the season have become increasingly visible, and kids sometimes expect to get presents on *both* days. In the weeks preceding Christmas the Plaza Mayor is filled with stalls selling Christmas trees, traditional cribs and other festive trinkets, department stores put on lavish seasonal displays, and Recoletos is packed for the annual crafts fair (great for buying presents). The

main Christmas celebrations take place on the night of Christmas Eve, which is when families in most of Spain have their traditional Christmas meal, at home. The streets are consequently empty, although things liven up a little after midnight, and many clubs are open all night. Christmas Day itself tends to be more a day for recovering.

Noche Vieja (New Year's Eve)
Puerta del Sol. Metro Sol/bus all routes to Puerta del Sol. **Date** 31 Dec. **Map** p309 E7.
As on Christmas Eve, many people start the evening with a meal with family or friends. The place to head to for those who don't stay in is the Puerta del Sol, where thousands gather beneath the clock for a communal countdown, fireworks and the grape-stuffing session that is the centre of a Spanish New Year's Eve – you eat one grape for each chime of midnight, to have good luck for the rest of the year. Then it's off to bars for the rest of the night (but be warned that drinks are much more expensive than usual).

Reyes* (Three Kings)
All over Madrid. **Date** 6 Jan.
On 5 January, the eve of the arrival of the Three Kings, there is an evening *Cabalgata* (parade) around the city, with hundreds of elaborate floats, from where costumed riders throw sweets to children in the crowd. Thousands of people gather to watch the parade, which is televised. Afterwards, adults, as on the other 'eves', enjoy yet another big dinner, while kids are tucked up in bed preparing for their big day on the 6th, when they finally get their presents.

ARCO
Feria de Madrid, Recinto Ferial Juan Carlos I. Metro Campo de las Naciones/bus 73, 122.
Information 91 722 50 00/www.arco.ifema.es.
Dates mid Feb.
The ARCO art fair attracts galleries from all over the world, providing a unique opportunity to see a huge range of work under one roof (*see p206*).

Carnaval
Various venues. **Date** the week before Lent (usually late Feb/early Mar).
The Carnival celebrations are opened with a speech by a famous artist or writer, followed by a parade, the route of which varies from year to year. In clubs and other venues there are music gigs, ribaldry, drinking, and a fair amount of dressing up, especially in gay clubs in Chueca (*see pp207-13*). There is a famous masked ball in the Círculo de Bellas Artes (*see p73*), but tickets are pricey and hard to come by. The end of Carnival on Ash Wednesday is marked by the loopy procession of the *Entierro de la Sardina* (Burial of the Sardine), a bizarre and ancient ritual in which the said fish is escorted around town in its tiny coffin, accompanied by an out-of-tune band, before being interred on Paseo de la Florida. This *fiesta* is the subject of a painting by Goya, now in the Real Academia de San Fernando (*see p99*).

Bullfighting

Essential drama, big business or just blood and sand – few things can provoke such passionate reactions, for and against.

Probably the one thing most people in the world know about Spain is that there is bullfighting. It is the activity that most sets the country apart, for good or ill. Foreigners have long been fascinated or repelled by it, regarding it as a symbol of the country's dark, exotic, mysterious nature.

It is, certainly, the extreme, dramatic spectacle so admired by writers like Hemingway; it can also be very vulgar, with lots of noise, raw humour and primary colours. Many Spaniards, for their part, see bullfighting as a regrettable hangover from a Spain locked into a tedious stereotype, something they'd rather not be associated with.

And yet, bullfighting has been intertwined with the country's culture for centuries, and is something from which it cannot easily be disentangled. It is thought to have originated in the Bronze Age Minoan civilisation in Crete. In Castile and Andalusia the bull is an ever-present symbol in traditional folklore, and bullfights of some kind have been held since at least the Middle Ages. Like sports that are an integral part of a nation's life such as cricket or baseball, it has inspired a vast amount of literature, from ultra-detailed press reports to one of the greatest works of modern Spanish poetry, García Lorca's *Llanto por Ignacio Sánchez Mejías*, an elegy for a bullfighter friend of the poet killed in the ring in 1934.

For years it was suggested that bullfighting was dying out. Not a bit of it. The 1990s saw it more in vogue than ever, and combined with modern marketing techniques to boot. At the ring, you can bump shoulders and rub knees with every strata of Madrid society, from the beret-wearing old villager to fashion models and young e-commerce entrepreneurs with slicked-back hair and sharp suits. Young *toreros* are treated like true celebs, and their love affairs and marriages – frequently to showbiz women – are often the lead stores in Spain's ever-popular gossip magazines.

One problem with bullfighting is in saying exactly what it is. It's not a sport, as there is no competition involved. It's more of a ritual, with certain set requirements.

How it is viewed by those who have grown up with it or become addicted to it is naturally very different from the way it's seen by those who simply find it revolting. One cultured *aficionado* has said that a *corrida* is a combination of *arte, ética y estética* – art (the skill the bullfighter needs), ethics (he must face up to the risk, and give the bull a fair chance of catching him, and if he doesn't will not be asked back) and aesthetics (the grace in movement that wins the greatest praise from the hyper-critical crowd). To put it another way, a bullfight is the ultimate fulfilment of the old English sporting adage that it ain't the winning but the taking part. Barring occasional incidents, the outcome is inevitable, but it is how the final victory is achieved, with what degree of courage, skill, cunning, even elegance, that is all-important. A Spanish expression of admiration is to say that somebody did something *a la torera* – with no other resources than nerve, flair, style, and not a little cheek.

Of course, you could say this is nothing but the sort of stuff that comes out of the end of a bull by the tail. But, such considerations aside, what keeps *aficionados*, Spanish and foreign, coming to the ring is that they find there's no other spectacle that gives them such a buzz, that's so gripping or even spine-chilling. For, in order for a *corrida* truly to be a demonstration of grace under pressure, there has to be a real element of danger for the bullfighter at every stage, no matter how formalised, or even corny, the event may appear.

WHAT HAPPENS

A bullfight is a complicated affair, and if you go to one it's advisable to have an idea of what you are going to see. There are two kinds: the most common, the *corrida de toros* in which the matador or *torero* is on foot, and the *corrida de rejoneo*, on horseback. Although the conventional *corrida*'s rules and rituals are now regarded almost as holy writ they were only established in the 18th century, when this relatively proletarian form of bullfighting first became dominant. The bullfights staged in the Plaza Mayor in imperial Madrid were mainly of the older, aristocratic *rejoneo* type. It is still practised today, but though very skilled is not regarded highly by hard-core *aficionados*.

Every aspect of the bullfight is determined by fixed rules, from the opening parade to the role of the *Presidente* of the *corrida* (in Madrid, usually a police inspector), who directs the various stages of the event by displaying a series of different-coloured handkerchiefs. The *corrida* consists of six sections, with three *toreros* alternating and killing two bulls each.

And while the bullfight goes on, for two hours or more, the running commentaries from fans munching on their tortilla bocadillos while the wine is passed back and forth, the raucous abuse they yell at the *torero* or the bull-breeder's mother, the cries of the beer and whisky hawkers and the lively *paso dobles* from the resident brass band, ensure a very special and thoroughly festive spirit.

Fighting bulls, *toros bravos*, usually weigh between 500 and 600 kilos (1,100-1,300lb). They are reared semi-wild on large ranches, and have little contact with a human on foot before their entrance into the ring. At midday before the fight they can be seen in the *apartado* outside the ring, when they are put into individual pens. When finally released into the ring, the animal's natural instinct is to charge and remove or kill all that moves before him. At this point the bull is too fast and strong for the bullfighter to be able to kill it in the strictly prescribed manner. It has to be weakened, and for the *torero* to get close enough he has to try to bring it under his control with the skill of his capework.

Each fight is divided into three sections called *tercios* (thirds). The first begins with the *torero* making *pases* or movements with a large pink cape to test out the temperament, strength and speed of the animal. This can seem one of the more innocent parts of the *corrida*, as if the two were playing. It is actually very dangerous, for at this point the bull still has all its strength and speed.

Next, still in the first *tercio*, lance-wielding *picadores* appear on padded horses, inciting the animal to charge and then piercing the neck muscle to force it to lower its head. This is the bloodiest part of the fight, and the one most frequently condemned by bullfighting's opponents. For *aficionados*, however, it's crucial in gauging the bull's spirit, on the basis of whether it returns to charge the *picador* and his horse despite being wounded and feeling pain.

The next *tercio*, possibly the most spectacular, involves the *banderillas*, long, multi-coloured barbed sticks. The *torero* and his three assistants (*banderilleros*) run towards or receive the charging bull, and then stab the *banderillas* into the back of its neck.

Finally, in the last third, comes the *faena de muleta*, the bullfighter's period alone with the bull, when he demonstrates his artistry in dominating the beast by making it follow a smaller red cape, the *muleta*. Immediately before making his first 'pass', the matador

dedicates the bull to somebody in the crowd, and then must complete the *faena* within 15 minutes. If not, the bull is returned to his pen. The *muleta* is draped over a stiff wooden stick and used with only one hand at a time, left-handed passes being considered superior to right-handed ones. The bull is wounded and weakened, but for this same reason is much more unpredictable. This culminates in the kill, the one moment when the ring falls silent. A 'good' kill, when the sword is plunged in through a precise area between the shoulder blades, neatly sectioning the aorta and causing the bull to drop in seconds, will be received rapturously by the crowd. In contrast, matadors will be booed and heckled deafeningly if the animal is seen to suffer through bungled attempts to get the sword in the right place.

More than in any other spectacle the crowd plays a vital part in bullfighting. They complain and criticise constantly. If, before the *tercio de picadores*, they think a bull is not up to scratch they can insist it be taken away by waving green handkerchiefs. It is also only through the crowd's insistent waving of white handkerchiefs that a *torero* is presented with the prized ear or, better, the tail of the bull he has killed. Likewise, if the bull has displayed remarkable courage, the crowd can demand it be pardoned, and granted a regal life back on the ranch thereafter.

STARS OF THE RING

If a good kill is far from certain, a good bullfight is also hard to come by, although for the first-time visitor this may not matter as it takes some experience to distinguish good from bad. For those involved, a truly good bullfight is as elusive as any masterpiece: the big names of the moment are more likely to give value for money, but it's notoriously impossible to guarantee.

Current figures of the *corrida* include the oddly dapper teenager Julián López, *El Juli*, José Tomás, Finito de Córdoba and the austere traditionalist Enrique Ponce. Another grand old man of the ring is Curro Romero, whose many eccentrically sub-standard performances only add to his legend when he suddenly hits form. The first woman to have had a real impact in the *corrida* in years, Cristina Sánchez, retired in 1999 in response, she said, to the machismo of male colleagues. However, another spirited young woman bullfighter, Mari Paz Vega, has managed to hold her own since her 1997 debut.

The standard of bullfighting is something that is constantly debated. It is now very much a part of modern Spain, moving billions of pesetas each year. There is much talk of 'decaffeination', with star *toreros* accused of influencing ranchers to breed weaker, more

The *aficionado*'s mecca, **Las Ventas**.

manageable bulls, and of horn-shaving, which affects the bull's judgement of distance and coordination. These complaints, though, are not new, and have been heard almost ever since bullfighting was invented. To know more of the history of bullfighting, visit the Museo Taurino, alongside the bullring (*see page 103*).

Going to a *corrida*

Corridas are held at Las Ventas every Sunday from March to October. Timings vary; some begin as early as 5-5.30pm, but a more usual time is 7pm. During the **Feria de San Isidro**, from May into June (*see page 186*), and the **Feria de Otoño**, beginning in late September, fights are held every day, always at 7pm. San Isidro is also preceded by another fair, the **Feria de la Comunidad**, which includes several *novilladas* for novice bullfighters.

Tickets go on sale only two days in advance, and it can be difficult to find out who is going to appear on a given day, except during San Isidro, when the programme is announced at least a month previously. Tickets can sometimes now be bought via Cajamadrid (*see page 171*) and some agencies, but most people buy them at the ring. There are many grades of ticket – the main division is between the cheap *sol* (sun) and *sombra* (shade), but some intermediate seats are *sol y sombra*. In a Madrid summer, it's very worth paying to be in the shade. The best seats, which are very expensive, are in *sombra* near

the front, the *barrera*. Probably the best price-comfort ratio is in *sol y sombra*, about halfway up. Wherever you sit, at whatever price, rent a cushion as you go in, or the cramped stone seats will give you pains for days afterwards. Some use them as ammunition to hurl at a below-par bullfighter, a practise that can earn the spectator swift removal from the ring and even a fine.

The ring in itself is only part of the ambience of Las Ventas. Prior to a fight the esplanade around the plaza is full of stalls selling sun-hats and tacky souvenirs, and Calle Alcalá and other streets nearby are full of bars that are steeped in bullfighting lore, where *aficionados* meet up. Los Timbales at Calle Alcalá 227 and El Paseíllo at Calle Francisco de Navacerrada 58 are only two of the best-known.

Plaza de Toros de Las Ventas

C/Alcalá 237 (91 726 48 00/91 361 13 61/www.las-ventas.com). Metro Ventas/bus 21, 38, 53, 146. **Box office** *Mar-Oct* 10am-2pm, 5-8pm Thur-Sun, & fight days; also Cajamadrid. **Tickets** 1,000-16,000ptas. **Credit** MC, V.

Bull fairs around Madrid

Villages and towns in the surrounding region also hold *corridas* every Sunday during the season. Many also hold bull fairs, with bullfights daily, during their annual *fiestas*. These small-town fairs often include an *encierro*, in which young bulls are run through the streets first thing in the morning, as in the most famous of such events, Pamplona's San Fermín. Have a care: bull-running requires a deal of skill, and untrained tourists should be aware that to join in might be extremely reckless. More than one has died doing so.

The fair in Valdemorillo, to the north west, offers the earliest bullfights of the year, in February, a rare opportunity to see a *corrida* in freezing cold. **Aranjuez** (*see page 257*) holds important bullfighting *ferias* in May and September, but the biggest month for bull fairs is August: **Chinchón** (*see page 258*) has fights in its historic Plaza Mayor, and a smaller event takes place in **Manzanares el Real** (*see page 267*). The most spectacular *encierro* close to Madrid is in San Sebastián de los Reyes, while the most prestigious fair is that in Colmenar Viejo. Dates vary slightly each year.

Bull fairs around Madrid

Colmenar Viejo (*information 91 845 00 53*). **Getting there** bus 721 from Plaza Castilla. **Feria** late Aug.
San Sebastián de los Reyes (*information 91 652 62 00*). **Getting there** bus 152, 154 from Plaza Castilla. **Feria** late Aug.
Valdemorillo (*information 91 897 73 60*). **Getting there** bus 641, 642 from Moncloa. **Feria** early Feb.

Arts & Entertainment

Children

Summer splashes, leafy parks and scary rides... Madrid may not be overly-equipped with entertainment for kids, but they still have a good time.

Despite a much-professed love of children, Spaniards, who already have the world's lowest birth rate, are having ever fewer of them. This, though, is not the explanation for the relative lack of special child-oriented facilities in Madrid. It has much more to do with the fact that children are seen as an integral part of social life, so that kids' rooms and separate menus run contrary to Spanish thinking. There is, though, a growing range of entertainment facilities for children, especially in summer.

Parents from northern Europe or North America have to re-think ideas on food and timetables when bringing children to Madrid. Lunch and dinner both come late, so that the late-afternoon *merienda* (snack) is necessary, as is a siesta, since in summer children are rarely asleep before 10pm. Children are welcome in most restaurants, but few offer children's menus or provide high chairs, so a buggy is very useful. Some that do provide both are those in the **Vip's** chain (*see page 161*), and the Hard Rock Café (*see page 132*), and fast-food outlets are other sources of child-friendly food. Traditional Spanish restaurants are also useful, as most will rustle up a plain hamburger, chips and other simple dishes on request. For pizza and food delivery, *see page 176*.

Sights & attractions

Of the big museums, shows at the **Reina Sofía** (*see page 97*) most often engage young imaginations. The **Palacio Real** is a hit with many kids (*see page 68*), as are the **Faro** observation tower and the **Teleférico** (*see page 85*).

Acuárium de Madrid

C/Maestro Victoria 8, Sol & Gran Vía (91 531 81 72). Metro Callao or Sol/bus all routes to Puerta del Sol. **Open** 11am-2pm, 5-9pm daily. **Admission** 575ptas; 375ptas under-8s. **Credit** (large groups only) MC, V. **Map** p309 E7.
From the outside, this is a pet shop, specialising in tropical fish; in the basement, though, there is a fascinating collection of fish, reptiles and spiders.

Cosmocaixa

C/Pintor Velázquez s/n, Alcobendas (91 484 52 00/902 22 30 40/www.fundacio.lacaixa.es). Bus 157, 151, 152, 153, 154, 156 from Plaza Castilla.

Open 10am-8pm Tue-Sun; closed Mon & 25 Dec, 1 Jan, 5 Jan. **Admission** 500ptas; 250ptas under-16s; 150ptas over-65s. **Credit** AmEx, MC, V.
This hands-on, interactive science museum, northeast of Madrid in Alcobendas, has been designed to make science fun and accessible for kids and adults alike. Visitors first see a reproduction of Foucault's Pendulum; there 's also an 'experimentarium' where processes can be tried out, and the *toca, toca* ('touch, touch') area for small kids, with animals to stroke.

IMAX Madrid

Parque Tierno Galván, Legazpi (91 467 48 00). Metro Méndez Alvaro/bus 62, 102, 148. **Shows** 11am-1pm, 5-11pm daily. **Admission** 1,000ptas; 800ptas Mon & over-65s; 1,500ptas for two sessions. *Telephone booking* via Servicaixa or Corte Inglés (*see p171*). **Credit** AmEx, MC, V
This giant-format cinema, in the same park as the Planetario (*see below*) on the south side of the city, mainly shows wildlife or scientific spectaculars, in Spanish, and so may only be of limited interest.

Museo de Cera (Wax Museum)

Paseo de Recoletos 41, Chueca (91 308 08 25). Metro Colón/bus all routes to Plaza de Colón. **Open** 10am-2.30pm, 4.30-8.30pm Mon-Fri; 10am-8.30pm Sat, Sun, public holidays. **Admission** 1,000ptas; 600ptas 4-10s, over-65s. *Tren del Terror* 500ptas; *Virtual Reality* 400ptas. **No credit cards**. **Map** p306 I4.
With a motley crew of (mainly Spanish) historical figures and celebrities and the gory 'Tortures of the Inquisition', this waxworks museum is a hoot. Some figures are lifelike; some (Margaret Thatcher) laughably grotesque. Recent additions are the popular *Tren del Terror* and a virtual reality simulator.

Planetario

Parque Tierno Galván, Legazpi (91 467 38 98). Metro Méndez Alvaro/bus 62, 102, 148. **Shows** *Mid Sept-mid June* 9.30am-1.45pm, 5-7.45pm Tue-Fri; 11am-1.45pm, 5-8.45pm Sat, Sun, public holidays. *Mid June-mid Sept* 11am-1.45pm, 5-7.45pm Tue-Sun, public holidays. **Admission** 500ptas; 200ptas 2-14s, over-65s; 375ptas groups. **No credit cards**.
Madrid's modern planetarium is in this relatively new park. Shows are in Spanish only, and a bit long (50min). There's a nice playground outside.

Parks & open spaces

In densely-populated central Madrid, squares are both necessary breathing spaces and playgrounds. The **Paseo del Prado** central

boulevard (*see page 59*) has safe wooden
climbing frames and slides; further afield, the
Plazas de Chamberí and **Olavide** in
Chamberí (*see page 86*) and **Dos de Mayo** in
Malasaña all have play areas for toddlers and
terrazas for adults, although Dos de Mayo on
weekend mornings is cluttered with litter from
the previous night's revels (*see page 232*). The
nearby **Plaza de las Comendadoras** has
a pleasant play area, with cafés alongside
where parents can enjoy an afternoon drink
(*see page 154*). Also, on Sunday mornings **Calle
Fuencarral** above Glorieta de Bilbao is closed
to traffic, and opened to bikes and skateboards.

Madrid's fine parks provide plenty of space
for kids to run wild in safety. Those with
perhaps most attractions are the **Retiro** (*see
page 83*) – a boating lake with cafés around its
edge, buskers, artists, puppet shows, tame red
squirrels, sports facilities and a good play area
(by the Puerta de Alcalá entrance); and the
vast **Casa de Campo** (*see page 84*), with
the Parque de Atracciones funfair, the Zoo,
the city's best public swimming pools (*see page
240*), and another boating lake with cafés (note
that parts of the Casa are a prostitution zone, so
be careful of 'leftovers' on paths). The **Parque
Juan Carlos I** (*see page 88*), accessible by
Metro, has an artificial river with catamaran
rides, a mini-train and a free *son et lumière*
show (*June-Sept* 10.30pm-midnight Thur-Sun).

The best way to get to the Casa de Campo is
with the **Teleférico** (*see page 85*) from Paseo
del Pintor Rosales, next to the lovely **Parque
del Oeste**. Near the cable-car terminal there is
the Bruin ice-cream parlour (*see page 153*).

The **Zoo-Aquarium**'s little beasts. *See p195.*

Outings

Madrid's answer to scorching summers are its
waterparks. Most rides are suited to older kids,
but there are usually special sections for small
children. For conventional pools, *see page 239*.

AquaMadrid

*Carretera de Barcelona (N-II), km 15.5, San Fernando
de Henares (91 673 10 13). Bus 281, 282, 284, 285
from Avda de América, also free bus from Avda de
América/by car N-II-A2/by train Cercanías C-1, C-2, C-
7a from Atocha.* **Open** *June-Sept* noon-8pm Mon-Fri;
11am-8pm Sat, Sun, public holidays. **Admission**
Mon-Fri 1,500ptas; 1,000ptas under-11s; *Sat, Sun,
public holidays* 1,800ptas; 1,400ptas under-11s. *After
4pm* all prices reduced by 300ptas. **Credit** MC, V.
Madrid's first waterpark offers giant water slides, a
big main pool, a pool for kids aged 4-6, another for
the 6-10s and a wave pool for budding surfers.

Aquasur

*Carretera de Andalucía (N-IV), km 44, Aranjuez (91
891 60 34). Bus 423, 423a from Estación Sur/
by car N-IV/by train Cercanías C-3 from Atocha.*

In Aranjuez, free bus from the station. **Open** *June-
Sept* 10.30am-8pm daily. **Admission** *Mon-Fri*
600ptas; 500ptas 4-9s; *Sat, Sun, public holidays*
1,500ptas; 1,100ptas 4-9s. **No credit cards.**
Aquasur, outside Aranjuez (*see p257*), is a whole
complex of fun things to do – the stars are a giant
pool with five slides, and a special children's pool.

Aquópolis

*Avda de la Dehesa, Villanueva de la Cañada (91
815 69 11). Bus 627 from Moncloa; also free
buses from Cuesta de San Vicente/by car Carretera
de La Coruña (N-VI), exit 41, then M503.* **Open**
mid June-mid Sept noon-9pm daily. **Admission**
1,975ptas; 1,300ptas 3-9s; 1,400ptas over-65s.
Credit AmEx, MC, V.
Towards El Escorial (*see p249*), this is one of the
largest waterparks in Europe, with all the usual
adventure lakes, wave machines and water slides.

Parque de Atracciones

*Casa de Campo (91 463 29 00/91 526 80 30).
Metro Batán/bus 33, 65 & special bus from Metro
Estrecho, Pacífico & Ventas, Sun, public holidays.*
Open *Oct-June* noon-dusk, Mon-Fri, Sun; noon-
1pm Sat. *July-Sept* noon-1am Mon-Thur, Sun;
noon-2am Fri, Sat. **Admission** 700ptas; *incl 2
rides* 1,400ptas; *under-7s incl 4 rides* 1,400ptas;
Supercalco (*all-inclusive ticket*) 3,000ptas; 1,775ptas
under-7s. *Advance booking* via Servicaixa (902 33
22 11). **No credit cards.**
This hugely popular funfair offers over 40 rides,
from the gentlest merry-go-round to the current
highlights, *Los Rápidos*, a white-water rafting ride,
and *Los Fiordos* (The Fjords), a boat ride ending in
a 15m (48ft) drop. The open-air auditorium offers
live music in summer. The fair gets packed on many
nights, and you may have to queue for some rides.

Safari de Madrid

*Aldea del Fresno, Carretera de Extremadura (N-V),
km. 32 (91 862 23 14). By car N-V to Navalcarnero,
then M-507 to Aldea del Fresno.* **Open** 10.30am-
sunset daily. **Admission** 1,600ptas; 1,000ptas 3-10s.
No credit cards.
This safari park 32km (20 miles) from Madrid must
be seen from inside a car, as the monkeys, lions, rhi-
nos, giraffes, elephants and tigers all roam around
freely. Included are the snake and reptile houses, the

aviary and lion-taming and other shows; for summer there's a swimming pool, a lake with pedalos, a go-kart track, mini-motorbikes and a giant slide.

Sport Hielo

Estación de Chamartín, C/Agustín de Foxá, Chamartín (91 315 63 08). Metro Chamartín/bus 5, 80. **Open** 5.30-9.30pm Thur; 5.30-10pm Fri; 11.30am-2pm, 5.30-10.30pm Sat, Sun, public holidays. Closed Mon-Wed, July, Aug. **Admission** (incl skate rental) 1,000ptas Thur, Sat & 11.30am-2pm Sun; 1,300ptas Fri, Sat, 5.30-10.30pm Sun. **No credit cards.**
One of only four ice-skating rinks in greater Madrid, above Chamartín station. Children from three years upwards are admitted; safety helmets can be hired.

Tren de la Fresa (Strawberry Train)

Estación de Atocha (902 22 88 22). Metro Atocha Renfe/bus all routes to Atocha. **Open** *Apr-July & 9 Sept-15 Oct* depart from Atocha 10am Sat, Sun, public holidays (return from Aranjuez 6.30pm). **Tickets** 3,250ptas; 2,000ptas 2-12s. **Credit** MC, V. **Map** p310 H10.
This lovely day-trip is a recreation of an outing of yesteryear, a leisurely steam train ride to Aranjuez (*see p257*). The price includes visits to the palaces and gardens, and some of Aranjuez's famed strawberries, served by hostesses in period costume. The trip is extremely popular in May and June.

Zoo-Aquarium de la Casa de Campo

Casa de Campo (91 512 37 70). Metro Batán/bus 33, 65 & special bus from Metro Estrecho, Pacífico & Ventas, Sun, public holidays. **Open** 10.30am-dusk (last entry 30min before closing time). **Admission** 1,655ptas; 1,335ptas under-8s. **No credit cards.**
Madrid's zoo has over 2,000 animals. Highlights include a parrot show, a dolphinarium, a giant tank of mean-looking sharks, and an immense net within which birds of prey can fly freely. There's also a children's zoo, a train ride and many snack bars.

Theatre

The Teatro Lara, Montacargas, Cuarta Pared, Sala Triángulo and Teatro Pradillo all present children's theatre in Spanish (*see pages 244-6*).

Sala San Pol

Plaza San Pol de Mar, Ribera de Manzanares (91 541 90 89). Metro Príncipe Pío/bus 41, 46, 75. **Shows** 6pm Sat, Sun, public holidays. Closed July-Aug. **Admission** 1,200ptas. **No credit cards.**
Madrid's official children's theatre, home to the very professional company *La Bicicleta.*

Teatro Municipal de Títeres del Retiro

Parque del Retiro. Metro Retiro/bus all routes to Puerta de Alcalá. **Shows** 6pm Sat, Sun, public holidays. *Titirilandia* mid July-mid Sept 7.30pm, 10.30pm Fri-Sun, public holidays. **Admission** free. **Map** p307 I7.
The open-air puppet theatre in the Retiro has weekend shows all year round. In summer, as part of the

Veranos de la Villa (*see p188*) it also offers the *Titirilandia* festival, featuring puppeteers from around the world. Puppetry-related exhibitions are held at the nearby Casa de Vacas (*see page 107*).

Events & *fiestas*

At **Christmastime** Spanish children leave out a shoe to receive presents from the Three Kings, on the night of 5 January; on **Reyes**, the next day, the Kings' arrival by helicopter in the Retiro is followed by a parade of giant floats to Sol and the Plaza Mayor, with the Kings throwing out sweets to children along the route.

During **Carnaval** (*see page 189*) special children's carnivals are organised, and every April **El día del niño** (day of the child) is held in Calle Bravo Murillo, north of Cuatro Caminos, when the street is taken over by bouncy castles, puppet shows, foam-spraying firemen, candy floss stalls and more. There are also kids' events in San Isidro and the summer *verbenas* (*see page 186 and 188*).

Childcare & babysitters

Ludotecas (play-centres) are places where parents can leave children in safety for a short time while they attend to other business. They can also, often, suggest reliable babysitters. The English Church, **St George's** (*see page 287*), has a regular English-speaking mothers' group, and local English-language magazines (*see page 290*) are good places to look for ads placed by English-speaking babysitters.

Centro de Recreo Infantil Dinopeppino

Calle Mártires de Alcalá 4, Malasaña & Conde Duque (91 559 22 04). Metro Ventura Rodríguez/bus 2, 44, 133, C. **Open** 4.30-8.30pm Mon-Fri; 11.30am-2pm, 4.30-8.30pm Sat, Sun, public holidays. **Admission** 800ptas per hr; 6,000ptas 10-hr ticket. **Credit** MC, V. **Map** p305 D3.
A spacious, well-equipped drop-off centre.

Escuela Infantil Olavide

C/Gonzalo de Córdoba 22, Chamberí (91 593 24 69). Metro Quevedo/bus 3, 37, 16, 61, 149. **Open** *Sept-July* 7.30am-9.30pm Mon-Fri; *Aug* 7.30am-6pm Mon-Fri. Closed Sat, Sun. **No credit cards.** **Map** p305 F2.
A well-regarded nursery school, some of whose staff speak English. Children can be left in their care for any length of time, from a few hours to a full day.

Gorongoro

Avda de Felipe II, 34, Salamanca (91 431 06 45). Metro Goya/bus 2, 15, 29, 61, C. **Open** 4.30-9pm Mon-Fri; 11.30am-2.30pm; 4.30-9pm Sat, Sun. *July-Aug* 6-9pm Mon-Fri; 11.30am-2.30pm, 6-9pm Sat; closed Sun. **Admission** *over-4s* 450ptas per 30min; *under-4s* 400ptas per 30min. **No credit cards.** **Map** p307 L5.
A well-equipped play centre just east of the Retiro.

Arts & Entertainment

Film

Spain's movie industry has big ambitions... or is it just in love with Hollywood?

Spain's love affair with the cinema shows no sign of cooling. Low prices and ample opportunities to see a wide range of movies make this a great city for film-lovers. A sure sign of the popularity of film in Spain is the construction here of some of the largest mega-multiplexes in Europe, especially in the fast-growing dormitory 'burbs to the north and west. Pozuelo has a 25-screen state-of-the-art complex, **Kinepolis**, and Saturday nights in towns like Aravaca and Las Rozas see massive traffic jams around multiplex car parks.

Mainly, they'll be watching dubbed Hollywood product, which takes over 75 per cent of the market. Spanish cinema has sought to adjust to this reality, by trying to blend local sensibilities with a US-style commercial appeal. Private TV companies and the State RTVE all finance film production, and the Spanish industry also takes part in Europudding co-productions, especially with France and Italy. Nevertheless, Spain is increasingly looking across the Atlantic, to do deals with Hollywood itself (*see page 197* **Hola Hollywood**).

On the face of it, this approach has been pretty successful, and Spain now looks to have one of the more commercially healthy film industries in Europe, with a steady flow of films that – while sometimes too commercially cute – combine imagination with strong box-office appeal. A new generation of auteur-directors emerged in the 1990s, such as Benito Zambrano, Alejandro Amenábar, Agustin Yáñez, Chus Gutiérrez, Enrique Gabriel, Salvador García Ruiz and Pablo Llorca. The Spanish media also pumped up Pedro Almodóvar's Oscar for *All About My Mother* as a cause for national celebration, and it may indeed open doors for some directors looking for American money.

VENUES

Despite the multiplex boom, the Gran Via remains Madrid's archetypal movie-avenue: massive cinemas – the Callao, the Palacio de la Música – are the landmarks of the street, and their publicity hoardings, hand-painted for each film, are one of the real sights of the city. Some are now multiplexes, while others retain their original 1-2,000-seater form. All attract capacity houses on Sunday nights for the dubbed international blockbusters they mostly screen.

While the biggest audiences are for dubbed movies, those who want to see non-Spanish films in their original language are not left out.

It's now quite common for Hollywood releases to be shown in English on at least one screen in the city during their first release. When a film is shown in its original language, with Spanish subtitles, this is indicated by **VO** (*versión original*) in newspapers and on cinema publicity. Specialist VO cinemas (and the official film theatre, the **Filmoteca**, which only shows films in VO) are reviewed here. Mercifully, all the cinemas listed here have air-conditioning.

TICKETS & TIMES

Newspapers and the *Guia del Ocio* (*see page 290*) are reliable sources of cinema schedules. Madrileños tend to go to the movies later than in other countries: the most popular screenings are at around 10-10.30pm, so 8pm shows are usually easier to get into. The busiest day is Sunday, when it's advisable to buy tickets in advance or at least arrive in good time. Several VO cinemas also have late (after midnight) shows on Fridays and Saturdays. Many cinemas charge lower prices for the first show in the afternoon, or have a reduced-price day, the *día del espectador* ('film-goer's day') once a week, usually on Monday or Wednesday.

Credit card booking has not arrived in most Madrid cinemas, but tickets to some larger venues can now be bought through savings bank ticket systems (*see page 171*).

VO cinemas

Alphaville

C/Martín de los Heros 14, Argüelles (91 559 38 36). Metro Plaza de España/bus all routes to Plaza de España. **Open** *box office* 4-11pm Mon-Thur, Sun; 4pm-1am Fri, Sat. **Late shows** *begin* 12.30-1am Fri, Sat. **Tickets** 850ptas; 550ptas Mon except public holidays. **Map** p304 C4.

This four-screener has won a loyal following since it opened in 1977. Its basement café was an in-vogue meeting point in its '80s heyday, as a venue for experimental screenings and theatre and music performances. The café is still sometimes used to host off-the-wall initiatives.

Bogart

C/Cedaceros 7, Huertas & Santa Ana (91 429 80 42). Metro Sevilla/bus all routes to Puerta del Sol. **Open** *box office* 4-10.45pm daily. **Tickets** 800ptas; 600ptas Tue except public holidays. **Map** p309 F7.

This recently reopened old movie house shows a lot of recent movies in VO, and is worth a visit if only for its slightly seedy, down-at-heel charm.

Hola Hollywood

A reflection of the increasing confidence of the Spanish film industry (or, perhaps, a strange lack of enough of it really to believe in itself) is its growing links to the great, big American one. Spain began courting Hollywood in the early '90s, largely through the efforts of filmmaker Fernando Trueba, who won an Oscar in 1994 for *Belle Epoque*. It was Trueba, a confirmed Hollywood fan, who brought Antonio Banderas and Melanie Griffith together in his uninspiring 1996 US co-production *Two Much*.

Since then Banderas, of course, has taken off to America, churning out any number of less-than-memorable vehicles, and a few good pictures thrown in for good measure. He is currently backing the building of a new cultural centre in Madrid. Meanwhile, his old friend Pedro Almodóvar won the foreign-language Oscar in 2000 with *All About My Mother*, after a determined year-long campaign based very much on the 'Hollywood we love you' approach of Roberto Benigni, 1999 Oscar-winner with *Life is Beautiful*. Almodóvar had previously cleaned up at the domestic awards – the Goya – and major European festivals, and, given the length of his Oscar acceptance speech, the boy from La Mancha was not exactly caught unawares by the award.

The Oscar also seems to have rehabilitated Almodóvar at home, after a few years in which critics said he had lost his flair. It has also opened doors in Hollywood. He is now making his first English-language film, an adaptation of Peter Dexter's *The Paperboy* – a sleazy mystery tale set in Florida.

Spain's latest eye-catching export to Holly-woodland is the attractive if vapid Penélope Cruz (pictured), who has worked with Trueba and Almodóvar. She got her break playing a small-town flirt in Bigas Luna's *Jamón Jamón* (1992), and has made over 20 films in Spain. After working with Almodóvar in *Live Flesh (Carne Trémula)*, she landed a part in Stephen Frears' *The High-Lo Country*, and then in Billy Bob Thornton's adaptation of *All the Pretty Horses*. She has yet to go much beyond stereotypical Mediterranean roles in any US movie, but her appearances on the cover of *Newsweek* and *Rolling Stone* were greeted as national events back home.

Whether Penélope or Pedro will really follow Antonio into the big time Stateside – and how far Banderas can go – is a matter of debate, but Spanish audiences are right behind them. It may once have been fashionable to be anti-American in Spain, but there's no glitz like Hollywood glitz.

California

C/Andrés Mellado 53, Moncloa (91 544 00 58).
Metro Islas Filipinas or Moncloa/bus 2, 12, 16,
61, C. **Open** box office 4-10.45pm daily.
Tickets 800ptas; 600ptas Wed except public
holidays. **Map** p304 C1.
This 500-seater near the university screens mostly
commercial films, but also some less standard fare.
It also encourages students to use it for English-
teaching purposes.

Cine Estudio de Bellas Artes

C/Marqués de Casa Riera 2, Huertas & Santa Ana
(91 360 54 00). Metro Banco de España/bus all
routes to Plaza de Cibeles. **Open** box office 4-10.30pm
daily. **Tickets** 500ptas; 400ptas members and youth
card holders. **Map** p310 G7.
After various guises the cinema at the Círculo de
Bellas Artes has opted for rep status, and features
varied film theatre-style seasons, a welcome alternative to the overcrowded **Filmoteca** (see below).

La Enana Marrón

Travesía de San Mateo 8, Chueca (91 308 14 97).
Metro Tribunal/bus 3, 40, 149. **Shows** 500ptas;
350ptas members. **Shows** 9.30pm Thur; 9pm, 11pm
Fri, Sat; 9pm Sun; closed Mon-Wed. **Map** p306 G4.
Set up by a group of independent filmmakers as a
forum for their work, the 'Brown Dwarf' is a delightful studio cinema showing retrospectives (Wim
Wenders, Cuban cinema), experimental movies,
shorts and repertory classics. A meeting place for
those moving up in the movie world, it also has
a unique membership system, with a range of
different rates and monthly pre-movie dinners.

Ideal Yelmo Cineplex

C/Doctor Cortezo 6, Lavapiés (91 369 25 18).
Metro Tirso de Molina/bus all routes to Puerta del
Sol. **Open** box office 4-11pm Mon-Thur, Sun; 4pm-
12.45am Fri, Sat. **Late shows** begin 12.15-1am Fri,
Sat. **Tickets** 850ptas; 600ptas Mon except public
holidays. **Map** p309 E8.
An eight-screen multiplex with a mix of Spanish
films, international hits and art-house movies in VO.
Very popular, with locals and foreigners.

Luna

C/Luna 2, Sol & Gran Vía (91 522 47 52). Metro
Callao/bus all routes to Plaza del Callao. **Open** box
office 4-10.45pm daily. **Tickets** 800ptas; 600ptas
Wed except public holidays. **Map** p309 E6.
This once run-down cinema has taken on a new
lease of life as a VO cinema, with an interesting selection of imported cinema.

Pequeño Cine Estudio

C/Magallanes 1,Chamberí (91 447 29 20). Metro
Quevedo/bus 16, 61, 149. **Open** box office 4.30-
10.30pm daily. **Tickets** 750ptas; 550ptas Mon except
public holidays; 550ptas over-65s, students Tue-Fri
first show except public holidays. **Map** p305 E2.
Opened in 1999, this intimate art-house cinema
has been packing 'em in with its diet of classic world
cinema, but sadly has no plans for late-nights.

Renoir Plaza de España

C/Martín de los Heros 12, Argüelles (phone line for
all Renoir branches 91 541 41 00). Metro Plaza de
España/bus all routes to Plaza de España. **Open** box
office 4-10.45pm Mon-Thur, Sun; 4pm-12.45am Fri,
Sat. **Late shows** begin 12.15-1am Fri, Sat. **Tickets**
850ptas; 600ptas over-65s, students first show Mon-
Fri except public holidays. **Map** p304 C4.
The enterprising Renoir chain has five modern VO
multiplexes in Madrid, and plans for more. This five-
screener was the first to open, in 1986. All Renoirs
are very comfortable, with first-rate sound and tech-
nical facilities. Good for late shows, too.
Branches: **Princesa** C/Princesa 3, Argüelles;
Renoir Cuatro Caminos C/Raimundo Fernández
Villaverde 10, Cuatro Caminos; **Renoir Princesa**
Pasaje Martín de los Heros, C/Princesa 5, Argüelles;
Renoir Retiro C/Narváez 42, El Retiro.

Rosales

C/Quintana 22, Argüelles (91 541 58 00). Metro
Ventura Rodríguez/bus 1, 44, 74, 133, C. **Open** box
office 4-10.30pm daily. **Tickets** 700ptas Mon-Fri;
750ptas Sat, Sun, public holidays; 500ptas Wed, over-
65s, students Mon-Fri. **Map** p304 C3.
A long-running VO art cinema. This 360-seat venue
sometimes stages theme weeks on directors or countries, and always gives out film notes.

The Filmoteca

Filmoteca Española (Cine Doré)

C/Santa Isabel 3, Lavapiés (91 369 21 18). Metro
Antón Martín/bus 6, 26, 32. **Open** box office 4.15-
10.30pm Tue-Sun; closed Mon. Bar-café 2pm-midnight
Tue-Sat; 4pm-midnight Sun; closed Mon. Bookshop
4.30-10.30pm Tue-Sun; closed Mon. **Tickets** 225ptas;
1,700ptas block ticket for 10 films. **Map** p309 F9.
Founded in 1953, Madrid's official film theatre has
lately expanded its role in restoring and preserving
the heritage of Spanish cinema. As well as its cinema, it has a bookshop and popular bar-cafés. In the
summer, films are shown in the open air in the rooftop bar. The Filmoteca has access to the archives of
other countries to feed its series on classic directors,
genres or the cinema traditions of different countries, and foreign films shown here are always in VO.

Open-air movies

Fescinal (Cine de Verano)

Parque de la Bombilla, Avda de Valladolid,
La Florida (91 541 37 21). Metro Príncipe Pío/bus
41, 46, 75. **Open** July-Sept from 10.15pm daily;
closed Oct-June. **Tickets** 550ptas;
400ptas over-65s, students; free under-5s.
As part of the city's **Veranos de la Villa** festival
(see p187), films are shown in an open-air venue,
with a double bill nightly through summer. Most
films screened are fairly mainstream, but more
unusual fare is included, some in VO. The giant
screen is set up in the Parque de la Bombilla, by the
river a little north of San Antonio de la Florida.

Flamenco

A feel for tradition is ever-present in Flamenco, but it's also one of Spain's most original and innovative modern art forms.

Flamenco is Spain's most distinctive art form, one of the things, like bullfighting, that makes the country's culture so unique. It is also something that has been widely misunderstood and caricatured, at home and abroad.

The swirling dresses, furious footwork and clattering castanets often served up to unwary tourists at hefty prices are no more than a sad parody of the real thing. Many Spaniards, too, have often seen flamenco music and dance as part of a hackneyed, kitschy and uncreative folkloric culture they would rather get away from. Under Franco, decaffeinated flamenco was an integral part of the regime's self-promotion campaigns, and even after the end of the dictatorship flamenco still seemed out of step with the new Spain's rush to prosperity and infatuation with all things modern. And, since the strongholds of the music are still very much among Spain's Gypsy communities, a degree of racism also played its part.

At the beginning of the 1980s there were almost no venues in Madrid regularly featuring quality live flamenco. This trend has been completely turned around in the last 20 years. A major factor has been a startling coincidence of new and imaginative talent – above all guitarists Paco de Lucía and Tomatito, and the singer Camarón de la Isla, one of the most extraordinary voices of the 20th century, whose death at just 41 in 1992 was a national catastrophe. They helped vindicate the music's finest traditions while continually breaking new ground, attracting entirely new audiences. New venues opened their doors, spearheading a flamenco resurgence.

Most flamenco venues today feature both traditional performers and what's called *nuevo flamenco*, New Flamenco. This has developed out of the innovations of Paco de Lucía and Camarón, and the subsequent experiments of young musicians, often themselves from Gypsy families – where they absorbed the music with their mothers' milk – but also open to a whole range of other musical influences. They are ready to blend traditional styles with blues, pop, jazz, rock, folk, salsa, Latin American styles and Arab music, and experiment with such unflamenco-like instruments as saxophones and electric bass. Far from succumbing to crossover blandness, though,

El Lebrijano as the temperature rises.

much of New Flamenco still has an unmistakable Gypsy edge.

The flamenco world has a deep sense of tradition, and *aficionados* argue endlessly over whether this kind of fusion represents a real advance for the music, or simply its dilution – even though the line has always been vague between flamenco and Spanish popular music in general. Another point at issue is how far flamenco can ever be open to *payos* (the Spanish Gypsy word for all non-Gypsies). The results of *nuevo flamenco* are uneven, but no one can deny that this opening up of flamenco can produce highly original, fresh and dynamic sounds.

THE BASIS – *CANTE*

The origins of flamenco can be traced back more than 500 years to the folk songs of Arab Andalusia. The late-medieval Gypsy immigration into Spain was, of course, the major factor in its development, but it also combines elements of Indian chants, Spanish-Jewish folk music and Middle Eastern, oriental and Latin American musical traditions and religious influences.

The essence of flamenco is the *cante jondo* or 'deep song': a voice, a guitar, a story to tell, and an audience to share in the telling. The guitar and singing are often accompanied by dancing, but good *cante* can always stand on its own. Guitar (always acoustic) and singer (the *cantaor* or *cantaora*) establish a taut communication, based on subtle rhythmic improvisation within the contours of the different styles, called *palos*. There are a great many of them, all richly inter-related, and differentiated by their intricate rhythmic patterns, chord structures, lyrical

José Mercé

José Soto Soto, one of the greats of contemporary flamenco, was born in Jerez, in Cádiz, in 1955, a year of good wine and great voices. He took his first steps in music in the choir of the Basilica of La Merced in Jerez, which was kept going through donations from a local Marqués, who paid for the boys' classes and their lunch in return for a demanding schedule that sometimes included three Masses a day. From that time comes José's stage name, Mercé, and his intense dislike of anything to do with churches. 'I've already heard enough Masses to last me a lifetime', he says. Mercé's CD *Del Amanecer* ('Dawn', 1999), has been one of the biggest-selling recent flamenco recordings.

Because of your voice and way of singing you're often compared to Camarón de la Isla.
Imitations are never any good, however much that might bother those who are always looking for replacements. Camarón was the genius of the century, like Paco de Lucía on the guitar. There'll be no one else like them. I was born with the gift of singing and I have my own way of doing things.

Your record Del Amanecer *has been a success, but didn't please the critics.*
The critics have drawn more attention to the record, and for that I'm grateful. Apart from that, I don't care what they say; everything that I do sounds like flamenco because I never lose sight of the roots.

Ever since the death of Camarón the experiments with flamenco have been going on without stopping. How do you see its future?
To transform flamenco you have to begin at the foundations, which are the basic *cantes*, and not with the roof. There are young musicians who want to conquer the world in a couple of days, and who aren't even capable of listening to older singers. Good things are boring, as Van Gogh found out. And if you've never been a *novillero*, how can you ever be a bullfighter?

Is it possible to keep up a passion for cante *when it's the way you earn your living?*
There are days when I'd pay money not to have to get up on stage, but, at the same time, I wouldn't know how to live without singing. I don't know how to do anything else. Tell me to knock in a nail and I might knock down the whole wall. It's on stage that I really express what I feel.

Some say a cantaor *only comes into his own after the age of 60.*
That's stupid: at 60 you should be at home in bed.

content and regional origin – *alegrías, bulerías, siguiriyas, soleares, tarantos, tientos, malagueñas, tangos* and *fandangos* are only the best-known.

Musicians play and sing within these recognised styles, but a real flamenco performance is still the most utterly spontaneous and improvised of music, each one unique and unrepeatable. The audience plays a crucial part in each performance. More than silence, what is demanded is rapt surrender to the artists' travails. *Cantaor* and guitarist always start quite cold, and it is only after a couple of songs that they really begin to get going, as in any conversation. Side-performers and the audience accompany the more rhythmically intense palos with intricate hand-clapping and shouts of *¡olé!*, – although this is one thing probably best left to the initiated.

The emotional repertory is far-ranging: from desperation to joyful celebration, a miner's lament, songs that speak of love, of solitude, of despair, of dire foreboding. Even the most ecstatic of *alegrías*, though, never seems to break away completely from the deep sense of pain and anguish that marks all *cante jondo*. Nor is the stark tragedy of a *siguiriya*'s deathly brooding ever without some element of cathartic relief.

Raw and honest, flamenco is an audacious music, full of risks and improvisation. Singers rely on plaintive wails, sobs and throaty murmurs to recount tales of personal or collective tribulation. In its most inspired moments, when what *aficionados* call the *duende* – roughly meaning 'spirit' or 'enchantment' – possesses performer and listener alike, the effect can be stunning; a primal emotion, an atavistic river of tears, seems to flow through the artists. Commanding performers can envelop the most varied of audiences with a sense of common humanity and shared fate.

STARS & NAMES TO WATCH

As a result of the flamenco resurgence Madrid, more than anywhere in the south, is now the best place in Spain to hear good flamenco. A sample of names to watch out for in the traditional field are José Mercé (*see page 200*), Carmen Linares, José Menese, Chano Lobato and Vicente Soto, among singers. The many fine younger singers include Duquende, Estrella Morente, Montse Cortés, Ginesa Ortega and Arcángel, but the sensation of recent years has been Niña Pastori. Leading guitarists are Paco de Lucía, Tomatito, Manolo Sanlúcar, Pepe Habichuela, Gerardo Núñez, Rafael Riqueni and Vicente Amigo.

Divisions between traditional and New Flamenco are never as precise as some people make out, and many musicians, like Paco de Lucía and Tomatito, work freely between both camps. Best-known of New Flamenco groups is Ketama, who combine flamenco with pop and salsa. Other acts to look out for are the jazz/flamenco mix of saxophonist-flautist Jorge Pardo, bassist Carles Benavent and pianist Chano Domínguez. Standing out among singers ready to experiment without losing touch with their roots are Diego Carrasco, Juan Peña *El Lebrijano*, a master in the fusion of flamenco with Arab music, and Enrique Morente, who made passions rise with his 1997 album *Omega*, mixing flamenco and hard rock.

Venues

For anyone new to flamenco the best introduction will be a session in a club such as La Soleá or Casa Patas. Note that, since spontaneity is the essence of flamenco, timekeeping is often imprecise. With flamenco so fashionable, several bars welcome the music: **El Burladero** doesn't host live acts, but is popular with young musicians, as is **Torito** (*see page 233*); **Cardamomo** (Wednesdays, *see page 227*) and **Los Gabrieles** (Thursdays, *see page 155*) both host regular live gigs. Look out too for flamenco nights in theatres, or outdoors in summer; **Colegio San Juan Evangelista** schedules flamenco shows five or six times a year. Other venues include **Sala Caracol** and **Clamores** (*see pages 221-2*).

Candela

C/del Olmo 2, Lavapiés (91 467 33 82). Metro Antón Martín/bus 6, 26, 32. **Open** 10pm-5.30am Mon-Thur; 10pm-6am Fri, Sat; closed Sun. **No credit cards. Map** p309 F9.

Although it does not programme live music, this bar is a cornerstone of the Madrid flamenco scene, simply because every flamenco artist seems to go there at some point in their off hours. The after-hours jam sessions in the cellar are legendary, but unfortunately they tend to be by 'invitation' only. Also, Candela is a good contact point for meeting guitarists willing to give private lessons. *See p229.*

Casa Patas

C/Cañizares 10, Lavapiés (91 369 04 96). Metro Antón Martín or Tirso de Molina/bus 6, 26, 32, 65. **Open** noon-5pm, 8pm-2am Mon-Thur; noon-5pm, 8pm-3am Fri, Sat; closed Sun. **Performances** 10.30pm Mon-Thur; midnight Fri, Sat. **Admission** 2,500ptas Mon-Thur; 3,000ptas. Fri, Sat. **Credit** AmEx, DC, MC, V. **Map** p309 E8

A pioneer of the flamenco upswing, a big, comfortable bar with a club space at the back where flamenco shows are staged most nights of the week. Patas is established as the city's most important flamenco specialist: it presents pretty much all of the best traditional flamenco singers and dancers, plus *nuevo flamenco*. The tapas are good, but pricey.

La Soleá

C/Cava Baja 27, Austrias (91 365 33 08). Metro La Latina/bus 17, 31, 35, 50, 65. **Open** 10pm-6am Mon-Sat; closed Sun. **Performances** 12.30am Mon-Sat. **No credit cards. Map** p309 D8.

This tiny bar, in the middle of Madrid's traditional restaurant area, has a house guitarist willing to accompany anyone wishing to test their luck in the art of flamenco singing. Anything can happen (and often does): you may hear a stirring recital by an outstanding artist who happens to come by, an inspired amateur, or just direly inept droning. The only sure thing is the good-natured atmosphere.

Suristán

C/de la Cruz 7, Huertas & Santa Ana (91 532 39 09). Metro Sevilla, Sol/bus all routes to Puerta del Sol. **Open** 10pm-4.30am Tue, Wed, Sun; 10.30pm-5.30am Fri, Sat; closed Mon. **Flamenco** 11pm Wed. **Admission** 1,000ptas. **Map** p309 E7.

One of the most innovative music venues in Madrid, Suristán programmes virtually every kind of music, but dedicates one night each week to flamenco, usually Wednesdays. The performers are mostly younger artists, in traditional and *nuevo flamenco*, and the audience is completely mixed, giving an atmosphere that makes it one of the best places to appreciate the range of modern flamenco. Check before going, as concert days can vary. *See also p221.*

Festivals

The number of regular flamenco-related events that are held in Madrid grows each year. In February-March comes the week-long **Festival Flamenco Cajamadrid**, in the Teatro Albéniz (*see page 243*). At the end of April, the Colegio San Juan Evangelista (*see page 222*) puts on an important gathering, the **Festival Flamenco por Tarantos**. Flamenco is also included in the programmes of the main city festivals such as **San Isidro** and the **Veranos de la Villa** (*see pages 186 and 188*).

Spain's most important purely flamenco festival, though, is the **Bienal** in Seville. The next one will be in September 2002; for information, contact Seville 95 421 83 83.

Arts & Entertainment

Bailes: Spanish dance

Spain is unique in Europe in possessing an entirely indigenous dance tradition that covers the range of sophistication from pure folk dance to very studied and refined techniques. Flamenco is only one of a great many styles; the differences between them can sometimes be hard to distinguish for newcomers, but devotees debate them passionately

Spanish dance styles enjoy huge commercial success outside Spain, and periodically produce superstars such as Joaquín Cortés, who has now launched himself as an actor alongside French supermodel Letitia Casta. Among other dancers setting the pace today are Antonio Canales and Javier Barón, and women like Sara Baras, La Yerbabuena and Belén Maya.

Performances by these and other quality dancers can frequently, if inconsistently, be seen in Madrid. Cortés tends to visit once a year, as does the polished and spectacular *Ballet Nacional de España*. Some theatres, such as the **Centro Cultural de la Villa** and the **Teatro de Madrid** (*see pages 243-4*), regularly host Spanish dance companies, and some always feature in the **Festival de Otoño** (*see page 188*). Very worth catching is the *Nuevo Ballet Español*, led by two of the best current male dancers, Angel Rojas and Carlos Rodríguez, who present traditional flamenco forms seen through modern eyes. For classes in Spanish dance, *see page 246*.

TABLAOS & SALAS ROCIERAS

Where people are most likely to see Spanish dance, though, is at a flamenco show, a *tablao*. There are several in Madrid, but those listed here are the ones where you are most likely to catch genuine, intense performances. As well as the show, you can dine or just drink; both are appallingly expensive, but if you stay till closing time you may get your money's worth of flamenco dance and music. The fun really starts about midnight, when most tourists go off to bed and the major artists appear; until then you may just get the kitsch jollity of the *cuadro de la casa* (the house musicians and dancers).

Also, as well as watching a Spanish dance show you can join in, by making for a *sala rociera* or Andaluz dance club for a bout of *sevillanas* and the odd rumba. For some prior preparation, many schools offer classes in these and other popular Spanish dances (*see page 246*).

Al Andalús

C/Capitán Haya, Chamartín (91 556 14 39). Metro Santiago Bernabéu/bus 5, 43, 149, 150. **Open** 10.30pm-6am Mon-Sat; closed Sun. **Flamenco shows** start 11pm, 1.30am. **Admission** free. **Credit** AmEx, DC, MC, V.
With *sala rociera* decor reminiscent of a *caseta* at the April Feria in Seville, this place offers a brassy live show, but the best part of it all is watching the mainly middle-aged public throw themselves into *sevillanas* till dawn. While there is no charge on the door, there is an obligatory minimum bar and tapas spend of 2,500ptas, Mon-Wed, 3,000ptas Thur-Sat.

Almonte

C/Juan Bravo 35, Salamanca (91 556 14 39). Metro Núñez de Balboa/bus 29, 51, 52, 61. **Open** 9pm-5am daily. **Admission** free. **Credit** AmEx, DC, MC, V. **Map** p307 K2.
On two floors, this striking combination of *sala rociera* and disco in Salamanca gets packed with upmarket, well-dressed 20-somethings letting their hair down to *sevillanas*. There is no live show, but a there's a minimum spend (2,000ptas).

Café de Chinitas

C/Torija 7, Sol & Gran Vía (91 547 15 01). Metro Santo Domingo/bus 44, 133, 147. **Open** 9pm-2am Mon-Sat; closed Sun. **Flamenco shows** from 10.30pm Mon-Sat. **Admission** *dinner & show* 10,250ptas; *drinks & show* 4,450ptas.
AmEx, DC, MC, V. **Map** p309 D6.
With a plush, nostalgic ambience that evokes a famous 19th-century flamenco locale of the same name, this is Madrid's most luxurious *tablao*, with a good *cuadro* and regular appearances by prestigious guest artists.

Corral de la Morería

C/de la Morería 17, Austrias (91 365 84 46). Metro La Latina/bus 17, 23, 35, 60. **Open** 9pm-2am daily. **Flamenco shows** from 10.45pm daily. **Admission** *dinner & show* 11,000ptas; *drinks & show* 4,300ptas. **Credit** AmEx, DC, MC, V. **Map** p308 C8.
Another of Madrid's more serious *tablaos*, but smaller and more rustic in style, and in the suitable setting of the one-time main street of the Arab quarter of medieval Madrid. As well as the house *cuadro*, shows often feature respected senior figures of the Madrid flamenco scene.

Galleries

A new, innovative attitude is showing itself as Madrid adjusts to new realities, and new publics.

Madrid's art world had a lean time in the late 1990s. For many galleries, survival was a matter of reorienting themselves toward showing market-friendly Spanish artists, whose work might be more conventional than the foreign names who were beginning to appear a decade ago, but had more appeal for a local public still unusued to spending money on adventurous art.

The role of Madrid's public exhibition spaces as a flagship for Spanish art has also much diminished. Critics blame the cultural policies of the *Partido Popular* – assorted cutbacks, reductions in sponsorship, and a signal failure to promote art to the same degree as was seen under the previous Socialist administration.

And yet, Madrid continues to host many private galleries that are very much in touch with the global art scene,and for visitors to the city a tour of its contemporary galleries can be a refreshing counter-weight to the historic art in the Prado and similar institutions. Some galleries have adopted an 'innovate or die' spirit, backing new artists and forging links with galleries abroad, while actively seeking new buyers. New galleries open up all the time.

The Ministry of Culture holds an annual show every September in the former Museo Español de Arte Contemporáneo in Moncloa, showcasing young Spanish artists, and the photography jamboree **PHotoEspaña** (*see page 186*) is another annual event that has really taken root. In fact, photography and related forms have rapidly gained ground in the Madrid art world, and photographers, such as prize-winning Isabel Muñoz and Enric Martí, are prominent among new talents on the scene.

The best source of information on what's on in galleries is the free monthly magazine *Guiarte*, available from galleries and tourist offices. The *Guía del Ocio* and local papers also have gallery listings and reviews (*see page 290*).

Commercial galleries

Madrid's art world has its own geography. Salamanca, above all Calle Claudio Coello, is the traditional centre of the upmarket gallery trade. Since the 1980s many newer galleries have sprung up across the Castellana, around Calle Génova and in Chueca, mostly in the classier part of the district near Calle Almirante. A crop

of adventurous galleries has also emerged further south, in Lavapiés and Atocha, around the magnet of the Reina Sofía. Most but not all private galleries close for the whole of August.

Huertas & Santa Ana

La Fábrica – PHotogaleríafax
C/Alameda 9 (91 360 13 20) Metro Atocha/bus 14, 27, 34, 37, 45. **Open** 11am-2pm, 5-8.30pm Tue-Sat; closed Mon, Sun & Aug. **Map** p310 G9.
Opened in 1998, this specialist in new photography aims to act as a forum for upcoming talent, but also attracts many of the best-known names in the field in Spain, such as ex-*Movida* figures Alberto García Alix or Ouka Lele. Very involved in PHotoEspaña, the Fábrica is now a much-sought-after exhibition space, and is among Madrid's most influential.

Lavapiés & Atocha

Angela Sacristán
C/Doctor Fourquet 6 (91 527 33 69) Metro Atocha/bus all routes to Atocha. **Open** 11am-2pm, 4.30-8pm Mon-Sat; closed Sun. **Map** p310 G9.
Representative of newer, more experimental trends, this tiny gallery switches happily from sculpture to photography and the odd installation.

Cruce
C/Argumosa 28 (91 528 77 83). Metro Atocha/bus all routes to Atocha. **Open** 5.30-9.30pm Tue-Sat; closed Sun. **Map** p309 F10
Run by an artists' collective, Cruce provides a space for meetings, workshops, book launches and a very variable roster of exhibitions. Joint projects are also taken on with galleries in other countries.

Ediciones Benveniste
C/Relatores 20, 1º (91 429 80 09/ www.benveniste.com). Metro Tirso de Molina/bus 6, 26, 32. **Open** 5-9pm Mon-Fri; closed Sat, Sun. **Map** p309 E8
This workshop/gallery, run by Danish copperplate printer Dan Benveniste, is located in an 18th-century convent, and has a nicely unsnooty feel. The ample space hosts four shows a year, mainly of non-Spanish artists. Opening times vary, so phone before visiting.

Espacio Fourquet
C/Doctor Fourquet 19 (91 530 81 39). Metro Atocha/bus all routes to Atocha. **Open** 10.30-2pm, 4.30-8.30pm Mon-Sat; 10am-2pm Sun. **Map** p310 G9.

Arts & Entertainment

Two faces of the consistently interesting **Masha Prieto** gallery. *See p205.*

The largest gallery space on a street that has become Madrid's cultural counterpoint to the upmarket and conservative venues of Claudio Coello. It shows sculpture, installations, video and photography.

EFTI (Escuela de Fotografía y Centro de Imágen)

C/Fuenterrabia 4-6 (91 552 99 99/www.efti.es). Metro Atocha or Menéndez Pelayo/bus 10, 14, 26, 32, C. **Open** 10am-2pm, 5pm-10pm Mon-Fri; 11am-2pm Sat. Closed Sun & Aug.

A photography school, EFTI also has a good sized exhibition space and organises several photography shows each year, presenting innovative work. The Hoffman Prizes, which showcase work by young photographers, are also held here annually.

Helga de Alvear

C/Doctor Fourquet 12 (91 468 05 06/ www.w3art.es/dealvear). Metro Atocha/bus all routes to Atocha. **Open** 11am-2pm, 5-9pm Tue-Sat. Closed Aug. **Map** p310 G9.

Helga de Alvear is one of the most respected gallery owners in the country, having worked with the late and highly influential Juana Mordó, and like her played a key role in opening up the Spanish art world to foreign artists such as Botero, César, David Hockney and Kandinsky. Her gallery continues to present the most innovative modern work from around the world.

Idearte

C/Doctor Drumen 3 (91 506 17 22). Metro Atocha/bus all routes to Atocha. **Open** 10am-2pm, 4.30-8pm Mon-Sat; 10am-2pm Sun. **Map** p310 H9.

Idearte has opted for a shopfront approach, and at first glance seems to offer little more than a touristy ragbag of accessible art, conveniently located next to the Reina Sofia. Venture in, however, and you'll find an interesting range of young artists represented. The helpful staff can arrange for you to visit artists at their studios in order to see more of their work.

Chueca & Calle Génova

Antonio Machón

C/Conde de Xiquena 8 (91 532 40 93/ www.antonio.machon.net). Metro Chueca/bus all routes to Paseo de Recoletos. **Open** 11am-2pm, 5.30-9pm Tue-Sat. Closed Mon, Sun & Aug. **Map** p306 H5.

Machón deals mainly with famous older artists such as Tàpies, Antonio Saura and Bonifacio, but also shows younger Spanish artists. He also publishes fine artists' books, combining a poetic component and illustrations by contemporary painters.

Dionís Bennassar

C/San Lorenzo 15 (91 319 69 72/ www.artemadrid.net). Metro Tribunal/bus 3, 37, 40, 149. **Open** 10am-2pm, 5-9pm Tue-Sat; closed Mon, Sun. **Map** p306 G4.

Firmly established in Mallorca, Bennassar has had a Madrid base since 1989. He mainly features young artists, but does not neglect better-known figures.

Elba Benítez

C/San Lorenzo 11 (91 308 04 68/ www.artnet.com/ebenitez.html). Metro Tribunal/ bus 3, 37, 40, 149. **Open** 11am-2pm, 5-9pm Tue-Sat; closed Mon, Sun & Aug. **Map** p306 G4.

In the courtyard of a 19th-century mansion, this gallery opened in 1990 with the dual aims of introducing major foreign artists to Spanish audiences and assisting young Spanish artists in gaining recognition. It has stuck to its gutsy brief, and remains one of Madrid's more interesting galleries.

Elvira González

C/General Castaños 9 (91 319 59 00/ galeriaeg@entorno.es). Metro Colón/bus all routes to Plaza de Colón. **Open** 10.30am-2pm, 5-9pm Mon-Fri; 11am-2pm, 6-9pm Sat. Closed Sat (June-Oct), Sun & Aug. **Map** p306 H4.

A true professional, Elvira González deals mostly in modern masters – Calder, Chillida, Léger, Picasso –

Arts & Entertainment

but also promotes some contemporary Spanish artists. Every exhibition held here is complemented by a special print edition of the same artist's work.

Estampa

C/Justiniano 6 (91 308 30 30/
galeriaestampa@teleline.es). Metro Alonso Martínez/
bus 3, 21, 37, 40, 149. **Open** 11am-2pm, 6-9pm
Tue-Sat; closed Mon, Sun & Aug. **Map** p306 H4.
A rather preciously run gallery that won its reputation by producing limited editions of small artist-made objects. Juan Hidalgo, Juan Bordes and Fernando Alamo are among those represented here.

Fúcares

C/Conde de Xiquena 12 (91 308 01 91/
galefucares@jazzfree.com). Metro Chueca/bus all
routes to Paseo de Recoletos. **Open** 11am-2pm, 5-9pm
Tue-Sat; closed Mon, Sun & Aug. **Map** p306 H5.
Norberto Dotor Pérez is a dedicated gallerist keen to promote young Spanish artists. His exhibitions bring together the different generations of artists he represents, so you can see established local names such as Javier Baldeón, Jesús Zurita and Abraham Lacalle along with the latest trends in the art world.

Galería Juana de Aizpuru

C/Barquillo 44, 1° (91 310 55 61). Metro Chueca/
bus 3, 37, 40, 149. **Open** 5-9pm Mon; 10am-2pm,
5-9pm Tue-Sat; closed Sun. **Map** p306 H5.
Juana de Aizpuru, one of the powerful women who have dominated the modern Madrid art world, opened this space in 1982. She has been a driving force in the international promotion of Spanish art, and ARCO (*see p206* **Art bazaars**) arose from one of her initiatives. About a third of the work here is by young Spanish artists; otherwise shows mainly feature better-known figures on the international scene.

Galería Metta

C/Marqués de la Ensenada 2 (91 319 02 30/
www.centrodearte.com/galerias). Metro Colón/bus all
routes to Colón, Recoletos. **Open** 11am-2pm, 5-9pm
Tue-Sat; closed Mon, Sun & Aug. **Map** p306 H4.
Opened in 1997, Metta has two fundamental aims – to promote young Spanish artists at fairs and galleries abroad, and to give exhibition space to foreign artists in Madrid. It also takes part in PHotoEspaña.

Galería Soledad Lorenzo

C/Orfila 5 (91 308 28 87/www.soledadlorenzo.com).
Metro Alonso Martínez/bus 3, 7, 21.
Open 5-9pm Mon; 11am-2pm, 5-9pm Tue-Sat; closed
Sun & Aug. **Map** p306 H4.
A powerful force in the Madrid art world, Lorenzo has a stable of established Spanish and foreign artists, from Miquel Barceló and José María Sicilia to Julian Schnabel, Ross Blechner and Anish Kapoor. As well as being one of the most prestigious in the city, the gallery itself is a very beautiful space.

Marlborough

C/Orfila 5 (91 319 14 14). Metro Alonso Martínez/
bus 3, 7, 21. **Open** 11am-2pm, 5-9pm Mon-Sat;
closed Sun & Aug. **Map** p306 H4.

International dealers with branches in London, New York and Tokyo. The Madrid gallery is in an ugly building, but thanks to US architect Richard Gluckman, an art space specialist, has a stunning interior. Previously criticised for resting on its laurels, Marlborough has opened up to new talent.

Masha Prieto

C/Belén 2 (91 319 53 71/mprietol@nexo.es). Metro
Chueca/bus 3, 37, 40, 149. **Open** 11am-2pm, 5-9pm
Tue-Sat; closed Mon, Sun & Aug. **Map** p306 H4.
A small space that tends to focus on the Spanish avant-garde. Regular names include Din Matamoro, Pablo Aizoiala and photographer Jaime Gorospe.

Moriarty

C/Almirante 5, 1°
(91 531 43 65/moriart@jazzfree.com).
Metro Chueca/bus all routes to Paseo de Recoletos.
Open 11am-2pm, 5.30-9pm Tue-Fri; 11am-2pm Sat.
Closed Mon, Sun & July, Aug. **Map** p306 H5.
Founded by Lola Moriarty in 1981, this gallery was a prime hang-out and showcase for artists on the *Movida* scene. Some names from the early days such as Alberto García Alix or Mireia Sentís can still be found here, but Moriarty has also promoted young artists such as Julio Jara, Ana Navarrete, Chema Madoz, Javier Utray and Paloma Muñoz.

Sen

C/Barquillo 43 (91 319 16 71). Metro Chueca/bus 3,
37, 40, 149. **Open** 11am-2pm, 5-9pm Tue-Fri; 11am-
2pm Sat; closed Mon, Sun & Aug. **Map** p306 H5.
Dedicated to contemporary figurative art, Sen is another *Movida*-related gallery, and played a big part in transforming the fringe work of Costus (responsible for the interior of legendary Malasaña bar La Vía Lactea) or Ceesepe into 'art'. It has expanded into a flat upstairs, and now has space in the basement for a permanent show of sculpture. It also produces editions of graphic art and sculpture.

Salamanca

Guillermo de Osma

C/Claudio Coello 4, 1° (91 435 59 36/
gdosma@ciberia.es). Metro Retiro/bus all routes
to Puerta de Alcalá. **Open** 10am-2pm, 4.30-8.30pm
Mon-Fri; noon-2pm Sat; closed Sun. **Map** p310 I6.
This influential gallery specialises in artists from the avant-garde movements of 1910-40; it's a curious place, but it knows what it's doing. The gallery only opens on Saturdays during some exhibitions.

Oliva Arauna

C/Claudio Coello 19 (91 435 18 08/
oarauna@hotmail.com). Metro Retiro or Serrano/
bus 1, 9, 19, 51, 74. **Open** 11am-2pm, 5-9pm
Tue-Sat; closed Mon, Sun & Aug. **Map** p307 I5.
Oliva Arauna has a strong interest in sculpture, photography and video. Two of Spain's best sculptors, Antoni Abad (who now dedicates himself mainly to video art) and José Herrera exhibit regularly, along with photographer Genín Andrada.

Art bazaars

Completely different in scale and aim, these events both open up the art scene, draw in the crowds and, in the case of ARCO, put contemporary art on the front page.

ARCO

Feria de Madrid (91 722 50 00/ www.arco.ifema.es). Metro Campo de las Naciones/bus 122. **Dates** 14-19 Feb 2001, 14-19 Feb 2002. **Open** 2-9pm Wed; noon-10pm Thur; noon-9pm Fri, Sat, Sun, Mon. **Admission** 3,500ptas Wed-Sat; 3,000ptas Sun, Mon. *Students* 2,000ptas Wed-Sat, Mon; 1,500ptas Sun.

Launched in 1981, Madrid's *Feria Internacional de Arte Contemporáneo* (known as ARCO), is one of the most important art fairs in Europe, and over the years has earned the respect of the international art brigade. It's now held at the gleaming **Feria de Madrid** trade fair site (see page 279). After the lean years of the 1990s, when many galleries stayed away, the number of participants has climbed back up to around 200. Each year ARCO focuses on a specific country – Britain, in 2001. There is a popular section devoted to electronics and multimedia, *ArcoCyber*, and the organisers also seem to be taking heed of Spain's underrepresented young artists, giving more space to 'emerging art'.

ARCO provides a great opportunity to get a broad perspective on the international art market: it's open to professionals and the general public, which gives it a less formal feel than some events elsewhere. This has not led to any compromise in quality, but does mean that it's absolutely packed. It's also worth noting that all work is for sale; check out what you are interested in, then go back late on the final day and make an offer. If you need to have anything shipped, ARCO has an official agent, **Transférex**, to take charge of all the formalities.

Art Supermarket/American Prints

C/Claudio Coello 16, Salamanca (91 577 91 55). Metro Retiro/bus all routes to Puerta de Alcalá. **Open** 5.30-9pm Mon; 11am-2pm, 5.30-9pm Tue-Sat; closed Sun. **Admission** free. **Map** p307 I5.

Normally a shop selling prints and posters rather than a gallery, American Prints hosts an 'art supermarket' from late November to mid-January each year. Works by around 80 artists, from up-and-comings to well-known names, are laid out as in a supermarket, for customers to pick up a basket and do their 'shopping'. Quality is variable, but you can find some gems. Prices usually start at around 7,000ptas for numbered prints.

Raquel Ponce

C/General Pardiñas 35 (91 576 83 21) Metro Núñez de Balboa/bus 29, 52. **Open** 10.30am-1.30pm, 5-9pm Tue-Sat; closed Mon, Sun & Aug. **Map** p307 K3.

The emphasis at this friendly and accessible small gallery is on affordable sculpture, much of it created with a strong sense of fun.

Tórculo

C/Claudio Coello 17 (91 575 86 86). Metro Retiro, Serrano/bus 1, 9, 19, 51, 74. **Open** 5-9pm Mon; 10am-2pm, 5-9pm Tue-Sat; closed Sun. **Map** p307 I5.

The Tórculo gallery, run by Carmen Ortiz, has been going since 1979, mainly showing Spanish artists. It also organises a range of other activities, conferences, concerts and literary discussions.

Elsewhere

Bassari

C/del Cristo 3, Malasaña & Conde Duque (91 541 33 60). Metro Noviciado/bus 2, 147. **Open** 11am-2pm, 5.30-8.30pm Mon-Fri; 11am-2pm Sat. **Map** p305 D4.

Named after an African tribe, Bassari seek to expand knowledge of African art and culture in all

its aspects in Spain. Exhibitions focus on different aspects and themes in traditional culture, art and ritual, or highlight ethnic groups or countries.

Estiarte

C/Almagro 44, Chamberí (91 308 15 70/ www.estiarte.com). Metro Rubén Darío/bus 7, 40, 147. **Open** 10.30am-2pm, 5-9pm Mon-Sat; closed Sun. **Map** p306 H2.

Specialists in original graphics, Estiarte represents many big names past and present – Miquel Barceló, Max Ernst, Calder, Chillida, Picasso, Piensa, José María Sicilia and Tàpies. A recent step has been to exhibit completely new work, always on paper.

Galería BAT – Alberto Cornejo

C/Rios Rosas 54, Cuatro Caminos (91 554 48 10/ bat.albertocornejo@artemadrid.net). Metro Rios Rosas/bus 5, 12, 45. **Open** 10am-2pm, 5.30-9pm Mon-Fri; 10.30am-2pm Sat; closed Sun.

BAT promotes, publishes and exhibits Spanish and international artists. A regular participant in art fairs in Spain and abroad, it has a large private collection with works by Chillida, Miró, Mompó, Picasso and Tàpies, as well as younger artists such as David Lechuga, Sadao Koshiba and Ouka Lele.

Arts & Entertainment

Gay & Lesbian

Gay is hip in Madrid, and the boom in the gay scene shows no sign of fading.

Gay and lesbian life in Madrid has come a long way in just a couple of decades. For years, it kept firmly in the closet. Then, in the early '80s, with the help of *la Movida* (*see page 25*), gays began to come out and thrive. Today the city's gay scene is one of the liveliest in Europe, and, what's more, has also become one of those most accepted by other people of all tendencies.

Gay restaurants have become a must among the fashionable straight crowd. Straight women love going out in gay neighbourhoods, because they have more fun and feel safe. In spring and summer the *terrazas* of Chueca are filled with people of all sorts of sexual preferences, without anyone bothering over much which is which. Maybe this is the distinguishing factor of gay life in Madrid: it's open to all.

PLANET CHUECA
You can't really talk about gay and lesbian life in Madrid without mentioning Chueca, the *barrio* at the centre of the scene, the 'pink hood' of Madrid. Chueca has its detractors, and has given rise to a discussion as to whether it's a gay ghetto, and whether it should be, or not. The rise in the crossover-fashionable status of Chueca as a hip place to be for gay and straight people has led some gays to wish it had remained more definedly, separately 'gay'; for others, though, this relaxed, no-barriers atmosphere is a key to the district's appeal. Call it what you like, this 'ghetto' is open to all.

A new style of life has flourished in this *barrio* under the rainbow colours of the gay flag. It's a symbol of tolerance. This has encouraged gays and lesbians not only to come here for Chueca's amenities but also to live here. Older inhabitants have welcomed the new 'colonists' warmly, in good part because, thanks to gay money and the non-gay business that has come in on the back of the gay scene, once run-down Chueca now has the fastest-growing economy of any neighbourhood in Madrid.

Even Madrid's conservative *Partido Popular* city council has invested in refurbishing buildings and squares, and cuts off traffic during **Gay Pride Week** around Gay Pride Day, 28 June. This is when Chueca comes most alive with colour, music and people. The high point is undoubtedly the Gay Parade on the Saturday, a multi-coloured march from Puerta de Alcalá to Puerta del Sol, followed by parties all over Chueca at night.

The angelic **Café Acuarela**. *See p208.*

In their socialising habits, Madrid's gays and lesbians tend to follow pretty much the same pattern as everybody else in the city. Rigorous social separatism is not a Spanish custom. This is why so many of Chueca's gay venues are 'mixed', places where gays and straight people can have fun together in total harmony. The common denominator is that gays feel comfortable in them and don't have to inhibit their behaviour. And, while Madrid has its exclusively gay venues (*see page 209*), in the same way that the trendy straight crowd has 'adopted' some gay venues, many gays and lesbians also enjoy visiting non-gay places.

Cafés & restaurants

Some of the most interesting new restaurants in Madrid in the last few years are also gay-run, and so gay-friendly – examples are **La Dame Noire**, **Divina la Cocina**, **Gula Gula** and **Star's Café** (*see chapter* **Restaurants**). All the cafés and restaurants listed below are in Chueca.

A Brasileira

C/Pelayo 49 (91 308 36 25). Metro Chueca/bus 3, 40, 149. **Open** 1-4pm, 8.30pm-midnight Mon-Thur, Sun; 1-4pm, 8.30pm-2am Fri, Sat. **Average** 3,500ptas. **Credit** MC, V. **Map** p306 G5.
With an interesting range of Brazilian food, this tiny, cosy restaurant is a great place to go for a quiet and intimate meal. Highly recommended.

Café Acuarela

C/Gravina 10 (91 522 21 43). Metro Chueca/bus 3, 37, 40, 149. **Open** 3pm-3am daily. **No credit cards. Map** p306 G5.
A special, very popular little café that's ideal for a quiet drink. The camp decor is an eclectic mix of baroque and other styles, filled with sofas, tables of all shapes and sizes, gilded angels, flowers and candles. Expect a mixed crowd – gay men, a lot of gay women, and a fair few non-gays.

Café Figueroa

C/Augusto Figueroa 17 (91 521 16 73). Metro Chueca/bus 3, 40, 149. **Open** noon-1am Mon-Thur; noon-2.30am Fri, Sat; 4pm-1am Sun. **No credit cards. Map** p306 G5.
Madrid's oldest gay café. It's still a good place to start the night – after dinner, that is – or to huddle on a cold night or shoot some pool upstairs.

Café La Troje

C/Pelayo 26 (91 522 62 18). Metro Chueca/bus 3, 40, 149. **Open** 5pm-2am Mon-Thur, Sun; 5pm-3am Fri, Sat. **No credit cards. Map** p306 G5.
A popular café, packed at weekends, that caters to a varied, amiable crowd. Service is good, and there are art exhibitions that change monthly.

Miranda

C/Barquillo 29 (91 521 29 46). Metro Chueca/bus 3, 40, 149. **Open** 9pm-12.30am Mon-Thur, Sun; 9pm-1am Fri, Sat. **Set menu** 2,900ptas. **Credit** MC, V. **Map** p310 G6.
Chicly-decorated Miranda serves great food that the staff describe it as 'creative gay cuisine'. One of the most popular recent openings in Chueca, it also has drag shows – as chic as the restaurant itself – on weekend nights. Good prices and service, and the waiters are cute to boot; it's often packed, so book ahead.

Sarrasín

C/Libertad 8 (91 532 73 48). Metro Chueca/bus 3, 37, 40, 149. **Open** 1-4pm, 9pm-midnight Mon-Sat; closed Sun. **Set menus** 1,250ptas lunch; 1,800ptas dinner. **Credit** MC, V. **Map** p306 G5.
Another very trendy Chueca eating-place, highly popular with the gay and non-gay crowds. It offers imaginative, well-priced food, nice decor and good service, so it's no wonder. *See also chapter* **Restaurants**.

La Sastrería

C/Hortaleza 74 (91 532 07 71). Metro Chueca/bus 3, 40, 149. **Open** 10am-2am Mon-Thur; 10am-3am Fri; 11am-3am Sat; 11am-2am Sun. **Credit** MC, V. **Map** p306 G4.

One of Chueca's biggest and most successful gay-run café-restaurants, decorated like a tailor's shop (hence the name), La Sastrería caters to gay men and lesbians, and is now also very popular with straight people. An excellent, relaxing place. *See also p151.*

Underwood Café

C/Infantas 32 (91 532 82 67). Metro Banco de España/bus all routes to Cibeles. **Open** noon-1.30am Mon-Thur, Sun; noon-2.30am Fri, Sat. **Credit** MC, V. **Map** p310 G6.
This cosy café is decorated to look like an old-fashioned newspaper pressroom. It has two separate spaces, where you can settle down for a coffee or snack, or come in after dinner for a *digestif*.

XXX Café

C/Clavel, corner C/Reina (91 532 84 15). Metro Gran Vía/bus all routes to Gran Vía. **Open** 1pm-1.30am Mon-Thur, Sun; 2pm-2.30am Fri, Sat. **Credit** MC, V. **Map** p309 F6.
A beautifully decorated, stylishly modern café. Big windows onto the street allow you to check out what's going on inside before you venture in, or see what's outside before you leave. It hosts some fun cabaret-drag shows on Fridays and Saturdays.

Clubs & *discobars*

Due to Ayuntamiento-imposed restrictions Madrid's nightlife is becoming a tad more sedate in the week, with many places closing around 2am. At weekends, though, the city still crams in a full 48 hours' partying. Madrileños love going from one place to another as the night goes on. So, don't be surprised if a place is empty one moment, and packed the next.

Unless otherwise stated, admission is free to the venues listed below; admission prices can be unpredictable, and those listed should be taken as guidelines. Note, too, that clubs open, close and change names with alarming frequency.

Chueca

Black & White

C/Libertad 34 (91 531 11 41). Metro Chueca/bus 3, 40, 149, N1, N18, N19, N20. **Open** 9pm-5am daily. **No credit cards. Map** p306 G5.
A long-running Madrid favourite. The top floor has shows at weekends, and is good for mingling with the crowd; the bottom floor has a small disco.

Liquid

C/Barquillo 8 (91 532 74 28). Metro Chueca/bus 3, 40, 149, N1, N18, N19. **Open** 9pm-3am Mon-Thur, Sun; 9pm-3am Fri, Sat. **No credit cards. Map** p306 H5.
Madrid's sleekiest, shiniest new gay venue, styled on the most cutting-edge New York bars, with VJs playing the latest music videos, projected on screens in two bar areas. Very popular with an attractive crowd, who queue around the block from 1am.

Priscilla

C/San Bartolomé 6 (no phone).
Metro Chueca, Gran Vía/bus 3, 40, 149.
Open 9pm-6am Mon-Thur; 9pm-8am Fri, Sat; closed
Sun. **No credit cards. Map** p309 F6.
A sister-venue to the Why Not? (*see below*). The
decor's not as kitsch, but the space is bigger, the
crowd is about the same, and the music is as good.

Ras

C/Barbieri 7 (91 522 43 17). Metro Chueca/bus 3,
40, 149, N1, N18, N19. **Open** 9.30pm-6am Mon-Sat;
closed Sun. **No credit cards. Map** p309 F6.
A buzzing Chueca venue since the '80s. Its decor has
changed a lot since then, though, and now looks like
something out of *Arabian Nights*. Great, hopping
music and a youngish crowd.

Rick's

C/Clavel 8 (no phone). Metro Gran Vía/bus all routes
to Gran Vía, N16, N17, N18. **Open** 11pm-6am daily.
No credit cards. Map p309 F6.
Really the all-time classic of Madrid gay nights:
Rick's hasn't changed for years, but is still at the centre of the action. With hi-energy disco music and a
gorgeous crowd, it's always full at weekends.

Why Not?

C/San Bartolomé 6 (91 523 05 81). Metro Chueca,
Gran Vía/bus 3, 40, 149, N19. **Open** 10.30pm-6am
Mon-Thur, 10.30pm-8am Fri, Sat; closed Sun. **No**
credit cards. Map p309 F6.
A classic example of how things have changed around
Chueca. It began life as a purely gay venue, but is now
one of the *barrio*'s most mixed bar-clubs. Whatever,
it's still a must on the gay scene, with a fun crowd, and
great music from the '60s, '70s and '80s.

Off-Chueca

Flamingo Club

C/Mesonero Romanos 13 (91 531 48 27). Metro
Callao/bus all routes to Plaza del Callao. **Open** *Cream*
midnight-6am Thur; *Goa After Club* 6-10am Sat, Sun.
Admission 1,000ptas, including one drink. **No**
credit cards. Map p309 E6.
The Flamingo, one of Madrid's best club venues,
hosts two mostly gay sessions. **Cream** on Thursday
nights (or rather Friday mornings) is a fun bash that
draws a great crowd; then on every weekend morning (and holidays) there's **Goa After Club**, the best
after-hours session in town, with progressive house
to take fun-seekers into daylight. Check also
www.tripfamily.com and www.interocio.es. For
other nights at the Flamingo, *see chapter* **Nightlife**.

La Lupe

C/Torrecilla del Leal 12, Lavapiés. (91 527 50 19).
Metro Antón Martín/bus 6, 26, 32, 57, N14.
Open 10pm-2am Mon-Thur, Sun; 10pm-3am Fri, Sat.
No credit cards. Map p309 F9.
This Lavapiés venue has been refurbished recent-
ly, but still attracts the same friendly, relaxed
crowd as before. The music is varied, and there are

shows at weekends. A place where people drop in
and spend a whole afternoon, playing cards or
other games while chatting.

El Mojito

C/Olmo 6, Lavapiés (no phone). Metro Antón
Martín/bus 6, 26, 32, 57, N14. **Open** 10pm-2.30am
Mon-Thur, Sun; 9pm-3.30am Fri, Sat. **No credit**
cards. Map p309 F9.
Another popular venue in Lavapiés. The decor is
wild; there are even Barbies hanging from lamps.
The music is fun and the drinks (especially *mojitos*,
Cuban rum cocktails) well priced. As at **La Lupe**
(*see above*), the crowd is relaxed and easygoing.

Ohm & Weekend

Bash Line, Plaza del Callao 4 (91 531 01 32/
www.tripfamily.com/ohm/www.tripfamily.com/weekend).
Metro Callao/bus all routes to Plaza del Callao. **Open**
Ohm midnight-6am Fri, Sat; *Weekend* midnight-5am
Sun. **Admission** 1,500ptas including one drink.
No credit cards. Map p309 D6.
The Bash disco on Plaza Callao hosts **Ohm** on Fridays
and Saturdays, a very cool, mainly gay session. The
music is hip house, and the venue an ideal size, with a
big floor that the crowd make the most of. Later on
Sundays it hosts **Weekend**, Ohm's 'tea dance', perfect for all those who don't let the fact it's Sunday get
in the way of having a good time. More house, and a
youngish crowd. *See chapter* **Nightlife**.

Shangay Tea Dance

Pasapoga, Gran Vía 37 (91 531 48 27
/www.tripfamily.com/shangay). Metro Callao/bus all
routes to Plaza del Callao. **Open** 10pm-3am Sun.
Admission 1,000ptas including one drink.
No credit cards. Map p309 E6.
One of the best Sunday tea dances in Madrid, a camp
institution, the Shangay has lately changed venues.
The old Pasapoga disco on the Gran Vía now turns
gay every Sunday night to host the Shangay's parties, shows, cabaret and disco session. The crowd is
very good-looking, and the music's great. Admission
is free before 10.30pm.

Tábata

C/Vergara 12, Los Austrias (91 547 97 35). Metro
Opera/bus 3, N13, N15. **Open** 10.30pm-5am Wed-Sat;
closed Mon, Tue, Sun. **No credit cards. Map** p308 C7.
Tábata is near the Palacio Real, and so the crowd is
smarter, and drinks pricier, than in Chueca. The
music (pop, dance and disco), though, is lively, and
there are fun shows and cabaret.

Exclusively male/hardcore

Cruising

C/Pérez Galdós 5, Chueca (91 521 51 43). Metro
Chueca/bus 3, 40, 149, N18, N19. **Open** 7pm-
1.30am daily. **No credit cards. Map** p306 G5.
A disco/club that's a real gay classic. Upstairs
there's a quieter pub area, and a room showing porn
videos; downstairs there's a big dancefloor and various backrooms. Scruffiness is part of its charm.

Arts & Entertainment

Eagle

C/Pelayo 30, Chueca (no phone).
Metro Chueca/bus 3, 40, 149. **Open** 10am-3am
daily. **No credit cards. Map** p306 G5.
A pretty seedy leather bar, where uniforms, fatigues
and boots are also *de rigueur*. Its leather parties get
pretty wild, so go for breakfast if you need something more sedate. Strangely enough, women are
allowed in sometimes, but from 10pm it's men-only.

New Leather Bar

C/Pelayo 42, Chueca (91 308 14 62). Metro
Chueca/bus 3, 40, 149, N19. **Open** 8pm-3am daily.
No credit cards. Map p306 G5.
A long-running, two-floor hangout. Leather parties
are held here, but despite the name it's not exclusively a leather bar. Steaming at weekends, though,
with hardcore parties on Thursdays and Fridays.

Olimpo

C/Aduana 21, Sol & Gran Vía (no phone/
www.interocio.es/olimpo). Metro Gran Vía, Sevilla/bus
all routes to Gran Vía. **Open** 10pm-5am Tue-Sun;
closed Mon. **No credit cards. Map** p309 F7.
This Pompeiian temple opens its doors to all those
who adore the body, good music, fun and... It has
one of Madrid's busiest backrooms.

Refugio

C/Doctor Cortezo 1, Lavapiés (91 369 40
38/www.interocio.es/refugio). Metro Tirso de
Molina/bus 6, 26, 32, 57, N14. **Open** midnight-6am
Mon-Thur; midnight-7am Fri, Sat; 9pm-2am Sun.
Admission 1,000ptas, including one drink.
No credit cards. Map p309 E8.
A very popular subterranean disco, renowned for
foam parties and its 'natural' (nude) night. It also
holds tea dances (Sundays), and cabaret shows. A
good-looking crowd, and a backroom.

Strong Center

C/Trujillos 7, Sol & Gran Vía (91 531 48 27).
Metro Opera/bus 3, 25, 39, N13, N15.
Open midnight-7am daily. **Admission** 1,000ptas.
No credit cards. Map p309 D7.
Madrid's seediest. It's a huge place, with a big dance-
floor (usually empty), and what is said to be the
biggest backroom in Spain (invariably packed).

Troyans

C/Pelayo 4, Chueca (91 521 73 58).
Metro Chueca/bus 3, 40, 149.
Open 9pm-3am Mon-Thur; 9pm-4am Fri, Sat.
No credit cards. Map p306 G5.
Leather parties on the first Thursday of each month;
Sunday is nude night, and there are two backrooms.

Saunas

Caldea

C/Valverde 32, Malasaña & Conde Duque (91 522
99 56). Metro Gran Vía/bus 3, 40, 149, N16, N17,
N18. **Open** 24hrs daily. **Admission** 1,500ptas. **No**
credit cards. Map p309 E6.

This new sauna – the only one in Madrid open round
the clock – has excellent facilities on two floors.
Recommended, especially at weekends.

Men

C/Pelayo 25, Chueca (91 531 25 83). Metro
Chueca/bus 3, 40, 149. **Open** 3.30pm-8am daily.
Admission 1,000ptas; 50% discount for men under
25. **No credit cards. Map** p306 G5.
A small sauna lacking facilities (there are only dry
and steam saunas), but in the heart of Chueca. Very
popular, especially on Sunday afternoons.

Paraíso Sauna

C/Norte 15, Malasaña & Conde Duque (91 522 42
32/www.interocio.es/paraiso). Metro Noviciado/bus
147, N16, N17, N18. **Admission** 1,600ptas; 50% discount for men under
25. **No credit cards. Map** p305 E4.
This spotlessly clean sauna used to be a flamenco
tablao, and has retained its suitably ditzy Andaluz-
fantasy decor. Also massage, UVA baths, bar, dark-
room, porn videos and good-looking customers.

Sauna Príncipe

C/Príncipe 15, Huertas & Santa Ana (91 429 39
49/www.interocio.es/principe). Metro Sevilla/bus all
routes to Puerta del Sol. **Open** 10am-1am daily.
Admission 1,600ptas, 50% discount for men under
25; ticket for 10 baths 12,000ptas. **No credit cards.**
Map p309 F8.
A clean, modern sauna with good facilities.

Accommodation

Hostal Hispano

C/Hortaleza 38, 2°A, Chueca (91 531 48 71/fax 91
521 87 80). Metro Gran Vía/bus all routes to Gran
Vía. **Rates** 4,475ptas single; 5,815ptas double.
Credit MC, V. **Map** p306 G5.
Hispano is a small, simple *hostal* in the centre of
town, right on the edge of the Chueca gay village,
and very reasonably priced. The clientele is mixed,
but gay people are always very well received, and
service is excellent.

Hostal Odesa

C/Hortaleza 38, 3°, Chueca (91 521 03 38).
Metro Gran Vía/bus all routes to Gran Vía.
Rates 3,000ptas single; 4,700ptas double. **Credit**
AmEx, DC, MC, V. **Map** p306 G5.
Madrid's first *hostal* aimed exclusively at the gay
community – both men and women. It's small, but
very clean and pleasant; the management also rents
small apartments, by the day or week.
Room services *TV.*

Hostal Sonsoles

C/Fuencarral 18, Chueca (91 532 75
23/m.g.d@mx3.redestb.es). Metro Gran Vía/bus all
routes to Gran Vía. **Rates** 4,000ptas single;
6,000ptas double. **Credit** MC, V. **Map** p309 E6.
A quaint but comfortable *hostal*, recently renovated
and perfectly placed for the Chueca scene.
Room services *Telephone. TV.*

Floral finery awaits at **Anthurium**.

Gay & lesbian shops

Anthurium

C/Pelayo 19, Chueca (91 522 69 29). Metro Chueca/bus 3, 40, 149. **Open** 10am-2pm, 5-9pm Mon-Sat; closed Sun. **Credit** AmEx, DC, MC, V. **Map** p306 G5.
This wonderful flower shop is a gay community favourite. The interior is lovely, with live piano music (usually in the afternoon), and all sorts of classic and exotic blooms. The window displays are something special, too, and staff are a delight.

Berkana

C/Gravina 11, Chueca (91 532 13 93). Metro Chueca/bus 3, 40, 149. **Open** 10.30am-2pm, 5-8.30pm Mon-Fri; noon-2pm, 5-8.30pm Sat; closed Sun. **Credit** AmEx, DC, MC, V. **Map** p306 G5.
Berkana was the first gay and lesbian bookshop in Madrid, and is now a gay community centre (for men and women) as well. There are books in English; staff are friendly and helpful. The recently-opened branch nearby, **Berkana Complementos**, specialises in gifts and attractive accessories.
Branch: **Berkana Complementos** C/Pelayo 23, Chueca (91 522 55 99).

Condonería-Tienda Erótica

C/Pelayo 46, Chueca (91 702 05 10). Metro Chueca/bus 3, 40, 149. **Open** 11am-2.30pm, 5-10pm Mon-Sat; closed Sun. **Credit** MC, V. **Map** p306 G5.
This new shop in Chueca sells all kinds of condoms, and erotic underwear and sundries. The decor and the space are great, and staff put you at your ease.

Lambda Viajes

C/Fuencarral 43, Malasaña & Conde Duque (91 532 78 33). Metro Chueca/bus 3, 37, 40, 149. **Open** 9.30am-2.30pm, 4.30-8pm Mon-Fri; 9.30am-2.30pm Sat; closed Sun. **Credit** MC, V. **Map** p306 G5.
A travel agency aimed at a gay clientele, which can book rooms in gay hotels throughout Spain and abroad. It also offers package trips to various destinations; staff speak English and French.

Serge K

C/San Gregorio 3, Chueca (91 319 04 53). Metro Chueca/bus 3, 40, 149. **Open** 10.30am-3pm, 4.30-8pm Mon-Fri 10.30am-3pm Sat; closed Sun. **Credit** MC, V. **Map** p306 G5.
One of the trendiest hairdresser's in Chueca, Serge K also does piercing and tanning. Very friendly.

Sex Shop Barco 43

C/del Barco 43, Malasaña & Conde Duque (91 531 49 88). Metro Gran Vía, Tribunal/bus 3, 40, 149. **Open** 10am-2pm, 4-10pm Mon-Sat; 4-10pm Sun. **No credit cards**. **Map** p309 E6.
The only exclusively gay sex shop in Madrid.

SR

C/Pelayo 7, Chueca (91 523 19 64). Metro Gran Vía, Chueca/bus 3, 40, 149. **Open** 11am-2pm, 5-9.30pm Mon-Sat; closed Sun. **Credit** AmEx, DC, MC, V.
Specialists for the leather (and similar) fan. Leatherwear, uniforms, rubber and SM gear, plus accessories from crucifixes to slings.

Contacts & information

Cogam (Coordinadora Gay de Madrid)

C/Fuencarral 37, Chueca (91 522 45 17). Metro Chueca, Tribunal/bus 3, 40, 149. **Open** 5-9pm Mon-Fri; closed Sat, Sun. **Map** p306 G5.
The largest gay and lesbian organisation in Madrid. It arranges Gay Pride week, campaigns for gay rights, and offers help on health issues, leisure activities and anything to do with the gay community.

Publications

Revista Mensual The most complete local gay magazine. Available from newsstands in central Madrid and in some clubs.
Shangay Express A free newspaper on gay and lesbian life in Madrid given out in clubs, cafés, **Berkana** bookshop and other shops.

Web pages

www.chueca.com Chueca's own web page, with information on activities, clubs, chats, organisations, and anything else around the neighbourhood.
www.hispagay.com One of the first gay websites in Spain, and one of the best: information on clubs, activities, events, gossip and so on.
www.yoentiendo.com Another gay website, providing contacts, chats and information

Arts & Entertainment

Lesbian Madrid

A few years ago the separation between gay men and lesbians in Chueca was well defined. However, little by little, as joint organisations have begun to operate and businesses owned by gay men and women have begun to prosper, this separation has diminished. In fact, many of Madrid's most popular lesbian venues – *terrazas* on the Plaza de Chueca such as La **Bohemia** and **Truco** (*see below*) – cater to men and women, as do many places run by gay men.

One of the biggest changes that has occurred in lesbian Madrid can be seen by comparing the secretiveness of past years and the openness of today. Nowadays the lesbian community has a noticeably laid-back attitude, and an apparent lack of political orientation, two things that attract the attention of foreign lesbians. This doesn't mean, though, that lesbians in Madrid don't feel there are rights to be won (in fact, they're more militant than gay men); it's just that the fight for lesbian rights doesn't colour all lesbian life, just as gay activism doesn't colour gay men's life here either.

Lesbian bars

Venues that are popular with gay men and straight women as well as lesbians include **Café Acuarela** and **La Sastrería** (*see page 208*) and **La Lupe** and **El Mojito** (*see page 209*).

Mixed venues

El Barberillo de Lavapiés

C/Salitre 43, Lavapiés (no phone). Metro Antón Martín, Lavapiés/bus 6, 26, 32. **Open** 9pm-2.30am Tue-Thur, Sun; 9pm-3.30am Fri, Sat; closed Mon. **No credit cards. Map** p309 F9.
This pleasant café in Lavapiés is a good place to have a pre- or after-dinner drink. Card and board games can be played, and there's interesting music.

Top gay bookstore **Berkana**. *See p212.*

La Bohemia

Plaza de Chueca 10, Chueca (no phone). Metro Chueca/bus 3, 40, 149. **Open** 8pm-3.30am daily. **No credit cards. Map** p306 G5.
This lesbian venue is best known for its summer *terraza* on the plaza, but it's popular at any time of year (especially at weekends). The music's fizzing too, prices are low, and there's a pool table.

Club Social de COGAM

C/Fuencarral 37, Chueca (91 522 45 17). Metro Chueca, Tribunal/bus 3, 40, 149. **Open** 5pm-midnight daily. **No credit cards. Map** p306 G5.
A café run by the gay and lesbian association COGAM (*see p212*), but most popular with women. A pleasant place to go for a drink and find out what's cooking on the political or social side of the scene.

Escape

C/Gravina 13, Chueca (no phone). Metro Chueca/bus 3, 40, 149. **Open** 8pm-5am Thur; midnight-6am Fri, Sat; closed Mon-Wed, Sun. **No credit cards. Map** p306 G5.
This club/disco opened as a lesbian venue but has since become highly mixed. However, it still has great music, and a very friendly crowd.

Truco

C/Gravina 10, Chueca (91 532 89 21). Metro Chueca/bus 3, 40, 149. **Open** 8pm-2.30am Mon-Thur, Sun; 9pm-5am Fri, Sat. **No credit cards. Map** p306 G5.
Amid the men's venues on Plaza de Chueca, this women's disco-pub-*terraza* has become enormously popular with a hip, lively crowd. The music is loud, and there's a fun vibe. The pool table is downstairs.

Women-only

These venues allow men in so long as they are accompanied by a gay woman.

Ambient

C/San Mateo 21,Chueca (no phone). Metro Tribunal/bus 3, 40, 149. **Open** 9pm-5am daily. Average 1,500ptas. **No credit cards. Map** p306 G4.
A friendly café with a warm, relaxing decor, tasty pizza and good music. There's also a pool table.

Medea

C/de la Cabeza 33, Lavapiés (no phone). Metro Antón Martín, Tirso de Molina/bus 6, 26, 32, 57. **Open** 11pm-5am Thur-Sat; closed Mon-Wed, Sun. **No credit cards. Map** p309 E9.
Considered by some the best-kept secret in Madrid, a long-successful lesbian club with a punchy disco, cabaret, pool table and a young crowd.

La Rosa

C/Tetuán 27, Sol & Gran Vía (no phone). Metro Sol/bus all routes to Puerta del Sol. **Open** 11pm-6am daily. **No credit cards. Map** p309 E7.
A more elegantly decorated lesbian club. Thursday night is cabaret night; at other times there's good music and a relaxed atmosphere.

Music:
Classical & Opera

Madrid's big music venues may be shrouded in polemic, but there are still plenty of interesting options for concertgoers.

It took forever, but the inauguration in late 1997 of Madrid's fabulous state-of-the-art opera house, the **Teatro Real**, was hailed as a landmark for the development of classical music in the city. Along with the **Teatro de la Zarzuela** and the **Auditorio Nacional de Música**, plus the less-splendid but always good **Teatro Monumental**, Madrid could now claim to have left the musical backwaters and placed itself firmly on the European musical map. The **Círculo de Bellas Artes** (*see page 73*) is also a significant music venue.

The redevelopment of the Teatro Real had been a tortuous process, subject to delays, setbacks and disasters, a rocketing budget and all manner of controversy. Since its inauguration the Real has been subject to close scrutiny, and in its first three years of operation has generated almost as much polemic as it did during its reconstruction.

Much had already been done during the 1980s to improve the dire situation of serious music in Madrid. The economic boom of that decade helped matters, and the opening in 1988 of the Auditorio Nacional gave musical life in the city an important boost. However, opera as a genre suffered from then on, owing mainly to the closure of the Real, during which time fans had to make do with the productions staged in the Teatro de la Zarzuela.

The early '90s were more difficult, as the post-1993 recession brought a drop in grants, sponsorship, commissions and audiences. Contemporary music was hardest hit, after a decade of tangible progress. Since 1996 the music world has been coming to terms with the policies of the *Partido Popular* government, pledged to austerity and encouraging private funding for the arts.

TICKETS

The state-funded venues, the Auditorio Nacional, and Teatro de la Zarzuela, as well as the theatres María Guerrero, and Teatro de la Comedia, have a joint ticketing system through which it's possible to buy tickets for all these venues at any one of them (*see also page 242*).

All provide free leaflets on their forthcoming programmes and are affiliated to the phone sales scheme operated by **Caja Madrid** (902 48 84 88). The Teatro Real does not participate in this scheme, but has a phone sales number, also operated by Caja Madrid (902 24 48 24). Tickets for large-scale concerts at the Auditorio can be hard to obtain as only a limited number are on open sale, but you can sometimes get standby tickets the day before. Ticket agencies can usually obtain opera and concert seats; for details of these and Caja Madrid and other phone booking systems, *see page 171*.

Concert seasons normally run from October to June. During the summer, and August in particular, many music venues virtually close down, and regular concerts are at a premium. The Teatro Real, though, has now begun to present a summer season, and it is possible to hear music at this time in many open-air performances as part of the city's festivals. Summer is also traditionally the main season for *zarzuela* (*see page 188* and *page 217* **Making light of things**).

Orchestras & ensembles

Grupo Círculo

Based at the Círculo de Bellas Artes (*see p73*), this 11-strong group has as musical director José Luis Temes, one of Madrid's leading contemporary musicians. They divide their time between performances and recording of Spanish contemporary music.

Orquesta y Coro de RTVE

Born out of the need to perform music for broadcasting, the excellent Spanish Radio and Television Orchestra began concert performances in 1965 in the Teatro de la Zarzuela. The founding director was Igor Markevitch and the orchestra has had, at different times, directors of the calibre of Antoni Ros Marbà, Enrique Asensio, who is now serving his second spell at the helm, and the Rumanian Sergiu Comissiona, from 1990 until 1998. It has made magnificent recordings of Spanish works, and a particularly successful Antología de la Zarzuela. It moved into its home at the newly revamped Teatro Monumental (*see p215*) in 1988. The varied

Mirella Freni with the **Orquesta Sinfónica**.

repertoire covers romantic classics, Spanish works and contemporary music. The associated Choir, led by the Hungarian Laszlo Heltay, is also highly rated.

Orquesta Nacional de España & Coro Nacional de España

The flagship of Spanish classical music over the last 50 years. The triple obligations of attracting public attention, creating basic repertoires and simultaneously enlarging them into new areas have often been too much for it to bear. Recently it has been marked by internal strife. Musicians, whose role is complicated by their position as state employees, went on strike in 1993 for the first time in the orchestra's history, and the musical director, Italian Aldo Ceccato, left the following year predicting a bleak future for the orchestra. Since then the ONE has performed under guest musical directors. At present there is still no permanent director, although Rafael Frühbeck de Burgos holds the position of Emeritus Director. Orchestra and choir have an excellent permanent home in the Auditorio Nacional, but funding cuts exacerbate their relative disarray.

Orquesta Sinfónica de Madrid

Unencumbered by extra-musical problems, this orchestra was founded in 1903. Its most famous director was the violinist Enrique Fernández Arbós, appointed in 1905 and in place for 30 years. He dominated the pre-war period so much that the orchestra became known as the Arbós. The orchestra's fortunes flagged after the Civil War, but in 1981 it was boosted by its (at the time) controversial appointment as resident orchestra at the Teatro de la Zarzuela (see p216). This move was opposed by Madrid's two other major orchestras, but the OSM justified the vote of confidence. In 1997 it took up temporary residence at the Teatro Real, initially until the end of the 1998-99 season. This agreement has now been extended to 2003, when the orchestra celebrates its centenary. Currently the orchestra is led by resident director Luis García Navarro, with Kurt Sanderling as honorary director and Cristóbal Halffter as associated composer. A professional choir was recently formed, which performs in productions at the Teatro Real.

Trio Mompou

Based in Madrid, and so named as a tribute to the late Catalan composer and master pianist Frederic Mompou, this contemporary chamber ensemble, headed by Luciano González Sarmiento, has a high reputation. Their repertoire includes over 100 works by almost every Spanish composer of the 20th century, and it frequently presents totally new work.

Venues

Auditorio Nacional de Música

C/Príncipe de Vergara 146, Prosperidad (91 337 01 00/www.auditorionacional.mcu.es). Metro Cruz del Rayo or Prosperidad/bus 1, 9, 16, 29, 51, 52, 73. **Open** *Box office* 5-7pm Mon; 10am-5pm Tue-Fri; 10am-1pm Sat. Closed Sun & Aug. **Main season** Oct-June. **Tickets** ONE concerts 1,000-4,500ptas Fri, Sat; 700-2,500 ptas Sun; other concerts vary.

The inauguration of this ugly building in 1988 put Madrid on the itineraries of the most important international conductors, soloists and orchestras, attracted by a new symphony hall rivalling the Berlin Philharmonie and Amsterdam Concertgebouw in capacity (2,000-plus in the main hall). Home to the Orquesta Nacional de España and its associated choir and the Joven Orquesta Nacional de España youth orchestra, it has, despite outward appearances, symphonic and chamber music halls that are light, comfortable and have excellent acoustics. It hosts an intensive concert programme during the relatively short season, with performances of some kind virtually every night. Other seasons or concert series run in parallel. The centrepiece season features the ONE with international guest conductors and soloists, with concerts at 7.30pm on Fridays and Saturdays and 11.30am on Sundays. Tickets for Sunday concerts are cheaper and go on sale just one hour in advance. Also, some extra tickets are made available four weeks in advance; there is a noticeboard outside the Sala de Cámara with information. Running parallel to the ONE season are three other series of concerts, taking place on various nights. One is the double series organised by Promoconcert; there is also the 'Ciclo de Conciertos Extraordinarios' organised by Juventudes Musicales de Madrid; and lastly there is the Liceo de Cámara, a chamber programme. Tickets for all three are only available if they have not already been taken by season-ticket holders. In this case they go on sale ten days before the concert.

Teatro Monumental

C/Atocha 65, Lavapiés (91 429 81 19). Metro Antón Martín/bus 6, 26, 32, 57. **Open** *Box office* 11am-2pm, 5-7pm daily. **Main season** Oct-May. **Tickets** 1,500-2,800ptas. **No credit cards.** **Map** p309 F8.

Much less lavish than Auditorio Nacional, the Teatro de la Zarzuela or the Teatro Real, the Monumental was smartened up just over a year ago. The main function of this theatre is to record concerts by the

RTVE Orchestra and Choir for broadcasting – something it does admirably well. It's a reasonably priced venue offering orchestral concerts, opera and *zarzuela*, and opens to the public for general rehearsals free of charge on Thursday mornings (though you must call first and get your name on a list as demand from school groups is pretty high).

Teatro Real

Plaza de Isabel II, Austrias (91 516 06 00/ www.teatro-real.com). Metro Opera/bus 3, 25, 33, 39. **Open** *Box office* 10am-1.30pm, 5.30-8pm Mon-Sat; closed Sun, also Caja Madrid . **Main season** Sept-July. **Tickets** 850-16,975ptas. *Visits* 500ptas; 300ptas concessions. **Visits** 1pm Tue-Fri; every 30min 10.30am-1.30pm Sat, Sun, public hols. **Map** p309 D7.
Madrid's opera house is possibly the most technologically advanced in Europe. First opened in 1850, the Real has had a long and chequered history and was in a fairly run-down state by the mid 1980s. When orchestral and symphonic activity moved to the Auditorio in 1988, the way was clear for rebuilding. The project took five years longer than planned and cost upwards of £80 million ($120 million) before finally opening in October 1997. Management now hopes to show that it was worth the wait. One of the main attractions is the splendid horseshoe shaped hall, while the stage itself is a true feat of engineering – up to six stage sets can be built and swung into place at any one time. The acoustics are so good that the quality of the sound is practically the same everywhere in the hall. The decor is lavish, and the eliptical main foyer has a feel of monumental roominess. A restaurant, café, numerous other spaces and the very latest in lighting all make the Real something Madrid can be proud of.
The Real's progress, however, has been under very close scrutiny throughout. Extra-musical problems are frequent, while, on the artistic side, reviews have been mixed – at times excellent and at others hypercritical. For many, the Real's lack of commitment to dance is inexcusable (in the 2000-1 season there are just three appearances by the Compañía Nacional de Danza), and even the opera programme, with a tight budget, often seems excessively dependent on visiting companies for a supposedly world-class house. In 2000-1 it features both home-produced works and visiting productions, with grand works by Mozart, Rossini, Verdi and Wagner and others by Spanish composers, among them a world première by Luis de Pablos. Varied, if limited, seasons of lyrical and symphonic concerts are also programmed. 2000 also saw the first summer festival in the theatre, almost exclusively of opera, which, hopefully, will continue in future years.

Teatro de la Zarzuela

C/Jovellanos 4, Huertas & Santa Ana (91 524 54 00). Metro Banco de España or Sevilla/bus all routes to C/Alcalá. **Open** *Box office* noon-6pm daily (noon-8pm performance days). **Main season** Sept-July. **Tickets** 1,800-13,200ptas. **Credit** AmEx, DC, V. **Map** p310 G7.

Another theatre with a chequered history, designed on the lines of Milan's Scala, this beautiful building was opened in 1856 in an attempt to boost the prestige of *zarzuela*. It was ravaged by fire in 1909, but later rebuilt. Callas sang here in 1958, and an annual opera festival began in 1964. For ten years it was Madrid's official opera house due to the closure of the Teatro Real in 1987, but now, unshackled of that responsibility, it can dedicate more resources to the genre from which it takes its name, *zarzuela* (productions are usually very good). Ballet is also scheduled, and the theatre presents an interesting range of operatic work, chamber pieces and modern works, as well as much-praised Lieder seasons and other music such as flamenco.

Institutions

Centro para la Difusión de la Música Contemporánea

Centro de Arte Reina Sofía, C/Santa Isabel 52, Lavapiés (91 467 50 62/http://cdmc.mcu.es). Metro Atocha/bus all routes to Atocha. **Main season** Oct-May. **Map** p310 G10.
Founded in 1983, this innovative music centre has been based at the Reina Sofía (*see p97*) since 1987. In its early stages the pressure of battling against musical conservatism nearly finished off its founder, composer Luis de Pablo, who left after only two years. However, thanks to his work the centre became established as the city's main focus for contemporary music. It gives 30 or so commissions annually to Spanish and foreign composers, which are premièred in four monthly concerts, three at the Reina Sofía and one in the chamber hall of the Auditorio Nacional. Other performances sometimes take place in the Círculo de Bellas Artes (*see p73*) and other venues.

Fundación Juan March

C/Castelló 77, Salamanca (91 435 42 40/ www.march.es). Metro Núñez de Balboa/bus 1, 9, 19, 29, 52, 74. **Main season** Oct-June. **Map** p307 K3.
The Fundación Juan March, a major player in many areas of the arts in Spain (*see also p108*), has provided financial support for new music since 1955. The small concert hall is in constant use, and its free concerts are recommended. The Foundation also organises concerts for young people and has an extensive Contemporary Music Library.

Festivals & other venues

Classical music programmes, albeit now rather frustrating ones, form part of the **Veranos de la Villa** and **Festival de Otoño** (*see page 188*). March and April sees the **Festival de Arte Sacro** (Sacred Art) in and around Madrid, featuring religious music, theatre, dance and poetry (information is available from tourist offices and the 012 phoneline).

Making light of things

Madrid is the home of *zarzuela*, Spain's very own form of light opera. Its distant origins date back to the Golden Age, in the entertainments staged for King Philip IV at the hunting lodge of La Zarzuela outside Madrid, but its current form developed from the 1830s onwards. It is comparable to the contemporary German *singspiel* or Viennese operetta, but has a distinctively Spanish musical idiom.

At the end of the 19th century *zarzuelas* dominated the entertainment world in Madrid, with ten different productions often playing at any one time. Their plots dealt not with great themes or heroic figures, but offered identifiable, comic and slightly bawdy scenes of local life. *Zarzuelas* helped to establish the *castizo* mythology of working-class Madrid (see page 184), with street-corner romances between flat-capped *chulos* and flashing-eyed, sassy *chulapas* in flowered shawls. The world of *zarzuela* became part of this mythology itself, singers were the era's jet set, and young aristocrats often had *las tiples*, the girls of the *zarzuela* chorus, as lovers.

The *zarzuela* repertoire includes some fine, sometimes subtle music. Tomás Bretón's *La Verbena de la Paloma*, Pablo Sorozábal's *La del Manojo de Rosas*, Ruperto Chapí's *La Revoltosa* and Lorente and Serrano's *La Dolorosa* are some of the classics. New *zarzuelas* were produced until the 1930s, but the Civil War and its aftermath dealt a blow to the genre's popularity and creativity.

Zarzuela nowadays struggles against the contempt of many serious music-lovers, who see it as opera's corny, kitsch poor relation. Nevertheless, it is a distinctively Madrileño art form, with a keen following and considerable official backing. Plácido Domingo, son of *zarzuela* singers, is a great fan, and has successfully recorded collections of *zarzuela* songs.

Where to find it

Madrid's main *zarzuela* season is in summer, from June to September, with an annual season in the **Centro Cultural de la Villa** (see page 243) and the open-air **La Corrala**, one of the surviving corridor-tenements once found throughout working-class Madrid (see page 78). The **Teatro de la Zarzuela** (see page 216) programmes several *zarzuelas* a season. *Zarzuela* buffs may also hear it sung in bars and restaurants such as the **Café Viena** (see page 153) and **La Castafiore** (see below).

La Corrala

C/Tribulete 12 & C/Sombrerete 13, Lavapiés (information 010). Metro Embajadores or Lavapiés/bus all routes to Embajadores. **Open** Box office 1hr before performance. **Performances** 10pm Tue-Sun; closed Mon. **Season** July, Aug. **Tickets** average 2,000ptas. **No credit cards.** **Map** p309 E10.

La Castafiore

C/Barquillo 30, Chueca (91 532 21 00). Metro Chueca/bus 37, 149. **Open** 2-4pm, 9.30pm-1am Mon-Sat; closed Sun. **Credit** MC, V. **Map** p306 H5. This café, tapas bar and restaurant offers the novelty of singing waiters: music students and professionals blend in with real waiters, and launch into an operatic aria at the drop of a hat during dinner.

La Fídula

C/Huertas 57, Huertas & Santa Ana (91 429 29 47). Metro Antón Martín/bus 6, 10, 14, 26, 27, 32, 34, 37, 45, 57. **Open** 7pm-3am Mon-Thur, Sun; 7pm-4am Fri, Sat. *July, Aug* opens at 8pm. **Map** p310 G8. This 'café-concert' presents small-ensemble music most nights of the week from September to June, and at weekends in summer. The performers are mostly music students, but often extremely good, and it's also pleasant just as a bar. The fare served up is increasingly diverse, and it's possible to catch jazz and tango as well these days.

Madrid offers many other opportunities to see concerts in unique and historic venues, sometimes for free. During July there is the **Clásicos en Verano** festival, of free concerts in churches and convents, and a programme mainly of baroque works is presented in the **Academia de Bellas Artes de San Fernando** (*see page 99*). Open-air summer concerts are often held in the **Centro Cultural Conde Duque** (*see page 107*), and also interesting are the irregular concerts at the **Residencia de Estudiantes** (*see page 109*).

Also, there are bars for most occasions in Madrid, and some host good music. The smart **Café Viena** (*see page 153*) has sessions every Monday where opera and *zarzuela* singers perform for enthusiastic diners, and the **Salón del Prado** (*see page 149*) hosts, among other performances, chamber music from October to June, starting around 11pm.

Music: Rock, Roots & Jazz

Though the number of venues in Madrid may be somewhat restricted, there's no end of musical styles to keep the loyal fans happy.

Madrid's music scene is somewhat village-like. There are still too few places offering live music, and the same acts tend to dominate the circuit all the time. Things have picked up over the last couple of years, but a clamp-down on licensing hours and noise levels have made it extremely difficult to open new venues. Perhaps the greatest contribution in recent years to the live music scene has come from the proliferation of Irish pubs, which offer a forum for rock, blues and folk outfits.

It must be said that apathy and lack of loyalty amongst Madrileños is in part to blame for the ease with which the conservative, Popular Party-run town hall has been able to limit the growth of the music scene. This is still a city where most people go out in large groups to socialise with each other, and are quite happy to wander from bar to bar talking amongst themselves, or to sit outside listening to ghetto blasters.

In the face of the relative absence of large venues, a handful of smaller places have taken on the job of keeping the music scene healthy. Thanks to the imaginative, open programmes of venues like **Suristán**, previously overlooked (often non-Spanish) types of music are in vogue; salsa, flamenco and African music are now enjoying unprecedented popularity. Today, if one word can sum up the atmosphere it is the fruitful concept *mestizaje*, Spanish for 'crossbreeding' or 'intermixing'. Flamenco, rock, Arab or Cuban music can all feature on different nights, and all have influence on local musicians. The international success of home-grown 'Latinos' such as Enrique Iglesias have spawned dozens of local copycats, while music from artists as varied as Santana, Monica Naranjo and Gloria Estefan all mix happily in many a bar and club. This free-flowing mingling has been reflected in two parallel trends – expanding creativity on the part of Spanish artists, and an explosion in the number of musicians from outside Spain who regularly play in Madrid. Cuba is dear to the heart of many Spanish music fans, and one of the most vibrant elements in the current scene is the

wealth of talent from the island that visits frequently. African artists have also found a small but enthusiastic public. Spanish musicians themselves have become increasingly open to outside influences, while at the same time looking to their own roots without many of the neuroses that tended to characterise previous generations. Flamenco, still basking in the fashionable status it acquired in the '90s, is still perhaps the most exciting current within Spanish music (*see pages 199-202*).

Cantautores, Spanish singer-songwriters more associated with the politicised '60s and '70s, are also enjoying a revival. A new generation of performers has revitalised the genre, adding rock, pop and Latin rhythms to the mix, while a wealth of smallish locales such as the **Café de la Palma** give a stage to singers like Ismael Serrano, Pablo Bicho and Jorge Drexler. Spain also still has – perhaps more than most non-English speaking European countries – its own bustling, traditional commercial music scene, *canción española*, which thrives in the face of international competition. It's also more to the taste of the local authorities. Older performers such as Rocio Jurado or Isabel Pantoja can be heard belting out their dramatic tunes on radios in shops and cafés all over Madrid, as well as at venues such as the **Parque de Atracciones** (*see page 223*). The boundaries of the genre – especially between it and flamenco – are always flexible, however, and there are also younger rock-influenced acts such as Rosario and Azúcar Moreno (a sister duo) that are massively popular.

VENUES AND PROGRAMMES

Madrid continues to suffer from a shortage of medium-sized, centrally located music venues, but the biggest recent addition to the scene has been with the conversion into a music venue of the bullring in the southern suburb of Leganés, **La Cubierta**, which now provides a great new setting for Spanish bands and non-stadium touring acts (*see page 220*). The hitch is its

Yes, I am a rock god. **Suristán** packs in the crowds six nights a week. *See p221.*

distance from the centre. Within the city, some venues with good facilities are **La Riviera**, **Suristán**, **Sala Caracol** and **Moby Dick** (all listed below). Big stadium concerts take place at Atlético Madrid's home, the **Vicente Calderón** (*see page 237*), or the **Palacio de los Deportes** (*see page 236*). Another venue that has seen top names recently is the **Palacio de Congresos** in the Castellana (*see page 279*), while the bullring, **Las Ventas**, makes an excellent outdoor concert space, and is used particularly during festivals. **San Isidro**, the **Veranos de la Villa** and many more of Madrid's annual events feature good live music. Although it was postponed in 2000 due to financial problems, in previous years the **Festimad** festival each May has done a lot to encourage local indie groups. The **May Day** celebrations, the **Fiesta Africana** in Getafe in July and the **Fiestas del Partido Comunista** in September are also good opportunities to see a wide range of locally based bands. For all these festivals – and more – *see chapter* **By Season**.

Venues listed in this chapter do not charge admission unless otherwise indicated. Small venues are usually free, but may charge a few hundred pesetas, with *consumición* (one drink) included. Where there is no admission charge, venues generally expect to make their money at the bar, so drinks usually cost more than they would elsewhere. Remember, too, that venues do not normally accept credit cards at the door.

Many places listed here combine live gigs or cabaret with DJ sessions; similarly, many venues featured in the **Nightlife** chapter (*see pages 224-235*) sometimes host live music, in particular **La Boca del Lobo** (pop-rock, singer-songwriters). Another venue worth checking out is the out-of-town **Estadio de la Comunidad de Madrid** (*see page 236*), which hosts macro-concerts by the likes of Bruce Springsteen.

Many gigs are sponsored by radio stations such as **Cadena Ser** or **Onda Cero**, which often give away promotional tickets. The *Guía del Ocio* and the 'Metrópoli' supplement of *El Mundo* (*see page 290*) both have listings of upcoming gigs, although they're not always comprehensive. Otherwise, concert information comes on flyposters and in fanzines, usually free from bars and music and fashion shops (*see pages 169 and 180*). Magazines to look for include *What Music?*, *Novedades*, *AB* and the irregular *Undersounds*. For ticket agencies, *see page 171*.

Rock/world music

Al'Laboratorio

C/Colón 14, Malasaña & Conde Duque (91 532 26 69). Metro Tribunal/bus 3, 40, 149. **Open** 9pm-3am Tue-Thur; 9pm-10am Fri-Sun; closed Mon. **Map** p305 F5.

Country and western decor combines with pop music at this lively, if dingy, two-floor Malasaña local. You won't find any big names here on Thursday, Friday and Saturday nights, but Al'Lab declares 'a passion for music' and encourages young groups by organising 'battle of the bands'-style contests.

Búho Real

C/Regueros 5, Chueca (no phone). Metro Alonso Martínez. **Open** 7pm-3am daily. **Map** p306 H4.
The music programming is ad hoc at this bar-cum-club that's popular among Madrid's early twenties crowd. Squeezed onto its tiny stage may be anything from aspiring local pop combos to singer-songwriters, taking in would-be-jazzers and even the odd talent night.

Café de la Palma

C/de la Palma 62, Malasaña & Conde Duque (91 522 50 31). Metro Noviciado/bus 147. **Open** 4pm-2.30am Mon-Thur, Sun; 4pm-3.30am Fri, Sat. **Admission** concert nights 300-1,500ptas. **Map** p305 E4.
This very popular bar has three separate areas, one of which serves as a performance space for a wide range of artists. High on the list are Madrid's new generation of singer-songwriters, but Cuban groups often play and the flamenco-crossover fraternity are also well represented. Tuesday nights brings story-telling (*cuentacuentos*), without music.

Chesterfield Café

C/Serrano Jover 5, Malasaña & Conde Duque (91 542 2817). Metro Argüelles/bus 1, 2, 21, 44, 133, C, N18. **Open** 1.30pm-3.30am daily. **Map** p304 C3.
Opened in 1997, with razzmatazz Americana decor, the Chesterfield is part of an ersatz-American chain that began in Paris and has now reached Moscow. Apart from offering food (Tex-Mex and Italian) and snacks at all times, the two-floor café hosts live gigs from Wednesday to Sunday at 11.30pm. Bands play mostly deeply innovative boogie rock: among the first artists billed were none other than hepcats Keanu Reeves and John 'you are the pits' McEnroe.

La Coquette

C/de las Hileras 14, Los Austrias (no phone). Metro Opera or Sol/bus 3, 25, 39, N13, N15. **Open** 8pm-2.30am daily. **Map** p309 D7.
Tucked away on a side street close to the Opera, La Coquette is also known as the Blues Bar, because it is Madrid's only bar dedicated to blues. Swiss-Spanish owner Albert has quite a record collection, and purists won't be disappointed. Old-school blues bands play from Tuesday to Thursday, and if you don't mind snogging students and hash smoke, you can enjoy well-intentioned if a bit ersatz Spanish harp-wailing. Drinks cost about 150ptas extra during performances.

La Cubierta de Leganés

C/Maestro 4, Leganés (91 689 87 15). Metro Oporto, then bus 484/by car N401 to Villaverde/Leganés exit. **Open** for details. **Admission** varies.
The southern suburb of Leganés has taken the bold move of partially covering the roof of its bullring,

Just your average night out.

thus allowing rock concerts throughout most of the year. AC/DC – after whom a street near the venue has been renamed, in acknowledgement of the popularity of the heavy-metal cult in Madrid's industrial fringe – inaugurated the venue in 2000, with The Cranberries, Chemical Brothers and Oasis among the early attractions. Beware – it's a long way from the nearest *Cercanías* station, and parking is impossible when there's a concert on. A taxi from the centre of Madrid will cost around 1,500ptas, but managing to get one back to town after the show could prove difficult.

Honky Tonk

C/Covarrubias 24, Chamberí (91 445 68 86). Metro Alonso Martínez/bus 3, 37, 147, 149, N19. **Open** 9pm-5am daily. **Map** p306 G3.
Going strong for more than a decade, and with a restaurant attached, the Honky Tonk offers local country, blues and rock acts every night of the week. The clientele are mainly 30-plus: it fills up after 2am and, while no strict dress code applies, if there's a queue the smartish have a better chance of getting in.

Kitty O'Shea's

C/Alcalá 57, Sol & Gran Vía (91 575 49 01). Metro Banco de España/bus all routes to Cibeles. **Open** noon-2am daily. **Map** p310 G7.
Once the legendary literary Café Lion, and now an Irish theme pub. The venue has hung on to its old-fashioned interior and has a good policy of

showcasing local talent. The music is often British and American blues and country, as well as Irish-oriented folk. *See also p147.*

Maravillas

C/San Vicente Ferrer 35, Malasaña & Conde Duque (91 523 30 71). Metro Bilbao or Tribunal/bus 3, 40, 149, N19. **Open** 9pm-6am Fri-Sun; closed Mon-Thur. **Map** p305 E4.

An 'alternative pop' club in the heart of Malasaña that usually offers live music (especially grunge, indie and Britpop-influenced bands) on Fridays and Saturdays. Watch out for posters announcing upcoming gigs. On non-gig nights, you can hear international indie sounds, and, usually, ambient and trance on Thursdays. The crowd is pretty young.

Moby Dick/The Irish Rover

Avda de Brasil 5 & 7, Chamartín (91 555 76 71). Metro Santiago Bernabéu/bus 5, 43, 126, N20. **Open** 10pm-3am Mon-Sat; closed Sun.

Decked out in fairly kitsch nautical-theme decor, with porthole windows and bottles dangling in nets, Moby Dick alternates between being a nightspot frequented by the *pijo* crowd and a live music joint with performances of pop, blues and rock. Many of the English-speaking bands on the Madrid circuit play here. Attached to it (Avda de Brasil 7) is the Irish Rover, a huge Irish theme pub featuring regular live Irish, folk and country music, as well as occasional theatre productions in English. There also no fewer than two *terrazas*, one out front and a garden at the back, which are shared by both bars, and add an extra dimension in summer.

La Riviera

Paseo bajo de la Virgen del Puerto s/n, near Puente de Segovia, Manzanares (91 365 24 15). Metro Príncipe Pío/bus 25, 31, 36, 39, N15, N16. **Open** midnight-6am Tue-Sun; closed Mon. **Admission** varies. **Map** p308 A8.

A disco next to the Manzanares, the Riviera is also Madrid's best bigger-than-club-size music venue, with good acoustics and several bars decorated in different styles. Part of its roof opens up in the summer, creating a very large *terraza*. The crowd tends to be trendy twenty- and thirtysomethings, and concerts have included Bob Dylan, James Brown, Blur, Patti Smith, Manu Dibango, Neneh Cherry, the Soweto String Quartet, Marilyn Manson, Ali Farka Touré and Massive Attack. It also attracts top salsa bands, and is often used for new record presentations, big PR functions and so on.

La Sala

Avda Nuestra Señora de Fátima 42, Carabanchel (91 462 77 89). Metro Carabanchel/bus 17, 35, N14. **Open** 7pm-5am daily. **Admission** varies.

Definitely not in the city centre, since this bar-venue is in the deeply unfashionable proletarian suburb of Carabanchel, but it's worth seeking out. It's really two bars in one: a typical Madrid bar at street level, with pool table, videos, pinball machines and loud music; and a purpose-built venue holding

around 300 people above, with excellent sound, lighting and atmosphere. There are live bands playing a range of styles most nights of the week; Spanish rock dominates.

Sala Caracol

C/Bernardino Obregón 18, Embajadores (91 527 35 94). Metro Embajadores/bus all routes to Embajadores. **Open** 9pm-3am Wed-Sun; closed Mon, Tue. **Admission** varies.

Once one of Madrid's foremost specialist flamenco venues, Caracol now presents a varied, multi-ethnic range of music from across the world. African and Cuban figure high on the agenda, but most recently rock in all its forms has carved out a niche. Cornershop and Catatonia have both visited. Still offers flamenco midweek.

Siroco

C/San Dimas 3, Malasaña & Conde Duque (91 593 30 70). Metro San Bernardo or Noviciado/bus 21, 147. **Open** 9.30pm-5.30am Tue-Sat; closed Sun. **Map** p305 E3.

Close to Cafe de la Palma on the fringes of Malasaña, Siroco is an unpretentious little place, with a bar upstairs and disco in the basement, which hosts local bands of the rock/pop/ funk/indie persuasion, and is often frequented by A&R types. It even has its own record label. It's also a popular club, with resident DJs offering many different styles of music. *See also p235.*

El Sol

C/Jardines 3, Sol & Gran Via (91 532 64 90). Metro Gran Via/bus all routes to Gran Via. **Open** 1.30-5am Tue-Thur; 1.30-5.30am Fri, Sat; closed Mon. **Admission** average 1,000ptas. **Map** p309 E7.

One of the melting pots of the *Movida* in the 1980s, this popular venue attracts Spanish and international acts of all styles (pop, funk, punk, rock, world music) thanks to its excellent acoustics and the proximity of the stage to the audience. It's a bit tatty – but in a likeable way – and one of a very few music venues in Madrid that still opens very late (arrive before 2.30am in order to avoid queues). DJs play often funk-oriented sessions at other times. *See also p226.*

Suristán

C/de la Cruz 7, Huertas & Santa Ana (91 532 39 09). Metro Sevilla or Sol/bus all routes to Puerta del Sol. **Open** 10pm-4.30am Tue, Wed, Sun; 10.30pm-5.30am Thur-Sat; closed Mon. **Map** p309 E7.

This medium-sized venue with ethnic decor still stands out from the crowd due to its pioneering approach to live music. Practically every night of the week you can experience a different musical style – from African music to rock, singer-songwriters, Brazilian and Cuban artists. Flamenco is a permanent speciality. The acoustics are good, but get there early for a decent view as the place packs out, and it doesn't exactly have the best layout. (Recorded) music is as varied as the amiable mixed crowd. *See also pp201 and 228.*

Vapor Blues

C/Doctor Esquerdo 52, Salamanca & the Retiro
(91 504 21 50). Metro Saínz de Baranda/bus 2,
30, 56,143, N7. **Open** noon-3am daily.
A pub-like bar, a little off the beaten track, with a
small room at the back, which from Thursday to
Sunday hosts pretty serious local R&B and blues
exponents. Look out for names such as Ñaco Goñ'
and Francisco Simón.

Jazz

Madrid has a vibrant jazz scene, with a devoted,
long-standing public. There are only about
five main venues that function throughout
the year, but two of them – **Café Central**
and **Clamores** – are absolutely top-notch.
The music also has its moment during the
autumn when the **Festival de Jazz de
Madrid** (see page 189), attracts a good many
heavyweights from the international circuit.

Café Central

Plaza del Angel 10, Huertas & Santa Ana (91 369
41 43). Metro Antón Martín, Sol/bus all routes to
Puerta del Sol. **Open** 1.30pm-2.30am Mon-Thur,
Sun; 1.30pm-3.30am Fri, Sat. **Admission** concert
nights 900-2,000ptas. **Map** p309 E8.
This beautiful high-ceilinged café/bar just off Plaza
Santa Ana was a mirror shop until its conversion
in the early '80s. Since then it has built a reputation
as Madrid's best jazz venue, and one of the best
in Europe. Leading international and Spanish
performers (George Adams, Don Pullen, Jorge
Pardo, Bob Sands) play in a relaxed atmosphere;
the wonderful Cuban bolero queen Lucrecia also
appears regularly.

Café Populart

C/Huertas 22, Huertas & Santa Ana (91 429 84
07). Metro Antón Martín/bus 6, 26, 32. **Open**
6pm-2.30am Mon-Thur, Sun; 6pm-3.30am Fri, Sat.
Map p309 F8.
A short walk from the Central, this former pottery
shop puts on a range of music from pure jazz and
blues to salsa and reggae. There are two sets
nightly at 10.30pm and 1am, and the atmosphere's
nicely relaxed and friendly, although if you really
want a good view you need to get there early.

Clamores

C/Alburquerque 14, Chamberí (91 445 79 38).
Metro Bilbao/bus 3, 21, 147, 149, N19. **Open** 6pm-
3am Mon-Thur, Sun; 6pm-4am Fri, Sat. **Admission**
concert nights 500-1,000ptas. **Map** p305 F3.
This premier jazz club – substantially bigger than
others in Madrid – hosts a sometimes bizarre range
of events that have included tango and karaoke
nights. The good-natured crowd plays ludo (yes,
ludo) in the early evening, and enjoys what Clamores
claims is Madrid's biggest selection of cava. The jazz
programme, though, is properly satisfying, and is
supplemented by pop, soul, blues, reggae and vari-

ous Latin American styles, including talented musi-
cians from Cuba. A frequent performer is Compay
Segundo, aged over 90, who played on Buena Vista
Social Club soundtrack with Ry Cooder.

Colegio Mayor
San Juan Evangelista

C/Gregorio del Amo 4, Moncloa (91 534 24 00).
Metro Metropolitano/bus 132, F, C. **Open** Oct-June
10pm Fri-Sun. July-Sept closed. **Admission** varies.
The music club in this student residence (open to,
and long popular with, non-students) has over many
years established a reputation as one of Madrid's
most discerning jazz venues. It also presents
concerts of classical and world music, and a festival
of flamenco (see pp199-202). The administration
does not go out of its way to sell itself, so you'll need
to look out for posters advertising gigs.

Dizzy Jazz

C/de la Luz 8, Las Matas (91 636 02 30/91 635
65 54). Cercanías C-8, C-10 to Las Matas, bus from
Moncloa to Las Matas, N-6 Carretera de A Coruña
exit Las Matas. **Open** 11pm-5am Fri, Sat; closed
Mon-Thur, Sun. **Admission** concert nights
1,000ptas.
Located a long way from town on the way to the
Guadarrama, Dizzy Jazz is a welcoming little spot
worth visiting if you're in the sierra. A frequent
performer is Brazilian Jayme Marqués.

Segundo Jazz

C/Comandante Zorita 8, Cuatro Caminos (91 554 94
37). Metro Cuatro Caminos or Nuevos Ministerios/
bus 3, 43, 149, N19. **Open** 7pm-4am daily.
Admission concert nights 500-1,000ptas.
There's a mixed bag of offerings at Segundo Jazz.
On Mondays it's '60s night, there's live jazz from
Tuesday to Saturday (unknowns midweek, local and
international acts on Fridays and Saturdays) and
cantautores on Sundays.

Triskel Tavern

C/San Vicente Ferrer 3, Malasaña & Conde Duque
(91 523 27 83). Metro Tribunal/bus 3, 40, 149,
N19. **Open** 6pm-3am Mon-Thur; noon-3am Fri-
Sun. **Map** p305 F4.
A popular Malasaña Irish pub that hosts a regular
Tuesday night jazz jam (about 11pm) with resident
bands. Strong guest performers have included
Jorge Pardo and Arturo Sándoval. As you might
expect, traditional Irish music often features on
other nights of the week.

Latin

For more Latin clubs, slightly less likely to
feature live bands, see chapter **Nightlife**.

Café del Foro

C/San Andrés 38, Malasaña & Conde Duque (91
445 37 52). Metro Bilbao or Tribunal/bus 3, 21,
147, 149, N19. **Open** 7pm-3am Mon-Thur, Sun;
7pm-4am Fri, Sat. **Map** p305 F4.

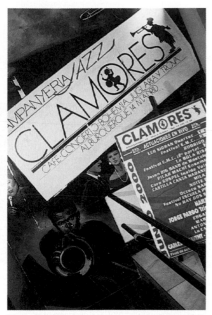

Clamores offers jazz and... ludo. *See p222.*

This cabaret club, in an old shopping arcade in Malasaña, is just the right side of cutesy, with an imitation star-lit sky painted above the stage. As often in Madrid, acts cover an eclectic range: magicians, hypnotists and comedians on Sunday and Monday nights; then salsa and merengue most of the week. Singer-songwriters, cabaret, theatre groups and pop bands also appear.

Café del Mercado
Ronda de Toledo 1, inside Mercado Puerta de Toledo, La Latina (91 365 87 39). Metro Puerta de Toledo/bus all routes to Puerta de Toledo. **Open** 10pm-4am daily. **Admission** average 1,200ptas incl 1 drink. **Map** p309 D10.
The café is located in the failed Mercado Puerta de Toledo development – an attempt to create a swish, ultra-modern shopping complex in a former fish market –but is unaffected by the problems surrounding it. Owner Seju Monzón lays on one of the most varied and interesting menus of Latin music in the city – maybe *merengue*, salsa, *bolero* and *chachachá*. Like a lot of the best places in town, it doesn't usually get going until well after midnight.

Galileo Galilei
C/Galileo 100, Chamberí (91 534 75 57). Metro Islas Filipinas or Quevedo/bus 2, 12, 16, 61. **Open** 6pm-3am Mon-Thur, Sun; 6pm-4.30am Fri, Sat **Admission** average 500-3,000ptas.
A sister club of Clamores (*see p222*), Galileo Galilei

presents all manner of artists from singer-songwriters to salsa bands, as well as occasional magic acts and stand-up comedy. In April the *Feria de Sevilla* comes to Madrid and fills the place with *sevillanas, fino* sherry and lots of shouting.

Oba-Oba
C/Jacometrezo 4, Sol & Gran Vía (no phone). Metro Callao/bus all routes to Plaza de Callao. **Open** 11pm-6am daily. **Admission** average 1,000ptas. **Map** p309 D6.
This friendly, thumping Brazilian bar pumps out samba until the sun comes up, with live music most nights of the week. It is packed with a good-time crowd from about 1am onwards. It's a cosy place, serving wonderful Caipirinhas.

La Toldería
C/Caños Viejos 3, La Latina (91 366 41 72). Metro La Latina/bus 3, 31, 65, 148, N13. **Open** 11pm-3am Tue-Sat; closed Sun. **Admission** average 1,000ptas. **Map** C8.
Latin American folk – not dance – music from throughout the continent is performed for a serious but appreciative audience. Some big names have appeared here over the years, among them Chavela Vargas and Mercedes Sosa. Three or four acts perform between about 12.30am and 3am. Not a place to let your hair down, and not cheap either.

Outdoor venues

In summer, Madrid comes alive after dark and out of doors. Balmy evenings and original and inspired locations can make this the best time of year to enjoy live music. The courtyards of the **Centro Cultural Conde Duque** (*see page 107*) make great performance spaces, usually as part of festivals (*see below*). The bullring at **Las Ventas** (*see page 192*) is also turned over to concerts in summer. During San Isidro, the park of **Las Vistillas** (*see page 70*) is a popular location for salsa and other dance acts.

Hipódromo de la Zarzuela
Carretera de La Coruña (N-VI), km 7.8 (91 307 01 40). Bus from Moncloa all routes to Aravaca/by car N-VI to El Pardo exit. **Open** *June-Sept* 9pm-5am Fri, Sat; closed Mon-Thur, Sun & Oct-May. **Admission** free; concerts from 500ptas.
Madrid's racecourse now mainly functions as a music venue. It's big enough to have hosted a Jean-Michel Jarre muzak extravaganza; the summer programme is eclectic, but worth checking out.

Parque de Atracciones
Casa de Campo (91 463 29 00). Metro Batán/bus 33. **Open** *see p194.* **Admission** 575ptas (entrance to park only).
All the fun of the fair and spectacular sunsets to boot. Summer gigs by Spanish family favourites and local rock bands are free with the entry ticket. Rides, though, cost more. *See also p194.*

Nightlife

Madrid's legendary seven-day weekends may be under pressure, but on the nights – or mornings – they do venture out, Madrileños sure as hell make up for it.

Madrid must be one of the only cities in the world where you're as likely to be stuck in a traffic jam at 4am as 4pm. The nightly rush hour leaves many a night owl fidgeting impatiently in a gridlocked taxi, or standing on a street corner trying to flag one down.

But what really differentiates Madrid from other party cities is the extent to which nightlife takes place on the street. Come rain or shine, from about 11pm onwards young and old alike claim the streets, chatting, checking each other out and wandering from bar to bar. They don't like to stay in any one place too long, and people will generally go out in a particular area, rather than to a specific venue. This makes finding your feet easy – just pick an area where you like the look of things, and wander around until you find a bar that takes your fancy.

Madrid may be famed for being a 24-hour party city, but things have changed since the debaucheries and lax (or to all intents and purposes non-existent) closing-time regime of the 1980s. The conservative *Partido Popular* city council has made much of promising to cut down on nightlife to make Madrid more peaceful for respectable citizens, and has been making slow but steady progress in its efforts to curtail licensing hours. Opinions vary widely as to how far these measures will be effective. Some see them as a study in bureaucratic impotence, Madrileños not being inclined to let anyone tell them when they have to go home.

However, the truth is that things ain't quite what they used to be, on weekdays especially, when there are fewer and fewer options available after 3am. On the clubbing scene, many after-hours parties, like the legendary Midday Sunday sessions, have shut down, and there has been a shift to out-of-town venues located in areas where there are no neighbours to annoy. Where it will all end is impossible to predict, but what can be said is that an 11pm have-your-glasses curfew will never happen.

THE MAP

One of the great things about Madrid as a city for going out is that the hub of the night-time round is situated in areas all within staggering distance of each other. For a pretty wide-ranging scene **Huertas** is a good place to start. The Plaza Santa Ana itself is the tourist's

El Burladero: passionate stuff. *See p227.*

favourite in Madrid, but the more local crowd will be found in bars in the streets around it. From there you can move on to **Lavapiés**, popular with a mixed bohemian crowd and the best place to hear drum'n'bass and *electrónica*.

Moving north a bit, **Malasaña** is great if puberty is still a novelty and you really have a liking for being out in the street all night (*see page 232* **Get your *litrona***). It's also home to Madrid's rock heartland, with unpretentious music bars. And if you head down Calle Espíritu Santo past the serious grunge, there are some more top places in **Conde Duque** around Calle de la Palma. **Chueca** is the centre of Madrid's gay scene (*see page 207*), but it's also The Place To Be for the studiously hip and trendy, parading their purchases from the Calle Fuencarral (*see page 169*). Just don't move too far north of Calle Fernando VI, which before midnight teems with teenagers.

If big disco-style venues are your thang then explore the triangle between **Sol**, Callao and Gran Vía, which has places of every shape and size to shake your tush. And, for dressing up big-style, head for **Salamanca** or up the Castellana to find Madrid's smartest venues.

RULES OF ENGAGEMENT

Rule *número uno* for out-of-towners is: Don't Go Out Too Early. Head out for your first beer at seven and you'll find yourself swaying back to your *hostal* before locals have even got their mascara on. Step out around nineish, have dinner and you'll be set up for a long night.

The real fun doesn't start till around midnight, when Madrileños head for *bares de copas*, or drinking, night bars.

Madrid's night-time terminology is tricky, and distinctions between types of hangouts are seriously blurry. **Bares de copas** and **discobares** may have a small dancefloor, and many of the hippest have DJs, although dancing is not necessarily on the agenda. However, they don't generally charge entry, but make up for it on drinks prices.

It's not until about 2am that most of the crowd thinks of going to actual club-style venues, with gorillas and ticket-entry at the door. Then, as the night is but young, it's time for **after-hours** places. These are the venues that the city council has been most keen to stamp out, but so far it hasn't succeeded.

As in most countries, Friday and Saturday are the big nights to hit the town, but Thursdays and Sundays can be lively too. Some clubs are known by the name of the venue, others by the name of the night; good places to find out about one-nighters are local guides like *AB* (in Spanish) or *InMadrid* (*see page 290*). If you hit town in August, bad luck, as many venue owners and DJs will have decamped to Ibiza. However, recently fewer places have closed in summer, so you could be lucky.

Los Austrias

El Barbú

C/Santiago 3 (91 542 56 98). Metro Opera or Sol/bus all routes to Puerta del Sol. **Open** 7pm-3am Tue-Sun; closed Mon *June, July* 9pm-3am Mon-Sat; closed Sun. Closed Aug. **No credit cards. Map** p309 D7.
A cavernous three-room locale offering a pretty varied mix of music for those who want to dance, although many opt for just chilling out and chatting on the comfy sofas. More of a starting point to a livelier destination, but definitely a good stop-off.

Kathmandú

C/Señores de Luzón 3 (91 541 52 53). Metro Sol/ bus all routes to Puerta del Sol. **Open** 11pm-5am Thur; 11pm-6am Fri, Sat; closed Mon-Wed. **Admission** 800-900ptas incl one drink. **No credit cards. Map** p308 C7.
In the early 1990s, Kathmandú was a mecca for unpretentious cool and the best in funk and acid jazz sounds. As the word got around, however, and the quantity of potential groovers brought the dancefloor to a swaying standstill, its original fans moved away. Nevertheless, it still plays a seductive mix of acid jazz, deep house, trip and hip hop. Come early or on Thursdays if you want to shake your stuff.

El Limbo

C/Bailén 39 (91 365 21 58). Metro La Latina/ bus 3, 60, 148, N13. **Open** 9pm-3.30am daily. **No credit cards. Map** p308 C8.

Words to know

Calimocho sickly tipple of cheap red wine and cola, commonly drunk on the street in litre plastic glasses.

Caña the standard small glass of beer, although it can range from a couple of gulpfuls to nearly double that in a *terraza*.

Doble Yes, double the size of beer. Also known as a *tubo* when it's in a long tumbler.

Copa a mix, as in a G&T (*gintonic*) or a rum and cola (a *cuba libre* or *cubata*). *Importaciones* (such as Scotch or Beefeater gin) are generally more expensive than Spanish brands.

Chupito a tiny Russian vodka-style glass; contents can range from a short shot of spirit to acrid herb liqueurs.

Caipirinhas and **Mojitos** the sophisticated choice – cocktails of Brazilian *cachaça* spirit and Cuban rum respectively, with lime and mint.

Guiri dumb foreigner, above all from the English-speaking world and northern Europe; in other words, sorry to say, you. Widely believed by Spaniards to be completely lacking in taste and basic bodily co-ordination.

Marcha energy, movement, excitement. What night owls go out looking for, or maybe wanting to work off. You can say of a good place *tiene mucha marcha*, it's got lots, and walk out of somewhere because *le falta marcha* (it hasn't any).

Pijos & **pijas** boys who wear polo shirts tucked into their trousers and sport well-combed hair, and girlies who dress up big time, with high heels and (nearly always) a fake tan. Found in Salamanca and anywhere else expensive. Not cool.

Located in Limboland far enough from the main nightlife routes not to attract too much passing trade, El Limbo is a well-kept secret, frequented by an upretentious crowd of locals and those in the know. Decked out like a retro living room, replete with fab wallpaper, velvet drapes, pot plants and '70s lighting, it has a small team of DJs spinning mainly funky house. Many punters prefer to hang around the elegant bar, maybe trying to get somewhere with the sexy bar girls.

El Viajero

Plaza de la Cebada 11 (91 366 90 64). Metro La Latina/bus 17, 18, 23, 35, 60. **Open** *bar* 1pm-3am Tue-Sat; 1-9pm Sun; closed Mon. **Credit** AmEx, DC, MC, V. **Map** p309 D9.

Is it a bar? Is it a restaurant? Is it a *terraza*? All three. The rooftop *terraza* is the perfect place for lounging away summer evenings, whereas the second-floor bar has DJs playing cool music from lounge to acid jazz, and a hip crowd dancing around an array of deep comfy sofas. Good Uruguayan and international food is served in the restaurant (*see p118*).

Sol & Gran Vía

Alien

C/Alcalá 44 (no phone). Metro Banco de España/ bus all routes to Cibeles. **Open** 6-10am Fri-Sun. **Admission** 1,500ptas. **No credit cards.** **Map** p310 G7.

If too much is never enough and at 6am you're still in motion, then Alien is the place to be. From Thursday to Saturday (or rather Friday to Sunday), swarms of shiny happy clubbers groove away in this After-venue to the best in progressive house and techno, until the DJ puts his decks away at 10am. Also an occasional venue for live bands.

Joy Eslava

C/Arenal 11 (91 366 37 33). Metro Opera or Sol/ bus all routes to Puerta del Sol. **Open** 11pm-6.30am Mon-Thur, Sun; 6.30pm-6.30am Fri, Sat. **Admission** 2,500ptas incl one drink; 800ptas Fri, Sat 6.30-11pm. **Credit** AmEx, MC, V. **Map** p309 D7.

Is this a disco or what? In an 1850s theatre in the very centre of Madrid, this is probably the city's most famous night-spot: the music has changed slightly with the years, but otherwise it remains the same ostentatiously glitzy disco, decked out in velvet and gold and attracting an untrendy crowd – men in smart suits, bejewelled ladies and gangs of girls on the razzle. Flamenco and salsa are brief interludes amid the disco music.

Mad Café

C/Virgen de los Peligros 4 (91 521 40 31). Metro Sevilla/bus all routes to Puerta del Sol. **Open** 1.30-5pm; 9pm-2.30am Mon-Fri, 9pm-2.30am Sat; closed Sun. **Credit** MC, V. **Map** p309 F7.

A little too knowing to be really mad, this is one of *the* places to see and be seen. Early on, the sleek chrome and steel ground floor is full of beautiful people enjoying cocktails or dinner to the loungey sounds of singer Paz Corral. Around midnight the pace picks up as folk shake their bon-bons to funk, disco and garage. When the weather's good there's a gorgeous fairy-light-draped *terraza* at the back.

Ohm

Bash Line, Plaza del Callao 4 (91 531 01 32/ www.tripfamily.com/ohm). Metro Callao/bus all routes to Plaza del Callao. **Open** midnight-6am Fri, Sat. **Admission** 1,500ptas incl one drink. **No credit cards. Map** p309 D6.

Named after the universal mantra of mantras, Ohm is one of Madrid's most popular club nights. Mainly gay but welcoming anyone up for dancing, it really gets going around 3am. With resident and guest DJs playing a full-on set of disco-house with a strong French influence, the dancefloor is a writhing mass of tight T-shirts and sweaty torsos. *See also p209.*

Top five: Clubs

Alien. See page 226.
Cocoon Clubland. See page 233.
Ohm. See page 226.
The Room. See page 227.
Sugar Hill. See page 233.

Palacio de Gaviria

C/Arenal 9 (91 526 60 69/91 526 60 70). Metro Sol/bus all routes to Puerta del Sol. **Open** 11pm-5.30am Mon-Sat; 9.30pm-2am Sun. **Admission** 1,500-2,500ptas incl one drink. **Credit** AmEx, MC, V. **Map** p309 D7.

Do believe the hype – this place is a real 19th-century palace, a beautiful space that's open to anyone with a decent pair of shoes and a well-stocked wallet. A staircase takes you up to the first-floor landing, and once there you have the run of a dozen or so rooms, all furnished in appropriately baroque style. Most of the rooms indulge a different musical style. The club also hosts international nights on Thursdays, organised by Forocio (*see p171*).

El Sol

C/Jardines 3 (91 532 64 90). Metro Gran Vía/bus all routes to Gran Vía. **Open** 1.30-5am Tue-Sat; closed Mon, Sun. **Admission** 1,000ptas. **No credit cards. Map** p309 E/F7.

The elder statesman of Madrid's clubs. On weekend nights it's a funk phenomenon that warms up late but, once hot, radiates an infectious party atmosphere. By 3.30am it's packed with sexy young things losing it to a varied mix of funk, acid jazz and hip hop. El Sol also hosts a varied mix of live music, often before the club sessions (*see p221*).

Soma

C/Leganitos 25 (no phone). Metro Plaza de España/ bus all routes to Plaza de España. **Open** 11pm-5.30am Tue-Sat; closed Mon, Sun. **No credit cards. Map** p309 D6.

A dark labyrinth of dimly lit tunnels wending between two chill-out bunkers and dance space, Soma is Madrid's mecca for a dedicated following of techno fans. Prestigious international DJs like Jeff Mills, Plastikman and Juan Atkins are among the guests who've graced the decks with their presence.

Weekend

Bash Line, Plaza del Callao 4 (91 531 01 32/ www.tripfamily.com/weekend). Metro Callao/bus all routes to Plaza del Callao. **Open** midnight-5am Sun. **Admission** 1,500ptas incl one drink. **No credit cards. Map** p309 D6.

For those who shun the idea of the Lord's Day as a

day of rest, Weekend proves that Sunday could well be the new Saturday. With resident DJ Roberto Rodriguez spinning the best in Latin house, you'll be dancing till daylight with a blend of fresh well-rested ravers and more frazzled party animals. Another mainly-gay night that draws a big crossover crowd (*see p209*).

Huertas & Santa Ana

Bar de la Comedia

C/Príncipe 16 (91 521 51 64). Metro Sevilla or Sol/ bus all routes to Puerta del Sol. **Open** 9pm-4am daily. **No credit cards. Map** p309 F8.

A crowded, fast-paced joint playing rap, rock and funk to a twentysomething crowd. It's mingling and drinking at the front, while dancing, if you can carve out a space, goes on at the back.

Beguin the Beguine

C/Moratín 27 (no phone). Metro Antón Martín/bus 6, 26, 32. **Open** 8pm-2.30am Mon-Thur, Sun; 8pm-3.30am Fri, Sat. **No credit cards. Map** p310 G8.

A cocktail den with a musty wooden interior, lined with dusty bottles, that makes a cosy environment in which to imbibe the tropical concoctions it serves up. They're not cheap, but big enough to share.

La Boca del Lobo

C/Echegaray 11 (91 429 70 13). Metro Sevilla or Sol/bus all routes to Puerta del Sol. **Open** 11pm-3am Mon-Thur, Sun; 11pm-3.30am Fri, Sat. **No credit cards. Map** p309 F8.

Having suffered under tightening licensing laws, this Bohemian intellectual dive is now firmly open again. Down a beer in the cramped foyer bar, shake a leg to the 'eclectic' sounds up top or catch a band playing anything from Cuban hip hop to serious soul in the basement. Also excellent off-the-wall film seasons, including an annual Blaxploitation fest.

El Burladero

C/Echegaray 19 (91 420 21 84). Metro Sevilla or Sol/bus all routes to Puerta del Sol. **Open** 8pm-3.30am daily. **No credit cards. Map** p309 F8.

Enjoy the queue at **The Room**.

A packed two-storey locale off Plaza Santa Ana that's regularly full of couples swinging each other round to flamenco, shouting *olé* and clapping. On the upper floor it's calmer, with a bit more space.

Cardamomo

C/Echegaray 15 (91 369 07 57). Metro Sevilla or Sol/bus all routes to Puerta del Sol. **Open** 9pm-4am daily. **No credit cards. Map** p309 F8.

If you've got any interest in flamenco or salsa, this is an essential stop. The dancing varies from eye-catchingly sensual to reassuringly clumsy. No one here gives a fig about such niceties, and the *gitano* flavour ensures the music can't be resisted for long.

Kapital

C/Atocha 125 (91 420 29 06). Metro Atocha/bus all routes to Atocha. **Open** *night session* midnight-6am Thur-Sat; *afternoon session* 6-11pm Fri-Sun; closed Mon-Wed. **Admission** 2,000ptas. **No credit cards. Map** p310 H9.

Madrid's superclub, Kapital boasts seven floors of disco decadence. It's a deliberately big, gadget-laden place – there's a cashpoint and a shop selling Kapital merchandise, and drinks can only be obtained at the bar by handing over a ticket bought from one of the many vending machines. The ground level hosts the main (house) dancefloor, with lasers and podiums where scantily clad dancers writhe. Up above there's a series of balconies, a karaoke bar, cinema and two more dancefloors, funk on the third and '70s disco on the fifth. Right at the top there's a *terraza*. Not cheap, but an experience. To complete its mega-disco feel it has 'early' sessions (ending at 11pm) for teens.

Matador

C/de la Cruz 39 (91 531 89 81). Metro Sol/bus all routes to Puerta del Sol. **Open** *Sept-June* 7pm-2.30am Mon; noon-2.30am Tue-Sun. *July, Aug* 7pm-2.30am daily. **No credit cards. Map** p309 E 7/8.

A camp temple to all things stereotypically Spanish, playing gypsy rumba and other Andalusian stuff and with a life-size, sequinned matador hanging from the ceiling. It's small, so the mixed clientele of natives and *guiris* often spills onto the street.

Oui

C/Cervantes 7 (no phone). Metro Antón Martín/ bus 10, 14, 27, 34, 37, N8-N12. **Open** 10pm-5.30am Wed-Sun; closed Mon, Tue. **No credit cards. Map** p309 F8.

This hip and happening Huertas hotspot is always packed to the rafters, but there's still room to groove or just chill out on one of the comfy banquettes. The music policy, which mixes a wide variety of sounds from Wednesday's smooth cocktail night to Saturday's more housey *Estación Norte*, is matched in eclecticism by the decor. A cool place.

The Room

C/Arlabán 7 (no phone). Metro Sevilla/bus all routes to Puerta del Sol. **Open** 1-6am Fri, Sat. Closed Aug. **Admission** 1,500ptas incl one drink. **No credit cards. Map** p309 F7.

Arts & Entertainment

Occupying the space that was once the Movida institution Stella, The Room is a party favourite among an up-for-it and out-of-it young crowd; queues go around the block from about 2-3am. The music is house, with a smattering of dancefloor classics. It tends to get seriously sweaty, probably because the dancefloor has just about the lowest ceiling in the whole of Madrid.

Suristán

C/de la Cruz 7 (91 532 39 09). Metro Sevilla or Sol/bus all routes to Puerta del Sol. **Open** 10pm-4.30am Tue, Wed, Sun; 10.30pm-5.30am Thur-Sat; closed Mon. **No credit cards. Map** p309 E7/8.
A buzzing space that's mainly a live venue devoted to world music, but which, after gigs, offers DJ sessions with a similarly wide range. The crowd is

The real tour

As in most cities, the club scene in Madrid is enigmatically fluid, with new nights opening and closing, and coming in and out of fashion with alarming frequency. Even those seemingly in the know have turned up for an after-hours at 6am only to find the place empty. The best way to keep up to date is to check out the flyers available in record and clothes shops, particularly on and around Calle Fuencarral, or pick up free magazines *AB* or *InMadrid*.

Music policies are often broad and unspecific: very few places want to limit themselves to a specific type of music beyond a broad categorisation like rock, house or electronic. Many clubs also have international DJs making regular guest appearances.

Below is one idea of how to squeeze the weekend dry; of course, it's in the nature of the beast that new places are always opening, while others as suddenly close.

Thursday

11.15pm After some Uruguayan meat and energy-giving carbs at **El Viajero** (see page 225), head to **Café del Nuncio** (see page 151) for a soothing cocktail.
12.15am Wander down to **El Mosquito** (see page 229) for a quickie and to check out the music.
1.30am Suitably revived, head over to **Oui** (see page 227) for cool sounds and a psychedelic atmosphere.
3.15am Decide to leave while the going's good, get a cab to **Kathmandú** (see page 225) for funk and acid jazz.
4.30am All that dancing's made you peckish. Get yourself over to **La Recoba** (see page 234) for pizza and a few beers for the road.
6am Call it a night, and stumble home and into bed. Not bad going – it's only 6.30am. Early.

Friday

11pm Start the night with some *raciones* in **El Poz Gordo** (see page 159).
midnight Move on to **El No. 1** (see page 234) for teas, juices and cocktails, but mind you dont't get too comfy in the armchairs.

1am A few drinks later, you're peckish again. Wander over to **La Ida** (see page 158).
2.15am Start walking over to Chueca, but you can't resist nipping into **El Baticano** (see page 233) for a *copa*. Elbow out some dancing space and get carried away in the general hilarity.
3.30am Finally drag yourself away and make it to **Camp** (see page 231), take in its groovy retro minimalism, and boogie some more downstairs.
4.30am Join the queue for **The Room** (see page 227), and eventually squeeze your way onto the dancefloor for some hands-in-the-air house.
6am Stay till closing time, then stagger out. Struggle over to **Chocolatería San Ginés** (see page 234) for reviving *chocolate* and *churros*.
7.15am Spend a good half hour trying to flag down a cab in Puerta del Sol, collapse into bed and wake up late Saturday afternoon.

Saturday/Sunday

1am Start in mellow mood and splurge on a cocktail in **Begin the Beguine** (see page 227).
1.45am Wander over to **La Ventura** (see page 229) for a quick hit of drum'n'bass.
2.30am Check out the music and the toilets in **La Boca del Lobo** (see page 227).
3.30am It's going to be a long night, so catch last orders and grab some big meat and in-house cabaret at **La Carreta** (see page 234).
4.30am Time to pump up the volume with a bit of techno, so get yourself over to **Long Play** (see page 232).
6am There's no stopping you now, so get over to **Alien** (see page 226) and wonder why everyone looks so wide awake.
10am On a roll, decide to take a cab up to **Space of Sound** (see page 235), grabbing a sandwich on the way. Get lost in the station complex trying to find the venue.
2.30pm Incapable of dancing any more, slope off to the Metro. Head back to your room, locate your passport and rely on the help of friends to get to the airport (just).

Arts & Entertainment

racially diverse and universally friendly. Somewhere to warm your ears and broaden your own musical horizons. Admission is not always charged outside of concert times. *See also p201* and *p221*.

Torero

C/de la Cruz 26 (91 523 11 29). Metro Sevilla or Sol/bus all routes to Puerta del Sol. **Open** 11pm-4.30am Tue; 11pm-5.30am Wed-Sat. Closed Mon, Sun. **No credit cards. Map** p309 E7/8.

Two straightbacked doormen bar the way to this famous Santa Ana nightspot. Getting in is free, but their job is to weed out trainer-clad riff-raff from the dressy majority. It's worth making the effort, though, as not many bars can compete with Torero's full-on party atmosphere. On the opulent ground floor the best Latin sounds hold sway, while in the cellar things rock to a more housey beat.

La Trocha

C/Huertas 55 (no phone). Metro Antón Martín/bus 6, 26, 27, 32, 45. **Open** 7pm-2.30am Mon-Thur, Sun; 7pm-3.30am Fri, Sat. **No credit cards. Map** p309 F8.

Smooth jazz and smoother drinks make this an ideal place to raise the tone of your night. There's no beer on tap, and everyone seems to drink *caipirinhas*. Genuinely refreshing.

La Latina, Rastro, Lavapiés

Candela

C/del Olmo 2 (91 467 33 82). Metro Antón Martín/bus 6, 26, 32. **Open** 10pm-5.30am Mon-Thur; 10pm-6am Fri, Sat; closed Sun. **No credit cards. Map** p309 F9.

With posters of flamenco stars lining the walls, and a flamenco soundtrack, the legendary and undisputedly unique Candela attracts a curious combination of *gitanos* and *guiris*, clapping and stamping their feet in time to the music (or not, as the case may be). Fills up in the small hours when the local competition have gone off to bed. *See p201.*

Deep

Ronda de Toledo 1 (mobile 607 774 668). Metro Puerta de Toledo/bus all routes to Puerta de Toledo. **Open** midnight-6.30am Fri, Sat; closed Mon-Thur, Sun. **Admission** 1,500ptas. **No credit cards. Map** p309 D10.

Anyone whose idea of a good night out is a little house, with an added dash of house, and then some more house, should get their dancing shoes on and head Deep down to Ronda de Toledo for a hands-in-the-air session. It has fine resident DJs and regular invited guests, and just about anyone who's anyone on the international scene, from Frankie Knuckles to David Morales, has performed here. Deep moves to Marbella for August, but the venue stays open.

El Juglar

C/Lavapiés 37 (91 467 10 32). Metro Lavapiés/bus 6, 26, 32. **Open** 9pm-3am Mon-Fri; noon-3.30am Sat; noon-3am Sun. **Admission** generally free, concerts average 500ptas. **No credit cards. Map** p309 E9.

A recent facelift has transformed the Juggler into a stylish and multi-faceted red brick and chrome bar/disco/venue. Although the backroom hosts regular concerts and performances of all kinds early in the evening, their real speciality is playing the best in world music, particularly African funk.

Kappa

C/del Olmo 26 (no phone). Metro Antón Martín/bus 6, 26, 32. **Open** 8.30pm-2am Tue-Thur, Sun; 8.30pm-3.30am Fri, Sat; closed Mon. **No credit cards. Map** p309 F9.

Recently done up to provide a more stylish atmosphere, Kappa still retains its warm, cosy charm, with deeply cushioned sofas, a soothing mix of ambient and trip hop and a mixed gay and non-gay crowd. It's a great place to sit down and chat, although at weekends DJs liven things up a little.

El Mosquito

C/Torrecilla del Leal 13 (no phone). Metro Antón Martín/bus 6, 26, 32. **Open** 8pm-2.30am Mon-Sat; 6pm-2.30am Sun. **No credit cards. Map** p309 F9.

'Musical and political' is how its friendly owner likes to describe this mixed gay- and non-gay bar in Lavapiés. Leaflets on the walls advertising demonstrations, exhibitions and performances make evident its commitment to gays, squatters and film and theatre groups; its musical claims are based on the quality of its DJs. Standard sounds include drum'n'bass, funk and techno.

La Ventura

C/Olmo 31 (91 468 04 51). Metro Antón Martín/bus 6, 26, 32, N12, N14. **Open** 10pm-5.30am Tue-Sat; closed Mon, Sun. **No credit cards. Map** p309 F9.

It would be easy to walk past La Ventura, as the owners still haven't managed to get a sign up. However, don't miss it if you want to hear some of Madrid's top DJs, AJs and KJs (answers on a postcard please) spin a mix of dub, *electrónica* and drum'n'bass. The predominantly young crowd are so laid-back they're horizontal – which is fine as there are ample floor cushions and sofas to crash on.

Chueca

Big Bamboo

C/Barquillo 42 (91 562 88 38). Metro Alonso Martínez/bus 3, 37, 40, 149, N19. **Open** 10pm-6am Tue-Thur; 10pm-7am Fri, Sat; closed Mon, Sun. **No credit cards. Map** p306 H5.

An institution in Madrid with those who are into the reggae vibe, but who are too busy feeling alright to notice that its menu rarely varies from pop reggae favourites and His Bobness. Fills up between midnight and 12.30am.

But

C/Barceló 11 (91 448 06 98). Metro Tribunal/bus 3, 40, 149, N19. **Open** 10.30pm-5am Mon, Tue, Thur; 7pm-5am Wed, Sun; midnight-5am Fri, Sat. **Admission** 1,000-1,500ptas incl one drink. **Credit** AmEx, MC, V. **Map** p306 G4.

Arts & Entertainment

Looking at the stars

One of the many delights of summer time in Madrid are the open-air bars and cafés or *terrazas* that spring up on streets and plazas city-wide as soon as the heat arrives. Some are busy by day or night (see page 150), while others have become nocturnal dance venues. Certain areas are favourites: **Plaza de Chueca**, centre of the gay scene, is filled with chairs, tables and revellers all summer long; **Calle Argumosa** is more low key and bohemian; the **Castellana** has the swankiest, and most expensive options, often with Spanish and European pop making it all but impossible to actually communicate. For outdoor dining, see page 120.

Bolero & Boulevard

Bolero Paseo de la Castellana 33, Chamberí (no phone); Boulevard Paseo de la Castellana 37, Chamberí (91 435 54 32). Metro Rubén Darío/bus 3, 25, 33, 39, 148, N1, N20. **Open** May-Sept 7pm-3/4am daily. Closed Oct-Apr. **Credit** AmEx, DC, MC, V. **Map** p306 I2.

Rising out of the greenery beside the Paseo de la Castellana like chic settlements in the jungle, these two big *terrazas*, which are separated by just a few hundred metres, are in fact two halves of the same bacchanalian beast. The atmosphere

is stunningly frivolous, a crush of coquettish, well-heeled people, chatting through Europop and eyeing up their peers.

El Eucalipto

C/Argumosa 4, Lavapiés (mobile 629 33 49 98). Metro Lavapiés/bus 6, 26, 32, 57, 27. **Open** 6pm-2am Mon-Sat; 1pm-2am Sun. **No credit cards. Map** p309 F10.

Tropical cocktails and music combine to make El Eucalipto one of the most popular of the *terrazas* along this tree-lined street, dubbed the *Costa Argumosa* because of its summer party atmosphere. The staff are famed for friendly service and great-quality *mojitos*.

La Vieja Estación

Estación de Atocha, Avda Ciudad de Barcelona, s/n, Atocha (91 539 93 30). Metro Atocha/bus all routes to Atocha. **Open** May-Sept 10pm-5am daily. Closed Oct-Apr. **Admission** 1,000-2,000ptas. **No credit cards. Map** p310 H10.

Madrid's biggest and most spectacular 'multi-*terraza*', in a gorge-like dip by Atocha station. It boasts an Argentinian restaurant, loads of bars, dancefloors, a karaoke space and a Chill Out room, which plays the same music as elsewhere. Fun, but expensive; however, there's sometimes a great after-hours on Sundays.

Occupying part of the same art deco building as Pachá (*see p232*), But is not a club, but a real dance hall – swirling with lush music and filled with a lively crowd of all ages. The dancing's often pretty good, and the moves range from ragtime to rumba, polka to paso doble. It's very popular with a 30-something crowd, but another fixture are its Wednesday and Sunday early-evening sessions for teens.

Camp

C/Marqués de Valdeiglesias 6 (no phone). Metro Banco de España/bus all routes to Gran Vía. **Open** 10pm-2.30am daily. **No credit cards. Map** p310 G6.

Camp is the operative word for this new beautiful people's bar in Chueca. However, despite the name and location, the crowd is mixed – the only common factor being their year-round tans and must-have wardrobes. The bar is on three levels, with a low-lit loungey basement, a main bar/restaurant area at ground-floor level and a hanging-out space up top. Decor is heavily retro, with funky original '60s plastic chairs from the US and Op Art tiles around the bar. And if it all gets too much, there are showers for cooling off.

Capote

C/Santa Teresa 3 (no phone). Metro Alonso Martínez/bus 3, 21,37, 40, 149, N19. **Open** 10pm-5am Mon-Thur, Sun; 10pm-6am Fri, Sat. **No credit cards. Map** p306 H4.

A disco-bar with a more discerning, and slightly older crowd, than the *pijo* youngsters who fill many of the Alonso Martínez bars. Cool decor, and competent DJs play mainly funk, soul, reggae and hip hop, tending towards more commercial sounds as the place fills up around 3am. Also live music some evenings.

El Clandestino

C/Barquillo 34 (no phone). Metro Chueca/bus 3, 37, 40, 149. **Open** 11pm-3.30am Mon-Sat; closed Sun. **No credit cards. Map** p306 H5.

Despite the name and the owners' intentions, the Clandestine bar hasn't managed to stay a secret for long. The bright bar upstairs serves tapas, while downstairs a creative mix of DJs play anything from party jazz to happy house, and funk to garage on Wednesday to Saturday. It often hosts concerts too. The clientele is almost as varied as the music, with grungy kids, fashion victims, *pijos* and rock fans.

Get your *litrona*

Madrid's nightlife isn't limited to actual venues. Local kids, especially those of a grungier outlook, take hanging around on street corners to a new dimension. With pocket money that doesn't extend to bar prices, they make their own entertainment, and hordes of teenagers descend on the city centre on weekend nights to take over whole squares with the *litrona scene*.

Plaza Dos de Mayo, **Plaza Barceló**, and in fact any of the open spaces of **Malasaña** are transformed on any given Friday or Saturday into one big open-air party, with bunches of kids sitting around all across the square. Refreshments are provided by the late-night, mostly Chinese-owned corner shops – litre bottles of beer (*litronas*, a name that has stuck to the whole phenomenon), cartons of cheap wine, bocadillos, and big plastic cola bottles into which are mixed wine or cheap spirits to create *calimochos* and bargain cocktails. Many shops also offer *minis* – actually industrial-sized plastic cups of spirit for ready mixing. To contain the necessaries, each circle of grungeophiles has its indispensable plastic bags. It's a bit like a rather low-key, spaced-out music festival, where none of the acts have turned up.

Dos de Mayo and the smaller Malasaña squares are the venues of choice for the real alternative-grunge crowd. Loud conversations take place to a backdrop of the inevitable bongos, and the sweet aroma of dope. Plaza Barceló caters to a slightly smarter set. Dressed-up girls in short skirts and boots swarm out of Tribunal Metro, trying to catch the eyes of the surrounding boys. Those with a little more cash might head off to But (see page 229) or other discos that offer early-evening teen sessions. At around 1.30am the crowds dissipate, most catching the last Metro home. As the night wears on all that is left is an astounding quantity of empty and broken bottles, cups, bags and cartons, cleaned up before dawn by efficient cleaners in preparation for the next onslaught.

Kingston's

C/Barquillo 29 (91 521 15 68). Metro Alonso Martínez or Chueca/bus 3, 37, 40, 149, N19. **Open** 11pm-5.30am daily. **Admission** 700ptas. **No credit cards. Map** p306 H5.

A place that likes to think of itself as a cut above other music bars in the area: the owner has dropped reggae from the playlist, explaining that it only attracted dopeheads. It now starts off with soul, moving to a funkier beat as the night progresses, and it attracts a slick, smartish crowd. Put your hands in the air and reach for the sky – the blue ceiling is daubed with fluffy clouds.

Long Play

Plaza Vázquez de Mella 2 (no phone). Metro Chueca or Gran Vía/bus all routes to Gran Vía. **Open** 10pm-5.30am Thur-Sat. **No credit cards. Map** p309 F6.

If you don't fancy being in bed before the sun comes up, you could do worse than fill in a few hours at 1,000-odd capacity Long Play. The main room downstairs vibrates to the sound of seriously pumping techno, spun by some of Madrid's top DJs. But if you're in a more chilled frame of mind, head upstairs to the old '50s ballroom and kick back to a super-cool mix of hip hop, funk and soul classics.

Pachá

C/Barceló 11 (91 447 01 28). Metro Tribunal/ bus 3, 40, 149, N19. **Open** midnight-6am Wed-Sat; also 7.30-11pm Fri, Sat. **Admission** Wed, Thur 1,500ptas; Fri, Sat 2,000ptas; 800ptas 7.30-11pm Fri, Sat. **Credit** AmEx, DC, MC, V. **Map** p306 G4.

Although it's related musically to its Ibiza namesake, Pachá is actually owned by the same people who run Joy Eslava (*see p226*). Inside it's big and camp, echoing to garage divas and house favourites and inspired by sensual dancers up on the stage. Populist in the best sense of the word, and, another plus, open till late.

Speakeasy

C/Fernando VI, 6 (no phone). Metro Alonso Martínez/bus 37, N19. **Open** 8.30pm-3.30am Wed-Sat; closed Mon, Tue, Sun. **Admission** (men) 1,000ptas. **No credit cards. Map** p306 H4.

This three-level place lets women in free, so it comes as no surprise that it's always packed to the rafters with thrifty girls and hopeful boys. There's a big dancefloor where people try and groove to naff Spanish pop, while below it there's a pub-style bar with pool and table football; the first floor is quieter and more intimate. Perennially popular with a noisy, young crowd.

Stars Café

C/Marqués de Valdeiglesias 5 (91 522 27 12).
Metro Banco de España/bus all routes to Cibeles.
Open 9am-2am Mon-Thur; 9am-3.30am Fri;
6.30pm-4am Sat; closed Sun. **Meals served**
2-4pm, 8.30pm-12.30am Mon-Fri; 8.30pm-12.30am
Sat. **Credit** AmEx, DC, MC, V. **Map** p305 E3/4.
The jewel in Chueca's mixed gay-fashionable crown,
this 'dance café', with its big windows overlooking
the street, has the feel of a vantage point from which
to view the night. Inside it's equally chic, all yellow
paint, Grecian columns, high ceilings, and the odd
sofa. A great, stylish venue, with bouncy, high-NRG
house to keep the people happy, and also good food.

Torito

C/Pelayo 4 (91 532 77 99). Metro Chueca/bus 3,
40, 149. **Open** 10pm-5am daily. **No credit cards.**
Map p306 G5.
A small, intimate and ever-so-kitsch bar in Chueca
playing only flamenco music. There's a whole bunch
of interesting clutter to look at, with every inch of
the red and black walls covered in photos, clippings,
bullfight memorabilia, and dismembered dolls. The
owners couldn't be more friendly.

Malasaña & Conde Duque

El Baticano

C/Colón 12 (91 522 53 19). Metro Tribunal/
bus 3, 40, 149. **Open** 10pm-3.30am daily.
No credit cards. Map p305 F5.
A haven for party creatures who don't want to leave
their good times for the weekends. A friendly, trendy
gay and straight crowd squeeze themselves into the
narrow bar, in a nightly competition to see who can
drink the most *copas* and dance the wildest to an
upbeat combination of house and disco.

Café Mercado Fuencarral

C/Fuencarral 46 (no phone). Metro Tribunal/
bus 3, 40, 149. **Open** 10am 2am Mon-Sat;
closed Sun. **No credit cards. Map** p305 F5.
The caff attached to the Shopping Mall with
Attitude (*see p169*) is the perfect place to parade

Head to **Deep** for full-on house. *See p229.*

your latest purchases. You're guaranteed to find any
number of amply pierced young things chilling out
and admiring each other's tattoos at any hour of the
day or night; exhibitions, cool music, cheap(ish)
drinks and good food are other attractions.

Cocoon Clubland

C/Amaniel 13 (91 354 63 45/www.mph-techno.com).
Metro Noviciado/bus 147, N18. **Open** midnight-5am
Fri, Sat. **Admission** 1,200-2,000ptas incl one drink.
No credit cards. Map p305 D4.
The times they are a-changin'. This venue (still confusingly with the name Midnight above the door)
was once home to three of Madrid's most central club
nights, Midnight, Nature and the Sunday after-hours
Midday, but these have all gone to a better life. All
is not lost, as it now resounds to the sounds of Cocoon
Clubland. With a range of top international DJs,
Cocoon is one of the best spots to wave your hands
in the air like you just don't care to techno, groove
beat and house. Also sleighted to start on Thursdays
is a freestyle and hip hop night. Watch this space.

Corto Maltés

C/San Andrés 11 (no phone). Metro Tribunal/
bus 3, 40, 149, N19. **Open** 9pm-3.30am daily.
No credit cards. Map p305 F3/4.
With a great location right on Plaza Dos de Mayo,
this colonnaded bar has a warm, balmy feel to it. Its
real strength, though, is its music, dance orientated
in a *barrio* over-endowed with guitar-fixated bars.

Flamingo

C/La Palma 11 (91 448 09 78). Metro Tribunal/
bus 3, 40, 149. **Open** 10pm-3am daily. **No credit
cards. Map** p305 F4.
Known to many as the heart of Madrid's rock'n'roll
scene, the Flamingo, despite not having a stage, is a
fave hangout for local musicos and record company
types and for those living on a diet of rock'n'roll (both
classic and indie) beer, long nights and good vibes.

Flamingo Club/Sugar Hill

*C/Mesonero Romanos 13 (91 531 48 27). Metro
Callao/bus all routes to Plaza del Callao.* **Open** *Sugar
Hill* midnight-5am Fri, Sat. **Admission** 1,000ptas,
incl one drink. **No credit cards. Map** p309 E6.
The funk soul brothers turn it up now. Lovers of the
Harlem sound needn't worry that following the closure of the much-loved Soul Kitchen they've got
nowhere to strut their stuff, as Sugar Hill now makes
merry in the same venue every Friday and Saturday.
A soulful mix of funky sounds and turned-up hip
hop, and in homage to its previous incarnation, the
temperature is definitely still hot, hot, hot. For the
ultra-popular gay nights at the Flamingo, *see p209*.

Maravillas

*C/San Vicente Ferrer 35 (91 523 30 71). Metro
Bilbao or Tribunal/bus 3, 40, 149, N19.* **Open** 9pm-
6am Fri-Sun; closed Mon-Thur. **Admission** free-
800ptas. **No credit cards. Map** p305 E/F4.
A favourite of indie fans, Maravillas plays the best
guitar-based music in town, specialising in Britpop

Arts & Entertainment

Those hunger pangs…

With so many people wandering the streets at night, Madrid naturally has plenty of places where night owls can stave off hunger. A great Spanish tradition are the *churrerrías* and *chocolaterías*, places where you can fill up with freshly made cups of hot chocolate and sweet cakes to dunk them in as the sun comes up.

Bar Farras

C/Mayor 28, Austrias (no phone). Metro Sol/bus all routes to Puerta del Sol. **Open** 8am-4am Mon-Fri; 2pm-8am Sat, Sun. **No credit cards. Map** p309 D7.
Nothing fancy, but this little bar, overseen by its plump, jovial owner Julio, turns out good *bocadillos* and *raciones* into the night for a mix of taxi drivers, ravers and insomniacs.

La Carreta

C/Barbieri 10, Chueca (91 532 70 42). Metro Chueca/bus 3, 40, 149, N19. **Open** 1-5pm, 8.30pm-5am daily. **Average** 3,000ptas. **Credit** AmEx, DC, MC, V. **Map** p305 E4.
This Argentinian restaurant in Chueca serves pasta, fish and lamb, and some of the best steak you'll ever eat. On Fridays and Saturdays between midnight and 4am it has shows that include dancing, tangos and stand-up comics.

Chocolatería San Ginés

Pasadizo de San Ginés 11, Austrias (91 365 65 46).Metro Sol/bus all routes to Puerta del Sol. **Open** 7pm-7am daily. **No credit cards. Map** p309 D7.
A Madrid institution, serving *churros y chocolate* (deep-fried batter sticks and thick hot chocolate) through the city nights since 1894. Watching the people in here, it's easy to be struck by the incongruity of the scene, with blue-rinsed old ladies sitting beside sweaty ravers. Tends to be packed from 4am to daylight.

La Farfalla

C/Santa María 17, Lavapiés (91 369 46 91). Metro Antón Martín/bus 6, 26, 32. **Open** 9pm-3.30am daily. **Average** 1,750ptas. **Credit** AmEx, V. **Map** p309 F8.
This basic but top-value restaurant is perfectly located for lining the stomachs of those moving out of Huertas civilisation and on to serious clubland. Chow down on mega pizzas, tasty pasta and some seriously big meat.

Laidy Pepa

C/San Lorenzo 5, Chueca (no phone). Metro Chueca/bus 3, 40, 149, N19. **Open** 11pm-5am daily. **Average** 1,500ptas. **No credit cards. Map** p306 G4.
This little place opens late and stays relatively empty for the first few hours, but once the bars and clubs begin to shut the hungry hordes arrivein search of its filling pasta dishes.

La Recoba

C/Magdalena 27, Lavapiés (91 369 39 88). Metro Antón Martín/bus 6, 26, 32. **Open** 9.30pm-5am daily. **Average** 2,000ptas. **Credit** MC, V. **Map** p309 E8.
If you're just not ready to go home yet, grab a table ain La Recoba and pack in a great pizza or crêpe, accompanied by live tango music and singing throughout the night.

---

and US indie bands, with some big beat and funk thrown in (but no heavy metal, despite the Malasaña location). Entrance policy varies: at the weekends there's sometimes an 800ptas charge, but most of the time it's free for all. Once mainly a live music venue, it now only has occasional concerts (*see p221*).

Morocco

C/Marqués de Leganés 7 (91 531 31 77). Metro Santo Domingo/bus 147, N17, N18. **Open** midnight-3am Thur; 9pm-5.30am Fri, Sat; closed Mon-Thur, Sun. **No credit cards. Map** p305 E5.
Previously owned by outspoken Spanish punk-rock chick and enfant terrible Alaska, Morocco is a good-time dive with DJs playing anything from '70s rock and pop to new electronic sounds, and especially as the night collapses into drunkenness, old sing-a-long faves like Frank Sinatra and Barry White.

El No. 1

C/de las Minas 1 (no phone). Metro Noviciado/bus 147. **Open** 6pm-2am Mon-Sat; 5pm-2am Sun. **No credit cards. Map** p305 E4.
If you're in need of a bit of calm this place is as mellow as it gets. A languid *tetería* just off Calle del Pez, it offers comfort and rejuvenation in the form of teas, fruit juices and cocktails, and living-room upholstery – big sofas and inviting armchairs. Of the two levels, upstairs is lighter, downstairs ultra violet. The owners have a penchant for classy Brazilian sounds, and give friendly service.

Radar

C/Amaniel 22 (no phone). Metro Noviciado or Plaza de España/bus all routes to Plaza de España. **Open** approx 8pm-4am Wed-Sun; closed Mon, Tue. **No credit cards. Map** p305 D4.

The most underground of Madrid's music bars. Its owner, a bespectacled techno-shaman called Seve, is devoted to non-commercial, futuristic music. Radar, however, indulges several different specialist audiences – noise, industrial, experimental, electronic techno, *electrónica*, dance and more. The bar itself is a purist's heaven – minimalist, not too packed and home to musicians and aficionados of fringe sounds.

Reflejos

C/Galileo 7 (no phone). Metro San Bernardo/bus 2, 21, 61, N18. **Open** 8pm-3.30am Thur-Sun; closed Mon-Wed. **No credit cards. Map** p305 D3.

A spot of Latino colour amidst the quiet of Calle Galileo. The Peruvian owner has turned it into an eclectic celebration of all things South American – dance, cuisine, shows and that famous indigenous ritual, um, stripping. On Thursdays there are dance lessons, Fridays see live salsa, Saturdays recorded dance music, and on Sundays there's Latino food available and shows to go with it.

Sala Mix

Mercado de Fuencarral, C/Fuencarral 45 (91 521 41 52). Metro Tribunal/bus 3, 40, 149. **Open** 10am-midnight Mon-Wed; 10am-2am Thur-Sat; closed Sun. **No credit cards. Map** p305 F5.

A venue/bar in the Mercado Fuencarral (*see p169*) offering an eclectic variety of entertainment for the eternally hip. Cinema, dance, theatre and performance all appear in this space, which aims to provide a forum for obscure or cutting-edge projects overlooked in other venues. A great place to start the night, chilling out to the music of young and up-and-coming DJs, and to check out what other events are going on. It often hosts one-nighters and one-off parties, in which case it stays open until about 6am.

Siroco

C/San Dimas 3 (91 593 30 70). Metro San Bernardo or Noviciado/bus 21, 147. **Open** 9.30pm-5.30am Tue-Sat; closed Sun, Mon. **No credit cards. Map** p305 E3/4.

One of the most relaxed and unpretentious clubs in Madrid, with a crowd encompassing '60s chicks in kinky boots and Cleopatra bobs to hardcore metal fans. The DJ sessions change every couple of months, but top nights include Bon y Em and the summer sensation Operación Bikini. What doesn't change, though, is the top DJ monikers: Ricky Marketing, Gud Lack and Watch TV. Also *the* place to see the best in new Madrileño independent music.

Tupperware

C/Corredera Alta de San Pablo 26 (no phone). Metro Tribunal/bus 3, 40, 149, N19. **Open** 8pm-3.30am daily. **No credit cards. Map** p305 F4.

A Malasaña institution, Tupperware has a constant good-time vibe that makes it stand out from the dozens of other music bars in the surrounding streets. The crowd's older, the atmosphere funkier and the decor stretches the boundaries between kitsch and tacky – inflatable dolls, fake fur-covered speakers and disgusting eyeballs on the ceiling.

Salamanca & the Retiro

Babylon

C/Recoletos 11 (696 83 93 80). Metro Banco de España/bus all routes to Cibeles. **Open** 9pm-3am Tue, Wed; midnight-6am Thur-Sat; 7pm-midnight Sun; closed Mon. **Admission** usually free. **No credit cards. Map** p310 H6.

The opening of a small basement-style club-bar offering sessions by some of the coolest DJs on the Madrid scene is a strange proposition in Salamanca, the *pijo* heartland. Through the week the menu features rock and blues (Tue, Wed), black music in Black is Black (Thur); techno in Offset (Fri) and funky natural grooves with hard US House in Da Joint (Sat). Sunday's chill out combines exhibitions with music to sit down with after a hard weekend.

Déjate Besar

C/Hermanos Bécquer 10 (no phone). Metro Rubén Darío. **Open** 11pm-3am Mon-Wed; 11pm-5.30am Thur-Sat; closed Sun. **No credit cards. Map** p307 I1.

Owned by radio presenter, DJ and fast-living man about town Jorge Albi, Déjate Besar or 'Let Yourself be Kissed' provides a late-night retreat for a curious and entertaining combination of local office workers loosening their ties, glammed-up girls and trendy young things. This '70s-style drinking and dancing den, decked out with tiger-print sofas, coloured lighting and movie star photos on the walls, offers a vibrant atmosphere any night of the week.

Rastatoo

C/Lagasca 120 (91 355 24 52). Metro Núñez de Balboa/bus 9, 19, 51, 61, N4. **Open** 10.30pm-3.30am daily. **No credit cards. Map** p307 J2.

In principle a reggae club serving Caribbean cocktails to get you into the swing, but Rastatoo's music policy is pretty varied, moving into faster grooves as the night wears on and the booze kicks in.

Chamartín

Space of Sound at Sala Macumba

Estación de Chamartín (91 733 35 05/902 10 40 28). Metro Chamartín/bus 5, 80, N20. **Open** *Space of Sound* 9am-6pm Sun. *Fun Club* 7pm-12.30am Sun. *Elite Club* midnight-6.30am Fri, Sat. *Elite afternoon* 7.30-11pm Fri. *Space of Sound light* 6-10pm Sat. **Admission** *Space of Sound* 1,000ptas; *Fun Club* 600ptas; *Elite Club* 1,400ptas; *Elite afternoon* 800ptas; *Space of Sound light* 500ptas. **No credit cards.**

If you're still wired on Sunday morning and have enough cash and energy after a night of revelry to afford the entry charge and transport yourself to the top of the Castellana for a hard core after-hours sesh, then get to Space of Sound. Many of its punters save themselves up for it, skipping out the Saturday night thing all together and arriving fresh and perky; for others, the atmosphere can be a bit too edgy and morning-after hostile.

Arts & Entertainment

Sport & Fitness

Football may be an endless cause for conversation, but Madrid also offers great opportunities to run, jump, swing a racket or just cool off with a swim.

The 1990s was a good decade for Spanish sport, and this, helped along by the advent of private, cable and satellite TV stations, has put spectator sports more in the public eye than ever before. Millions follow the successes and near-misses of Spanish sporting heroes – tennis stars such as Arantxa Sánchez Vicario and Alex Corretja, Miguel Indurain and the ONCE and Kelme cycling teams, or motorcycle racers Alex Crivillé and Carlos Checa. In football, Barcelona and Real Madrid both brought the European Cup back to Spain, although the Spanish national squad has been a constant disappointment in major tournaments.

Participation in sport has grown too, and facilities have improved. Crowded central Madrid is not overly endowed with sports halls, but you don't have to go far to find somewhere to work out, jog, or swim. For activities in the countryside outside Madrid, *see pages 271-2.*

Spectator sports

Athletics/*atletismo*

Sports authorities in Spain have been keen to build on recent Olympic successes, and have given athletics a major boost by investing large amounts in the stadium and sports complex in Canillejas, in eastern Madrid. Indoor events are also held in the **Palacio de Deportes** (*see below*), in particular the *Trofeo Memorial Cagigal* international meeting each February.

Estadio de la Comunidad de Madrid

Avda de Arcentales s/n, Canillejas (91 580 51 80/ information 012). Metro Las Musas/bus 38, 48, 140. This striking stadium, inaugurated in 1994, has world-class indoor and outdoor facilities. Several important national athletics events are held here annually, and occasional international meetings. It is sometimes known as the *Estadio de Canillejas.* Admission prices vary for different events.

Maratón Popular de Madrid

Information *MAPOMA, C/Linneo 4, Manzanares (91 366 97 01). Metro Puerta del Angel/bus 25, 31, 36, 50.* **Open** 10am-2pm, 5-7pm Mon-Fri; closed Sat, Sun.
Madrid's marathon, on the last Sunday in April, is more a fun run than an outing for serious runners, but is nonetheless very well attended. The course usually finishes in the Retiro or Plaza de Cibeles. The previous Sunday there is another road race, the *20 Kilómetros de Madrid*, organised by **Agrupación Deportiva Maratón** (91 521 79 83).

Basketball/*baloncesto*

A highly popular sport in Spain, second only to football. Madrid has two teams that play at the top of the Spanish league and in European competitions: **Adecco Estudiantes** (91 562 40 22/www.clubestudiantes.com), recent winners of the Spanish Cup, and the many-times champion **Real Madrid** (part of the football club; 91 398 43 00/www.realmadrid.es). Both play at the **Palacio de Deportes**, which is also used for many other indoor sports.

Palacio de Deportes de Madrid

Avda Felipe II, Salamanca (91 401 91 00/ information 012). Metro Goya/bus 30, 56, 71, C. **Ticket office** 11am-2pm, 5-8pm daily, depending on match. **Tickets** 1,000-3,000ptas. **No credit cards**. The season runs from September to early May, but hots up in April with the league play-offs, when one of the Madrid teams almost inevitably clashes with one of their great rivals from the Barcelona area.

Cycling/*ciclismo*

La Vuelta de España (Tour of Spain) goes around the country in September, ending in Madrid on the third weekend of the month with five laps of the Castellana, between Plaza de Castilla and the Estadio Bernabéu. Follow the tour on the Net, in English, at www.sportec.com.

Football/*fútbol*

Football in Madrid has been turned upside down lately as one of the city's grand old clubs, **Atlético de Madrid**, culminated a dramatic 1999-2000 season by dropping down to Division Two, while the doughty plebs of **Rayo Vallecano**, Madrid's 'unknown' team, actually finished mid-table in the big league and got into the UEFA Cup via a fair-play draw. Aristocrats **Real Madrid**, meanwhile, carried off their eighth European Championship.

The football season normally runs from September to May. Real and Rayo usually play at 5pm on Sundays, but some games are played on Saturday evenings (at 8.30pm), and there are

Arts & Entertainment

often midweek cup or European games. While Atlético is in the Second Division it will play at 5pm on Saturdays. Tickets are available from the clubs and some agencies, but not, as yet, savings banks (*see page 171*). Shirts and fan-junk can also be bought at sports shops such as Supporters Shop (*see page 182*). *See also page 238* **Football (gone) crazy...**

Atlético de Madrid

Estadio Vicente Calderón, Paseo de llos Melancólicos s/n, Manzanares (91 366 47 07/shop 91 366 82 37/www.at-madrid.es). **Open** *Ticket office* 11am-2pm, 5-8pm daily; from 11am till kick-off on match days. *Shop* 9.30am-2pm, 5-8pm Mon-Fri; also on match days. **Tickets** 1,000-1,500ptas. **Credit** *tickets* MC, V; *shop* **no credit cards.**

Atlético's stadium on the banks of the Manzanares, famous for its atmosphere, seats 57,000, and promises emotion as *El Atleti* attempt to return to the First Division. Relegation to the Second, however, has obliged the club to cut its prices drastically, so admission is now cheap; the basic ticket (1,000ptas for most games) affords decent views from behind either goal, while 1,500ptas seats are along the side. You can also pick up an *Atleti* shirt for 9,000ptas, from the club shop (by door 4). Tickets are usually on sale from the Wednesday before the match.

Rayo Vallecano

Nuevo Estadio de Vallecas Teresa Rivero, Avda del Payaso Fofó s/n, Vallecas (91 478 22 53/shop 91 477 73 57/www.rayovallecano.es). *Metro Portazgo/ bus 54, 58, 103, 136.* **Open** *Ticket office* 5.30-8.30pm daily, depending on match; *shop* 10am-1.30pm, 5-8pm Mon-Fri; closed Sat, Sun. **Tickets** 2,000-5,000ptas; 500ptas under-12s. **Credit** *both* V.

This 15,500-capacity stadium, recently renamed after the club's 'Presidenta', Chairwoman Teresa Rivero, is where Rayo's loyal and loopy followers are looking forward to an unprecedented second consecutive season in the top flight. They will even have European action to enjoy, in the UEFA Cup. At he club shop you can acquire cool Rayo shirts (resembling a Red Stripe beer can) for a modest 8,500ptas. For more on seeing Rayo, *see p87* **Viva Vallecas.**

Real Madrid

Estadio Santiago Bernabéu, Paseo de la Castellana 144, Chamartín (91 398 43 00/shop 91 458 69 25/ www.realmadrid,es). *Metro Santiago Bernabéu/ bus 5, 14, 27, 120, 150.* **Open** *Ticket office* 6-9pm daily, depending on match. *Shop* 10am-9pm Mon-Sat; 11am-8pm Sun & match days. **Tickets** 2,500-11,500ptas. **No credit cards.**

This giant stadium, enlarged a few years ago, holds 'only' 75,000, since it was converted into an all-seater ground in 1998. It is often used to host cup finals and internationals. Since the conversion the imbecilic hooligan element *Ultrasur*, who used to occupy the *Fondo Sur* (south end), now hang out in

the *gallinero* ('chicken run') in the upper east stand: if you don't want trouble, go elsewhere. As the stadium is so huge, cheaper tickets may only get you a poor view, so go for the middle-range. Official shirts cost 10,000ptas, more with a name and number, at the **Todo Real Madrid** shop (91 344 14 14/91 458 74 22), next to the stadium. *See also p64.*

Motor sport

Circuito del Jarama

Carretera de Burgos (N-I), km 27, San Sebastián de los Reyes (91 657 08 75). *Bus 171 from Plaza de Castilla to Ciudad Santo Domingo/by car N-I to Fuente del Fresno.*

This track hosted the Spanish Grand Prix until 1992, when the race moved to the Catalunya circuit near Barcelona. Its calendar is now rather diminished, but it still hosts several motorcycling meets a year and, for true motor-freaks, the European Truck Racing Championship in early October.

Active sports

Billiards & pool/*billares*

Academia de Billar

C/Pelayo 39, patio, Chueca (91 308 42 52). *Metro Chueca/bus 3, 37, 40, 149.* **Open** 11am-10pm (approx) daily. **Admission** *Tables* 1,000ptas per hr. *Classes* 1,800ptas per hr. **No credit cards.** **Map** p306 G5.

In a decrepit old patio in the heart of Chueca resides this wonderful little billiard hall-cum-academy. The affable, bearded Don Julio offers classes in Spanish billiards (*billar*), but only if you are 'polite and intelligent'; there are two tables for playing and practising, open all day every day of the year.

Bowling/*boleras*

Star Bowl Azca

Paseo de la Castellana 77, Tetuán (91 555 76 26). *Metro Nuevos Ministerios/bus all routes to Nuevos Ministerios.* **Open** 11am-12.30am Mon-Thur, Sun; 11am-2.30am Fri, Sat. **Admission** *before 5pm* 450ptas, *after 5pm* 525ptas Mon, Tue, Thur, Sun; 375ptas all day Wed; *before 5pm* 475tas, *after 5pm* 600ptas Fri, Sat. Unlimited games (incl shoe rental) 1,000ptas daily. *Shoe hire* 150ptas. **Credit** V.

Although it's located in the heart of the business district, within the AZCA complex (*see p64*), this well-equipped 16-lane bowling alley has a pleasantly relaxed atmosphere, and attracts a varied public.

Football/*fútbol*

English Football League

The EFL began in the early 1990s, and now includes mixed-nationality or wholly Spanish, or Peruvian, teams. Five-a-side indoor (*fútbol sala*) games are on

Arts & Entertainment

Football (gone) crazy…

The 1999-2000 season threw up some great surprises in what had perhaps been the most predictable league in Europe, traditionally dominated by Real Madrid and Barcelona to the extent that they have shared two-thirds of all league titles between them. A completely new name was inscribed on the trophy, that of Deportivo de La Coruña. Little Alavés, meanwhile, qualified for the UEFA Cup only two years after returning to the First Division, as did Madrid's own humble Rayo Vallecano. The biggest shock was the relegation of Atlético de Madrid, in a Dantesque season that came just four years after its greatest moment ever, the 1996 double year.

Spanish teams fared well in Europe – Real Madrid, Barcelona and Valencia all reached the Champions' League semi-finals, for Real to beat Valencia in the first-ever final between teams from the same country. But Spain's international team once again flopped when faced with a major tournament, Euro 2000.

Football is passionately debated in Spain, and all these events have provoked much high-decibel discussion in cafés throughout the country. How, people ask, can Barcelona, with half the Dutch national squad, Figo and Rivaldo, and Real, with players such as Roberto Carlos and Raúl (pictured) and capable of turning over Manchester United at Old Trafford, both perform so badly in a league that *Depor* won with one of the lowest percentage point totals ever, and how can Spanish teams do so well in Europe while the national squad falters so consistently?

Many blame the 'invasion' of the Spanish league by foreign players, which, they say, hampers the development of Spanish players while the big clubs spend obscene amounts on foreign stars in pursuit of European glory, downgrading the domestic league. Real recently splashed out £40 million ($60 milliion) on Portuguese midfielder Luis Figo, forcing Barcelona to content Rivaldo and keep him from wandering by making him the best-paid player in the world, on £85,000 ($127,000) a week. Interestingly, the highest scorer in the league was a Spaniard, Salva, a product of Sevilla's youth squad, who managed 27 goals for Racing de Santander.

THE HIGH AND THE LOW

In Madrid, each stadium offers the visitor a different experience. **Real Madrid**'s Bernabéu has a greater density of stars than anywhere else in Spain (except Barcelona's Camp Nou, of course), and exudes grandeur. This is to be expected from the club with more European cups (eight) in its trophy room than any other, plus 27 domestic league titles. Here nothing short of winning is ever acceptable, the Champions' League is an obsession and failure inevitably means a radical shake-up. In recent elections, Florentino Pérez ousted Chairman Lorenzo Sanz, who had presided over two Champions' League triumphs, and devoured several coaches.

Rayo Vallecano, meanwhile, has just become Madrid's 'second' First Division club. Traditionally a humble club that yo-yos

Sundays from noon to 5-6pm at the **Colegio del Niño Jesús**, just east of the Retiro (Metro Ibiza/Map p311 K8). A weekly broadsheet, *The Pink'Un*, and website (http://ourworld.compuserve.com/home-pages/robraabe), gives information, results and gossip. Teams are often looking for players, so if you fancy your chances, call League secretary Paul Flint (91 504 63 74/pflint@worldonline.es). If you prefer full-scale eleven-a-side, call Dave Weston (91 844 37 69/weston@correo.cop.es) or John McLaughlin (91 459 95 28).

Golf

Golf clubs around Madrid tend to be quite exclusive, and are expensive for non-members.

Club de Campo Villa de Madrid

Carretera de Castilla, km 2 (91 550 08 40). Bus 84 from Moncloa. **Open** 8am-10pm daily. **Rates**

1,750ptas club entry, plus 6,225ptas course fee Mon-Fri; 3,500ptas club entry, plus 11,800ptas course fee Sat, Sun. **Credit** V.

The best-equipped course in the area, with 36 holes and a driving range. Unsurprisingly, it's very expensive. The lavishly equipped country club also offers squash, tennis, clay pigeon and range shooting, hockey pitches, polo, horse riding and a swimming pool. Hire of clubs will cost another 2,675ptas.

Horse riding/*hípica*

For information riding and trekking trips into the Guadarrama north of Madrid, *see page 272.*

Glen Horse

Soto el Real, Carretera a Guadalix km 1.5 (91 852 70 35/mobile 607 703 726). Bus 726 from Plaza de Castilla/by car Carretera de Colmenar M607, M611

between the first and second grades, Rayo finished a respectable ninth in its most successful season ever. Rayo is a symbol of Vallecas, and seeing a game there is a world away from the heights of the Bernabéu. Its small stadium is possibly the only ground in Spain where you will see together banners with images of Che Guevara, marihuana leaves, anarchist emblems and the hammer and sickle (see page 87 **Viva Vallecas**).

Atlético de Madrid, meanwhile, have been involved in a bizarre and tortuous melodrama. Owned by the always-polemical construction magnate Jesus Gil y Gil, also Mayor of Marbella, *El Atleti* started going downhill within two years of winning the double in 1996, despite the arrival (and departure) of several prestigious coaches. The club lived its blackest moments ever prior to Christmas 1999, when it was placed in the hands of a court administrator due to allegations of financial irregularities against Gil and his board. This chaos contributed to a downhill spiral on the pitch, culminating in relegation for the first time in 64 years. By the start of the 2000-1 season its legal problems had largely been sorted out, but *Atleti* faced a hard struggle to regain First Division status. Nevertheless, bumper crowds were expected, and season ticket sales were higher than ever. Atlético fans seemed to face the prospect of local derbies against teams of the standing of Getafe or Leganés with stoicism, and maybe a slightly perverse enthusiasm.

to Soto, then M608 to Guadalix. **Open** 10am-8pm Tue-Sun; varies according to sunset; Sat, Sun classes am only; closed Mon. **Rates** *classes & excursions* 2,000ptas per hr groups; 2,500ptas per hr (negotiable) individuals. **No credit cards**. This school and trekking centre offers beginners and experienced riders classes and treks of varying lengths around La Morcuera peak, between Soto el Real and Miraflores. English is spoken, and they are committed to ethical treatment of their animals.

Jogging & running/*footing*

There is a set jogging route in the **Retiro** (*see page 83*). The **Casa de Campo** (*see page 84*), is an excellent place to jog because the air is better; in summer, go first thing (before 9am), while it is still fresh. For longish straight runs, try the **Parque del Oeste** (*see page 86*).

Squash

Gimnasio Argüelles

C/Andres Mellado 21-23, Moncloa (91 549 00 40). *Metro Argüelles.* **Open** 8am-11am Mon-Fri; 9am-3pm Sat, Sun. *Sept-June, July* closed Sun. *Aug* open Tue, Wed, Thur only. **Rates** 1,200ptas 30min; 2,400ptas 1hr. **No credit cards**. **Map** p304 C2.
A squash club and gym open to non-members.

Swimming pools/*piscinas*

Far from the sea and with summer temperatures reaching 40°C, Madrid, thankfully, has many swimming pools. Public pools are run by the city (*Ayuntamiento*), or regional authorities (*Comunidad de Madrid, CAM*). Each body has its own separate pricing and ticket systems. For more sports centres that

When the heat's up, head for the wonderful waters of **Piscinas Casa de Campo**.

also have pools attached, *see page 241*. There are also several waterparks around Madrid, which are fun for kids (*see page 194*). For more hotels with pools, *see page 49* **Best pools**.

City-run open-air pools

Piscinas Casa de Campo, Avda del Angel s/n (91 463 00 50). Metro Lago/bus 31, 33, 36, 39. **Open** *May-mid Sept* 10.30am-8pm daily. **Admission** 520ptas; 130-235ptas concessions; voucher for 20 admissions 880-7,800ptas. **No credit cards**.

The best – and most popular – of the public pools are the ones in the Casa de Campo (*see p84*), where there is an indoor pool (closed July-Aug), and three open-air pools: Olympic standard, a children's pool and one intermediate-size. They are attractively landscaped, with a café area; topless sunbathing is allowed, and there is an informal gay area. The pools are crowded at weekends, but usually more relaxed in the week. Of the other pools, the Barrio del Pilar and La Elipa have nude sunbathing areas, and the latter has water chutes; the Casa del Campo and Concepción have good disabled access. All the city pools have the same hours and prices, but other pools open for summer on 15 May rather than 1 May. There are several more pools around Madrid; leaflets available at city sports centres (*see p241*) have details of all of them.

Other pools: Barrio del Pilar C/Monforte de Lemos (91 314 79 43). Metro Barrio del Pilar/bus 134, 137; **Concepción** C/José del Hierro (91 403 90 20). Metro Barrio de la Concepción or Quintana/bus 21, 48, 146; **La Elipa** Parque de La Elipa, C/O'Donnell s/n (91 430 35 11). Metro Estrella/bus 71, 110, 113; **Moratalaz** C/Valdebernardo s/n (91 772 71 00) Metro Pavones/bus 8, 32, 71.

City-run indoor pools

Piscina La Latina, Plaza de La Cebada 1 (91 365 80 31). Metro La Latina/bus 17, 18, 23, 35, 60. **Open** 8am-7pm Mon-Fri; 10am-9pm Sat, Sun, public holidays. Closed Aug. **Admission** 500ptas; 125-225ptas concessions; voucher for 20 admissions 850-7,500ptas. **No credit cards**. **Map** p309 D9.

The city has several indoor pools, most of which open all year except August (hours may vary). Full information is available from sports centres (*see p241*). La Latina is the only pool in central Madrid; Chamartín is Olympic-standard.

Other pools: Chamartín Plaza del Perú s/n (91 350 12 23). Metro Pío XII/bus 16, 29, 150.

Canal de Isabel II

Avda de las Islas Filipinas 54 (91 533 96 42). Metro Islas Filipinas/bus 2, 3, 12, 37, 149. **Open** 8am-10pm daily. *Swimming pool late May-early Sept* 11am-8pm. **Admission** *Swimming pool* 480ptas Mon-Fri; 530ptas, Sat, Sun, public holidays; 240ptas concessions daily; voucher for 10 admissions 4,165ptas; 20 admissions 7,185ptas, full summer 10,420ptas. **No credit cards**.

Run by the CAM, not the city council, this lovely complex has an Olympic-size pool, a children's pool, tennis and *frontón* courts, and a bar and restaurant. It also has good wheelchair access facilities.

Hotel Emperador

Gran Vía 53, Sol & Gran Vía (91 547 28 00). Metro Gran Vía/bus all routes to Gran Vía. **Open** *June-Sept* 11am-9pm daily. **Admission** *average* 3,000ptas Mon-Fri; 4,000ptas Sat, Sun, public holidays. **Credit** AmEx, DC, MC, V. **Map** p309 E6.

One of the most spectacular pools in Madrid, on the

Arts & Entertainment

roof of the Emperador hotel, open to non-residents at a price. The terrace has fabulous views over central Madrid. *See p41.*

Hotel Eurobuilding
C/Padre Damián 23, Chamartín (91 345 45 00).
Metro Cuzco/bus 5, 27, 40, 150. **Open** *June-Sept*
11am-8am daily. **Admission** 3,480ptas. **Credit**
AmEx, DC, MC, V.
Another hotel with excellent indoor and outdoor pools open to non-residents, but expensive. *See p43.*

Piscina Club Stella
C/Arturo Soria 231, Ciudad Lineal (91 359 16 32).
Metro Arturo Soria/bus 11, 70, 120, 122, 201.
Open *June-mid Sept* 11am-8pm daily. **Admission**
Mon-Fri 1,000ptas; 550ptas children; *Sat* 1,200ptas;
550ptas children; *Sun & public holidays* 1,400ptas;
750ptas children. **No credit cards.**
A private swimming club open to non-members, with a 1930s art deco pool and clubhouse.

Tennis/*tenis*

Many city sports centres (*see right*) have clay or tarmac courts for hire. At municipal *polideportivos*, court hire costs 675ptas per hour, plus a 155ptas reservation fee. The Barrio del Pilar, Concepción and La Elipa swimming pools also have tennis courts for hire, and the Canal de Isabel II has courts for 650ptas per hour (*see page 240*). More expensive than these is the top-notch private Club de Tenis de Chamartín (C/Federico Salmón 2, 91 345 25 00) where temporary monthly membership costs 41,800ptas.

Fitness

Gyms & fitness centres/ *gimnasios*

Some hotels have agreements with private health clubs for guests to use their facilities.

Bodhidharma
C/Moratines 18, Embajadores (91 517 28 16).
Metro Embajadores/bus all routes to Embajadores.
Open 8am-11pm Mon-Fri; 9am-2pm, 6-10pm Sat;
10am-3pm Sun. **Rates** 8,300ptas per mth; 20,600ptas
per 3mths. **Credit** AmEx, MC, V.
A well-equipped mixed health club with sauna, weights, exercise machines and aerobics classes.

Votre Ligne
C/Lagasca 88, 1º, Salamanca (91 576 40 00).
Metro Núñez de Balboa/bus 1, 9, 74. **Open** 8am-
9.30pm Mon-Fri; 10am-2pm Sat; closed Sun.
Rates 15,000ptas per mth; 108,000ptas per yr.
Credit AmEx, MC, V. **Map** p307 J3.
A lush women-only facility offering, as well as a gym and aerobics classes, a sauna, jacuzzis, a pool, massage, beauticians and other services. The associated

El Presidente club offers similar luxury for men. Both offer special rates for non-members in summer.
Branch: El Presidente C/Profesor Waksman 3 (91 458 67 59).

Sports centres/*polideportivos*

Madrid has 45 city-run *Polideportivos* (sports centres). At any of them you can pick up a map and a guide to the facilities available at each municipal centre. Facilities range from lavish, including pools and tennis courts, to a gym and little else. All have the same basic entrance fees, but there may be extra charges for some facilities. The most central *polideportivo* for obtaining leaflets and information is **La Chopera** in the Retiro.

Estadio Vallehermoso
Avda de las Islas Filipinas 10 (91 534 77 23/
information 012). *Metro Islas Filipinas/bus 2, 12.*
Open 8am-9.30pm daily. *Swimming pool* 11am-8pm
daily. **Admission** *Swimming pool* 480ptas Mon-Fri;
530ptas Sat, Sun, public holidays. *Season ticket* 10
admissions 4,165ptas; 20 admissions 7,185ptas;
10,420ptas all summer. **No credit cards.**
This athletics stadium and multi-purpose sports centre, run by the *Comunidad*, offers an indoor sports hall, gym, a football pitch, an open-air swimming pool and more. It's also good for jogging.

Parque de Ocío La Ermita – Paidesport Center
C/Sepúlveda 3, Virgen del Puerto (91 470 01 11).
Metro Puerta del Angel/bus 17, 25, 138, 500.
Open 9am-11pm Mon-Fri; 10am-8pm Sat; 10am-
3pm Sun. **Admission** *Tennis, squash* from
1,000ptas 30min. *Swimming pool* 1,600ptas per
day. **No credit cards.**
This enormous private sports centre caters for practically all needs, and membership is not required. As well as racket courts and an open-air pool, it has a gym and weights room and indoor sports hall; there is also sports tuition, especially for children.

Polideportivo de la Chopera
Parque del Retiro (91 420 11 54). *Metro Atocha/bus all*
routes to Atocha. **Open** 8am-10pm daily. **Admission**
varies according to facilities used. **Map** p310 I9.
Near the entrance to the Retiro behind the Museo del Prado, this attractive centre has two sand-surface football pitches (for eleven-a-side and seven-a-side), as well as tarmac courts, adaptable for five-a-side games, tennis and basketball.

Disabled sports facilities

The city sports institute is slowly adapting its *polideportivos* to allow full access for disabled users, but this programme is not yet complete. The majority of indoor swimming pools have been adapted, and many outdoor pools have ramps and full-access changing rooms.

Arts & Entertainment

Theatre & Dance

Though not totally out of the woods after years dogged by controversy, the capital's performing arts scene is still something to be proud of.

The performing arts in Madrid offer a varied panorama with great optimism in some areas, timid hope in others and some downright sombre zones. The commercial theatre world is enjoying a boom, while the dance scene, against tremendous odds, is still holding its own and playing a dignified role.

Politics and economics have much to do with this situation. In terms of commercial theatre, smart impresarios have seen a niche in the market with more disposable income. They have revamped certain Gran Vía cinemas (which were originally theatres anyway), invested in super productions, marketed them in a sophisticated way and achieved more backsides on seats than has been managed for a long time. Musicals, a genre that nobody would have bet a peseta on a few years back, have enjoyed huge success.

Theatre-goers are also showing renewed interest in text-based work too, as shown by the huge success of *Art*, which packed the **Teatro Marquina** for two and a half seasons.

With no national theatre company as such, the officially backed *Centro Dramático Nacional*, based at the magnificent **Teatro María Guerrero**, and *Compañía Nacional de Teatro Clásico*, specialising in Golden Age dramatists, at the **Teatro de la Comedia**, play this role. Serious drama regularly fills houses, showing that it's not just commercial theatre that's viable.The fringe, partially subsidised, is lively and enterprising and offers a wide variety of work – some good, some bad, but often worth seeing.

THE DANCE SCENE

The dance world in Madrid is less buoyant but nonetheless offers its loyal public considerable variety. Two major national dance companies are based in Madrid: the much-lauded *Compañía Nacional de Danza*, featuring contemporary productions, and the *Ballet Nacional de España*, specialists in Spanish dance. Madrid is also home to the regional government's flagship company, the *Ballet de la Comunidad de Madrid*, whose repertoire is much more classical under the artistic direction of Victor Ullate. The *CNT*, formerly the *Ballet Lírico*, is run by the dynamic dancer-choreographer Nacho Duato, who stopped

dancing himself in 1996. He shook up the company completely, renamed it and embraced a more contemporary style. The *Ballet Nacional* now has at its helm Aída Gómez, its youngest-ever director, and performs to rave reviews worldwide. Ullate's company smartly filled the gap in classical ballet vacated by the *CNT* under Duato. Neither the *CNT* nor the *Ballet Nacional* appear frequently in Madrid. However, the *CNT* performs two or three times at the **Teatro Real** and occasionally at the **Teatro de Madrid**, and the *Ballet Nacional* comes once a year to the **Teatro de la Zarzuela**. More frequent are appearances by Ullate's company in the **Teatro Albéniz** and the **Teatro de Madrid**.

Outside of the major circuit, the situation for contemporary dance is not easy, but its exponents fight on with admirable energy and enthusiasm.The regional government is committed to helping companies find a permanent base and is negotiating with cultural institutions in smaller towns to find homes for them. The recently unveiled plans to build a large theatre and choreographic centre in Chamberí, still two or three years away, should also give dance a boost. Only two permanent contemporary companies exist in Madrid, both outstanding. The lively *10 y 10* and hard-working *Provisional Danza* appear regularly in Madrid and tour more widely. Initiatives by independent choreographers include the showcase *Desviaciones* ('Deviations') mini-festival at **Cuarta Pared**, combining dance and performance art.

VENUES, SEASONS & TICKETS

The city's top theatres are the **María Guerrero**, the **Comedia**, the **Español**, and the much-praised **La Abadía**. The **Teatro Real** and **Teatro de la Zarzuela** both present Spanish and international dance companies, although their commitment to dance is clearly secondary. Practically the only large venue almost exclusively devoted to dance is the **Teatro de Madrid**, while the **Teatro Albéniz** also features dance frequently. The main season for both is from September to June, but some theatres now continue working in summer, in some cases presenting open-air works as part of the

Veranos de la Villa festival (*see page 188*). The **Festival de Otoño** (*see page 188*) is also an important part of the annual cultural calendar. Other exciting events are the fringe festival **La Alternativa** (*see page 184*), and **Madrid en Danza** (*see page 187*), with its wide variety of styles.

Theatres are usually closed on Mondays, although some programme other events. The *Guía del Ocio* and *El Mundo*'s Friday supplement *Metrópoli* carry listings (*see page 290*), as does the *ABC*'s Friday listings magazine and *El País' Tentaciones*, although its information is less complete. Many theatres have a *día del espectador* ('theatre-goer's day', usually Wednesday) when prices are reduced, and many offer children's shows.

The State theatres – the **Comedia, María Guerrero, Teatro de la Zarzuela** and **Auditorio Nacional** (*see page 215*) – have a joint ticketing system whereby tickets for all can be bought at any one of them. All operate via the **Caja Madrid** telesales service (902 48 84 88). Tickets for other theatres can be purchased ahead from box offices, and in most cases can also be bought in advance through savings banks including Caja Madrid, the **Caja de Cataluña** (24-hour telesales service, Tel-Entradas, 902 10 12 12), or through **El Corte Inglés**' own tickets line (902 40 02 22). For full information on telesales, *see page 171*.

Mainstream theatres

Centro Cultural de la Villa

Jardines del Descubrimiento, Plaza de Colón, Salamanca & the Retiro (91 575 60 80/91 575 64 96). Metro Colón/bus all routes to Plaza de Colón. **Open** *Box office* 11am-1.30pm, 5-6pm Tue-Sun; closed Mon; also Caja de Cataluña. **Tickets** 1,000 2,500ptas. **No credit cards. Map** p306 I4.

This comfortable venue in Plaza de Colón, owned and run by the city council, offers concerts, children's theatre and quality popular theatre as well as productions by smaller ballet companies, Spanish dance and contemporary work. It also stages a Latin American theatre festival every autumn, a puppet season for children, and *zarzuela* in summer (*see p217* **Making light of things**). *See also p107*.

Círculo de Bellas Artes

C/Marqués de Casa Riera 2, Huertas & Santa Ana (91 532 44 37/91 532 44 38). Metro Banco de España or Sevilla/bus all routes to Plaza de Cibeles. **Open** *Box office* 11.30am-1.30pm, 5pm until performance Tue-Sun; closed Mon; also Caja Madrid. **Tickets** 1,700-3,000ptas. **No credit cards. Map** p310 G7.

A multi-faceted arts centre that hosts much more than theatre, the Círculo was once home to Valle-Inclán's company. Today it offers several interesting theatre productions every year, plus

dramatised readings, opera and puppet shows for children. There's also a theatre festival in November (*see p73*).

Sala Mirador

C/Doctor Fourquet 31, La Latina, Rastro, Lavapiés (91 528 95 01). Metro Atocha or Lavapiés/bus all routes to Atocha. **Open** *Box office* 1hr before performance Fri, Sat; closed Mon-Thur, Sun. **Tickets** 1,500-2,500ptas. **No credit cards. Map** p310 G10.

Worth visiting for the unique entrance alone: an old-fashioned Madrid patio. Productions are varied, and have included dance, children's shows and a recent one-man show of *Fresa y Chocolate*.

Teatro de la Abadía

C/Fernández de los Ríos 42, Chamberí (91 448 16 27/91 448 11 81). Metro Quevedo/bus 2, 16, 61. **Open** *Box office* 5-9pm Tue-Sat; 5-8pm Sun; closed Mon; also Caja de Cataluña. **Tickets** 1,900-3,000ptas; reduced price concessions & Wed. **Credit** V. **Map** p305 D1.

One of Madrid's newest and most beautiful theatres, the Abadía has received major awards. Among the outstanding productions performed have been works by Valle-Inclán, Cervantes, Shakespeare, Brecht, Lorca, Ionesco, Beckett, and Lope de Vega.

Teatro Albéniz

C/Paz 11, Los Austrias (91 531 83 11). Metro Sol/bus all routes to Puerta del Sol. **Open** *Box office* 11.30am-1pm, 5.30-9pm daily; also Caja Madrid. **Tickets** 3,500ptas; reduced price concessions and groups. **Credit** V. **Map** p309 E8.

Privately owned but managed by the Comunidad de Madrid, the Albéniz stages a wide variety of quality drama and a good selection of dance, both classical and contemporary. Alicia Alonso's Cuban Ballet have an annual spot in late summer. The Albéniz is also the principal venue for the Festival de Otoño (*see p188*) and concerts are frequently programmed.

Teatro Alfil

C/del Pez 10, Malasaña & Conde Duque (91 521 45 41). Metro Callao or Noviciado/bus 147. **Open** *Box office* 1hr before performance Tue-Sun; closed Mon & Aug; also Caja Madrid. **Tickets** 1,500-2,500ptas; reduced price students & groups. **No credit cards. Map** p305 E5.

The Alfil has survived attempts to close it down, and since 1996 has been under new management. So far, the risky programming seems to be paying off – the Festival Internacional de Teatro de Humor was held successfully in 1997 and '98. Comedy and stand-up comedians are increasingly the mainstay too.

Teatro de Cámara

C/San Cosme y San Damián 3, La Latina, Rastro, Lavapiés (91 527 09 54). Metro Antón Martín or Lavapiés/bus 6, 26, 32. **Open** *Box office* 30min before performance Thur-Sun; closed Mon-Wed; also Caja de Cataluña and FNAC. *Performances* Oct-June Thur-Sun; July-Sept Wed-Sun. **Tickets** 1,500ptas; reduced price concessions & Thur (Wed July-Sept). **No credit cards. Map** p309 F9.

A small but highly regarded independent repertory theatre presenting worldwide drama by major writers, with a particular interest in Russian works. Chekhov is a mainstay but Spanish Golden Age writers also feature regularly.

Teatro de la Comedia (Compañía Nacional de Teatro Clásico)

C/Príncipe 14, Huertas & Santa Ana (91 521 49 31). Metro Sevilla or Sol/bus all routes to Puerta del Sol. **Open** Box office 11.30am-1.30pm, 5.30-6.30pm Mon, Tue, Thur-Sun; closed Wed; also Caja Madrid. **Tickets** 1,300-2,600ptas; reduced price Thur. **Credit** AmEx, DC, MC, V. **Map** p309 F8.

Classic Spanish theatre at its best. Under director Adolfo Marsillach, the CNTC, dedicated to preserving the heritage of Golden Age theatre, became one of the most highly respected and most vital Spanish companies. Marsillach resigned in 1996 (due to the unfavourable cultural climate emerging under the PP). There are upwards of three productions a year, plus occasional French or English plays.

Teatro Español

C/Príncipe 25, Huertas & Santa Ana (91 429 62 97). Metro Sevilla or Sol/bus all routes to Puerta del Sol. **Open** Box office 11.30am-1.30pm, 5-7pm Tue-Sun; closed Mon; also Caja de Cataluña. **Tickets** 200-2,500ptas; reduced price Wed. **No credit cards**. **Map** p309 F8.

This site has housed a theatre since 1583, when the Corral del Príncipe, in which many of Lope de Vega's works were premièred, opened. The current theatre, which replaced it in 1745, is the most beautiful in Madrid. It now presents mainly 20th-century Spanish drama, along with new work and international classics such as Cyrano de Bergerac.

Teatro Lara

Corredera Baja de San Pablo 15, Malasaña & Conde Duque (91 521 05 52). Metro Callao/bus all routes to Plaza del Callao. **Open** Box office 11.30am-1pm, 5pm until start of performance Tue-Sun; closed Mon; also Caja de Cataluña. **Tickets** 1,800-3,500ptas; discounts Wed, Thur, also for groups (91 548 99 80). **No credit cards**. **Map** p305 F5.

After being closed for many years, this jewel of 19th-century theatre architecture was rescued and reopened in 1996. Since reopening, it has offered a wide mix. Try to take the kids to one of the excellent children's matinées.

Teatro de Madrid

Avda de la Ilustración s/n, Barrio del Pilar (91 740 52 74). Metro Barrio del Pilar/bus all routes to Barrio del Pilar, La Vaguada. **Open** Box office 5.30-9pm Tue-Thur; 11.30am-1.30pm, 5.30-9pm Fri-Sun; closed Mon; also Caja Madrid. **Tickets** 1,000-3,000ptas; reduced price groups and Wed & Sun. **Credit** MC, V. This modern public theatre, managed privately, has lavish facilities, is really the only dance-oriented theatre in Madrid and is home to the exciting Nuevo Ballet Flamenco. It presents a mixture of ballet, Spanish dance and high-budget drama, and some children's shows around Christmas time. High-calibre Spanish and international dance companies regularly appear, among them Compañía Nacional de Danza, the Ballet de la Comunidad de Madrid and internationally known groups such as Momix, DV8 Physical Theatre and the Batsheva Dance Company.

Teatro María Guerrero (Centro Dramático Nacional)

C/Tamayo y Baus 4, Chueca (91 319 47 69). Metro Colón/bus all routes to Plaza de Colón. **Open** Box office 11.30am-1.30pm, 5pm until performance Tue-Sun, advance sales only until 6pm; closed Mon; also Caja Madrid. **Tickets** 1,600-2,600ptas. **Credit** AmEx, MC, V. **Map** p306 H5.

The base for Spain's Centro Dramático Nacional, which presents both international and contemporary Spanish drama in high-quality productions. Politicking has affected the management of the theatre in recent times but the programming is still top-class. In the last couple of years there have been well-received productions of Lorca's La Casa de Bernarda Alba and Buero Vallejo's La Fundación, and Albert Boadella's Els Joglars presented their particular take on the life of Dalí in Daaalí. The 1885 theatre has a beautiful interior, and was thoroughly renovated a couple of seasons ago to include wheelchair access.

Teatro Marquina

C/Prim 11, Chueca (91 532 31 86). Metro Banco de España or Colón/bus all routes to Paseo de Recoletos, Colón. **Open** Box office 11.30am-until performance Tue-Sun; closed Mon; also El Corte Inglés. **Tickets** 3,300ptas, Wed reduced price. **No credit cards**. **Map** p306 H5.

After a refurbishment, the Marquina reopened in 1997. Since the beginning of 1998-9 season it has housed a long-running version of Yasmina Reza's worldwide hit Art, directed by and starring the prestigious Catalan actor Josep Maria Flotats.

Teatro Nuevo Apolo

Plaza de Tirso de Molina 1, La Latina, Rastro, Lavapiés (91 369 06 37/902 11 50 18). Metro Tirso de Molina/bus 6, 26, 32, 65. **Open** Box office 11.30am-1.30pm, 5pm until performance Tue-Sun; closed Mon; also Caja Madrid. **Tickets** 1,000-5,000ptas, Wed reduced price. **No credit cards**. **Map** p309 E8.

Madrid's venue for big musical and a variety of Dance spectaculars: the Nuevo Apolo has recently been visited by Joaquín Cortés, and Russian clown Slava Polounine with his award-winning show.

Fringe/alternative

El Canto de la Cabra

C/San Gregorio 8, Chueca (91 310 42 22). Metro Chueca/bus 3, 40, 149. **Open** Box office 1hr before performance Thur-Sun; closed Mon-Wed; also Caja Madrid. Performances Sept-June Thur-Sun 9pm; July, Aug Wed-Sun 10pm. **Tickets** 1,700ptas; 1,200ptas Wed, Sun, concessions. **No credit cards**. **Map** p306 G5.

Going for gold

With many plots taken and adapted from history, folklore and the Bible, Spanish Golden Age drama offers the spectator a dazzling variety of plays, frequently starring dynamic women, wily comic servants and their inept masters. Topics such as the deceptiveness of appearances, the nature of reality and the question of honour crop up time and time again, even in *entremeses* (short comic sketches performed between the first two acts) and *autos* (religious plays).

Towards the end of the 16th century, demand in the capital for theatre was so that Philip II had two permanent open-air theatres built. These *corrales* provided space for all sections of Madrid society, ranging from rowdy groundling to royalty. **Lope de Vega**'s (1562-1635) verse treatise *Arte Nuevo de Hacer Comedias* (1609) was his recipe for success, establishing the rules that playwrights would follow for years to come: whatever the subject matter, the *comedia* (play) was to have three acts, be written in verse, and blend comic and serious elements to satisfy all tastes.

The prolific Lope's plays roar along at a terrific pace due to the flair of his verse. Historical drama (*Fuente Ovejuna*), urban comedy (*La Discreta Enamorada*), and folkloric tragedy (the magnificent *El Caballero de Olmedo*) are just three strings to his bow.

In addition to Lopean themes of love and honour, the friar **Tirso de Molina** (c.1584-1648) brought religious questions to the stage in his effort to 'teach through entertainment'. His *El Condenado por Desconfiado* is a superb study of the burning question of free-will and fate, while *El Burlador de Sevilla* marks the first appearance of the Don Juan story. Tirso's comedies also contain food for thought: *Don Gil de las Calzas Verdes* and *El Vergonzoso en el Palacio* are witty examinations of the deceptiveness of appearances.

Golden Age drama reached its peak with **Calderón de la Barca** (1600-81). The question of honour – so popular with the crowd that Lope mentions it in *Arte Nuevo* – permeates both his more serious plays (*A secreto agravio, Secreta Venganza*; *El alcalde de Zalamea*) and *comedies* such as *La Dama Duende*, (a performance by the **Compañía Nacional de Teatro Clásico** is pictured). Calderón's greatest achievement, *La Vida es Sueño*, manages to combine metaphysical reflection and analysis of kingship with the more usual *comedia* fare.

One of the more experimental venues, 'The Goat's Bleat' programmes work by contemporary Spanish and foreign writers. With a capacity of 70, it is cosy and intimate. Outdoor performances in summer.

Cuarta Pared

C/Ercilla 17, Arganzuela (91 517 23 17). Metro Embajadores/bus all routes to Embajadores. **Open** *Box office* 1hr before performance Thur-Sun; closed Mon-Wed & Aug; also Caja Madrid. **Tickets** 800-1,200ptas. **No credit cards.**
This reasonably sized venue presents quality contemporary productions, both from home and abroad, plus excellent cutting-edge contemporary dance. It also houses theatre workshops, courses and children's plays, for which it recently won an award.

Ensayo 100

C/Raimundo Lulio 20, Chamberí (91 447 94 86). Metro Iglesia/bus 3, 37, 40, 147. **Open** *Box office* 2hrs before performance Thur-Sun; closed Mon-Wed; also Caja Madrid. **Tickets** 2,000ptas, reduced price young carnet, over 65s. **No credit cards.** **Map** p306 G2.

The fare here is generally intellectual, and the attitude totally professional; the company's director, Argentinian Jorge Eines, is highly regarded.

El Montacargas

C/Antillón 19, Puerta del Angel (91 526 11 73). Metro Puerta del Angel/bus 31, 33, 39, 65, 138. **Open** *Box office* 30min before performance Thur-Sun. **Tickets** 1,500ptas; reduced price Sun 6pm for children. **No credit cards.**
This sparky cultural association hosts kids' shows (Sunday, 6pm), *café-teatro* (cabaret) and a range of workshops and other activities as well as its theatre programme, which is suitably unpredictable.

Sala Triángulo

C/Zurita 20, La Latina, Rastro, Lavapiés (91 530 68 91). Metro Antón Martín or Lavapiés/bus 6, 26, 32. **Open** *Box office* 30min before performance Thur-Sun; closed Mon-Wed; also Caja Madrid. **Tickets** 1,500ptas. **No credit cards. Map** p309 F9.
One of the best fringe venues, the Triángulo has hosted almost every theatrical movement at some point, and is a good showcase for new writing and

young actors. Be sure to keep an eye out for the Alternativa festival in late winter-early spring, an international festival of avant-garde theatre (*see p184*), as well as the regular children's shows and *café-teatro* (cabaret).

Teatro de las Aguas

C/Aguas 8, Los Austrias (91 366 96 42). Metro La Latina/bus 17, 18, 23, 35, 60. **Open** *Box office* 1hr before performance Wed-Sat; closed Mon, Tue, Sun. **Tickets** 1,000ptas. **No credit cards. Map** p308 C9.
A tiny space that has not been going long, and has made its niche with a mix of small productions. Look out for English-language shows.

Teatro Estudio de Madrid

C/Cabeza 14, La Latina, Rastro, Lavapiés (91 539 64 47). Metro Tirso de Molina/bus 6, 26, 32, 65. **Open** *Box office* 1hr before performance Fri-Sun; closed Mon-Thur. **Tickets** 1,200ptas. **Map** p309 E9.
A tiny fringe theatre (capacity 50) that makes a suitably intense venue for solo shows or two-handers. Short pieces by Dario Fo are a regular feature.

Teatro Pradillo

C/Doctor Fourquet 31, La Latina, Rastro, Lavapiés (91 528 95 01). Metro Atocha or Lavapiés/bus all routes to Atocha. **Open** *Box office* 1hr before performance Fri, Sat; closed Mon-Thur, Sun; also Caja Madrid. **Tickets** 1,500-2,500ptas. **No credit cards. Map** p310 G9/10.
This is an intimate studio theatre with a good space for dance: the daring experimental work staged here has often been highly praised. It also presents theatre for adults and children, including puppet shows, flamenco and English-language theatre.

Carmen Roche

C/del Roble 22, Tetuán (91 579 08 05). Metro Tetuán/bus 3, 66, 124. **Open** 9.30am-10pm Mon-Fri; closed Sat, Sun.
Highly regarded school with a range of classes for students of all levels: classical, Spanish, contemporary, jazz, ballroom, *sevillanas*. Also exercise classes.

Centro Coreográfico La Ventilla/ 10 y 10 Danza

C/Carmen Montoya 12, Chamartín (91 315 32 72). Metro Ventilla/bus all routes to Plaza de Castilla. **Open** 10am-4pm Mon-Fri; closed Sat, Sun.
This studio is the base of the 10 y 10 company, directed by Pedro Berdayes and Mónica Ründe. There is a contemporary class at 10-11.30am daily. Afterwards the company rehearses, and students can often stay and watch. Rehearsal space available.

Centro de Danza Karen Taft

C/Libertad 15, Chueca (91 522 84 40). Metro Chueca/bus 3, 40, 149. **Open** *Oct-June* 9am-10pm Mon-Fri. *July-Sept* 10am-10pm Mon-Thur intensive groups. **Map** p306 G5.

The groundbreaking **10 y 10**.

One of the foremost schools in Spain, with classes in classical and modern techniques, in addition to flamenco and tap.

Estudio de Carmen Senra

C/Apolonio Morales 11 (91 359 16 47). Metro Plaza de Castilla/bus 14, 150. **Open** 10am-10pm Mon-Fri; closed Sat, Sun.
Madrid's most important studio for contemporary dance, offering classes in various styles, including jazz, flamenco, ballroom and pre-dance for children.

Estudios Amor de Dios

C/Fray Luis de León 13 (91 530 16 61). Metro Embajadores/bus all routes to Plaza de Embajadores. **Open** 10am-10pm Mon-Fri; 10am-3pm Sat; closed Sun.
The nerve centre of Madrid's flamenco dance scene, packed with students eager to learn from prestigious artists but often in financial straits. Classes in all the Spanish styles and techniques, and studios for hire.

Certamen de Coreográfia de Danza Española y Flamenco

Information *Producciones Maga (91 547 69 79).* **Date** July.
Held over three days at the Albéniz (*see p243*), this competition is a great opportunity to spot new trends and talents in Spanish dance.

Certamen Coreográfico de Madrid

Information *Paso a Dos, C/Tutor 18 (91 547 69 79/91 365 70 37).* **Date** late Nov.
A national platform for new work in contemporary dance and ballet. Lately it has been staged in the Círculo de Bellas Artes last year (*see p243*).

Desviaciones

Information *Sala Cuarta Pared (see p245).* **Date** Oct.
This short festival of experimental and contemporary dance takes place at the Cuarta Pared (*see p245*).

Día Internacional de la Danza

Information *Asociación de Profesionales de la Danza (91 420 32 32).* **Date** 29 Apr-1 May.
International Dance Day, 29 April, is celebrated with a Gala at the Teatro Albéniz. The programme features about every important name in Spanish dance.

Trips Out of Town

Getting Started

Head for the hills, they're closer than you think.

By bus

Most of the companies that run inter-city coach services to and from Madrid operate from the **Estación Sur de Autobuses**, Calle Méndez Alvaro (Metro and *Cercanías* Méndez Alvaro). It is some way south-east of the city centre; to get there by Metro, take line 1 (pale blue) to Pacífico, and change to line 6 (grey).

A single phone line (**91 468 42 00**) handles all enquiries, but companies also have their own lines (if the main number is engaged and you have a local Yellow Pages, look up *Autocares*: ads often show the companies' routes).

However, buses for many places listed in these chapters – especially some closer to the city within the *Comunidad de Madrid* – don't leave from the Estación Sur but from their companies' own depots or terminal points around the city, close to the main highways that lead to their destinations.

For regional buses to most routes north of Madrid, use the **Plaza Castilla** terminal; for the north-west, the streets around **Moncloa** Metro; for the south-east, Avda del Mediterráneo, next to **Conde de Casal** Metro; and for most routes north-east, **Avenida de América**. Further details of current services are available from tourist offices, on map 4 of the *Consorcio de Transportes* series (for services within the *Comunidad*) and on the regional transport website, www.ctm-madrid.es. Local tour companies also offer guided trips to many destinations. For details, *see page 60*.

By car

The infamous six roads, numbered in Roman numerals N-I to N-VI, which are the driver's sole normal way out of Madrid, can all be reached from the M-30 or the outlying M-40 ring road. For the eastern Guadarrama and the Sierra Pobre, the **N-I** (Carretera de Burgos) is the main road. For Alcalá de Henares, take the **N-II** Barcelona road, and for Chinchón, the **N-III** towards Valencia. The **N-401** to Toledo can be reached from either the M-30 or the N-IV, and the route toward El Escorial, Segovia, Avila and Salamanca is the **N-VI** north-west, the Carretera de La Coruña. For more on driving and car hire, *see page 277*.

Driving around Madrid can be an appalling experience at times when the whole city decides to go somewhere. On some weekends there are bottlenecks as far as Talavera de la Reina, 120km out on the N-V. For safety and/or your sanity's sake avoid leaving the city on Friday evenings. The real teeth-grinder is the return trip on Sundays: dead in the water from mid-afternoon till well past midnight. Immense back-ups and a substantial crop of accidents are also dismally predictable on long weekends and at the beginning and end of August.

By train

Alcalá, Aranjuez, El Escorial and many towns towards the Guadarrama are on the *Cercanías* local rail network (*see p276, and map, page 315*). At main RENFE (Spanish Railways) stations *Cercanías* platforms are signposted separately. Services to other destinations leave from the main-line stations, **Chamartín** and **Atocha**, although many trains also stop between them at Nuevos Ministerios and Recoletos *Cercanías* stations. Some towns, especially those on *Cercanías* lines, have frequent rail services; for others, particularly **Segovia**, buses are quicker and more frequent. One other thing to note is that the excellent AVE high-speed trains to Seville, with services almost hourly from Atocha, make a weekend or even a day trip to Andalusia a comfortable possibility, and according to when you travel there are often very good low-price fare deals.

RENFE information

902 24 02 02/www.renfe.es.
Open *information* 24hrs, *reservations* 5am-11.30pm daily. **Credit** AmEx, DC, MC, V.
Tickets for long-distance services can be booked by phone with a credit card. English is spoken, and tickets can be delivered to a hotel or address in Madrid for a small extra charge.

RENFE central sales office

C/Alcalá 44 (no phone).
Metro Banco de España/bus all routes to Cibeles.
Open 9.30am-8pm Mon-Fri; closed Sat, Sun.
Credit AmEx, DC, MC, V. **Map** p310 G7.
Train information and tickets for the AVE and all RENFE long-distance services are available in central Madrid from this office, a short walk from Plaza de Cibeles. It does not handle phone enquiries, which go through the central number (*see above*).

Castilian Towns

Ancient alleyways, royal palaces, lush gardens and gutsy country cooking: the historic towns around Madrid are an essential part of any visit to the city.

The essence of austerity: **El Escorial.**

Still a relatively compact city, Madrid offers old-world towns and unspoiled countryside within 40 kilometres (25 miles) of the Puerta del Sol. The areas north and west have the most spectacular landscapes, with the three main Sierras (*see page 263*). The country to the south and east is flatter and less dramatic, but full of fascinating places – among them Aranjuez, Chinchón and, above all, Toledo. Far more historic than Madrid itself, they nevertheless still retain the pleasant feel of living, functioning towns.

El Escorial

Take **El Escorial** as you will: Philip's folly, the forbidding barracks of fanaticism, a megalomaniac's monument to himself. Foreigners have never thought much of this immense monastery-mausoleum, dreamt up by the same king who gave us the Invincible Armada. Writers have seen it virtually as the Inquisition in stone. But it's hard not to conclude that this is one of the most extraordinary structures ever built by man.

The statistics are staggering: 2,675 windows, 1,200 doors, 16 inner courtyards, 24 kilometres (15 miles) of passageways and 86 staircases. Its architects, Juan Bautista de Toledo and Juan de Herrera, built it on a rectangular pattern to represent the gridiron on which the martyr Saint Laurence was roasted to death. What makes it so imposing is the monumentality and coldness of all that Guadarrama granite and the un-Spanish frugality of ornamentation.

Philip II – dour, devout and shy – required a resting place for his father where a community of monks could pray for the eternal repose of his lineage. He also needed somewhere to go to commune privately with God the Father – the two father figures were a little mixed up in his mind. Hence, he chose to combine a palace (a bare, unhedonistic one), a monastery and a royal tomb in one. All but two Spanish sovereigns and their consorts lie in the jasper, gold and marble mausoleum beneath the basilica, the *Panteón de los Reyes*, designed by Gian Battista Crescenzi in the 1620s.

Walk this way

The best place from which to get an overview of El Escorial is **La Silla de Felipe II** (Philip II's Chair), a rocky promontory from which the King watched the progress of his great edifice. This vantage point also provides a splendid view of the leafy oak forests and *dehesa* pasturelands of Castile. With your back to the main façade of the monastery, turn left to leave the esplanade by the **Puerto de la Cruz Verde** and take the track heading left through the oak woods at **Las Herrerías**. Cross the M-505, to come to an asphalt track that leads to La Silla. From the **Ermita de la Vírgen de Gracia**, follow the red-and-white markings of the GR10 long-distance footpath. To La Silla and back takes about two and a half hours, on easy, shaded paths.

If you have six or seven hours to spare, you can always follow the classic **Cumbres Escurialenses** route. It's traditionally walked on 10 August, the day of Saint Laurence (San Lorenzo). From La Silla, continue north to the **Collado de Entrecabezas**, then follow the spur north and east to the peak of **Abantos** (1,754 metres/5,756 feet), before dropping back down to El Escorial from **Puerto de Malagón**. The path is clear, but takes you over five peaks.

A good walk for the less ambitious, and those tied to public transport, involves getting off the train to El Escorial at the previous stop, **Las Zorreras**, and walking to the town through rolling pastureland, a two-hour walk that criss-crosses the rail track. A picnic along the way makes a perfect break. From the station, head north along the right side of the track for half an hour, passing houses. The road eventually peters out, but the path continues, heading right up a dirt track. On the brow of the hill to the right there is an abandoned cottage. Follow the path to a footbridge over the rail track, and continue through a series of gates, with the peak of Abantos above El Escorial straight ahead. The path crosses the railway track again after about another half-hour, and passes through some farm buildings. It emerges at the bottom of El Escorial, past a marble factory. Turn right past the petrol station to continue uphill to the monastery, or follow signs for *Estación FFCC* to return to Madrid. If you try any of these walks, be sure to take water with you. For more walks, *see pages 263-72*.

Philip's austere apartments are above the altar of the vast grey basilica, with a *jalousie* window so he didn't miss Mass when bedridden. Otherwise, he amused himself with his art collection, including a huge El Greco and works by Bosch, Titian and the Flemish masters (the best pictures are now in the Prado, but several, including Titian's *Last Supper* and El Greco's *Adoration of the Name of Jesus*, are still here). He could also browse beneath the barrel-vaulted ceiling of the magnificent library, whose 50,000 volumes rival the Vatican's holdings.

After the Spanish Habsburgs inbred themselves to extinction, their Bourbon successors made little use of the Escorial, except for hunting-mad cuckold Charles IV. The **Palacio de los Borbones**, the apartments that he had remodelled to his taste – light, airy, and in a fluffy neo-classical style completely at odds with the gloomy corridors of Philip's palace – contain many superb tapestries designed by Goya and his contemporaries. This area was closed for restoration for years, but can now be visited with guided tours on certain days. In the gardens of the monastery is Charles IV's summerhouse, the **Casita del Príncipe**, reopened recently after restoration, and visitable at weekends, with prior reservation (call the main palace number).

Away from the monastery, El Escorial is really two towns – the mountain village built up around Philip's grand pile, officially **San Lorenzo de El Escorial**, and the plain town around the train station at the bottom of the hill, **El Escorial** proper. A popular summer and weekend stop for Madrileños, San Lorenzo retains the feel of a mountain village, and out of season can be a delight. Just north of the grey expanse of the monastery esplanade, in Plaza San Lorenzo, is another contrasting 18th-century building, Charles III's dainty **Real Coliseo** theatre (*see page 244*). Further into the village there's an old-world cinema, the Teatro Variedades, on Calle Las Pozas, and the streets off Calle del Rey are worth exploring for bars and restaurants. San Lorenzo also makes a fine base for walks in the Guadarrama (*see page 250* **Walk this way**).

Monasterio de San Lorenzo El Real de El Escorial

91 890 59 02/3/4. **Open** *Apr-Sept* 10am-6pm Tue-Sun *Oct-Mar* 10am-5pm Tue-Sun; closed Mon. **Admission** 1,000ptas; 500ptas concessions; Wed free for EU citizens; *guided tours* 100ptas extra. **Palacio de los Borbones** *Guided tours only* 4pm, 5pm, 6pm Fri; 10am, 11am, noon, 5pm, 6pm Sat. **Admission** 600ptas; 450ptas concessions. **Casita del Príncipe** *Guided tours only* 10.30am-1pm, 3.30-6.30pm Sat, Sun. **Admission** 500ptas; 350ptas concessions. **No credit cards**.
Reservations are essential for the Palacio and Casita tours, at least 24 hours in advance.

Where to stay & eat

Fonda Genara (Plaza San Lorenzo 2,
91 890 43 57, set lunch 1,250ptas) is a pretty,
comfortable restaurant with good-value
Castilian fare. Entered via a likeable bar, in
an arcade next to the Real Coliseo, the dining
room has period furnishings and old playbills
around the walls. A short walk from the square
on Calle del Rey will lead you to **Mesón Las
Rejas** (C/Xavier Cabello La Piedra 2, 91 890
63 59, average 2,000ptas), an unpretentious
place with a quiet terrace. Up above San
Lorenzo in the Abantos district, **Horizontal**
(Camino Horizontal, 91 890 38 10, average
3,500ptas) offers outdoor eating in summer
and a warm welcome in winter. If you stay
over in San Lorenzo, try the **Parilla
Príncipe** (C/Floridablanca 6, 91 890 16 11,
rates 8,000ptas, set lunch 2,500ptas), in an 18th-
century palace with a hotel on the upper floors,
and classic sierra cooking available below.

Getting there

By bus

Herranz (91 890 41 22) buses 661 and 664 leave from
Moncloa to San Lorenzo (55 min), at least every two
hours 7.15am-10pm (9am-9.30pm Sat; 9am-11pm
Sun, holidays). Last return is at 9pm (8pm Sat,
10pm Sun, holidays).

By car

N-VI/A6 to Guadarrama, and San Lorenzo is a left
turn (south) on the M-600 (50km/31 miles).

By train

Cercanías C-8a, 27 trains from Atocha 5.48am-
11.33pm, Mon-Fri; every hour Sat, Sun. Last
return 10.17pm daily. Trains run to El Escorial
town, from where it's a 2km (1¼-mile) walk or bus
ride uphill to San Lorenzo and the monastery.
The bus is much more direct.

Tourist information

Oficina de Turismo

C/Floridablanca 10 (91 890 15 54). **Open** 10am-
2pm, 3-5pm Mon-Fri; 10am-2pm Sat; closed Sun.
Cuesta de Grimaldi (no phone) **Open** 10am-
7pm daily.

El Valle de los Caídos

The 'Valley of the Fallen', Franco's vast
monument (officially) to the dead on his own
side in the Spanish Civil War, lies a little north
of El Escorial off the Guadarrama road. It may
theoretically commemorate all the nationalist
war dead, but you won't find any imposing
lists of names here, as in most collective war
memorials; in the whole place the only names
shown are two, those of Franco himself and José
Antonio Primo de Rivera, the rich boy founder
of the Falange, conveniently dead (and so no
rival to the dictator) long before the mausoleum
was begun. It is thus, really, nothing other than
one of the most megalomaniac monuments ever
created by one man to himself, worthy of Hitler,
Stalin or Ceaucescu.

Opinions differ as to whether Franco had
already decided that this should be his final
resting place when he had chain gangs of
Republican prisoners labour to quarry this giant
cavern out of the rock. Nobody knows how many
died in the process, but it must be
a bitter irony to their families to think they rest
alongside the dictator beneath a basilica laden
with gargantuan examples of the unadulterated
kitsch so dear to the totalitarian mindset, topped
by a 152 metres (500 foot) high stone cross,
visible for 50 kilometres (31 miles). Inside, it's
one huge, converging tunnel, each chamber
slightly smaller than the last and ending finally
in the tomb, with effects worthy of a Hollywood
horror movie set. The whole thing is so bizarre
you can almost forget to dislike it. If you want
the total fascist experience, go on 18 July,
anniversary of the 1936 military uprising, or
better still on 20 November, Franco's deathday.

El Valle de los Caídos

Open *Oct-Mar* 10am-6pm Tue-Sun. *Apr-Sept*
9.30am-7pm Tue-Sun. Closed Mon & some
holidays. **Admission** 800ptas; 350ptas
concessions. **No credit cards.**

Getting there

By car

The Valle de los Caídos is 13km/8miles north of San
Lorenzo de El Escorial, and reached via a turn off the
M-600 between San Lorenzo and the Guadarrama
exit off the N-VI/A6.

Avila

The highest and coldest corner of Old Castile,
capital of a nut-brown province consisting of
seven parts mountain to one part tufted rock.
If it weren't for its medieval walls, who would
come to Avila? The saintly among us, maybe,
for the city is also famous for the dour piety of
its inhabitants.

Had Avila ever known real prosperity and
change before the 1980s we probably would
have lost the walls. It didn't, and there they
are, a perfectly preserved mile and a half of
them, with 88 watchtowers and nine gates,
still encircling most of the town. There is a
superb view of the walls from the Salamanca

road, outside the westernmost gate of the old city, Puerta del Puente. The **walls** (open 10am-6pm Tue-Sun; admission 200ptas; 100ptas under-14s) can be climbed at two points, by the Puerta del Alcazar, just south of the cathedral, and the Puerta de San Vicente, to the north.

The medieval city is stately and elegant, not least the stark, fortified **Cathedral** (open 10am-1pm, 3.30-5pm daily; admission 250ptas) embedded in the walls. There's no mistaking its 12th-century origins, although the main portal is full-blown Gothic. Another stylistic hybrid, **San Vicente**, rivals the cathedral in size and grandeur. In contrast, outside the walls are the pure Romanesque **San Andrés** church

and the palatial 16th-century **Santo Tomás** monastery, wherein lie the bones of the son Ferdinand and Isabella had hoped would succeed them. These are only a few of the historic buildings in this city of convents and churches.

Avila was settled by the knights who had a hand in chucking out the Moors in 1089, one year before work began on the walls, so noble palaces are also plentiful. The city is most famous, however, as the home of Saint Teresa, greatest of Spanish mystics, and a reformer, administrator, brilliant writer and self-assured woman of the Renaissance. Kitschy souvenirs apart, she is remembered with a little exhibit in

El Pardo

Six kilometres (four miles) north of Madrid, the village of El Pardo has managed to avoid becoming a dormitory adjunct to the capital, and retains an air of rural calm. Not far from the Palacio de la Zarzuela, main residence of the royal family, it houses many barracks and military installations. It's best known to Spaniards, though, for the **Real Palacio de El Pardo**, long the residence of General Franco.

Like Aranjuez and the Escorial, this was one of the ring of royal residences that surrounded Madrid. The hunting estate of El Pardo was what first attracted the Emperor Charles V to Madrid; a palace was built there for Philip II, but it was damaged by fire and rebuilt by Francesco Sabatini in the 18th century. Fernando VI made much use of it as a hunting lodge. Since Franco's passing in 1975 it has been used to house foreign heads of state on official visits, but part of it is normally open to the public. There are fine displays of Spanish tapestries, some designed by Goya, and Franco's cabinet rooms; the *Generalísimo*'s plain, gloomy office gives an immediate insight into the dry little man who ran Spain for four decades. The ornate theatre, built for Charles IV's Italian wife María Luisa, is where film buff Franco used to watch flicks with his chums before deciding on their suitability for the great unwashed.

Whether because many people assume it is closed, or due to its Francoist associations, El Pardo is the least visited of the royal residences. Outside in the fresh air, the palace can best be savoured from a distance. This is not as easy as one would wish, as much of the magnificent surrounding

parkland is closed to the public. It's a superb stretch of hills and woodland, remarkably untouched due to its royal/dictatorial status, and extremely rich in bird- and wildlife such as deer and imperial eagles. Game features prominently in the village's popular restaurants.

Real Palacio de El Pardo

91 542 00 59. **Open** *Oct-Mar* 10.30am-5pm Mon-Sat; 9.30am-1.30pm Sun. *Apr-Sept* 10.30am-6pm Mon-Sat; 9.30am-1.40pm Sun. Closed during official visits. **Admission** 800ptas; 400ptas concessions; Wed free for EU citizens. **No credit cards**.

Where to eat

Next to the palace and a string of other game-centred restaurants, **El Gamo** (Avda de la Guardia 6, 91 376 03 27, set lunch 2,000ptas) stands out for the quality of its food, such as local venison, and scrambled eggs with wild mushrooms. On the same street at no.29 is **La Marquesita** (91 376 03 77, average 3,500ptas). An open fire and the feel of an old hunting lodge make this a fine winter stop-off.

Getting there

By bus

Bus 601 from Moncloa (services every 10-15min, 6.30am midnight daily). The last return is at 12.30am, and the journey time 25min.

By car

M-30 to El Pardo-M-40 exit, then the C601.

A great survivor, Segovia's imposing Roman **Aqueduct**.

an annexe to the **San Juan Bautista** church, with manuscripts and relics, including a couple of knucklebones – but not the mummified arm that Franco had at his bedside in his last days.

Where to stay & eat

Avila and its province are renowned for distinct culinary specialities: steaks (*chuletón de Avila*) from the native Iberian breed of black cattle (the same kind that's fought in rings), and haricot beans, *judías*. They're both staples in the town's restaurants. **Mesón del Rastro** (Plaza del Rastro 1, 920 21 12 18, average 5,000ptas) is a reliable choice; **El Molino de la Losa** (Bajada de la Losa 12, 920 21 11 02, average 5,000ptas) is a simulacrum of an old grain mill, on the banks of the Adaja river. It's great if the weather lets you sit outside, especially at night when the walls are lit up. The other eatables inseparable from Avila are *yemas*, ultra-rich sweets made from egg yolks and supposedly once made by Santa Teresa herself, which are offered in pretty packages by any number of shops in the old town.

Avila is a quiet, ancient town, but makes an atmospheric place for a stopover thanks, above all, to its special hotels, all in beautiful converted Renaissance palaces. The delightful **Parador Raimundo de Borgoña** (C/Marqués de Canales de Chozas 2, 920 21 13 40, rates 10,000-16,000ptas) is the official *parador* (*see page 257*), and has an especially fine restaurant; **Hostería de Bracamonte** (C/Bracamonte 6 (920 25 12 80, rates 12,000-18,500ptas) is the smallest, and most intimate; the **Palacio de Valderrábanos** (Plaza de la Catedral 9, 920 21 10 23, rates 9,000-17,000ptas), on the plaza facing the cathedral, has extra grandeur.

Getting there

By bus
Larrea (91 530 48 00) from Estación Sur; three buses daily. Journey time 1hr 45min.

By car
N-VI/A6 to Villacastín, then N110 (113km/70 miles).

By train
16 trains daily from Chamartin or Atocha 6.40am-8.32pm. Last return at 10.16pm. Journey time (*Regional Exprés* services) 1hr 30min.

Tourist information

Oficina de Turismo
Plaza de la Catedral 4 (920 21 13 87). **Open** 9am-2pm, 5-7pm Mon-Fri; 10am-2pm, 5-8pm Sat, Sun.

Segovia & around

Despite the hordes of tourists and Madrileño day-trippers who take over the place in summer and on Sundays, **Segovia** is still very much its own town. Wander its back streets, up towards the Alcázar, and you'll find atmospheric corners, and bars frequented only by locals.

The Roman **Aqueduct** comes first, since all approaches to the old city, which stands high on a bluff over the diminished Eresma river, bring you almost within touching distance of its double-decker span. The unsightly braces around some of its 163 arches were put up when the whole thing seemed about to collapse due to erosion caused by vibration and exhaust fumes. It was probably built early in the second century AD – no date was recorded by Roman chroniclers. As is evident, the rough-hewn blocks mesh perfectly without need of mortar. Generations of guidebooks have reported that it still carries water, but it hasn't done so for years.

Steps ascend the wall where the Roman span splices into the hill, or you can spiral up the streets that channel traffic up and down. Buttresses flying brazenly, the **Cathedral** (open daily) stands to the left of the arcaded **Plaza Mayor**. It looks like a graceful piece of medieval Gothic, but was actually built in this anachronistic style to replace a predecessor destroyed in the *Comunero* rising of 1521.

Second only to eating yourself silly on suckling pig or roast lamb, the attraction of Segovia is in wandering the narrow streets between the Plaza Mayor and the Alcázar, especially those on the outer ramparts with views over the vast dry plains of Castile. From the north-east flank you can see a Romanesque gem, the **Iglesia de Vera Cruz**, built by the Templars with loot from the Crusades. It's a long walk out there, but well worth a close look.

Within the old town, the church of **San Esteban** is easy to spot because of its striking belltower and segment of cloister. A dozen more churches and convents from the 12th to the 16th centuries are likewise within reach. **San Millán** is first-rate Romanesque, with an elaborately carved wooden ceiling. As for secular buildings, the **Casa de los Picos**, with waffle-iron studs on its façade, is found amid the shopping streets downhill from the cathedral.

The **Alcázar** juts out where the city's rocky plinth forms a sharp natural prow, its ramparts making an acute angle over the abyss into which a negligent nursemaid once dropped a 14th-century heir to the Castilian throne. Its towers and turrets give it a flamboyantly un-Spanish fairytale look – a perfect model for any Disney castles – but the attractive bits weren't added until the 19th century. The Army (which owns the place) has filled its chambers with a rather haphazard selection of weaponry, armour, tapestries and works of art, so that paying visitors might have something to see.

So much for the scenery. What hordes of city folk come to Segovia to do each weekend, though, is to eat. The city is the capital of Castilian cuisine, and roasts of lamb (*cordero asado*) and suckling pig (*cochinillo*) are the star dishes for Sunday lunch in Segovia's traditional *mesones*, their walls covered with photos of distinguished former clients.

Spaniards like their meat crisp on the outside, excruciatingly tender but well done within. The best Segovia piglets are *lechones*, nurtured with the milk of barley-fed mothers, and just 21 days old when they go into a brick baker's oven. The

Carnivores' haven, **Restaurante José María**.

late Cándido (*see below*) originated the stunt whereby pork is sliced with the edge of a plate to show how tender it is.

Lamb is also eaten young, and sometimes suckled by two ewes to produce superior meat. As a rule, a quarter-lamb serving two is cooked in a dry earthenware dish rotated according to a secret ritual. Some roasters baste their lamb with pork drippings, but eschew herbs, garlic or salt so as not to interfere with the flavour of the smoke from holly, oak and other fragrant woods. Don't expect *any* vegetables to eat with it; that would be an insult to the meat.

Alcázar de Segovia

921 46 07 59. **Open** *Oct-April* 10am-6pm daily, *May-Sept* 10am-7pm daily. **Admission** 400ptas; free-275ptas concessions; free Tue. **No credit cards.**

Where to stay & eat

Cándido (Plaza Azoguejo 5, 921 42 81 03, average 6,000ptas) is where Orson Welles wolfed down an entire roast piggy and called out for more. Its famous founder, Cándido himself, died a few years ago; the restaurant is now very touristy, and its cooking no better, nor worse, than that of other places nearby, only more expensive. Go for pork, not the lamb. For Castilian cooking with a fancy twist, head for **Mesón del Duque** (C/Cervantes 12, 921 43 05 37, average 5,000ptas). After their roast lamb everyone gets a cholesterol-dissolving slug of brandy on the house. Consistently good, with excellent *cochinillo* and the best lamb in town, is **Restaurante José María** (C/Cronista Lecea

11, 921 46 11 11, average 5,000ptas). After your gargantuan meat-feast, take the time to wander the backstreets in search of a digestive drink.

If you stay the night, you can't get much more atmospheric than **Los Linajes** (C/Dr Velasco 9, 921 46 04 75, rates 8,000-12,000ptas), a 13th-century palace with beamed ceilings, antiques in the rooms and a lush patio.

Getting there

By bus
La Sepulvedana (91 530 48 00) buses run from Paseo de la Florida 11. There are over 30 buses 6.30am-9pm, Mon-Fri, and 20 services Sat, Sun. Last return is at 8pm Mon-Sat, 9pm Sun. Journey time (direct services) 1hr 15min.

By car
N-VI/A6 to Guadarrama, then the N603 (90km/56 miles); or the Navacerrada road from Guadarrama (a slow mountain road).

By train
Eight *Regional* trains daily from Atocha or Chamartín, but be warned: it's a slow journey (2hrs).

Tourist information

Oficina de Turismo
Plaza Mayor 10 (921 46 03 34). **Open** 10am-2pm, 5-8pm daily.

La Granja

About 11 kilometres (7 miles) from Segovia, back towards Madrid on the N601, lies **La Granja de San Ildefonso**, the former hunting estate where Philip V built a scaled-down version of the palace where he spent his childhood, Versailles, to remind him of home. His wife Isabella Farnese, equally out of place in Madrid, added many Italianate touches.

The King liked gardens – even though he was told that a French garden would never take in the harsh sierra – and classical statuary by the hundredweight, arranged around splashing fountains. He imported trees and plants from his dominions to 'improve' the mountain pine groves – look out for the giant California sequoia towering outside the chapel, in semi-tropical company. Nymphs and goddesses cavort in every corner, but nowadays normally without cascades of spray around them, because of the ongoing drought. The palace itself is another that has benefited from major recent restoration work to return it to its full opulence, and has a dazzling collection of cut-glass chandeliers, and one entire wing displaying a mere selection of Spanish and Flemish tapestries from the royal collections.

From the grounds of La Granja there's a spectacular hike over the sierra to **El Paular** and **Rascafría** (*see page 266*). The village of San Ildefonso is often overlooked, but has its own charm, and if you have transport offers an alternative to staying in Segovia itself. Of its bars, **La Fundición** in Plazuela la Calandra is a treat in winter, with a roaring open fire.

Palacio Real de La Granja de San Ildefonso
921 47 00 19. **Open** *Palace* Apr, May 10am-1.30pm, 3-5pm Tue-Fri; 10am-6pm Sat, Sun, holidays; June-Sept 10am-6pm Tue-Sun; Oct-Mar 10am-1.30pm, 5-7pm Tue-Sat; 10am-2pm Sun, holidays. Closed Mon. *Gardens* June-Sept 10am-9pm daily; *Oct-May* 10am-6pm daily. *Fountains operate June-Sept* at 5.30pm Sat, Sun only. **Admission** *Palace* 800ptas; 350ptas concessions. *Gardens* 325ptas; 250ptas concessions. *Both* Wed free for EU citizens. **No credit cards**.

Where to stay & eat

You won't find any roast lamb or suckling pig at **Casa Zaca** (C/Embajadores 6, 921 47 00 87, average 4,000ptas). This family-run restaurant, in business since 1940, is open only for lunch, and you must book in advance. The huge portions of 'home-style' cooking include chunky casseroles and braised ox tongue. **Hostal Las Fuentes** (C/Padre Claret 6, 921 47 10 24, rates 6,500-10,000ptas) is a beautifully restored house with quiet rooms looking down to Segovia or into a flower-filled courtyard.

Getting there

By bus
La Sepulvedana (91 530 48 00) from Estación Sur or Paseo de la Florida 11; there's one bus at 9.30am, Sun only, with return at 7.30pm.

By car
N-VI to Collado Villalba, then M-601 north (78km/48 miles).

Ríofrío

The palace of Ríofrío has cause to feel slighted; despite their proximity, the day is just not long enough to see La Granja and then move on to this purely Italian residence, built for Philip V's widow Isabella Farnese in 1754. It was built in the middle of the best deer-hunting country near Madrid, and later sovereigns also came to this beautiful estate to blast away to their hearts' content.

If hundreds of antlered skulls are to your liking, the hunting museum might appeal. You can also see the chambers where a

Trips Out of Town

La Granja de San Ildefonso, Philip V's Versailles in the Sierra. *See p255*.

heartbroken King Alfonso XII nursed his grief after Mercedes, his bride of a few months, died while still in her teens.

Palacio de Ríofrío

921 47 00 19. **Open** *Oct-May* 10am-1pm, 3-5pm Tue-Sun; closed Mon. *June-Sept* 10am-6pm Tue-Sun; closed Mon. **Admission** 800ptas; 350ptas concessions. Wed free for EU citizens. **No credit cards**.

Getting there

By car

The palace is south-west of Segovia, on the SG-724 side road between the N110 and N603 (90km/56 miles from Madrid).

By train

Segovia trains (*see above*) stop at La Losa village, about 2km (1¼ miles) from Ríofrio.

Alcalá de Henares

Alcalá de Henares lies just 31 kilometres (19 miles) east of Madrid along the N-II Barcelona road. Although its name is Arabic in origin (*Al-khala Nahar*, the Moorish city-fort located here), excavations have shown that this privileged site on the banks of the Henares river has been home to homo sapiens since paleolithic times. Carthaginians, Romans and Visigoths all settled here before the Moors arrived.

Now more or less a subsidiary-city of Madrid, Alcalá once surpassed the capital in cultural importance thanks to its university, founded in 1498 by Cardinal Cisneros, Queen Isabella's mentor and the most influential leader the Spanish Church has ever had. The Universidad Complutense (*Complutum* was the Roman name for the city) was one of the most important in Europe; one of its greatest achievements was the Polyglot Bible, commissioned by Cisneros, a colossal work of scholarship with the text in several languages. Cervantes was also born in Alcalá, in 1547. When the university was moved to Madrid in 1836 the town fell into decline; the university was reopened in 1977, in an attempt to bring back some of the ambience that made Alcalá special for over three centuries.

This effort has paid off, and Alcalá is an interesting place to spend a day, its streets lined with the *Colegios Mayores*, built in the 16th and 17th centuries as student residences, but which now house hotels, restaurants and sections of the modern university. Most impressive of all is the **Colegio de San Ildefonso** on Plaza San Diego, built in 1537-53 and now once again the university rectorate, justly famous for its spectacular Renaissance carved façade and lofty three-tiered patio.

Plaza San Diego connects with the centre of town, the Plaza de Cervantes, lined by cafés and historic buildings such as the **Casa Consistorial** (town hall) and the **Capilla de Oidor**, a 15th-century chapel, now used for exhibitions, which contains a reconstruction (from the same stones) of the Roman font in which Cervantes was baptised. Leading off from the plaza is the historic main street, the **Calle Mayor**, with shaded arcades all along its length, and which after 7pm fills with locals taking their evening stroll. A walk down the street will take you to the **Casa Natal de Cervantes** (open 10.15am-1.30pm, 4-6.30pm Tue-Sun, admission free), a reconstruction of his birthplace; in the street alongside it a plaque marks the home of a later distinguished resident of Alcalá, Manuel Azaña, President of the Spanish Republic defeated in 1939. Next door to the Casa de Cervantes there is also the 1483 **Hospital de Antezana**, with a wonderful plant-shrouded Castilian patio that takes you right back to the Golden Age. There is plenty more to be discovered in a wander around Alcalá's streets.

Trips Out of Town

Where to stay & eat

The **Hostería del Estudiante** (C/de los Colegios 3, 91 888 03 30, rates 10,000-16,000ptas, restaurant average 4,500ptas) is the closest *parador* (*see below*) to Madrid. Occupying an impressive Golden Age *Colegio*, it also has an admired restaurant. Otherwise, **El Palco de Cervantes** (C/Cervantes 2, 91 880 67 78, average 4,000ptas), offers modern Castilian food; nearby, **Las Columnas del 40** (C/Mayor 40, 91 878 90 40; set lunch 900ptas) is a good budget choice. Alcalá is so close to Madrid that it's a very easy day trip, but as well as the *parador* there's the **Hotel Bedel** (Plaza de San Diego 6, 91 889 37 00, rates 9,000ptas), with a view of the San Ildefonso façade from some rooms.

The Paradors

None of the 84 *Paradores Nacionales* dotted around Spain is in Madrid itself. However, **Alcalá de Henares**, **Chinchón**, **Toledo** and other places around the city all boast fine examples of this state-run chain of luxury hotels, with a policy of taking over the most historic building in town – castles, monasteries, palaces – or, failing that, one with the best views of it. All *Paradores* have been beautifully restored. More than just a room for the night, a stay in a *Parador* can make a trip a real experience.

Paradores are not budget hotels (naturally), but with a bit of planning a stay in one can be a not-too-expensive treat. Rates vary, and some *paradores* have higher standards than others: Gredos is around 15,000ptas a night, while Segovia weighs in at 22,000ptas. However, discounts are available for stays of two nights or more on a half-board basis. Rooms can be booked through the chain's local agents around the world (Keytel International, 020 7616 0300, in the UK; Marketing Ahead, 1 800 223 1356, in the USA and Canada), but note that it is cheaper if you book direct through the www.parador.es website. It's a good idea, though, to follow up your online request with at least one call to the (English-speaking) central office in Madrid.

Reservations

Central de Reservas, C/Requena 3 (91 516 66 66/www.parador.es). Metro Opera/bus 3, 25, 33, 39, 148. English spoken.

Getting there

By bus

Continental Auto (91 356 23 07) buses 223 and 223A leave from Metro Cartagena about every 10min, 6.05am-11pm Mon-Sat, less frequently Sun.

By car

N-II/A2, a 25min drive (31km/19 miles).

By train

Cercanías C-2, C-7a; at least five trains an hour each way 5.10am-11.30pm daily. From the station it's a 10min walk to the centre (go straight down Paseo de la Estación).

Tourist information

Oficina de Turismo

Callejón Santa María 1 (91 889 26 94). **Open** *Sept-June* 10am-2pm, 4-6.30pm daily. *July, Aug* 10am-2pm, 5-7pm Tue-Sun; closed Mon.

Aranjuez & Chinchón

Just 45 kilometres (28 miles) south of Madrid, **Aranjuez** is an oasis in the arid plains of central Spain. Famous for its royal palace, asparagus and giant strawberries, it sits in a wide valley formed by the Jarama and Tajo (Tagus) rivers. The area has been inhabited since prehistoric times, and has seen Romans and Moors come and go. Aranjuez reached its greatest splendour, however, between the 17th and 19th centuries, when its palace served as the official spring residence of the Kings and Queens of Spain and their Court.

The mixed baroque and classical **Real Palacio** and its gardens have dominated life here for centuries. When the Court came to town in the spring, the village's population of 6,000 increased four fold. First built for Philip II in the 1560s, the palace was greatly enlarged in the 1770s by Charles III, who had Francesco Sabatini add a further two wings. Despite all this architectural fiddling, it is surprisingly harmonious. Inside are lavish salons (the Throne Room, the Dress Museum, the extraordinary Porcelain Room) filled with treasures. The gardens that inspired Rodrigo's *Concierto de Aranjuez* lie between the palace and the River Tagus, and are wonderful places for a stroll. Some sections (the **Jardín de la Isla** and **Jardín del Príncipe**) were laid out in the 16th century. A restoration programme has done wonders to return flora and fountains to their original splendour.

The **Casita del Labrador** is worth a visit in itself. In the middle of the gardens, this rococo fancy was built in 1803 as an indulgence for silly King Charles IV. Inside there are painted ceilings, tapestry-lined walls, and porcelain and marble floors, some of them embedded with Roman mosaics brought from Mérida in Extremadura. The *Casita* can only be visited with guided tours: places are limited, and in great demand at weekends, so make sure you book ahead or get there early in order to reserve a slot for the same day.

Real Palacio de Aranjuez

91 891 13 44. **Open** *Palaces* 10am-6.15pm Tue-Sun; closed Mon. *Gardens* Oct-Mar 10am-7.30pm daily; Apr-Sept 8am-8.30pm daily. **Admission** *Palace* 800ptas; 350ptas concessions. *Casita del Labrador (guided tours only)* 600ptas; 350ptas concessions. *Casa de Marinos* 425ptas; 325ptas concessions. *Gardens* free. All free Wed for EU citizens. **No credit cards**.

Where to eat

In the centre of town, near the main square, **Casa José** (C/Abastos 32, 91 891 14 88, set lunch 3,500ptas) is regarded by many as the finest south of Madrid. International cuisine is given a skilfully distinctive slant here with fresh local produce, such as asparagus and strawberries. Also recommended, for traditional Castilian fare, is **El Molino de Aranjuez** (C/Príncipe 21, 91 892 42 33, average 5,000ptas). There is an attractive campsite in Aranjuez, **Soto del Castillo** (*see page 53*).

Getting there

By bus

Autominibus (91 530 46 06) 423, 423a from Estación Sur, hourly 8am-10pm Mon-Fri, 8am-9pm Sat, 9am-10pm Sun. Last return 7pm Mon-Sat, 8pm Sun.

By car

N-IV, then M-305 (47km/29 miles).

By train

Cercanías C-3 from Atocha, trains every 15-20min 5am-9pm, every two hours until 11.55pm, Mon-Fri, with a reduced service at weekends. Last return 11.34pm. For a special treat, especially for families, the steam-powered 'Strawberry Train' (*Tren de la Fresa*) runs on summer weekends and holidays (*see p195*).

Tourist information

Oficina de Turismo

Plaza del Puente (91 891 04 27). **Open** *Oct-June* 10am-1pm, 3-5pm Tue-Sun. *July-Sept* 10am-2pm, 4-6pm Tue-Sun; closed Mon.

Chinchón

A little east of Aranjuez and 45 kilometres (28 miles) out of Madrid lies Chinchón, one of the most picturesque towns in the province. It's a popular weekend getaway for Madrileños, who fill its *mesones* for lunch and dinner.

Winters are cold in this part of Castile, and Chinchón is known for its *anís*, an aniseed spirit popular with Spanish workers for getting their motors running on frosty mornings. It's most famous, though, for its grand town square, the **Plaza Mayor**. An oft-filmed and unforgettable setting for bullfights during local *fiestas* in June and August, the plaza is a giant amphitheatre ringed by three-storey, wooden balcony-lined houses that are centuries old. The whole is overlooked by the impressive town church.

Mesones abound in this town of fewer than 5,000 inhabitants. Several have tables on balconies overlooking the Plaza Mayor, and many have splendid dining rooms lined with *tinajas*, the baked-clay casks formerly used for storing wine, or impressive wine cellars (*bodegas*, or *cuevas* as they are called in Chinchón) where you can try the strong red.

A good place to sample *anís* is at the splendid **Parador**; even teetotallers enjoy a walk through its Moorish-style gardens. The ruins of a medieval castle, burned by Napoleon's troops and later used as an *anís* distillery, can be seen (from the outside) on a hill west of the town.

Where to stay & eat

Mesón La Cerca (C/Cerca 9, 91 893 55 65, set lunch 2,500ptas) has fine traditional fare at good prices, or tuck into roast lamb and bean stews while enjoying the view over the plaza at **Mesón de la Virreina** (Plaza Mayor 28, 91 894 00 15, average 3,500ptas). The town also has one of the most attractive *paradores*, the **Parador de Chinchón** (Avda Generalísimo 1, 91 894 08 36, rates 10,000-16,000ptas), in a 17th-century former Augustinian convent, with delicious gardens and a restaurant where you can sample such specialities as venison with truffles and sweet, eggy puddings.

Getting there

By bus

La Veloz (91 409 76 02) bus 337 from Conde de Casal Metro. Buses every hour on the hour 7am-10pm Mon-Fri, 8am-9pm Sat, and every 1hr 30min, 9am-10.30pm Sun. Last return 7.30pm Mon-Sat, 9pm Sun. Journey time about an hour.

By car

N-III, then M-311, or N-IV/M-404 (45km/28 miles).

Toledo

Just an hour's journey south of Madrid, Toledo
bears little relation to its late-coming neighbour.
Madrid did not even exist when Toledo was
capital of Visigothic Spain (AD 567-711). Toledo
has been Muslim, Jewish and very Christian, all
at the same time. The fruitful cohabitation of
the three great religions in Toledo in the last
300 years of the first millennium AD is unique
in the Western world. It was a centre for
Mozárabes (Christians who lived under Muslim
rule with a semi-Arabic liturgy), and later the
Mudéjares, Muslims who did the reverse
after the Christian conquest. At one time it
was also the most important centre of Jewish
scholarship anywhere in the world.

Toledo today is very much a must-see for
visitors to Madrid, and sometimes struggles
to absorb its busloads of day trippers.
Nevertheless, it's still very worth the
journey: the old city is a magical, up-and-
down maze of narrow, often very steep alleys,
many without name-signs, so that getting lost
at least once is near inevitable, and part of the
fascination (the free maps available from the

tourist offices are a great help). The best
way to avoid the crowds is to visit midweek –
Mondays are especially quiet, but note that
most of the major sights are closed – or out of
season. Most importantly, if you can, take the
time to stay overnight. As night falls, after the
tours have gone, you'll find yourself largely
alone to wander Toledo's alleys and hidden
corners, its abrupt contrasts of light and shade.
Next day, make the effort to get up early and
feel the city slowly come to life.

THE BISAGRA TO THE CATHEDRAL

Whether you stay here or just come for the day,
a logical place to begin exploring is the 11th-
century **Puerta de Bisagra** (1, on the map,
see left) on the north side of the old city, the
only remaining Moorish gate in the medieval
walls and the point of entry if you come from
Madrid by bus, car or train (next to it there is
also a tourist office). Before going into the old
city proper, walk back a little way down the
main street up to the walls to the **Museo
Duque de Lerma** (2; C/Cardenal Tavera 2,
925 22 04 51, open 10.30am-1.30pm, 3.30-6pm
daily, admission 500ptas). Housed in the 1541
Hospital de Tavera, with a fine chapel and
Renaissance courtyards, it has works by
Tintoretto, Zurbarán and,
of course, El Greco – just
the first you will see in his
adopted home.

There is an 'alternative',
little-appreciated route
from the Puerta de Bisagra
into town, to take which
you turn right (looking at
the gate), along Calle
Alfonso VI and Paseo de
Recaredo, and so get a fine
view of the outside of the
walls before entering the
old city at **Puerta
del Cambrón** (3). It's
little-known in good
part because it seems so
natural to head uphill
through the Bisagra itself.
Behind the gate, the
superb *Mudéjar* brick
church of **Santiago del
Arrabal** (4) stands out,
with an impressive tower.
Part of it was once a
mosque, but after the
Christian conquest it was
rebuilt as a church.

The maze of streets on
either side as you head up
Calle Real del Arrabal was

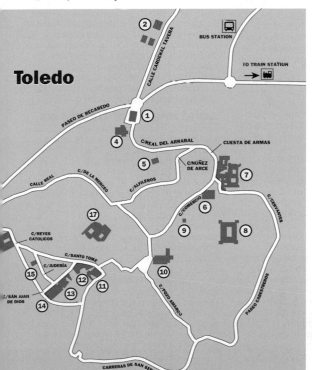

Toledo

Trips Out of Town

Santiago del Arrabal. *See p259.*

the *Arrabal* – an area originally outside the Christian city. Off to the right in Calle Cristo de la Luz there is a tenth-century mosque that is the oldest surviving building in Toledo, the **Mezquita Cristo de la Luz (5)**, built in 999. It is kept locked, but its main features are easily visible from the street.

Real de Arrabal leads into Cuesta de Armas, which in turn winds round to the centre of the city, the **Plaza de Zocodover (6)**. Lined with café tables for most of the year, it has even managed discreetly to incorporate a McDonalds without losing its provincial charm. By the plaza is the magnificent Renaissance **Hospital de Santa Cruz (7**; C/Miguel de Cervantes 3, 925 22 10 36, open 10am-6pm Mon-Sat, 10am-2pm Sun, admission 200ptas), now a museum, with works by El Greco and Ribera and superb tapestries.

After a drink in one of the Zocodover's cafés to take in the local scene, there are several options. Very visible from the plaza is the **Alcázar (8**; 925 22 30 38, open 9.30am-2.30pm Mon-Sun; admission 200ptas), the enormous fortress that towers over the city. Built on the highest point of Toledo, this was the scene of a two-month siege after the outbreak of the Civil War in 1936, when supporters of the military uprising barricaded themselves inside.They

were relieved only when General Franco and his troops arrived from Seville, and the Alcázar acquired a special place in Francoist mythology. It now houses a military museum that, despite 25 years of democracy, is still a monument to the fortress's defenders; in future, it will probably also house the very sizeable collection of the Museo del Ejército in Madrid.

Alternatively, if you go on from the Zocodover up the nearest thing to a main street in the old town, Calle del Comercio – passing, off to the left in Calle Tornerías, the **Mezquita de las Tornerías (9)**, a beautiful 11th-century mosque imaginatively restored as an art and craft gallery – you eventually emerge into Toledo's second main square, the **Plaza del Ayuntamiento**, with the 16th-century town hall itself (with a tourist office), the **Palacio Arzobispal** (Archbishop's Palace) and the **Cathedral (10**; 925 22 22 41, open 10.30am-7pm Mon-Sat, 2-7pm Sun, admission 400ptas).

A walk all around the cathedral is a good way to get your bearings, and a feel of the neighbourhood. Completed one year after Columbus discovered America, work upon it had begun 250 years earlier, and a Christian church is said to have been founded here in the first century AD by Saint Eugene, first Bishop of Toledo. Outside, a 91m- (298ft-) high tower, flying buttresses and enormous doors catch the eye; inside, the dark, cavernous space is divided into five naves, supported by 88 columns. Perhaps its most extraordinary feature is the **Choir**, carved with scenes from the Bible and of the fall of Granada. Also unforgettable is the **Transparente**, a baroque *trompe-l'oeil* side chapel painted by Narciso Tomé in 1732.

SANTO TOMÉ & THE SYNAGOGUES

On Plaza del Ayuntamiento, signs for the *Casa del Greco* indicate the way to more narrow alleys that soon lead you to Plaza del Salvador, and one of the most visited parts of Toledo. The first major building you reach is the **Taller del Moro (11**; 925 22 44 00, open 10am-2pm, 4-6pm Tue-Sat, 10am-2pm Sun, admission 100ptas), a *Mudéjar* workshop that now houses exhibitions of Toledo craftsmanship; nearby on Calle Santo Tomé (and throughout the old city), there are plenty of shops offering Toledo's most famous artisan food product, marzipan. Behind the *Taller* down Calle San Juan de Dios, camera-packing crowds lead you straight to the church of **Santo Tomé (12**; 925 25 60 98, open *Oct-June* 10am-6pm daily; *July-Sept* 10am-7pm daily, admission 200ptas), with its beautiful *Mudéjar* tower and, inside, El Greco's *Entierro del Conde de Orgaz*. Almost beside it is the **Casa-Museo de El Greco (13)** itself. It has never actually been confirmed that the artist lived here, but it's an attractive reconstruction of a Toledan home of that era, with several works by him. It has been closed for some time for restoration, but it's worth checking whether it's open.

This area was once the *Judería*, the Jewish quarter of medieval Toledo, and contains some of the finest works of Jewish-*mudéjar* architecture. The Jewish presence in Toledo has been much easier to appreciate since extensive restoration work was carried out for 1992, as an act of atonement on the 500th anniversary of the expulsion of Jews from Spain. At the end of Calle San Juan de Dios, past the Casa de El Greco, is the **Sinagoga del Tránsito (14)**, built in 1357 and used as a church after 1492, which today houses a fascinating museum of Sephardic Jewish culture, the **Museo Sefardí** (925 22 36 65, open 10am-2pm, 4-6pm Tue-Sat, 10am-2pm Sun, admission 400ptas). This is now another of the city's most visited sites; the museum aside, the synagogue is a remarkable mix of ornate Moorish columns, Gothic touches and Hebrew inscriptions.

At the opposite end of the very narrow Calle de la Judería is the second of the surviving medieval synagogues, the **Sinagoga de Santa María la Blanca (15**; 925 22 72 57, open *Oct-June* 10am-2pm, 3.30-6pm, *July-Sept*

The millennial **Mezquita Cristo de la Luz.**

10am-2pm, 3.30-7pm, daily, admission 200ptas). Its simple interior, dominated by a series of horseshoe arches, is extremely beautiful, in spite of the intromission of a baroque altar, added when it was used as a church. Behind it, at Calle del Angel 15, there is a lovely bookshop dedicated to matters Jewish, the **Casa de Jacob**, and further down the same street there is a great old shop selling handmade lamps and glassware.

The main street of the *Judería* is now, ironically, called Calle de los Reyes Católicos, upon which, very near Santa María la Blanca, there looms up the very Christian **Monasterio de San Juan de los Reyes (16**; 925 22 83 02, open *Oct-June* 10am-2pm, 3.30-6pm, *July-Sept* 10am-2pm, 3.30-7pm daily, admission 200ptas). Built for Ferdinand and Isabella themselves, it has a dramatic Gothic cloister.

The labyrinth of streets to the east has fewer monuments, but is great for aimless wandering. A walk up the streets opposite San Juan de los Reyes will, with twists and turns, lead you to the **Iglesia de San Román (17**; open 10am-2pm, 4-6pm Tue-Sat, 10am-2pm Sun, admission 100ptas), which houses a rag-bag collection of Visigothic finds. A further meander away to the north is **Plaza de la Merced**, with the headquarters of the regional government of Castilla-La Mancha, **Casa Rata**, a traditional marzipan and sweets shop, and a likeable bar, **Abracadabra**. Leave the square by Calle Buzones to take in the lovely Calle Santa Clara before heading back to the Zocodover.

Other options include a walk around the south side of the walls, finishing at Paseo del Tránsito, close to the Museo Sefardi, where there is a park that's a lovely place to sit and watch the sunset while deciding where to have dinner. For another great view, back over the whole city, head out of town over the River Tagus by the Puente de San Martín, and turn right along the Carretera de Piedrabuena.

Where to eat

Toledo is full of restaurants that look like tacky tourist traps, but are often actually (perhaps surprisingly) pretty good. Definitely not tacky, and located up one of the streets that winds off to the right as you climb up from Puerta de Bisagra, is **La Abadía** (C/Núñez de Arce 3, 925 25 11 40, average 3,500ptas), mainly frequented by locals, and occupying part of an old bishop's palace. There's a cosy bar with imported beers by the entrance, and modern cuisine as well as the traditional favourites of game and partridge. In the same street is the internationally renowned **Marcial & Pedro** (C/Núñez del Arce 11, 925 22 07 00, average

5,000ptas), famous above all for its game, but which also has imaginative starters, fine fish and a good wine list. In the very centre of the old town is **Alex** (C/Amador de los Ríos 10, 925 22 39 63, average 3,000ptas), which nevertheless allows you to eat outside in a tree-lined courtyard. It has well-priced traditional *Toledano* fare: rabbit, game, partridge, and decent wines. Nearby, **Mesón Palacios** (C/Alfonso X el Sabio 3, 925 21 59 22, set lunch 1,000ptas) is a good budget choice.

    Asador Adolfo (C/Granada 6, 925 22 73 21, average 5,000ptas) is one of the best-known traditional restaurants in the city. Its fame rests on superbly-prepared roast meats, local specialities such as game and partridge, and impeccable service. **Placido** (Santo Tomé 6, 925 22 26 03, average 4,000ptas) is another good upscale choice. In a former convent school, it offers a choice of eating areas: inside, in a courtyard, or in its own olive grove – and rich traditional dishes. Also in a pretty courtyard is the **Corral de Don Diego** (Corral de Don Diego 5, 925 23 35 52, set menu 2,000ptas), between the Alcázar and the synagogues. It looks touristy, but the food's good (if a little overpriced), and it's a treat to sit outside here on a summer evening. Finally, just outside the walls by the Puerta del Cambrón, is **Pedro** (Bajada de San Martín 1, 925 21 58 07, closed Aug, set menu 995ptas), a straightforward locals' bar with bargain local dishes.

Where to stay

The première accommodation in Toledo is that found at the **Parador Conde de Orgaz** (Paseo de los Cigarrales, 925 22 18 50, rates 10,000-18,500ptas), the luxurious *parador*, with a fine restaurant and a wonderful pool. You'll need a car or a cab to get from there into town, but it's worth it for the superb views over the city. Almost as impressive is the **Hostal del Cardenal** (Paseo de Recaredo 24, 925 22 49 00, rates 12,500-16,000ptas), which occupies an 18th-century former palace built into the Puerta de Bisagra. The downside is that its views are mostly over the new town, but the building is wonderful, and delightfully cool in summer; the restaurant is just as superb, with a lovely terrace in the palace garden.

    The best hotel inside the old city is the **Alfonso VI** (General Moscardó 2, 985 22 26 00, rates 12,000-17,500ptas), close to the Alcázar. Ask for one of the rooms with great views out of Toledo toward the south. **Hostal Madrid** (C/Marqués de Mendigorri 7, 925 22 11 14, rates 7,000-9,500ptas), is a good cheaper option. Clean, well looked after, and with air-conditioning, it has more lovely views from some of its rooms.

Life in the **Plaza de Zocodover**. *See p260.*

Getting there

By bus

Galeano Continental from Estación Sur (91 527 29 61), departures every 2hr from 6.30am, last return at 10pm, Mon-Sat; first bus from Madrid at 8.30pm, last return at 11.30pm, Sun, holidays. There are direct (on the hour) and local (on the 2hr) services; journey time direct is 50min. From the new bus station it's a 5-10min walk to the Puerta de Bisagra, or there are cabs to take you the rest of the way.

By car

N-401 off the M-30, a fast road (70km/44 miles).

By train

From Atocha, ten trains each day roughly every two hours, 7am-8.25pm Mon-Sat, eight trains 8.30am-8.25pm Sat, Sun. Last return 8.56pm daily. The train is more pleasant than the bus, but a little more expensive; from Toledo's neat 1920s neo-*mudéjar* station, take local bus 6 to the Puerta de Bisagra, or face a long uphill walk.

Tourist information

Oficina Municipal de Turismo

Plaza del Ayuntamiento (925 25 40 30).
Open 4.30-7pm Mon, 10.30am-2.30pm, 4.30-7pm Tue-Sun.

Oficina de Turismo

Puerta de Bisagra (925 22 08 43).
Open *Oct-June* 9am-6pm Mon-Fri, 9am-7pm Sat, 9am-3pm Sun. *July-Sept* 9am-7pm Mon-Sat, 9am-3pm-Sun.

Trips Out of Town

The Sierras

For a real change of air and scenery, take advantage of the magnificent ring of mountains around Madrid.

From Las Vistillas, just south of the Palacio Real, and many other places in central Madrid, it's very easy to see the giant peaks of the Guadarrama, the massive mountain screen that runs across the northern and western horizon. It's an often-repeated fact that, with an altitude of 650 metres (2,135 feet), Madrid is the highest capital in Europe, but it's less appreciated that it is also one of the European cities closest to high mountain ranges. In less than an hour's journey from the city it's possible to be amid superb mountain scenery, with any number of walks to choose from, from gentle strolls to routes for serious mountaineers. Many outdoor sports are also available (*see pages 271-2*).

The standard common-sense rules for mountain walking apply in the Sierras. It's essential to have local maps and know how to use them, and also useful to carry a compass. For good places to buy maps and walking guides in Madrid, *see page 163*. Summer temperatures are high and the sun intense, so high-factor suncream, sunglasses and a hat are indispensable. In winter, temperatures drop below freezing and there can be dangerous patches of ice and snow. Only experienced walkers should try the higher walks in winter. Also, weather in the mountains is notoriously changeable: check forecasts before you go.

Be sure to buy food and water in Madrid or on the way before your walk. Water is often scarce in the mountains, and you'll need an adequate supply.

Sierra de Guadarrama

The Guadarrama, sometimes just called the Sierra de Madrid, runs from El Escorial (*see page 249*) in the south-west to Somosierra in the north-east, and separates the two Castilian *mesetas*. These mountains have for centuries been appreciated for their clear air, abundance of springs and forests and wealth of game and other wildlife. Many Madrileños have second homes in the Sierra, and many others regularly travel the 50 kilometres (31 miles) there to enjoy walking, climbing, skiing and

other activities away from the big city. The following is only a selection of the many walks possible in the area. The regional government has produced some easy-to-use free walking maps in English, available at the tourist office at Mercado Puerta de Toledo (*see page 287*).

Puerto de Guadarrama

Also known as the Alto de los Leones, the Guadarrama pass has formed part of the main route from Madrid to Valladolid and the north-east for centuries. It was a battlefront during the Civil War, and Hemingway chose to set much of his *For Whom the Bell Tolls* there. The nearest public transport to the pass is the train station at Tablada, three kilometres (two miles) below the Puerto on the Madrid side.

Guadarrama to Peguerinos

Once you've walked or otherwise made your way up to the main pass, it's possible to walk, cycle or, if you have an off-road vehicle, drive along a dirt track south-west for 30km (19 miles) to the remote village of **Peguerinos**, from where there are buses and a fully paved road to El Escorial. The track (signposted) veers off to the left as you come up the hill from the village of **Guadarrama**, among a jumble of radio towers and satellite dishes. Before leaving Guadarrama, check out the timewarp café **Casa Hilario**, with excellent views westward over the valley of San Rafael, and great-value rolls for picnics. Set back from the road on the brow of a hill are Casa Hilario's original premises, which date back to a time when getting this far out of Madrid on the way to Segovia merited a stopover for lunch. The track to Peguerinos also leads to several campsites.

Peña del Arcipreste de Hita

Another good walk runs north of the Puerto. From Tablada station, walk up 2km (1¼ miles) – not all the way to the pass – to km 56, and take a well-marked forestry track on the right to the **Peña del Arcipreste de Hita** (1,527m/5,010ft), a crag declared a 'natural monument' in honour of Juan Ruiz, Archpriest of Hita and author of the *Libro del Buen Amor*, a bawdy 14th-century classic. The track eventually descends again, to reach the station at Cercedilla. This walk takes about three hours, passing pines bent into fantastic shapes by the wind, and panoramic views of the valley to the south.

Trips Out of Town

Where to stay & eat

Camping La Nava (908 11 20 38, closed Nov-Mar), four kilometres (2½ miles) from the Puerto, and **Valle de Enmedio** (no phone), 11 kilometres (6½ miles) along the track, are two good campsites on the Peguerinos road. For food, it has to be **Casa Hilario** (no phone, average 1,500ptas), on the crest of the pass.

Getting there

By bus

There are no buses to Puerto de Guadarrama. To get back after a walk, Larrea route 684 runs from Cercedilla to Moncloa (last return, 6.45pm daily); to get back from Peguerinos, take the 665 to San Lorenzo de El Escorial and go on from there (*see p249*).

By car

N-VI to Puerto de Guadarrama (55km/34 miles). To get back from Peguerinos, go via El Escorial, 23km (14 miles) away. From Cercedilla, take the M-995 to the N-VI.

By train

For Tablada, there are trains on the Segovia line from Atocha and Chamartín. To get back, *Cercanías* C-8b runs hourly from Cercedilla, until 10.40pm daily.

The little mountain town of **Cercedilla** stands at the foot of a valley that leads up to the pass that forms the oldest-known route across the Sierra, the **Puerto de la Fuenfría** (1,796 metres/5,895 feet). Along the valley there is a *Calzada Romana* (Roman Road), which dates back to the first century AD, with two fine Roman bridges at El Descalzo and Enmedio. The pass is also an important junction of modern footpaths, and has been thoughtfully developed with a range of walks to suit all abilities and timescales. It is also possible to hire horses to explore the area.

Cercedilla is a charming town, its income boosted in summer as affluent Madrileños take up residence in their mountain retreats, and others just trek up on the train to escape the city heat. Even in winter, an overnight stay is worthwhile, especially if you want to try any of the longer walks possible nearby.

The most leisurely excursion from Cercedilla is on the narrow-gauge *Cercanías* line (C-9) that runs through fine scenery up to the Cotos ski station, a charming way to get up to and beyond the Puerto de Navacerrada (*see page 265*), especially when it's snowing. Alternatively, from the *Cercanías* station in Cercedilla, a 45-minute walk up the M-966 (the main road in front of you)

will bring you to a stretch of open woodland, **Las Dehesas**, with an **information centre** that's an essential port of call for visitors to the valley, with good free maps, some in English, and often some English-speaking staff. Las Dehesas, especially the part further up near the Casa Cirilo restaurant, is a very popular picnic spot, with natural spring swimming pools nearby.

The *Calzada Romana* to Fuenfría

A good walk to try in an afternoon is the one through the woods from the information centre up to Puerto de la Fuenfría, returning via Collado Ventoso, which takes about two hours. Check details on the information centre maps. The Roman road, well or poorly conserved by turns, climbs steep slopes to reach the pass; follow signposts for the *Calzada Romana*, and carry on for about 20 minutes until you reach a large map, carved in wood, which shows the key landmarks and different walks (graded by colour). From there, continue to the next Roman bridge, the Puente de Enmedio, where the path turns to the right, to go left again before continuing up to the Puerto. A track to the right climbs in about 30 minutes to **Collado Ventoso**, with great views across the pines of the Fuenfría valley. The giant peak ahead of you is the **Siete Picos** (*see page 265*). Turn right down the signposted *Camino de Schmid* to return to the wooden map and Las Dehesas.

Walking alternatives

A very easy walk is the one along the road that follows the C-9 rail line all the way from Cercedilla up past **Camorritos**: a round trip of about 8km (five miles); just follow the rail track from the station. Experienced walkers might prefer the 14 kilometre (8½ mile) round trip on the *Camino Schmid*, or take the *Mujer Muerta*, which takes about nine hours – again, visit the information centre for maps, or get walking guides in Madrid (*see page 163*).

Where to stay & eat

Casa Gómez (C/Emilio Serrano 40, 91 852 01 46, average 2,000ptas), opposite Cercedilla station, is a simple restaurant with good-quality meals; excellent tapas, plus roast lamb or suckling pig, can be had at **El Chivo Loco** (C/Pontezuela 23, 91 852 34 39, average 2,500ptas), in the square behind the town hall.

Of places to stay in Cercedilla, **Hostal Longinos** (C/Emilio Serrano 71, 91 852 15 11, rates 8,000-12,000ptas), just up the main street from the station, is the most attractive; booking ahead is a must in summer. On the same street at no.3, **Hostal El Frontón** (91 852 39 80, rates 5,000-8,000ptas) is simpler, but fine for a night. There are two **youth hostels**, both near Las Dehesas – **Albergue Las Dehesas** (91 852 01 35, rates 1,200-1,700ptas) and **Albergue La Castora** (91 852 03 34, same rates).

Stunning hills at **Cercedilla**. *See p264.*

Getting there

By bus
Larrea bus 684 runs hourly from Moncloa to Cercedilla and back.

By car
N-VI to Guadarrama, then M-995 to Cercedilla, and M-966 to Puerto de la Fuenfría (56km/35 miles).

By train
Cercanías C-8b to Cercedilla; trains hourly. Going back, the last train leaves Cercedilla at 10.37pm.

Tourist information

Centro de Información Valle de la Fuenfría
Carretera de las Dehesas, km 2, Cercedilla (91 852 22 13). **Open** 9am-6pm daily.

Puerto de Navacerrada

The pass of **Navacerrada** (1,860 metres/6,104 feet) is, with **Cotos** and **Valdesquí** to the north-east, the main skiing centre of the Sierra. Outside the winter season, the ski station offers other activities (*see page 271*), and there are great mountain walks nearby.

Los Siete Picos
This is a magnificent walk along one of the Sierra's main ridges, through the seven granite peaks, the *Siete Picos*, that run west towards Cercedilla. There are superb views over the pine forests of Valsaín, home to much of the area's wildlife. From the *Cercanías* station at Navacerrada, walk to the top of the pass, where the main road goes on to Segovia and another turns off for Cotos and Valdesquí, to the right; the path is to the left, signposted to the *telesilla* or ski lift. From here you can reach the very highest of the *Siete Picos* (2,138m/7,016ft) in an hour and a half; from there, head on down to Cercedilla, following the path until the saddle between the fifth and sixth peaks; once there, dip down and south towards Camorritos. This takes about 4-5 hours.

Navacerrada to Fuenfría
Another route from Navacerrada (5hrs or more), is to follow the path signposted as *Camino Schmid* by the **Venta Arias** café, towards a military residence known as *El Chalet de Aviación*. Shortly before you reach it a path turns left into the pine forests, indicated by yellow signs. It meanders up through the forest for about an hour, to meet another path signed in yellow on the right, which will take you to the Fuenfría pass. Further along there are two more options: a shorter route back to the road to Navacerrada, or a longer path that goes to Fuenfría or to Navacerrada via the *Siete Picos*. This is a well-walked route, and even in winter one meets other hikers who can tell you if you're on the right track.

La Cuerda Larga
'The Long Cord' is a much longer walk in the opposite direction, eastwards from Navacerrada to the Puerto de la Morcuera (1,800m/5,908ft), finishing by Miraflores de la Sierra. For the most part the path is above 2,000 m/6,560 ft; there are panoramic views to the south of La Pedriza and its ever-present griffon vultures, and over pine forests in the Valle de Lozoya to the north. The whole route takes 7hrs: the path is clear enough, if hard going at times.

Where to stay & eat

La Fonda Real (Carretera de Madrid km 52.5, 91 856 03 05, rates 12,000-18,000ptas) is a restored 18th-century lodge below Navacerrada pass, with wonderful views. It also has a fine restaurant, with Castilian staples, a log fire in winter and a splendid terrace in summer. The youth hostel, the **Albergue Alvaro Iglesias** (91 852 38 87, rates 1,200-1,700ptas), has good facilities and a beautiful location.

Getting there

By bus

Larrea (91 530 48 00) bus 691 from Moncloa, once every two hours. If returning from Miraflores de la Sierra, Colmenarejo bus 725 bus runs to Plaza Castilla; the last bus is at 8.10pm Mon-Fri, 9.55pm Sat, 9pm Sun.

By car

N-VI to Collado Villalba, then M-601 to Puerto de Navacerrada (57km/36 miles). To get back from Cercedilla, *see p265*.

By train

Cercanías C-8b to Cercedilla, then C-9 to Puerto de Navacerrada. There are four trains daily Mon-Fri, hourly Sat, Sun. The last C-8b train back from Cercedilla is at about 7.30pm. From Miraflores de la Sierra, trains on the Burgos line run to Charmartín.

Tourist information

Edificio Deporte y Montaña

Puerto de Navacerrada (91 852 33 02/ www.puertonavacerra.com). **Open** 9am-6pm daily.

Valle de Lozoya

The **Valle de Lozoya** is a magnificent broad mountain valley that runs north-east, parallel to the main ridge of the Sierra, from the pass of Puerto de los Cotos (1,830 metres/6,006 feet), north-east of Navacerrada. There are two popular ways into it: by train, to Cotos, at the very end of the narrow-gauge *Cercanías* line (C-9) from Cercedilla, and by road, whether from Navacerrada, continuing over the Puerto de los Cotos on the M-604, or directly from Madrid via Colmenar Viejo and Miraflores de la Sierra. The village of **Rascafría** at the western end of the valley and **Monasterio de El Paular** are both well worth a visit. The Benedictine monastery, a short way south of the village, dates back to the 14th century and is still partly occupied by monks, even though most of it is now a hotel. The monastery entrance can be visited.

El Palero

There is a very pleasant, quite easy downhill walk (about 3hrs) from the **Puerto de los Cotos** to El Paular, via the *El Palero* route. This is one of the historic paths of the Sierra; it's now part of the GR10 long-distance path, marked in red and white. From Cotos, follow the M-604 road downhill for about

Ponder eternity at the monastery of **El Paular**.

0.5km to the **Casa Marcelino** café, on the left, to find the clearly signposted path. On the way down you cross pine forests at the head of the Lozoya valley, refuge of the last roe deer in the Sierra, and any number of streams and springs. The path follows the larger stream of La Umbria to bring you to the road again, where you turn left for the monastery, under a kilometre away. A little way further on there are some natural swimming pools at **Las Presillas**. On summer weekends they can get crowded, but they still make a perfect stop-off and picnic point.

El Paular to La Granja

There is also an ancient path right across the Sierra between El Paular and the palace of **La Granja** (*see page 255*), through Rascafría. To find it, walk west out of the village of Rascafría, past the new schools, and cross the dense oak woods, looking out for wild boar. Climb up to the Puerto del Reventón (2,034m/6,675ft), and continue downhill on the Segovia side until you reach pines again and the gardens of La Granja. The paths are poorly marked, but the walk is not hard-going. The whole hike takes about five hours.

Trips Out of Town

Peñalara

Serious walkers can tackle the highest peak in the Guadarrama, **Peñalara** (2,430m/7,970ft), reachable from Puerto de los Cotos. It's not too difficult to get to the top in about three hours, but the climb is quite steep and rocky. From Cotos station (which in winter offers hot soup and food), walk up under the Zabala chairlift (or take the lift), pass the peak of Dos Hermanas and continue to the main summit, from where you can see the southernmost point of the Sierra and north to Lozoya; to get back, walk down in an arc, north past Risco Claveles and the lakes of Laguna de Los Pájaros and Laguna Grande until you reach Puerto de los Cotos. A less taxing alternative, especially for summer, is just to walk up to the Laguna Grande, leaving the main path and following signs to the Zabala mountain refuge. The lake is behind it. Even in August the water is freezing, but after a walk it's very much worth a dip.

Where to stay & eat

Briscas (Plaza España 13, 91 869 12 26, average 2,000ptas) is a great-value restaurant in Rascafría's main square, with a lively terrace in summer. **Hostal Rosaly** (Avda del Valle 39, 91 869 12 13, rates 5,000-10,000ptas) is a low-key family-run hotel, with horses to hire.

It's also possible to stay amid the (austere) splendour of El Valle de El Paular. The 58-room **Santa María del Paular**, (91 869 10 11, rates 7,500-14,500ptas), occupies the former monastery cloister; its simply-furnished rooms still have a monastic air, but it's delightfully peaceful, and offers a choice of two restaurants. Male readers (only) seeking a place of contemplation can stay alongside at the **Monastery** itself (91 869 14 25) for 2,000ptas a night – for a minimum three nights' stay, and a maximum of ten. There is also a youth hostel at El Paular, the **Albergue Juvenil Los Batanes** (91 869 15 11, rates 1,200-1,700ptas).

Getting there

By bus

To or from Rascafría, take La Castellana bus 194, which leaves Madrid from Plaza Castilla, at 2.30pm, 6pm Mon-Fri, 8am, 6pm, Sat, 8am Sun. The last bus back is at 5pm Mon-Fri, 10.30pm Sat, 6pm Sun.

By car

For Puerto de los Cotos, take the N-VI to Collado-Villalba, M-601 to Puerto de Navacerrada, then M-604 (64km/40 miles). For Rascafría, go via Cotos, or the M-607 to Colmenar Viejo, M-609 to Soto del Real, M-611 to Rascafría (80km/50 miles).

By train

For Puerto de los Cotos, take the *Cercanías* C-8b to Cercedilla, then line C-9 to Cotos; four trains daily Mon-Fri, hourly Sat, Sun.

Manzanares el Real & La Pedriza

La Pedriza is a wild region of scattered and stacked granitic rock, south of the main Sierra. It surrounds the upper Manzanares – good for swimming at this level – and overlooks the Santillana reservoir. Its inaccessible crags are home to the Sierra's biggest colony of griffon vultures, protected in the Parque Regional de la Cuenca Alta del Manzanares.

The main base for visiting the area is **Manzanares el Real**, on the banks of the reservoir, a popular place for second homes. A pleasant town, with ultra-relaxing cafés around its small squares, it has a dramatic landmark in the 15th-century **Castillo de Manzanares el Real**, once the stronghold of the Mendozas, one of the most powerful aristocratic clans of medieval Castile (91 580 23 06, open 10am-2pm, 4-8pm Tue-Sun, closed Mon, admission 350ptas). Much of its interior is the product of recent restoration work, but the castle retains a fascinating mix of late Gothic and *Mudéjar* features, especially in the courtyard and the beautiful upper gallery, with a spectacular outlook over the valley.

El Yelmo

The outstanding natural landmark of La Pedriza is **El Yelmo** (1,716m/5,630ft), a huge dome-shaped rock above the town. From the Plaza Mayor in Manzanares el Real, head up the main street, Calle Risco, as far as a concreted river bed, and veer right up Calle Las Peñas; the path starts by the Café Julián. It takes about three hours to get to the foot of El Yelmo, from where you can scramble up a wide, easy chimney to the top. The return walk to Manzanares takes about one and a half hours.

The circuit of La Pedriza

It's also possible to 'do' a circuit of La Pedriza in about five or six hours. From Manzanares el Real, head up the road signposted to **Canto Cochino** (4km/2½ miles), a somewhat chaotic car-parking area, with a couple of bars, where the nature park begins. Getting out of the car park can be a bit complicated, but afterwards the path is easy to follow. It eventually joins the GR10, with red and white markings, to follow the river and zigzag to gain height before more or less levelling off for most of the walk. Along the way there's **El Tolmo**, a granite tower usually covered in rock climbers, **Collado de la Dehesilla**, with fine views across the park's mountains and, at the halfway point after about three hours, a giant rock known as **La Cara**, with wonderful vistas over Madrid. Going down on the final stretch you'll also come to the foot of **El Yelmo**, with drinking water close by. From here it's a gradual walk downhill, often meeting walkers and climbers taking the direct route to the Yelmo.

Where to stay & eat

In La Pedriza, off the path to El Yelmo above Manzanares el Real, a hot meal and a comfy bed can be found to rejuvenate weary legs at the small but well-appointed **El Tranco** (91 853 00 63, rates 6,000-9,000ptas). Book ahead on summer weekends. Another option is **La Fresneda** campsite (*see page 53*).

Getting there

By bus

Colmenarejo 724 from Plaza Castilla, buses approx hourly 7.20am-9.40pm Mon-Fri, 8.45am-9.30pm Sat, 8am-8pm Sun. The last return is at 9.45pm Mon-Fri, 7.55pm Sat, 9pm Sun.

By car

Take the M-607 to Colmenar Viejo, then the M-609 to Soto del Real and turn west onto the M-608 for Manzanares el Real (53km/33 miles).

Sierra Pobre

East of the N-I (the Carretera de Burgos) and beginning about 60 kilometres (37 miles) north of Madrid is the so-called *Sierra Pobre*, the Poor Sierra, running north-east toward Guadalajara. It is only *pobre* compared with the Guadarrama to the west, and inasmuch as its relative isolation has restricted the local economy, so that some villages have been all but abandoned. However, it is less discovered and perhaps more 'authentic' than the main Sierra, and its rolling, at times forbidding hills and peaks host some of the region's finest deciduous forests. Even at the height of summer the area is never crowded, and in spring and autumn its woods are a delight.

Buitrago de Lozoya is the main town. Its old centre dates back to the Middle Ages, and a walk around the walls – the inner part of which survives from Arab times – is essential. More surprising is that Buitrago has a **Picasso Museum** in its town hall, consisting of some 60 works, especially on bullfighting themes and mostly from his later years, which the great (and bald) man donated to his hairdresser and friend Eugenio Arias, a native of the town.

Decent roads now run round the villages of the Sierra, but there are still some with no direct bus from Madrid; however, from Buitrago a variety of microbuses run into the hills. Another option is to hire a bike in Madrid, take it on the bus and tour the Sierra from Buitrago. **Buitrabike** (91 868 07 19) is a cycle club in Buitrago that organises guided trips.

Among the first places of interest after Buitrago is **Montejo de la Sierra**, 16 kilometres (10 miles) to the north-east, and

a good central point for excursions on foot. The jewel in its crown is a magnificent beech forest, the most westerly in Europe. It can be visited with guided tours, run from the **Centro de Recursos de Alta Montaña** information centre, on the east side of Montejo on the road towards the remote village of **La Hiruela** (1,477 metres/4,847 feet). Note that it's usually necessary to book places well ahead. This is also popular mountain biking country, and the same centre has information on walking and cycling routes. An easy-to-follow bike route from Montejo, taking about three and a half hours, is along a dirt track that cuts off the La Hiruela road uphill towards Puerto de Cardoso and Cardoso de la Sierra, in the province of Guadalajara, before turning back to descend again to Montejo. On the way there are superb views north to the Ayllón mountains, and the 2,129-metre (6,985-foot) **Peña Cebollera**.

Further south, at the bottom of a magnificent valley in the very heart of the Sierra Pobre, lies **Puebla de la Sierra**. With a population of just 77, this mountain hamlet represents a trip back into the past of rural Spain, only 100 kilometres from Madrid. Much of it has been restored, and it makes an ideal base for walks to the surrounding reservoirs. Information is available at the Parador de la Puebla – not an official *Parador* – in the centre of the village.

About 25 kilometres (16 miles) south-west of Puebla (as the crow flies, not as the road winds) is **El Berrueco**, with a 13th-century church, and close to the huge El Atazar reservoir. **El Atazar** village is the starting point for more walks, and a range of water sports can be tried at the reservoir. **Patones**, on the southern edge of the Sierra, is reached via the Torrelaguna road off the N-I from Madrid. Once on the verge of being abandoned, the two villages of Patones (**de Arriba** and **de Abajo**) have been extensively restored, and many of their ancient slate houses are now restaurants or holiday homes. A road north-east from Patones leads in 12 kilometres (7½ miles) to the **Cueva del Reguerillo**, with prehistoric cave paintings.

Museo Picasso

Plaza Picasso, Buitrago de Lozoya (91 868 00 56). **Open** 11am-2pm, 4-6pm Tue-Fri; 10am-2.30pm, 3.30-6.30pm Sat; 10am-2.30pm Sun, holidays; closed Mon. **Admission** free.

Where to stay & eat

Buitrago has the **Hostal Madrid-Paris** (Avda Madrid 23, 91 868 11 26, rates 7,000ptas), an old stone house with 25 bargain rooms and

Storks are an image of rural Castile.

a great-value restaurant. For old-fashioned food in surroundings to match, try **Asador Jubel** (C/Real 33, 91 868 03 09, average 1,500ptas).

In Montejo de la Sierra, **Hotel Montejo** (Vereda del Zarzal, 91 869 71 25, rates 5,000ptas) has great views and rooms. For eating, **Mesón del Hayedo** (C/del Turco, 91 869 70 23, average 1,500ptas) is small, crowded and lively.

Puebla de la Sierra offers **El Parador de la Puebla** (Plaza Carlos Ruiz 2, 91 869 72 56, rates 6,500ptas). It only has five rooms, so book. Other houses in the village let rooms: ask around. Patones has **El Tiempo Perdido** (Travesía del Ayuntamiento 7, 91 843 21 52, rates 23,000ptas). This restored five-room house is a hillbilly heaven; a bit expensive, but it's a privilege to stay here. The **renovated school buildings** in C/Escuelas (91 843 20 26, rates 5,000ptas) are cheaper, and for food you can't beat the old-world charm of **El Rey de Patones** (C/Asas, 91 843 20 37, average 2,000ptas).

Getting there

By bus
Continental bus 191 runs to Buitrago; the 196 also goes to Buitrago and Acebeda via El Berrueco, and the 199 to Montejo de la Sierra via El Berrueco (very infrequent). All run from Plaza Castilla. The 191 leaves every two hours from 8am; last return from Buitrago 6pm Mon-Sat, 8pm Sun. Many local microbus services run from Buitrago.

By car
N-I north direct to Buitrago de Lozoya (75km/47 miles), or turn right in Venturada (51km/32 miles; signposted to Torrelaguna) for Patones, or just north of La Cabrera (62km/39 miles) for El Berrueco.

Tourist information

Centro de Recursos de Alta Montaña
91 869 70 58. **Open** 9am-6pm Mon-Thur; 9am-10pm Fri; 9am-9pm Sat; 9am-4pm Sun.

Centro de Turismo de la Sierra Norte
La Cabrera (91 868 86 98). **Open** *mid-Sept-May* 9am-5pm daily. *June-mid Sept* 9am-2pm, 3-7pm Mon-Fri; 10am-2pm, 4-7pm Sat, Sun.
The tourist office for the whole area is in La Cabrera, 15km (9 miles) south of Buitrago. Buitrago town hall also has a lot of information on activities in the Sierra, on the floor above the Picasso Museum.

Sierra de Gredos

The craggy peaks and lush valleys of the Sierra de Gredos – the part of Spain's central *cordillera* straddling southern Avila – were remote and little known until two decades ago. When roads brought them within an easy drive from Madrid, the Gredos became a playground, and walkers, climbers, campers, mountain bikers, hang-gliders, fishermen, hunters, swimmers, skiers and city-dwellers simply in search of peace now flock in all year round.

Where and how you go depends on the time of year: in summer, the reservoirs are full of swimmers and windsurfers, while above them walkers camp or sleep in mountain refuges; in winter, roads may be blocked by snow. May and June are the ideal months, and in any season it's always better to go there midweek, if you can.

From Madrid, the best route into the Gredos is the M-501, the country road via Brunete. Plan to spend at least two days in the Sierra to make a visit worthwhile, as the journey from Madrid (133 kilometres/83 miles to Arenas de San Pedro) easily takes three hours.

The Gredos runs roughly from the River Alberche in the east to the Aravalle valley in the west. It divides into three sections. In the eastern triangle between **San Martín de Valdeiglesias**, **Cebreros** and the pass at **Puerto del Pico** (the area most accessible by bus from Madrid), the land climbs from the mild Valle del Tiétar through bare hills to the first real peaks at the Puerto. Here, a dramatically steep stretch of Roman road drops south into the delicious valley of **Mombeltrán**, with a medieval castle, 16th-century church and pretty surrounding villages. Another sight in this area, just west of San Martín near **El Tiemblo**, are the mysterious **Guisando** bulls – huge stone sculptures of unknown, pre-Roman origin. The woods around El Tiemblo, full of wild flowers, are unmissable. Other stop-offs could be the reservoirs of **San Juan** or **Burguillo**, both crowded on summer weekends, peaceful at other times. **Cebreros** is a small wine-making town.

The heart of the Sierra is the massif centred on the **Pico Almanzor**, protected since 1905 as a royal hunting ground (the *Coto Real*) – a forerunner of today's nature reserve. Serious climbing is concentrated around **Los Galayos** to the south, a series of spectacular rock needles. For walkers there are plenty of paths too, from north and south. Here you can find the rare Gredos mountain goats running around below the peaks, while eagles, vultures and kites cruise the thermals overhead.

The main bases here are, to the south, **Arenas de San Pedro** – jumping-off point for Los Galayos – which bulges with tourists at peak times, and 18 kilometres (11 miles) further west, **Candeleda**, less picturesque but less crowded. South of Arenas near Ramacastañas there are caves at **Cuevas del Aguila**, with bizarre rock formations. The northern access points are the cooler villages near the River Tormes, such as **Hoyocasero**, **Navarredonda de Gredos** and **Hoyos del Espino**, from where a road cuts 12 kilometres (7½ miles) into the centre of Gredos by the Almanzor peak. This valley, with cattle pastures and pine forests beside the river, is a prime area for horse-riding and fishing. From the end of the road there's a great two- to five-hour walk (in good weather) up to dazzling mountain lakes at the **Circo de Gredos**.

The western Gredos is dominated by the **Tormantos** mountains and, in particular, the **Covacha** peak. To the south runs the valley of **La Vera**, with half-timbered villages known in Spain for their tobacco and paprika. In the autumn, strings of dried peppers hang off the wooden balconies. Above **Cuacos de Yuste** is the monastery of **Yuste**, where Charles V retired from the world to die. It's a humble monument, but as rewarding as the grander model his son Philip II built at El Escorial.

On the north side of these westerly mountains is **El Barco de Avila**, with a 14th-century church and 15th-century castle. However, Barco is most famous for the quality of its dried beans (*judías* and larger *judiones*), which are privileged with a *denominación de origen*. Many, therefore, come here to tuck in at the town's restaurants. A short drive west is **Hervas**, a preserved hill village with a Jewish quarter, and further on is the medieval city of **Plasencia**, on the River Jerte, which has a superb double cathedral.

Whatever your interests, to make the most of Gredos you need a good map and a walking guide (there are no local tourist offices). So far all guides are in Spanish. *Las Sierras de Gredos y Béjar*, by Rafael Serra (Anaya Ecoguía series), is very useful, with good maps and itineraries.

Where to stay & eat

Apart from beans, the other omnipresent food of the province of Avila is steak, from Iberian black cattle (*see page 253*). Convinced carnivores are well catered for, but others can find the options limited.

Heading west from Madrid, in Mombeltrán, **Hostal Albuquerque** (Parque de la Soledad, 920 38 60 32, rates 3,000-5,000ptas) is an atmospheric *hostal*. It's an excellent base for exploring the valley, with good basic cooking.

Navarredonda is the location of the **Parador de Gredos** (920 34 80 48, rates 10,000-15,000ptas). The first-ever *Parador* (*see page 257*), this grey stone hunting lodge in a superb location was opened in 1928 by Alfonso XIII, and is now an atmospheric old hotel with creaking floors. There's also a good restaurant. A cheaper but excellent alternative is the **Venta Rasquilla** (920 34 82 21, rates 4,000ptas, restaurant average 1,500ptas), a traditional roadside inn at the point where the Navarredonda road meets the N-502, with some of the best local steaks at bargain prices. Navacepeda de Tormes has the **Hostal Capra Hispánica** (Carretera de Avila 40, 920 34 91 77, rates 3,000-5,000ptas), an informal small *hostal* with bar and restaurant.

The best base in the western Gredos is the **Hotel Manila** (Carretera de Plasencia, 920 34 08 44, rates 6,600-8,950ptas) in El Barco de Avila. It also organises riding, walking, mountain biking and so on, and has a campsite. Of the town's clutch of restaurants, one of the best is **Casa Lucio** (C/de la Pasión 3, 920 34 07 59), just off the main plaza; if you want to buy any of the famous beans, head for **Legumbres Coronado**, a little shop on the plaza itself.

To the south west, Losar de la Vera has the **Hotel Carlos V** (Avda de Extremadura 45, 927 57 06 36, rates 7,000ptas), with mountain views. But, for a treat it must be the **Parador Carlos V** in Jarandilla de la Vera (Avda García Prieto 1, 927 56 01 17, rates 14,000-15,000ptas), where rooms overlook the Renaissance courtyard of this former castle of the counts of Oropesa.

Getting there

By bus

Cevasa (91 539 31 32) buses 551 run from Estación Sur to San Martín de Valdeiglesias, El Tiemblo/Burguillo and Cebreros. Buses leave about every two hours, with a last return 6.30pm, 8.30pm Sun. Many more Gredos services run from Avila.

By car

The main route is the N-V to Alcorcón, then M-501. San Martín is 65km/40 miles from Madrid.

Worth the climb: **La Pedriza**. *See p267.*

Take to the hills

A few of the many ways to get more from a trip to the Madrid sierras. For travel book shops with local guides, maps and more information about these and other activities, *see page 163.*

Adventure

Escuela de Supervivencia
C/Valenzuela 8, Barrio del Retiro (91 532 50 72). Metro Banco de España/bus all routes to Cibeles. **Open** 9.30am-1.30pm, 4-7.30pm Mon-Sat; closed Sun. **Map** p310 H7.
Bored with nightlife? Try a weekend survival course in Gredos (in winter). Small groups have to survive outdoors, with a minimum of supplies.

Climbing & mountaineering

Escuela Madrileña de Alta Montaña
C/Apodaca 16, 1° (91 593 80 74). Metro Tribunal/bus 3, 37, 40, 149. **Open** 10.30am-2pm, 6-8pm Mon-Thur; 10.30am-2pm Fri; closed Sat, Sun. *July, Aug* 10.30am-2pm Mon-Fri; closed Sat, Sun. **Map** p306 G4.
Mountaineering and climbing classes at all levels; the school also arranges membership of the local mountaineering federation, which is based here.

Espacio Acción
C/Santa Casilda 12, Delicias (91 473 93 16). Metro Puerta de Toledo/bus 17. **Open** 10am-2pm, 4-7.30pm Mon-Fri; closed Sat, Sun.
Internationally recognised guides who organise activities including rock climbing in La Pedriza (or, if you prefer, Kazakhstan) and winter sports.

Estacíon del Puerto de Navacerrada
Edificio Deporte y Montaña, Puerto de Navacerrada (91 852 33 02).
Madrid office: C/Sagasta 13, 5°, Chueca (91 594 30 34). Metro Alonso Martínez/bus 3, 7, 21, 37, 40. **Open** 9am-6pm Mon-Thur; 9am-3pm Fri; closed Sat, Sun. **Map** p306 G3.
Outside the ski season, the Navacerrada ski station offers activities including mountain biking, climbing, mountain walks and tours. Also a good source of information on other facilities in the Sierras.

Guided walks

Arawak Viajes
C/Peñuelas 12, Embajadores (91 474 25 24). Metro Acacias/bus all routes to Embajadores. **Open** 10am-2pm, 5-9pm Mon-Sat; closed Sun. **Credit** MC, V.
A small agency with young staff that offers a big choice of one- and two-day group walking tours near Madrid at weekends, plus longer trips and activity courses. Prices are low (from 2,000ptas for one-day trips), and some routes are designed for families with children. It also functions as a general travel agency. **Branch**: C/Floridablanca 2, San Lorenzo de El Escorial (91 890 27 69).

Azimut
C/Jardines 3, 4°, 7ª, Sol & Gran Vía (91 521 42 84). Metro Gran Vía or Sol/bus all routes to Puerta del Sol. **Open** 5-9pm Mon-Fri; closed Sat, Sun. **No credit cards. Map** p309 E/F7.
One- and two-day walking tours on many weekends. One-day trips mostly go to the Guadarrama and areas near Madrid; prices include a guide, maps, transport, board, accommodation and insurance.

Haciendo Huella
C/José Abascal 32, Chamberí (91 593 04 41). Metro Gregorio Marañón/bus 3, 12, 37, 149. **Open** 9am-2.30pm, 4.30-7.30pm Mon-Fri; closed Sat, Sun. **No credit cards.**
A professional agency that organises one-, two-day and longer group walking tours. One day trips are mostly to the Guadarrama; Gredos features on longer excursions. Prices include guide, transport, board and lodging (half-board) and insurance.

OPADE
C/Colmenares 9, Chueca (91 521 57 66). Metro Banco de España/bus all routes to Cibeles. **Open** 10am-2pm, 4-8pm Mon-Fri; 10am-2pm Sat; closed Sun. **No credit cards. Map** p310 G6.
Walking excursions in the Guadarrama and Gredos, as well as white-water rafting, canoeing, windsurfing and pony-trekking.

Pangea
C/Melilla 10, Delicias (91 517 28 39). Metro Pirámides/bus 34, 36, 116, 118, 119. **Open** 10am-2pm, 4-8pm Mon-Fri; 10am-1.30pm Sat; closed Sun. **No credit cards.**
This co-operative organises small group trips to some of the lesser-known areas around Madrid such as La Pedriza and the Sierra Pobre: bike trips, walks, and climbing (at your own risk).

Hang-gliding

De Madrid al Cielo
Avda del Mediterráneo 35, Atocha (91 552 8433). Metro Conde Casal/bus 14, 32, 63. **Open** by appointment.
Hang-gliding courses for beginners, as well as week-end trips to the Sierra.

Trips Out of Town

Horse riding

Las Palomas

Club Hípico, Carretera de Colmenar Viejo km 28.9 (908 728 795/91 803 31 76). By bus 721, 724, 725, 726 from Plaza de Castilla/by car Carretera de Colmenar Viejo. **Open** 10am-2pm, 6-8pm Tue-Sun; closed Mon.

Offers riding courses for all levels, and accompanied one-day to one-week treks in the Guadarrama.

La Pasá

Urbanización La Cabezuela, Cercedilla (91 852 21 21/ 989 43 76 38). By bus Larrea 684 from Moncloa; by car N-VI to Guadarrama, M-622 to Cercedilla, M-966 to Puerto de la Fuenfría; by train Cercanías C-8b. **Open** by appointment.

Horse and pony treks in the Guadarrama from Cercedilla up to Navacerrada or Rascafría, across to Segovia or whichever route suits you, for around 6,000ptas a day. No experience is necessary. Very busy on summer weekends; call ahead to arrange times and discuss possible routes.

Mountain biking

A very handy Spanish-language guide to routes all around Madrid, with good maps, is *Bicicleta de Montaña por la Comunidad de Madrid*, by Miguel Angel Delgado (El Senderista). For more on bike hire in Madrid, *see page 279.*

Bicibus

Puerta del Sol 14 (91 522 45 01). Metro Sol/bus all routes to Puerta del Sol. **Open** 9.30am-1.30pm, 4.30-8pm Mon-Fri; 10am-1.30pm Sat; closed Sun. **Credit** AmEx, MC, V. **Map** p309 E7.

Two-day and longer trips for small groups into the Guadarrama or further afield. Two-day trips start at 8,000ptas, and include tour leader, insurance, transport, lodging and breakfast. Also bikes for hire in Madrid, from around 1,200ptas a day.

Bicimanía

C/Palencia 20, Cuatro Caminos (91 533 11 89). Metro Alvarado/bus 3, 43, 64, 66, 124, 127. **Open** 10am-2pm, 5-8.30pm Mon-Fri; closed Sat, Sun. **Credit** AmEx, MC, V.

Organised group excursions through the year. Prices start at about 1,000ptas, which includes a tour leader and a light snack on the trip.

Karacol Sport

C/Tortosa 8, Atocha (91 539 96 33). Metro Atocha/bus all routes to Atocha. **Open** 10.30am-8pm Mon-Wed, Fri; 10.30am-10pm Thur; 10.30am-2pm Sat except Aug; closed Sun. **Credit** MC, V.

A big hire shop that runs group trips throughout the year. Prices start at about 7,000ptas, including bike hire, tour leader, insurance, transport and back-up vehicle, plus half-board and lodging on longer trips. *See also p279.*

Branch: C/Montera 32 (91 532 90 73).

Skiing

ATUDEM Phoneline

(91 350 20 20).

Recorded information (in Spanish only) on snow conditions at ski resorts. Of the four resorts near Madrid, **Valcotos** (91 563 60 31) has the prettiest setting, and **Valdesquí** (91 570 96 98) usually has the best snow. **La Pinilla** (921 55 03 04) is directly north of Madrid near Riaza; the others are in the central Guadarrama. There is hotel accommodation only at **Puerto de Navacerrada** (91 852 33 02). All-in package trips to these resorts can be booked at any travel agency in Madrid. These ski stations offer limited skiing only and are of little interest to intermediate or advanced skiers, but are great for day trips out of Madrid, and the pleasure of swinging up on a chairlift with the city to the south is undeniable.

Club Pokhara

C/Profesor Waksman 11, Chamartín (91 458 61 29). Metro Cuzco/27, 40, 126, 147. **Open** 10am-2pm, 5-8pm Mon-Fri; closed Sun.

Half travel agency, half sports club, Pokhara organises skiing trips and even ski-board classes in the sierra, and other parts of Spain.

Water sports

The reservoirs that ring Madrid offer a welcome break from soaring summer temperatures. The largest is **San Juan**, in Gredos (*see page 269*). As well as 'beaches', San Juan has many places to eat. Several water sports clubs are based there, but there is nowhere for casual visitors to hire equipment. **Valmayor** reservoir towards El Escorial has more accessible facilities.

Escuela de Agua Bravas 'Los Gancheros'

C/Cuesta Negra 44, Las Musas (91 306 72 78/ 989 42 97 28). Metro Las Musas/bus 38, 140. **Open** *information* 10am-11pm Mon-Fri; closed Sat, Sun. **Credit** MC, V.

A pioneer in the field, Iñaki San José runs one-day kayak and canoe trips through white-water sections of an 80km (50 mile) stretch of the upper Tagus. Starts at Cifuentes, north-east of Madrid. English spoken.

Nortesport

Instalaciones Náuticas del Embalse del Atazar, Cervera de Buitrago (91 868 71 53). **Open** 11am-9pm daily. **Credit** MC, V.

Canoeing, windsurf, and sailing at this reservoir in the Sierra Pobre (*see p268*). In spring and autumn it also organises hikes and bikes.

Sport Natura

Avda Donostiarra 4, El Carmen (91 403 61 61). Metro El Carmen/bus 21, 48, 146. **Open** 9am-2pm, 4-7pm Mon-Fri; closed Sat, Sun. **No credit cards.**

Windsurfing, sailing, paragliding, caving and rafting classes and group trips, mostly in Gredos.

Directory

Directory

Getting Around

Unless you're in a real hurry, the best way to get around Madrid is often on foot. Most of the main attractions are within walking distance of the main axes of Puerta del Sol, Plaza Mayor, Gran Vía and the Castellana (with its older stages, the Paseos del Prado and Recoletos). The Puerta del Sol is the historic centre of the city, and the main hub of the bus and Metro systems. Street numbers in Madrid all run outwards from Sol. The Paseo del Prado runs along the east side of the old city and continues through Paseo de Recoletos into the great avenue of the Castellana, leading to the business areas of north Madrid. Drivers become familiar with the M-30, the inner motorway that skirts the city centre in a loop to the south, and the M-40, an outer ring-road forming a full circle around Madrid.

For when you need to travel quickly, Madrid has a cheap, efficient public transport system. For transport outside Madrid, *see page 248.*
Note: all transport and taxi fares are subject to revision each January.

Arriving & leaving

By air

Madrid's **Barajas Airport** is 16km (10 miles) east of the city on the A2 motorway. A major extension programme is underway at Barajas, important parts of which are now in place. A Richard Rogers-designed new main building is already open, and a third runway should be in use by mid-2001. While work goes on, though, travellers can expect occasional delays.

The very long Barajas main terminal building is split into three sections. All non-Spanish airlines and flights on Spanish airlines from non-Schengen-area countries (such as Britain and the USA, *see page 282*) use Terminal 1 (**T-1**); most domestic flights and Spanish airlines' flights from Schengen countries use **T-2**; some local flights and the Madrid-Barcelona air shuttle use **T-3**. In T-1 and T-2 there are 24-hour exchange facilities and ATM machines, a tourist office (in T-1 only; *see page 287*), hotel booking desks (*see page 37*) and a rail reservations desk (in T-1 only).

For airport information, call **902 35 35 70** or 91 393 60 00, or check www.anea.es. All phone lines are open 24 hours daily. To get from the airport into town there is now a Metro connection as well as buses and taxis. However, this is not necessarily an automatic advantage.

Airport bus

Plaza de Colón Terminal (91 431 61 92/information 91 406 88 10). Metro Colón or Serrano/bus all routes to Plaza de Colón. **Map** p306 I4.
The special airport bus runs between T-1 and T-2 at Barajas and the Plaza de Colón, and takes between 30min and 1hr, depending on the traffic. There are six stops en route, including one at Avda de América which can provide a handy Metro connection. The Colón bus terminal is underneath the square, and has a taxi rank; to get from there to Colón Metro, go up to street level and cross the Castellana by the underpass at the corner of Calle Goya. First buses of the day leave Colón at 4.45am, and Barajas at 5.45am; they run every 10min, 7am 11pm, and about every 15min at other times. Last buses nightly leave Barajas at 2am, and Colón at 1.30am. A single ticket costs 385ptas. The airport buses are not accessible to wheelchairs.

Metro from the airport

The Metro now provides the cheapest means of getting to central Madrid, but also the slowest. The Aeropuerto station is between T-2 and T-3, which means that if, as is very likely, you arrive at T-1 you have a 10-15 minute walk to get there. From the airport there are two stops on Metro line 8 (pink) to Mar de Cristal, where you must change to line 4 (brown) in the direction of Argüelles. To get to the Puerta del Sol, change again at Goya (after 10 stops) onto line 2 (red, direction Cuatro Caminos), from where there are 5 more stops to Sol. **Note that this can take 50min-1hr**, or more at peak times. In future line 8 will continue to Nuevos Ministerios, which will cut this time considerably, but this line will not be open until 2003. If you do take the Metro, save money by buying a *metrobús* ticket at the airport station (*see p277*).

Taxis from the airport

A taxi to central Madrid from Barajas (depending very much on traffic) should cost about 2,500ptas to Plaza de Colón or 3,000ptas to Puerta del Sol, including a 400ptas special airport supplement. There are further supplements at night, on Sundays and for each item of luggage placed in the car boot. Taxis are abundant at Barajas, sometime too much so: some drivers specialise in hanging round the airport, and may try a variety of scams, such as taking passengers by the longest possible route. To avoid them, use only taxis from the well-signposted official ranks outside each terminal, and ignore drivers who approach you inside the building. Check the meter is at the current minimum fare (*see p276*) when you begin the journey. It's also a good idea, to avoid unwanted 'tours' to check a map first, and have a landmark in mind in the area to which you should be going. For more on taxis, *see p276*.

Airlines

Aer Lingus 91 541 41 16/ www.aerlingus.ie.
American Airlines 91 453 14 00/ 901 10 00 01/www.aa.com.
British Airways 902 11 13 33/ www.british-airways.com.
easyJet 902 29 99 92/ www.easyjet.com.
Go 901 33 35 00/www.go-fly.com.
Iberia (902 40 05 00/www.iberia.com).

Directory

By bus

Virtually all international and long-distance coach services to Madrid terminate at the **Estación Sur de Autobuses**, C/Méndez Alvaro (information 91 468 42 00; bus companies also have their own lines, *see page 248*), to the south of central Madrid. It is next to Metro and *Cercanías* (local train) stations, both called Méndez Alvaro; bus 148 also runs from there to the city centre (Plaza del Callao). Taxi fares from the bus station carry a 150ptas supplement.

By train

Spanish national railways (RENFE) has two main stations in Madrid. Trains from France, Catalonia and northern Spain, and most of those from Portugal arrive at **Chamartín**, on the north side of the city, some distance from the centre. High-speed AVE trains from Seville, express services from Lisbon and trains from southern and eastern Spain arrive at **Atocha**, at the southern end of the Paseo del Prado. There are exchange facilities at both stations, and a tourist office at Chamartín (*see page 287*). Atocha is also the main hub of RENFE's local (*Cercanías*) rail lines for the Madrid area (*see page 276*).

Both Chamartín and Atocha are on the Metro. Line 10 runs from Chamartín to the city centre, but **note** that from late 2000 to spring 2001, due to the Metro building programme (*see right*), southbound trains will run only as far as Gregorio Marañón; during this time it will be more convenient to change onto line 1 at Plaza de Castilla. Atocha Renfe (the train station; not the same Metro as Atocha) is four Metro stops from Sol on line 1. A taxi fare to the centre from Chamartín should be about 1,800ptas, including a 150ptas station supplement. There are extra supplements at night, on Sundays and for luggage. The

same need for caution with cabs at the airport (*see page 274*) applies with drivers touting for fares at main rail stations.

For more information on all rail services, *see page 248*.

RENFE Information

902 24 02 02/www.renfe.es.
Open *information* 24hrs, *reservations* 5am-11.50pm, daily.
Estación de Atocha
Glorieta del Emperador Carlos V. Metro Atocha Renfe/bus all routes to Atocha. **Map** p310 H10.
Estación de Chamartín *C/Agustín de Foxá. Metro Chamartín/bus 5, 80.*

Left luggage

Barajas airport

Terminals T-1 & T-2. **Open** 24hrs daily. **Rates** 425ptas first 24hrs; 530/740ptas per day thereafter, according to size of locker. Coin-operated lockers; anything left for more than two weeks will be removed from the locker and kept in a separate storeroom, for 210ptas per day plus a 5,300ptas surcharge.

Estación Sur (buses)

Open 6.30am-midnight Mon-Sat; closed Sun. **Rates** 175ptas per day. A staffed office, which is sometimes open on Sundays.

RENFE train stations

Open *Chamartín* 8am-9pm, *Atocha* 6.30am-10.30pm, daily. **Rates** 300ptas first 24hrs; 400-600ptas per day thereafter, according to size of locker. Coin-operated lockers.

Maps

Metro and central-area street maps are included at the back of this Guide. Metro maps are also available at all Metro stations: ask for *'un plano del Metro'*. The Consorcio de Transportes, the regional transport authority, publishes good free maps, especially the *Plano de los Transportes del Centro de Madrid*, from which the maps in this Guide are taken. It should be available at tourist offices, Metro stations and bus information kiosks (ask for a transport map, rather than the inferior street map tourist offices often give out). For good shops to buy maps, *see page 163*.

Public transport

For transport for disabled travellers, *see page 283*.

Metro

The Metro is the quickest and simplest means of travelling to most parts of the city. Each of its 11 lines is identified by a number and a colour on maps and at stations. Metro stations also make essential reference points, and 'Metro Sevilla', 'Metro Goya' and so on will often be given to you as tags with addresses.

The Metro is open from 6am to 1.30am daily (a plan to extend services to 2.30am on Fridays and Saturdays is under discussion, so it's worth checking). Tickets are available at all stations from coin-operated machines and staffed ticket booths (*see page 277*). **Take the right ticket**). Trains run every three to five minutes during weekdays, and about every ten minutes after 11pm and on Sundays. The Metro can get packed in rush hours (7.30-9.30am, 1-2.30pm, 7.30-9pm), but is rarely crowded at other times.

BUILDING SCHEMES

The Metro is in the midst of an ongoing expansion programme. The north-south line 10 (dark blue) is now being extended south to Alcorcón, where it will meet a new circle line (the *Metrosur*) serving the suburbs of Alcorcón, Leganés, Getafe, Fuenlabrada and Móstoles, due to enter service in 2002. The airport line (line 8, pink) will be extended to Nuevos Ministerios by 2003, to provide a fast shuttle service. While work on all such projects goes on services on some lines will be disrupted at different times. **From late 2000 to spring 2001 there will be no service on line 10 between Gregorio Marañón and Campamento, and on line 2 from Banco de España to Ventas.**

In some cases extra buses will be provided to compensate. Information on any further work will be found in leaflets distributed at all Metro stations.

Metro information

C/Cavanilles 58 (91 552 59 09/www.metromadrid.es). Metro Conde de Casal/bus 10, 56. **Open** 8am-2.30pm Mon-Fri; closed Sat, Sun.

Buses

Run by the Empresa Municipal de Transportes (EMT). For fare and ticket information, *see page 277* **Take the right ticket.**

EMT Information

C/Alcántara 24, Salamanca (91 406 88 10). Metro Lista/bus 1, 21, 26, 53, 146. **Open** 8am-1.30pm Mon-Fri; closed Sat, Sun.
EMT Kiosks
Puerta del Sol, Plaza de Cibeles. **Open** 8am-8pm Mon-Fri; closed Sat, Sun. **Map** p309 E7, p310 H7.

Taking the bus

Route timings vary, but most run from about 6am to 11.30pm daily, with buses every 10-15min on each route (more frequently on more popular routes). At other times night buses operate. Due to the many one-way systems buses don't always follow the same route in each direction, so a bus map is handy. You board buses at the front, and get off via the middle or rear doors. The fare is the same for each journey, however far you go. Officially, there is a limit to how much luggage passengers can take on city buses: to some extent this depends on each driver, but travellers with suitcases can find they are not allowed to board.

Useful routes

2 From Moncloa to Plaza de España, then along Gran Via to Cibeles, the Retiro and Plaza Manuel Becerra.
3 From Puerta de Toledo up Gran Via de San Francisco and C/Mayor to Sol, then up C/Hortaleza to Cuatro Caminos and the Estadio Bernabéu.
5 From Puerta del Sol via the Plaza de Cibeles, Plaza de Colón and the Castellana to Chamartín station.
14 From Conde de Casal along Paseo Reina Cristina to Atocha, then along Paseo del Prado, Recoletos and the Castellana to Chamartín.
27 A frequent service all the way up and down the Castellana between Atocha and Plaza Castilla.
C The 'Circular' route runs in a wide circuit around the city, via Atocha, Embajadores, Plaza de España, Moncloa, Cuatro Caminos, Plaza Manuel Becerra and the Retiro.

Night buses

Between midnight and around 5am there are 20 night routes in operation, N1 to N20, called *Búho* ('owl') buses. All begin from Plaza de Cibeles and run out to the suburbs, and are numbered in a clockwise sequence; thus, N1 runs north to Manoteras, N2 a little further east to Hortaleza, and so on. The N18 runs along the Gran Via to Moncloa and Tetuán; the N20 along the length of the Castellana to Fuencarral. On Friday and Saturday night buses run every 25 minutes on all routes till 5.15am; on other nights, they run every half-hour from midnight to 3am, and every hour after that. Tickets and fares are the same as for daytime services.

Cercanías/local trains

The *Cercanías* or local network of Spanish Railways (RENFE) for the Madrid area consists of 11 lines – not numbered 1-11, since some divide into branches – centred on Atocha. Several stations connect with Metro lines. They are most useful for trips to the suburbs, or to the Guadarrama and towns near Madrid such as Aranjuez or Alcalá de Henares. Also, though, lines C-7a and C-7b combine (with one change at Príncipe Pio) to form a circle line within Madrid that is quicker than the Metro for some journeys, and the RENFE line between Chamartín and Atocha is the fastest link between the two main stations. *Cercanías* lines run from 5-6am to midnight-1am daily, with trains on most lines about every 15-30 minutes. Fares vary by distance, but the lines are included in the monthly season ticket (*see page 277* **Take the right ticket**). A map of the *Cercanías* network is on *page 315* of this Guide.

Taxis

Madrid taxis are white, with a diagonal red stripe on the front doors. The city has over 15,000 taxis, so they are rarely hard to find, except maybe late at night when it's raining heavily. They are also relatively cheap. When a taxi is free there is a

Libre ('Free') sign behind the windscreen, and a green light on the roof. If there is also a sign with the name of a district in red, this means the driver is on his way home, and not obliged to take you anywhere that isn't near that route.

There are taxi ranks, marked by a blue sign with a white T, at many places in the central area. At the airport and rail and bus stations, it's always best to take a taxi from the official ranks (*see page 274*); within Madrid, though, those in the know prefer to flag cabs down in the street when possible, to avoid the risk of scams occasionally tried on by some cab drivers who spend all their time waiting at ranks.

Fares

Official fare rates and supplements are shown inside each cab, on the right-hand sunvisor and/or the rear windows. Currently the minimum fare is 190ptas, and that is what the meter should show when you first set off. Within the main tariff zone (A, covering the whole of Madrid city) the fare will then increase at a rate of 85ptas per kilometre, or on a time rate if you are travelling at under 20kph. The minimum fare is the same at all times, but the additional charge increases at a higher rate at night (11pm-6am) and on Sundays and public holidays, and there are extra supplements for trips starting from the bus and train stations (150ptas), to and from the trade fair complex (150ptas), to and from the airport (400ptas), and for each item of luggage placed in the car boot (50ptas). Also, the fare rate is higher for journeys to suburban towns in the outer tariff zone (zone B).

Receipts & complaints

Sección de Autotaxi y Vehículos de Alquiler, Ayuntamiento de Madrid, C/Vallehermoso 1, 28015 Madrid (91 588 96 31). **Open** 9am-2pm Mon-Fri; closed Sat, Sun. **Map** p305 D3.
Taxi drivers provide receipts on request – ask for *'un recibo, por favor'*. If you think you've been overcharged or have any other complaint, insist the receipt is made out in full, with details of the journey and the driver's signature. Make a note of the taxi number, displayed on a plaque on the dashboard. Take or send the receipt, keeping a copy, with a complaints form to the city taxi office at the address above. The form is included in the Taxi Information leaflet available from tourist offices.

Take the right ticket

Single tickets both for the
Metro, which are available
from all stations, and city
buses, bought only from the
driver on board, cost
135ptas. Unless you really
are just passing through,
though, buying tickets this
way wastes time and money.
It's much better to use the
multi-journey **metrobús**
ticket, which can be used on
both systems. Valid for ten
journeys, they can be shared
between two or more people.
  Current price of the
metrobús is 705ptas. They
are available from automatic
machines and ticket booths
at Metro stations, and
tobacco shops (*estancos*,
see page 287) and the EMT
information kiosks (see page
276). On the Metro, you
insert the ticket into the
machine at the gate through

to the platform, which
cancels one unit for each
trip, and will reject expired
tickets. There is no checking
or collection of tickets at
station exits. On buses, the
metrobús should be inserted
arrow-downwards into the
blue and yellow machine just
behind the driver. Metrobús
tickets cannot be bought on
the bus itself.

Abonos – season tickets

Anyone spending a few
weeks in Madrid might be
interested in getting a
monthly season ticket (*abono
transportes*). Unlike the
metrobús, it is valid for
Cercanías trains as well as
the Metro and city buses,
giving unlimited travel within
a specified area. A one-
month ticket for zone A

(virtually the whole of Madrid-
city) currently costs
4,620ptas, and there are
substantial reductions for
people under 21 or over 65.
Your first *abono* must be
obtained with an identity
card, available only from
estancos, for which you will
need two passport-size
photos and have to fill in a
brief form. In succeeding
months you can buy tickets
(*cupones*) to revalidate the
card from Metro stations and
EMT kiosks as well as
estancos. Note, though, that
an *abono* is valid for an
actual calendar month, not
for 30 days from date of
purchase, so that if your stay
runs across two months
buying one may not be
particularly economical,
unless you qualify for one of
the different age discounts.

Phone cabs

You can call for a cab from any
of the companies listed below.
Operators will rarely speak
much English, but as a
direction to the driver try to
give the name of the street and
a restaurant or bar that makes
a suitable place to wait, or
position yourself near a street
corner and say, for example,
'*Sagasta, esquina Larra*'
('Sagasta, corner [of] Larra').
The operator will also ask you
your name.
  Phone cabs start the meter
from the point when a call is
answered. A very few cabs will
take credit cards.

Taxi companies
Radio-Taxi Asociación Gremial
91 447 51 80.
Radio-Taxi Independiente
91 405 12 13/91 405 55 00.
Radio Teléfono Taxi/Euro Taxi
91 547 85 00/91 547 82 00.
Teletaxi 91 371 21 31/91 371 37 11.

Driving

Driving in Madrid may be a
little wilder than you're used to.
Jams, snarl-ups and slow speed
bumps are common. In Madrid
itself driving is rarely a quick
way of getting anywhere
(although a scooter can be
handy for those brave enough to
face the traffic), but a car is an
asset for trips outside the city
(*see page 248*). If you drive here,
bear these points in mind:
● You can drive here with a
valid driving licence from most
countries, but an international
licence, available in Britain from
the AA or RAC, is also useful.
● Keep your licence, vehicle
documents and insurance
papers with you at all times.
● It is obligatory to wear seat
belts at all times, and note that
in Spain you must have two,
not just one, warning triangles
in your car.

● Children under 14 may not
travel in the front of a car.
● Speeding fines imposed on
motorways (*autopistas*) and
highways are paid on the spot.
● Do not leave anything of
value, including a car radio, in
your car, and do not leave bags
or coats in view on the seats.
Take all luggage into your
hotel when you park.
● In general drivers go as fast
as they can irrespective of the
speed limit. At traffic lights
many will follow through on
the amber light as it changes
between green and red. Do not
stop sharply when you see a
light begin to change, as the
driver behind will not expect it
and could run into your back.
● When oncoming drivers
flash lights at you it means they
will **not** slow down (contrary to
British practice). On main
highways, the flashing of lights
is usually a helpful warning
there's a speed trap ahead.

Car & motorbike hire

Most companies have a minimum age limit (usually 21) and require you to have had a licence for over a year. You will also need a credit card, or have to leave a big cash deposit. Check if IVA (VAT) at 16 per cent, unlimited mileage and full insurance are included; it's always advisable to take out full, rather than minimum, insurance. Price structures vary a lot, with good weekend deals.

Econocar

C/Felix Boix, 2, Chamartín (91 359 14 03/aguseconocar@jazz.com. Metro Plaza Castilla. **Open** 9am-2pm, 4-8pm Mon-Fri; 9.30am-1.30pm Sat; closed Sun. **Credit** AmEx, MC, V.
A small, efficient local company with good rates (Peugeot 106 for 36,000ptas per week, all included) and, better still, bargain weekday and weekend offers at all times. Prices rise in July-August.

Europcar

Avda del Partenón 16-18 (91 722 62 26/reservations 901 10 20 20). Metro Campo de las Naciones/bus 122. **Open** 8.30am-2pm, 4.30-8pm Mon-Fri; closed Sat, Sun. **Credit** AmEx, DC, MC, V.
An Opel Corsa costs 46,609ptas for a week, all inclusive. 'Weekend' deals (five days, which can be Wed-Mon or Thur-Tue) are 28,000ptas.
Branches: Barajas airport (91 393 72 35); Atocha station (91 530 01 94); Chamartín station (91 323 17 21); C/San Leonardo 8 (91 541 88 92); C/Orense 29 (91 555 99 30).

Motoalquiler

C/Conde Duque 13. Malasaña & Conde Duque (91 542 06 57). Metro Noviciado, Plaza de España/bus all routes to Plaza de España. **Open** 8am-1.30pm, 5-8pm Mon-Fri; 9-11am Sat; closed Sun, and Sat July, Aug. **Credit** AmEx, DC, MC, V. **Map** p305 D4.
Motorcycle specialists: a Vespa costs 5,000ptas a day, 23,000ptas a week; a Yamaha 250cc 12,000ptas/40,000ptas; there are also big road bikes.

National-Atesa

Paseo de la Castellana 130 (902 10 01 01). Metro Santiago Bernabéu/bus 27, 40, 147, 150. **Open** *Sept-June* 7.30am-2.30pm, 3.30-6pm Mon-Thur; 7.30am-2.30pm Fri; *July, Aug* 7.30am-3.30pm Mon-Fri; closed Sat, Sun. **Credit** AmEx, DC, MC, V.
A Citroën Saxo costs 40,600ptas (incl insurance, tax, unlimited mileage) for a week, 16,913ptas for a weekend.
Branch: Barajas airport (91 393 72 32).

PlanCar

C/Embajadores 173, South of centre (91 530 27 23). Metro Legazpi/bus 6, 18, 78, 148. **Open** 9am-2pm, 4.30-8.30pm Mon-Fri; 9am-1.30pm Sat; closed Sun. **Credit** AmEx, V.
A local agency well placed for anyone in the south of the city. A Ford Focus costs 55,000ptas a week.

Breakdown services

If you take a car to Spain it's advisable to join an organisation such as the AA or RAC, or the AAA in the US. They have reciprocal arrangements with the local equivalent, **RACE**.

RACE (Real Automóvil Club de España)

C/José Abascal 10, Chamberí (freephone 900 11 22 22/information 91 593 33 33/office 91 549 74 00). Metro Alonso Cano/bus 3, 12, 37, 149. **Open** *office* 8.30am-5.30pm Mon-Fri; closed Sat, Sun.
The RACE has English-speaking staff and will send immediate breakdown assistance. If you are outside Madrid, call the emergency freephone number, but you will be referred on to a local number. Repairs are carried out on the spot when possible; if not, your vehicle will be towed to the nearest suitable garage. Members of foreign affiliated organisations are not charged for call-outs, but non-members pay around 7,000ptas for the basic breakdown service. The RACE also provides a range of other services.

Parking

For car-owning Madrileños parking is a daily trauma. The Municipal Police give out tickets readily (many locals never pay them). Be careful not to park in front of doorways with the sign '*Vado Permanente*', indicating an entry with 24-hour right of access. Parking is banned in most main streets in the centre, but in side streets the **ORA** system applies.

ORA

The main features of ORA (*Operación Regulación Aparcamiento*) are: within the central ORA zone (roughly between Moncloa, C/José Abascal, C/Doctor Esquerdo and Atocha), residents park for free if they have an annual sticker. From 9am to 8pm (9am to 3pm in August), non-residents can also park with a special card, *ZER*,

valid for up to two hours; after then a new card must be used, and the car parked in a new spot. Cars parked in the ORA zone without a card can be towed away (*see below*). ZER cards are bought from *estancos* and newsstands, cost 160ptas and should be displayed behind the windscreen. All streets in this zone that do not have additional restrictions signposted are ORA parking areas. In other zones time allowances are a bit more generous.

Car parks

Central car parks *Plaza de las Cortes, Plaza Santa Ana, C/Sevilla, Plaza Jacinto Benavente, Plaza Mayor, C/Descalzas Reales, C/Tudescos, Plaza de España.* **Open** 24hrs daily. **Rates** 130ptas for first 30 min; 110ptas each subsequent half-hour; 2,220ptas 24hrs. There are some 30 municipal car parks around Madrid, indicated by a white 'P'-on-blue sign. It's especially recommendable to use a car park if your car has foreign plates.

Towing away & car pounds

91 345 00 50. **Open** 24hrs daily.
Main pounds: *Plaza del Carmen, Sol & Gran Vía. Metro Sol/bus all routes to Puerta del Sol.* **Map** p309 E7; *Avda de Alfonso XIII, 135, Chamartín. Metro Colombia/bus 7, 40, 52.*
If your car seems to have been towed away by the Municipal Police, call the central number and quote your car number plate to be told which of the car pounds your vehicle has gone to. Staff do not normally speak English. It will cost 14,000ptas to recover your vehicle, plus 130ptas for the first hour and 115ptas per hour after that, timed from the moment it was towed away.

Petrol

Unleaded petrol is *sin plomo*; regular is *súper*, and diesel fuel is *gas-oil*.

24-hour petrol stations

All are open 24 hours daily.
Atocha: Repsol junction of Paseo de Infanta Isabel and Avda Ciudad de Barcelona, next to Atocha station. **Credit** AmEx, MC, V. **Map** p310 I10.
Campsa: Paseo de Santa María de la Cabeza 18, on southward exit from Glorieta del Emperador Carlos V. **Credit** AmEx, MC, V. **Map** p310 H10. Both have 24-hour shops on site.
Avda de América: Repsol C/María de Molina 21. **Credit** AmEx, MC, V. **Map** p307 K1.
Salamanca: Repsol C/Goya 24, junction C/Núñez de Balboa. **Credit** AmEx, DC, MC, V. **Map** p307 J4.
Cuatro Caminos: Carba C/Ríos Rosas 1, by C/Bravo Murillo. **Credit** AmEx, MC, V.

Cycling

Heavy and aggressive traffic and a lack of cycle lanes on any of the central streets of the city (there are a few in parks and by the river) means that cycling is never an enjoyable means of getting around Madrid. Bikes are popular, though, for trips to the larger city parks (Retiro, Casa de Campo) and the Madrid Sierras. Bikes can be carried for no extra charge on some *Cercanías* lines and on the Metro at weekends and on public holidays.

Cycle hire shops often ask that you leave proof of identity (take a photocopy to avoid having to leave your passport) and a cash deposit. For biking tours out of town, *see page 272*.

Karacol Sport

C/Tortosa 8, Atocha (91 539 96 33/ www.karakol.com). Metro Atocha/ bus all routes to Atocha. **Open** 10.30am-8pm Mon, Tue, Wed, Fri; 10.30am-10pm Thur; 10.30am-2pm Sat (Aug closed Sat). Closed Sun. **Credit** MC, V. Mountain bikes from 2,000ptas a day, with 5,000ptas deposit and ID. A weekend deal (Fri-Mon) costs less – 4,000ptas – with the same deposit. The shop also runs tours (*see p272*). **Branch:** C/Montera 32 (91 532 90 73).

Resources A-Z

Business

Anyone wanting to conduct business in Madrid needs to familiarise themselves with some of the intricacies of Spanish and EU legislation. Chambers of Commerce, consulates and a good *gestoría* can help you in getting started.

Institutions/info

The American Club

Edificio España, Gran Vía 88, 9ª, Sol & Gran Vía (91 547 78 02). Metro Plaza de España/bus all routes to Plaza de España. **Map** p305 D4. A meeting point for the US business community and guests.

Bolsa de Comercio (Stock Exchange)

Plaza de la Lealtad 1 (91 589 26 00/ 91 589 16 59/ www.go-spain.com/acm bolsamadrid.es). Metro Banco de España/bus 10, 14, 27, 34. **Open** 10am-5pm Mon-Fri; closed Sat, Sun. **Map** p310 H7.

Cámara de Comercio e Industria de Madrid

Plaza de la Independencia 1, Salamanca (91 538 35 00). Metro Banco de España or Retiro/bus all routes to Puerta de Alcalá. **Open** 8.30am-2.30pm, 4.30-6.30pm Mon-Thur; 8.30am-2.30pm Fri; closed Sat, Sun. **Map** p310 H6. The Chamber of Commerce provides a useful information service for foreign investors in Madrid.

Instituto Español de Comercio Exterior

Paseo de la Castellana 14, Salamanca (91 349 61 00/www.icex.es). Metro Colón/bus all routes to Plaza de Colón. **Open** *Oct-May* 8.30am-5.30pm Mon-Fri; *June-Sept* 8am-3pm Mon-Fri; closed Sat, Sun. **Map** p306 I4.

The state-run ICEX (Spanish Institute for Foreign Trade) has an excellent information service to aid small- to medium-sized businesses.

Conference services

IFEMA/Feria de Madrid

Recinto Ferial Juan Carlos I, Northern suburbs (91 722 51 80). Metro Campo de las Naciones/bus 73, 122. **Open** *office* 9.30am-6.30pm Mon-Fri; closed Sat, Sun.
Madrid's lavish state-of-the-art trade fair centre, north-east of the city near the airport, opened in 1991. It has eight main pavilions, a 600-seater auditorium and many smaller facilities, plus 20 catering outlets and 14,000 parking spaces. By the entrance is the **Palacio Municipal de Congresos**, a 2,000-capacity conference hall. Among the many events hosted by the Feria are the ARCO art fair (*see p206*) and Madrid Fashion Week (both in Feb).

Oficina de Congresos de Madrid

C/Mayor 69, Austrias (91 588 29 00/www.munimadrid.es). Metro Sol or Opera/bus 3, 148. **Open** *Oct-May* 8am-3pm, 4-6pm Mon-Thur; 8am-3pm Fri; *June-Sept* 8.30am-2.30pm Mon-Fri; closed Sat, Sun. **Map** p308 C8.
An office of the city council to assist organisations or individuals wishing to hold a conference or similar event in Madrid, and facilitate contacts with venues and service companies.

Palacio de Exposiciones y Congresos

Paseo de la Castellana 99 (91 337 81 00/www.madridconventioncentre.com). Metro Santiago Bernabéu/bus 27, 43, 147, 149, 150. **Open** 9am-2.30pm, 4.30-7pm Mon-Fri; closed Sat, Sun.
Longer established than the Feria, with a dramatic Miró frieze across the façade, and used for several major international conferences. It has conference rooms and galleries of all sizes; facilities are excellent.

Recintos Feriales de la Casa de Campo

Avda de Portugal, Casa de Campo (91 463 63 34). Metro Lago/bus 31, 33, 36, 39. **Open** *Sept-July* 8am-3pm Mon-Fri; closed Sat, Sun. *Aug* 8am-2pm Mon-Fri; closed Sat, Sun.
An attractive site with three halls and open-air space in the Casa de Campo.

Gestorías/admin aid

A *gestoría* is a very Spanish institution, combining the functions of lawyer, bookkeeper, business adviser and general aid with bureaucracy. They can be very helpful in taking you through paperwork and seeing short cuts that foreigners are often unaware of. Most local residents employ a *gestor* at some point. English is spoken at the *gestorías* listed here.

Gestoría Calvo Canga

C/Serrano 27, Salamanca (91 577 07 09). Metro Serrano/bus all routes to Plaza de Colón. **Open** 9am-2pm, 5-8pm Mon-Fri; closed Sat, Sun. **Map** p307 I4. General *gestoría* dealing with labour law, tax, accounts and residency.

Gestoría Cavanna

C/Hermosilla 4, Salamanca (91 431 86 67). Metro Colón/bus all routes to Plaza de Colón. **Open** *Sept-June* 9am-1.30pm, 5-7.30pm, *July, Aug* 9am-1.30pm Mon-Fri; closed Sat, Sun. **Map** p306 I4. Tax and employment law specialists.

Work Manager

C/Bravo Murillo 9, Chamberí (91 593 96 22/wmanager@arrakis.es). Metro Quevedo/bus 16, 37, 61, 149. **Open** *Sept-July* 10am-8pm, *Aug* 10am-2.30pm Mon-Fri; closed Sat, Sun. **Map** p305 E2.
A friendly and efficient women-run *gestoría* that gives comprehensible advice on all kinds of legal and bureaucratic problems, at decent rates.

Directory

Translators

Lernout & Hauspie

Torre Europa, Paseo de la Castellana 95 (91 456 71 00/www.lhsl.com).
Metro Nuevos Ministerios/bus 5, 27, 40, 149, 150. **Open** 8.30am-8.30pm Mon-Fri; closed Sat, Sun.
A professional translation agency.

Traductores Jurados (Official translators)

Concepción Pardo de Vera
C/Costa Brava 20 (91 734 23 31).
Polidioma *C/Espronceda 33 (91 554 47 00/polidioma@bitmailer.net).*
In Spain, official and other bodies often demand that foreign documents be translated by legally certified translators. Call for an appointment; rates are higher than for other translators. Some consulates also provide these services; *see p283.*

Communications

Internet & email

There are now plenty of cybercafés and easy-access Net centres in Madrid. For other computer services, *see page 281.*

Café Comercial Cibercafé

Glorieta de Bilbao 7, Malasaña (91 521 56 55/ www.intervia.com/comercial). Metro Bilbao/bus 3, 21, 40, 147, 149.
Open 8.30pm-12.45am Mon-Thur, Sun; 8.30pm-1.45am Fri, Sat. **No credit cards. Map** p305 F3.
The classic Café Comercial now has a basic Netcafé in an upstairs room, with bargain email access (25ptas for 2min, 500ptas for 1hr). *See also p157.*

Cestein

C/Leganitos 11, Sol & Gran Vía (91 548 27 75/www.cestein.es). Metro Santo Domingo or Plaza de España/bus all routes to Plaza de España. **Open** 8am-10pm Mon-Fri; 10am-2pm Sat; closed Sun. **No credit cards. Map** p309 D6.
Efficient Net centre with better-than-usual hard- and software (including Macs), offering office services, Net and mail access (400ptas for 30min, less for mutiple sessions) and temporary email addresses (1,000ptas/month).

Vortex

C/Ave María 20, Lavapiés (91 506 05 71/vortexmadrid@yahoo.com). Metro Antón Martín/bus 6, 26, 32.
Open 10am-midnight daily. **No credit cards. Map** p309 F9.

A small, cheap (500ptas/1hr) but well-run Net-and email centre, centrally located in Lavapiés. The downside is that it can get crowded.

WORKcenter

C/Alberto Aguilera 1, Malasaña (91 448 78 77/902 11 50 11/ www.workcenter.es). Metro San Bernardo/bus 21, 147. **Open** 24hrs daily. **Credit** MC, V. **Map** p305 E3.
An open-access office centre that aims to meet a whole range of needs. You can send or receive faxes and emails, access the Net, work on a computer, print from a disk, make copies or get ID photos. It also offers a variety of courses, and sells stationery.
Branch: C/Reina Mercedes 9 (91 533 35 95).

Www.call.home

Plaza Puerta de Moros 2, La Latina (91 354 01 04/ www.callhomeshops.com). Metro La Latina/bus 6, 17, 13, 35. **Open** 10am-11pm Mon-Fri; 11am-11pm Sat, Sun. **Credit** MC, V. **Map** p308 C9.
A mini-chain of youth-oriented Net centre-cafés that offer Internet access, email (including temporary addresses), games, printers, scanners and other office services, plus discount phone calls.
Branches: Paseo de Juan XXIII, 22, Moncloa (91 533 44 07); C/Carmen Sánchez Carrascosa 7, Chamartín (91 323 24 82).

Local access numbers

AOL 91 534 93 45.
BT 91 270 02 00.
Compuserve 91 395 65 00.

Mail

If you just need normal-rate stamps, it's always easier to buy them in an *estanco* (tobacco shop; *see page 287*).

Palacio de Comunicaciones

Plaza de Cibeles (91 521 65 00/ information 902 19 71 97/ www.correos.es). Metro Banco de España/bus all routes to Cibeles.
Open 8.30am-9.30pm Mon-Fri; 9.30am-9.30pm Sat; 8.30am-2pm Sun. **Map** p310 H7.
In the magnificent central post office, all manner of postal services are available at separate windows around the main hall: parcel post, telegrams, telex and so on. Faxes can be sent and received at all post offices, but their rates are expensive, so it's better to use a private fax bureau. There is an information desk near the main entrance. Note that

within the general opening times not all services are available at all times. Mail sent Poste Restante (General Delivery) should be addressed to *Lista de Correos, 28000 Madrid, Spain.* To collect it, go to windows 17-20 with your passport. For express post, say you want to send a letter *urgente.* For more on the building itself, *see p63.*
Other city centre post offices
(open 9am-2pm Mon-Fri; closed Sat, Sun): El Corte Inglés, C/Preciados 1-4, Sol & Gran Via; Gran Vía de San Francisco 13, La Latina; C/Mejia Lequerica 7, Chueca; C/Hermosilla 103, Salamanca.

Postal rates & postboxes

Letters and postcards up to 20g cost 35ptas within Spain, 70ptas to Europe and North Africa, 115ptas to the Americas and some of Africa and Asia and 155ptas to South-east Asia and Australasia. Cards and letters to other European countries generally arrive in 3-4 days, to North America in about a week. Aerogrammes (*Aerogramas*) cost 80ptas to all destinations. Normal postboxes are yellow, with two horizontal red stripes. There are also a few special red postboxes for urgent mail, with hourly collections.

Postal Exprés

Available at all post offices, this is an efficient express mail system with next-day delivery within Spain of packages up to 1kg (2.2lb), for 815-1,600ptas, according to the distance.

Telephones

Since the Spanish national phone company (*Telefónica*) was privatised other companies now compete with it in some areas, but it still dominates the field. *Telefónica* charges are relatively high, especially for international calls. Calls are cheaper after 10pm and before 8am, Monday to Saturday, and all day on Sundays and public holidays.

Phone numbers

It is necessary to dial provincial area codes with all phone numbers in Spain, even within the same area. Hence, all normal numbers in the Madrid area are preceded by *91*, whether you're calling within Madrid, from elsewhere in Spain or from abroad. Numbers beginning *900* are freephone lines; *901, 902* or *906* numbers are special-rate services. Spanish mobile phone numbers all begin with a *6*; calling to a mobile costs a minimum of 200ptas from a public phone.

Emergencies

Madrid has a general emergency number – **112** – to call for the police, ambulance or other emergency services. Some staff speak English, French and/or German. You can also call the relevant services direct. For more on police forces, see page 286.

Ambulancia/Ambulance 061/092/91 335 45 45
Bomberos/Fire service 080
Policía Municipal/City Police 092
Policía Nacional/National Police 091
Guardia Civil 062/91 533 53 00/91 537 31 00

Emergency repairs

The electricity company you need to call will be indicated on the electricity meter.
Electricity: Unión Fenosa (91 406 80 00);
Iberdrola (91 364 88 88)
Butane Gas: Repsol Butano (901 10 01 00/901 12 12 12)
Gas: Gas Natural (900 75 07 50/900 76 07 60)
Water: Canal de Isabel II (901 51 65 16/901 51 25 12)

Public phones

The most common model of public phone accepts coins, phonecards and credit cards, and has a digital display with instructions in several languages. The minimum charge for a local call is currently 25ptas. If you use larger coins, this type of phone gives you credit to make further calls without having to reinsert your money. If you're likely to make more than one or two calls it's better to get a phonecard, available for 1,000, 2,000 or 5,000ptas from post offices or estancos. There are some older-model phones around, with which you insert the coins into a slot at the top before dialling; coins drop when the call is answered. For a local call you need at least five duros (5pta coins) and will not get change if you put in 50 or 100ptas coins.

Most bars and cafés have a phone for public use. They usually accept 5 and 25ptas coins, but in some bars they're set to take only 25ptas pieces, an illegal but not-uncommon practice.

International & long-distance calls

To make an international call from any phone, dial **00**, wait for a continuous tone and then dial the country code: **Australia** 61; **Canada** 1; **Irish Republic** 353; **New Zealand** 64; **United Kingdom** 44; **USA** 1; followed by the area code (omitting the first zero in UK codes) and individual number. To call Madrid from abroad, dial the international code (00 in most countries), then 34 for Spain (and the 91 for Madrid).

Phone centres

At phone centres (locutorios) you are allotted a booth and pay at the counter when you have finished all your calls, thus avoiding the need for pocketloads of change. As well as the main Telefónica centre in the Gran Via there are several private locutorios such as those of Sol Telecom, which as well as phone and fax services provide email access, money exchange and facilities for sending and receiving money. Their cheap rates begin at 6pm; branch opening hours vary.
Telefónica phone centre Gran Vía 30, Sol & Gran Via. Metro Gran Via/bus all routes to Gran Via. **Open** 9am-midnight Mon-Sat; noon-midnight Sun, public holidays. **Credit** AmEx, MC, V. **Map** p309 E6.
Sol Telecom Puerta del Sol 6 (91 531 03 82). Metro Sol/bus all routes to Puerta del Sol. **Open** 9am-10.30pm daily. **Credit** MC, V. **Map** p309 E7.
Other central branches Plaza del Callao 1, Sol & Gran Via (91 532 79 77); Gran Via 84, Sol & Gran Vía (91 559 79 77).

Mobile phones

Anyone taking a mobile phone with them to Spain should always check with their home phone provider on current compatibility, as conditions and the level of charges are constantly changing. Spain's main operators are Telefónica, Airtel and Retevisión (Amena). They all work on 900 and 1800 GSM; digital systems are to be introduced in 2001. For further information check www.gsmworld.com/gsminfo.

Operator services
Normally in Spanish only.
National directory enquiries 1003
International directory enquiries 025
International operator Europe & North Africa 1008; Rest of World 1005
Telephone breakdowns 1002
Time 093
Weather information Madrid 906 36 53 28; national 906 36 53 65.
Alarm calls 096
Once the message has finished (when it starts repeating itself), key in the number you are calling from followed by the time at which you wish to be woken, in four figures, ie 0830 if you want to be called at 8.30am.
General information 098
A local information service provided by Telefónica, with information on duty pharmacies in Madrid. Otherwise, it is less reliable than the 010 line (see p287).

Computers/IT

For Net centres, see page 280.

Bitmailer

C/Juan Bravo 51, Salamanca (91 402 15 51/www.bitmailer.com). Metro Diego de León/bus 26, 29, 52, C. **Open** 8am-7pm Mon-Fri; closed Sat, Sun. **Credit** V. **Map** p307 K2. An Internet service provider with a helpful and efficient back-up service. Unlimited Net access costs 3,500ptas per month (19,900ptas per year) plus tax. Also software for sale.

Data Rent

C/Montearagón 3 (91 759 62 42/datarent@datarent.es). Metro Arturo Soria/bus 9, 70, 72, 87, 201. **Open** Sept-June 9am-2pm, 4-7pm Mon-Fri; closed Sat, Sun; July, Aug 8am-3pm Mon-Fri; closed Sat, Sun. **Credit** V, MC. PCs, printers, OHP projectors and other equipment for rent by the day, the week or the month.

Courier services

Cheapest way of sending small packages within Spain is via **Postal Exprés**, available at all post offices (see page 281).

DHL

902 12 24 24/www.dhl.com. **Open** phoneline 24hrs daily; pick ups & deliveries 9am-8pm Mon-Sat. **Credit** V. One of the most expensive of the international courier companies, but also one of the most reliable. All business is done by phone.

MFR
Distribución Urgente

Avda del Manzanares 202 (91 476 71 61/www.motorecado.com). Bus 23, 79, 123. **Open** 8am-8pm Mon-Fri; closed Sat, Sun. **No credit cards.**
Deliveries within Madrid from 998ptas for 5kg (11lb), but service is fast. Call by 6pm for same-day delivery; outside office hours there is a 50% surcharge. They also collect luggage from hotels to take to the airport and rail stations, and have long-distance services.

RUM

C/Galileo 91, Moncloa (91 535 38 16). Metro Quevedo/bus 2, 12, 16, 61. **Open** 9am-7pm Mon-Fri; closed Sat, Sun. **No credit cards. Map** p305 D1.
An efficient local courier company, with motorbikes and vans. Delivery of up to 3kg (6.6lb) within Madrid costs 450ptas for non-account customers.

Trébol

C/Esperanza 3, Lavapiés (91 530 32 32). Metro Lavapiés/bus 6, 26, 32. **Open** *Sept-July* 9am-8pm, *Aug* 9am-3pm Mon-Fri; closed Sat, Sun. **No credit cards. Map** p309 F9.
An all-cycle courier company giving fast service at low prices. Deliveries under 2kg (4.4lb) within the M-30 cost 395ptas, up to 5kg (11lb) 1,000ptas, with occasional discounts. There is also a competitive long-distance courier service.

Customs & immigration

EU residents do not have to declare goods imported into Spain from other EU countries for their personal use if tax has been paid in the country of origin. However, Customs officers can question whether large amounts of any item really are for your own use, and random checks are made for drugs. Quantities accepted as being for personal use include:

● up to 800 cigarettes, 400 small cigars, 200 cigars and 1kg of loose tobacco

● 10 litres of spirits (over 22% alcohol), 90 litres of wine (under 22%) and 110 litres of beer

Limits for non-EU residents and goods brought from outside the EU:

● 200 cigarettes or 100 small cigars or 50 cigars or 250 grams (8.82 ounces) of tobacco

● 1 litre of spirits (over 22% alcohol) or 2 litres of fortified wine (under 22% alcohol)

● 50 grams (1.76 ounces) of perfume

There are no restrictions on cameras, watches or electrical goods, within reasonable limits, and visitors can also carry up to 1 million pesetas in cash. Non-EU residents can also reclaim Value Added Tax (IVA) paid on some large purchases when they leave Spain. For details, *see page 160.*

IMMIGRATION & VISAS

Spain is one of the European Union countries within the Schengen agreement, with many shared immigration procedures and reduced border controls between each other (others are Portugal, France, Luxembourg, Belgium, Holland, Germany, Austria, Italy and Greece). To enter a Schengen country most EU nationals need only show their national ID card, but British, Irish and all non-EU citizens must have full passports.

Additional visas are not needed by US, Canadian, Australian and New Zealand citizens for stays of up to three months. Citizens of South Africa and some other countries do need a visa to enter Spain and the Schengen area. They can be obtained from Spanish consulates in other European countries as well as in your home country (or from those of other Schengen countries you visit).

EU citizens hoping to work, study or live long-term in Spain are required to obtain a residency card (*tarjeta de residencia*), for which you need to register with the police shortly after your arrival. Non-EU nationals who aim to work in Spain or study here for more than three months should, officially, have the relevant visa before entering the country. For more on living in Spain, *see page 289.*

Disabled travellers

Madrid is not yet a city where disabled people, especially wheelchair users, get around freely, although the situation is gradually improving. Access to public transport is patchy; buses and taxis are the most accessible forms of transport.

There is no general guide to accessibility in the city. Recent legislation requires all public buildings to be fully accessible by 2003, but in practice the law is more demanding with new than existing buildings. Thanks to ONCE (Spain's lottery-funded organisation for the blind) more has been done on behalf of blind and partially sighted people. Most street crossings in the centre have knobbled paving and low kerbs.

Coordinadora de Minusválidos Físicos de Madrid (COMFM)

C/Ríos Rosas 54, Chamberí (91 535 06 19). Metro Ríos Rosas/bus 3, 12, 37, 45, 147. **Open** 9am-3pm Mon-Fri; closed Sat, Sun.
An organisation for disability groups that collects information on access and facilities. Another local organisation (FAMCM) has a (Spanish-only) website, *www.servicom.es/famma.*

Sights & museums

Madrid's big three museums (the **Prado**, the **Reina Sofía**, the **Thyssen**) all have ramps, lifts and full access facilities. Wheelchair users and others with mobility problems can visit the **Palacio Real** with the aid of a lift (no reservations necessary), and the **Ermita de San Antonio de la Florida** has relatively few steps to negotiate (*see pages 68, 69*).

All or in some cases most parts of the venues listed below are accessible by ramp and/or lift (for their details, *see pages 89-109*). Monuments still near-inaccessible include the Royal Monasteries of the **Descalzas** and the **Encarnación** (*see page 74*) and the **Casa-Museo de Lope de Vega.**

Museums

Colección Permanente del ICO; Museo Africano; Museo del Aire; Museo de América; Museo Arqueológico Nacional; Museo Cerralbo; Museo de la Ciudad; Museo del Ejército (partial access); Museo Lázaro Galdiano; Museo de la Real Academia de Bellas Artes de San Fernando; Museo Romántico; Museo de San Isidro; Museo Tiflológico (a special museum for the blind and partially sighted).

Exhibition spaces

Casa de América; Centro Cultural Casa de Vacas; Centro Conde Duque; Centro Cultural de la Villa; Instituto de México; Sala del Canal de Isabel II.

Transport access

Buses

There are seats reserved for people with mobility problems behind the driver on most buses. Buses on many routes (including **3**, Puerta de Toledo-Cuatro Caminos; **5**, Sol-Chamartín, and **14**, Atocha-Chamartín), are now of the *Piso Bajo* ('Low Floor') type, with low doors and spaces for wheelchairs.

Metro & rail stations

The Metro expansion programme includes the provision of access at all new stations, and so those on recently built lines (line 8 to the airport, the Gregorio Marañón interchange, line 7 to Pitis, some others) all have good lifts. However, older stations in the city centre generally have a lot of steps, and only a very few have lifts, so changing lines and exiting once on the Metro is still a problem. Adapting these older stations will take time. The Metro map on p316 of this Guide and the free maps available at Metro stations indicate stations with lifts.

Of the main-line rail stations, Atocha has good access, but Chamartín has stairs to the Metro and is accessible to wheelchairs only with assistance, which must be requested from station authorities. *Cercanías* trains have very limited access, but some new stations such as Méndez Alvaro (by Estación Sur coach station) have lifts connecting Metro, train and bus stations.

Taxis

Special taxis adapted for wheelchairs can be called through **Euro-Taxi** on 91 547 82 00/86 00. This is also a general cab service, so make clear you want an adapted model (ask for *un Eurotaxi*). The number of such taxis in Madrid is growing but still limited, and the waiting time can be up to 30min. Fares are the same as for standard cabs, but since they may have to come from far away the cost can be quite high, as the meter is started as soon as a request is received.

Embassies

For a full list look in the local phone book under *Embajadas*.

American Embassy

C/Serrano 75, Salamanca (91 587 22 00/www.embusa.es). Metro Rubén Darío/bus 9, 19, 51, 61. **Open** *phoneline* 24hrs daily; *office* 9am-1pm Mon-Fri; closed Sat, Sun. **Map** p307 I2.

Australian Embassy

Plaza del Descubridor Diego de Ordás 3, Chamberí (91 441 93 00/emergency phoneline 900 99 61 99/ www.emaustralia.es). Metro Ríos Rosas/bus 3, 12, 37, 45, 149. **Open** 8.30am-2pm, 3-5pm Mon-Thur; 8.30am-2.15pm Fri; closed Sat, Sun.

British Embassy

C/Fernando el Santo 16, Chamberí (91 308 06 18/www.ukinspain.com). Metro Alonso Martínez/bus 7, 21, 147. **Open** 9am-1.30pm, 3-6pm Mon-Fri; closed Sat, Sun. **Map** p306 H3. **British Consulate** *C/Marqués de la Ensenada 16, Chueca (906 42 34 56). Metro Colón/bus all routes to Plaza de Colón.* **Open** 8am-2.30pm Mon-Fri; closed Sat, Sun. **Map** p306 H4.

Canadian Embassy

C/Núñez de Balboa 35, Salamanca (91 423 32 50/www.canada-es.org). Metro Velázquez/bus 1, 9, 19, 51, 74. **Open** *phoneline* 8.30am-1pm,2-5pm, *office* 9am-12.30pm, Mon-Fri; closed Sat, Sun. **Map** p307 J4.

Irish Embassy

Paseo de la Castellana 46 (91 576 35 00/embajada.irlanda@ran.es). Metro Rubén Darío /bus 5, 27, 15, 150. **Open** 10am-2pm Mon-Fri; closed Sat, Sun. **Map** p306 I3.

New Zealand Embassy

Plaza de la Lealtad 2 (91 523 02 26). Metro Retiro or Banco de España/bus all routes to Plaza de la Lealtad. **Open** 9am-1.30pm, 2.30-5.30pm Mon-Fri; closed Sat, Sun. **Map** p310 H7.

Health

All visitors can obtain emergency care through the Spanish national health service, the *Seguridad Social*. EU citizens are entitled to basic attention for free if they have an E111 form (if you can get one sent or faxed within four days, you will still be exempt from charges). Many medicines will be charged for. In non emergency situations, short-term visitors usually find it

more convenient to use travel insurance and private clinics rather than the state system.

Emergencies

In a medical emergency the best thing to do is go to the *urgencias* (accident and emergency) department of any of the major hospitals. All are open 24 hours daily. In the centre, go to the Clínico or Gregorio Marañón.

If you have no E111 or other insurance, you can still be seen at the Marañón. Alternatively, go to a *Casa de Socorro*, where you will be given first aid, and if necessary referred to a hospital. Most open 24 hours daily.

Ambulances

There are several emergency lines for calling an ambulance: usually the best to use is **061**, but you can also try the general emergency line (112), the Red Cross (*Cruz Roja*, 91 522 22 22) or the city SAMUR service (via the Municipal Police, on 092).

Casas de socorro (emergency centres)

Gran Vía area *C/Navas de Tolosa 10 (91 588 96 60). Metro Callao/bus all routes to Callao.* **Map** p309 D7.
Huertas/Atocha area *C/Gobernador 39 (91 420 30 03/91 420 36 03). Metro Antón Martín or Atocha/bus all routes to Atocha.* **Map** p310 G9.
Retiro area *C/Reyes Magos 19 (91 501 70 65). Metro Conde de Casal/ bus C, 20, 26, 63.* **Map** p311 K9.
Salamanca *C/Montesa 22 (91 588 51 00). Metro Manuel Becerra/bus 1, 43, 53, 74, C.*

Hospitals

Ciudad Sanitaria La Paz *Paseo de la Castellana 261, Chamartín (91 358 26 00/91 727 70 00). Metro Begoña/ bus 66, 67, 124, 132, 135.*
The largest city hospital, in north Madrid near Plaza Castilla.
Hospital Clínico San Carlos *Plaza de Cristo Rey, Moncloa (91 330 30 00). Metro Moncloa/bus 1, 12, 44, C.* Enter from Calle Isaac Peral, just off the Plaza de Cristo Rey.
Hospital General Gregorio Marañón *C/Dr Esquerdo 46, Salamanca (91 586 80 00). Metro Ibiza or O'Donnell/bus 2, 28, 143, C.* The *Urgencias* entrance is in C/Ibiza.
Hospital Ramón y Cajal *Carretera de Colmenar Viejo, km 9.1, Northern suburbs (91 336 80 00). Train Cercanías lines C-7, C-8 to Ramón y Cajal/bus 124, 135.*
Also on the northern edge of the city.

Directory

Private health care

Unidad Médica Anglo-Americana

C/Conde de Aranda 1, Salamanca
(91 435 18 23). Metro Retiro/bus all
routes to Puerta de Alcalá. **Open**
Sept-July 9am-8pm Mon-Fri; 10am-
1pm Sat; closed Sun; Aug 10am-4pm
Mon-Fri; closed Sat, Sun. **Credit**
AmEx, MC, V. **Map** p310 I6.
A British-American clinic with a full
range of services, including dentistry.
Staff make house and hotel calls.

AIDS/HIV

Centro Dermatológico de la Comunidad

C/Sandoval 7, Chamberí (91 445 23
28). Metro San Bernardo/bus 21,
147. **Open** 9am-noon Mon-Fri;
closed Sat, Sun. **Map** p305 E3.
An official clinic that carries out free,
confidential HIV tests.

Fundacíon Anti-SIDA

C/Juan Montalvo 6, Moncloa
(freephone 900 11 10 00/91 536 15
00). Metro Guzmán el Bueno/bus 2,
44, 45, 128, C. **Open** 10am-8pm
Mon-Fri; closed Sat, Sun.
The best organisation for support and
advice about HIV and AIDS.

Alternative medicine

Instituto de Medicina Integral

Plaza de la Independencia 4,
Salamanca (91 576 26 49). Metro
Banco de España or Retiro/bus all
routes to Puerta de Alcalá. **Open**
8.30am-2pm, 5-8pm Mon-Fri; 9am-
2pm Sat; closed Sun. **No credit
cards**. **Map** p310 H6.
Acupuncture, homeopathy and other
complementary medicine. The clinic
has English-speaking practitioners.

Contraception & women's health

Condoms (profilácticos or
condones) are available from
most pharmacies, and vending
machines and supermarkets.

Clínica Duratón

C/Colegiata 4, Austrias (91 429 77
69). Metro Tirso de Molina/bus 6,
17, 23, 25, 50, 65. **Open** Sept-July
9.30am-1.30pm, 4.30-8.30pm; Aug
4.30-8.30pm, Mon-Fri; closed Sat,
Sun. **Map** p309 D8.
Family planning centre run by
women doctors and staff.

Espacio de Salud Entre Nosotras

Avda Alfonso XIII, 118, Chamartín
(91 519 56 78). Metro Colombia/bus
7, 11, 40. **Open** 10am-1pm Mon-
Thur; closed Fri-Sun.
A feminist medical association
offering free advice and counselling.

Dentists

See also **Private health care**.

Clínica Dental Cisne

C/Magallanes 18, Chamberí
(91 446 32 21/24hr emergencies
mobile 629 98 86 87). Metro
Quevedo/bus 16, 37, 61, 149. **Open**
10am-1.30pm, 3-8pm Mon, Thur; 2-
8pm Tue, Wed, Fri; closed Sat, Sun.
Credit MC, V. **Map** p305 E2.
British dentist Dr Ian Daniel is based
at this clinic. Consultations cost
4,000ptas. Hours may vary in summer,
and it sometimes closes in August.
Dentistry is not covered by the E111
form, so you must pay all charges.

Pharmacies

Pharmacies (farmacias) are
signalled by large green, usually
flashing, crosses, and are
plentiful in central Madrid.
Pharmacies within the official
system of the College of
Pharmacies are normally open
9.30am to 2pm, 5 to 8pm,
Monday to Saturday. At other
times a duty rota operates.
Every pharmacy has a list of the
College's farmacias de guardia
(duty pharmacies) for that day
posted outside the door, with the
nearest ones highlighted (many
now have a computerised, push-
button panel). Duty pharmacies
for the whole city are also listed
in local newspapers, and
information is available on the
010 and 098 phonelines.

At night duty pharmacies
may look as if they are closed,
and you may have to knock on
the shutters to be served.

Currently there are also two
24-hour pharmacies in Madrid,
open every day of the year:

Farmacia Central

Paseo de Santa María de la Cabeza
64, Embajadores (91 473 06 72).
Metro Palos de la Frontera/bus 6,
55, 59, 78, 85. **No credit cards**.
South of Glorieta de Embajadores.

Farmacia Lastra

C/Conde de Peñalver 27, Salamanca
(91 402 43 63). Metro Goya/
bus 1, 26, 61, 74. **Credit** AmEx, DC,
MC, V. **Map** p307 L4.
A handy standby, on the east side of
Salamanca.

Insurance

EU nationals are entitled to use
the Spanish state health service,
provided they have an E111
form, which in Britain can be
obtained from post offices,
health centres and Social
Security offices. This will cover
you for emergencies, but for
short-term visitors it's often
simpler to avoid dealing with
the state bureaucracy and take
out private travel insurance
before departure, particularly as
this will also cover you for
stolen or lost cash or valuables
as well as medical costs.

Some non-EU countries also
have reciprocal health-care
agreements with Spain, but,
again, for most travellers it will
be more convenient to have
private travel insurance for all
eventualities before arriving in
the country. For more on all
health services, see page 283.

Libraries

For a full list, check Bibliotecas
in the local Yellow Pages.

Ateneo Científico y Literario de Madrid

C/del Prado 21, Huertas (91 429 17
50). Metro Antón Martín/bus 6, 9,
26, 32. **Open** 9am-1am Mon-Sat;
9am-10pm Sun. **Map** p309 F8.
A literary and philosophical club
founded in 1820, Madrid's Ateneo has
often been a focal point in the city's
cultural life. It also has the second-
largest library in Spain, with the
advantage of being open when others
are closed. Anyone staying in Madrid
long enough might want to take out
membership (15,000ptas per year).
Members have access to talks, cultural
events and other activities.

Biblioteca Nacional

Paseo de Recoletos 20, (91 580 78 00/
www.bne.es). Metro Colón/bus all
routes to Plaza de Colón. **Open** 9am-
9pm Mon-Fri; 9am-2pm Sat; closed
Sun. **Map** p306 I5.

Spain's national library has early books and manuscripts on display (in the Museo del Libro), and is also the home of the **Hemeroteca Nacional**, the national newspaper library. To use the library regularly you need accreditation from a university or similar institution, but a one-day pass is quite easy to obtain (take a passport or residency card).

Biblioteca Pedro Salinas

Glorieta de la Puerta de Toledo 1, La Latina (91 366 54 07). Metro Puerta de Toledo/bus all routes to Puerta de Toledo. **Open** 8.30am-8.45pm Mon-Fri; 9am-2pm Sat; closed Sun, & Sat July-Sept. **Map** p308 C10.
The most attractive and convenient of Madrid's public libraries. Books can be taken out on loan.

Hemeroteca Municipal

C/Conde Duque 9-11, Conde Duque (91 588 57 71). Metro Noviciado/bus all routes to Plaza de España. **Open** *Oct-June* 9am-9pm, *July, Sept* 9am-8pm, *Aug* 9am-1pm Mon-Fri; closed Sat, Sun. **Map** p305 D4.
The city newspaper library is one of several institutions housed in the Centro Conde Duque. To be admitted you need a researchers' card, for which you need to provide a copy of your passport and two ID photos.

Lost property

Airport & rail stations

If you lose something land-side of check-in at Barajas Airport, report the loss to the *Aviación Civil* office in the relevant terminal, or call 91 393 60 00. If you think you've mislaid anything on the RENFE rail network, look for the *Atención al Viajero* desk or *Jefe de Estación* office at the main station nearest to where your property went astray. For information by phone on lost property call the main RENFE information number (902 24 02 02). In all cases, ask for '*Objetos Perdidos*'.

EMT (city buses)

EMT *C/Alcántara 24, Salamanca (91 406 88 43). Metro Lista/bus 1, 21, 26, 53, 146.*
For any items lost on city or airport buses.

Metro/taxis/municipal lost property office

Negociado de Objetos Perdidos, Plaza de Legazpi 7 (91 588 43 46/44). Metro Legazpi/bus all routes to Legazpi. **Open** *Oct-June* 9am-2pm, *July-Sept* 9am-1.30pm Mon-Fri; closed Sat, Sun. This office mainly receives articles found on the Metro or in taxis, but if you're lucky, something lost in the street may turn up here.

Money

For the time being, Spain's everyday currency is the *peseta*, abbreviated to *ptas*. There are coins for 1, 5, 10, 25 (with a hole in the centre), 50, 100, 200 and 500ptas. A 5pta coin is called a *duro*. Notes are green 1,000ptas, 2,000 (red), 5,000 (brown) and 10,000ptas (blue).

THE EURO

In Spain, however, as in 11 other EU countries, local money is technically now only one outward form of the future European currency, the *euro*. It is already the reserve currency for banking, and euro-prices appear next to peseta ones in most shops, on receipts and so on. All 12 euro-zone currencies have fixed exchange rates with the euro and each other; one euro equals 166.386ptas.

The euro-era proper really begins on 1 January 2002, when euro notes and coins finally appear on the street. There will then be a six-month transition period, when both currencies will be in circulation. Banks, bureaux de change and ATM machines will (officially) dispense euros only, with the idea that the peseta will rapidly fade from use.

Anyone travelling to Spain in the first half of 2002, therefore, is advised to take euros (or use an ATM), but, given the mix-ups that will come with the changeover (especially in small shops) it will still be a good idea to have some pesetas; banks say they will still give out pesetas over the counter if customers insist on it. After 30 June 2002 your pesetas will be officially worthless, but you will be able to exchange them in banks. For queries on the euro in Spain, ring 902 11 20 02.

Banks & exchange

Banks and savings banks (*cajas de ahorros*) readily accept cash and travellers' cheques (you must show your passport). Commission rates vary a lot between banks, and it's worth shopping around before changing money; also, given the rates charged by Spanish banks the cheapest way to get money is often through an ATM machine by credit card rather than with travellers' cheques (*see below*). It is always quicker to change money at larger bank offices than at local branches.

There are many small bureau de change (*cambio*), particularly on the Gran Vía. Exchange rates are usually worse than in banks.

Bank hours

Banks and savings banks normally open 9am-2pm, Monday to Friday. Between 1 October and 31 May many branches also open from 9am to 1pm on Saturdays. Hours vary a little between different banks, and some open slightly earlier or later, while some have branches that stay open until around 5pm one day a week. Savings banks often open late on Thursday afternoons, but are less likely to open on Saturdays. All banks are closed on public holidays.

Out-of-hours services

Outside normal hours you can change money at the **airport** (terminals T-1 and T-2, 24hrs), at the main train stations (**Atocha**, 9am-9pm, **Chamartín**, 8am-10pm, daily), in **El Corte Inglés** (*see p160*), in hotels, at private *cambios* and at the places below. At the airport, Chamartín and outside some banks in Gran Vía and Puerta del Sol there are automatic cash exchange machines that accept notes in major currencies, in good condition (but avoid the ones at Gran Vía and Puerta del Sol late night).

American Express

Plaza de las Cortes 2, Huertas (91 572 03 03). Metro Banco de España/bus 9, 14, 27, 37, 45. **Open** 9am-5.30pm Mon-Fri; 9am-noon Sat; closed Sun. **Map** p310 G8.
The usual AmEx services, and an ATM for AmEx cards. Money can be transferred from AmEx offices worldwide in 24 hours..
Branch: C/Francisco Gervás 10, Tetuán (91 572 03 03); closed Sat.

Western Union Money Transfer

Change Express, Gran Vía 16, Sol & Gran Vía (91 542 81 80/900 63 36 33). Metro Gran Vía/bus all routes to Gran Vía. **Open** 8am-11.30pm daily. **Map** p309 F6.

Change Express is the local Western Union agent: the quickest if not the cheapest way to have money sent from abroad. Commission is paid by the sender.
Branches: Gran Via 25, 46, 51 & 53, Sol & Gran Via; Plaza Cánovas del Castillo 5, Huertas.

Chequepoint
Puerta del Sol 8 (91 521 67 02).
Metro Sol/bus all routes to Puerta del Sol. **Open** 9am-midnight daily.
Map p309 E7.
An international exchange company. Opening hours vary between offices. **Main branches**: C/Preciados 7, Sol & Gran Via (91 531 02 60); Plaza de Callao 4, Sol & Gran Via (91 532 29 22); open 24hrs daily.

Credit cards

Major credit and charge cards are accepted in most hotels, shops, restaurants and for many other services. You can also withdraw cash with major cards from most bank ATM machines, which provide instructions in different languages.

Exchange rates and handling fees often work out to be more favourable for card withdrawals than with cash or travellers' cheque transactions. Banks will also advance cash against credit cards over the counter, but much prefer you to use an ATM.

Lost or stolen cards
All lines have English-speaking staff and are open 24hrs daily.
American Express 91 572 03 20.
AmEx travellers' cheques
freephone 900 99 44 26.
Diners' Club 91 701 59 00.
Mastercard 91 519 21 00;
freephone 900 97 12 31.
Visa 91 519 60 00;
freephones 900 97 44 45/900 99 12 16.

Opening times

Today not many Madrileños will take a nap for their afternoon *siesta*, but they do operate to a distinctive schedule. Foreigners who fail to adapt to (or even recognise) this often complain the place is dead when they try to go for a walk at 4pm, without realising that the same streets might be bustling three to four hours later, or even after 1am.

Shop hours are flexible, but most smaller shops open from 9.30-10am to 2pm, and 5-5.30 to 8-8.30pm, Monday to Saturday, although many stay closed on Saturday afternoons. Food markets open earlier, at 8-9am. In summer many shops open and close slightly later in the afternoons. Summer schedules usually apply through July and August. Major stores and malls are open 10am to 9pm without a break, Monday to Saturday (for the vexed question of Sunday shopping, *see page 160*).

Madrileños still eat, drink and go out and stay out later than their neighbours in virtually every other European country. Most restaurants are open 1 to 4pm, and 9pm to midnight, and you'll find it hard to get a full evening meal before 9pm. Many restaurants, especially in the city centre, close on Sundays, and some restaurants and shops close for the whole of August.

Police & crime

Street crime is no more a problem in Madrid than in other major cities, but there are naturally parts of the city where you need to be extra careful. You should of course avoid empty, unlit streets at night, particularly in the old city. On the other hand, on weekend nights in popular areas such as Huertas or Calle Fernando VI the number of people in the street creates a sense of security that's often hard to find late-night in more northerly cities.

Pickpocketing or bag-snatching are more likely than mugging here. Places to be on your guard are the Puerta del Sol, the Plaza Mayor, the Plaza Santa Ana and above all the Rastro; watch out, too, on the Metro. The area around the junction of Gran Via and Calle Montera is a centre of street prostitution, and can feel uncomfortable at night. Most recently, the Lavapiés district has acquired a bad reputation

for street crime, especially bag snatching and muggings. This has developed alongside the growth in racial tensions in the area (*see pages 28-9*), as robberies are often attributed to young, homeless North African illegal immigrants. Extra care is needed here at all times, especially around the junction of C/Mesón de Paredes and C/Cabestreros.

Street thieves, however, often prey very deliberately on the unwary, and their chances can be limited greatly by the following simple precautions.

● When sitting in a café, above all at an outside table, **never** leave a bag or coat on the floor, on the back of a chair or on a chair where you cannot see it clearly. If in doubt, keep it on your lap.
● Give the impression of knowing what's going on around you, and without getting paranoid, watch out to see if you are being followed.
● Wear shoulder bags pulled to the front, not at your back. Keep the bag closed and keep a hand on top of it.
● Avoid pulling out big-denomination notes to pay for things, especially in the street at night; try not to get large notes when changing money.
● Be aware that street thieves often work in pairs or groups; if someone hassles you for money or to buy something in the street, or pulls out a map and asks you for directions, keep walking, as this can be a ruse to distract you so that the 'partner' can get at your bag. This is often done pretty crudely, and so not hard to recognise.

Police forces

Spain has several police forces. In Madrid the most important are the local *Policía Municipal*, in navy and pale blue, and the *Policía Nacional*, in darker blue and white uniforms (or all-blue combat gear). Each force has its own responsibilities, although they overlap. *Municipales* are principally concerned with traffic and parking problems and local regulations. The force with primary responsibility for dealing with crime are the *Nacionales*. The *Guardia Civil*, in green, are responsible, among other things, for policing inter-city highways, and Customs.

Reporting a crime

If you are robbed or attacked, you should report the incident as soon as possible at the nearest *Policía Nacional* station (*comisaría*). If you report a crime you will be asked to make an official statement (*denuncia*). It is unlikely anything you have lost will be recovered, but you need the *denuncia* to make an insurance claim. A very few officers speak some English.

Jefatura de Policía

C/Leganitos 19, Sol & Gran Via (91 541 71 60). Metro Santo Domingo, Plaza de España/bus all routes to Gran Via. **Map** p309 D6.
The *Policía Nacional* headquarters for central Madrid, near Plaza de España. Some other police stations in the city centre are listed below; all are open 24hrs daily.
Puerta del Sol *inside Metro Sol, by C/Carretas exit (91 521 09 11). Metro Sol/bus all routes to Puerta del Sol.* **Map** p309 E7.
Huertas/Retiro *C/Huertas 76 (91 249 09 94). Metro Antón Martín/bus 14, 27, 34, 37.* **Map** p310 G8.
The most convenient station for any incidents that occur around Huertas and the main art museums.
Chamberí *C/Rafael Calvo 33 (91 322 32 78). Metro Iglesia/bus 3, 16, 40, 61, 147.* **Map** p306 H2.

Religious services

Anglican & Protestant

Saint George's (British Embassy Church) *C/Núñez de Balboa 43, Salamanca (91 576 51 09). Metro Velázquez/bus 1, 9, 19, 21, 51, 74.*
Services *Sept-June* 7.30pm Wed; 10.30am Fri; 8.30am, 10am, 11.15am Sun; *July, Aug* 8.30am, 11.15am Sun. **Map** p307 J3.
Community Church *C/de la Viña 3, Moncloa (91 730 03 49). Metro Metropolitano/bus 132, C, F.* **Services** 11am Sun.

Catholic (in English)

Our Lady of Mercy
Avenida Alfonso XIII , 165 (91 533 59 35). Metro Pío XII/bus 29, 150.
English Mass 11am Sun.
Sunday Schools for adults and children, and a special children's Mass.

Jewish

Sinagoga de Madrid *C/Balmes 3 (91 591 31 31). Metro Iglesia/bus 3, 16, 61, 149.* **Prayers** 8am, 8pm Mon-Fri, 9.15am Sat, 9am Sun. **Map** p306 G1.
A Sephardic congregation.

Muslim

Centro Cultural Islámico de Madrid *C/Salvador de Madariaga 4 (91 326 26 10). Metro Barrio de la Concepción/bus 53.* **Open** 10am-8pm Mon-Thur, Sat, Sun; 4-8pm Fri.
One of the largest Islamic centres in Europe. As well as a mosque it houses a social centre and other services.

Tourist information

City and regional authority (*Comunidad de Madrid*) tourist offices all provide similar basic information on Madrid and its region, plus free maps (*see also page 275*). The city also runs a phone information line for local citizens, **010**, that can be very useful to visitors. Tourist offices do not make hotel bookings but can advise on vacancies; for booking agencies, *see page 37*.

Useful publications free at tourist offices in Spanish and English are *En Madrid*, an events guide, and the monthly *Vive Madrid*. Full information on what's on at any time is in local papers, listings magazines and local English-language magazines (*see page 290*). For useful websites, *see page 293*.

Oficina Municipal de Turismo

Plaza Mayor 3, Austrias (91 588 16 36). Metro Sol/bus all routes to Puerta del Sol. **Open** 10am-8pm Mon-Fri; 10am-2pm, 3-8pm Sat; 10am-3pm Sun. **Map** p309 D8.
The city office is also the departure point for walking tours (*see p61*).

Oficinas de Información Turística

C/Duque de Medinaceli 2, Huertas (91 429 49 51). Metro Banco de España/bus 9, 14, 27, 34, 45. **Open** 9am-7pm Mon-Fri; 9am-1pm Sat; closed Sun. **Map** p310 G8.
Hours vary slighty between offices.
Branch offices: Barajas Airport Terminal 1 (91 305 86 56); Chamartín Station, near platform 20 (91 315 99 76); Mercado Puerta de Toledo (91 364 18 76).

Summer information officers

During July and August pairs of young information guides, in bright yellow and blue uniforms, are sent by the city *Patronato de Turismo* to roam the central area ready to answer enquiries in a courageous variety of languages (10am-3pm, 4-9pm daily). They also staff information stands at Puerta del Sol, Plaza del Callao, Plaza Mayor, by the Palacio Real and by the Prado.

010 phoneline

Open 8am-9pm Mon-Fri; 9am-2pm Sat; closed Sun.
A city-run information line that will answer enquiries of any and every kind on Madrid, and particularly on events promoted by the city council. Calls are accepted in French and English, but you may have to wait for an English-speaking operator. From outside Madrid, call 91 540 40 10/40. There is also a tourist information line, 901 30 06 00, which, though, usually has more limited information.

Useful points

Addresses

Individual flats in apartment blocks have traditionally been identified by the abbreviations *izq* (*izquierda*, left) or *dcha* (*derecha*, right) after the floor number (C/del Prado 221, 5ª dcha); in newer buildings they may be shown more simply (C/del Prado 223, 4B). If a building has no street number (usually because it's too big, like a station or hospital), it is written *s/n* (*sin número*).

Electricity

The standard current in Spain is now 220v, but a few old buildings still have 125v circuits, so check before using electrical equipment in older hotels. Plugs are all of the two-round-pin type. The 220v current works fine with British 240v products, with a plug adaptor, available at El Corte Inglés (*see p160*). With US 110v appliances you will need a current transformer.

Estancos (tobacco shops)

Although no longer as ubiquitous as they once were, the tobacco shop or *estanco* (identified by a brown and yellow sign with the word *tabacos*) is still an important Spanish institution. Their main role, as the sign suggests, is to supply tobacco-related products, but they are also places to buy postage stamps, phonecards and *metrobús* and monthly *abono* bus and Metro tickets. *Estancos* are also the only places where you can obtain the official money vouchers (*papel de estado*) needed in dealings with Spanish bureaucracy. Some also have photocopiers.

Queuing

Although it may not be immediately visible, Spaniards have a highly developed queuing culture. In small shops and at market stalls people may not be standing in line, but they generally have a clear idea of when it is their turn. One common practice is to ask when you first arrive, to no one in particular, '*¿Quién da la vez?*' or '*¿Quién es el último/la última?*' ('Who's last?'); see who nods back at you, and follow on after them. Say '*yo*' ('me') to the next person who asks the same question.

Smoking

Most adult Spaniards still smoke – a lot. It is very unusual to find non-smoking areas in restaurants or bars, although smoking bans in cinemas, theatres and on main-line trains are generally respected. Smoking is officially banned throughout the Metro system, but many people take this to mean on trains only, and not station platforms. For more on buying tobacco, *see pages 158, 182*.

Time

Spain is one hour ahead of British time, and six hours ahead of US EST. Changes to and from summer time now happen on the same nights in the UK and Spain. Hence, when it's 6pm in Madrid, it's 5pm in London and, usually, noon in New York.

Tipping

Tipping is less generalised than it once was in Spain. There are no fixed rules, nor any expectation of a set ten per cent or more, and many Spaniards tip very little. It is still customary to leave around five to ten per cent for a waiter in a restaurant, up to and rarely over 500ptas, and many people also leave some coins in a bar, maybe part or all of the usual change. It's also usual to tip hotel porters and toilet attendants. In taxis a usual tip is around five per cent; more is given for longer journeys, or if a driver has helped with luggage.

Toilets

Public toilets are scarce. There are some with an attendant in the Retiro, by the lake, at Chamartín and Atocha stations and in the Paseo del Prado. At several locations there are pay-on-entry cubicles that cost 25ptas. Apart from that, head for bars, cafés, big stores or fast-food restaurants.

Water

Madrid's water no longer comes from the fast-flowing streams that earned the city its name, but local tap water is good and safe to drink, with none of the chlorine taste that you get in some Spanish cities. There are occasional water shortages in summer, and signs posted in hotels urge guests to avoid wasting water.

When to go

A good way to appreciate Madrid is to visit during one of the city's *fiestas* (*see pages 184-9*). Hotel prices are a little higher in July/August, and lowest in February/March and October/November. The dry, mountain climate of Madrid has been described as 'six months of winter (*invierno*) and three months of hell (*infierno*)'. This is a gross exaggeration, but the weather does tend to extremes.

Spring

Average temperatures 6.5-18.5 °C (43.7-65.3 °F). One of the most pleasant times of year, with moderate sunshine and clear skies, and occasional bursts of rain. Pavement cafés fill the streets from Eastertime, and late spring and early summer is one of the liveliest times in Madrid. May is dominated by the city's biggest fiesta, San Isidro.

Summer

Average temperatures 15.5-30.5 °C (59.9-86.9 °F). June and early July are another time when Madrid is at its best. Temperatures usually only approach 40°C (104°F) from mid-July to mid-August. In the midsummer heat activity winds down, and many people become semi-nocturnal, so that streets can be silent at 4pm but bustling after midnight. Traditionally, anyone who can do so has left the city for the whole of August. This means it's uncrowded, but many places are closed (it's hard to do much in such heat anyway). One solution is to be up early (or see the night through), as the early morning air can be so fresh you could drink it. For those who stay in Madrid there are some great traditional fiestas. Lately the August exodus has been smaller, with more places staying open. After mid-August the peak of the heat passes, and things are more pleasant.

Autumn/Fall

Average temperatures 7.5 -20.5 °C (45.5-68.9 °F). The weather is lovely, especially in September. The return from holidays is greeted by new arts programmes, and the football season. Most cafés take in their pavement tables at the end of October.

Winter

Average temperatures 0.5-10.5 °C (32.9-50.9 °F). January is the coldest month: temperatures can drop to freezing, and snow is not unknown, although the air is usually more crisp than wet. A busy time culturally, and Madrileños still go out, if less than at other times of year.

Holidays

On public holidays (*fiestas*), virtually all shops, banks and offices, and many bars and restaurants, are closed. There is a near-normal public transport service, except on Christmas Day and New Year's Day, and many museums are open, with Sunday hours. When a holiday falls on a Tuesday or Thursday many people still take the day before or after the weekend off as well, in a long weekend called a *puente* (bridge). Many places are also closed for the whole of Easter Week. For the city's festivals, *see pages 184-9*. The usual official holidays are:
New Year's Day/*Año Nuevo* 1 Jan; **Three Kings/*Reyes Magos*** 6 Jan; **Good Friday/*Viernes Santa*;** May **(Labour) Day/*Fiesta del Trabajo*** 1 May; **Madrid Day/*Día de la Comunidad de Madrid*** 2 May; **San Isidro** 15 May; **Virgen de la Paloma** 15 Aug; **Discovery of America/*Día de la Hispanidad*** 12 Oct; **All Saints' Day/*Todos los Santos*** 1 Nov; **Virgen de la Almudena** 9 Nov; **Constitution Day/*Día de la Constitución*** 6 Dec; **Immaculate Conception/ *La Inmaculada*** 8 Dec; **Christmas Day/*Navidad*** 25 Dec.

Women

Centro de la Mujer

C/Barquillo 44, Chueca (91 319 36 89). Metro Chueca/bus 3, 37, 40. **Open** 4-8pm Mon-Fri; closed Sat, Sun. **Map** p306 H5.
A women's centre used by a variety of independent organisations.

Dirección General de la Mujer

Plaza Carlos Trías Beltrán 7 (91 580 37 73/www.comadrid.es/dgmujer). Metro Santiago Bernabéu/bus 27, 43, 149. **Open** 9am-2pm Mon-Fri; closed Sat, Sun.
Information, advice and other services.

Instituto de la Mujer

C/Condesa de Venadito 34, La Concepción (91 347 80 00). Metro Barrio de la Concepción/bus 11, 53. **Open** 9am-2pm, 4-6pm Mon-Thur; 9am-2pm Fri; closed Sat, Sun.
A government organisation that acts as an umbrella for many other bodies, with a useful information service. At C/Génova 11, Chueca (91 391 58 80), theInstitute has a legal advice office.

Living & Working in Madrid

Foreigners, especially from the EU, now work in a variety of fields in Madrid, but for new arrivals the best chances of finding work are still in English teaching and/or translation. To teach, it's advisable to have a relevant qualification. Private work is available; to get your first students, try placing ads at the **British Institute** (C/Miguel Angel 1, Chamberí, 91 337 35 01), English bookshops (*see page 162*) or in the English-language press (*see page 290*).

If you stay and work here there are bureaucratic hurdles to negotiate; you can maybe ignore them for a while, but in the long run this is counter-productive. If you come here contracted from your country of origin, papers should be dealt with by your employer. The quickest way to deal with the Spanish State's love of form-filling is to resort to one of the agencies called *gestorías*. For English-speaking *gestorías*, see page 279.

Paperwork

The Interior Ministry has a freephone line for immigration enquiries, 900 15 00 00, and a website at *www.mir.es*.

EU CITIZENS

All EU nationals have the right to live, work and study in Spain, but must become legally resident, with a residency card (*tarjeta de residencia*), if they stay for more than three months. If you have work lined up, you can begin the process. Take the necessary documents (*see below*) to the **Comisaría de Extranjería** and fill in the application form. You will be given another form to pay 990ptas into a Ministry bank account, which must be paid before they begin processing the request, and a number to call to check when to collect your card (a month or so later). The *tarjeta*

will show your *NIE* (*Número de Identificación de Extranjero*, identification number as a foreigner). You will normally be given a five-year residency card.

When you apply, if you are going to work as an employee (*de cuenta ajena*), you need to show a contract or firm offer of work (which can be part-time and with no fixed duration). Other necessities are: passport, four passport photographs and photocopies of all documents. Other papers (proof of address) are sometimes requested as well.

If you aim to be freelance or self-employed (*autónomo/a* or *trabajador por cuenta propia*), more papers are needed. Most people find it near-indispensable to get a *gestor* at this point (this costs about 10,000ptas). First you need a *Número de Identificación Fiscal* or *NIF* (tax code), which as a foreigner is the same as your *NIE* (*see above*). This can be obtained, prior to the main residency application, from a Comisaría de Extranjería or a local tax office (*Delegación de Hacienda*). Once you have a *NIF* you can open a bank account, request a phone line, be paid by other businesses and so on. You also need to register with the tax and social security offices; in future you will have to pay contributions and make tax declarations, and this is one stage in particular when the advice of a good *gestor* can save significant amounts of money. With this done you apply for a residency card at the Comisaría de Extranjería, with the same documents as an employee.

NON-EU CITIZENS

Immigration laws have relaxed greatly for EU nationals, but have tightened for people from the rest of the world. White-skinned non-Europeans suffer less than Africans and Asians, but for all non-EU citizens it's best to keep papers in order.

First-time applicants officially need a special visa, obtained from a Spanish consulate in your home country, although you can start the ball rolling in Spain if you don't mind making at least one trip back home. This, and the length of the process, means that good legal advice is especially important. You must present a variety of documents to the consulate, who pass copies on to the Labour Ministry in Madrid. Only when it approves them will the consulate issue a special visa, which allows you, back in Spain, to apply for a residency permit with similar procedures as for European citizens (*see above*).

Comisarías de Extranjería

For EU citizens *Comisaría de Tetuán, Pasaje Maestros Ladrilleros 2* (91 571 92 00) *Metro Valdeacederas/ bus 42, 49, 124, 125.* **Open** 9am-2pm Mon-Fri; closed Sat, Sun.
For non-EU citizens *C/Moratín 43* (91 429 09 94). *Metro Antón Martín/ bus 10, 14, 27, 34, 37, 45.* **Open** 9am-2pm Mon-Fri; closed Sat, Sun. Once a residency card has been issued it can be collected from another *comisaría*, at C/Madrazo 9 (91 521 93 50), near Cibeles.

Students

Students who stay in Spain over three months, including EU citizens, also officially require a residency card, and students on full-time courses may find it creates problems if they do not obtain one. To do so, you take to the Comisaría de Extranjería confirmation of enrolment on a recognised course; proof of income for the duration of the course, currently estimated at a minimum of 800,000ptas for a 12-month period; and proof of health insurance status, private or public.

Renting a flat

The price of buying a flat in Madrid rocketed at the end of the '90s, but rents surprisingly stayed relatively stable. It is possible to find a one-bedroom flat with balcony for around 75,000ptas (£280/$450) a month, and if you share large properties are available for 190,000ptas (£710/$1,150).

Places to look for flat ads are the ads magazine *Segundamano* and the English-language press (*see below*). Another option is to choose an area and look for '*Se alquila*' ('To rent') signs in windows and doorways.

Contratos de alquiler (rental agreements) generally cover a five-year period, within which a landlord can only raise the rent each year in line with inflation, set in the official price index (*IPC*). Landlords often ask for the equivalent of one month's rent as a *fianza* (deposit) and/or

a month's rent in advance before allowing you into a flat. Details of contracts (especially on responsibility for repairs) vary a lot, and don't sign a *contrato* unless you're fully confident of your Spanish and/or a lawyer or *gestor* has looked at it. For residents rent is tax deductible.

Media

The press

A good place to look for or to place small ads of all kinds is *Segundamano*, published three times a week. *The Broadsheet* and *InMadrid* (*see below*) also have useful classified pages.

ABC
Remarkably conservative in outlook and style, but the preferred paper of Madrid's most respectable citizens. However, its journalists also have a reputation for a higher level of basic professionalism than others in town.

Marca & As
Two great sports-only papers that reflect Spain's obsession with football (and some other sports). *Marca* is frequently the bestselling daily paper.

El Mundo
Now a bastion of the new right associated with the Aznar government, this populist paper made its name by unearthing many corruption scandals under the Socialists during the 1990s. It has good supplements, especially Friday's *Metrópoli* listings magazine.

El País
Founded in 1976, the liberal *El País* is a symbol of post-Franco Spain, the established paper of record. Very critical of the *Partido Popular*, in national and local government, it also carries good daily information on Madrid, and useful supplements.

¡Hola!, Pronto, Diez Minutos & Semana
A gateway into Spanish life, or at least into conversations in bus queues or hairdressers' – the *prensa del corazón* or 'press of the heart', mags dedicated to chronicling the triumphs, disasters, affairs, homes, surgical interventions and other happenings of Spanish and international celebrity-meat. An ongoing national soap opera, with a cast of thousands; gossip is one area in which Spain leads the world.

English-language

The Broadsheet
A glossy free monthly available from tourist offices, pubs, anglophone businesses, language schools, VO cinemas, and some kiosks. Articles on all aspects of life in Madrid and Spain, and useful classified and ad pages.

InMadrid
Hipper, more youth-oriented free monthly that you can find in pubs, restaurants, bookshops, universities, language schools and tourist offices, with good articles on the Madrid scene and listings information, events, reviews and small ads.

Foreign newspapers
Most kiosks around Sol, Gran Via, Calle Alcalá and the Castellana, and all *Vip's* stores (*see p161*) have a wide selection of international newspapers.

Listings/what's on

Local papers carry daily film and theatre programme details, and the Friday supplements of *El Mundo* (**Metrópoli**) and *El País* (**Tentaciones**) give fuller information, reviews and so on.

Guía del Ocio
Published every Friday, the standby local listings magazine with cinema, arts, entertainment, nightlife and restaurant listings, and a good galleries section. It also now has an online ticket sales service (*see p171*). However, Madrid social life often works by word-of-mouth, so the *Guía* can miss out on last-minute changes.

Music & style mags
Undersounds is a music monthly, mainly sold in music shops and at festivals, that's good for information on the club scene. Two free mags to look out for, found in many bars, shops and so on, are the clubbers' zine *AB* and the smarter monthly *Cartel*.

TV

Non-Spanish films and shows on some channels can be seen undubbed on stereo TVs; look for *VO* in listings and a *Dual* symbol at the top of the screen.

TVE 1 (La Primera)
Flagship channel of state broadcaster RTVE: professional if predictable, it has lost heavily to the independents.

TVE 2 (La Dos)
RTVE's serious, 'minority channel'. Classic movies sometimes appear late night on La 2 in the original language.

Antena 3
A private channel, current leader in the ratings war. The secret of its success is an emphasis on family entertainment mixed with late-night salaciousness.

Tele 5
Also private, a byword for tackiness, Tele 5 fights Antena 3 head-to-head for ratings. Lately it has had a more hip look, but is still celebrity-obsessed.

Telemadrid
Madrid's own station. Good for live football on Saturday nights.

Canal +
A classier-than-most channel available to subscribers with a decoder, although many hotels, bars and cafés now receive it. Live football is a mainstay.

Radio

Radio Nacional de España stations to listen for include **RNE-2** (96.5 FM, classical music) and **RNE-3** (93.2 FM, rocky and ravey, and more alternative after dark). There are dozens of other local stations. **BBC World Service** can be found in the evenings on 12095 kHz short wave.

Students

A growing number of foreigners study in Madrid, whether on language or Erasmus-scheme courses. Foreign students staying more than three months require a residency permit; non-EU students may also need a visa (*see page 289*).

Consejería de Educación y Cultura

Gran Vía 10, Sol & Gran Vía (91 580 42 42). Metro Sevilla/bus all routes to Gran Vía. **Open** 9am-3pm Mon-Fri; closed Sat, Sun. **Map** p309 F6.
Regional government office with details of courses, grants and other facilities. Resident foreigners under 26 can obtain the *Tarjeta Joven* youth card, giving a range of discounts.

Instituto de la Juventud

C/Ortega y Gasset 71, Salamanca (91 347 77 00/www.mtas.es/injuve). Metro Lista/bus 1, 74. **Open** *Sept-June* 9am-2pm, 4-6pm Mon-Fri; 9am-2pm Sat; closed Sun; *July, Aug* 9am-2pm, 4-6pm Mon-Fri; closed Sat, Sun. **Map** p307 I3.
An official youth information centre providing advice and information on courses, educational exchanges and student and youth activities.

TIVE

C/Fernando el Católico 88, Moncloa (91 543 02 08/www.comadrid.es). Metro Moncloa/bus 1, 16, 44, 61, C. **Open** 9am-2pm Mon-Fri; *info only* 9am-noon Sat; closed Sun. **Credit** V. **Map** p304 C2.
Comunidad-run student and youth travel agency that issues student and youth hostel cards, and has discount air, rail and coach tickets available to anyone under 26, or students up to 30.

Universities

Erasmus, Socrates & Lingua programmes

Information in the UK:
UK Socrates and Erasmus Council, R&D Building, The University, Canterbury, Kent CT2 7PD (01227 762 712/www.erasmus.ac.uk).
The **Erasmus** student-exchange scheme and **Lingua** project (for language learning) are the main parts of the EU's **Socrates** programme to help students move freely between member states. Madrid universities have exchanges set up with many British and Irish colleges, covering a range of subjects. To be eligible you must be studying at an exchange institution; they are open to students

from the second year onwards, and prospective applicants should contact their college's Erasmus co-ordinator.

Universidad de Alcalá de Henares

Plaza de San Diego, Alcalá de Henares, 28071 (91 885 40 03/www.uah.es). **Open** *office* 9am-2pm, 4-6pm Mon-Thur, 9am-2pm Fri; closed Sat, Sun.
Seat of Madrid's oldest university, founded in 1498 and moved to the city in 1836; the university reopened in Alcalá (*see p256*) in 1977.

Universidad Autónoma de Madrid

Ciudad Universitaria de Cantoblanco, Carretera de Colmenar km15, 28049 Madrid. (91 397 51 00/www.uam.es). **Open** *office* 9am-2pm, 4-6pm Mon-Fri; closed Sat, Sun.
Founded in 1968 in the city's northern suburbs, the UAM now competes in prestige with the Complutense.

Universidad Carlos III

C/Madrid 126, Getafe, 28903 Madrid (91 624 95 00/98 39/www.uc3m.es). **Open** *office* 9am-2pm, 4-6pm Mon-Fri; closed Sat, Sun.
Madrid's newest university, with campuses in Getafe and Leganés, and a growing number of Erasmus students.

Universidad Complutense de Madrid

Avda de Séneca 2, Moncloa (91 394 10 00/www.ucm.es). **Open** *office* 9am-2pm, 4-6pm Mon-Fri; 9am-1am Sat; closed Sun.
Madrid's main university derives its title from the Latin for Alcalá de Henares, its original home. The current site, the *Ciudad Universitaria*, was opened in 1928, became a Civil War battlefield, and was rebuilt under the Franco regime to become the sprawling compound of today. Home to 130,000 students, 3,000 from abroad.

Language learning

University courses

Universidad Autónoma de Madrid

Servicio de Idiomas, Universidad Autónoma de Madrid, pabellón A, Ciudad Universitaria de Cantoblanco, Carretera de Colmenar km15, 28049 Madrid (91 397 46 33/www.uam.es). **Open** *office* 9.30am-2.30pm Mon-Fri; closed Sat, Sun.
All-year and summer courses; fees are slightly lower than at the Complutense.

Universidad Complutense de Madrid

Secretaría de Cursos para Extranjeros, Facultad de Filosofía y Letras, Ciudad Universitaria, 28040 Madrid (91 394 53 25/www.ucm.es/info/cextran). **Open** (office) *Sept-June* 10am-1pm, 3-6pm, *July* 10am-1pm only, Mon-Fri; closed Sat, Sun & Aug.
Courses for foreign students are held in the academic year and in summer. Higher-level students can study linguistics, literature and culture; there are also intensive language courses. Accommodation is not provided. Spanish for foreigners is also offered in the college year (not in summer) at the Universidad de Alcalá de Henares.

Language schools

Escuela Oficial de Idiomas

C/Jesús Maestro s/n, Moncloa (91 533 58 05). Metro Guzmán el Bueno/bus 2, 12, 44. **Open** *Sept-June* 10am-1pm, 4-7pm Mon-Fri; closed Sat, Sun.
This government-run school offers courses in Spanish and several other languages during the academic year (no summer courses). There are several other centres around Madrid; call for a full list. Admission is problematic, as fees are low, and demand is very high. Registration is in the first two weeks of September; to have the best chance of getting in it can be worth camping out by the school the previous night, and putting up with incredible queues.

Idiomas XXI

C/Bárbara de Braganza 12, Chueca (91 319 41 73/www.ddnet.es/idiomasXXI) Metro Colón/bus 3, 37, 40, 149. **Open** 9am-8pm Mon-Fri; closed Sat, Sun.
Small-group Spanish courses using dynamic modern methods: longer-term and intensive courses at all levels.

International House

C/Zurbano 8, Chamberí (91 310 13 14/ ihmadrid.es). Metro Alonso Martínez/ bus 3, 7, 21. **Open** 9am-8.30pm Mon-Fri; closed Sat, Sun. **Map** p306 H3.
Varied Spanish courses at all levels, all year, with full-time and short courses.

Tandem

C/Marqués de Cubas 8, Huertas (91 532 27 15/www.tandem-madrid.com). Metro Banco de España/bus all routes to Cibeles. **Open** 9am-2pm, 5-8pm Mon-Fri; closed Sat, Sun. **Map** p310 G7.
Imaginative courses in English, German and Spanish, with intensive and other programmes. Tandem can also arrange accommodation.

Directory

Essential Vocabulary

Like other Latin languages, Spanish has different familiar and polite forms of the second person (you). Many young people now use the familiar *tú* form most of the time; for foreigners, though, it's always advisable to use the more polite *usted* with people you do not know, and certainly with anyone over 50. In the phrases listed here all verbs are given in the *usted* form. For help in making your way through menus, *see chapters* **Restaurants** *and* **Tapas**.

Pronunciation

c, before an **i** or an **e**, and **z** are like **th** in **th**in.
c in all other cases is as in **c**at.
g, before an **i** or an **e**, and **j** are pronounced with a guttural **h**-sound that does not exist in English – like **ch** in Scottish lo**ch**, but much harder.
g in all other cases is pronounced as in **g**et.
h at the beginning of a word is normally silent.
ll is pronounced almost like a **y**.
ñ is like **ny** in ca**ny**on.
A single **r** at the beginning of a word and **rr** elsewhere are heavily rolled.

Basics

hello *hola*; **hello** (when answering the phone) *hola, diga*
good morning, good day *buenos días*; **good afternoon, good evening** *buenas tardes*; **good evening** (after dark), **good night** *buenas noches*
goodbye/see you later *adiós/hasta luego*
please *por favor*; **thank you** (very much) *(muchas) gracias*
you're welcome *de nada*
do you speak English? *¿habla inglés?*
I don't speak Spanish *no hablo español*
I don't understand *no entiendo*
what's your name? *¿cómo se llama?*
speak more slowly, please *hable más despacio, por favor*
wait a moment *espere un momento*
Sir/Mr *señor (sr)*; **Madam/Mrs** *señora (sra)*; **Miss** *señorita (srta)*
excuse me/sorry *perdón*
excuse me, please *oiga* (the standard way to attract someone's attention, politely; literally 'hear me')

OK/fine/(or to a waiter) **that's enough** *vale*
where is... *¿dónde está...?*
why? *¿porqué?*; **when?** *¿cuándo?*; **who?** *¿quién?*; **what?** *¿qué?*; **where?** *¿dónde?*; **how?** *¿cómo?*
who is it? *¿quién es?*
is/are there any... *¿hay...?*
very *muy*; **and** *y*; **or** *o*
with *con*; **without** *sin*
open *abierto*; **closed** *cerrado*
what time does it open/close? *¿a qué hora abre/cierra?*
pull (on signs) *tirar*; **push** *empujar*
I would like... *quiero...* (literally, 'I want...'); **how many would you like?** *¿cuántos quiere?*
I like *me gusta*
I don't like *no me gusta*
good *bueno/a*; **bad** *malo/a*; **well/badly** *bien/mal*; **small** *pequeño/a*; **big** *gran, grande*; **expensive** *caro/a*; **cheap** *barato/a*; **hot** (food, drink) *caliente*; **cold** *frío/a*
something *algo*; **nothing** *nada*
more/less *más/menos*
more or less *más o menos*
the bill/check, please *la cuenta, por favor*
how much is it? *¿cuánto es?*
do you have any change? *¿tiene cambio?*
price *precio*; **free** *gratis*
discount *descuento*
bank *banco*; **to rent** *alquilar*; **(for) rent, rental** *(en) alquiler*; **post office** *correos*; **stamp** *sello*; **postcard** *postal*; **toilet** *los servicios*

Getting around

airport *aeropuerto*; **railway station** *estación de ferrocarril/estación de RENFE* (Spanish Railways);
Metro station *estación de Metro*
entrance *entrada*; **exit** *salida*
car *coche*; **bus** *autobús*; **train** *tren*
a ticket *un billete*; **return** *de ida y vuelta*; **bus stop** *parada de autobús*;
the next stop *la próxima parada*
excuse me, do you know the way to...? *¿oiga, señor/señora/etc, sabe como llegar a...?*
left *izquierda*; **right** *derecha*
here *aquí*; **there** *allí*
straight on *recto*; **to the end of the street** *al final de la calle*
as far as *hasta*; **towards** *hacia*
near *cerca*; **far** *lejos*

Accommodation

do you have a double/single room for tonight/one week? *¿tiene una habitación doble/para una persona para esta noche/una semana?*
where is the car park? *¿dónde está el parking?*

we have a reservation *tenemos reserva*
an inside/outside room *una habitación interior/exterior*
with/without bathroom *con/sin baño*; **shower** *ducha*
double bed *cama de matrimonio*; **with twin beds** *con dos camas*
breakfast included *desayuno incluido*
air-conditioning *aire acondicionado*; **lift** *ascensor*; **swimming pool** *piscina*

Time

morning *la mañana*; **midday** *mediodía*; **afternoon/evening** *la tarde*; **night** *la noche*; **late night/early morning** (roughly 1-6am) *la madrugada*
now *ahora*; **later** *más tarde*
yesterday *ayer*; **today** *hoy*; **tomorrow** *mañana*; **tomorrow morning** *mañana por la mañana*
early *temprano*; **late** *tarde*
delay *retraso*; **delayed** *retrasado*
at what time...? *¿a qué hora...?*
in an hour *en una hora*
the bus will take 2 hours (to get there) *el autobús tardará dos horas (en llegar)*
at 2 *a las dos*; **at 8pm** *a las ocho de la tarde*; **at 1.30** *a la una y media*
at 5.15 *a las cinco y cuarto*; **at 22.30** *a veintidós treinta*

Numbers

0 *cero*; 1 *un, uno, una*; 2 *dos*; 3 *tres*; 4 *cuatro*; 5 *cinco*; 6 *seis*; 7 *siete*; 8 *ocho*; 9 *nueve*; 10 *diez*; 11 *once*; 12 *doce*; 13 *trece*; 14 *catorce*; 15 *quince*; 16 *dieciséis*; 17 *diecisiete*; 18 *dieciocho*; 19 *diecinueve*; 20 *veinte*; 21 *veintiuno*; 22 *veintidós*; 30 *treinta*; 40 *cuarenta*; 50 *cincuenta*; 60 *sesenta*; 70 *setenta*; 80 *ochenta*; 90 *noventa*; 100 *cien*; 1,000 *mil*; 1,000,000 *un millón*

Days, months & seasons

Monday *lunes*; **Tuesday** *martes*; **Wednesday** *miércoles*; **Thursday** *jueves*; **Friday** *viernes*; **Saturday** *sábado*; **Sunday** *domingo*
January *enero*; **February** *febrero*; **March** *marzo*; **April** *abril*; **May** *mayo*; **June** *junio*; **July** *julio*; **August** *agosto*; **September** *septiembre*; **October** *octubre*; **November** *noviembre*; **December** *diciembre*
spring *primavera*; **summer** *verano*; **autumn/fall** *otoño*; **winter** *invierno*

Further Reference

Reading

Art & architecture

Jonathan Brown *Velázquez: Painter and Courtier* The most comprehensive study in English.
JH Elliott & Jonathan Brown *A Palace for a King: The Buen Retiro and the Court of Philip IV* A vivid reconstruction of the life, culture and spectacle of the Habsburg Court, and the grandest of Madrid's palaces.
Francisco de Goya *Disasters of War; Disparates, or the Proverbs; Los Caprichos* Dover Books publish good-value, high-quality reproductions of Goya's three most remarkable series of etchings.
Michael Jacobs *Madrid Observed* A lively survey by one of the best current foreign writers on Spain. A good walking companion.
Angus Mitchell *Spain: Interiors, Gardens, Architecture, Landscape* Lavishly illustrated.

Food & drink

Christine Boyle & Chris Nawrat *Spain and Portugal* In the Traveller's Food and Wine Guide series, a pocket-sized handbook and glossary.
Penelope Casas *Food and Wines of Spain* Informative general guide.

History, politics, culture

Fernand Braudel *The Mediterranean and the Mediterranean World in the Age of Philip II* (two vols). Huge, multi-faceted study of society, economics and culture during Spain's Golden Age. There is a one-volume edition, *The Mediterranean*.
JH Elliott *Imperial Spain, 1469-1716* The standard history.
RA Fletcher *Moorish Spain* Varied account of a little-known period in European history.
Ronald Fraser *Blood of Spain* An oral history of the Spanish Civil War, the most vivid and human account of Spain's great crisis.
Juan Lalaguna *A Traveller's History of Spain* Handy introduction.
Ian Gibson *Fire in the Blood* Idiosyncratic vision of modern Spain by Lorca's biographer.
David Gilmour *Cities of Spain* With an informative, impressionistic chapter on Madrid.
John Hooper *The New Spaniards* The best survey of post-1975 Spain, updated to cover the changes in the country in the 1990s.

Paul Preston *Franco* A massive and exhaustive biography. The same author's *The Spanish Civil War* is a good concise account of the war.
Hugh Thomas, ed *Madrid, A Traveller's Companion* A great anthology of writings on Madrid from the Middle Ages to the 1930s, by authors as varied as Casanova, Pérez Galdós and the Duke of Wellington.

Literature

Pedro Almodóvar *Patty Diphusa Stories and Other Writings* Frothy, disposable, but full of the sparky, sexy atmosphere of *Movida* Madrid.
Camilo José Cela *The Hive* Nobel-prizewinner Cela's sardonic masterpiece on Madrid in the aftermath of the Civil War.
Miguel de Cervantes *Don Quixote* The great classic of Golden-Century Spain, although the Don only actually visits Madrid very briefly. Cervantes' shorter pieces are collected together as *Exemplary Stories*.
Antonio Múñoz Molina *Prince of Shadows* A psychological thriller based on the legacy of the recent past in modern Madrid.
Benito Pérez Galdós *Fortunata y Jacinta* The masterwork of Spain's great 19th-century novelist, a story of love and class of great depth set amid the political conflicts of 1860s Madrid.
Arturo Pérez Reverte *The Fencing Master, The Flanders Road* and *The Club Dumas* (also published as *The Dumas Club*) Elegant, unconventional mystery novels by one of the most lauded of current Spanish writers.
Francisco de Quevedo, & anon (Penguin edition) *Two Spanish Picaresque Novels* The anonymous *Lazarillo de Tormes* and Quevedo's 1626 *El Buscón* (translated as 'The Swindler'), an earthy masterpiece, the second-greatest work of classical Spanish prose and an essential text on the 'Golden Century'. And a lot shorter than *Quijote*.

Music

Camarón de la Isla *Potro de Rabia y de Miel* One of the last recordings made by the most legendary figure of modern flamenco before he died, with Paco de Lucía on guitar.
Corazón Loco: 40 Joyas del Pop Español Excellent intro to the perky, occasionally daft and sometimes pretty cool soundtrack of modern Madrid.
Plácido Domingo *Romanzas de Zarzuelas* One of several recordings by Domingo of lush tunes from *Zarzuelas* that have played a big part in the revival of Madrid's own comic operas.

Ray Heredia *Quien no corre, vuela* One of the most original new-flamenco performers.
Los Jovenes Flamencos Several CDs in this series, bringing together all the best *nuevo flamenco* artists of the last 15 years, have been issued by the Nuevos Medios label. One at least is available outside Spain with the title *The Young Flamencos*.
El Lebrijano, con la Orquesta Arábigo Andaluza *Casablanca* Fascinating crossover recording by flamenco *cantaor* El Lebrijano with Moroccan musicians using traditional themes from Muslim Andalusia.
Carmen Linares *Antología* Classic flamenco themes sung by one of the best younger *cantaoras*. Another CD, *Carmen Linares, Cantaora*, may be more widely available outside Spain.
Paco de Lucía *Luzía*, or any of the many recordings by the greatest of modern flamenco guitarists.
José Mercé *Del Amanecer* Fine performances by *cantaor* Mercé, with Vicente Amigo on guitar.
Joaquín Sabina *Pongamos que hablo de Madrid* Sabina is a cool and witty *chanteur* of modern Madrid.
Radio Tarifa *Temporal* Brilliant, sharp-edged, funkily eclectic flamenco-pop from an Andalusia-based band.
Tomatito *Guitarra Gitana* Spectacular recordings by an exceptional Gypsy flamenco guitarist, former accompanist of Camarón.

Madrid online

www.munimadrid.es The Madrid *Ayuntamiento*'s functional website, with some information in English.
www.comadrid.es Equivalent site of the *Comunidad*: practical information on local services, in Spanish only.
www.ctm-madrid.es Madrid transport information (Spanish only).
www.renfe.es Spanish Railways' site, with online booking.
www.madridandbeyond.com A British-run Madrid-based company offering tailor-made tours, city breaks, hotel booking and personalised travel services in Madrid and Spain.
http://malika.iem.csic.es/˜grant/ madi.html 'Guide to Madrid' site put together by American Grant Langdon, with plenty of useful links.
http://madrid.lanetro.com Hippest and best of the local Spanish-language events and listings sites, with news on music, clubs, restaurants, films and more in and around Madrid, even though it's often hard to access. Two others, **www.repamadrid.com** and **www.webmadrid.com**, are more efficient, but less interesting.
For more Madrid links, check the Madrid page of **www.timeout.com**.

Index

Advertisers' Index

Maps

Key to symbols

 Metro entrance

 Bus route

 End of bus route

 Night bus terminus

 Airport bus route

 Coach depot

 Mainline rail station

 Cercanías local rail station

 AVE high-speed train

 Tourist information

Advertisers' Index

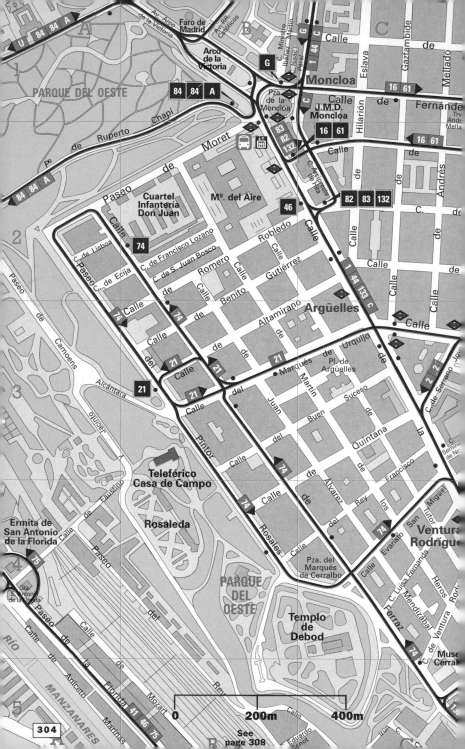

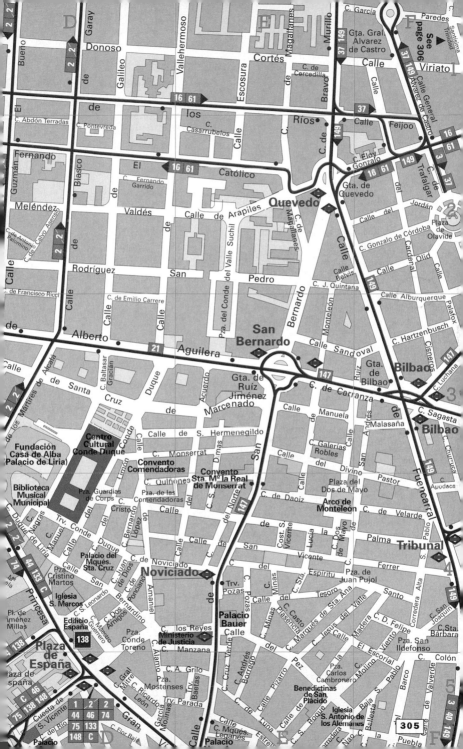

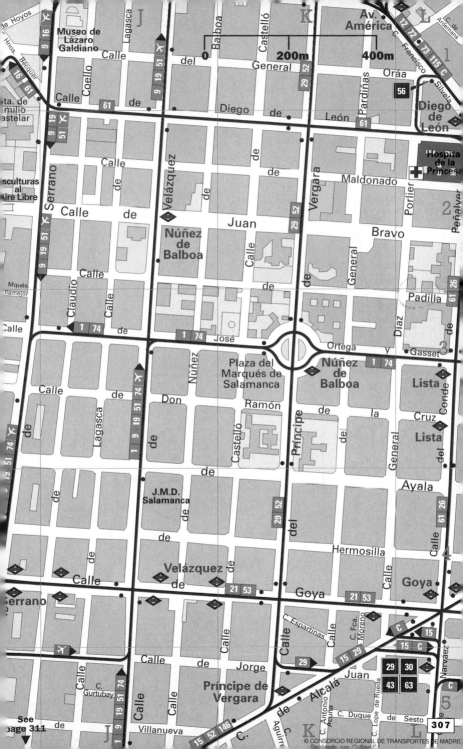

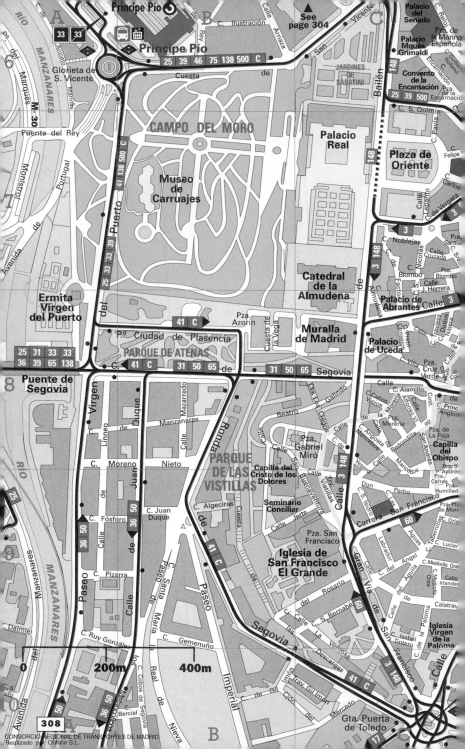

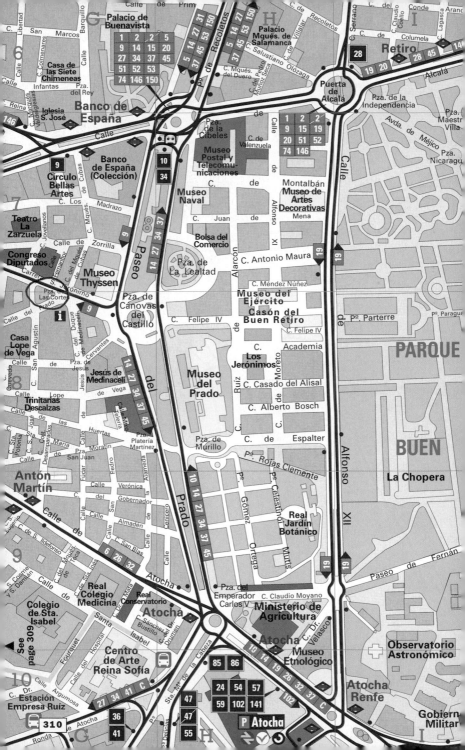

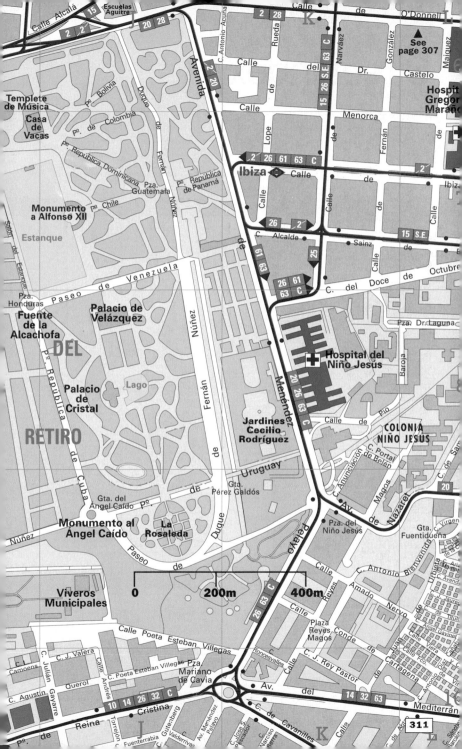

Street Index

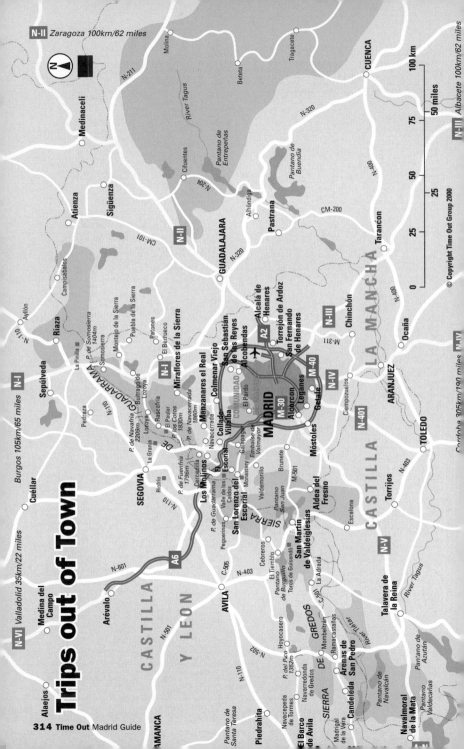

Trips out of Town

Cercanías/Local trains

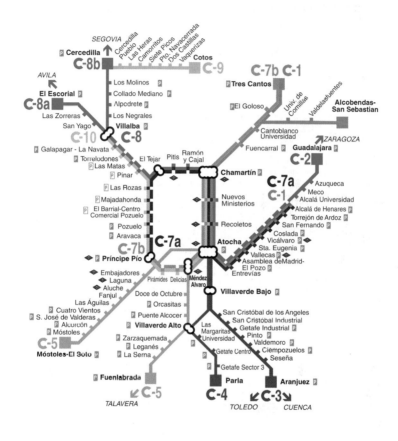

Line interchange ◆ **Metro connection** P **Parking** P **Free parking**

Metro